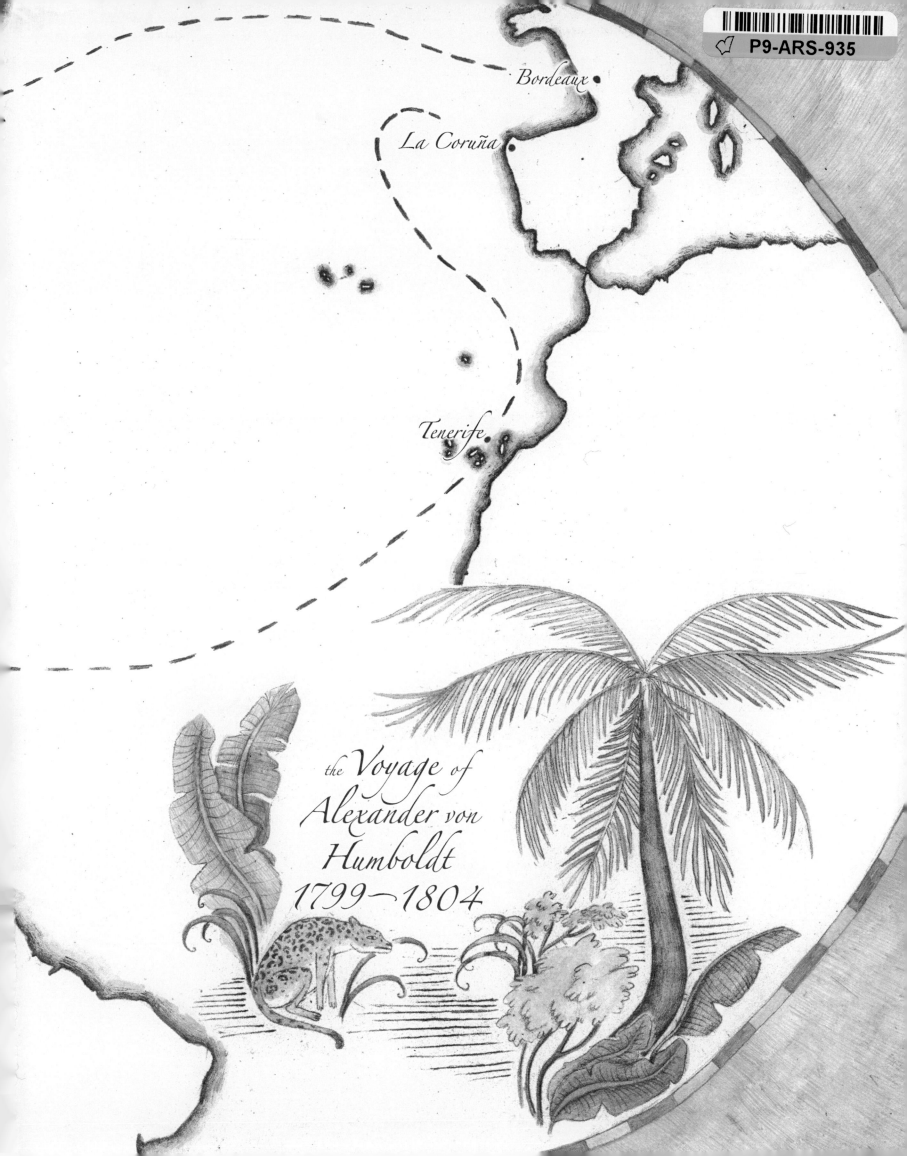

Bordeaux •

La Coruña •

Tenerife •

the *Voyage of*
Alexander von
Humboldt
1799—1804

ALSO BY ANDREA WULF

The Invention of Nature: Alexander von Humboldt's New World

Chasing Venus: The Race to Measure the Heavens

Founding Gardeners: The Revolutionary Generation, Nature,
and the Shaping of the American Nation

The Brother Gardeners: Botany, Empire, and the Birth of
an Obsession

This Other Eden: Seven Gardens and 300 Years of English History
(with Emma Gieben-Gamal)

THE
ADVENTURES
OF
ALEXANDER
VON
HUMBOLDT

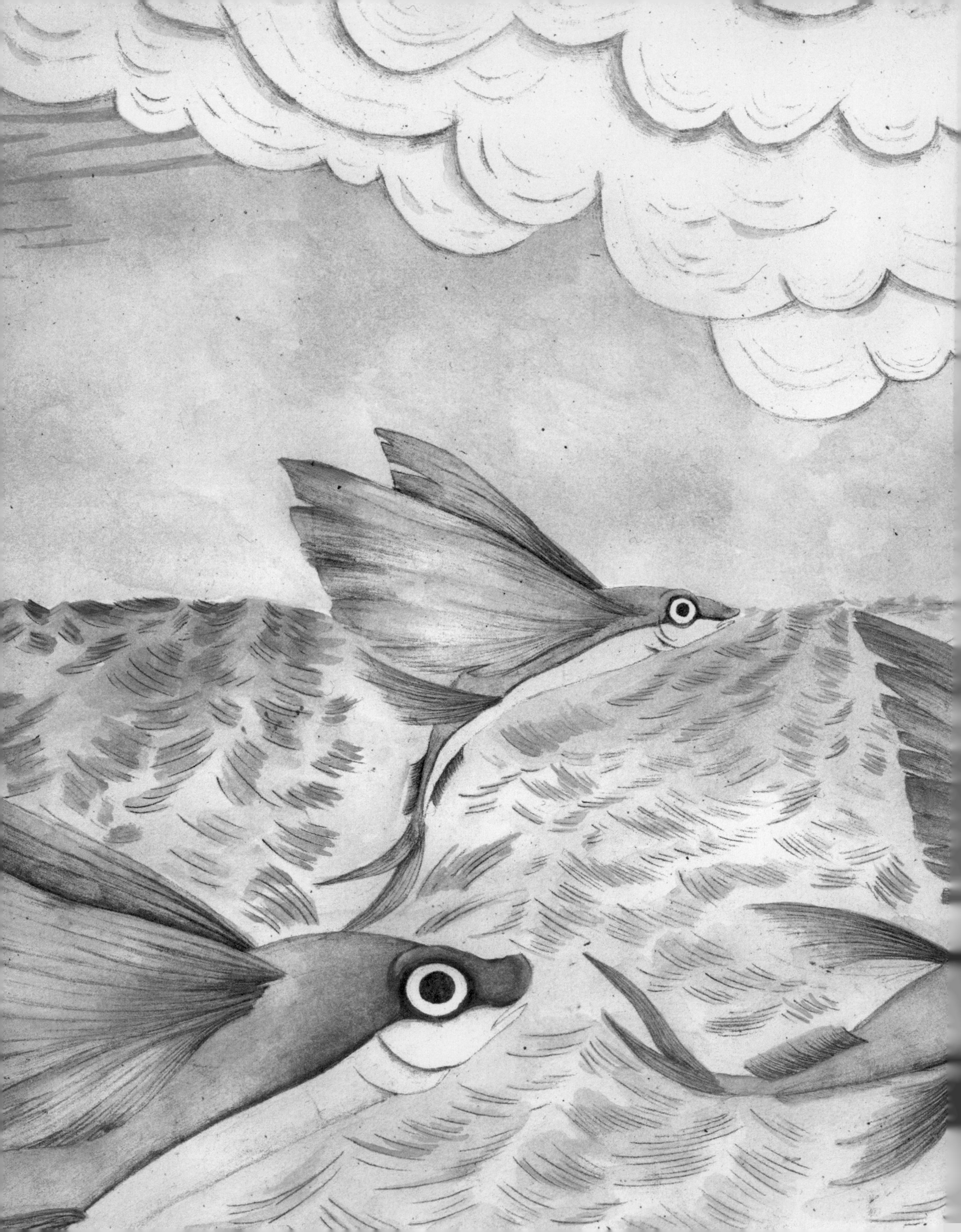

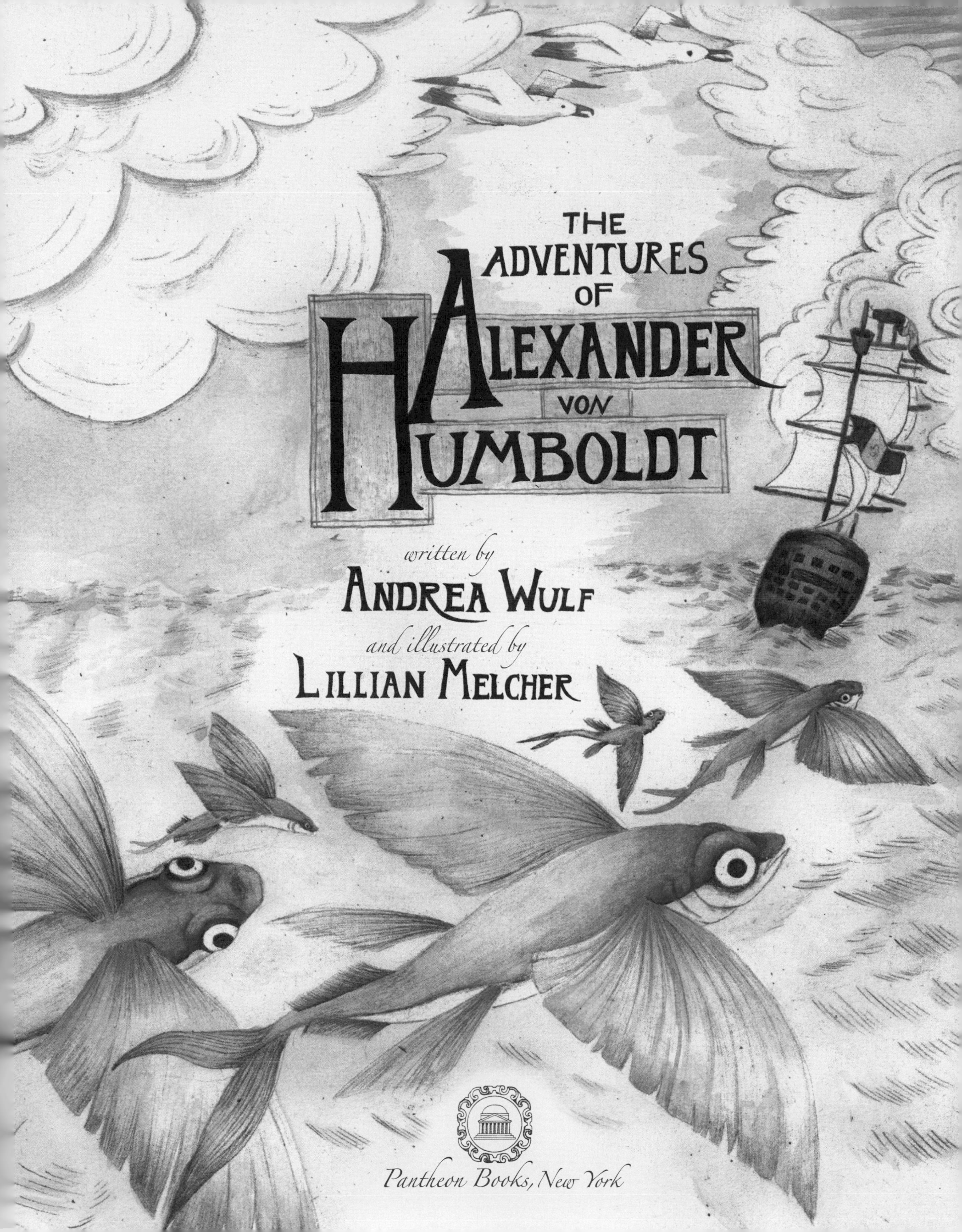

The Adventures of Alexander von Humboldt

written by

Andrea Wulf

and illustrated by

Lillian Melcher

Pantheon Books, New York

PUBLISHED IN THE UNITED STATES BY PANTHEON BOOKS, A DIVISION OF PENGUIN RANDOM HOUSE LLC, NEW YORK, AND DISTRIBUTED IN CANADA BY RANDOM HOUSE OF CANADA, A DIVISION OF PENGUIN RANDOM HOUSE CANADA LIMITED, TORONTO.

PANTHEON BOOKS AND COLOPHON ARE REGISTERED TRADEMARKS OF PENGUIN RANDOM HOUSE LLC.

LIBRARY OF CONGRESS CATALOGING-IN-PUBLICATION DATA
NAMES: WULF, ANDREA, AUTHOR. MELCHER, LILLIAN, ILLUSTRATOR.
TITLE: THE ADVENTURES OF ALEXANDER VON HUMBOLDT / ANDREA WULF ; ILLUSTRATED BY LILLIAN MELCHER.
DESCRIPTION: FIRST EDITION. NEW YORK : PANTHEON BOOKS, 2019
IDENTIFIERS: LCCN 2018032020.
ISBN 9781524747374 (HARDCOVER : ALK. PAPER).
ISBN 9781524747381 (EBOOK)
SUBJECTS: LCSH: HUMBOLDT, ALEXANDER VON, 1769-1859—TRAVEL—SOUTH AMERICA—COMIC BOOKS, STRIPS, ETC. SCIENTISTS—GERMANY—BIOGRAPHY—COMIC BOOKS, STRIPS, ETC. SCIENTIFIC EXPEDITIONS—SOUTH AMERICA—HISTORY—COMIC BOOKS, STRIPS, ETC.
CLASSIFICATION: LCC Q143.H9 W848 2019 | DDC 508.092 [B]—DC23 | LC RECORD AVAILABLE AT LCCN.LOC.GOV/2018032020

WWW.PANTHEONBOOKS.COM

JACKET ILLUSTRATION BY LILLIAN MELCHER
PRINTED IN CHINA
FIRST EDITION
9 8 7 6 5 4 3 2 1

to Thomas &
to Jen and Doug

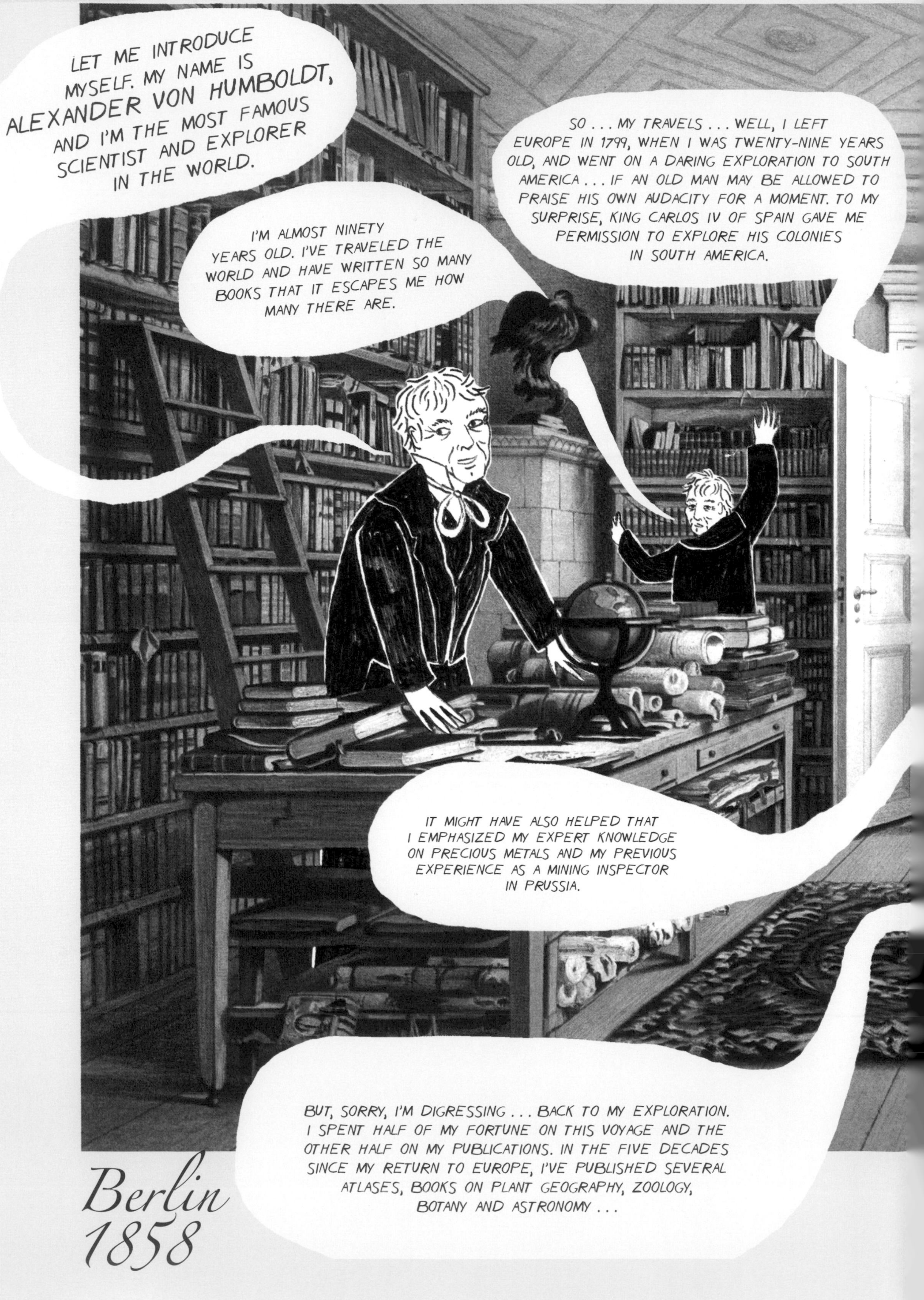
LET ME INTRODUCE MYSELF. MY NAME IS ALEXANDER VON HUMBOLDT, AND I'M THE MOST FAMOUS SCIENTIST AND EXPLORER IN THE WORLD.
I'M ALMOST NINETY YEARS OLD. I'VE TRAVELED THE WORLD AND HAVE WRITTEN SO MANY BOOKS THAT IT ESCAPES ME HOW MANY THERE ARE.
SO . . . MY TRAVELS . . . WELL, I LEFT EUROPE IN 1799, WHEN I WAS TWENTY-NINE YEARS OLD, AND WENT ON A DARING EXPLORATION TO SOUTH AMERICA . . . IF AN OLD MAN MAY BE ALLOWED TO PRAISE HIS OWN AUDACITY FOR A MOMENT. TO MY SURPRISE, KING CARLOS IV OF SPAIN GAVE ME PERMISSION TO EXPLORE HIS COLONIES IN SOUTH AMERICA.
IT MIGHT HAVE ALSO HELPED THAT I EMPHASIZED MY EXPERT KNOWLEDGE ON PRECIOUS METALS AND MY PREVIOUS EXPERIENCE AS A MINING INSPECTOR IN PRUSSIA.
BUT, SORRY, I'M DIGRESSING . . . BACK TO MY EXPLORATION. I SPENT HALF OF MY FORTUNE ON THIS VOYAGE AND THE OTHER HALF ON MY PUBLICATIONS. IN THE FIVE DECADES SINCE MY RETURN TO EUROPE, I'VE PUBLISHED SEVERAL ATLASES, BOOKS ON PLANT GEOGRAPHY, ZOOLOGY, BOTANY AND ASTRONOMY . . .

Berlin 1858

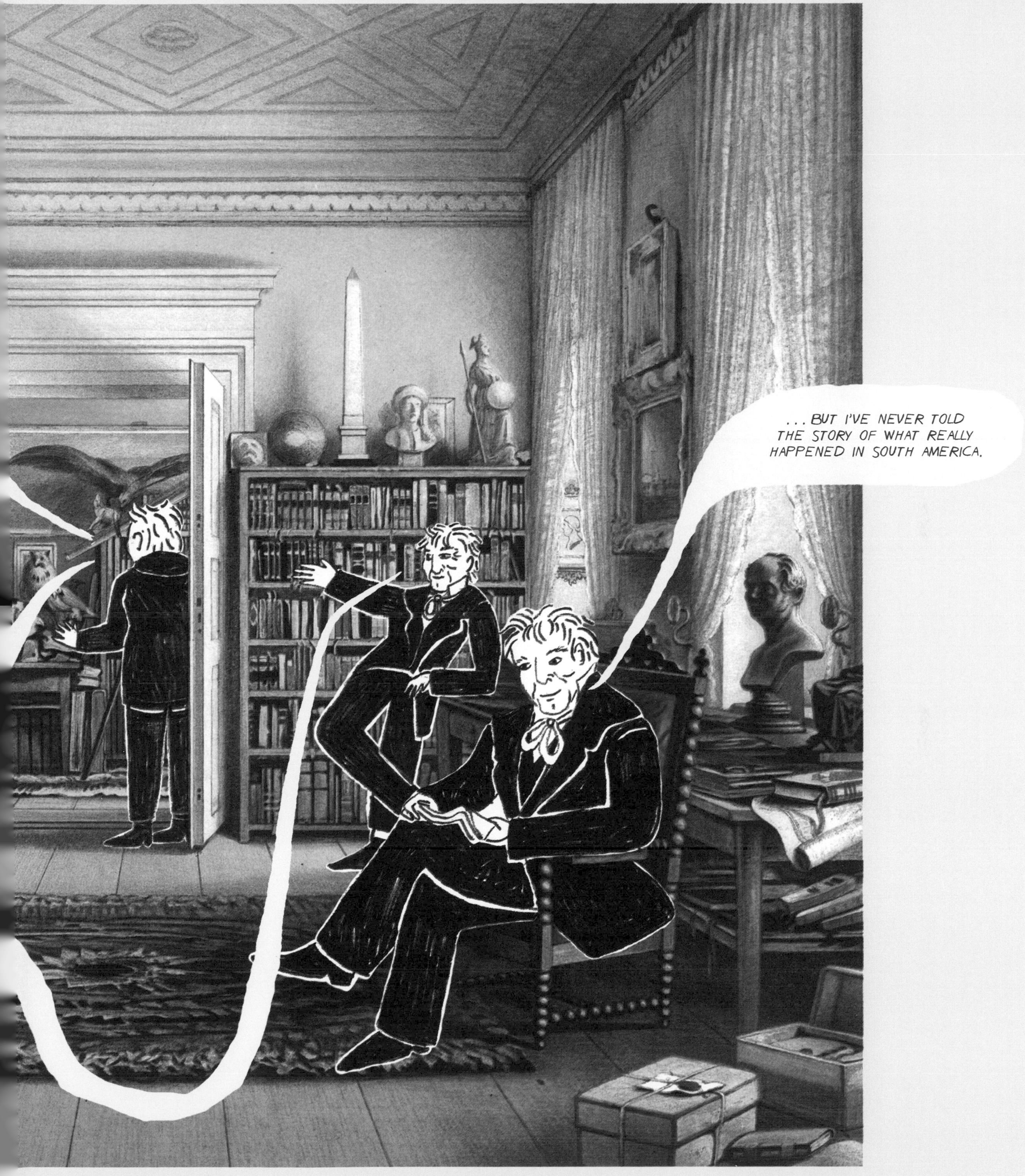
. . . BUT I'VE NEVER TOLD THE STORY OF WHAT REALLY HAPPENED IN SOUTH AMERICA.

I AM GLAD TO LEAVE . . .

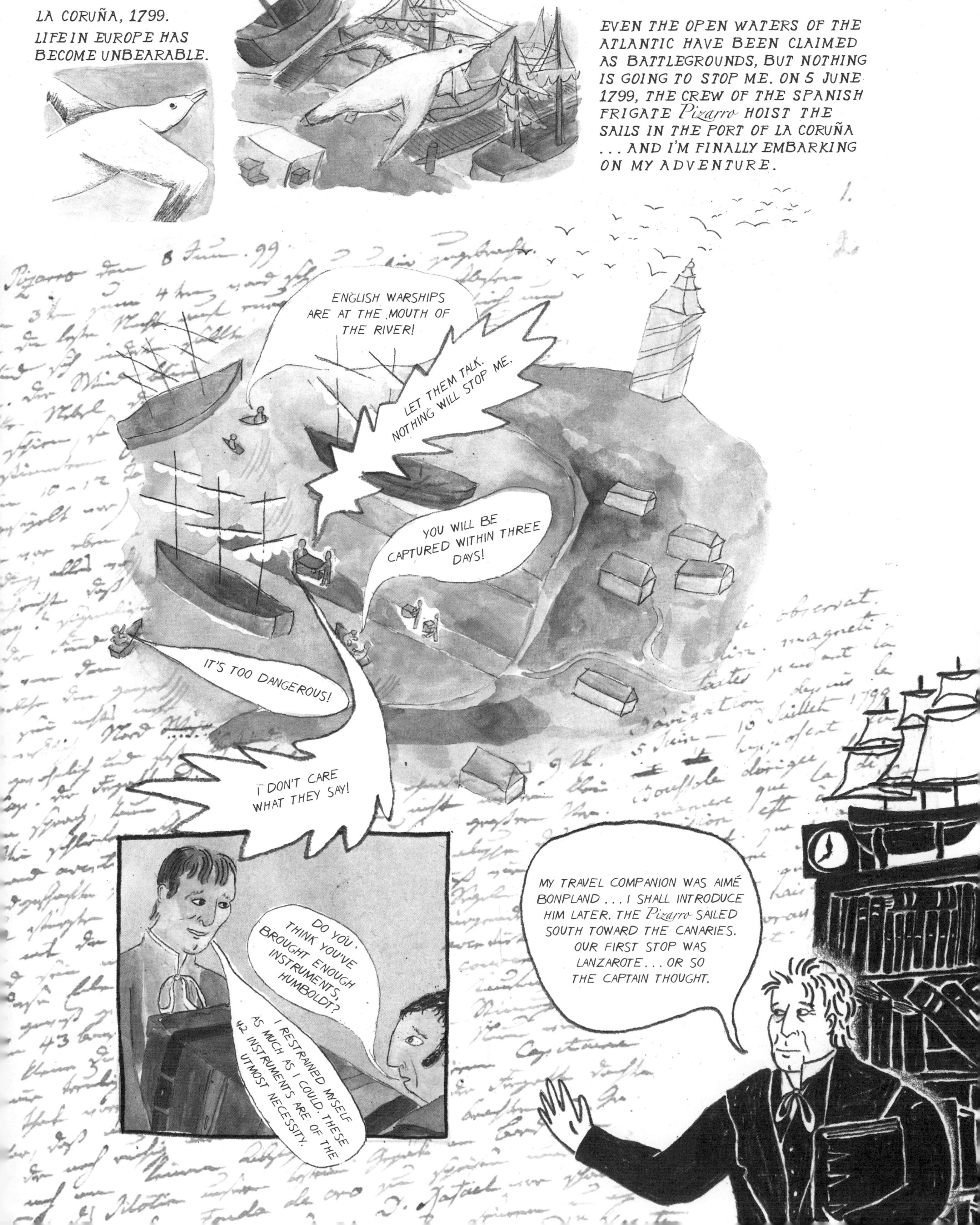
LA CORUÑA, 1799. LIFE IN EUROPE HAS BECOME UNBEARABLE.
EVEN THE OPEN WATERS OF THE ATLANTIC HAVE BEEN CLAIMED AS BATTLEGROUNDS, BUT NOTHING IS GOING TO STOP ME. ON 5 JUNE 1799, THE CREW OF THE SPANISH FRIGATE *Pizarro* HOIST THE SAILS IN THE PORT OF LA CORUÑA . . . AND I'M FINALLY EMBARKING ON MY ADVENTURE.
ENGLISH WARSHIPS ARE AT THE MOUTH OF THE RIVER!
LET THEM TALK. NOTHING WILL STOP ME.
YOU WILL BE CAPTURED WITHIN THREE DAYS!
IT'S TOO DANGEROUS!
I DON'T CARE WHAT THEY SAY!
DO YOU THINK YOU'VE BROUGHT ENOUGH INSTRUMENTS, HUMBOLDT?
I RESTRAINED MYSELF AS MUCH AS I COULD. THESE 42 INSTRUMENTS ARE OF THE UTMOST NECESSITY.
MY TRAVEL COMPANION WAS AIMÉ BONPLAND . . . I SHALL INTRODUCE HIM LATER. THE *Pizarro* SAILED SOUTH TOWARD THE CANARIES. OUR FIRST STOP WAS LANZAROTE . . . OR SO THE CAPTAIN THOUGHT.

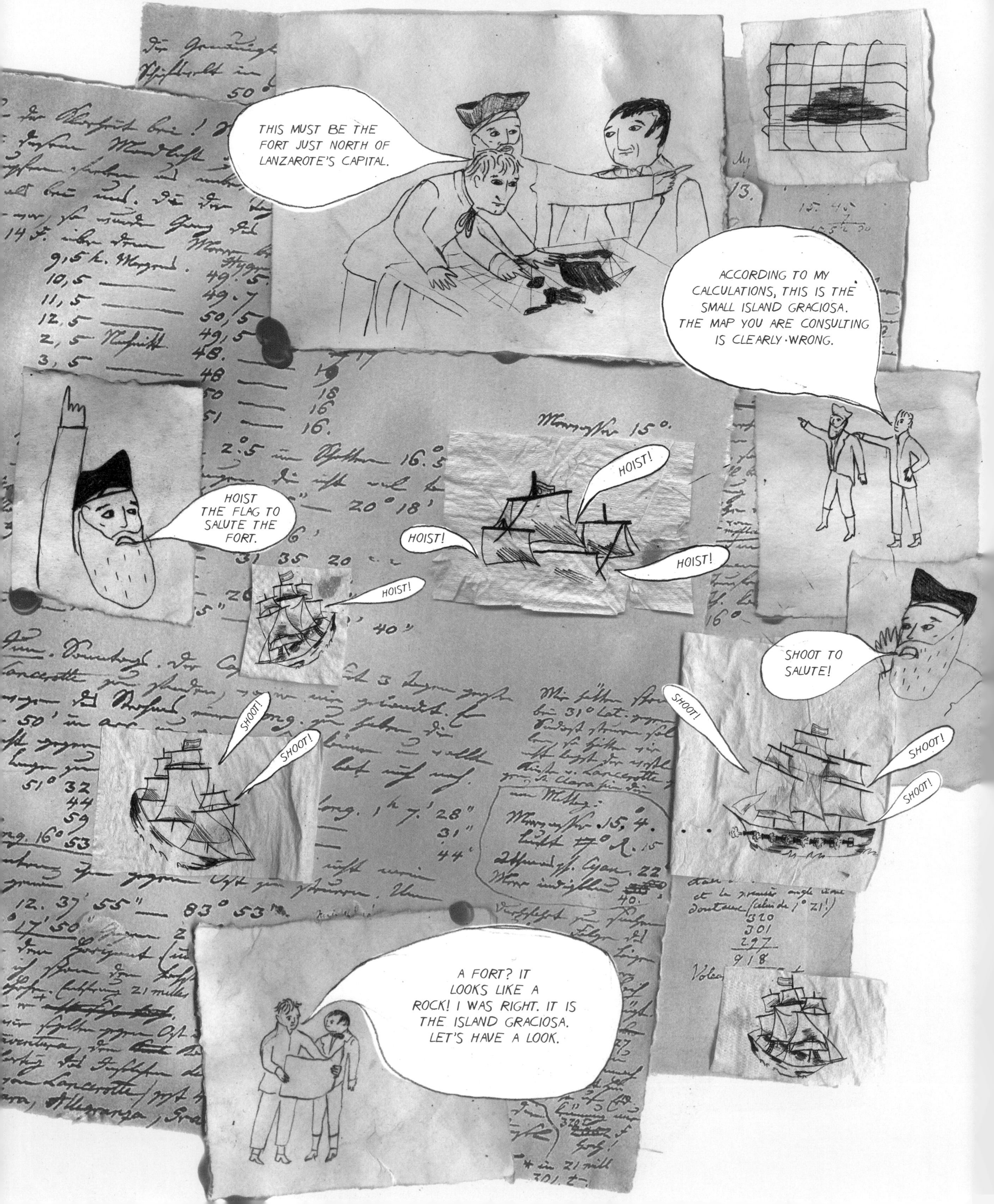
THIS MUST BE THE FORT JUST NORTH OF LANZAROTE'S CAPITAL.
ACCORDING TO MY CALCULATIONS, THIS IS THE SMALL ISLAND GRACIOSA. THE MAP YOU ARE CONSULTING IS CLEARLY WRONG.
HOIST THE FLAG TO SALUTE THE FORT.
HOIST!
HOIST!
HOIST!
HOIST!
SHOOT TO SALUTE!
SHOOT!
SHOOT!
SHOOT!
SHOOT!
SHOOT!
A FORT? IT LOOKS LIKE A ROCK! I WAS RIGHT. IT IS THE ISLAND GRACIOSA. LET'S HAVE A LOOK.

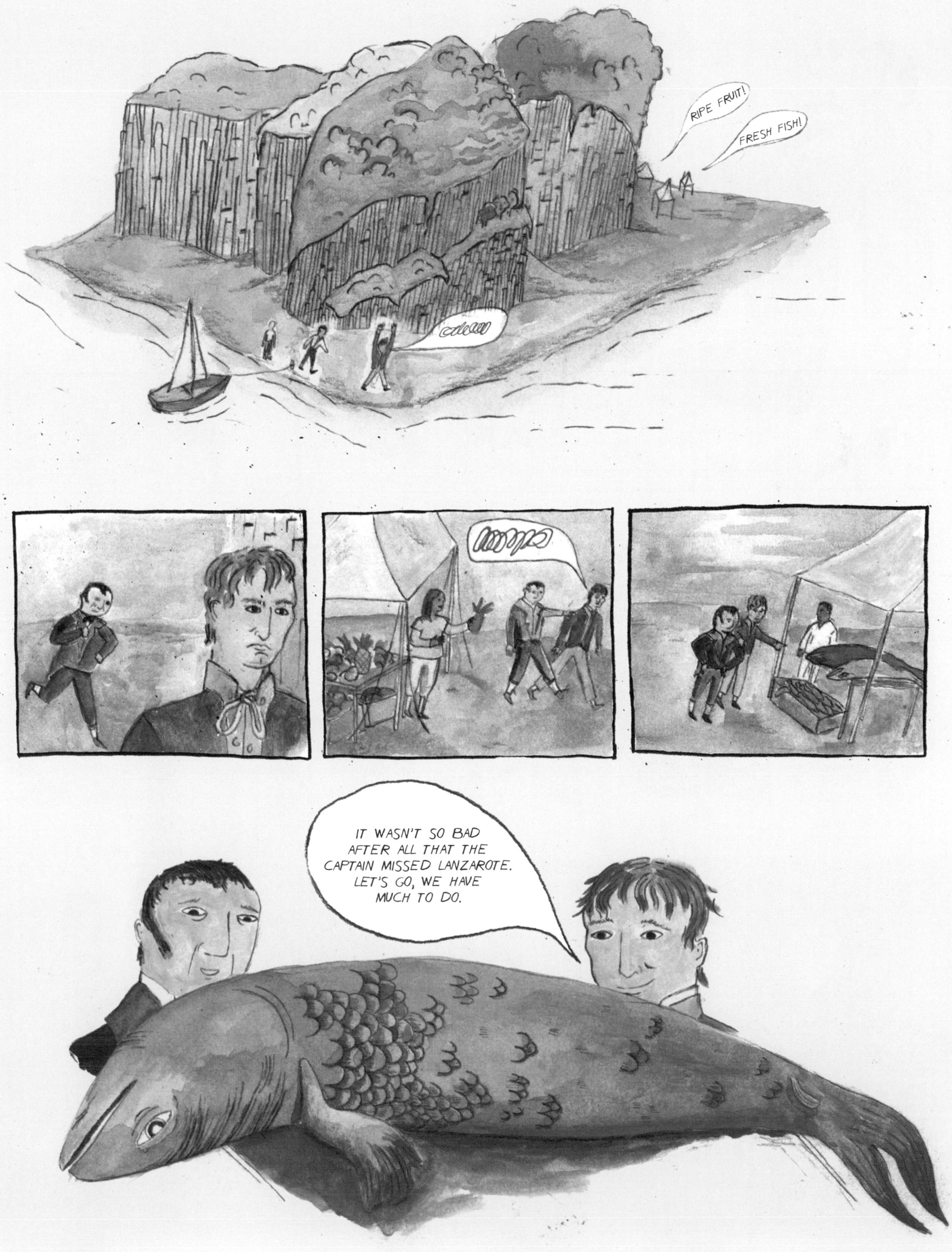
RIPE FRUIT!
FRESH FISH!
IT WASN'T SO BAD AFTER ALL THAT THE CAPTAIN MISSED LANZAROTE. LET'S GO, WE HAVE MUCH TO DO.

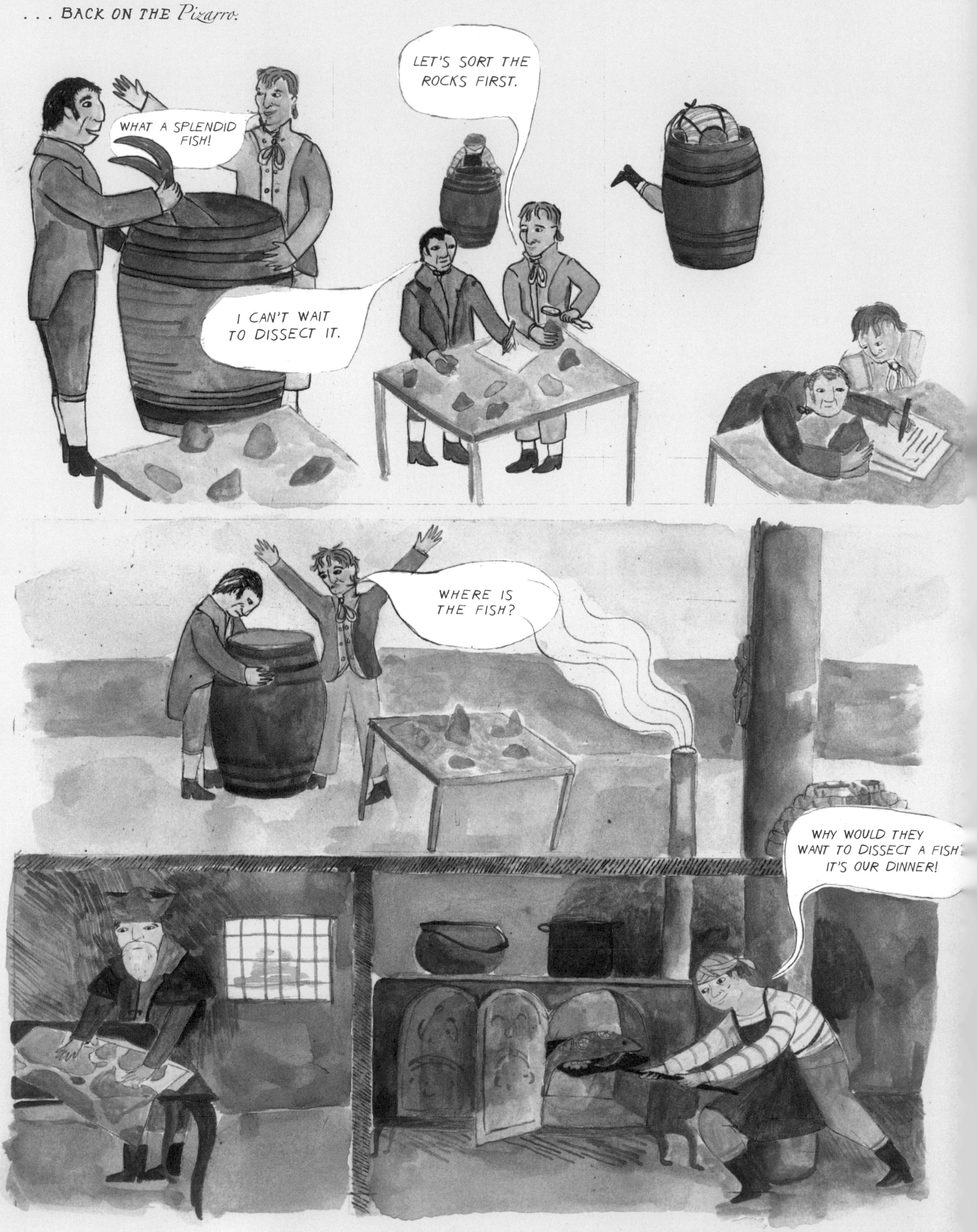
. . . BACK ON THE *Pizarro*:
WHAT A SPLENDID FISH!
LET'S SORT THE ROCKS FIRST.
I CAN'T WAIT TO DISSECT IT.
WHERE IS THE FISH?
WHY WOULD THEY WANT TO DISSECT A FISH
IT'S OUR DINNER!

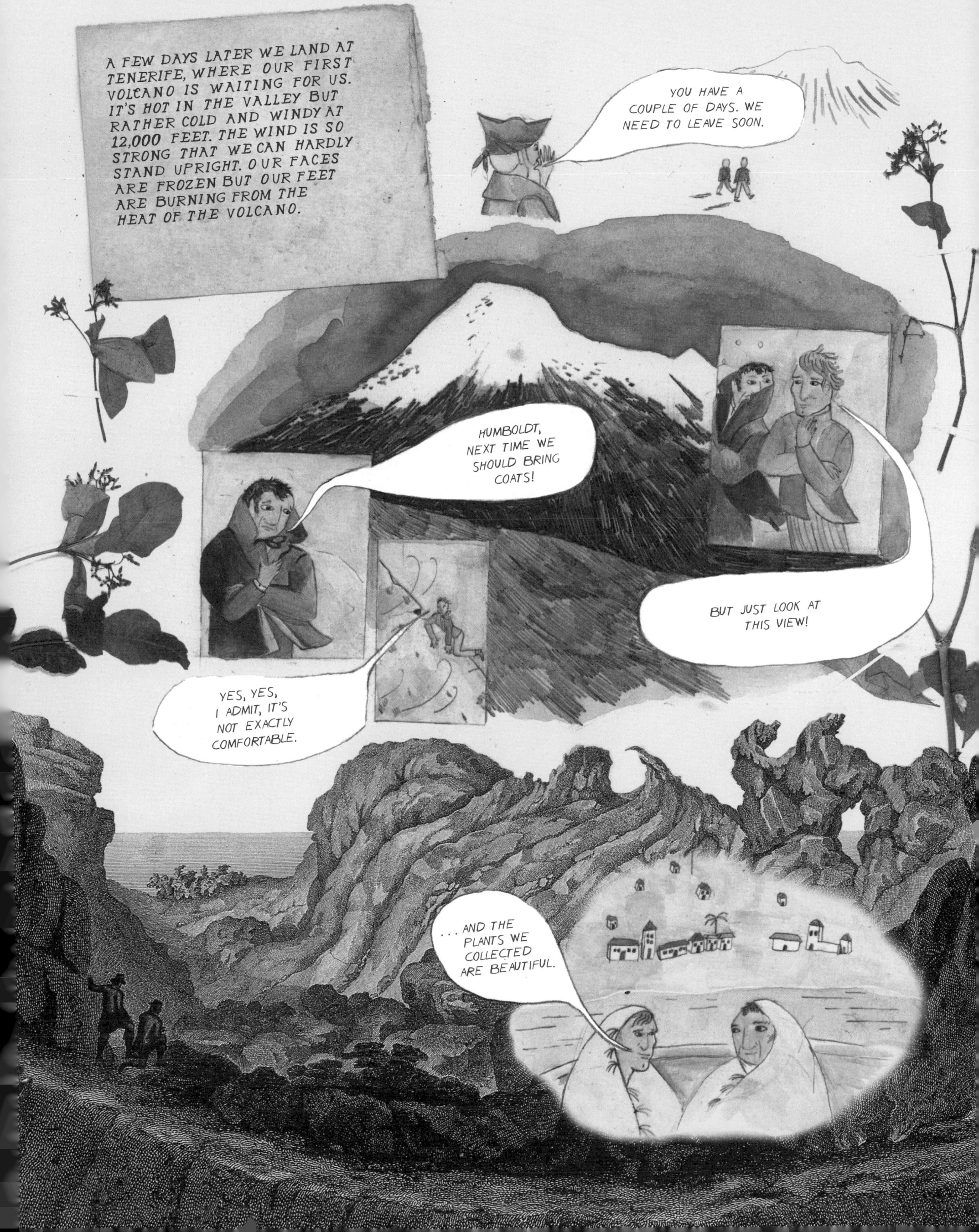
A FEW DAYS LATER WE LAND AT TENERIFE, WHERE OUR FIRST VOLCANO IS WAITING FOR US. IT'S HOT IN THE VALLEY BUT RATHER COLD AND WINDY AT 12,000 FEET. THE WIND IS SO STRONG THAT WE CAN HARDLY STAND UPRIGHT. OUR FACES ARE FROZEN BUT OUR FEET ARE BURNING FROM THE HEAT OF THE VOLCANO.
YOU HAVE A COUPLE OF DAYS. WE NEED TO LEAVE SOON.
HUMBOLDT, NEXT TIME WE SHOULD BRING COATS!
YES, YES, I ADMIT, IT'S NOT EXACTLY COMFORTABLE.
BUT JUST LOOK AT THIS VIEW!
... AND THE PLANTS WE COLLECTED ARE BEAUTIFUL.

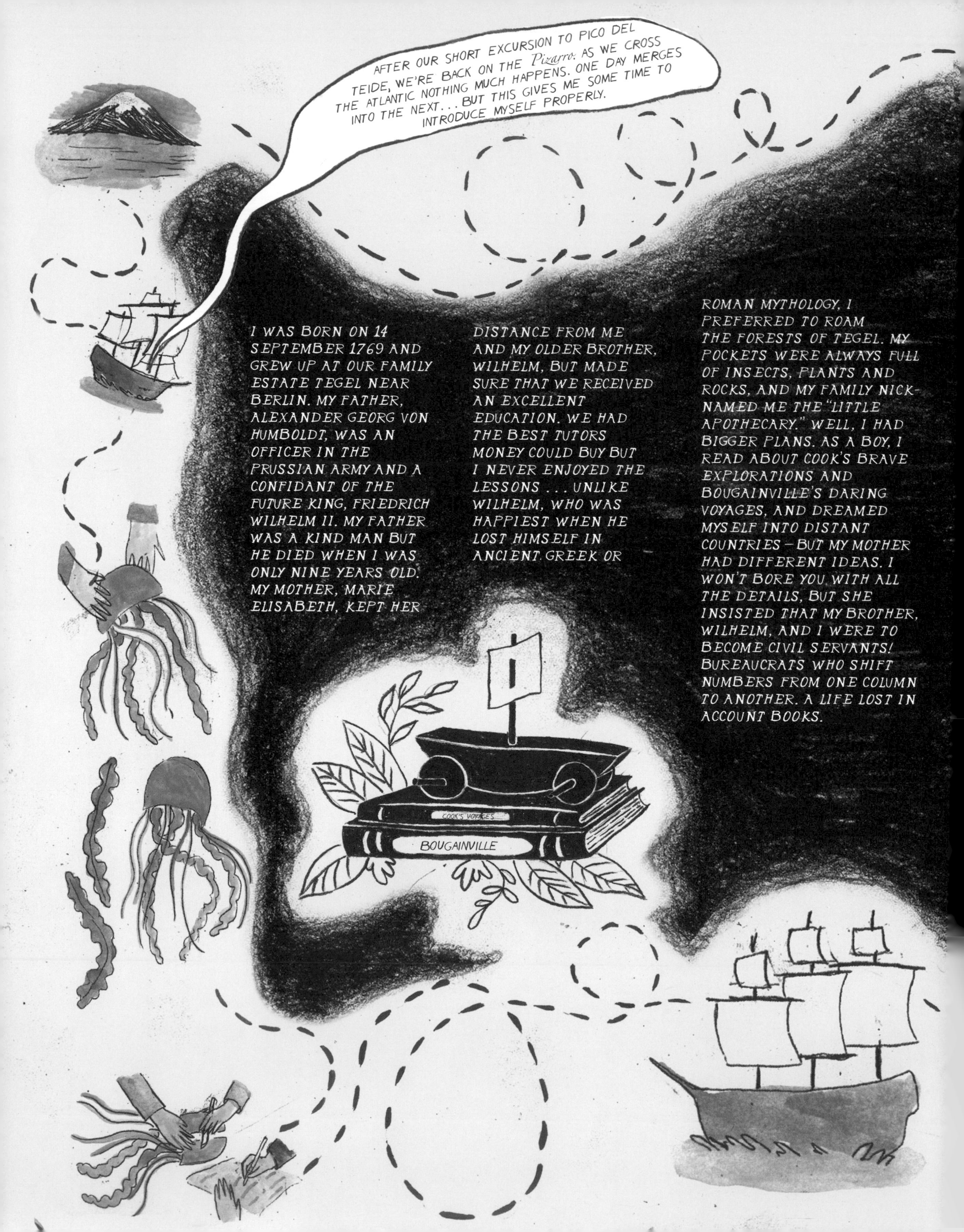
AFTER OUR SHORT EXCURSION TO PICO DEL TEIDE, WE'RE BACK ON THE *Pizarro*. AS WE CROSS THE ATLANTIC NOTHING MUCH HAPPENS. ONE DAY MERGES INTO THE NEXT . . . BUT THIS GIVES ME SOME TIME TO INTRODUCE MYSELF PROPERLY.
I WAS BORN ON 14 SEPTEMBER 1769 AND GREW UP AT OUR FAMILY ESTATE TEGEL NEAR BERLIN. MY FATHER, ALEXANDER GEORG VON HUMBOLDT, WAS AN OFFICER IN THE PRUSSIAN ARMY AND A CONFIDANT OF THE FUTURE KING, FRIEDRICH WILHELM II. MY FATHER WAS A KIND MAN BUT HE DIED WHEN I WAS ONLY NINE YEARS OLD. MY MOTHER, MARIE ELISABETH, KEPT HER DISTANCE FROM ME AND MY OLDER BROTHER, WILHELM, BUT MADE SURE THAT WE RECEIVED AN EXCELLENT EDUCATION. WE HAD THE BEST TUTORS MONEY COULD BUY BUT I NEVER ENJOYED THE LESSONS . . . UNLIKE WILHELM, WHO WAS HAPPIEST WHEN HE LOST HIMSELF IN ANCIENT GREEK OR ROMAN MYTHOLOGY, I PREFERRED TO ROAM THE FORESTS OF TEGEL. MY POCKETS WERE ALWAYS FULL OF INSECTS, PLANTS AND ROCKS, AND MY FAMILY NICKNAMED ME THE "LITTLE APOTHECARY." WELL, I HAD BIGGER PLANS. AS A BOY, I READ ABOUT COOK'S BRAVE EXPLORATIONS AND BOUGAINVILLE'S DARING VOYAGES, AND DREAMED MYSELF INTO DISTANT COUNTRIES – BUT MY MOTHER HAD DIFFERENT IDEAS. I WON'T BORE YOU WITH ALL THE DETAILS, BUT SHE INSISTED THAT MY BROTHER, WILHELM, AND I WERE TO BECOME CIVIL SERVANTS! BUREAUCRATS WHO SHIFT NUMBERS FROM ONE COLUMN TO ANOTHER. A LIFE LOST IN ACCOUNT BOOKS.
COOK'S VOYAGES
BOUGAINVILLE

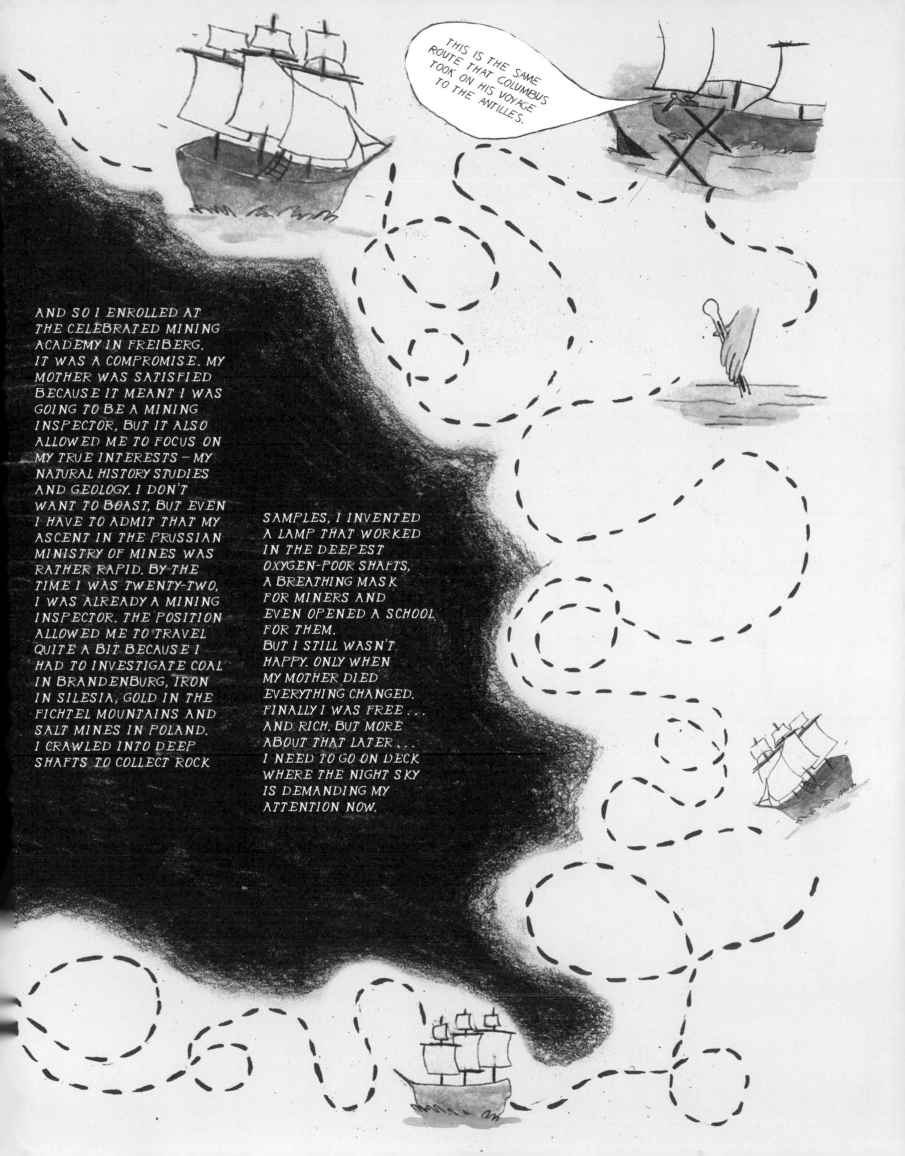

THIS IS THE SAME ROUTE THAT COLUMBUS TOOK ON HIS VOYAGE TO THE ANTILLES.

AND SO I ENROLLED AT THE CELEBRATED MINING ACADEMY IN FREIBERG. IT WAS A COMPROMISE. MY MOTHER WAS SATISFIED BECAUSE IT MEANT I WAS GOING TO BE A MINING INSPECTOR, BUT IT ALSO ALLOWED ME TO FOCUS ON MY TRUE INTERESTS — MY NATURAL HISTORY STUDIES AND GEOLOGY. I DON'T WANT TO BOAST, BUT EVEN I HAVE TO ADMIT THAT MY ASCENT IN THE PRUSSIAN MINISTRY OF MINES WAS RATHER RAPID. BY THE TIME I WAS TWENTY-TWO, I WAS ALREADY A MINING INSPECTOR. THE POSITION ALLOWED ME TO TRAVEL QUITE A BIT BECAUSE I HAD TO INVESTIGATE COAL IN BRANDENBURG, IRON IN SILESIA, GOLD IN THE FICHTEL MOUNTAINS AND SALT MINES IN POLAND. I CRAWLED INTO DEEP SHAFTS TO COLLECT ROCK SAMPLES, I INVENTED A LAMP THAT WORKED IN THE DEEPEST OXYGEN-POOR SHAFTS, A BREATHING MASK FOR MINERS AND EVEN OPENED A SCHOOL FOR THEM. BUT I STILL WASN'T HAPPY. ONLY WHEN MY MOTHER DIED EVERYTHING CHANGED. FINALLY I WAS FREE ... AND RICH. BUT MORE ABOUT THAT LATER ... I NEED TO GO ON DECK WHERE THE NIGHT SKY IS DEMANDING MY ATTENTION NOW.

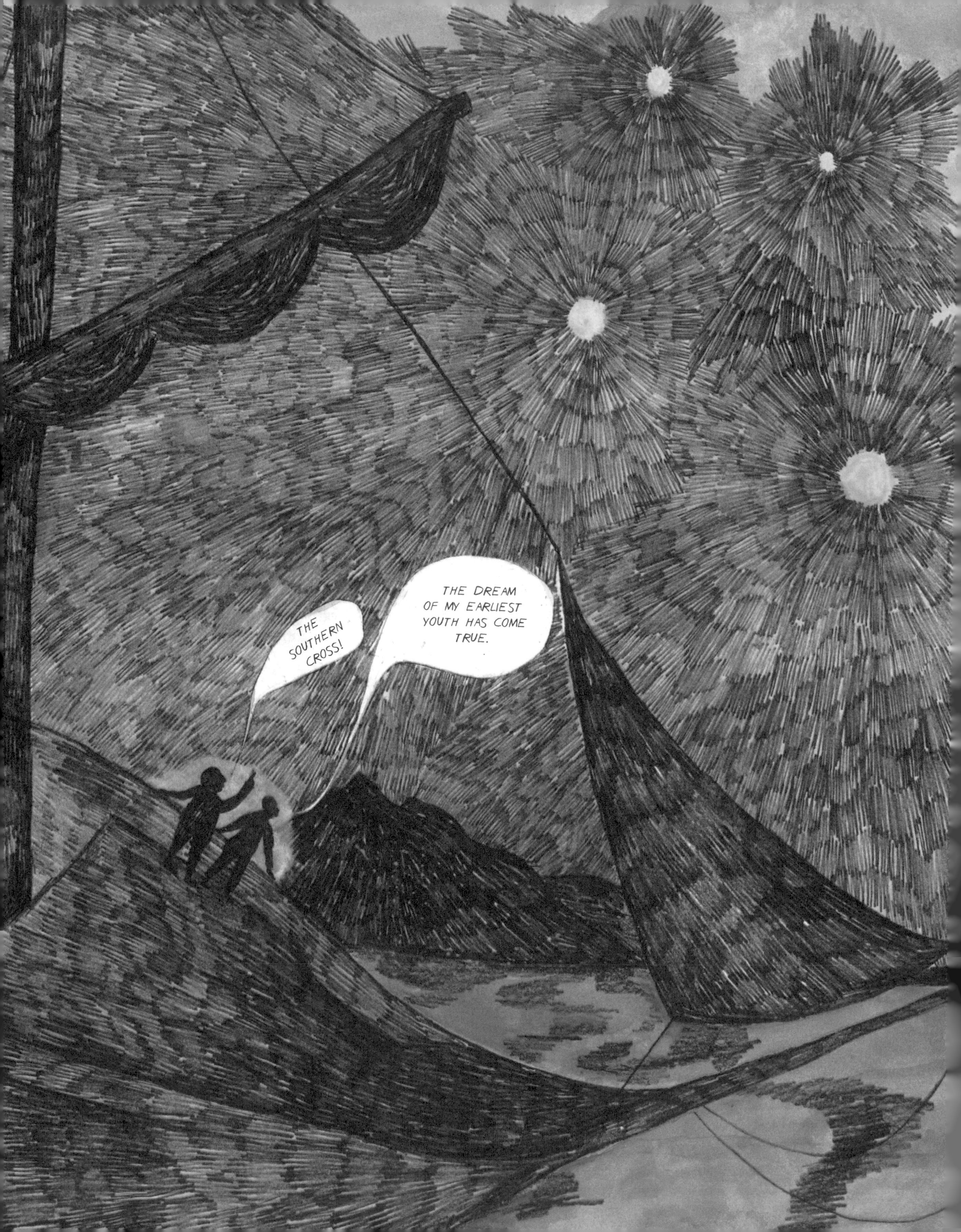
THE SOUTHERN CROSS!
THE DREAM OF MY EARLIEST YOUTH HAS COME TRUE.

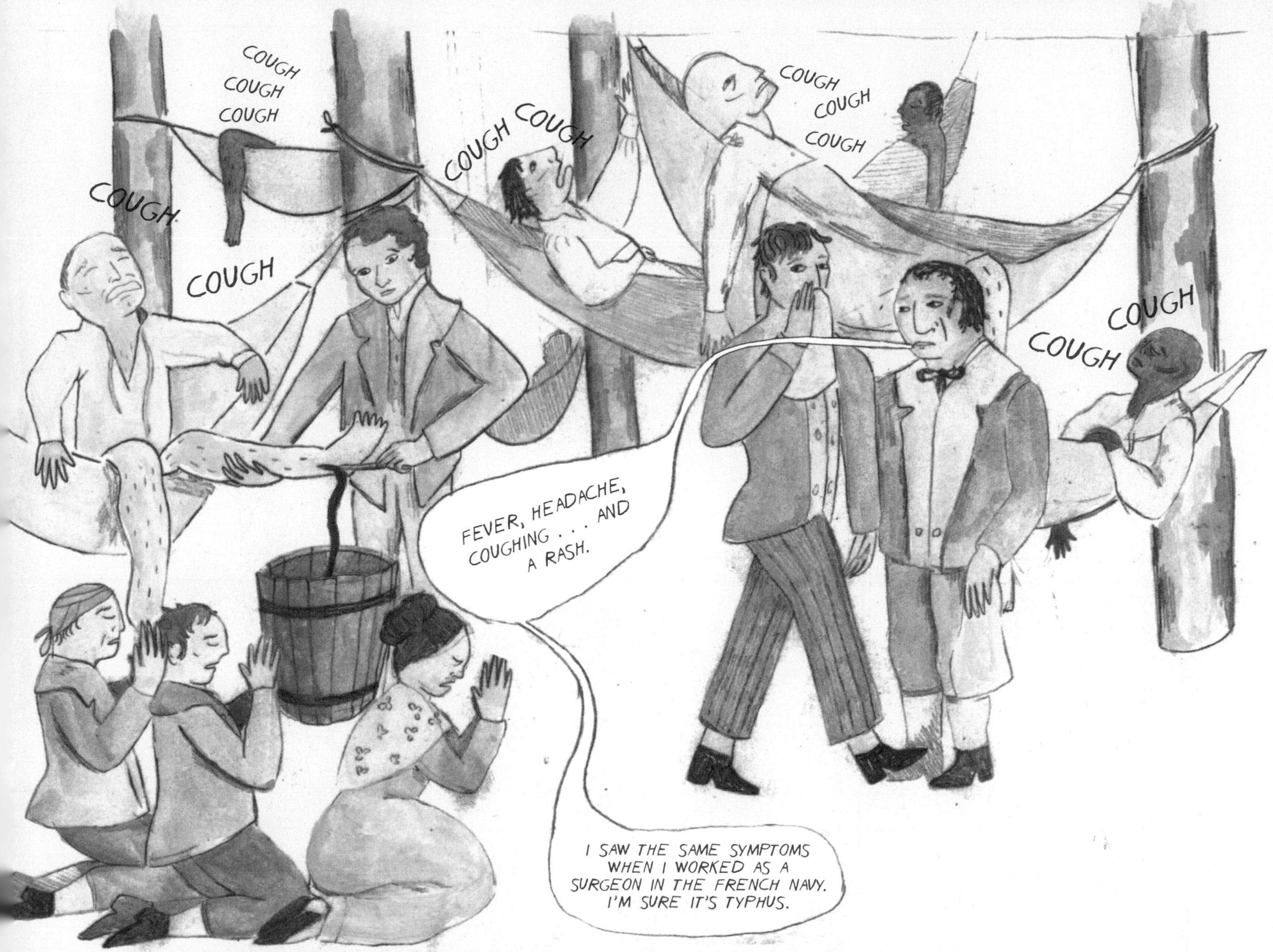
COUGH COUGH COUGH
COUGH
COUGH
COUGH COUGH
COUGH COUGH COUGH
COUGH COUGH
FEVER, HEADACHE, COUGHING . . . AND A RASH.
I SAW THE SAME SYMPTOMS WHEN I WORKED AS A SURGEON IN THE FRENCH NAVY. I'M SURE IT'S TYPHUS.

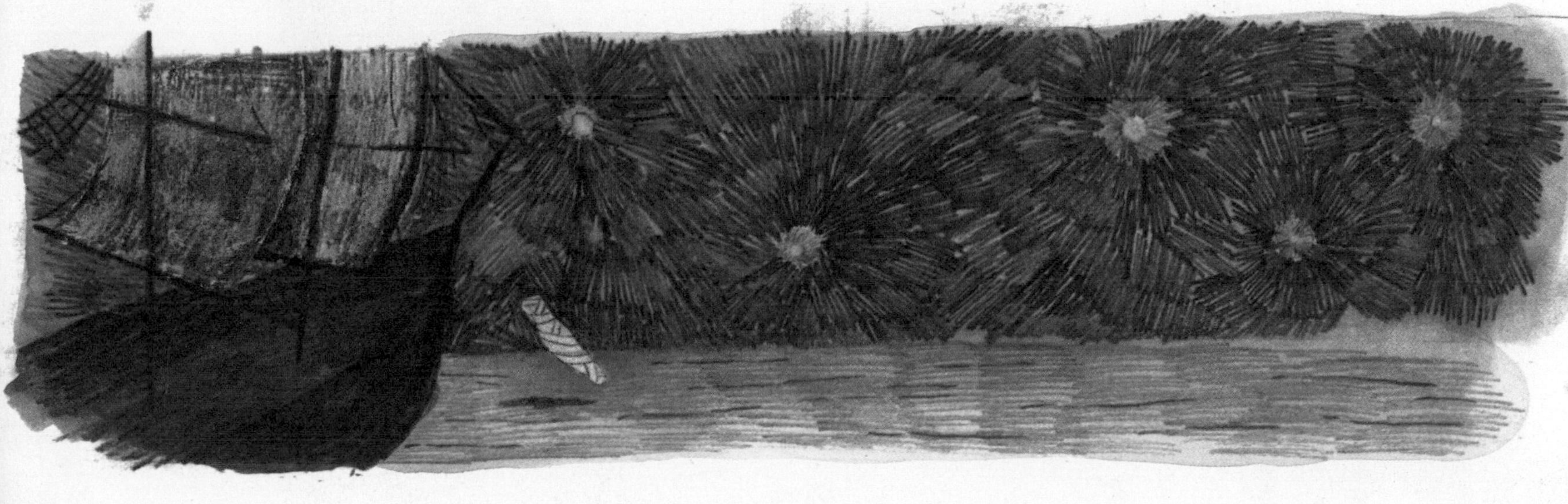

WHEN THE FIRST PASSENGER DIES, OUR CAPTAIN CHANGES COURSE AND SAILS TO THE NEAREST PORT – CUMANÁ IN THE CAPTAINCY GENERAL OF VENEZUELA. IT'S TIME TO BEGIN MY ADVENTURES.

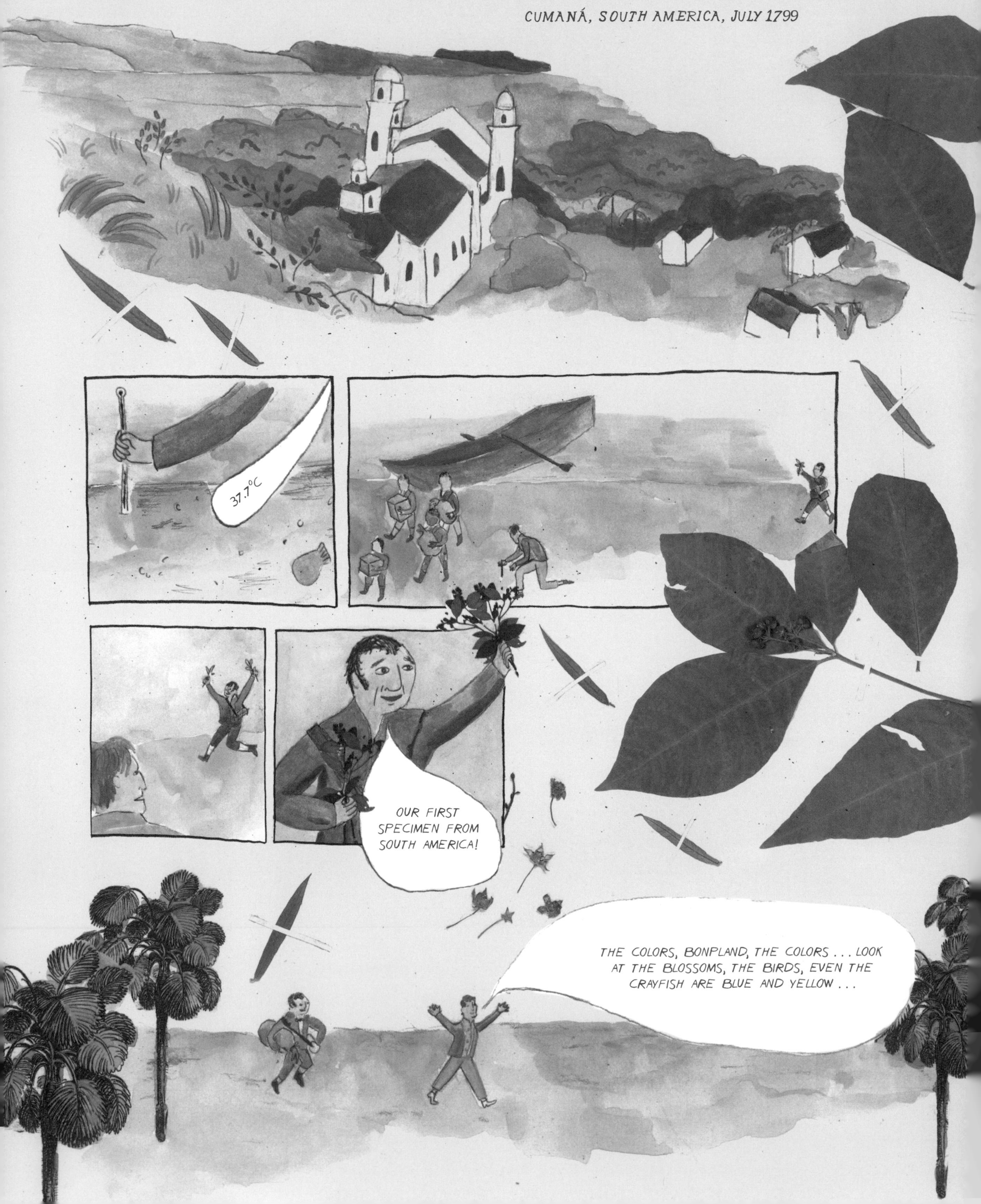
CUMANÁ, SOUTH AMERICA, JULY 1799
37.7°C
OUR FIRST SPECIMEN FROM SOUTH AMERICA!
THE COLORS, BONPLAND, THE COLORS . . . LOOK AT THE BLOSSOMS, THE BIRDS, EVEN THE CRAYFISH ARE BLUE AND YELLOW . . .

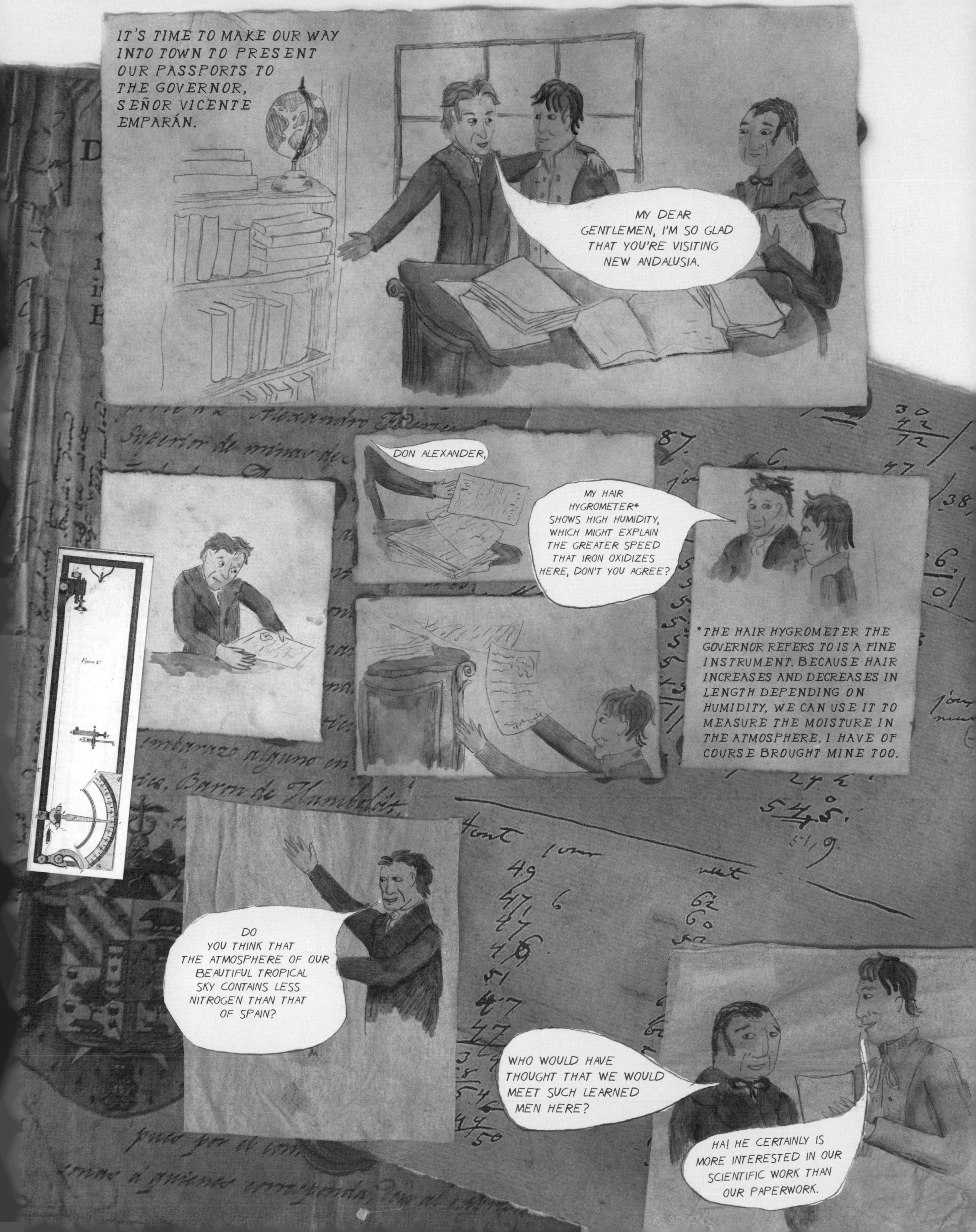
IT'S TIME TO MAKE OUR WAY INTO TOWN TO PRESENT OUR PASSPORTS TO THE GOVERNOR, SEÑOR VICENTE EMPARÁN.
MY DEAR GENTLEMEN, I'M SO GLAD THAT YOU'RE VISITING NEW ANDALUSIA.
DON ALEXANDER,
MY HAIR HYGROMETER* SHOWS HIGH HUMIDITY, WHICH MIGHT EXPLAIN THE GREATER SPEED THAT IRON OXIDIZES HERE, DON'T YOU AGREE?
*THE HAIR HYGROMETER THE GOVERNOR REFERS TO IS A FINE INSTRUMENT. BECAUSE HAIR INCREASES AND DECREASES IN LENGTH DEPENDING ON HUMIDITY, WE CAN USE IT TO MEASURE THE MOISTURE IN THE ATMOSPHERE. I HAVE OF COURSE BROUGHT MINE TOO.
DO YOU THINK THAT THE ATMOSPHERE OF OUR BEAUTIFUL TROPICAL SKY CONTAINS LESS NITROGEN THAN THAT OF SPAIN?
WHO WOULD HAVE THOUGHT THAT WE WOULD MEET SUCH LEARNED MEN HERE?
HA! HE CERTAINLY IS MORE INTERESTED IN OUR SCIENTIFIC WORK THAN OUR PAPERWORK.

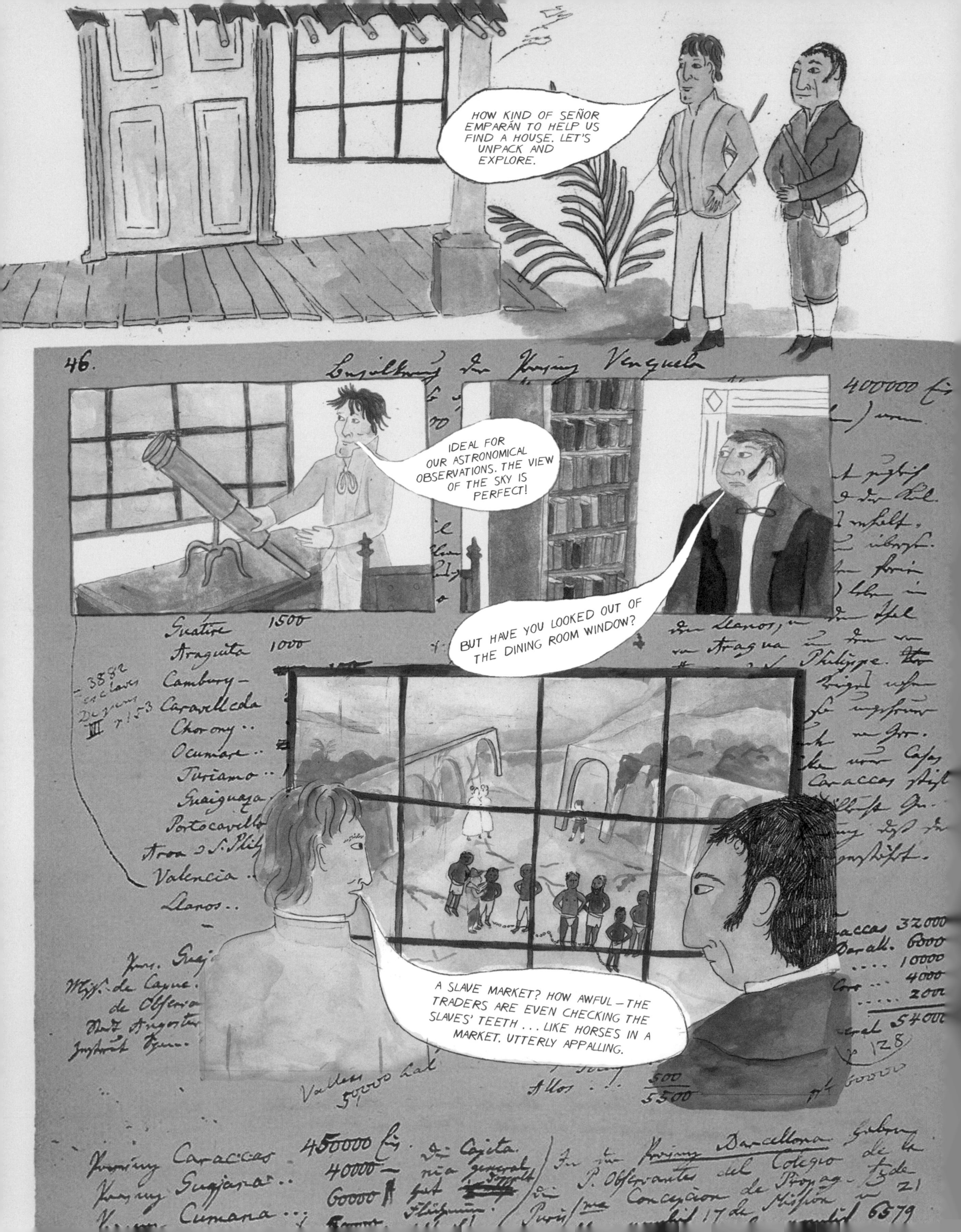
HOW KIND OF SEÑOR EMPARÁN TO HELP US FIND A HOUSE. LET'S UNPACK AND EXPLORE.
IDEAL FOR OUR ASTRONOMICAL OBSERVATIONS. THE VIEW OF THE SKY IS PERFECT!
BUT HAVE YOU LOOKED OUT OF THE DINING ROOM WINDOW?
A SLAVE MARKET? HOW AWFUL—THE TRADERS ARE EVEN CHECKING THE SLAVES' TEETH . . . LIKE HORSES IN A MARKET. UTTERLY APPALLING.

CUMANÁ WAS FOUNDED IN THE EARLY 16TH CENTURY AND IS ONE OF THE OLDEST EUROPEAN SETTLEMENTS IN SOUTH AMERICA. THE CITY IS PART OF THE VAST SPANISH EMPIRE THAT STRETCHES FROM CALIFORNIA ALL THE WAY TO THE SOUTHERN TIP OF CHILE. CUMANÁ BELONGS TO THE CAPTAINCY GENERAL OF VENEZUELA. ITS 15,000 INHABITANTS ARE MADE UP OF SPANIARDS, MESTIZOS, SLAVES, INDIANS AND CREOLES OR CRIOLLOS – WHITE COLONISTS OF SPANISH DESCENT BORN IN SOUTH AMERICA. SOME OF THE CRIOLLOS ARE VERY WEALTHY, BUT THEY ARE NONETHELESS EXCLUDED FROM THE HIGHEST ADMINISTRATIVE AND MILITARY POSITIONS. THE CITY WAS ALMOST DESTROYED BY AN EARTHQUAKE IN 1797, ONLY EIGHTEEN MONTHS BEFORE WE ARRIVE, AND WHEREVER WE LOOK, WE CAN STILL SEE HOUSES IN RUINS. I'LL TALK MORE ABOUT EARTHQUAKES LATER, BUT FOR NOW, LET ME JUST TELL YOU THAT BONPLAND AND I ARE OVERWHELMED BY THE NATURAL WORLD JUST OUTSIDE THE CITY.

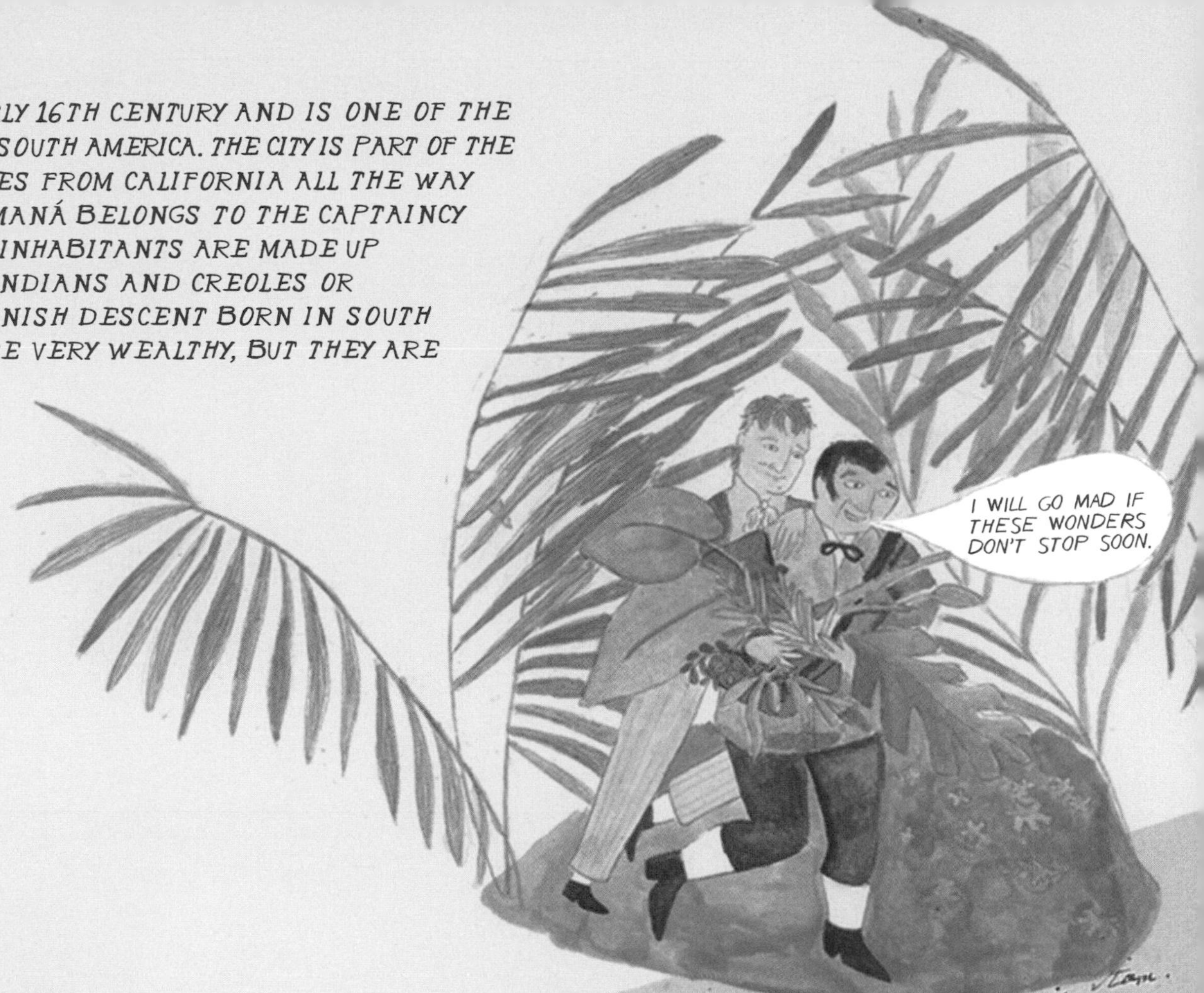
I WILL GO MAD IF THESE WONDERS DON'T STOP SOON.

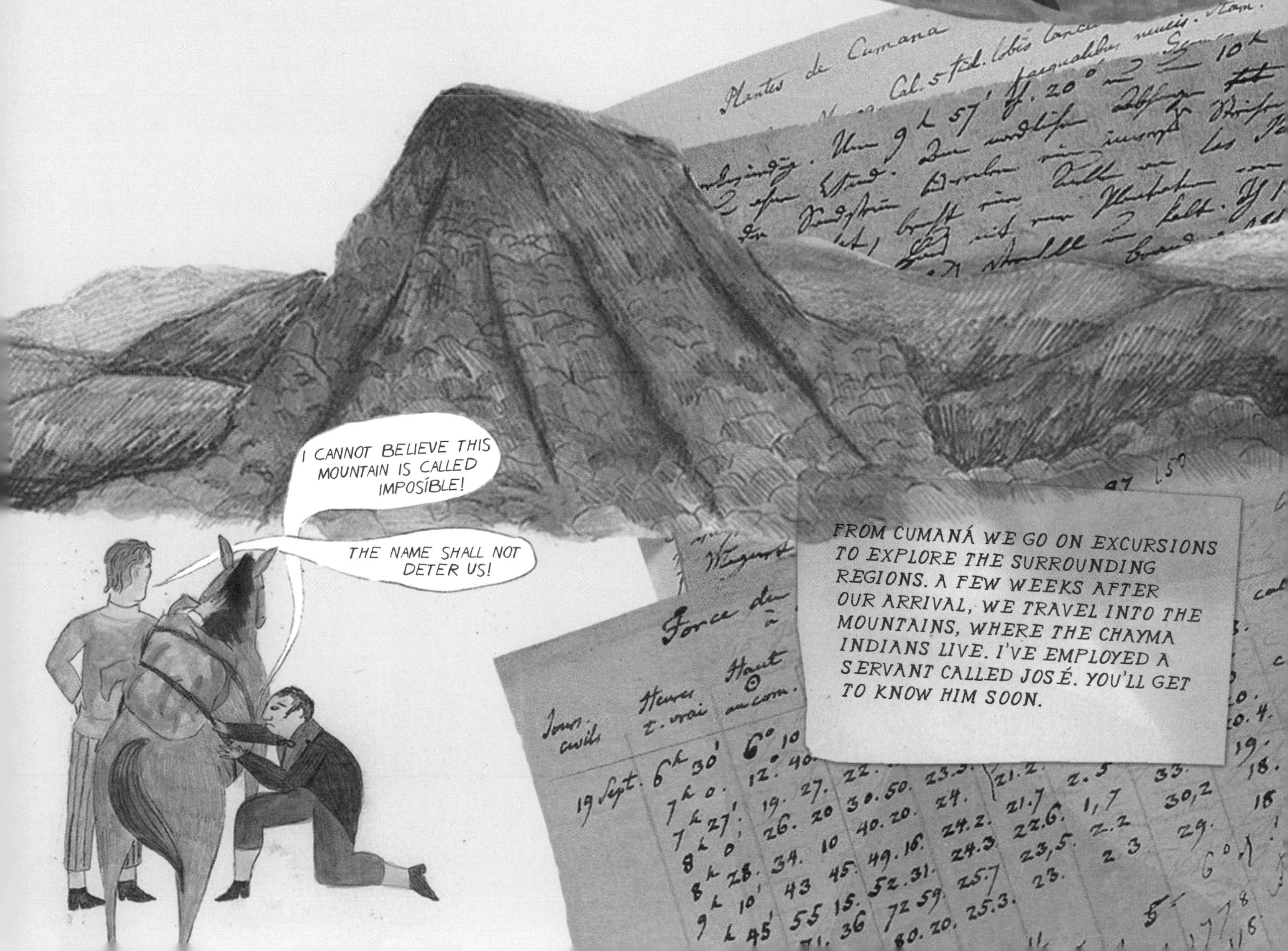
I CANNOT BELIEVE THIS MOUNTAIN IS CALLED IMPOSÍBLE!
THE NAME SHALL NOT DETER US!
FROM CUMANÁ WE GO ON EXCURSIONS TO EXPLORE THE SURROUNDING REGIONS. A FEW WEEKS AFTER OUR ARRIVAL, WE TRAVEL INTO THE MOUNTAINS, WHERE THE CHAYMA INDIANS LIVE. I'VE EMPLOYED A SERVANT CALLED JOSÉ. YOU'LL GET TO KNOW HIM SOON.
Plantes de Cumana

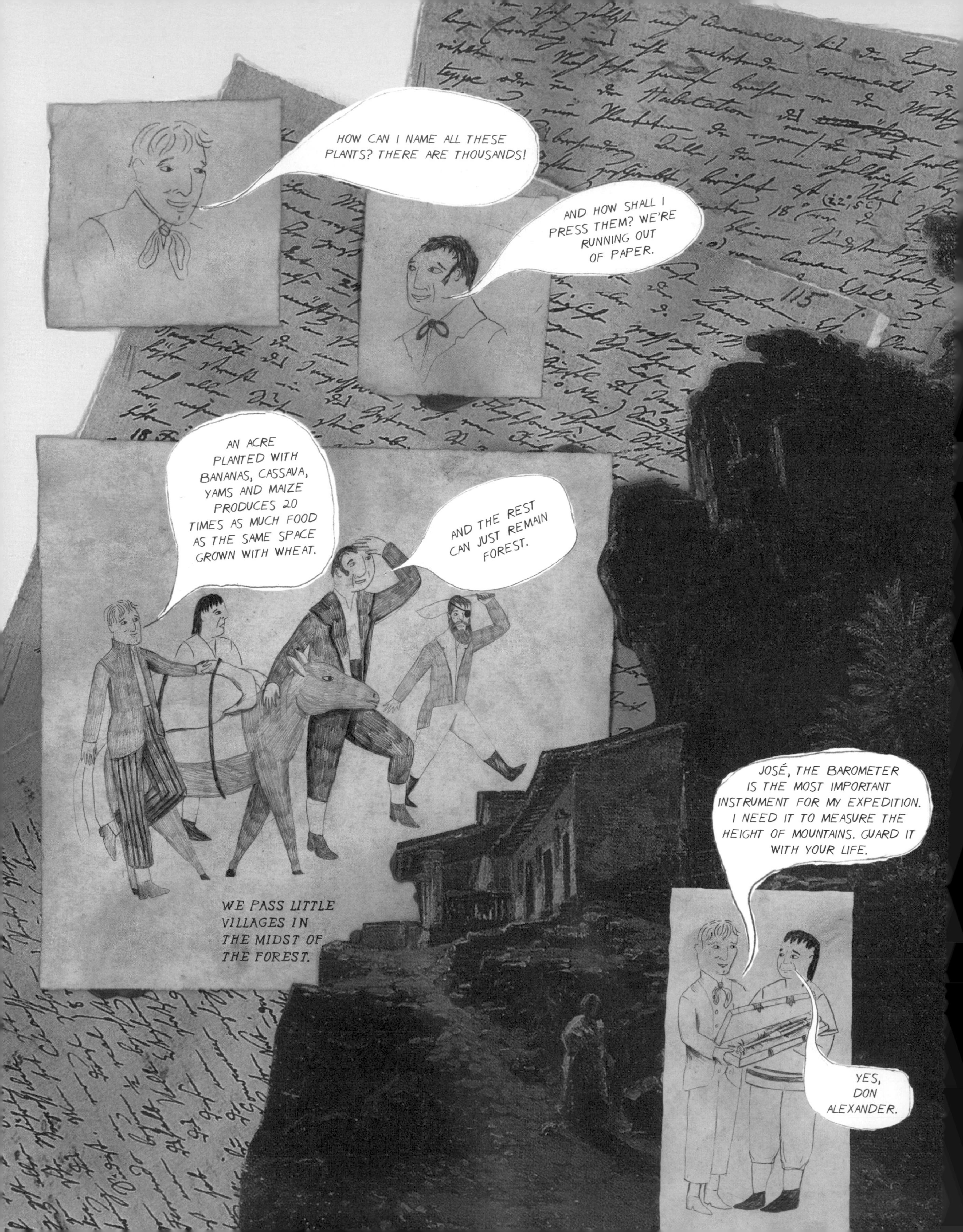
HOW CAN I NAME ALL THESE PLANTS? THERE ARE THOUSANDS!
AND HOW SHALL I PRESS THEM? WE'RE RUNNING OUT OF PAPER.
AN ACRE PLANTED WITH BANANAS, CASSAVA, YAMS AND MAIZE PRODUCES 20 TIMES AS MUCH FOOD AS THE SAME SPACE GROWN WITH WHEAT.
AND THE REST CAN JUST REMAIN FOREST.
WE PASS LITTLE VILLAGES IN THE MIDST OF THE FOREST.
JOSÉ, THE BAROMETER IS THE MOST IMPORTANT INSTRUMENT FOR MY EXPEDITION. I NEED IT TO MEASURE THE HEIGHT OF MOUNTAINS. GUARD IT WITH YOUR LIFE.
YES, DON ALEXANDER.

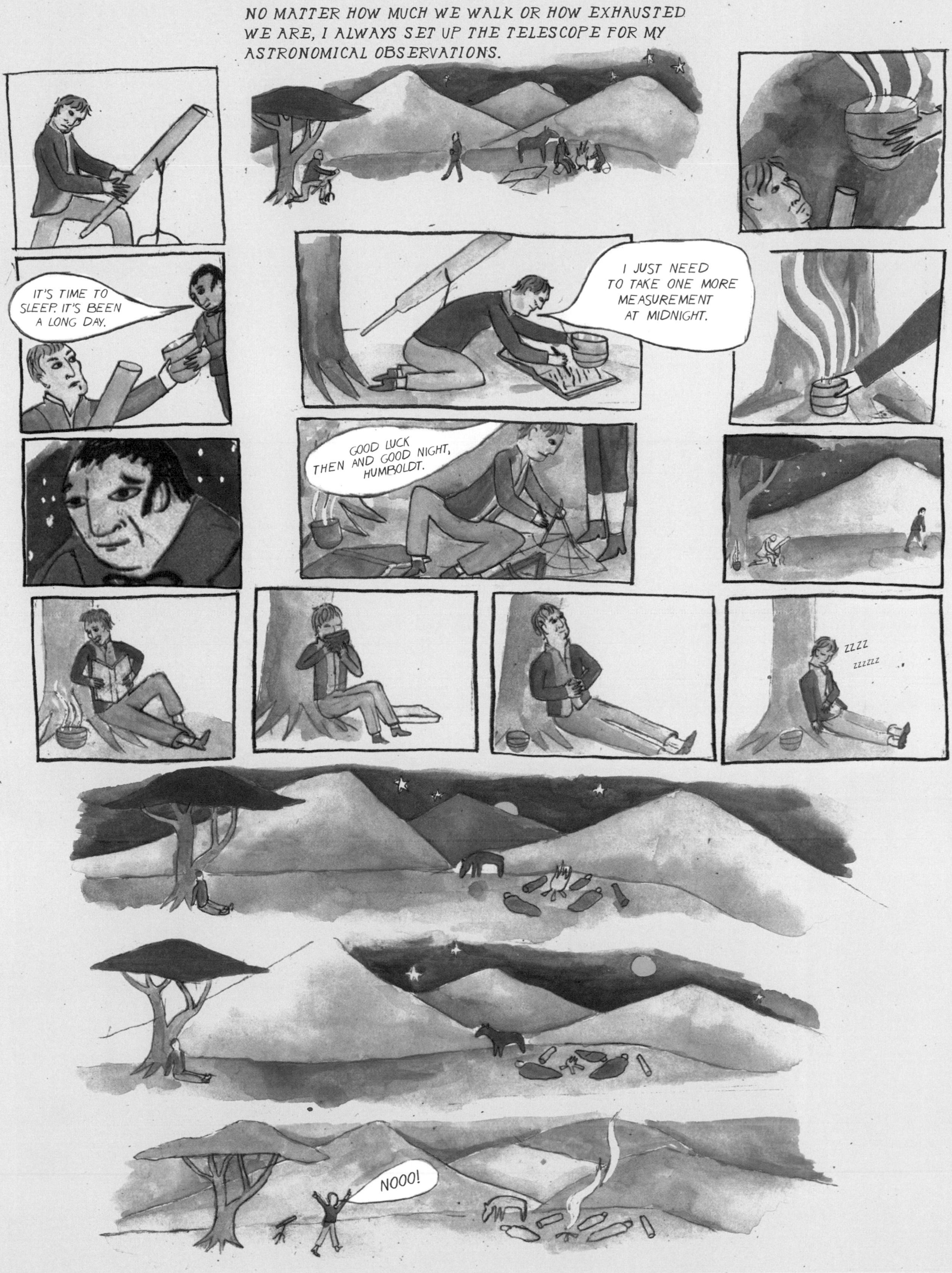
NO MATTER HOW MUCH WE WALK OR HOW EXHAUSTED WE ARE, I ALWAYS SET UP THE TELESCOPE FOR MY ASTRONOMICAL OBSERVATIONS.
IT'S TIME TO SLEEP. IT'S BEEN A LONG DAY.
I JUST NEED TO TAKE ONE MORE MEASUREMENT AT MIDNIGHT.
GOOD LUCK THEN AND GOOD NIGHT, HUMBOLDT.
ZZZZ
ZZZZZ
NOOO!

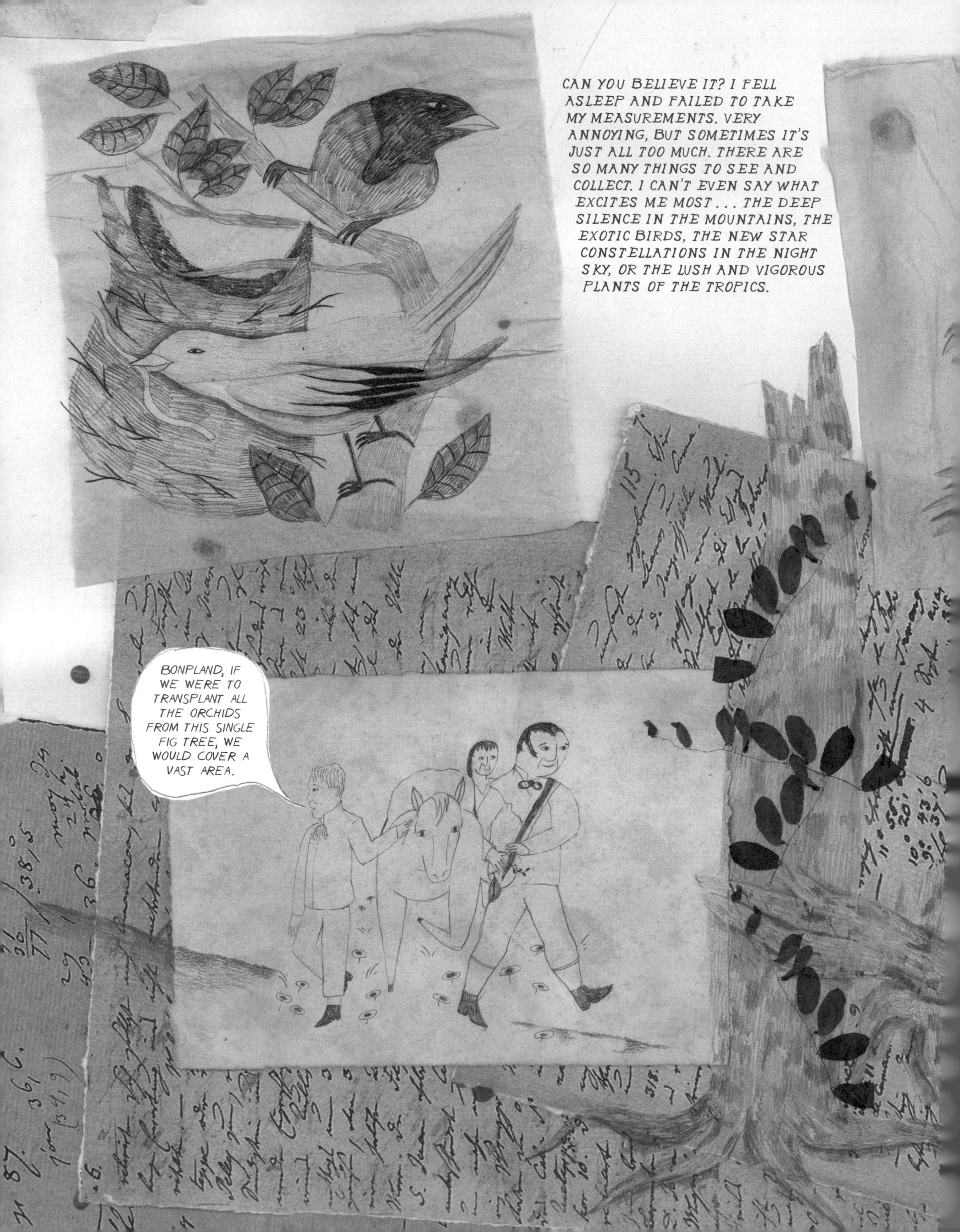
CAN YOU BELIEVE IT? I FELL ASLEEP AND FAILED TO TAKE MY MEASUREMENTS. VERY ANNOYING, BUT SOMETIMES IT'S JUST ALL TOO MUCH. THERE ARE SO MANY THINGS TO SEE AND COLLECT. I CAN'T EVEN SAY WHAT EXCITES ME MOST . . . THE DEEP SILENCE IN THE MOUNTAINS, THE EXOTIC BIRDS, THE NEW STAR CONSTELLATIONS IN THE NIGHT SKY, OR THE LUSH AND VIGOROUS PLANTS OF THE TROPICS.
BONPLAND, IF WE WERE TO TRANSPLANT ALL THE ORCHIDS FROM THIS SINGLE FIG TREE, WE WOULD COVER A VAST AREA.

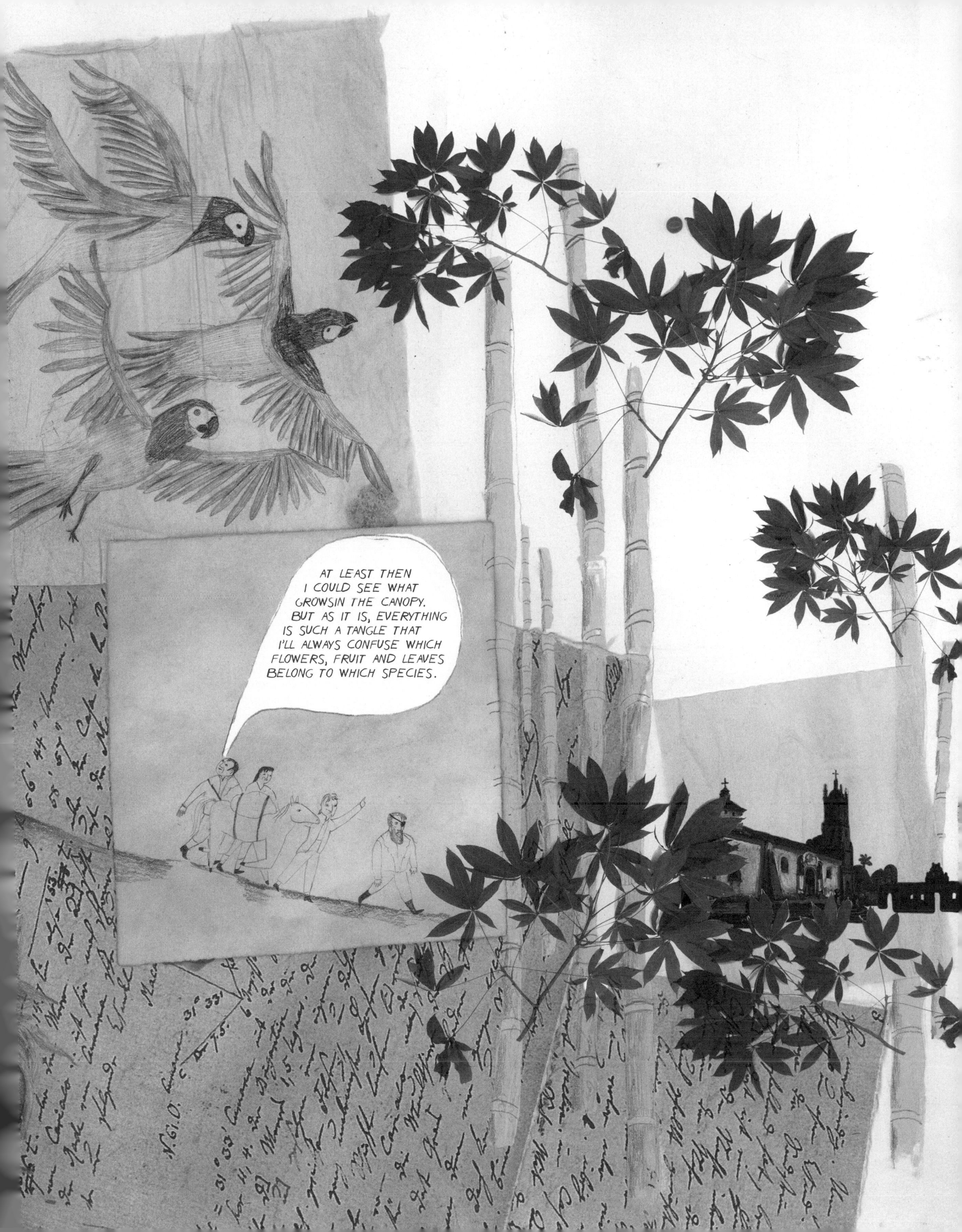
AT LEAST THEN I COULD SEE WHAT GROWSIN THE CANOPY. BUT AS IT IS, EVERYTHING IS SUCH A TANGLE THAT I'LL ALWAYS CONFUSE WHICH FLOWERS, FRUIT AND LEAVES BELONG TO WHICH SPECIES.

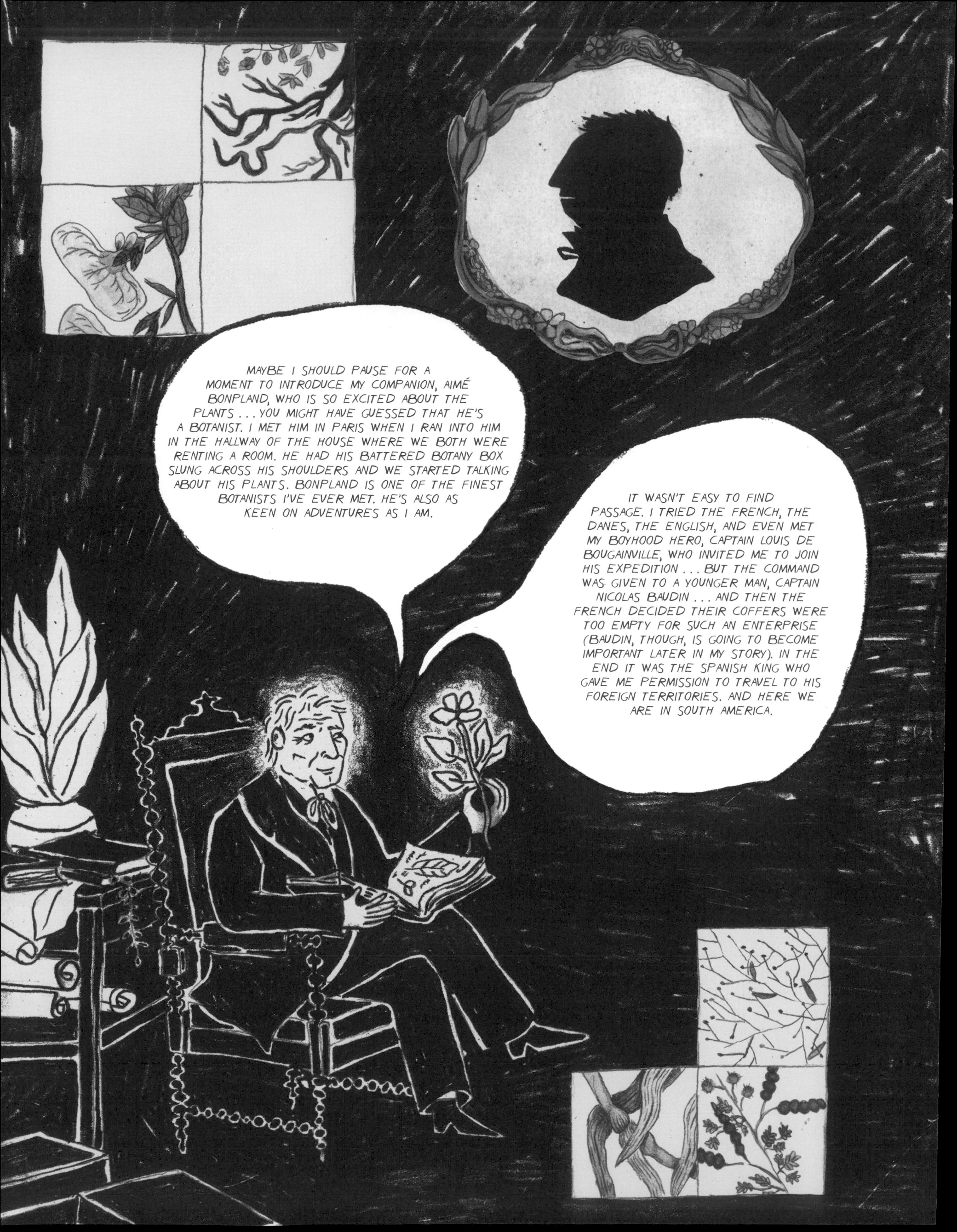
MAYBE I SHOULD PAUSE FOR A MOMENT TO INTRODUCE MY COMPANION, AIMÉ BONPLAND, WHO IS SO EXCITED ABOUT THE PLANTS . . . YOU MIGHT HAVE GUESSED THAT HE'S A BOTANIST. I MET HIM IN PARIS WHEN I RAN INTO HIM IN THE HALLWAY OF THE HOUSE WHERE WE BOTH WERE RENTING A ROOM. HE HAD HIS BATTERED BOTANY BOX SLUNG ACROSS HIS SHOULDERS AND WE STARTED TALKING ABOUT HIS PLANTS. BONPLAND IS ONE OF THE FINEST BOTANISTS I'VE EVER MET. HE'S ALSO AS KEEN ON ADVENTURES AS I AM.
IT WASN'T EASY TO FIND PASSAGE. I TRIED THE FRENCH, THE DANES, THE ENGLISH, AND EVEN MET MY BOYHOOD HERO, CAPTAIN LOUIS DE BOUGAINVILLE, WHO INVITED ME TO JOIN HIS EXPEDITION . . . BUT THE COMMAND WAS GIVEN TO A YOUNGER MAN, CAPTAIN NICOLAS BAUDIN . . . AND THEN THE FRENCH DECIDED THEIR COFFERS WERE TOO EMPTY FOR SUCH AN ENTERPRISE (BAUDIN, THOUGH, IS GOING TO BECOME IMPORTANT LATER IN MY STORY). IN THE END IT WAS THE SPANISH KING WHO GAVE ME PERMISSION TO TRAVEL TO HIS FOREIGN TERRITORIES. AND HERE WE ARE IN SOUTH AMERICA.

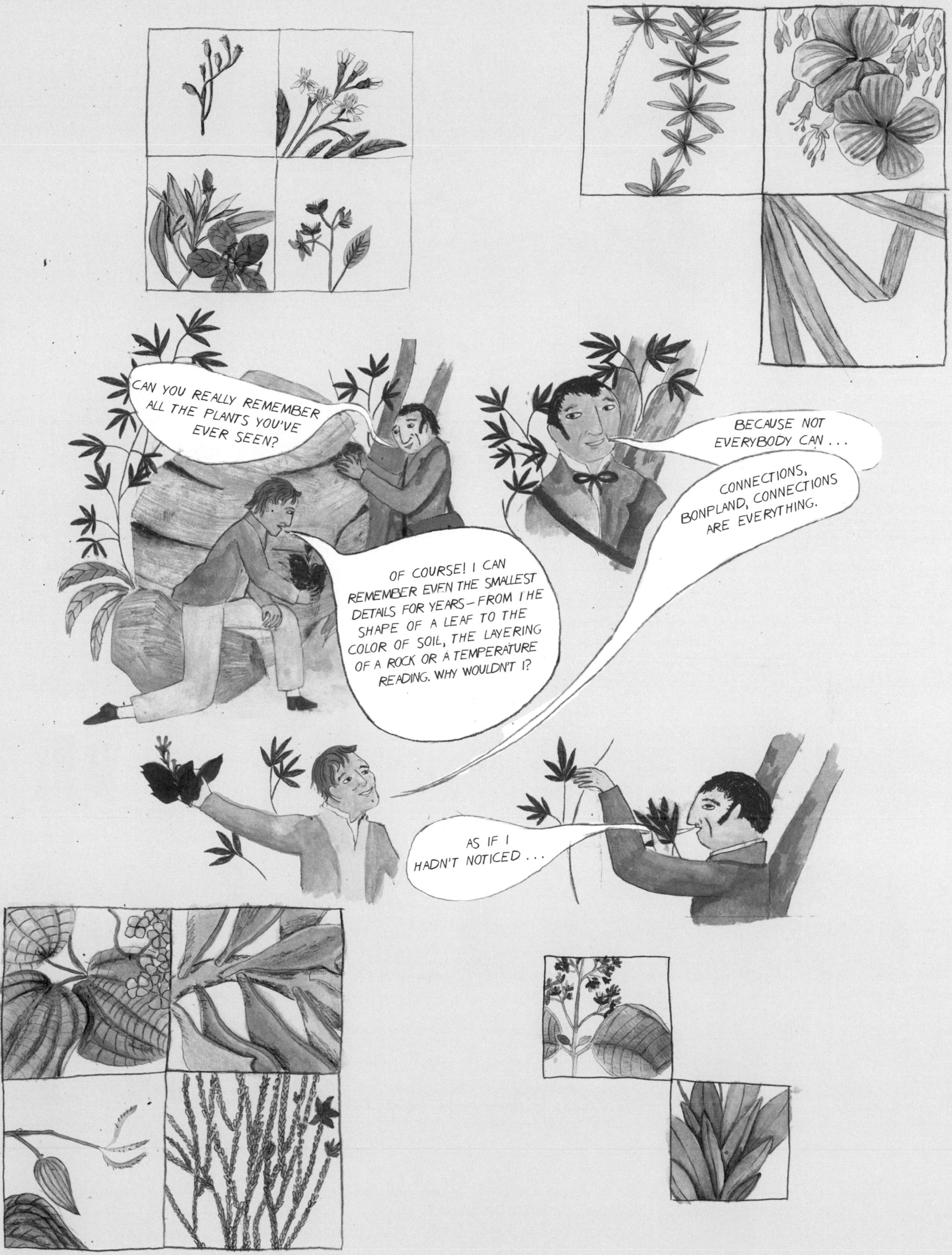
CAN YOU REALLY REMEMBER ALL THE PLANTS YOU'VE EVER SEEN?
OF COURSE! I CAN REMEMBER EVEN THE SMALLEST DETAILS FOR YEARS—FROM THE SHAPE OF A LEAF TO THE COLOR OF SOIL, THE LAYERING OF A ROCK OR A TEMPERATURE READING. WHY WOULDN'T I?
BECAUSE NOT EVERYBODY CAN . . .
CONNECTIONS, BONPLAND, CONNECTIONS ARE EVERYTHING.
AS IF I HADN'T NOTICED . . .

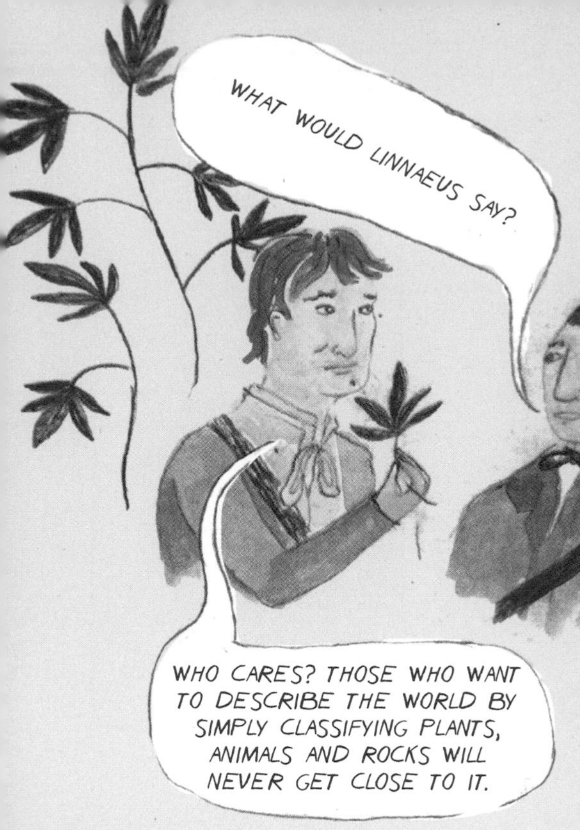
WHAT WOULD LINNAEUS SAY?
WHO CARES? THOSE WHO WANT TO DESCRIBE THE WORLD BY SIMPLY CLASSIFYING PLANTS, ANIMALS AND ROCKS WILL NEVER GET CLOSE TO IT.

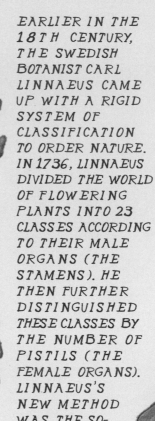

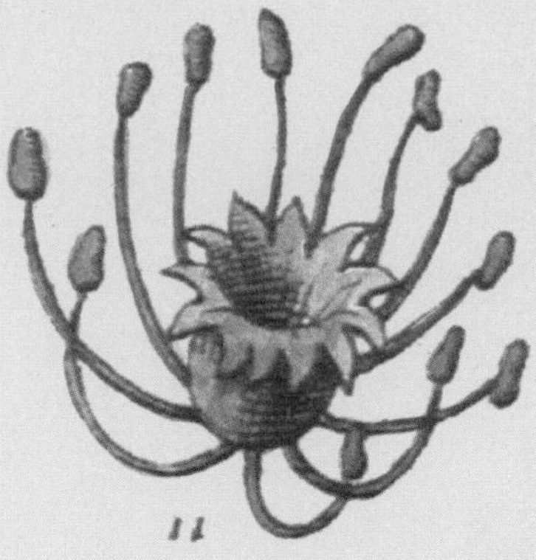
11

EARLIER IN THE 18TH CENTURY, THE SWEDISH BOTANIST CARL LINNAEUS CAME UP WITH A RIGID SYSTEM OF CLASSIFICATION TO ORDER NATURE. IN 1736, LINNAEUS DIVIDED THE WORLD OF FLOWERING PLANTS INTO 23 CLASSES ACCORDING TO THEIR MALE ORGANS (THE STAMENS). HE THEN FURTHER DISTINGUISHED THESE CLASSES BY THE NUMBER OF PISTILS (THE FEMALE ORGANS). LINNAEUS'S NEW METHOD WAS THE SO-CALLED "SEXUAL SYSTEM."

THERE ARE OTHER SYSTEMS BASED ON THE SHAPE OF LEAVES, FRUITS AND BLOSSOMS, FOR EXAMPLE. DON'T GET ME WRONG, TAXONOMY IS CERTAINLY IMPORTANT WHEN IT COMES TO SORTING PLANT SPECIMENS, BUT I HAVE OTHER AND BIGGER IDEAS.

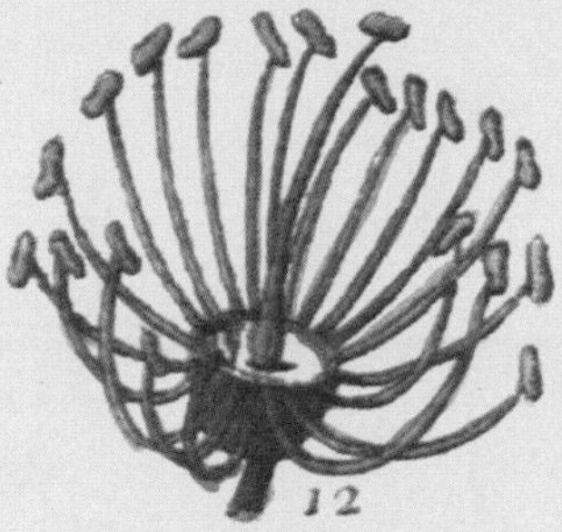
12

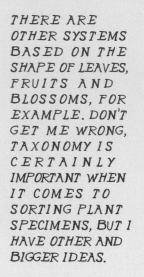

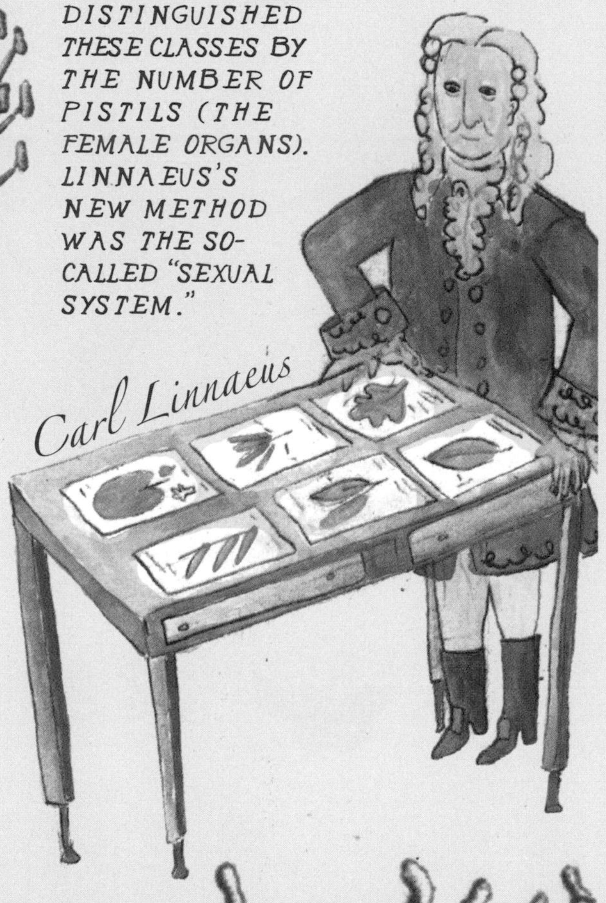
Carl Linnaeus

I TRAVELED THE WORLD FROM EUROPE TO SOUTH AMERICA AND LATER EVEN TO THE ALTAI MOUNTAINS IN RUSSIA IN PURSUIT OF THESE CONNECTIONS. IN THE ANDES I SAW A MOSS THAT REMINDED ME OF A SPECIES FROM THE FORESTS IN NORTHERN GERMANY. ON THE MOUNTAINS NEAR CARACAS I EXAMINED RHODODENDRON-LIKE PLANTS—ALPINE ROSE TREES, I LIKE TO CALL THEM—WHICH ARE LIKE THOSE FROM THE SWISS ALPS. IN MEXICO, I FOUND PINES, CYPRESSES AND OAKS SIMILAR TO THOSE THAT GROW IN CANADA. THIS MIGHT NOT SOUND ALL THAT REVOLUTIONARY, BUT IT WAS AT THE TIME. NO ONE ELSE WAS DISCUSSING GLOBAL VEGETATION AND CLIMATE ZONES.

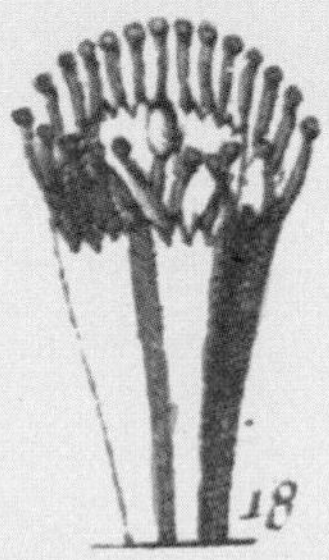
18

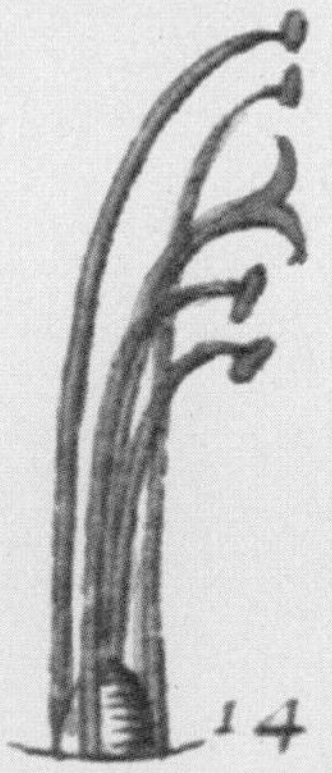
14

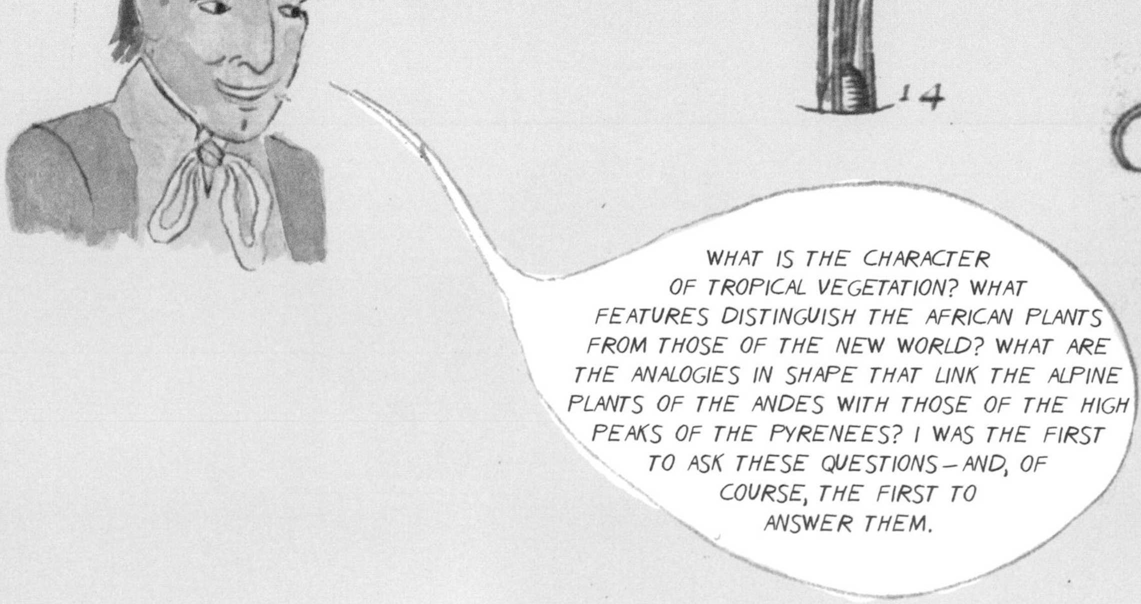
WHAT IS THE CHARACTER OF TROPICAL VEGETATION? WHAT FEATURES DISTINGUISH THE AFRICAN PLANTS FROM THOSE OF THE NEW WORLD? WHAT ARE THE ANALOGIES IN SHAPE THAT LINK THE ALPINE PLANTS OF THE ANDES WITH THOSE OF THE HIGH PEAKS OF THE PYRENEES? I WAS THE FIRST TO ASK THESE QUESTIONS—AND, OF COURSE, THE FIRST TO ANSWER THEM.

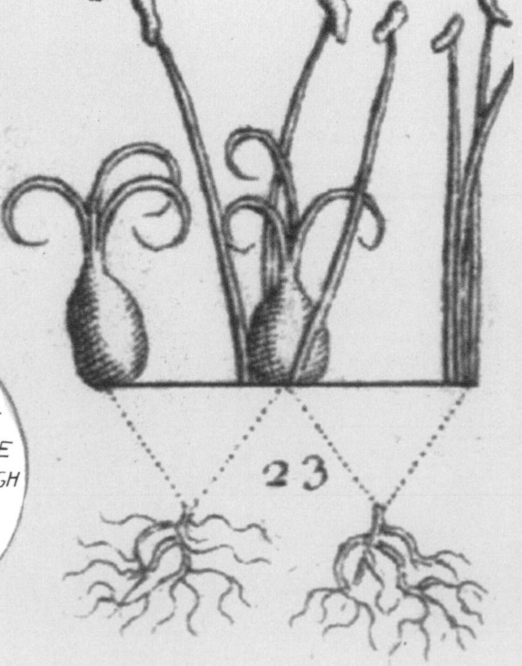
23

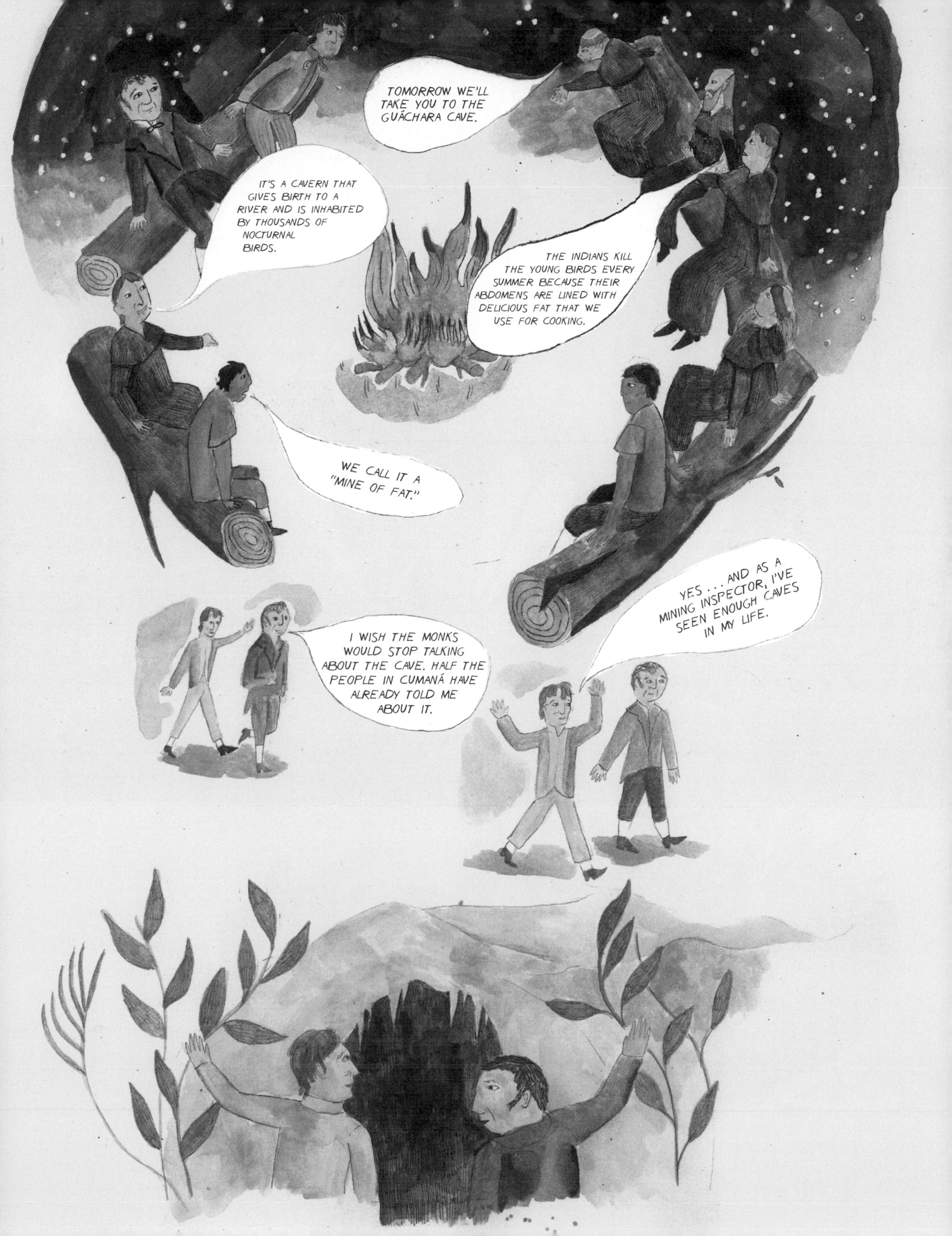
TOMORROW WE'LL TAKE YOU TO THE GUÁCHARA CAVE.
IT'S A CAVERN THAT GIVES BIRTH TO A RIVER AND IS INHABITED BY THOUSANDS OF NOCTURNAL BIRDS.
THE INDIANS KILL THE YOUNG BIRDS EVERY SUMMER BECAUSE THEIR ABDOMENS ARE LINED WITH DELICIOUS FAT THAT WE USE FOR COOKING.
WE CALL IT A "MINE OF FAT."
I WISH THE MONKS WOULD STOP TALKING ABOUT THE CAVE. HALF THE PEOPLE IN CUMANÁ HAVE ALREADY TOLD ME ABOUT IT.
YES . . . AND AS A MINING INSPECTOR, I'VE SEEN ENOUGH CAVES IN MY LIFE.

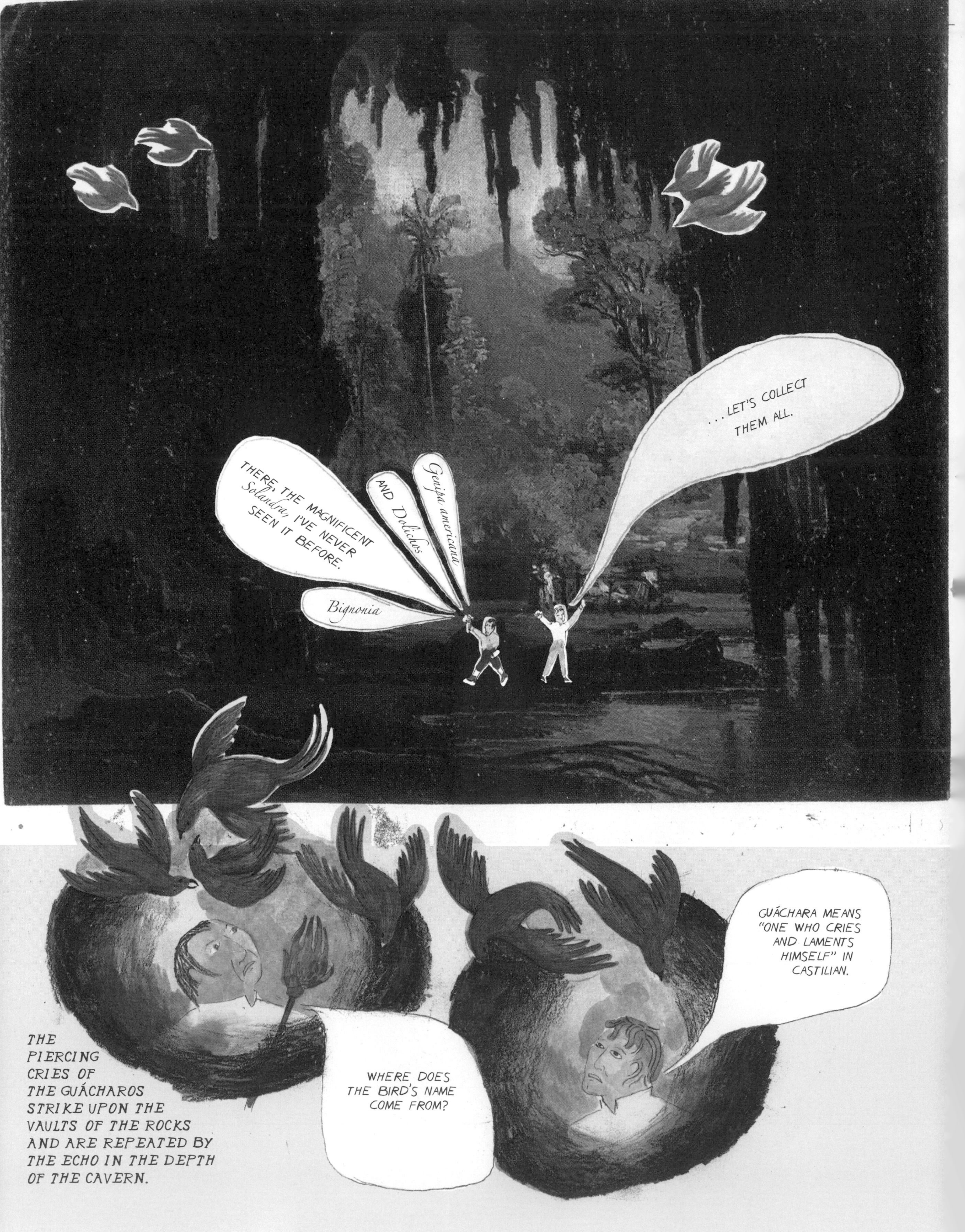
THERE THE MAGNIFICENT Solandra, I'VE NEVER SEEN IT BEFORE.
AND Dolichos
Genipa americana
Bignonia
. . . LET'S COLLECT THEM ALL.
THE PIERCING CRIES OF THE GUÁCHAROS STRIKE UPON THE VAULTS OF THE ROCKS AND ARE REPEATED BY THE ECHO IN THE DEPTH OF THE CAVERN.
WHERE DOES THE BIRD'S NAME COME FROM?
GUÁCHARA MEANS "ONE WHO CRIES AND LAMENTS HIMSELF" IN CASTILIAN.

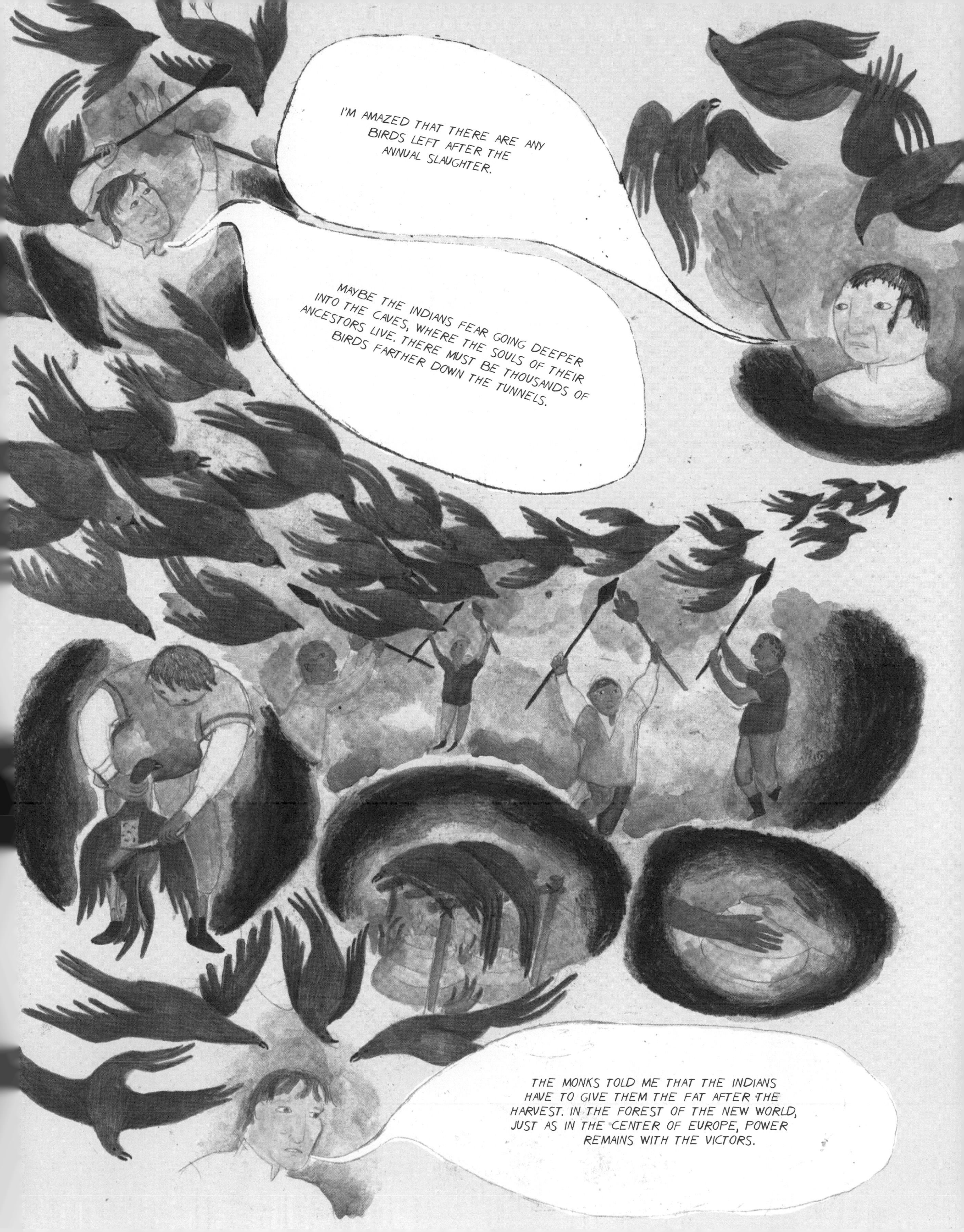
I'M AMAZED THAT THERE ARE ANY BIRDS LEFT AFTER THE ANNUAL SLAUGHTER.
MAYBE THE INDIANS FEAR GOING DEEPER INTO THE CAVES, WHERE THE SOULS OF THEIR ANCESTORS LIVE. THERE MUST BE THOUSANDS OF BIRDS FARTHER DOWN THE TUNNELS.
THE MONKS TOLD ME THAT THE INDIANS HAVE TO GIVE THEM THE FAT AFTER THE HARVEST. IN THE FOREST OF THE NEW WORLD, JUST AS IN THE CENTER OF EUROPE, POWER REMAINS WITH THE VICTORS.

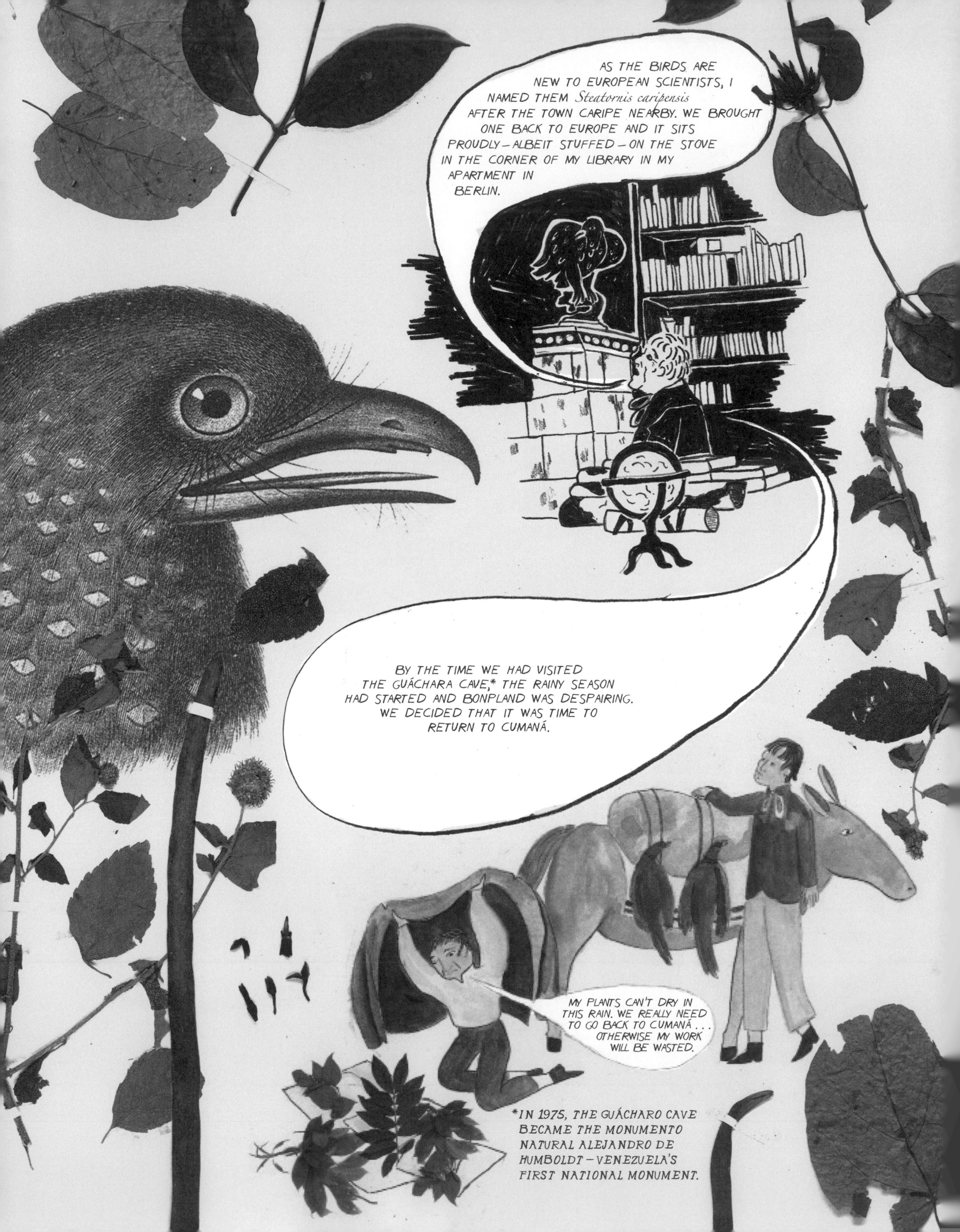
AS THE BIRDS ARE NEW TO EUROPEAN SCIENTISTS, I NAMED THEM *Steatornis caripensis* AFTER THE TOWN CARIPE NEARBY. WE BROUGHT ONE BACK TO EUROPE AND IT SITS PROUDLY—ALBEIT STUFFED—ON THE STOVE IN THE CORNER OF MY LIBRARY IN MY APARTMENT IN BERLIN.
BY THE TIME WE HAD VISITED THE GUÁCHARA CAVE,* THE RAINY SEASON HAD STARTED AND BONPLAND WAS DESPAIRING. WE DECIDED THAT IT WAS TIME TO RETURN TO CUMANÁ.
MY PLANTS CAN'T DRY IN THIS RAIN. WE REALLY NEED TO GO BACK TO CUMANÁ . . . OTHERWISE MY WORK WILL BE WASTED.
*IN 1975, THE GUÁCHARO CAVE BECAME THE MONUMENTO NATURAL ALEJANDRO DE HUMBOLDT—VENEZUELA'S FIRST NATIONAL MONUMENT.

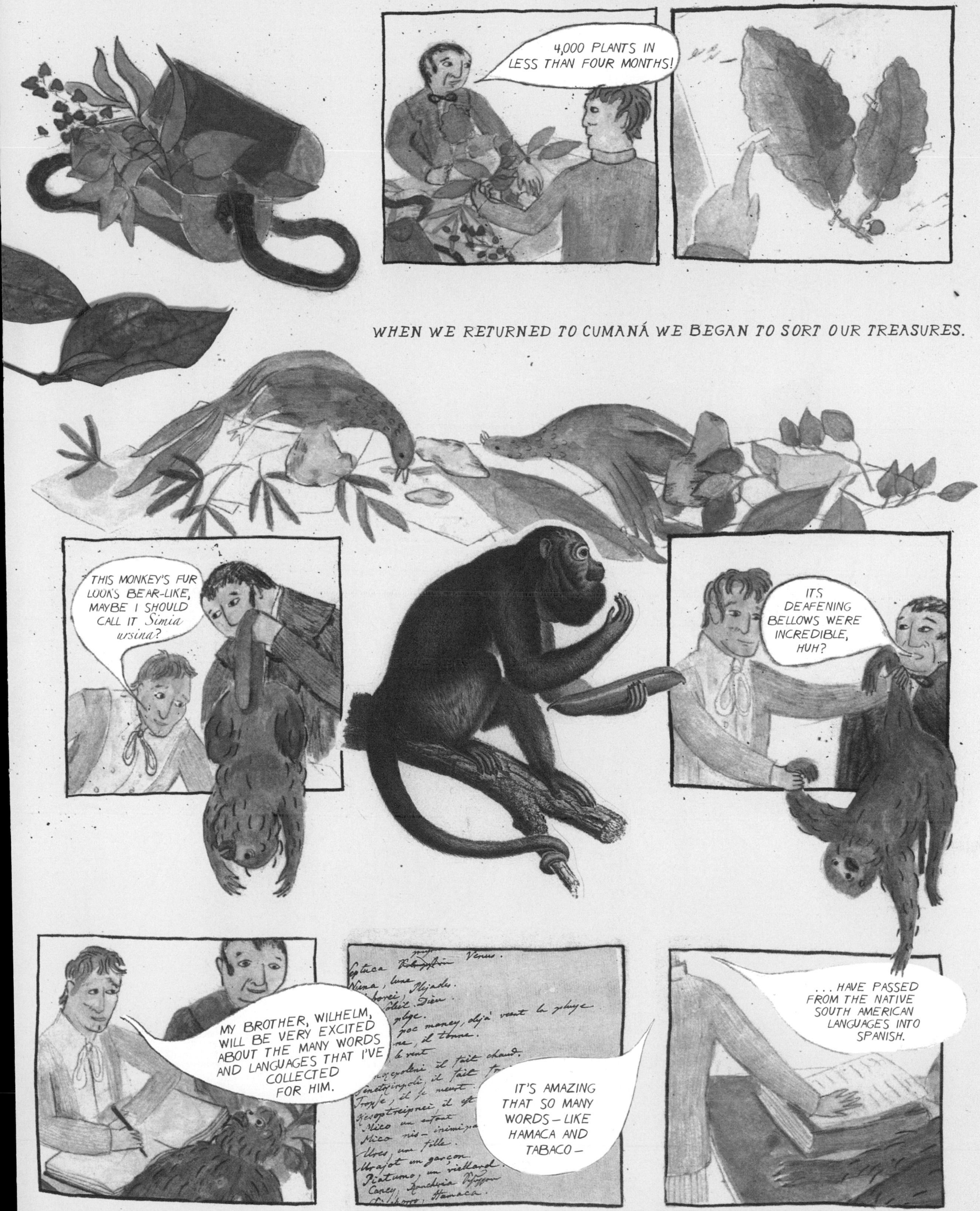
4,000 PLANTS IN LESS THAN FOUR MONTHS!
WHEN WE RETURNED TO CUMANÁ WE BEGAN TO SORT OUR TREASURES.
THIS MONKEY'S FUR LOOKS BEAR-LIKE, MAYBE I SHOULD CALL IT *Simia ursina*?
ITS DEAFENING BELLOWS WERE INCREDIBLE, HUH?
MY BROTHER, WILHELM, WILL BE VERY EXCITED ABOUT THE MANY WORDS AND LANGUAGES THAT I'VE COLLECTED FOR HIM.
IT'S AMAZING THAT SO MANY WORDS—LIKE HAMACA AND TABACO—
...HAVE PASSED FROM THE NATIVE SOUTH AMERICAN LANGUAGES INTO SPANISH.

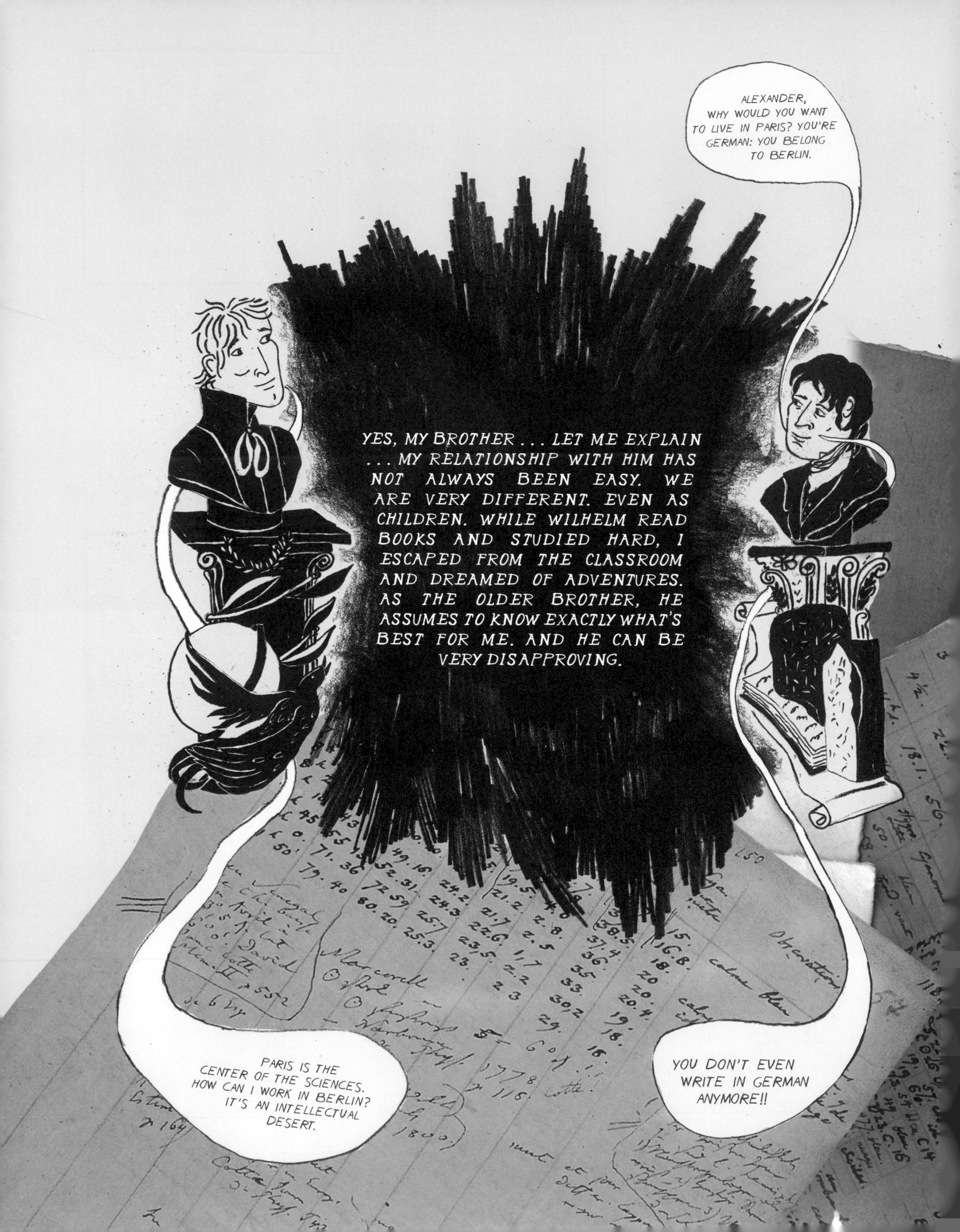
YES, MY BROTHER . . . LET ME EXPLAIN . . . MY RELATIONSHIP WITH HIM HAS NOT ALWAYS BEEN EASY. WE ARE VERY DIFFERENT. EVEN AS CHILDREN. WHILE WILHELM READ BOOKS AND STUDIED HARD, I ESCAPED FROM THE CLASSROOM AND DREAMED OF ADVENTURES. AS THE OLDER BROTHER, HE ASSUMES TO KNOW EXACTLY WHAT'S BEST FOR ME. AND HE CAN BE VERY DISAPPROVING.
ALEXANDER, WHY WOULD YOU WANT TO LIVE IN PARIS? YOU'RE GERMAN: YOU BELONG TO BERLIN.
PARIS IS THE CENTER OF THE SCIENCES. HOW CAN I WORK IN BERLIN? IT'S AN INTELLECTUAL DESERT.
YOU DON'T EVEN WRITE IN GERMAN ANYMORE!!

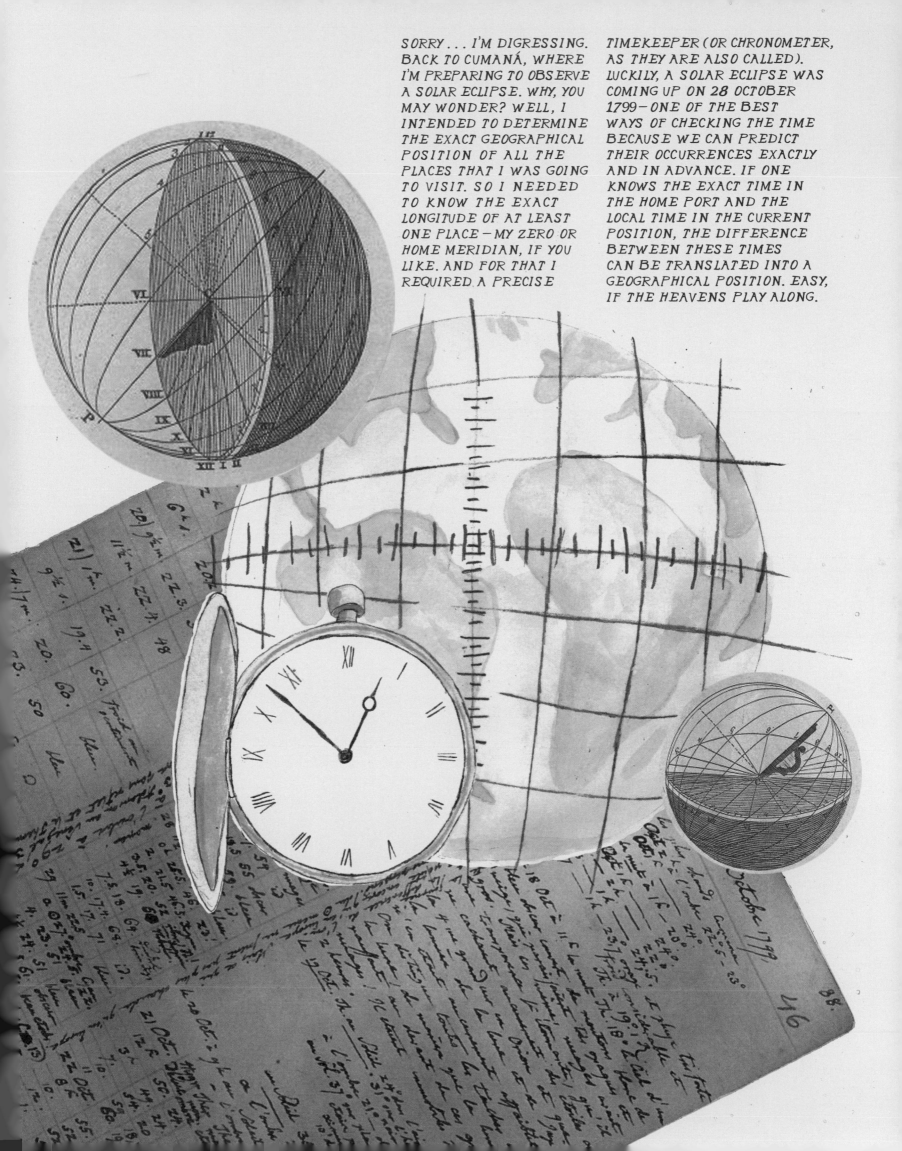

SORRY . . . I'M DIGRESSING. BACK TO CUMANÁ, WHERE I'M PREPARING TO OBSERVE A SOLAR ECLIPSE. WHY, YOU MAY WONDER? WELL, I INTENDED TO DETERMINE THE EXACT GEOGRAPHICAL POSITION OF ALL THE PLACES THAT I WAS GOING TO VISIT. SO I NEEDED TO KNOW THE EXACT LONGITUDE OF AT LEAST ONE PLACE — MY ZERO OR HOME MERIDIAN, IF YOU LIKE. AND FOR THAT I REQUIRED A PRECISE TIMEKEEPER (OR CHRONOMETER, AS THEY ARE ALSO CALLED). LUCKILY, A SOLAR ECLIPSE WAS COMING UP ON 28 OCTOBER 1799 — ONE OF THE BEST WAYS OF CHECKING THE TIME BECAUSE WE CAN PREDICT THEIR OCCURRENCES EXACTLY AND IN ADVANCE. IF ONE KNOWS THE EXACT TIME IN THE HOME PORT AND THE LOCAL TIME IN THE CURRENT POSITION, THE DIFFERENCE BETWEEN THESE TIMES CAN BE TRANSLATED INTO A GEOGRAPHICAL POSITION. EASY, IF THE HEAVENS PLAY ALONG.

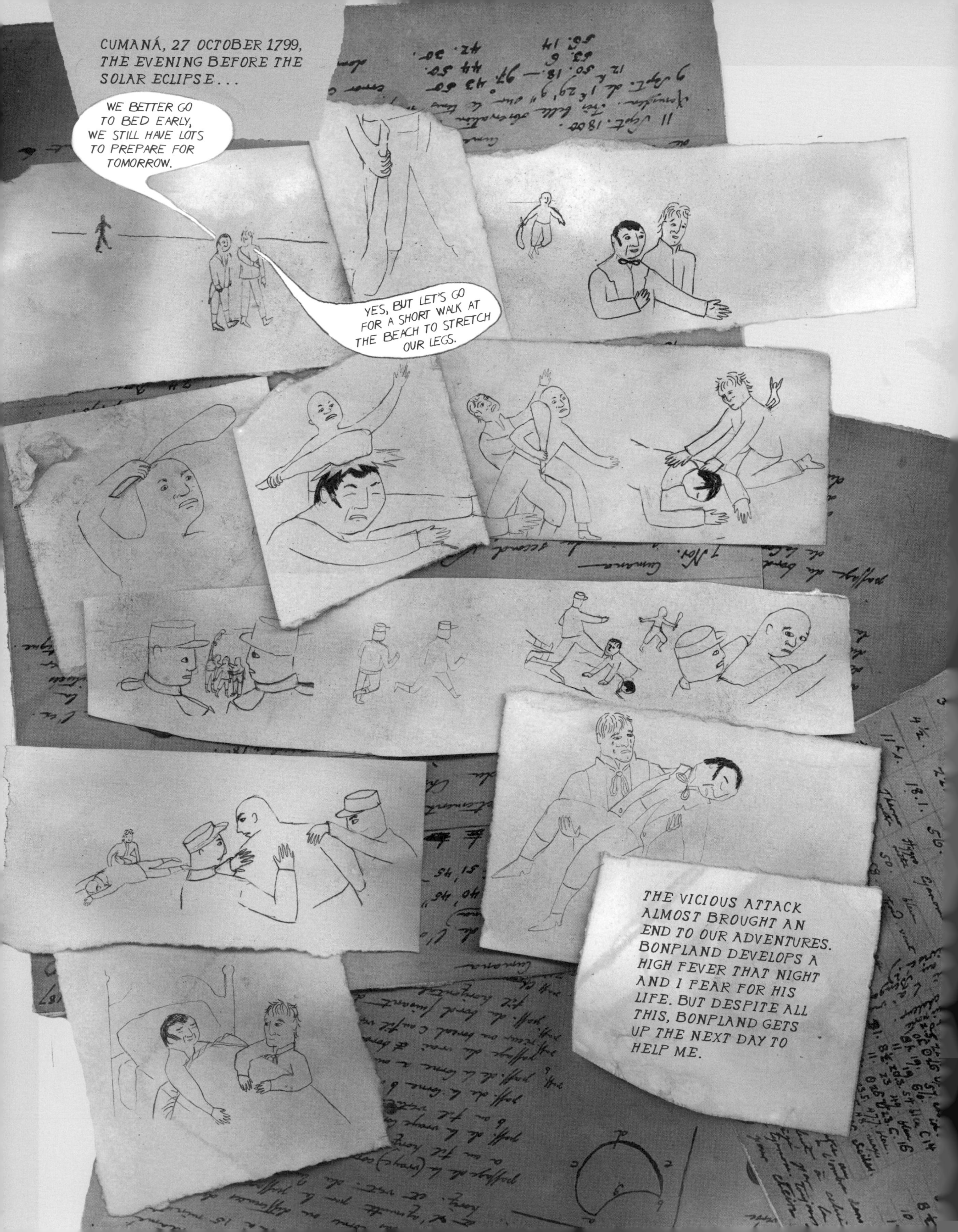
CUMANÁ, 27 OCTOBER 1799, THE EVENING BEFORE THE SOLAR ECLIPSE...
WE BETTER GO TO BED EARLY, WE STILL HAVE LOTS TO PREPARE FOR TOMORROW.
YES, BUT LET'S GO FOR A SHORT WALK AT THE BEACH TO STRETCH OUR LEGS.
THE VICIOUS ATTACK ALMOST BROUGHT AN END TO OUR ADVENTURES. BONPLAND DEVELOPS A HIGH FEVER THAT NIGHT AND I FEAR FOR HIS LIFE. BUT DESPITE ALL THIS, BONPLAND GETS UP THE NEXT DAY TO HELP ME.

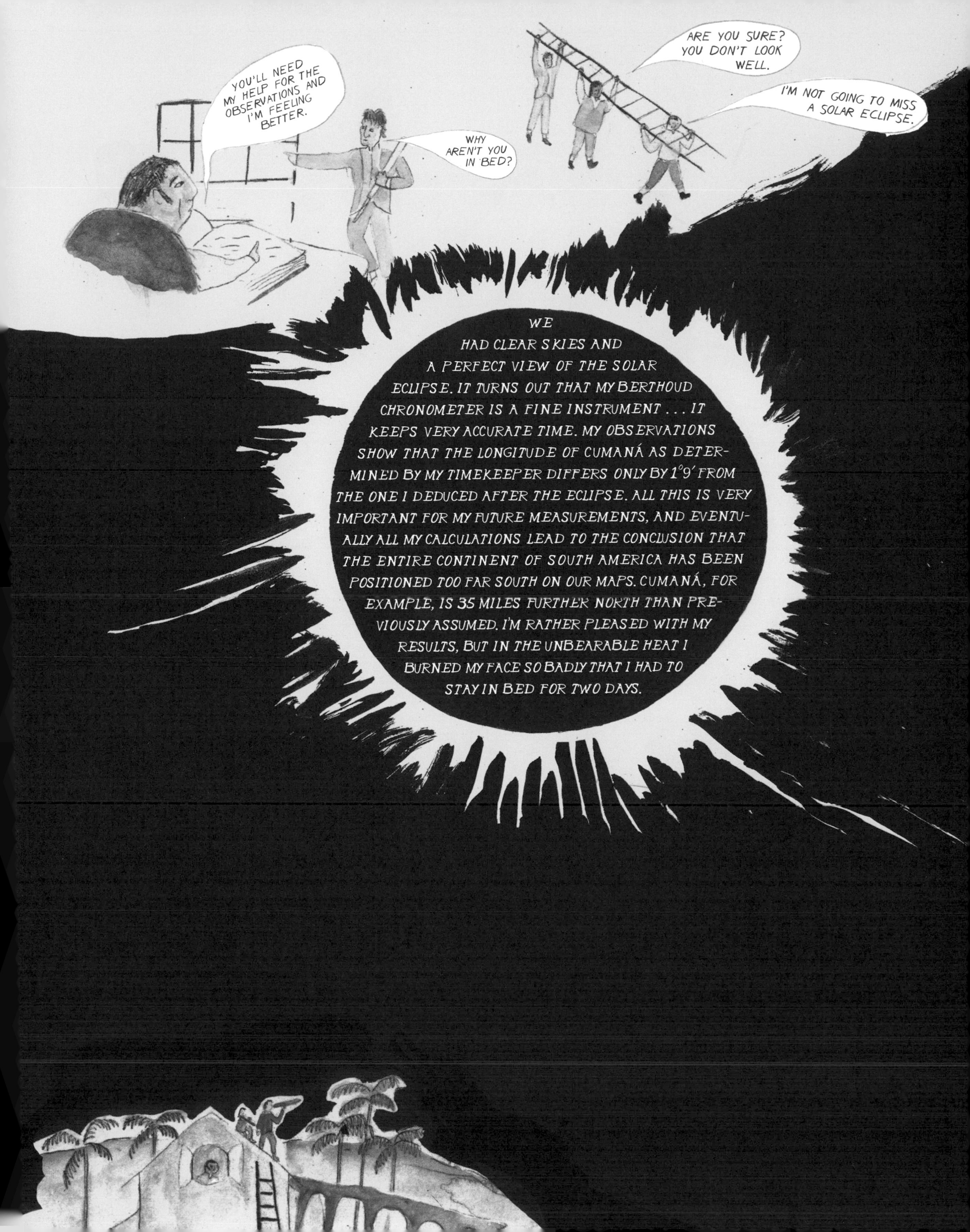
YOU'LL NEED MY HELP FOR THE OBSERVATIONS AND I'M FEELING BETTER.
WHY AREN'T YOU IN BED?
ARE YOU SURE? YOU DON'T LOOK WELL.
I'M NOT GOING TO MISS A SOLAR ECLIPSE.
WE HAD CLEAR SKIES AND A PERFECT VIEW OF THE SOLAR ECLIPSE. IT TURNS OUT THAT MY BERTHOUD CHRONOMETER IS A FINE INSTRUMENT . . . IT KEEPS VERY ACCURATE TIME. MY OBSERVATIONS SHOW THAT THE LONGITUDE OF CUMANÁ AS DETERMINED BY MY TIMEKEEPER DIFFERS ONLY BY 1°9′ FROM THE ONE I DEDUCED AFTER THE ECLIPSE. ALL THIS IS VERY IMPORTANT FOR MY FUTURE MEASUREMENTS, AND EVENTUALLY ALL MY CALCULATIONS LEAD TO THE CONCLUSION THAT THE ENTIRE CONTINENT OF SOUTH AMERICA HAS BEEN POSITIONED TOO FAR SOUTH ON OUR MAPS. CUMANÁ, FOR EXAMPLE, IS 35 MILES FURTHER NORTH THAN PREVIOUSLY ASSUMED. I'M RATHER PLEASED WITH MY RESULTS, BUT IN THE UNBEARABLE HEAT I BURNED MY FACE SO BADLY THAT I HAD TO STAY IN BED FOR TWO DAYS.

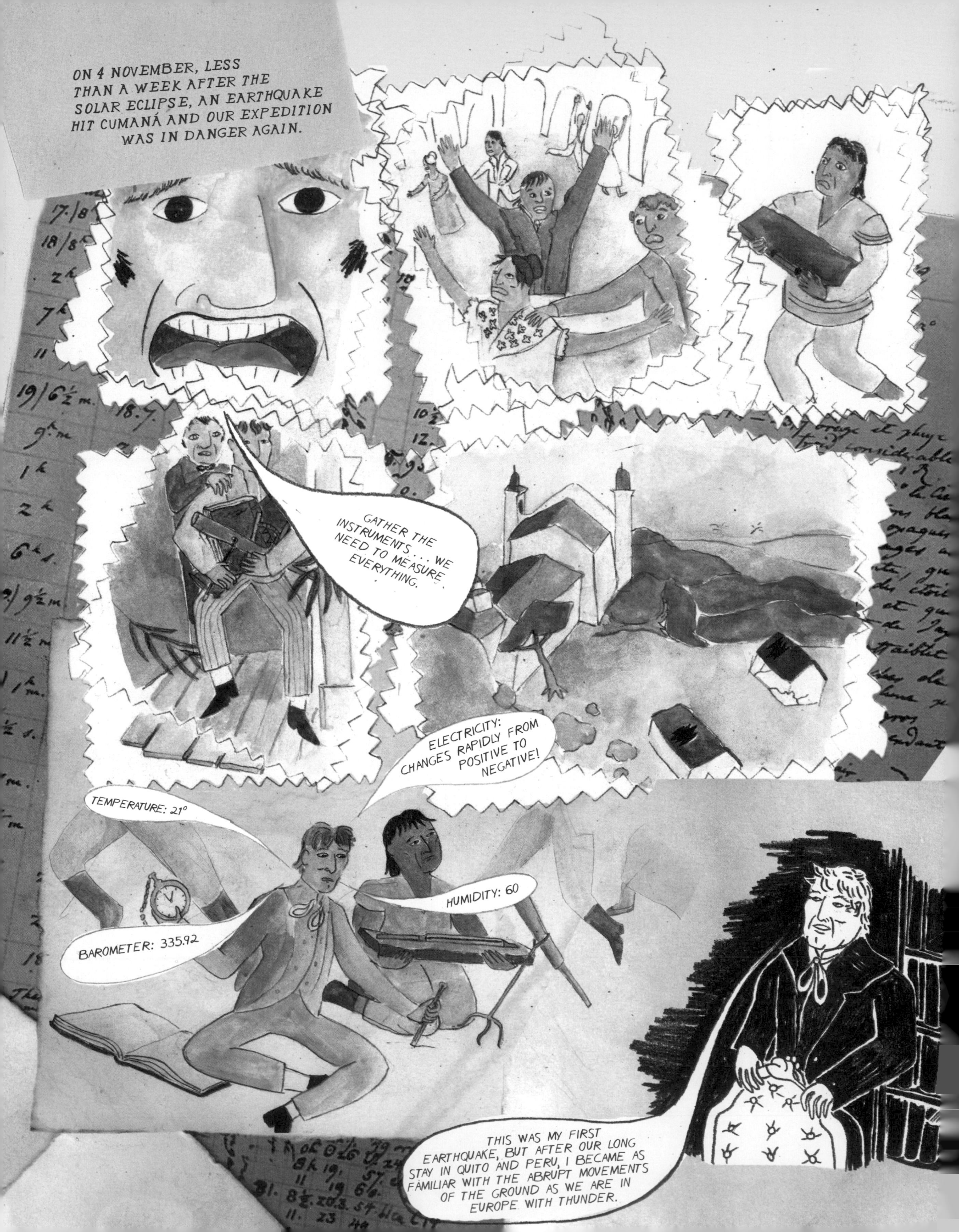
ON 4 NOVEMBER, LESS THAN A WEEK AFTER THE SOLAR ECLIPSE, AN EARTHQUAKE HIT CUMANÁ AND OUR EXPEDITION WAS IN DANGER AGAIN.
GATHER THE INSTRUMENTS . . . WE NEED TO MEASURE EVERYTHING.
ELECTRICITY: CHANGES RAPIDLY FROM POSITIVE TO NEGATIVE!
TEMPERATURE: 21°
HUMIDITY: 60
BAROMETER: 335.92
THIS WAS MY FIRST EARTHQUAKE, BUT AFTER OUR LONG STAY IN QUITO AND PERU, I BECAME AS FAMILIAR WITH THE ABRUPT MOVEMENTS OF THE GROUND AS WE ARE IN EUROPE WITH THUNDER.

A FEW DAYS LATER, THERE IS MORE EXCITEMENT IN CUMANÁ . . .

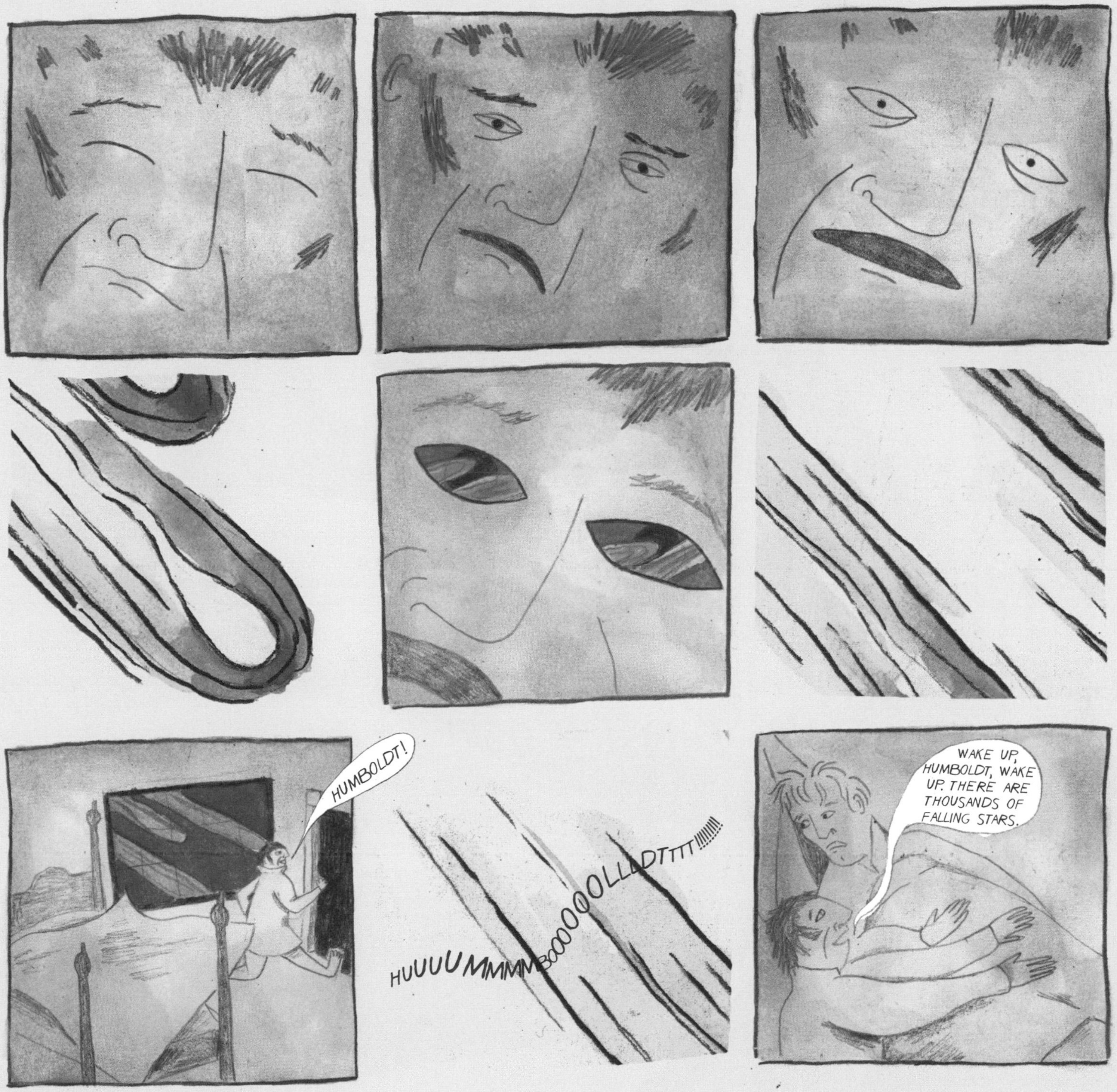
HUMBOLDT!
HUUUUMMMMBOOOOOOLLLDTTTT!!!!!!
WAKE UP, HUMBOLDT, WAKE UP. THERE ARE THOUSANDS OF FALLING STARS.

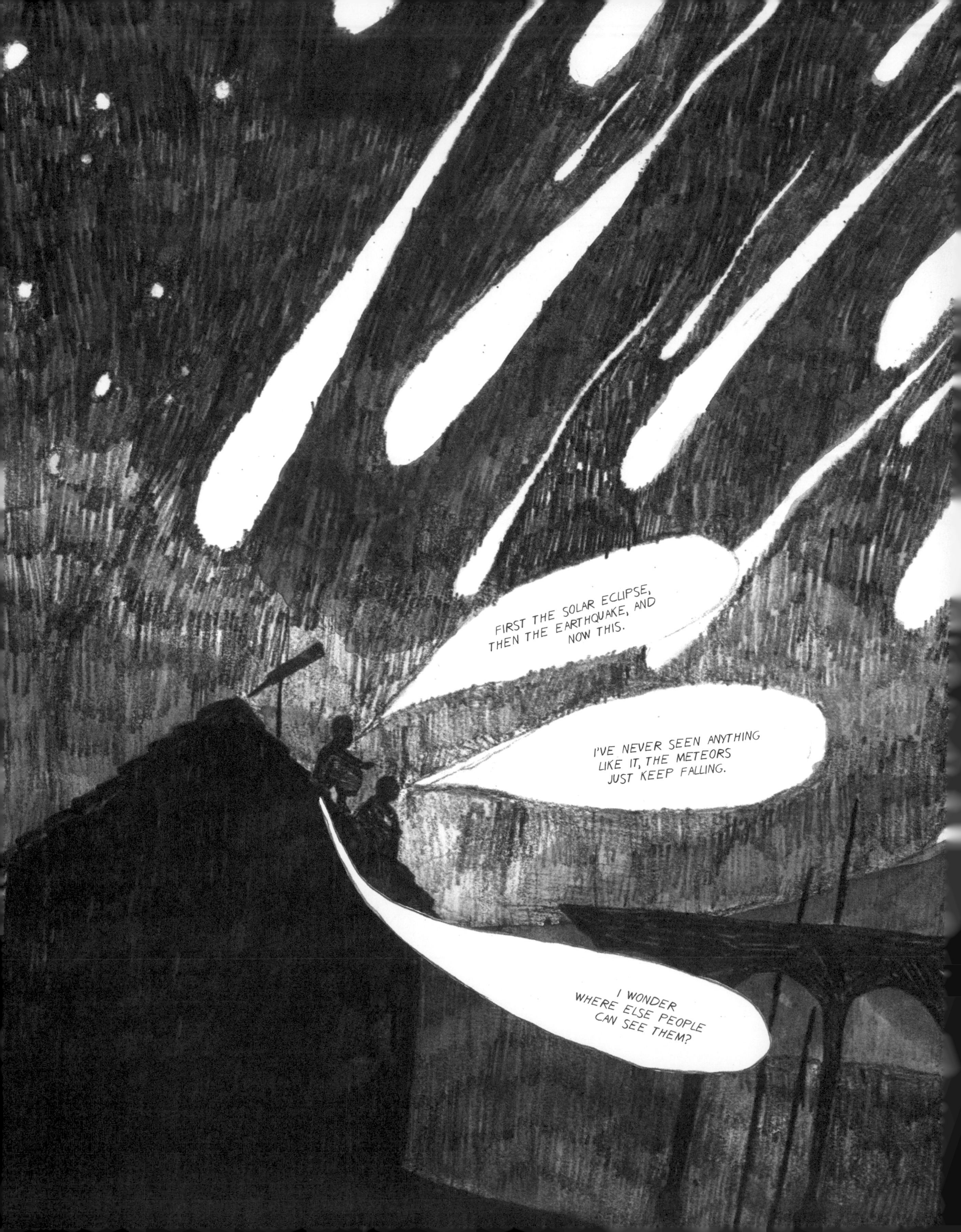
FIRST THE SOLAR ECLIPSE, THEN THE EARTHQUAKE, AND NOW THIS.
I'VE NEVER SEEN ANYTHING LIKE IT, THE METEORS JUST KEEP FALLING.
I WONDER WHERE ELSE PEOPLE CAN SEE THEM?

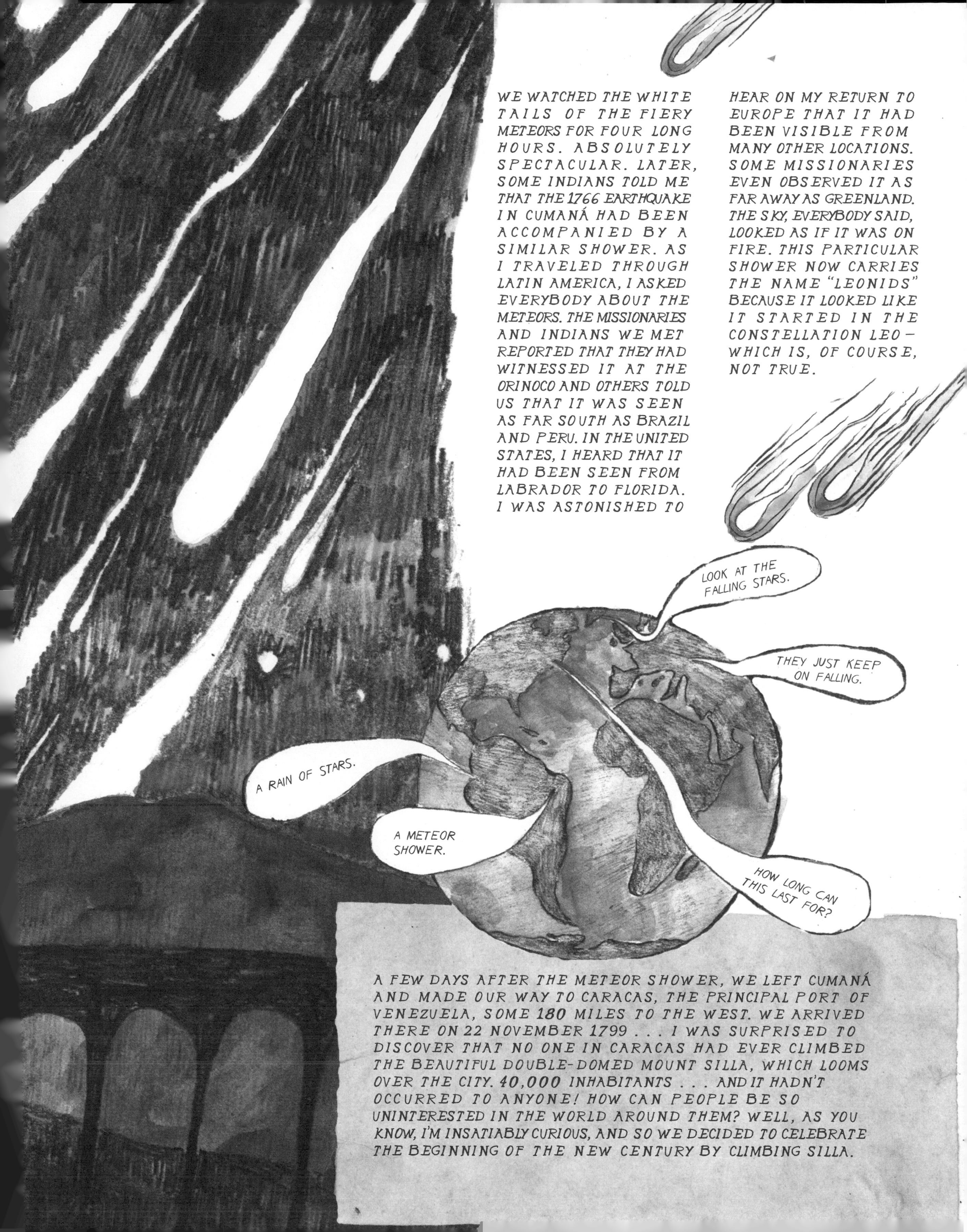
WE WATCHED THE WHITE TAILS OF THE FIERY METEORS FOR FOUR LONG HOURS. ABSOLUTELY SPECTACULAR. LATER, SOME INDIANS TOLD ME THAT THE 1766 EARTHQUAKE IN CUMANÁ HAD BEEN ACCOMPANIED BY A SIMILAR SHOWER. AS I TRAVELED THROUGH LATIN AMERICA, I ASKED EVERYBODY ABOUT THE METEORS. THE MISSIONARIES AND INDIANS WE MET REPORTED THAT THEY HAD WITNESSED IT AT THE ORINOCO AND OTHERS TOLD US THAT IT WAS SEEN AS FAR SOUTH AS BRAZIL AND PERU. IN THE UNITED STATES, I HEARD THAT IT HAD BEEN SEEN FROM LABRADOR TO FLORIDA. I WAS ASTONISHED TO HEAR ON MY RETURN TO EUROPE THAT IT HAD BEEN VISIBLE FROM MANY OTHER LOCATIONS. SOME MISSIONARIES EVEN OBSERVED IT AS FAR AWAY AS GREENLAND. THE SKY, EVERYBODY SAID, LOOKED AS IF IT WAS ON FIRE. THIS PARTICULAR SHOWER NOW CARRIES THE NAME "LEONIDS" BECAUSE IT LOOKED LIKE IT STARTED IN THE CONSTELLATION LEO— WHICH IS, OF COURSE, NOT TRUE.
LOOK AT THE FALLING STARS.
THEY JUST KEEP ON FALLING.
A RAIN OF STARS.
A METEOR SHOWER.
HOW LONG CAN THIS LAST FOR?
A FEW DAYS AFTER THE METEOR SHOWER, WE LEFT CUMANÁ AND MADE OUR WAY TO CARACAS, THE PRINCIPAL PORT OF VENEZUELA, SOME 180 MILES TO THE WEST. WE ARRIVED THERE ON 22 NOVEMBER 1799 . . . I WAS SURPRISED TO DISCOVER THAT NO ONE IN CARACAS HAD EVER CLIMBED THE BEAUTIFUL DOUBLE-DOMED MOUNT SILLA, WHICH LOOMS OVER THE CITY. 40,000 INHABITANTS . . . AND IT HADN'T OCCURRED TO ANYONE! HOW CAN PEOPLE BE SO UNINTERESTED IN THE WORLD AROUND THEM? WELL, AS YOU KNOW, I'M INSATIABLY CURIOUS, AND SO WE DECIDED TO CELEBRATE THE BEGINNING OF THE NEW CENTURY BY CLIMBING SILLA.

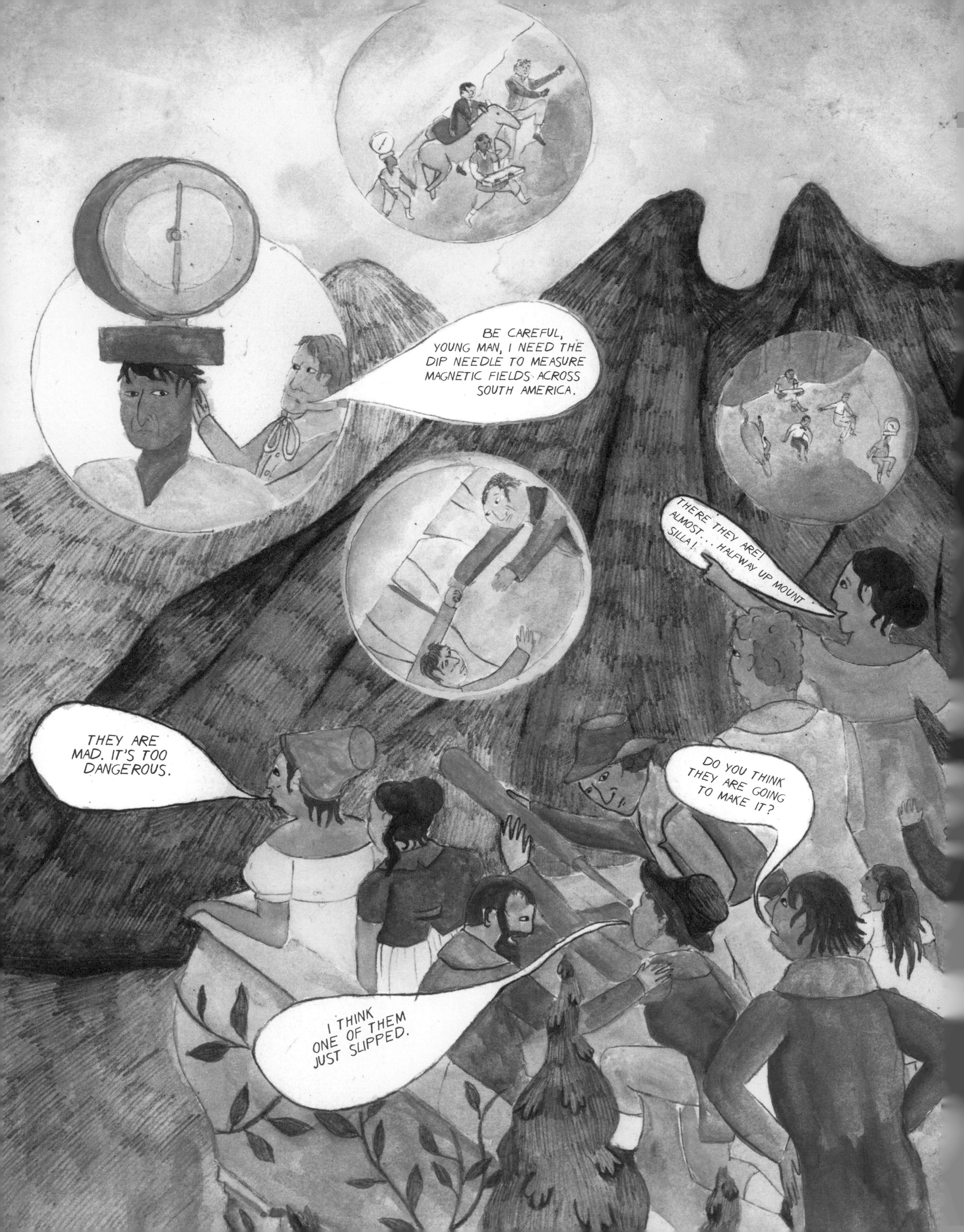
BE CAREFUL, YOUNG MAN, I NEED THE DIP NEEDLE TO MEASURE MAGNETIC FIELDS ACROSS SOUTH AMERICA.
THERE THEY ARE! ALMOST... HALFWAY UP MOUNT SILLA!
THEY ARE MAD. IT'S TOO DANGEROUS.
DO YOU THINK THEY ARE GOING TO MAKE IT?
I THINK ONE OF THEM JUST SLIPPED.

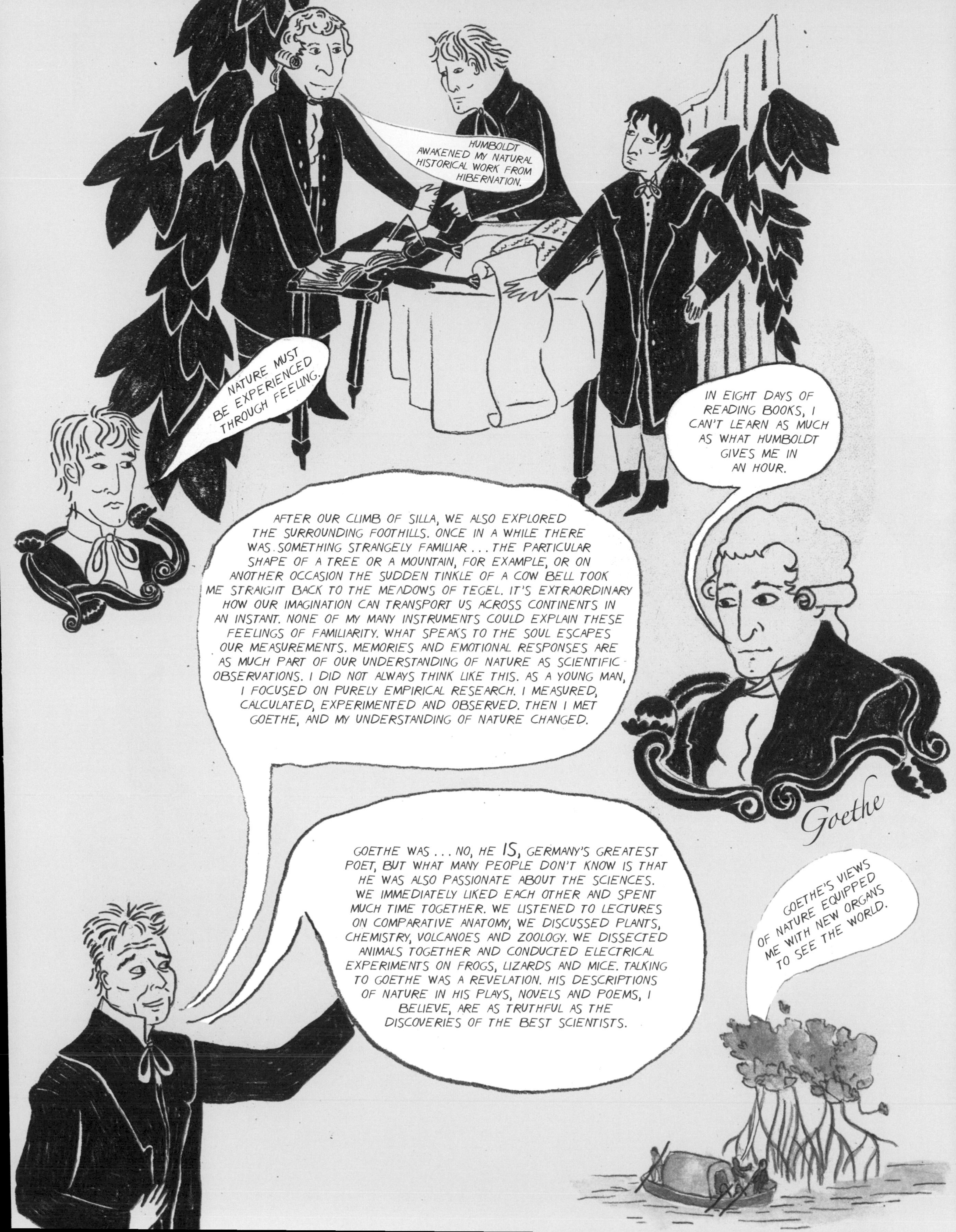
HUMBOLDT AWAKENED MY NATURAL HISTORICAL WORK FROM HIBERNATION.
NATURE MUST BE EXPERIENCED THROUGH FEELING.
IN EIGHT DAYS OF READING BOOKS, I CAN'T LEARN AS MUCH AS WHAT HUMBOLDT GIVES ME IN AN HOUR.
AFTER OUR CLIMB OF SILLA, WE ALSO EXPLORED THE SURROUNDING FOOTHILLS. ONCE IN A WHILE THERE WAS SOMETHING STRANGELY FAMILIAR . . . THE PARTICULAR SHAPE OF A TREE OR A MOUNTAIN, FOR EXAMPLE, OR ON ANOTHER OCCASION THE SUDDEN TINKLE OF A COW BELL TOOK ME STRAIGHT BACK TO THE MEADOWS OF TEGEL. IT'S EXTRAORDINARY HOW OUR IMAGINATION CAN TRANSPORT US ACROSS CONTINENTS IN AN INSTANT. NONE OF MY MANY INSTRUMENTS COULD EXPLAIN THESE FEELINGS OF FAMILIARITY. WHAT SPEAKS TO THE SOUL ESCAPES OUR MEASUREMENTS. MEMORIES AND EMOTIONAL RESPONSES ARE AS MUCH PART OF OUR UNDERSTANDING OF NATURE AS SCIENTIFIC OBSERVATIONS. I DID NOT ALWAYS THINK LIKE THIS. AS A YOUNG MAN, I FOCUSED ON PURELY EMPIRICAL RESEARCH. I MEASURED, CALCULATED, EXPERIMENTED AND OBSERVED. THEN I MET GOETHE, AND MY UNDERSTANDING OF NATURE CHANGED.
Goethe
GOETHE WAS . . . NO, HE IS, GERMANY'S GREATEST POET, BUT WHAT MANY PEOPLE DON'T KNOW IS THAT HE WAS ALSO PASSIONATE ABOUT THE SCIENCES. WE IMMEDIATELY LIKED EACH OTHER AND SPENT MUCH TIME TOGETHER. WE LISTENED TO LECTURES ON COMPARATIVE ANATOMY, WE DISCUSSED PLANTS, CHEMISTRY, VOLCANOES AND ZOOLOGY. WE DISSECTED ANIMALS TOGETHER AND CONDUCTED ELECTRICAL EXPERIMENTS ON FROGS, LIZARDS AND MICE. TALKING TO GOETHE WAS A REVELATION. HIS DESCRIPTIONS OF NATURE IN HIS PLAYS, NOVELS AND POEMS, I BELIEVE, ARE AS TRUTHFUL AS THE DISCOVERIES OF THE BEST SCIENTISTS.
GOETHE'S VIEWS OF NATURE EQUIPPED ME WITH NEW ORGANS TO SEE THE WORLD.

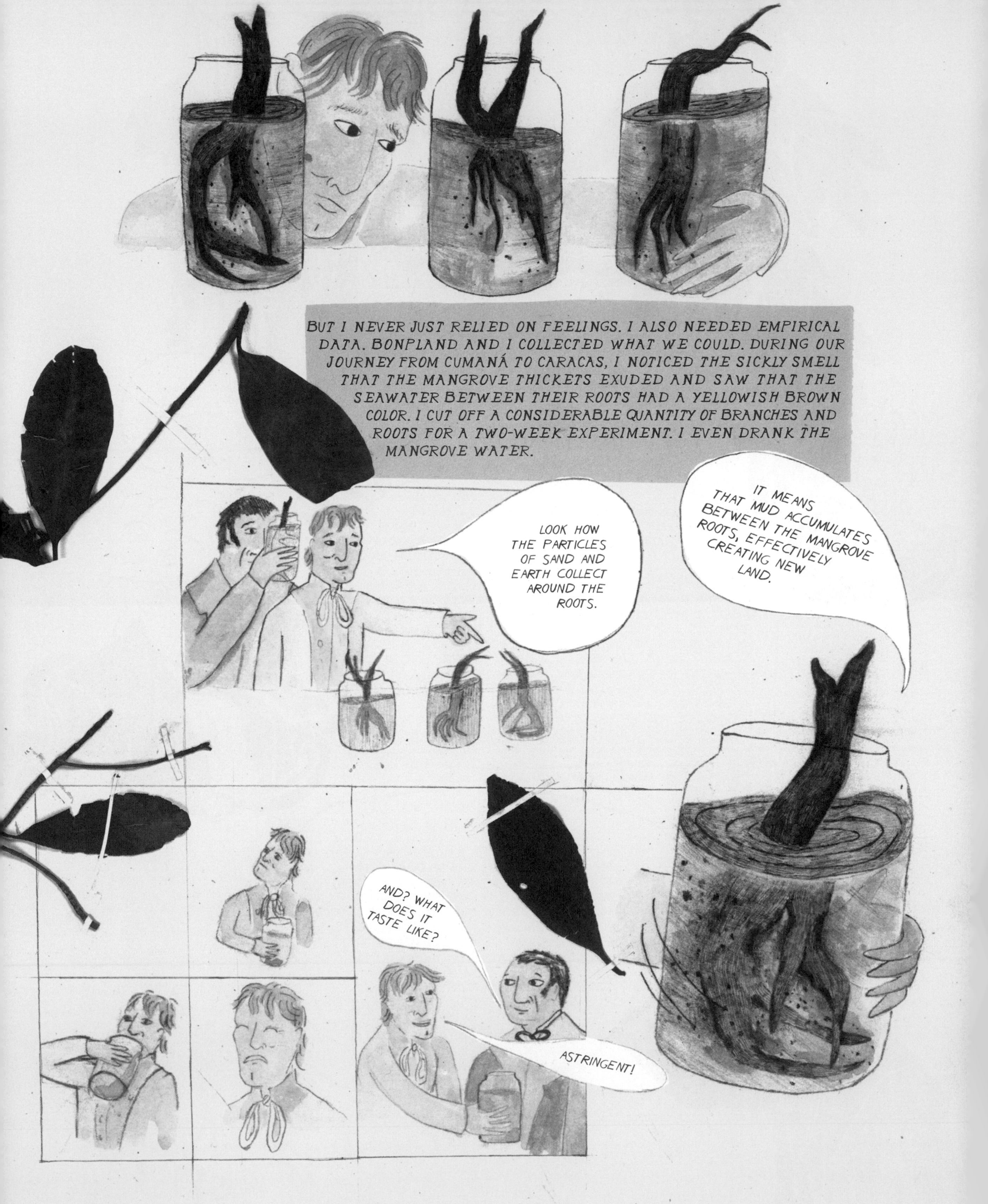
BUT I NEVER JUST RELIED ON FEELINGS. I ALSO NEEDED EMPIRICAL DATA. BONPLAND AND I COLLECTED WHAT WE COULD. DURING OUR JOURNEY FROM CUMANÁ TO CARACAS, I NOTICED THE SICKLY SMELL THAT THE MANGROVE THICKETS EXUDED AND SAW THAT THE SEAWATER BETWEEN THEIR ROOTS HAD A YELLOWISH BROWN COLOR. I CUT OFF A CONSIDERABLE QUANTITY OF BRANCHES AND ROOTS FOR A TWO-WEEK EXPERIMENT. I EVEN DRANK THE MANGROVE WATER.
LOOK HOW THE PARTICLES OF SAND AND EARTH COLLECT AROUND THE ROOTS.
IT MEANS THAT MUD ACCUMULATES BETWEEN THE MANGROVE ROOTS, EFFECTIVELY CREATING NEW LAND.
AND? WHAT DOES IT TASTE LIKE?
ASTRINGENT!

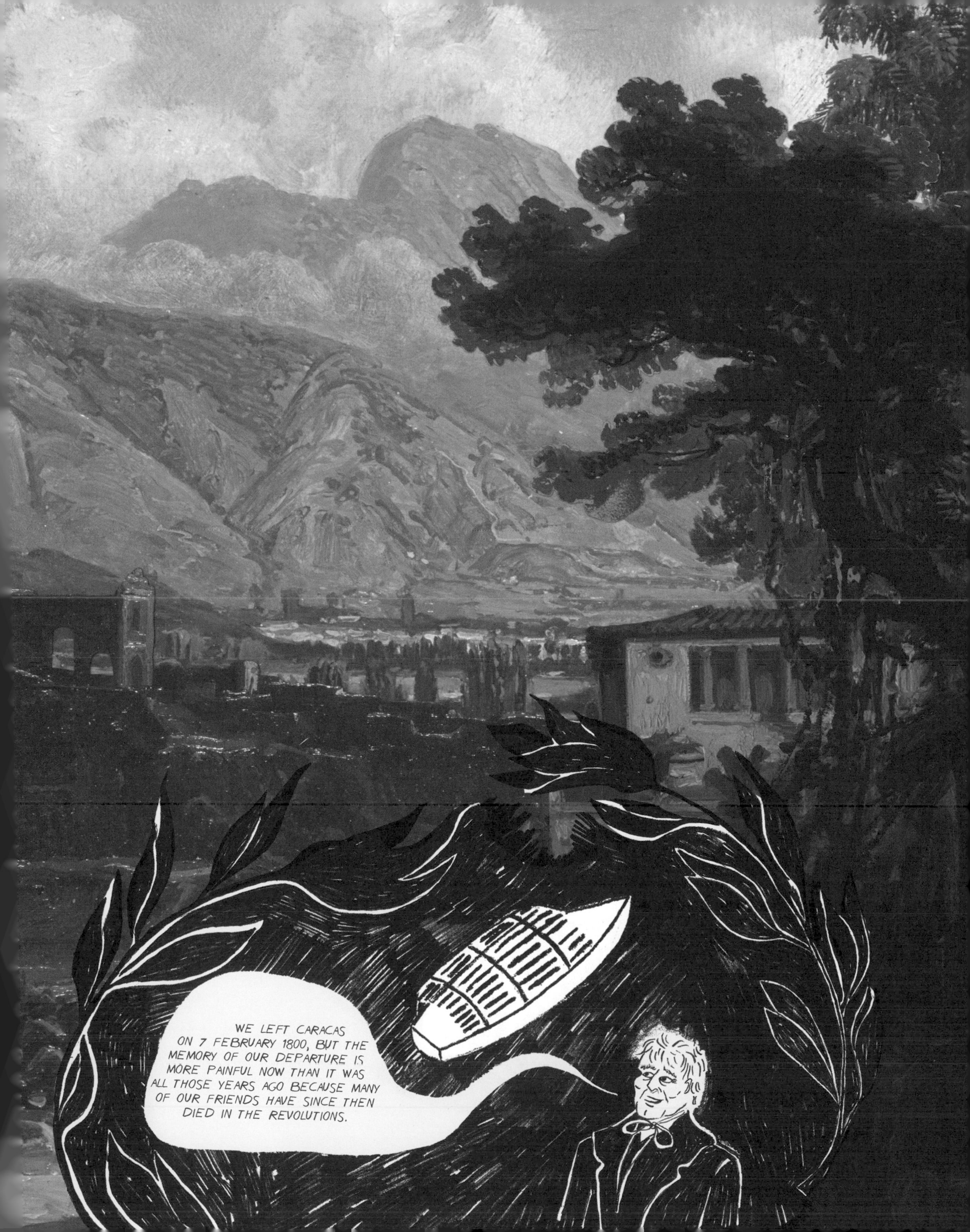
WE LEFT CARACAS ON 7 FEBRUARY 1800, BUT THE MEMORY OF OUR DEPARTURE IS MORE PAINFUL NOW THAN IT WAS ALL THOSE YEARS AGO BECAUSE MANY OF OUR FRIENDS HAVE SINCE THEN DIED IN THE REVOLUTIONS.

WHEREVER I WENT IN SOUTH AMERICA, I HEARD PEOPLE COMPLAINING ABOUT THE TYRANNIES OF COLONIAL RULE – MOSTLY THEIR GRIEVANCES WERE WHISPERED FOR FEAR OF THE AUTHORITIES . . . ONLY SOME SPOKE OPENLY AGAINST THE SPANIARDS. IT WOULD TAKE ANOTHER DECADE FOR THEM TO FIGHT. THE MAN WHO LED THE REVOLUTIONS WAS AN OLD FRIEND, SIMÓN BOLÍVAR. THEY CALLED HIM LATER "EL LIBERTADOR." I WAS INTRODUCED TO BOLÍVAR IN AUTUMN 1804, JUST A FEW WEEKS AFTER MY RETURN FROM SOUTH AMERICA. HE WAS YOUNG – TWENTY-ONE, IF MY MEMORY SERVES ME RIGHT, AND THE SON OF ONE OF CARACAS'S WEALTHIEST CRIOLLO FAMILIES. WE MET IN PARIS, WHERE WE WERE HOMESICK FOR THE GLORIES OF VENEZUELA. WE TALKED ABOUT THE GREAT RAPIDS OF THE ORINOCO AND THE SOARING PEAKS OF THE ANDES BUT ALSO ABOUT POLITICS AND REVOLUTIONS. BACK THEN, I THOUGHT YOUNG BOLÍVAR WAS A DREAMER WITH A BRILLIANT IMAGINATION – PASSIONATE, YES, BUT I DID NOT SEE HIM AS THE FUTURE LEADER OF A REVOLUTION.

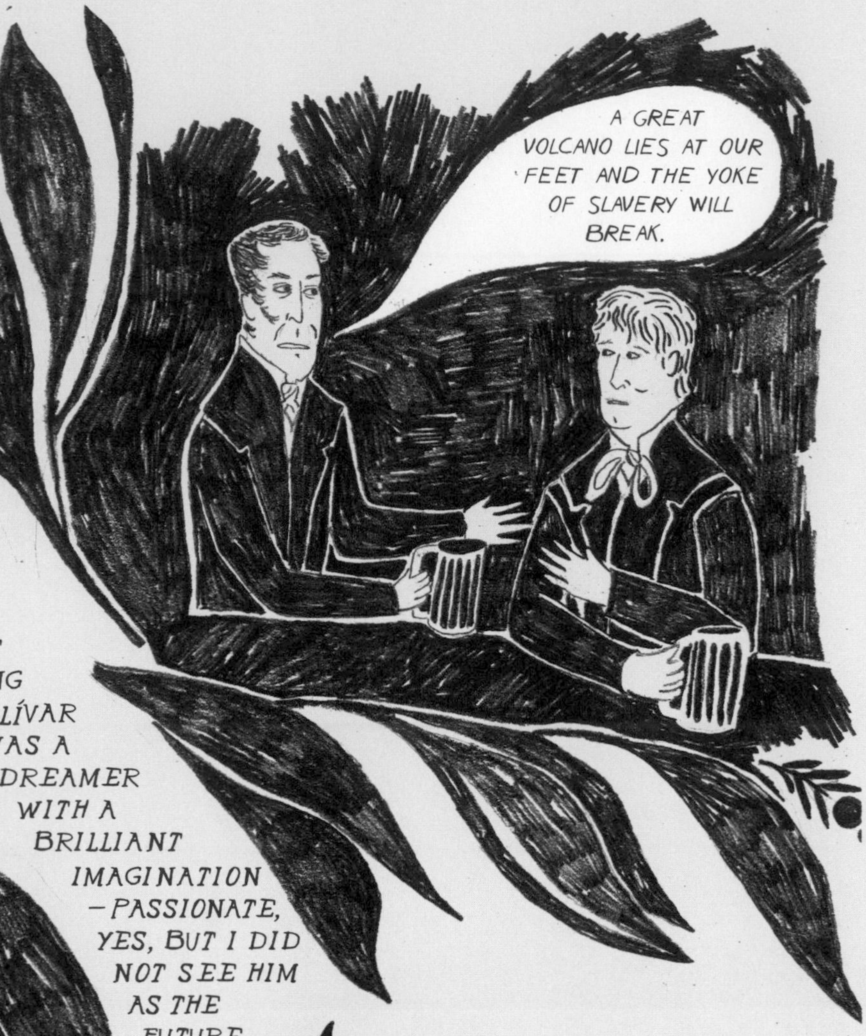
A GREAT VOLCANO LIES AT OUR FEET AND THE YOKE OF SLAVERY WILL BREAK.

I WAS WRONG. I'VE BEEN TOLD THAT MY DESCRIPTIONS OF SOUTH AMERICA MIGHT HAVE HELPED TO INVIGORATE HIS REVOLUTION, AS IF MY DESCRIPTIONS OF NATURE AND PEOPLE MADE THE COLONISTS APPRECIATE HOW UNIQUE AND MAGNIFICENT THEIR CONTINENT WAS. BOLÍVAR HIMSELF WAS INSPIRED BY MY WRITING.

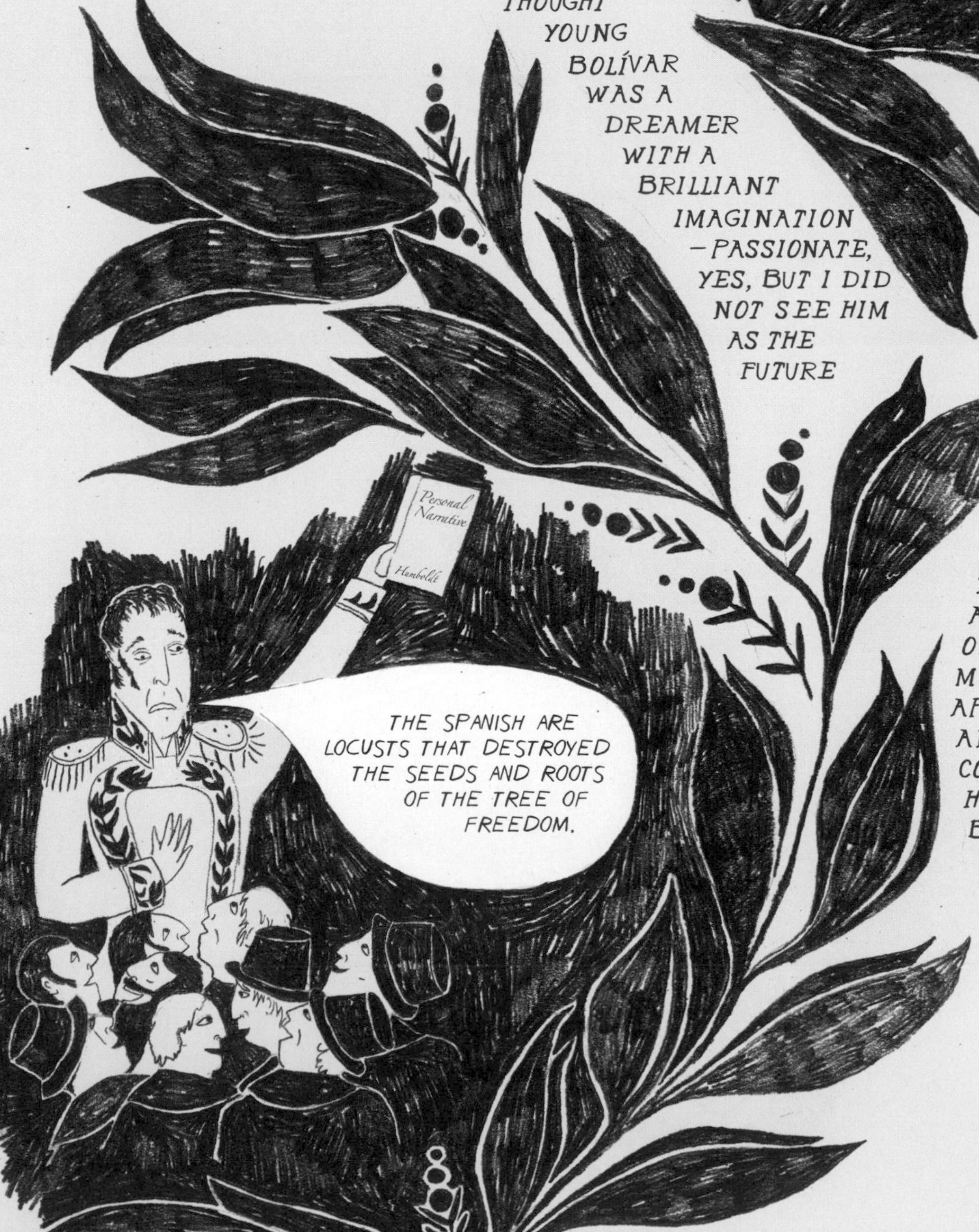
Personal Narrative
Humboldt
THE SPANISH ARE LOCUSTS THAT DESTROYED THE SEEDS AND ROOTS OF THE TREE OF FREEDOM.

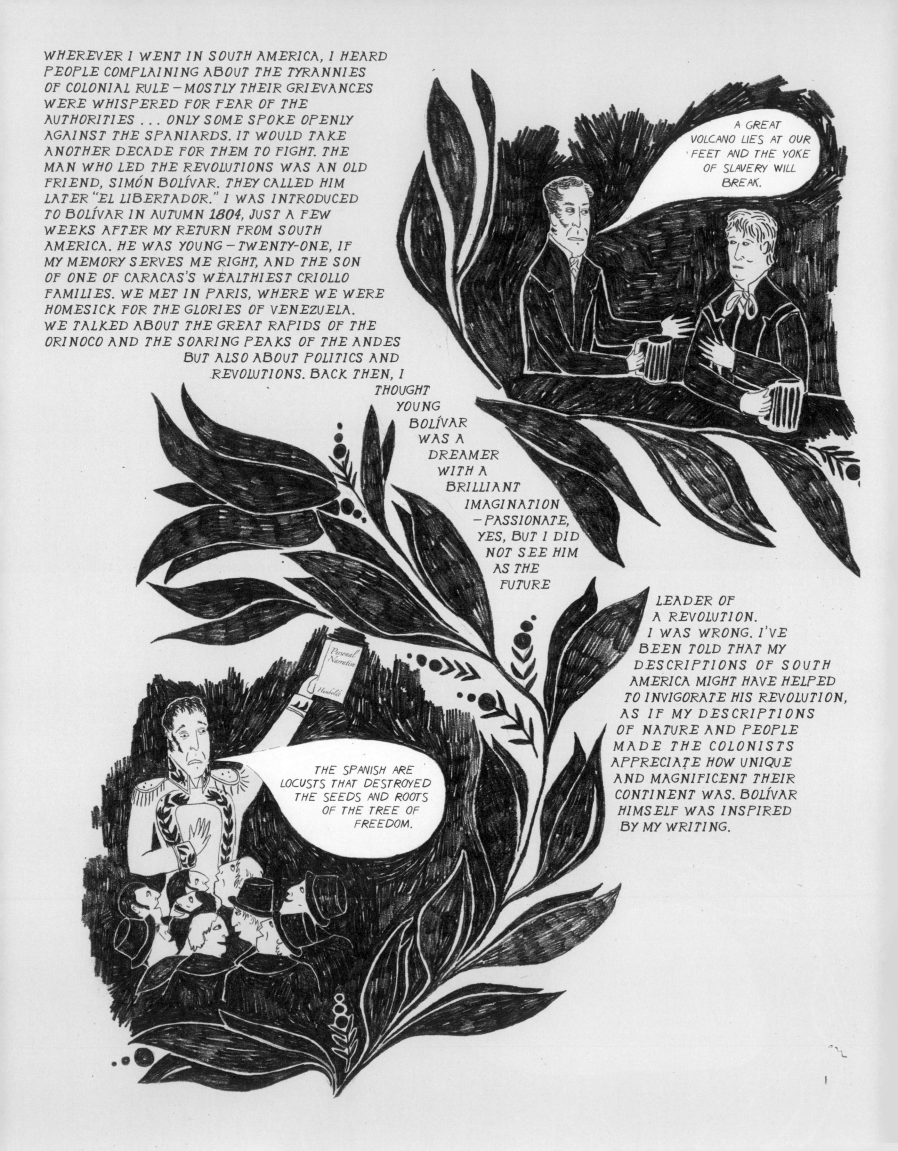

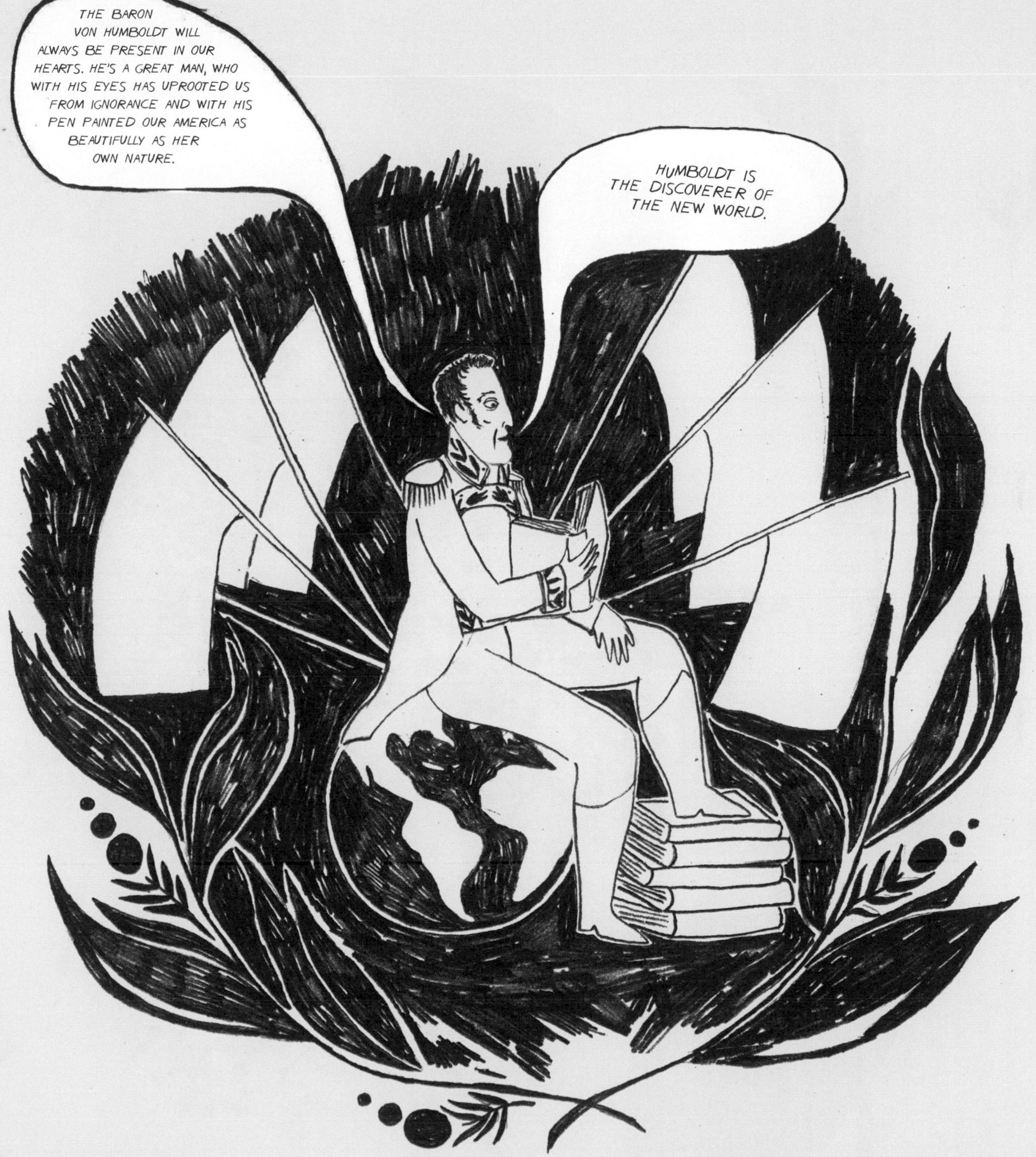
THE BARON VON HUMBOLDT WILL ALWAYS BE PRESENT IN OUR HEARTS. HE'S A GREAT MAN, WHO WITH HIS EYES HAS UPROOTED US FROM IGNORANCE AND WITH HIS PEN PAINTED OUR AMERICA AS BEAUTIFULLY AS HER OWN NATURE.
HUMBOLDT IS THE DISCOVERER OF THE NEW WORLD.

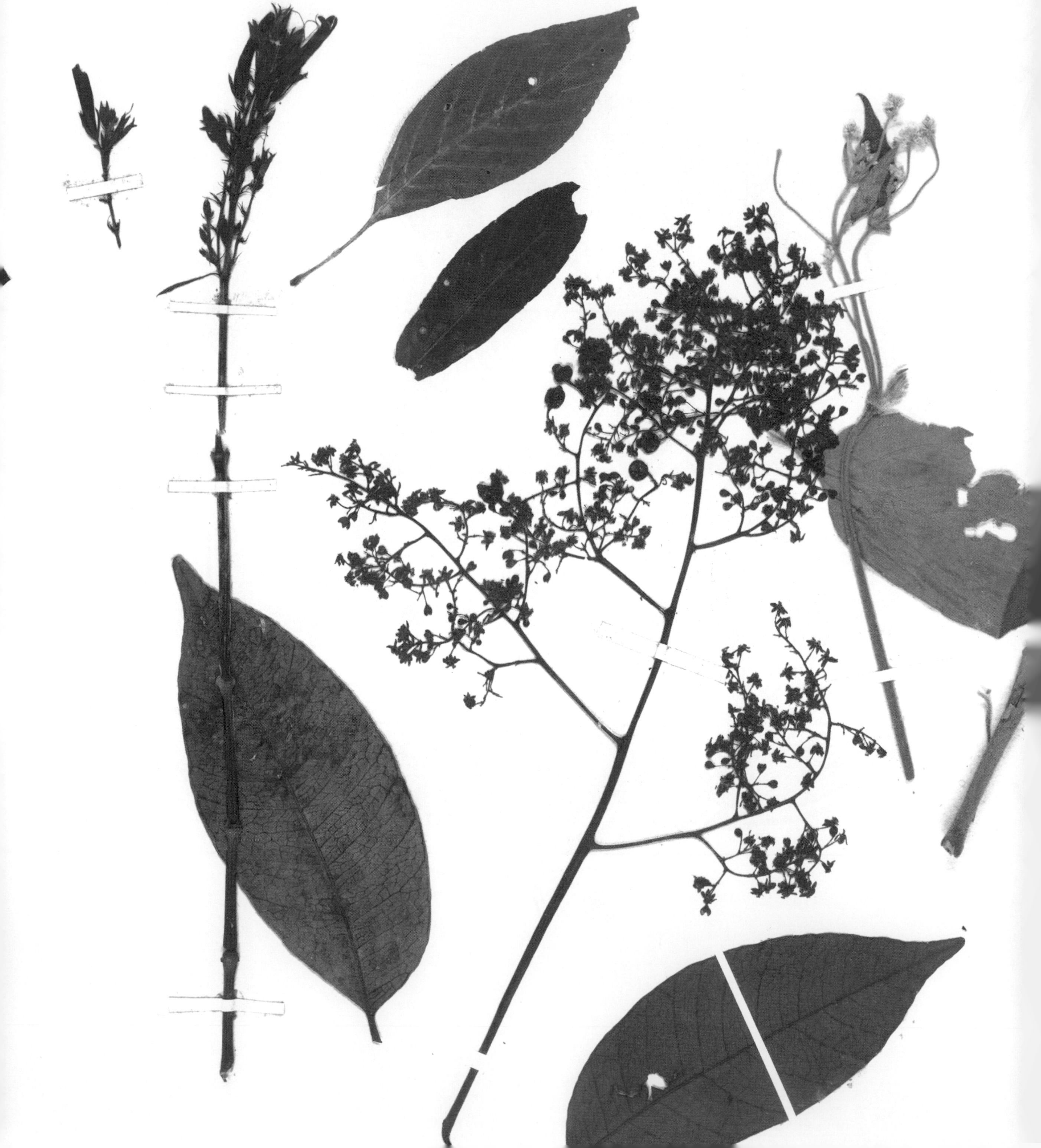

AS WE TRAVELED THROUGH SOUTH AMERICA, WE TOOK DETOURS WHENEVER WE HEARD OF SOMETHING INTERESTING. I INTENDED TO EXPLORE THE ORINOCO AND ITS NETWORK OF TRIBUTARIES — BUT INSTEAD OF GOING SOUTH, WE FIRST TURNED WEST TO LAKE VALENCIA AND THE LUSH VALLEY OF ARAGUA, ONE OF THE WEALTHIEST AGRICULTURAL REGIONS IN THE COLONIES.

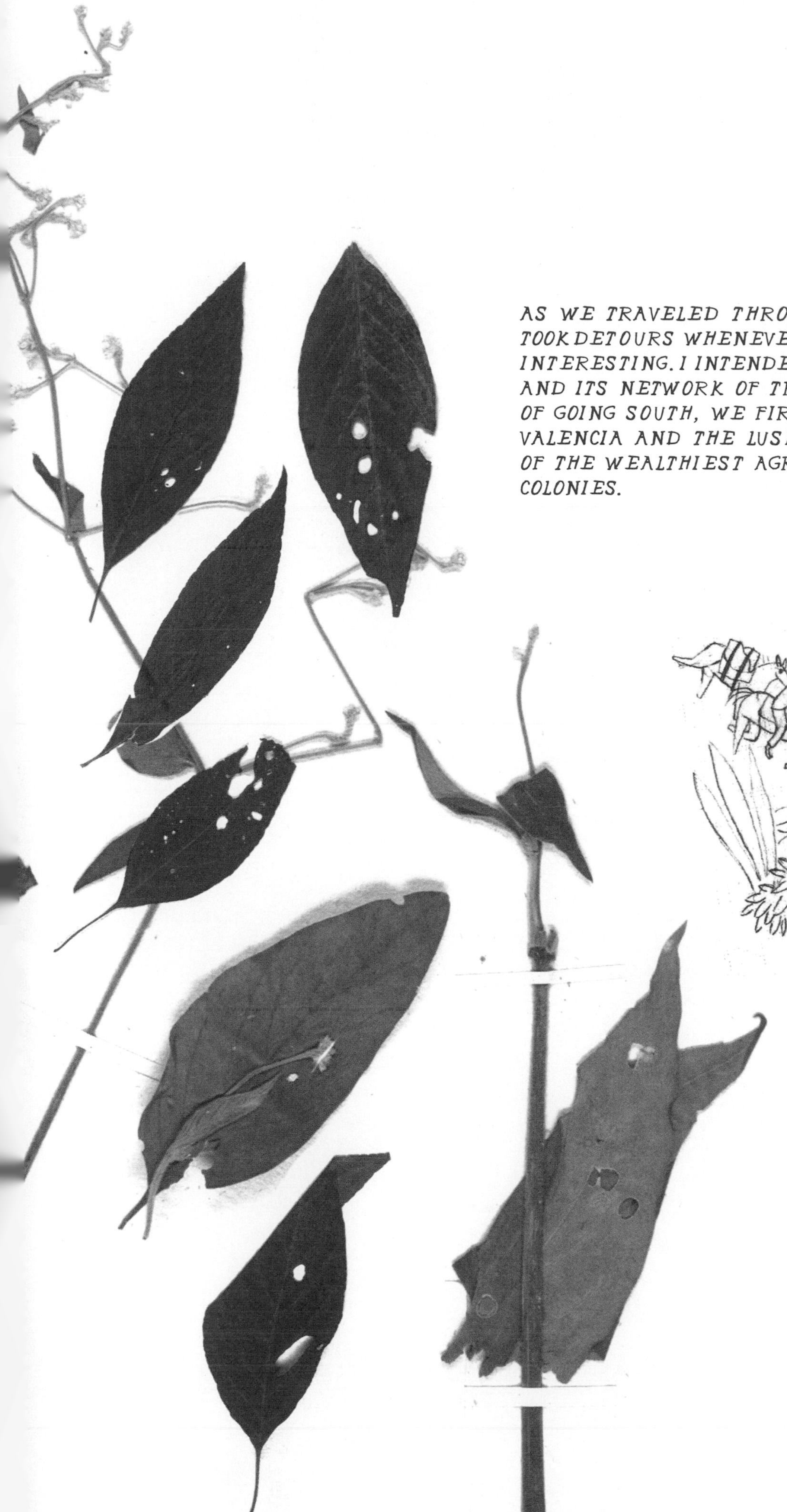

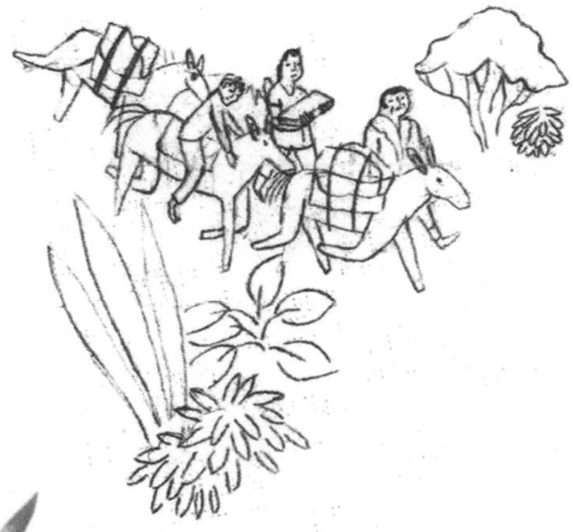

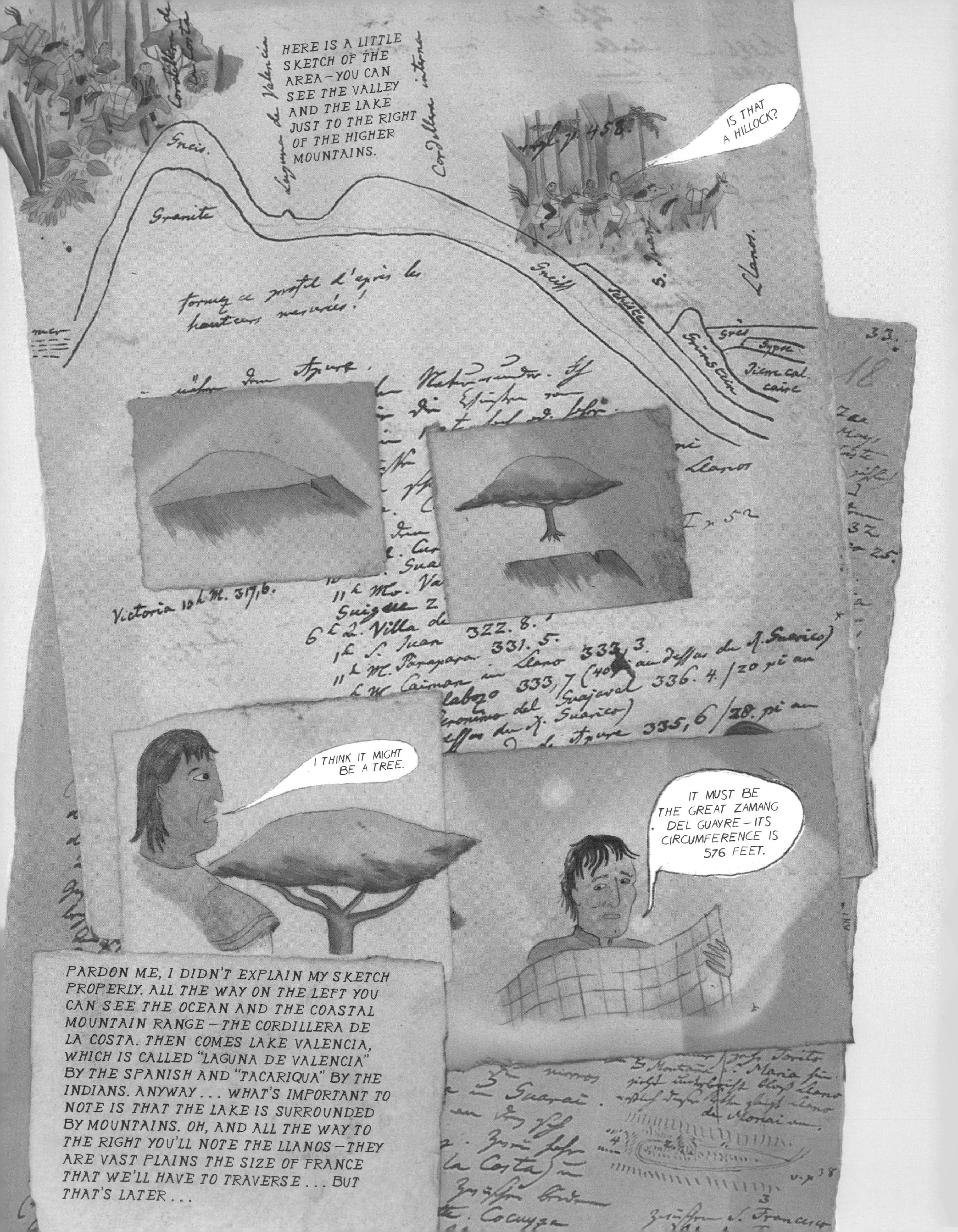
HERE IS A LITTLE SKETCH OF THE AREA—YOU CAN SEE THE VALLEY AND THE LAKE JUST TO THE RIGHT OF THE HIGHER MOUNTAINS.
IS THAT A HILLOCK?
I THINK IT MIGHT BE A TREE.
IT MUST BE THE GREAT ZAMANG DEL GUAYRE—ITS CIRCUMFERENCE IS 576 FEET.
PARDON ME, I DIDN'T EXPLAIN MY SKETCH PROPERLY. ALL THE WAY ON THE LEFT YOU CAN SEE THE OCEAN AND THE COASTAL MOUNTAIN RANGE—THE CORDILLERA DE LA COSTA. THEN COMES LAKE VALENCIA, WHICH IS CALLED "LAGUNA DE VALENCIA" BY THE SPANISH AND "TACARIQUA" BY THE INDIANS. ANYWAY . . . WHAT'S IMPORTANT TO NOTE IS THAT THE LAKE IS SURROUNDED BY MOUNTAINS. OH, AND ALL THE WAY TO THE RIGHT YOU'LL NOTE THE LLANOS—THEY ARE VAST PLAINS THE SIZE OF FRANCE THAT WE'LL HAVE TO TRAVERSE . . . BUT THAT'S LATER . . .

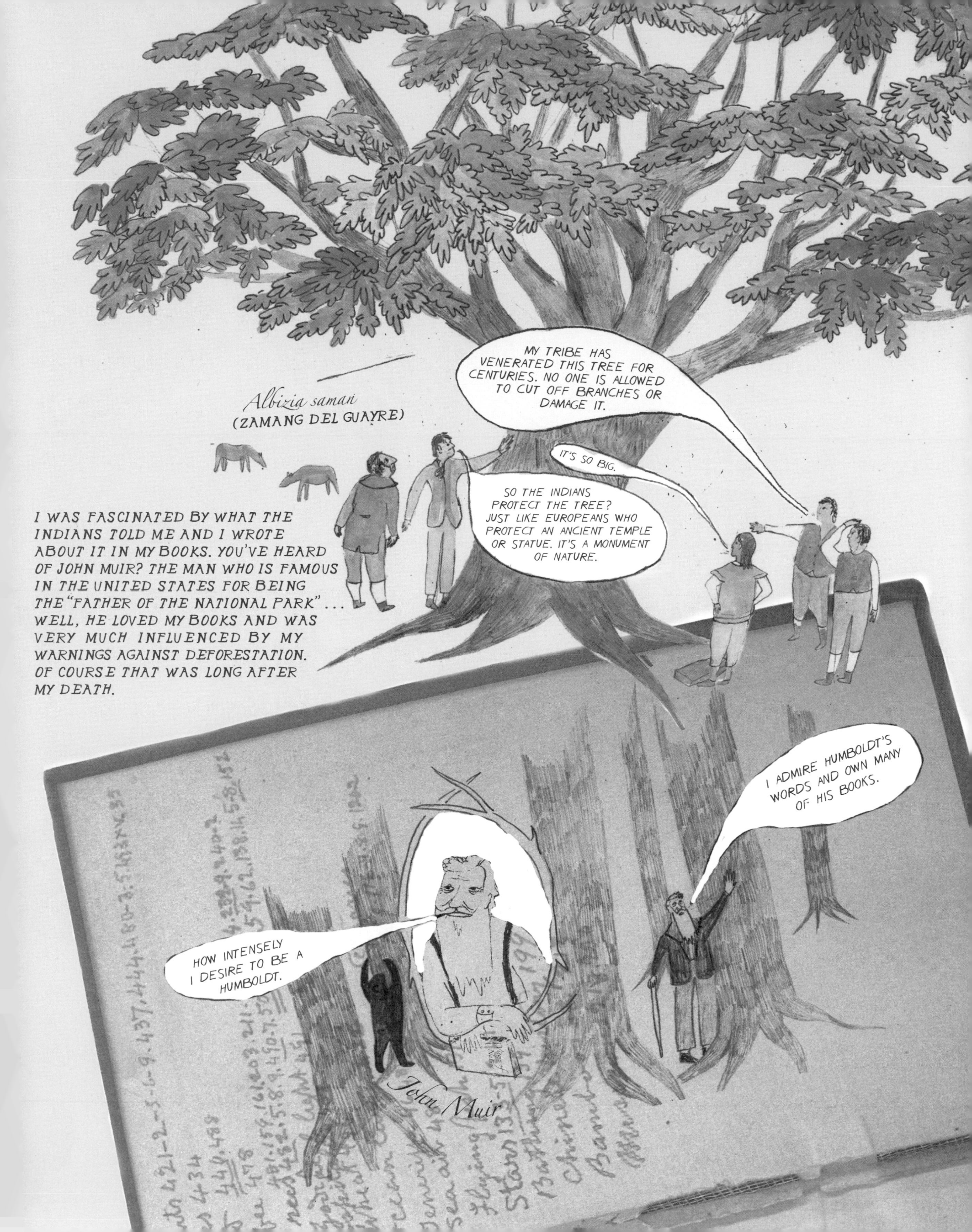

Albizia saman
(ZAMANG DEL GUAYRE)
MY TRIBE HAS VENERATED THIS TREE FOR CENTURIES. NO ONE IS ALLOWED TO CUT OFF BRANCHES OR DAMAGE IT.
IT'S SO BIG.
SO THE INDIANS PROTECT THE TREE? JUST LIKE EUROPEANS WHO PROTECT AN ANCIENT TEMPLE OR STATUE. IT'S A MONUMENT OF NATURE.
I WAS FASCINATED BY WHAT THE INDIANS TOLD ME AND I WROTE ABOUT IT IN MY BOOKS. YOU'VE HEARD OF JOHN MUIR? THE MAN WHO IS FAMOUS IN THE UNITED STATES FOR BEING THE "FATHER OF THE NATIONAL PARK" . . . WELL, HE LOVED MY BOOKS AND WAS VERY MUCH INFLUENCED BY MY WARNINGS AGAINST DEFORESTATION. OF COURSE THAT WAS LONG AFTER MY DEATH.
I ADMIRE HUMBOLDT'S WORDS AND OWN MANY OF HIS BOOKS.
HOW INTENSELY I DESIRE TO BE A HUMBOLDT.
John Muir

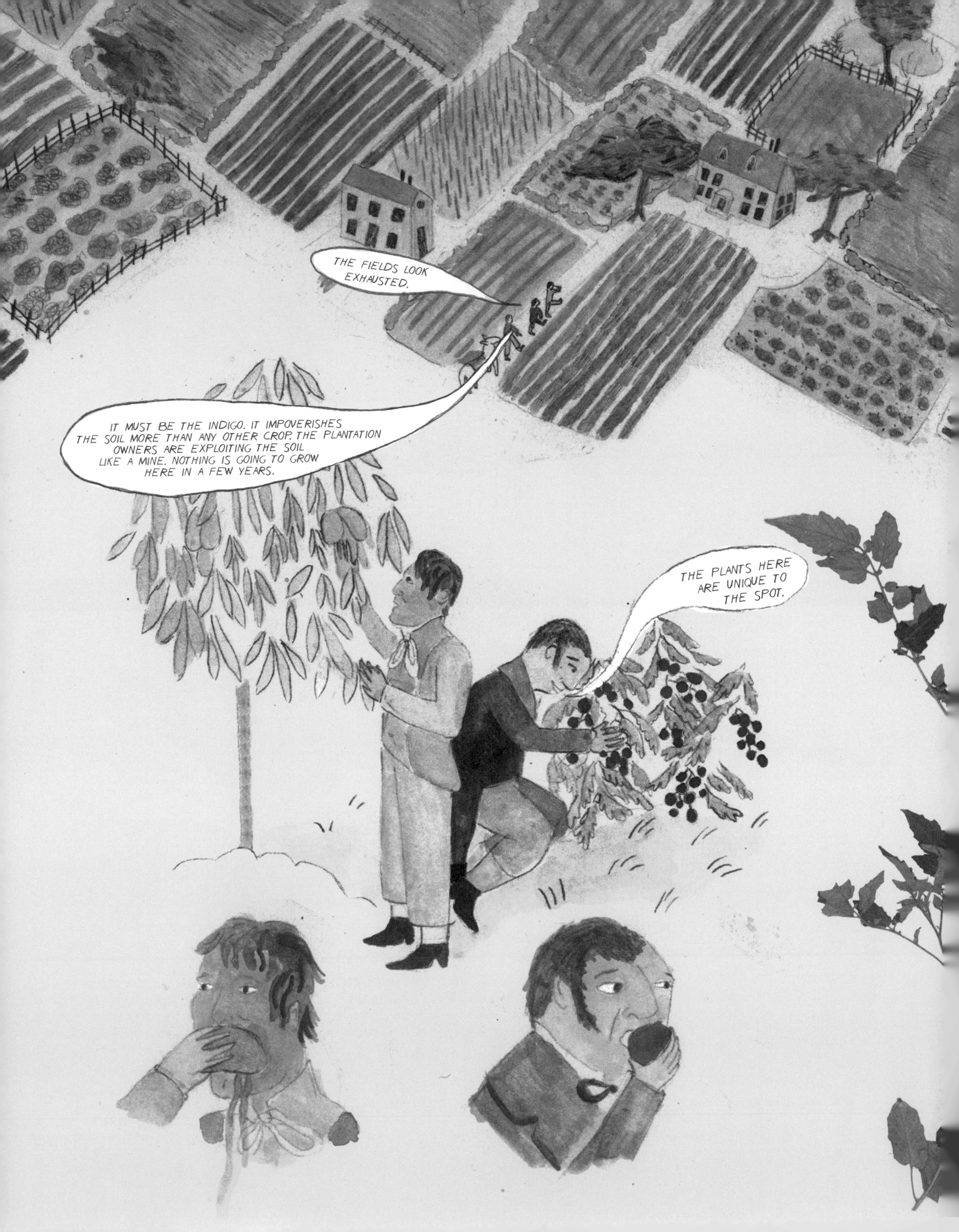
THE FIELDS LOOK EXHAUSTED.
IT MUST BE THE INDIGO. IT IMPOVERISHES THE SOIL MORE THAN ANY OTHER CROP. THE PLANTATION OWNERS ARE EXPLOITING THE SOIL LIKE A MINE. NOTHING IS GOING TO GROW HERE IN A FEW YEARS.
THE PLANTS HERE ARE UNIQUE TO THE SPOT.

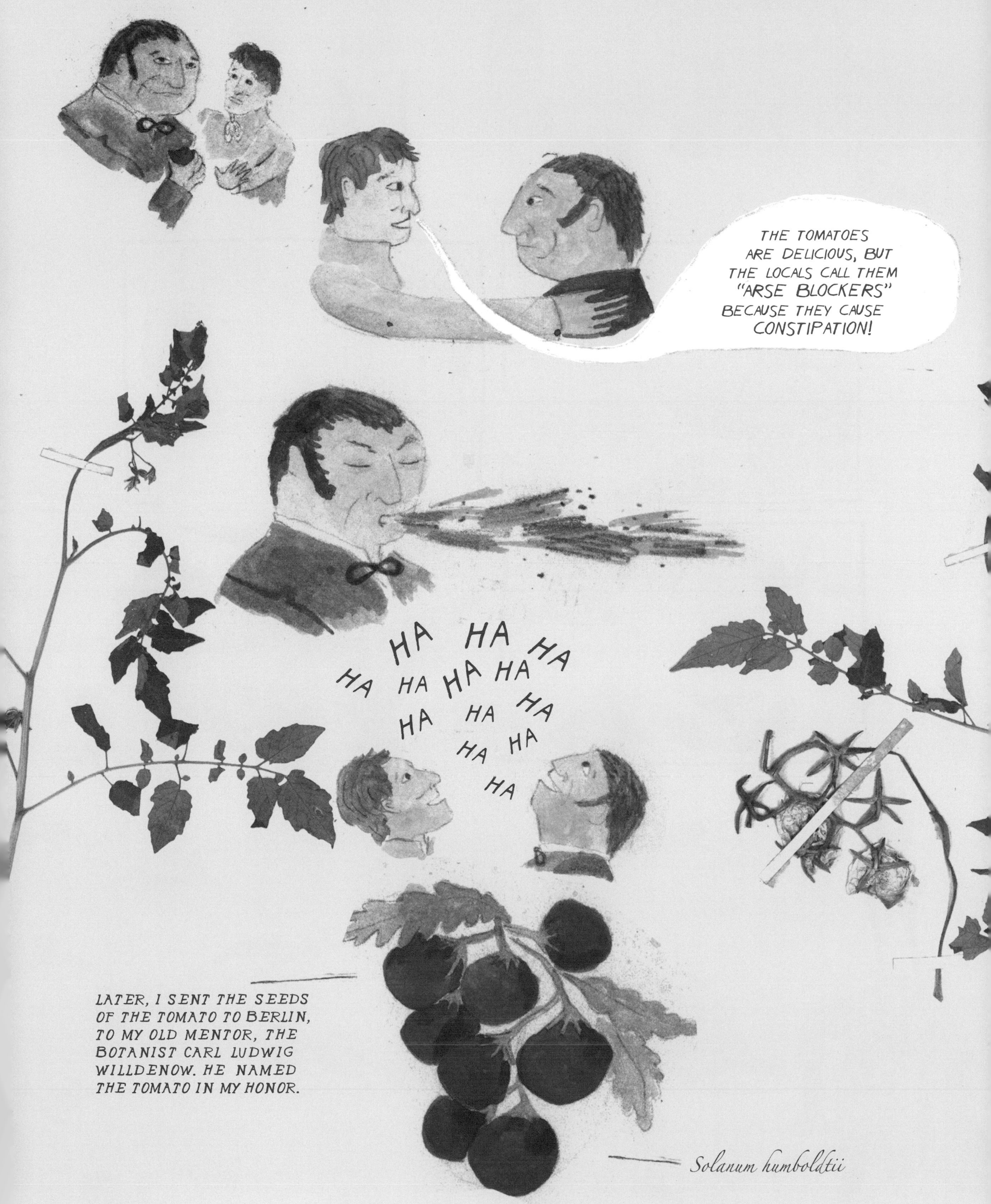
THE TOMATOES ARE DELICIOUS, BUT THE LOCALS CALL THEM "ARSE BLOCKERS" BECAUSE THEY CAUSE CONSTIPATION!
HA HA HA HA HA HA HA HA HA HA HA HA HA
LATER, I SENT THE SEEDS OF THE TOMATO TO BERLIN, TO MY OLD MENTOR, THE BOTANIST CARL LUDWIG WILLDENOW. HE NAMED THE TOMATO IN MY HONOR.
Solanum humboldtii

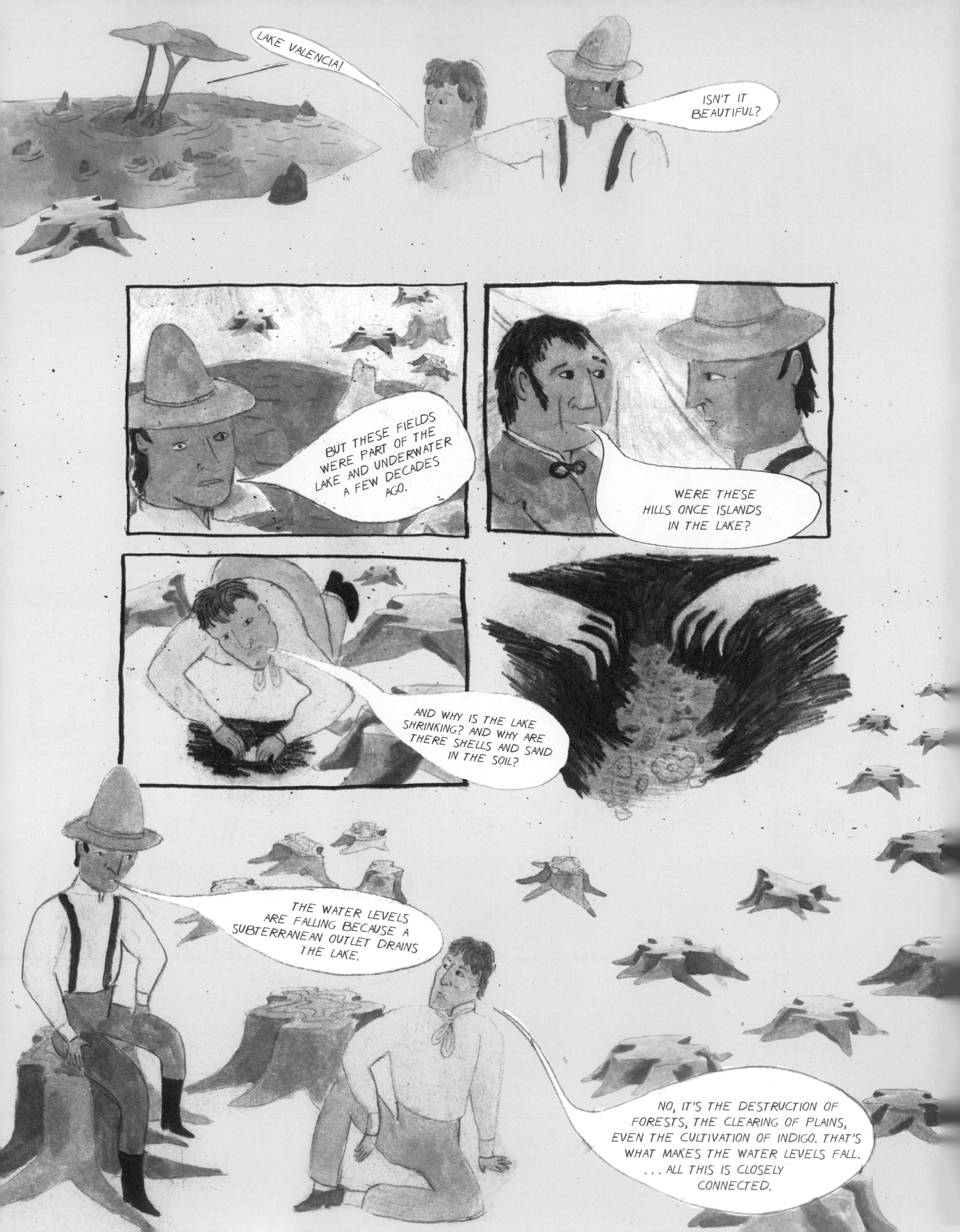
LAKE VALENCIA!
ISN'T IT BEAUTIFUL?
BUT THESE FIELDS WERE PART OF THE LAKE AND UNDERWATER A FEW DECADES AGO.
WERE THESE HILLS ONCE ISLANDS IN THE LAKE?
AND WHY IS THE LAKE SHRINKING? AND WHY ARE THERE SHELLS AND SAND IN THE SOIL?
THE WATER LEVELS ARE FALLING BECAUSE A SUBTERRANEAN OUTLET DRAINS THE LAKE.
NO, IT'S THE DESTRUCTION OF FORESTS, THE CLEARING OF PLAINS, EVEN THE CULTIVATION OF INDIGO. THAT'S WHAT MAKES THE WATER LEVELS FALL. ... ALL THIS IS CLOSELY CONNECTED.

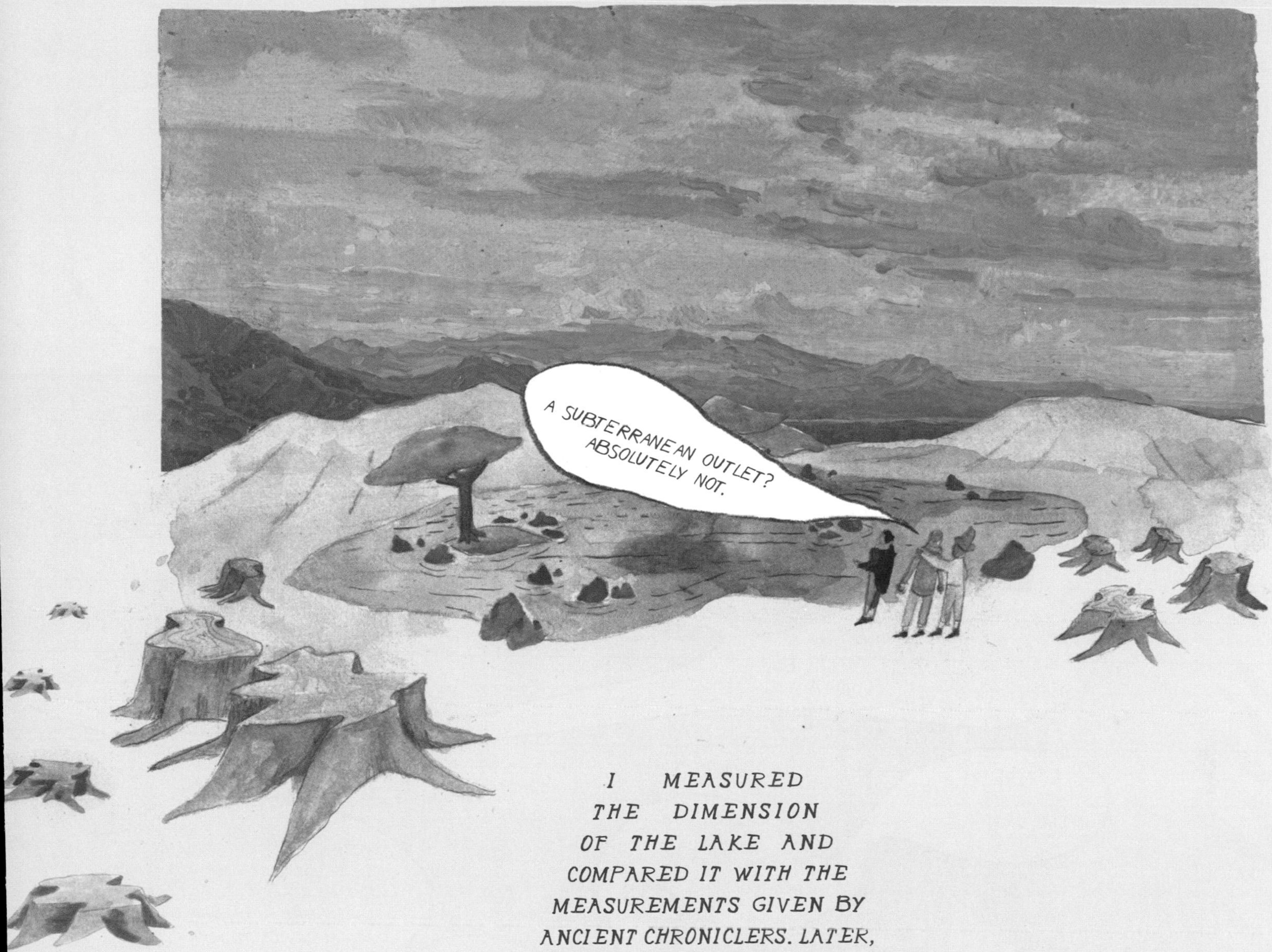
A SUBTERRANEAN OUTLET? ABSOLUTELY NOT.

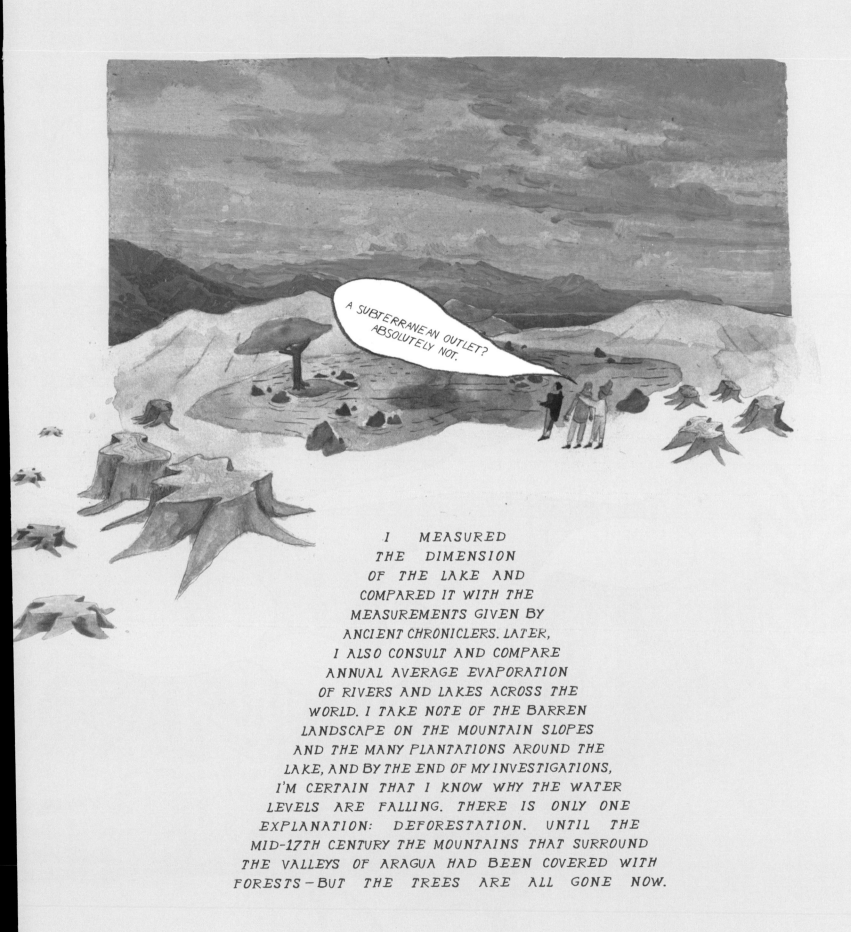

I MEASURED THE DIMENSION OF THE LAKE AND COMPARED IT WITH THE MEASUREMENTS GIVEN BY ANCIENT CHRONICLERS. LATER, I ALSO CONSULT AND COMPARE ANNUAL AVERAGE EVAPORATION OF RIVERS AND LAKES ACROSS THE WORLD. I TAKE NOTE OF THE BARREN LANDSCAPE ON THE MOUNTAIN SLOPES AND THE MANY PLANTATIONS AROUND THE LAKE, AND BY THE END OF MY INVESTIGATIONS, I'M CERTAIN THAT I KNOW WHY THE WATER LEVELS ARE FALLING. THERE IS ONLY ONE EXPLANATION: DEFORESTATION. UNTIL THE MID-17TH CENTURY THE MOUNTAINS THAT SURROUND THE VALLEYS OF ARAGUA HAD BEEN COVERED WITH FORESTS—BUT THE TREES ARE ALL GONE NOW.

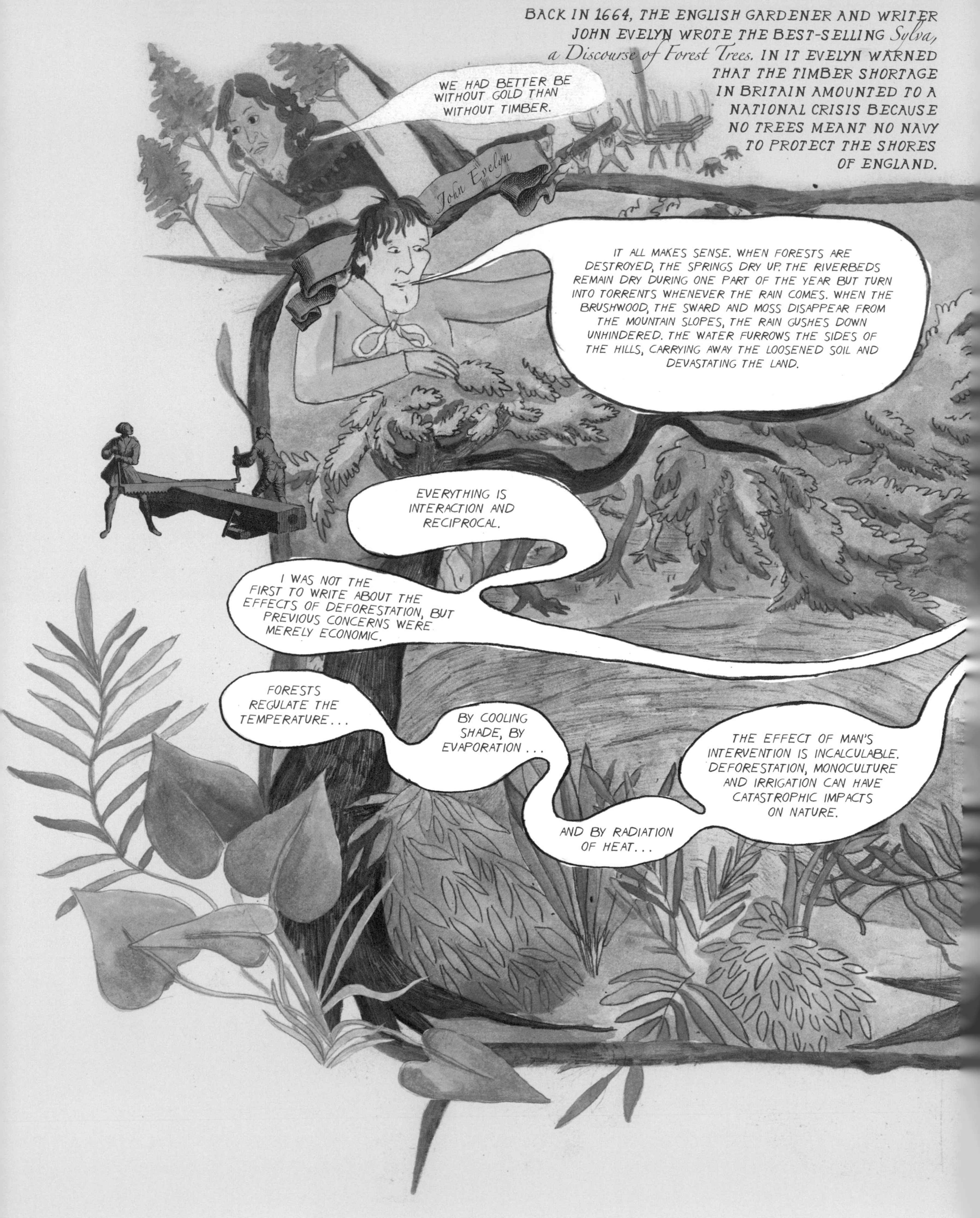
BACK IN 1664, THE ENGLISH GARDENER AND WRITER JOHN EVELYN WROTE THE BEST-SELLING *Sylva, a Discourse of Forest Trees.* IN IT EVELYN WARNED THAT THE TIMBER SHORTAGE IN BRITAIN AMOUNTED TO A NATIONAL CRISIS BECAUSE NO TREES MEANT NO NAVY TO PROTECT THE SHORES OF ENGLAND.
WE HAD BETTER BE WITHOUT GOLD THAN WITHOUT TIMBER.
John Evelyn
IT ALL MAKES SENSE. WHEN FORESTS ARE DESTROYED, THE SPRINGS DRY UP. THE RIVERBEDS REMAIN DRY DURING ONE PART OF THE YEAR BUT TURN INTO TORRENTS WHENEVER THE RAIN COMES. WHEN THE BRUSHWOOD, THE SWARD AND MOSS DISAPPEAR FROM THE MOUNTAIN SLOPES, THE RAIN GUSHES DOWN UNHINDERED. THE WATER FURROWS THE SIDES OF THE HILLS, CARRYING AWAY THE LOOSENED SOIL AND DEVASTATING THE LAND.
EVERYTHING IS INTERACTION AND RECIPROCAL.
I WAS NOT THE FIRST TO WRITE ABOUT THE EFFECTS OF DEFORESTATION, BUT PREVIOUS CONCERNS WERE MERELY ECONOMIC.
FORESTS REGULATE THE TEMPERATURE...
BY COOLING SHADE, BY EVAPORATION...
AND BY RADIATION OF HEAT...
THE EFFECT OF MAN'S INTERVENTION IS INCALCULABLE. DEFORESTATION, MONOCULTURE AND IRRIGATION CAN HAVE CATASTROPHIC IMPACTS ON NATURE.

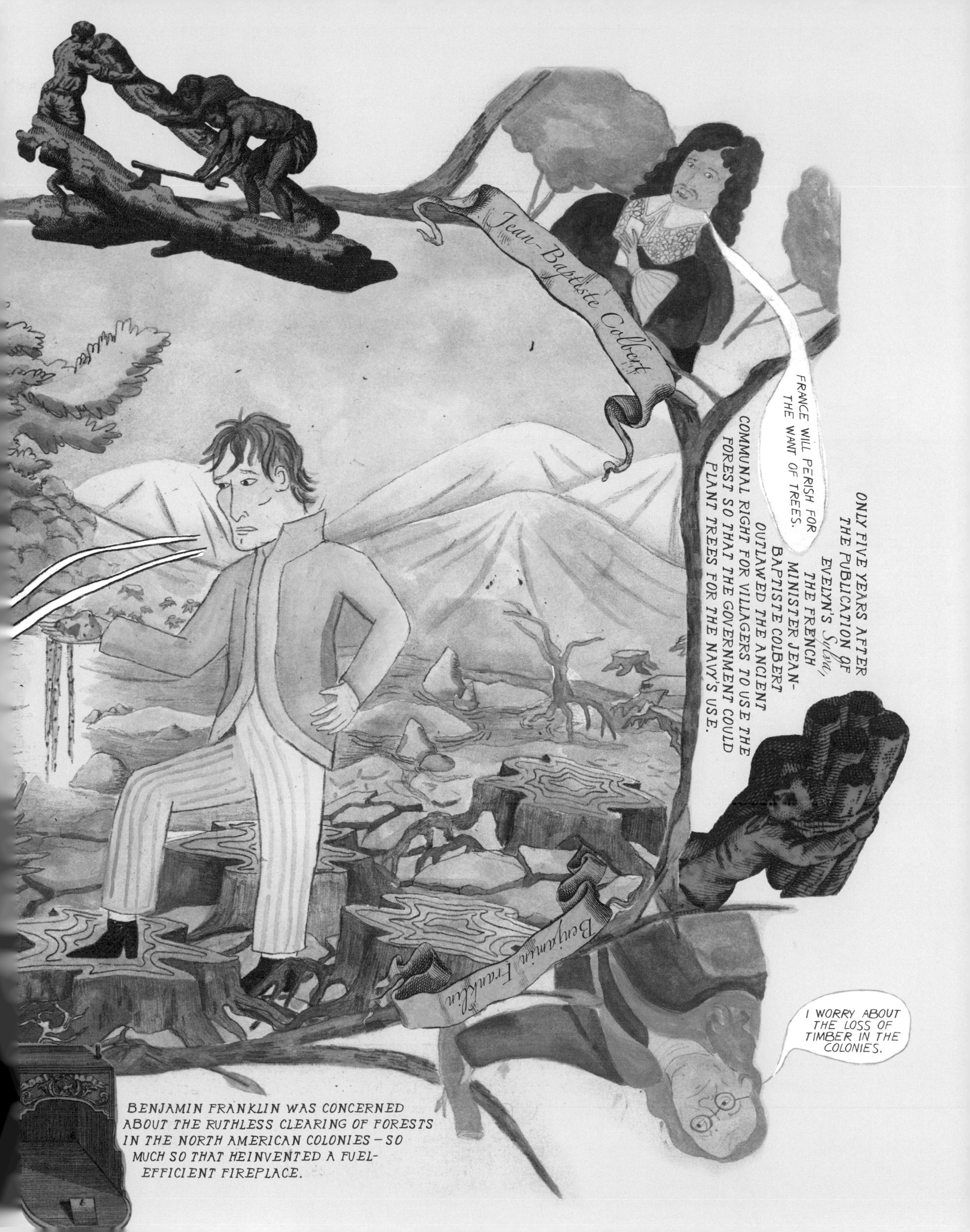
Jean-Baptiste Colbert
ONLY FIVE YEARS AFTER THE PUBLICATION OF EVELYN'S Sylva, THE FRENCH MINISTER JEAN-BAPTISTE COLBERT OUTLAWED THE ANCIENT COMMUNAL RIGHT FOR VILLAGERS TO USE THE FOREST SO THAT THE GOVERNMENT COULD PLANT TREES FOR THE NAVY'S USE.
FRANCE WILL PERISH FOR THE WANT OF TREES.
Benjamin Franklin
I WORRY ABOUT THE LOSS OF TIMBER IN THE COLONIES.
BENJAMIN FRANKLIN WAS CONCERNED ABOUT THE RUTHLESS CLEARING OF FORESTS IN THE NORTH AMERICAN COLONIES – SO MUCH SO THAT HEINVENTED A FUEL-EFFICIENT FIREPLACE.

MY WARNINGS ABOUT THE EFFECTS OF DEFORESTATION WERE A RADICAL CHANGE FROM THE HUMAN-CENTERED PERSPECTIVE THAT HAD RULED HUMANKIND'S APPROACH TO NATURE FOR MILLENNIA.

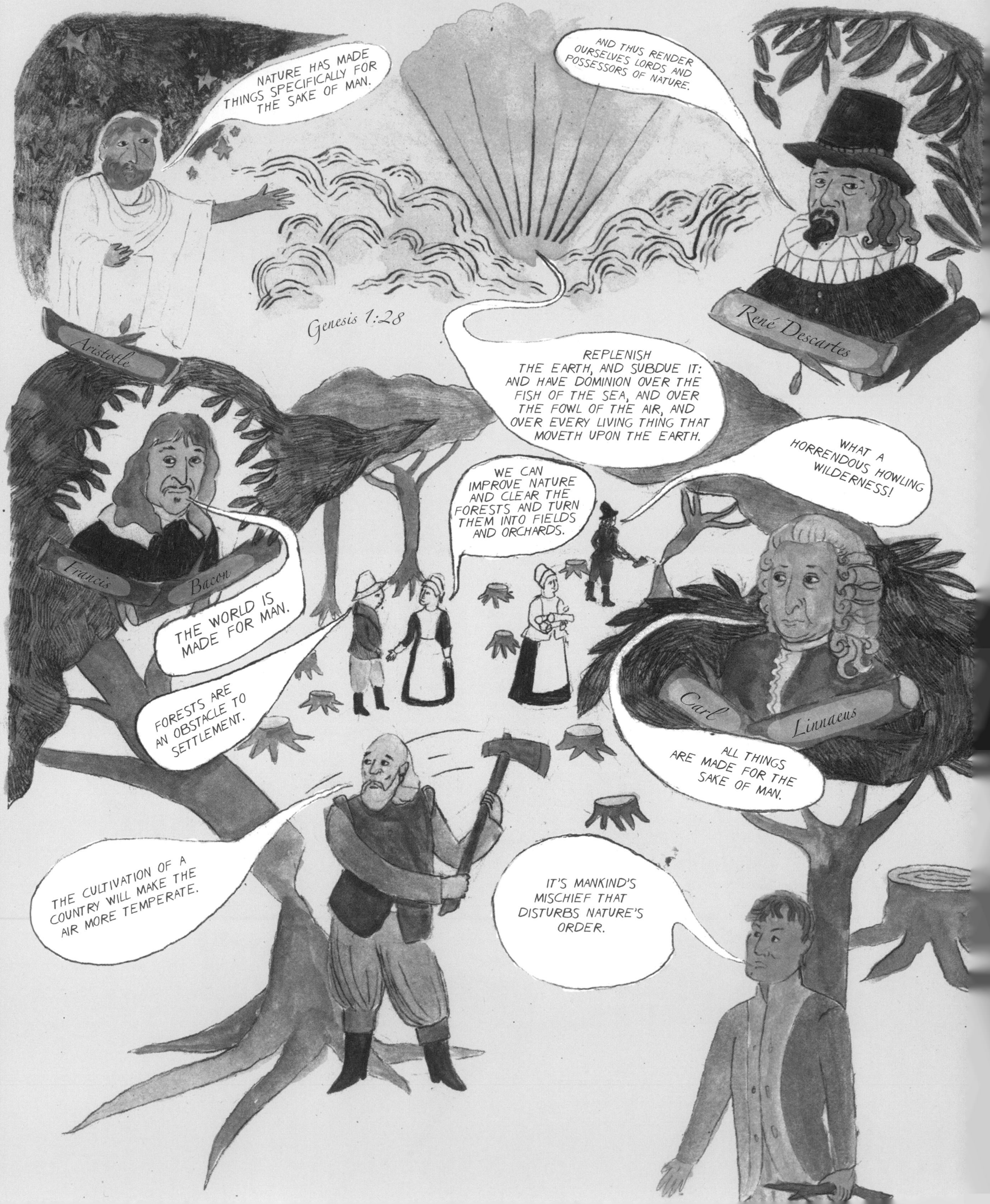
NATURE HAS MADE THINGS SPECIFICALLY FOR THE SAKE OF MAN.
Aristotle
Genesis 1:28
AND THUS RENDER OURSELVES LORDS AND POSSESSORS OF NATURE.
René Descartes
REPLENISH THE EARTH, AND SUBDUE IT: AND HAVE DOMINION OVER THE FISH OF THE SEA, AND OVER THE FOWL OF THE AIR, AND OVER EVERY LIVING THING THAT MOVETH UPON THE EARTH.
Francis Bacon
THE WORLD IS MADE FOR MAN.
WE CAN IMPROVE NATURE AND CLEAR THE FORESTS AND TURN THEM INTO FIELDS AND ORCHARDS.
WHAT A HORRENDOUS HOWLING WILDERNESS!
FORESTS ARE AN OBSTACLE TO SETTLEMENT.
Carl Linnaeus
ALL THINGS ARE MADE FOR THE SAKE OF MAN.
THE CULTIVATION OF A COUNTRY WILL MAKE THE AIR MORE TEMPERATE.
IT'S MANKIND'S MISCHIEF THAT DISTURBS NATURE'S ORDER.

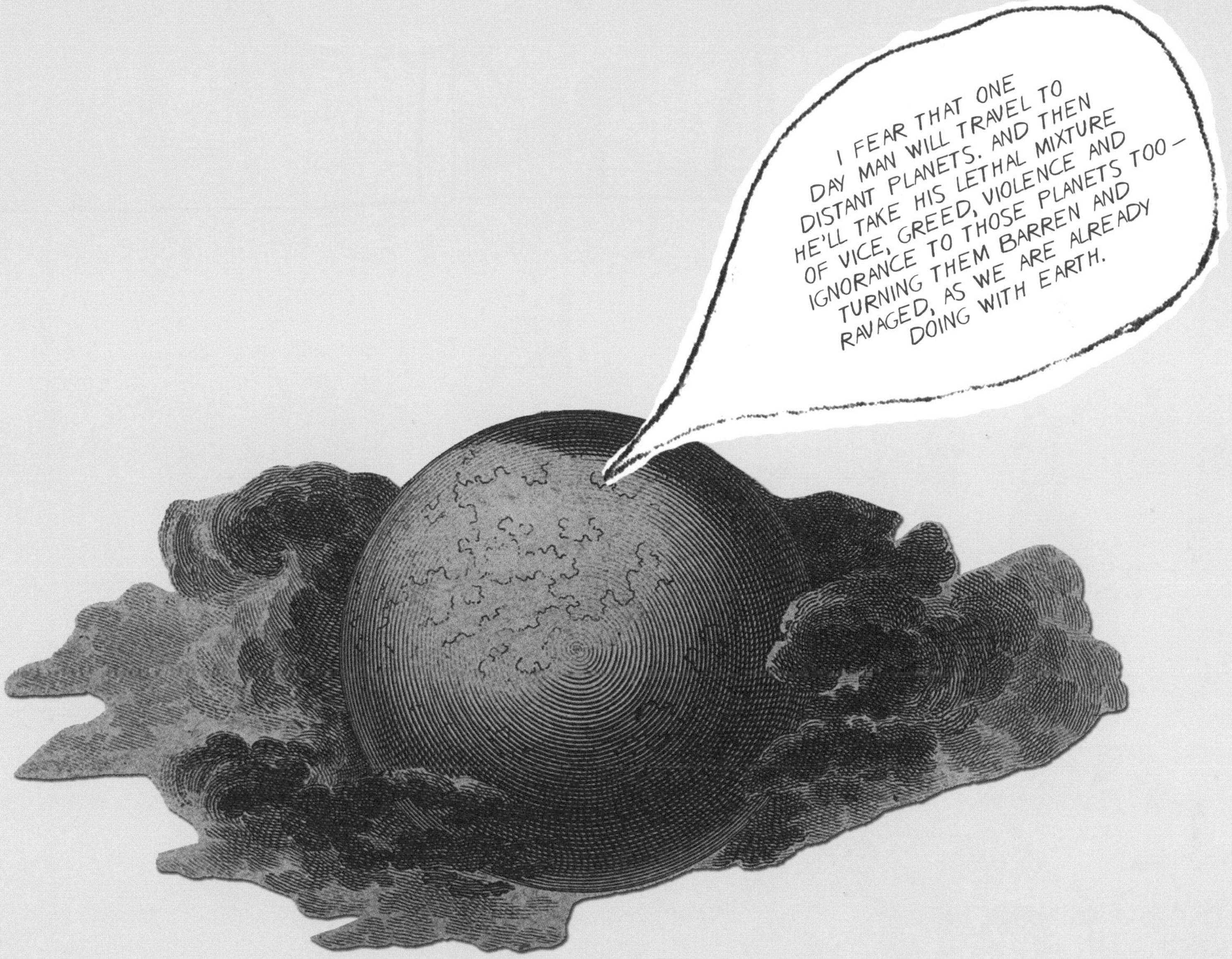
I FEAR THAT ONE DAY MAN WILL TRAVEL TO DISTANT PLANETS. AND THEN HE'LL TAKE HIS LETHAL MIXTURE OF VICE, GREED, VIOLENCE AND IGNORANCE TO THOSE PLANETS TOO— TURNING THEM BARREN AND RAVAGED, AS WE ARE ALREADY DOING WITH EARTH.

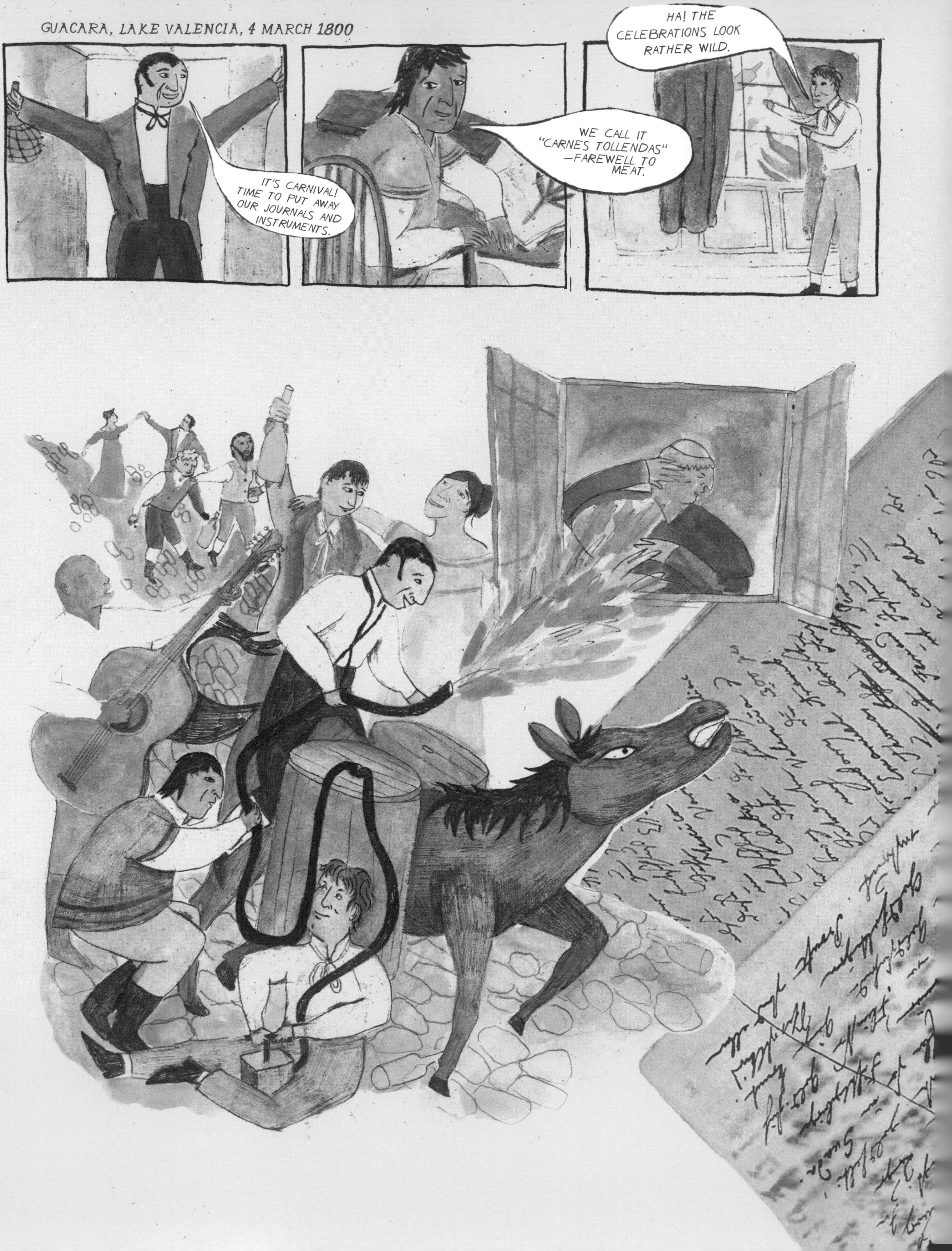
GUACARA, LAKE VALENCIA, 4 MARCH 1800
IT'S CARNIVAL! TIME TO PUT AWAY OUR JOURNALS AND INSTRUMENTS.
WE CALL IT "CARNES TOLLENDAS" —FAREWELL TO MEAT.
HA! THE CELEBRATIONS LOOK RATHER WILD.

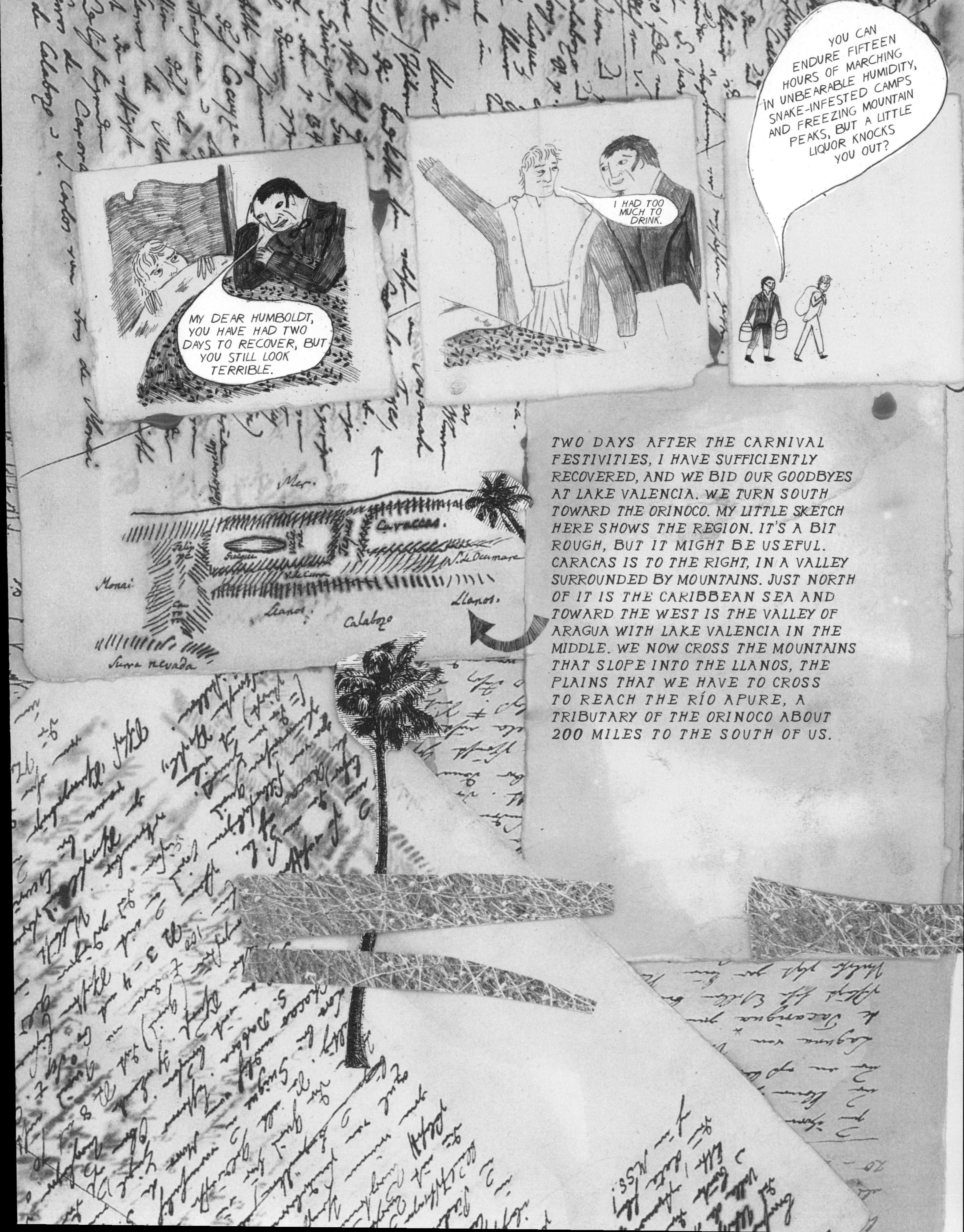
MY DEAR HUMBOLDT, YOU HAVE HAD TWO DAYS TO RECOVER, BUT YOU STILL LOOK TERRIBLE.
I HAD TOO MUCH TO DRINK.
YOU CAN ENDURE FIFTEEN HOURS OF MARCHING IN UNBEARABLE HUMIDITY, SNAKE-INFESTED CAMPS AND FREEZING MOUNTAIN PEAKS, BUT A LITTLE LIQUOR KNOCKS YOU OUT?
Mer.
Caraccas.
Llanos.
Calabozo
TWO DAYS AFTER THE CARNIVAL FESTIVITIES, I HAVE SUFFICIENTLY RECOVERED, AND WE BID OUR GOODBYES AT LAKE VALENCIA. WE TURN SOUTH TOWARD THE ORINOCO. MY LITTLE SKETCH HERE SHOWS THE REGION. IT'S A BIT ROUGH, BUT IT MIGHT BE USEFUL. CARACAS IS TO THE RIGHT, IN A VALLEY SURROUNDED BY MOUNTAINS. JUST NORTH OF IT IS THE CARIBBEAN SEA AND TOWARD THE WEST IS THE VALLEY OF ARAGUA WITH LAKE VALENCIA IN THE MIDDLE. WE NOW CROSS THE MOUNTAINS THAT SLOPE INTO THE LLANOS, THE PLAINS THAT WE HAVE TO CROSS TO REACH THE RÍO APURE, A TRIBUTARY OF THE ORINOCO ABOUT 200 MILES TO THE SOUTH OF US.

IN THE LLANOS WE'RE PLUNGED INTO A VAST SOLITUDE.

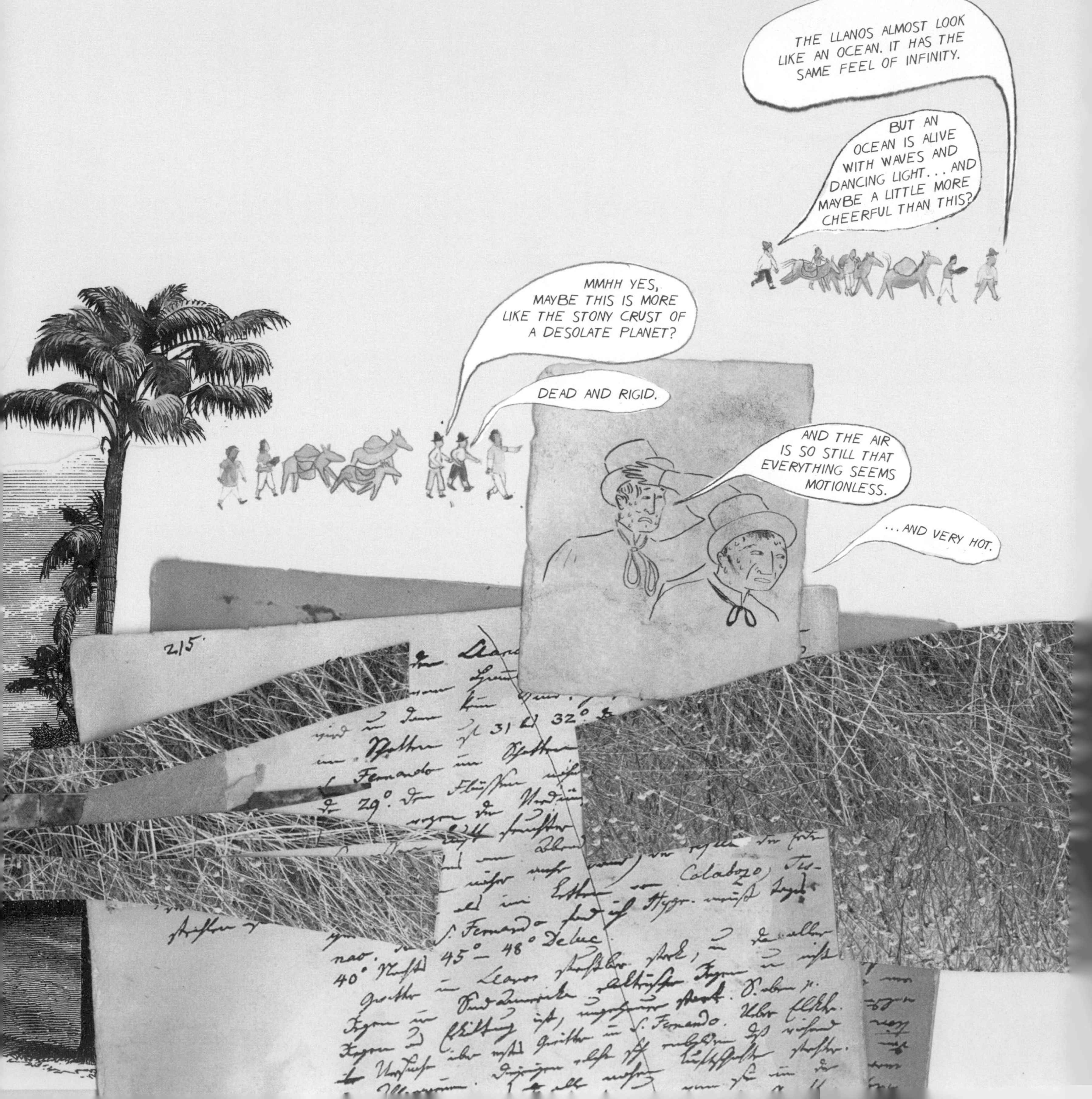
THE LLANOS ALMOST LOOK LIKE AN OCEAN. IT HAS THE SAME FEEL OF INFINITY.
BUT AN OCEAN IS ALIVE WITH WAVES AND DANCING LIGHT... AND MAYBE A LITTLE MORE CHEERFUL THAN THIS?
MMHH YES, MAYBE THIS IS MORE LIKE THE STONY CRUST OF A DESOLATE PLANET?
DEAD AND RIGID.
AND THE AIR IS SO STILL THAT EVERYTHING SEEMS MOTIONLESS.
...AND VERY HOT.

50°C
WE SHOULD TRAVEL AT NIGHT.
THERE IS NO SHADE WHERE WE CAN REST DURING THE DAY.
IF YOU STUFF LEAVES INTO YOUR HATS, IT WILL PROTECT AND INSULATE YOU FROM THE SUN.

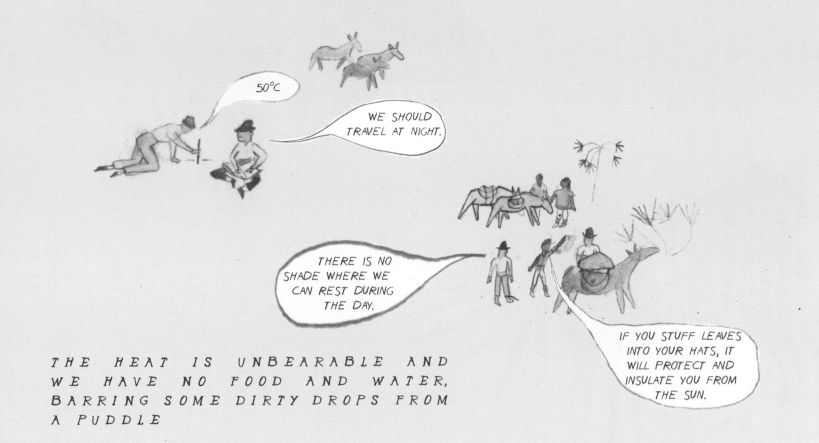

THE HEAT IS UNBEARABLE AND WE HAVE NO FOOD AND WATER, BARRING SOME DIRTY DROPS FROM A PUDDLE

JOSÉ, IS THE BAROMETER SAFE?

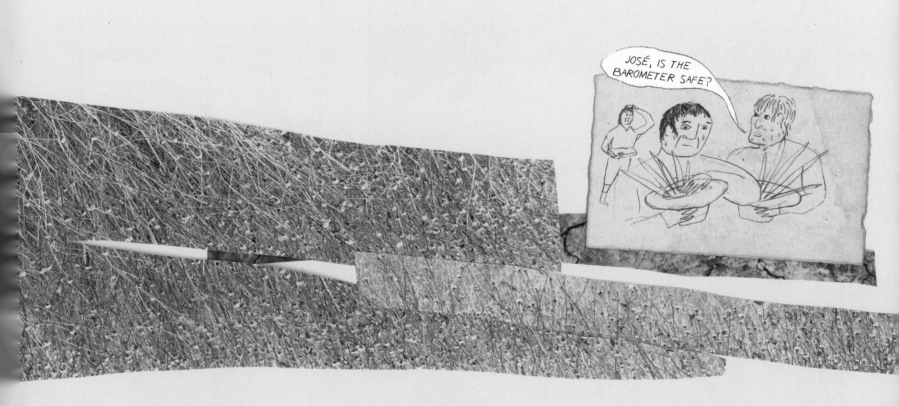

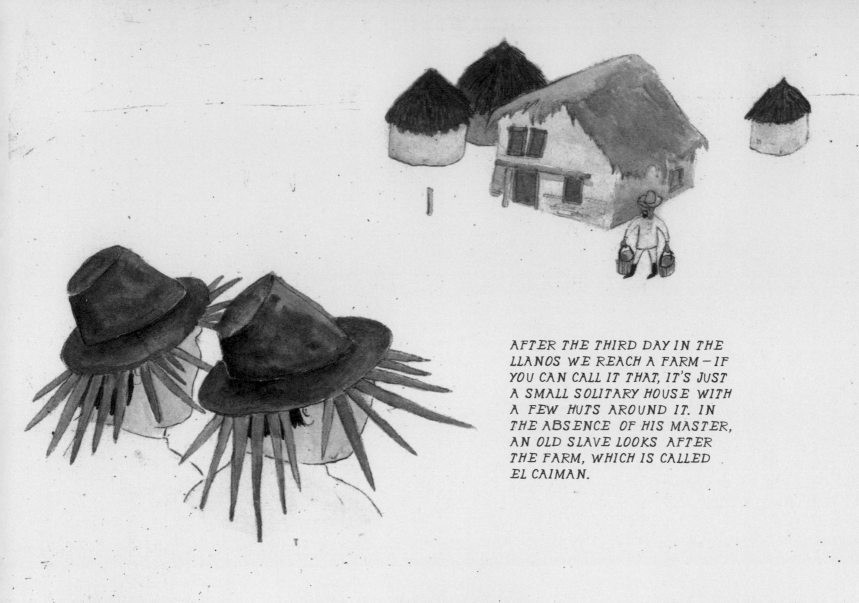

AFTER THE THIRD DAY IN THE
LLANOS WE REACH A FARM — IF
YOU CAN CALL IT THAT, IT'S JUST
A SMALL SOLITARY HOUSE WITH
A FEW HUTS AROUND IT. IN
THE ABSENCE OF HIS MASTER,
AN OLD SLAVE LOOKS AFTER
THE FARM, WHICH IS CALLED
EL CAIMAN.

GOOD MAN,
WE HAD A LONG DAY,
MIGHT YOU HAVE SOME
MILK FOR US?

NO,
I DON'T.

MAYBE YOU
HAVE SOME WATER
THEN?

OVER THERE
IN THE BARREL, BUT YOU
BETTER COVER YOUR CUP
WITH CLOTH WHEN
YOU DRINK.

WHY?

SO YOU DON'T
SWALLOW THE MUD.

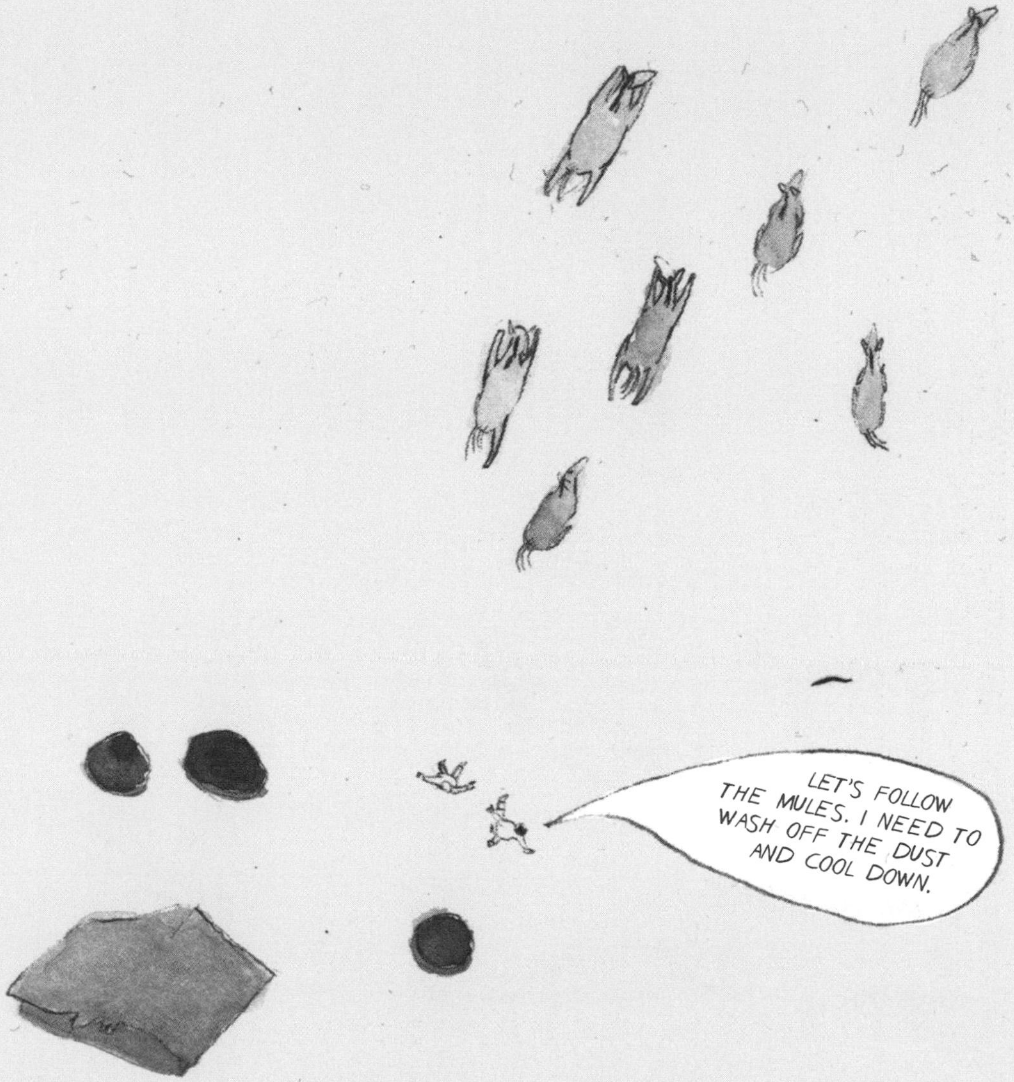
LET'S FOLLOW THE MULES. I NEED TO WASH OFF THE DUST AND COOL DOWN.

THE MULES RUSH INTO THE SAVANNAH. THEIR TAILS RAISED, THEIR HEADS THROWN BACK, STOPPING FROM TIME TO TIME. THEIR LOUD NEIGHING ANNOUNCES THE PRESENCE OF WATER.

AFTER A MILE WE FIND A MUDDY POOL.

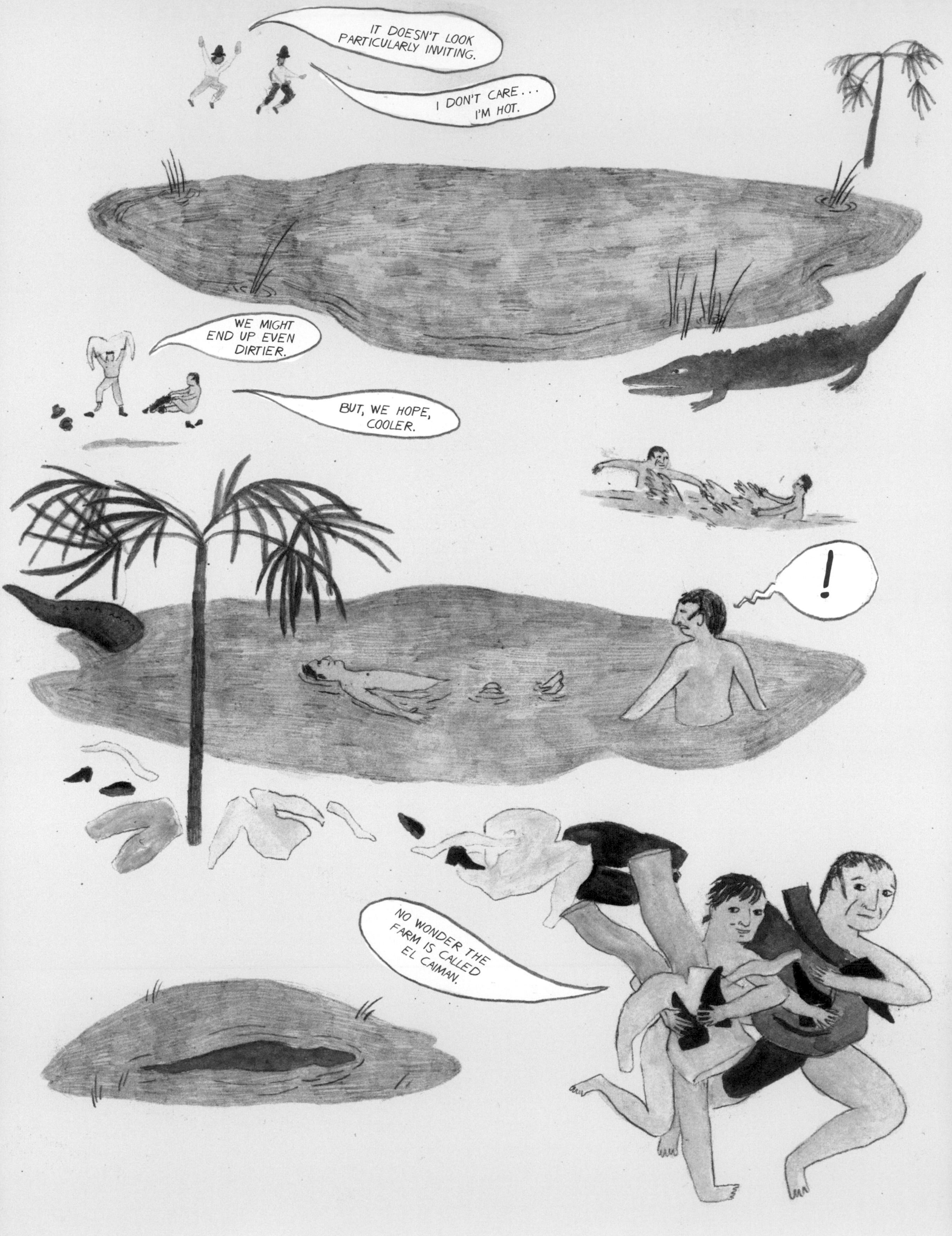
IT DOESN'T LOOK PARTICULARLY INVITING.
I DON'T CARE . . . I'M HOT.
WE MIGHT END UP EVEN DIRTIER.
BUT, WE HOPE, COOLER.
!
NO WONDER THE FARM IS CALLED EL CAIMAN.

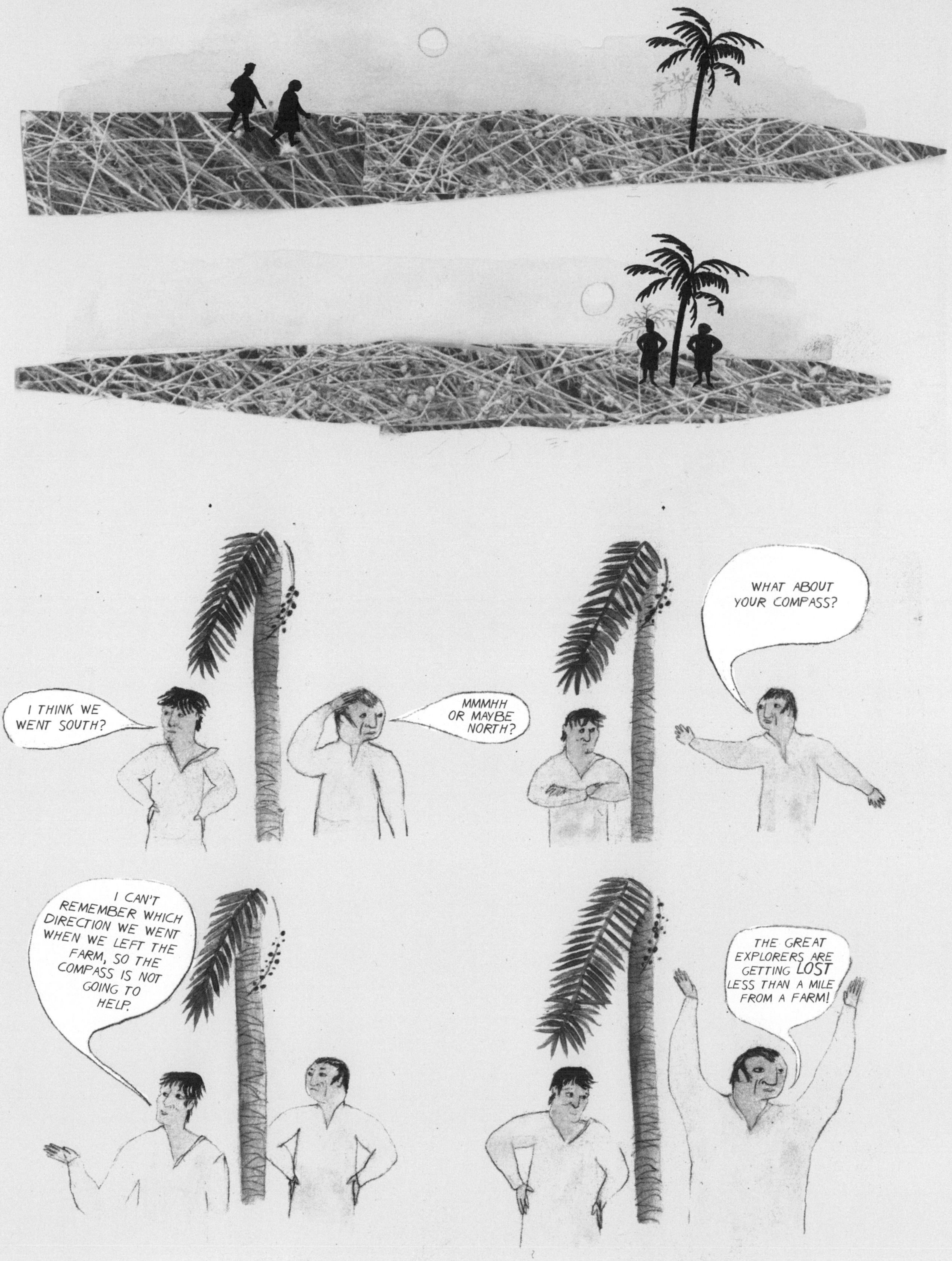
I THINK WE WENT SOUTH?
MMMHH OR MAYBE NORTH?
WHAT ABOUT YOUR COMPASS?
I CAN'T REMEMBER WHICH DIRECTION WE WENT WHEN WE LEFT THE FARM, SO THE COMPASS IS NOT GOING TO HELP.
THE GREAT EXPLORERS ARE GETTING LOST LESS THAN A MILE FROM A FARM!

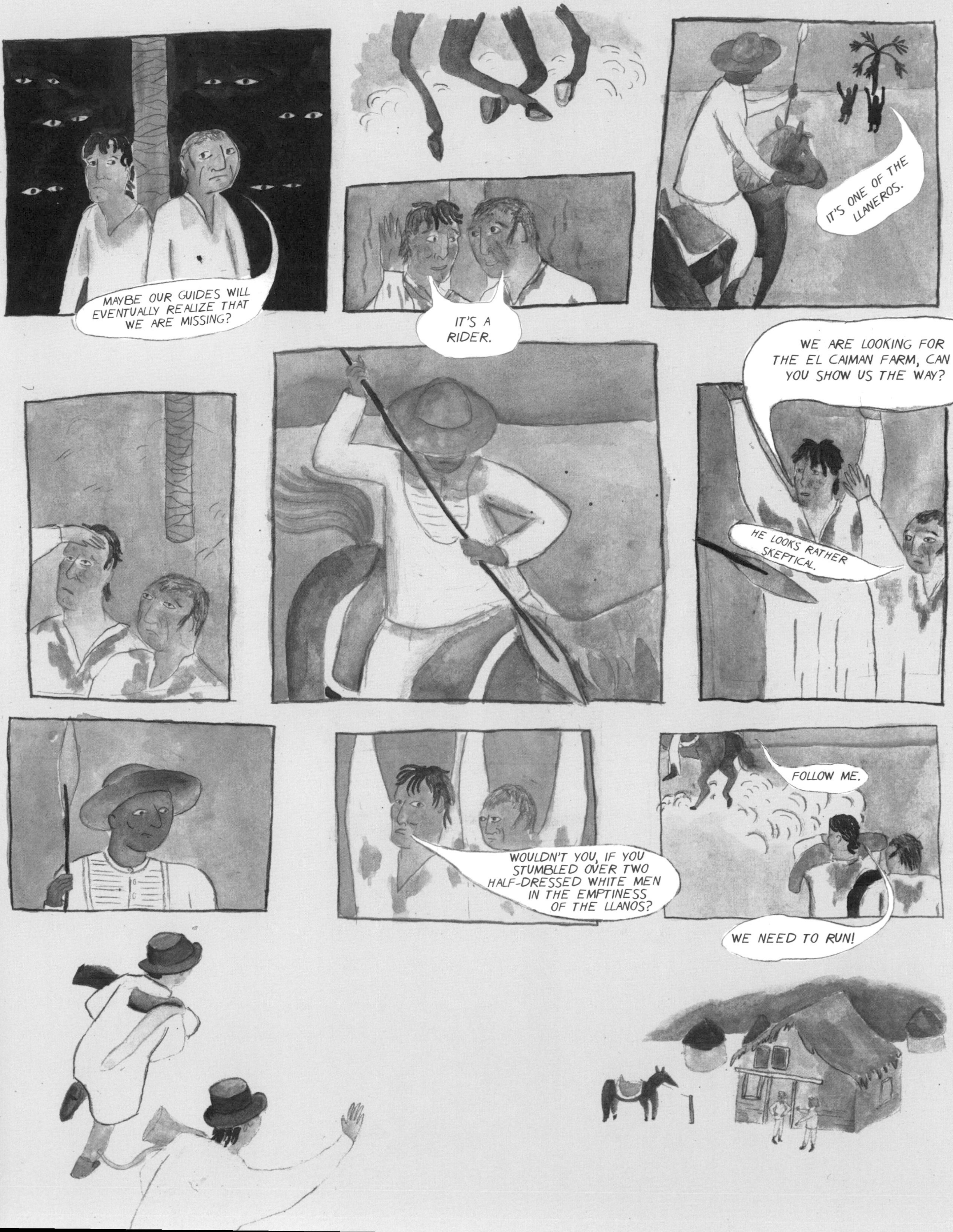
MAYBE OUR GUIDES WILL EVENTUALLY REALIZE THAT WE ARE MISSING?
IT'S A RIDER.
IT'S ONE OF THE LLANEROS.
WE ARE LOOKING FOR THE EL CAIMAN FARM, CAN YOU SHOW US THE WAY?
HE LOOKS RATHER SKEPTICAL.
WOULDN'T YOU, IF YOU STUMBLED OVER TWO HALF-DRESSED WHITE MEN IN THE EMPTINESS OF THE LLANOS?
FOLLOW ME.
WE NEED TO RUN!

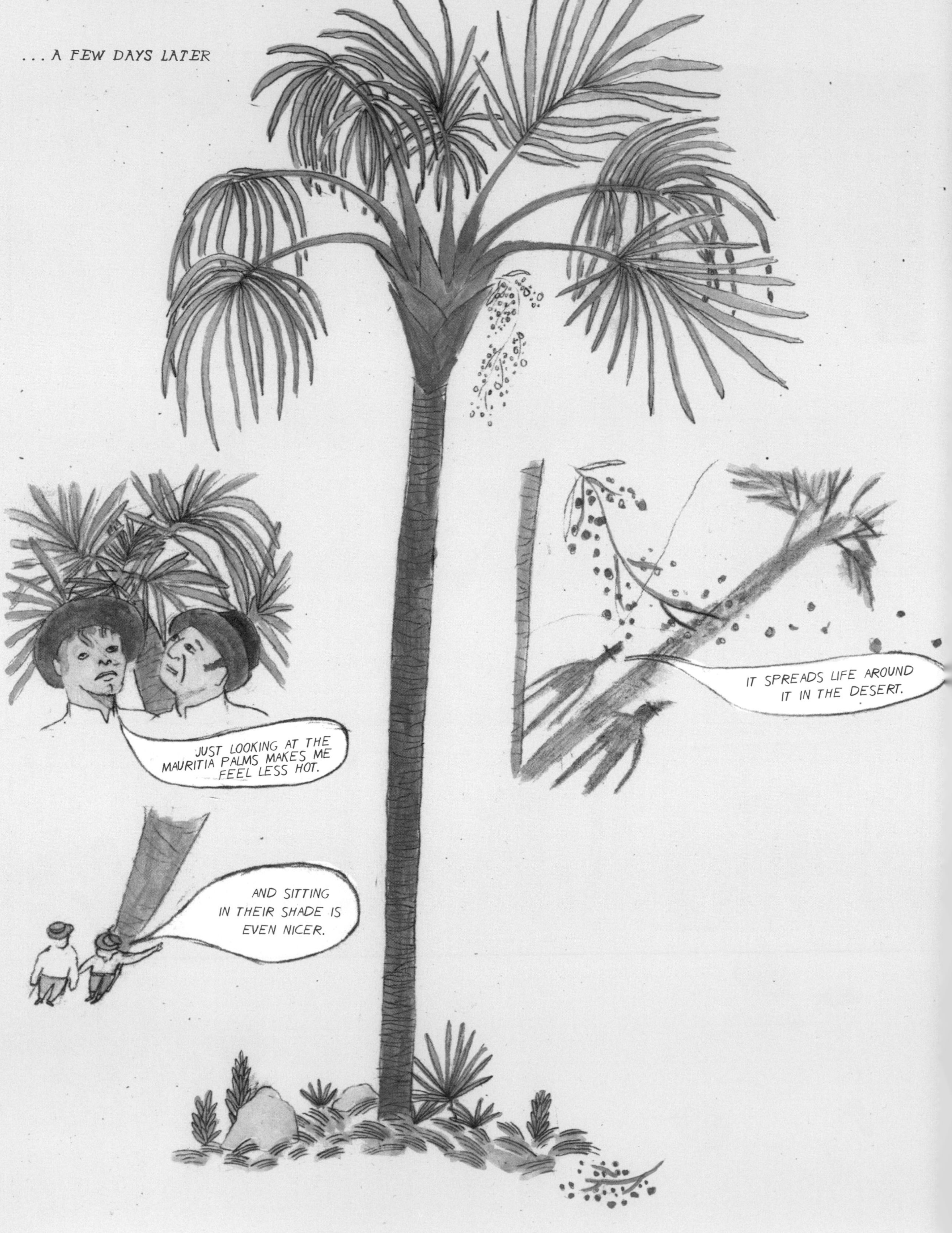
. . . A FEW DAYS LATER
JUST LOOKING AT THE MAURITIA PALMS MAKES ME FEEL LESS HOT.
AND SITTING IN THEIR SHADE IS EVEN NICER.
IT SPREADS LIFE AROUND IT IN THE DESERT.

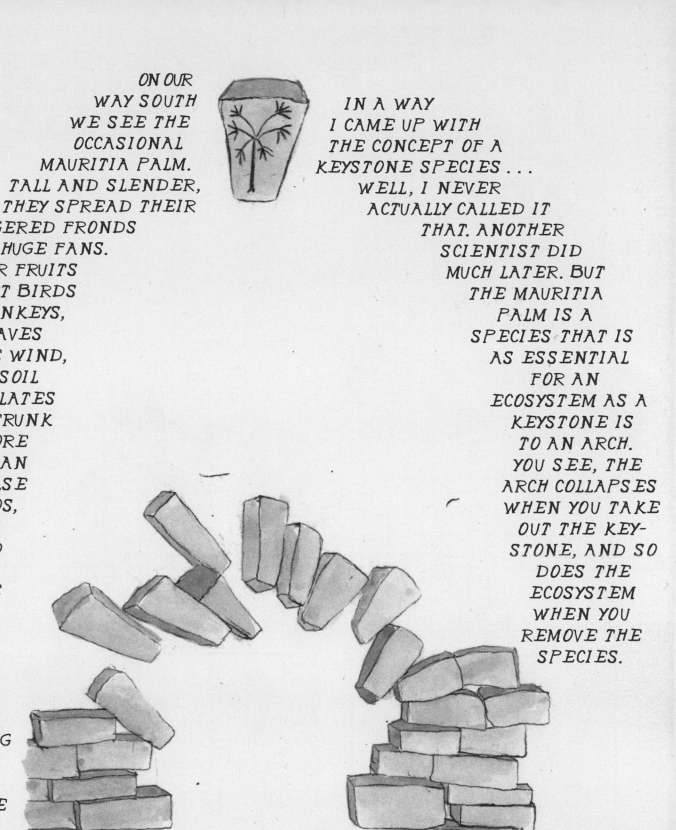

ON OUR
WAY SOUTH
WE SEE THE
OCCASIONAL
MAURITIA PALM.
TALL AND SLENDER,
THEY SPREAD THEIR
FINGERED FRONDS
LIKE HUGE FANS.
THEIR FRUITS
ATTRACT BIRDS
AND MONKEYS,
THE LEAVES
SHIELD THE WIND,
AND THE SOIL
THAT ACCUMULATES
AROUND ITS TRUNK
RETAINS MORE
MOISTURE THAN
ANYWHERE ELSE
IN THE LLANOS,
SHELTERING
INSECTS AND
WORMS.
PEOPLE MAKE
BASKETS,
THREADS,
HAMMOCKS,
NETS, ROOFS
AND CLOTHING,
AND EVEN A
VERY REFRESHING
FERMENTED
LIQUOR FROM IT.
IT'S A TRUE TREE
OF LIFE —
A PERFECT
SYMBOL OF
NATURE AS
A LIVING
ORGANISM.

IN A WAY
I CAME UP WITH
THE CONCEPT OF A
KEYSTONE SPECIES . . .
WELL, I NEVER
ACTUALLY CALLED IT
THAT. ANOTHER
SCIENTIST DID
MUCH LATER. BUT
THE MAURITIA
PALM IS A
SPECIES THAT IS
AS ESSENTIAL
FOR AN
ECOSYSTEM AS A
KEYSTONE IS
TO AN ARCH.
YOU SEE, THE
ARCH COLLAPSES
WHEN YOU TAKE
OUT THE KEY-
STONE, AND SO
DOES THE
ECOSYSTEM
WHEN YOU
REMOVE THE
SPECIES.

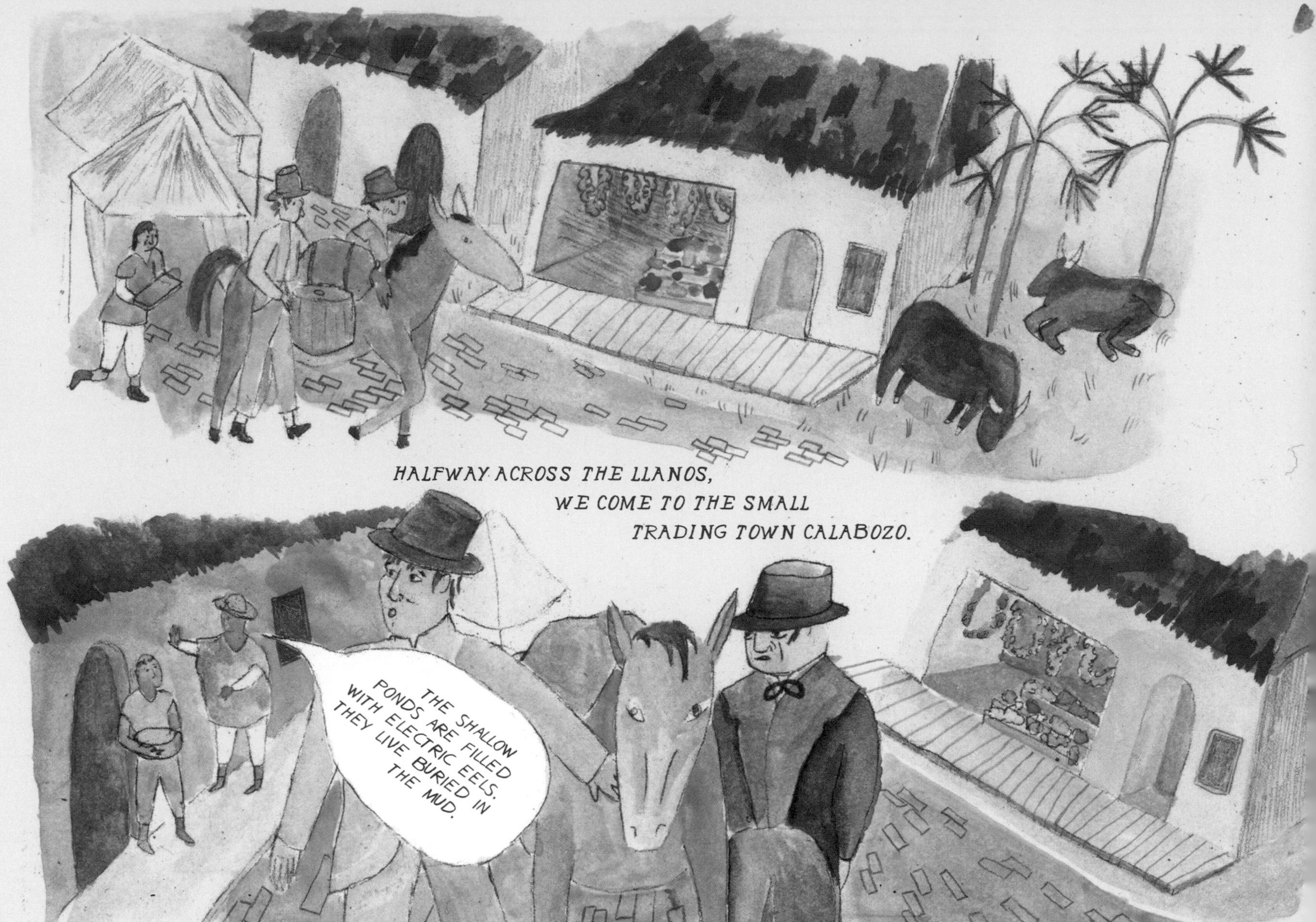
HALFWAY ACROSS THE LLANOS,
WE COME TO THE SMALL
TRADING TOWN CALABOZO.
THE SHALLOW PONDS ARE FILLED WITH ELECTRIC EELS. THEY LIVE BURIED IN THE MUD.
I ALWAYS WANTED TO EXAMINE THESE EXTRAORDINARY FISH.
THEY CAN DELIVER ELECTRIC SHOCKS OF MORE THAN 600 VOLTS.

BACK IN GERMANY, I HAD BEEN OBSESSED WITH SO-CALLED "ANIMAL ELECTRICITY." I CONDUCTED **4,000** EXPERIMENTS IN WHICH I CUT, PRODDED, POKED AND ELECTROCUTED FROGS, MICE AND LIZARDS.

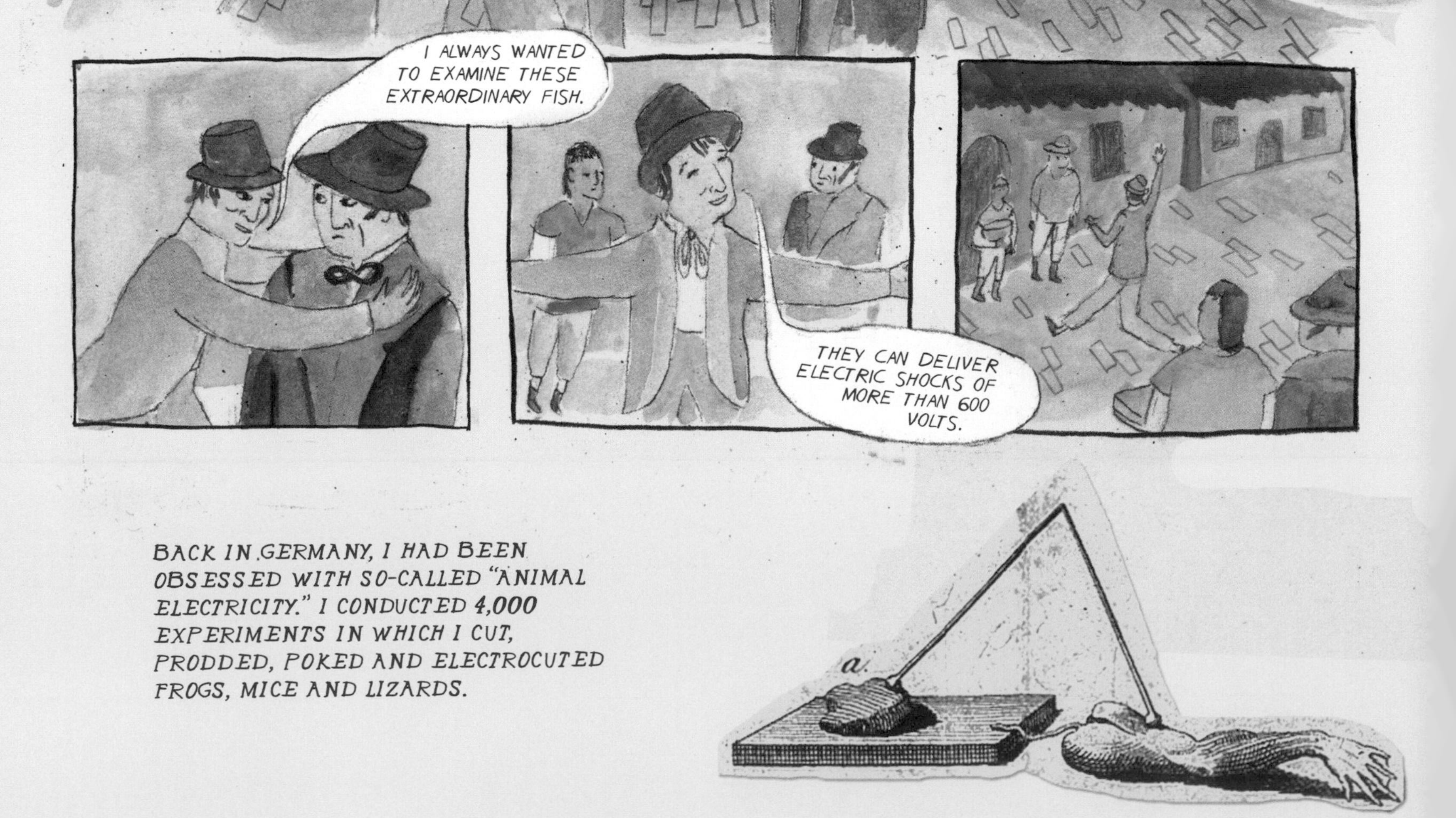
a.

YOU FEEL SORRY FOR THE ANIMALS? WHAT ABOUT ME? WITH A SCALPEL I MADE INCISIONS ON MY ARMS AND TORSO IN WHICH I RUBBED CHEMICALS AND ACIDS. I STUCK METALS, WIRES AND ELECTRODES ON AND IN MY SKIN AND NOTED EVERY CONVULSION AND BURNING. MY BODY WAS COVERED IN BLOOD-FILLED WELTS FOR WEEKS BUT THE EXPERIMENTS WENT SPLENDIDLY.

I WAS INTERESTED IN THE QUESTION, IS THERE A "FORCE" IN MATTER? UNLIKE ISAAC NEWTON, WHO BELIEVED THAT MATTER WAS ESSENTIALLY INERT, I BELIEVE QUITE THE OPPOSITE. NEWTON IS UNDOUBTEDLY ONE OF THE GREATEST SCIENTISTS WHO HAS EVER LIVED, BUT IN THIS CASE, HE WAS WRONG. I THINK. NATURE IS NOT JUST A MECHANICAL SYSTEM BUT A LIVING ORGANISM.

IN THE 1790S, MY FRIEND GOETHE AND I SPENT A GREAT MANY DAYS LOCKED IN THE ANATOMY THEATER. ONE TIME WE EVEN DISSECTED A DEAD FARMER AND HIS WIFE. THEY HAD BEEN STRUCK BY LIGHTNING . . . BUT THAT'S ANOTHER STORY. WE WANTED TO UNDERSTAND THE STRANGE FORCES THAT MIGHT SHAPE AND ANIMATE MATTER.

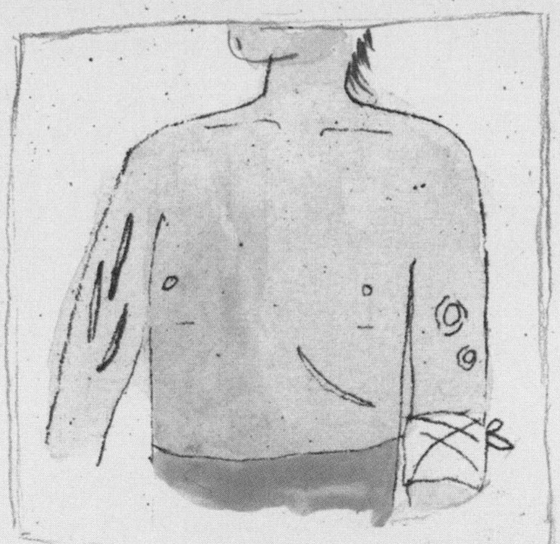

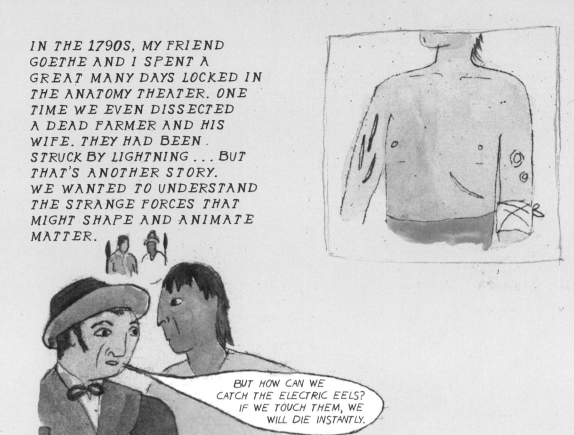

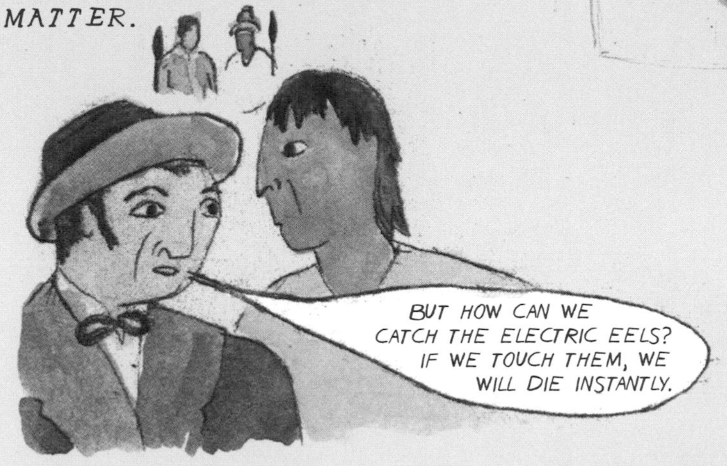
BUT HOW CAN WE CATCH THE ELECTRIC EELS? IF WE TOUCH THEM, WE WILL DIE INSTANTLY.

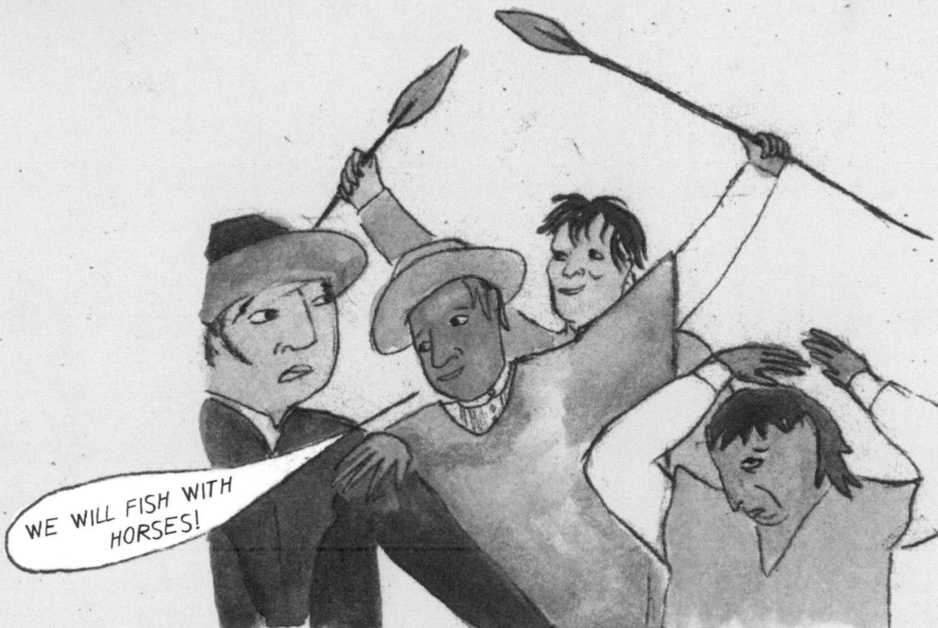
WE WILL FISH WITH HORSES!

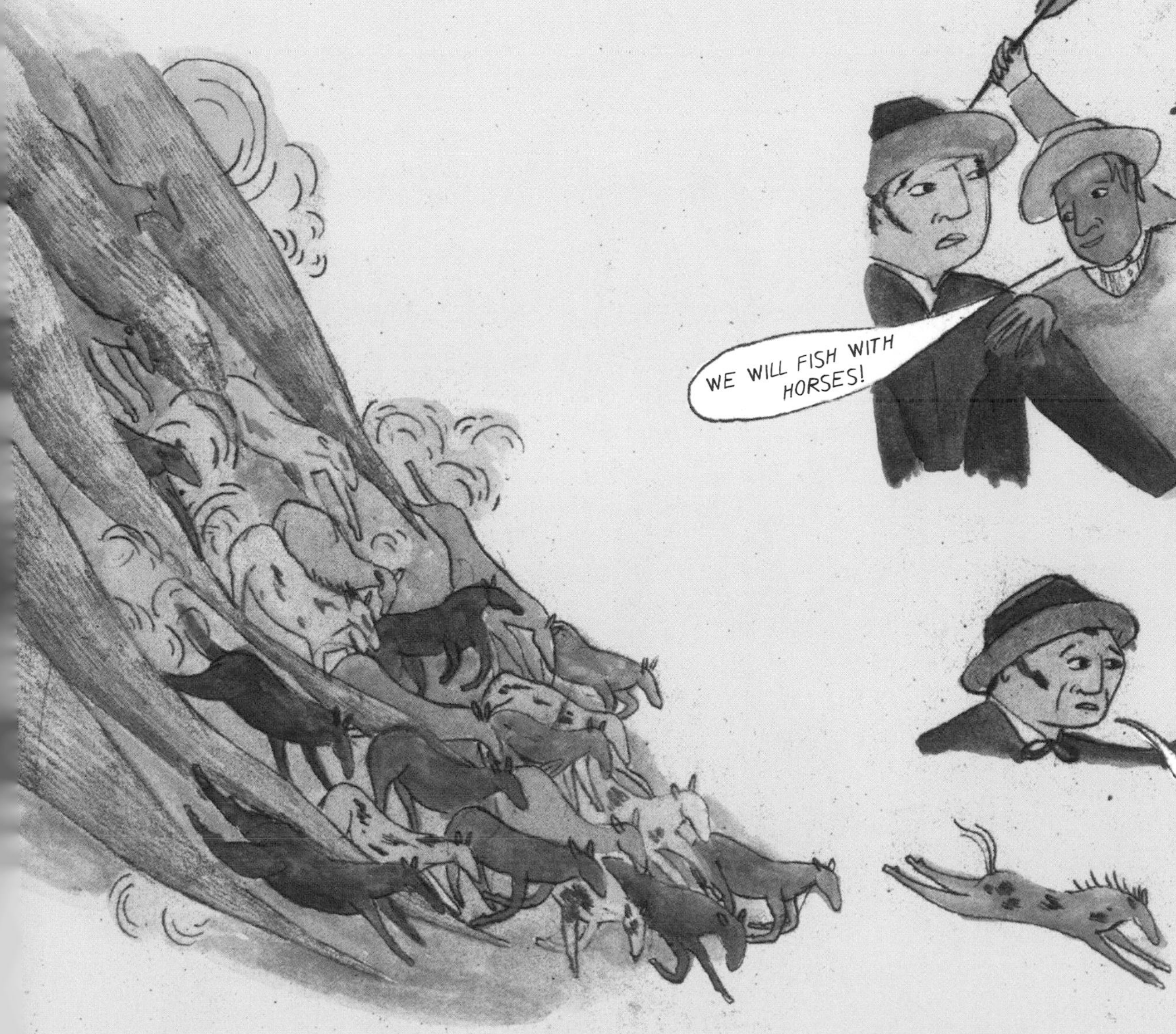

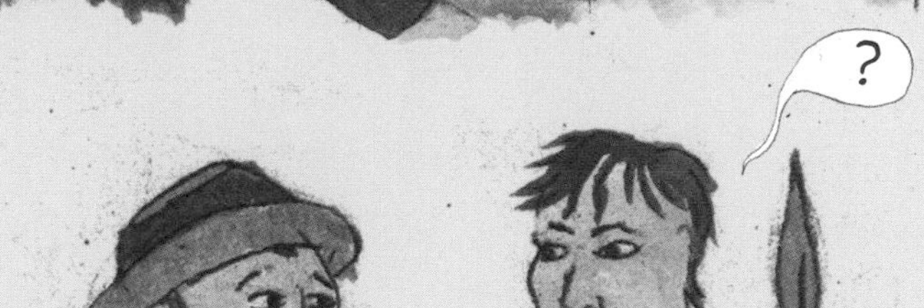
?
WHAT DO THEY MEAN?

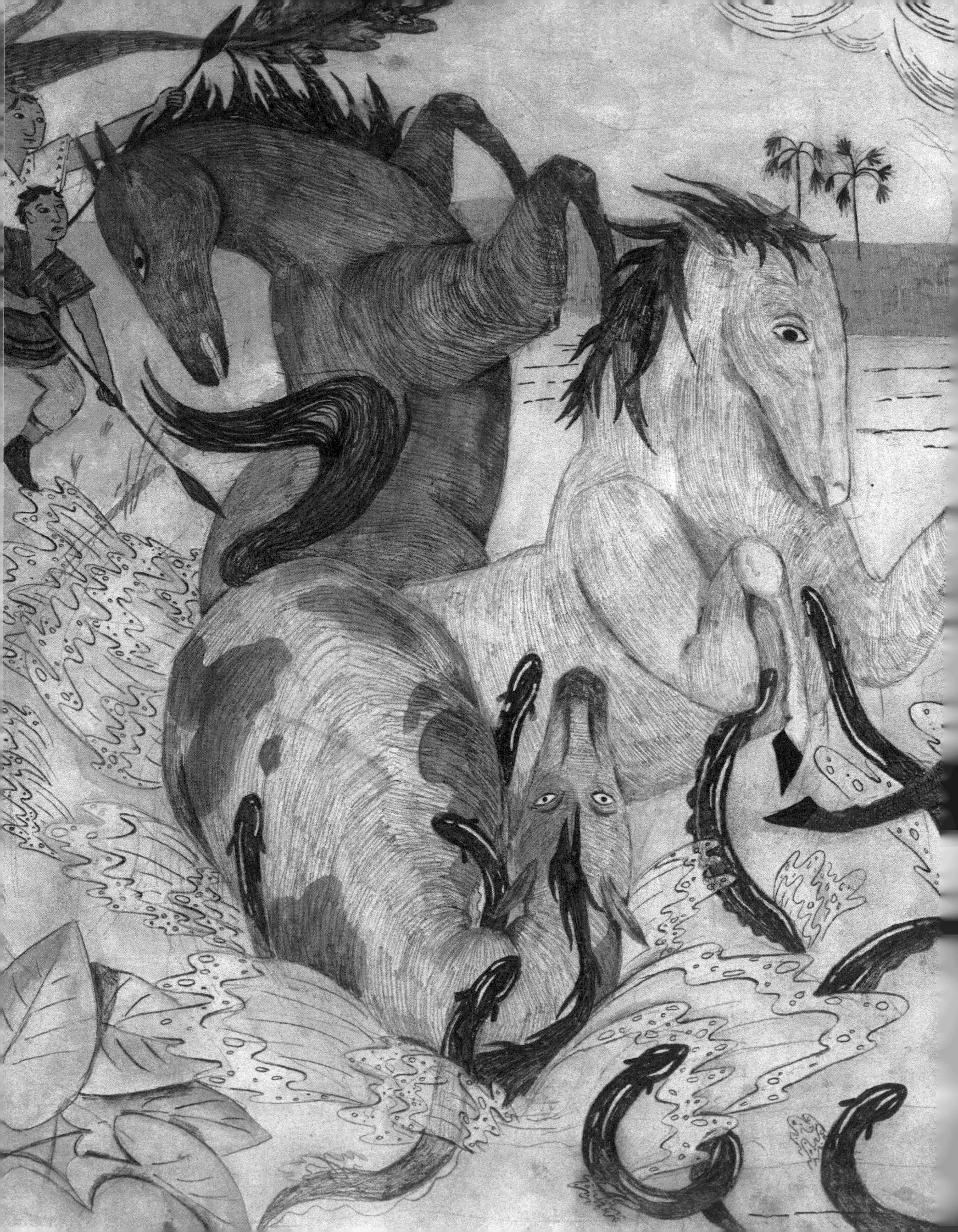

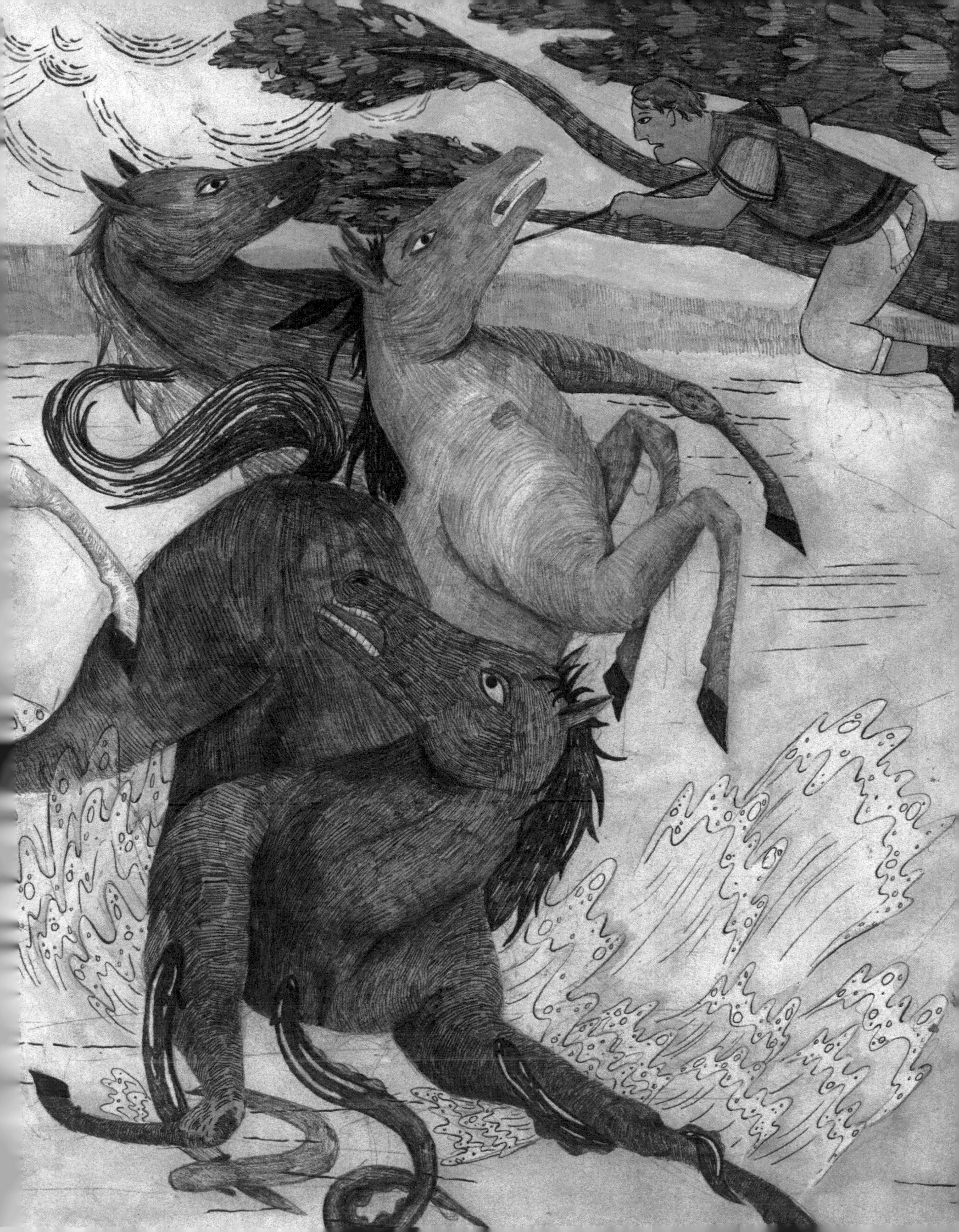

AS THE HORSES ARE DRIVEN INTO THE POND, THE EELS THRASH AGAINST THEIR BELLIES AND BEGIN TO TIRE. THE STRENGTH OF THEIR SHOCKS DIMINISHES, AND THE LLANEROS SUCCEED IN CATCHING FIVE OF THEM FOR US TO EXAMINE. FOR THE NEXT FOUR HOURS WE CONDUCT A SERIES OF EXPERIMENTS.

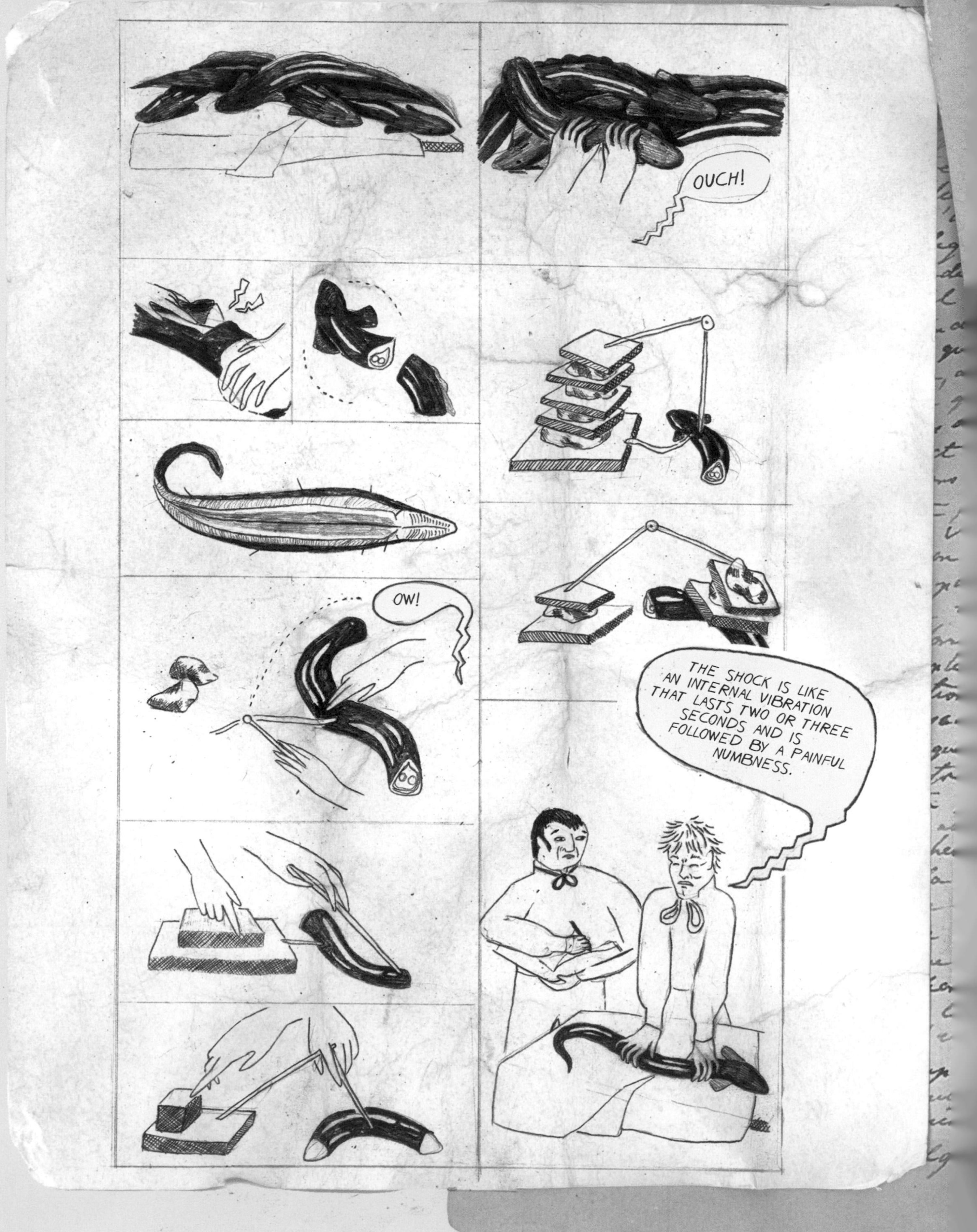
OUCH!
OW!
THE SHOCK IS LIKE AN INTERNAL VIBRATION THAT LASTS TWO OR THREE SECONDS AND IS FOLLOWED BY A PAINFUL NUMBNESS.

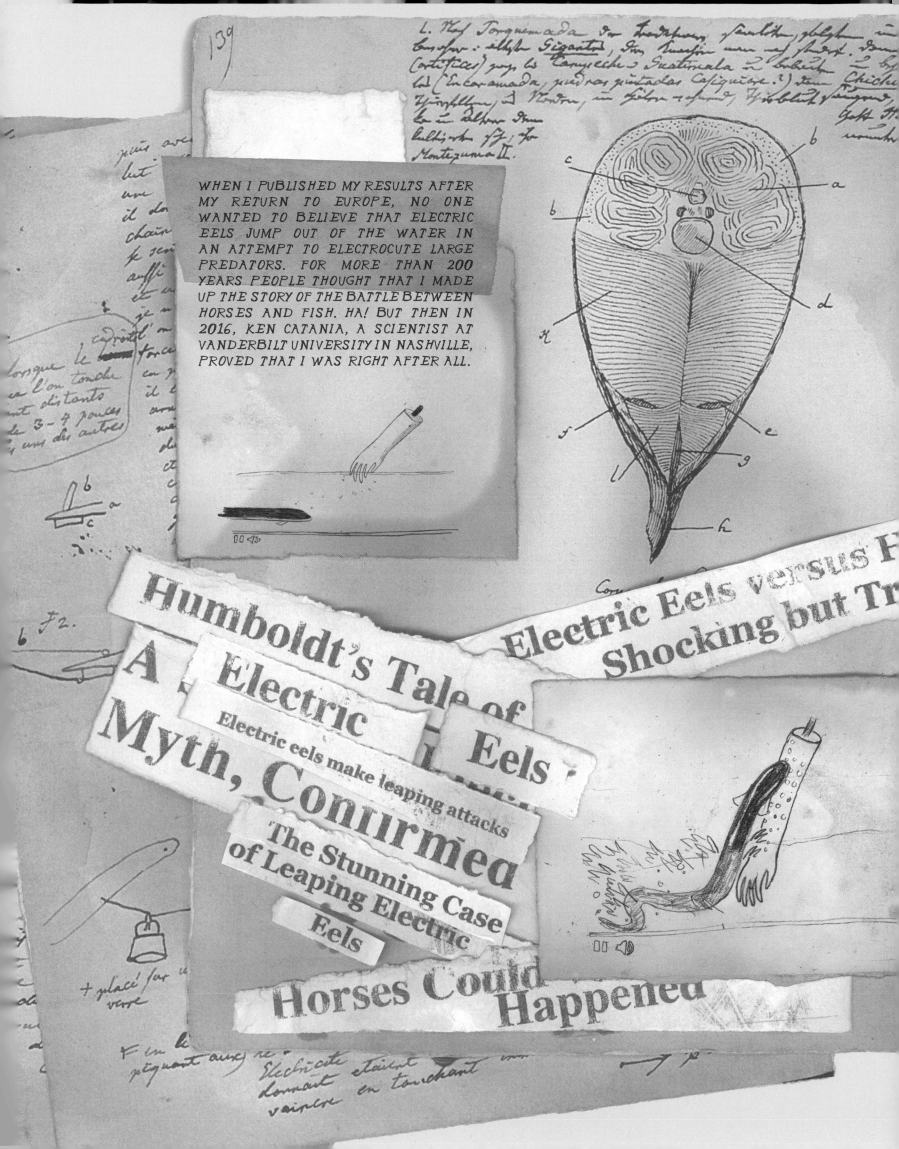

WHEN I PUBLISHED MY RESULTS AFTER MY RETURN TO EUROPE, NO ONE WANTED TO BELIEVE THAT ELECTRIC EELS JUMP OUT OF THE WATER IN AN ATTEMPT TO ELECTROCUTE LARGE PREDATORS. FOR MORE THAN 200 YEARS PEOPLE THOUGHT THAT I MADE UP THE STORY OF THE BATTLE BETWEEN HORSES AND FISH. HA! BUT THEN IN 2016, KEN CATANIA, A SCIENTIST AT VANDERBILT UNIVERSITY IN NASHVILLE, PROVED THAT I WAS RIGHT AFTER ALL.

Humboldt's Tale of

A

Myth, Confirmed

Electric

Eels

Electric eels make leaping attacks

The Stunning Case of Leaping Electric Eels

Electric Eels versus H

Shocking but Tr

Horses Could

Happened

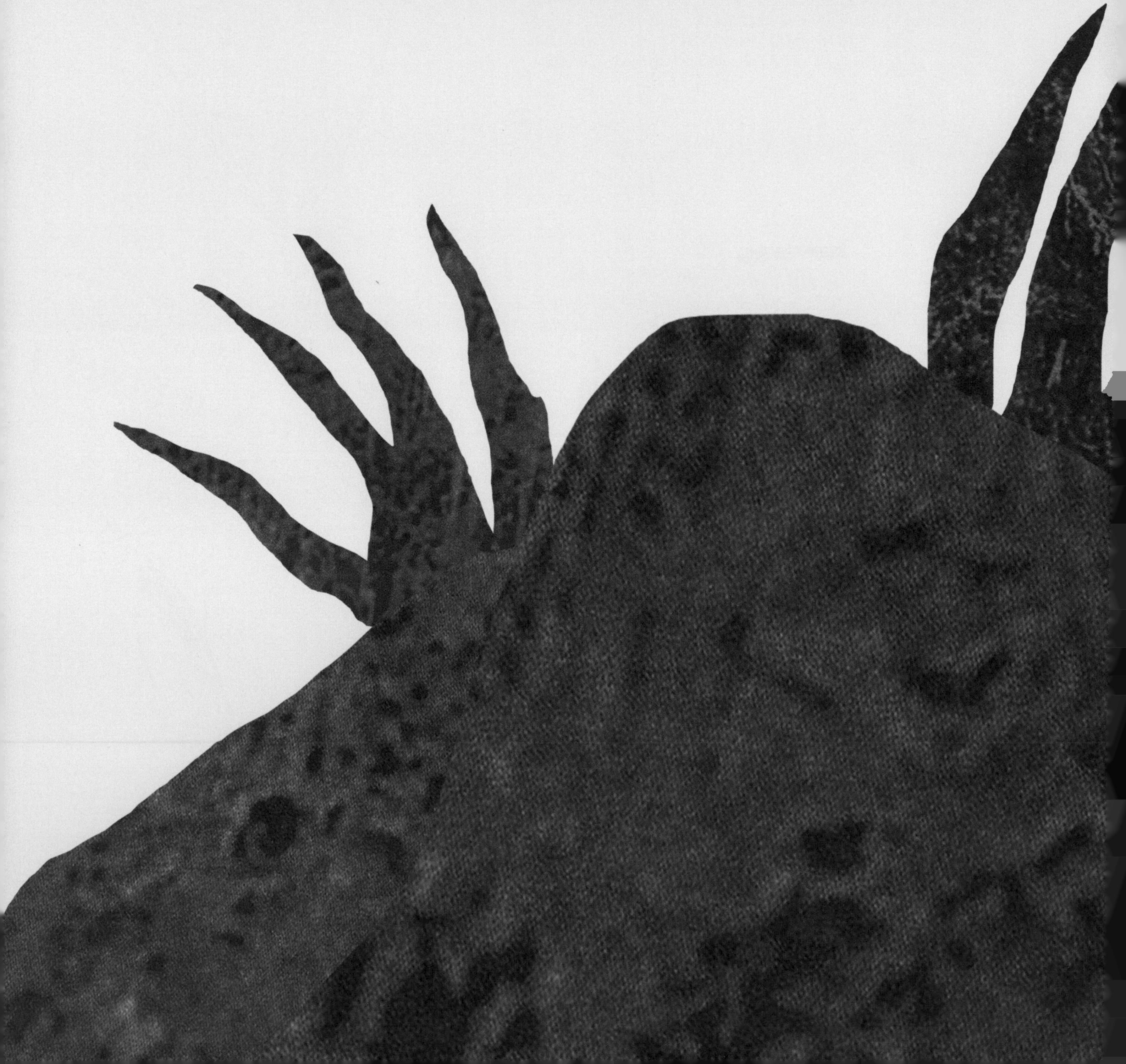

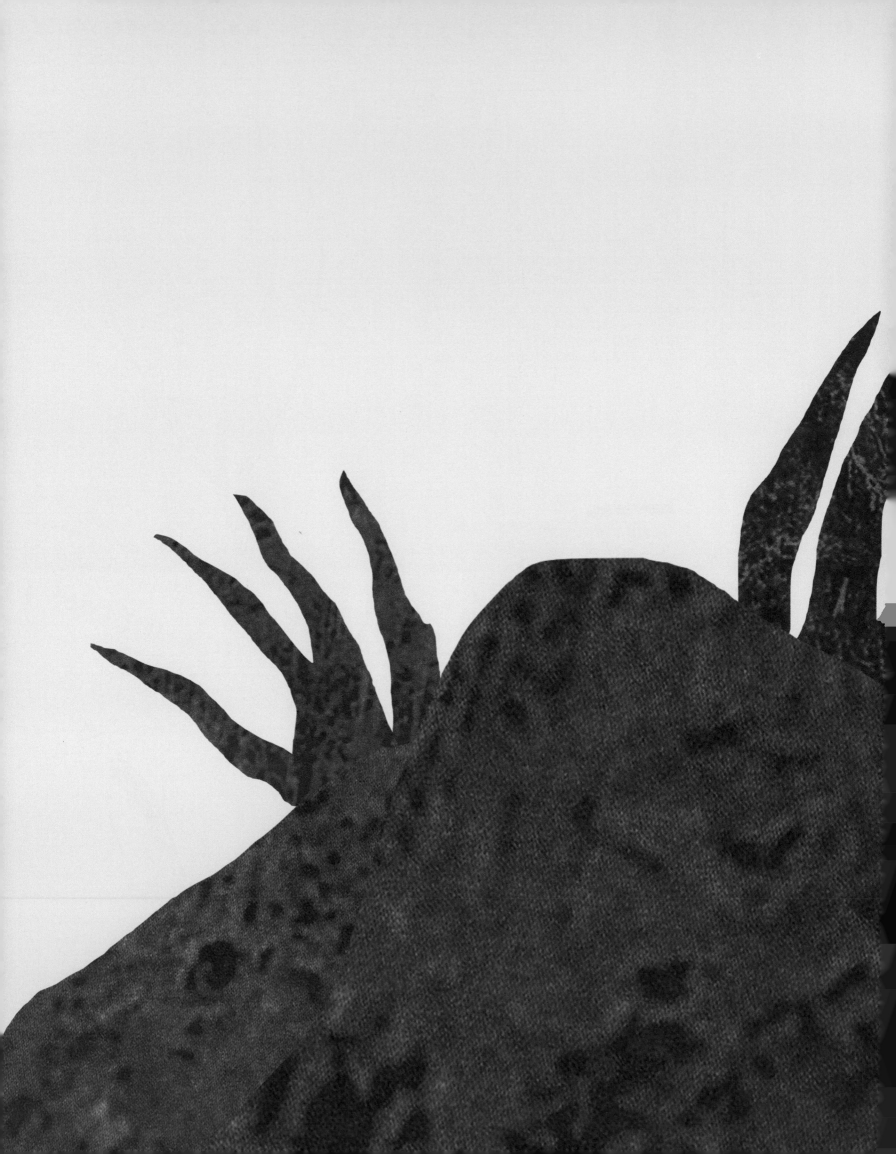

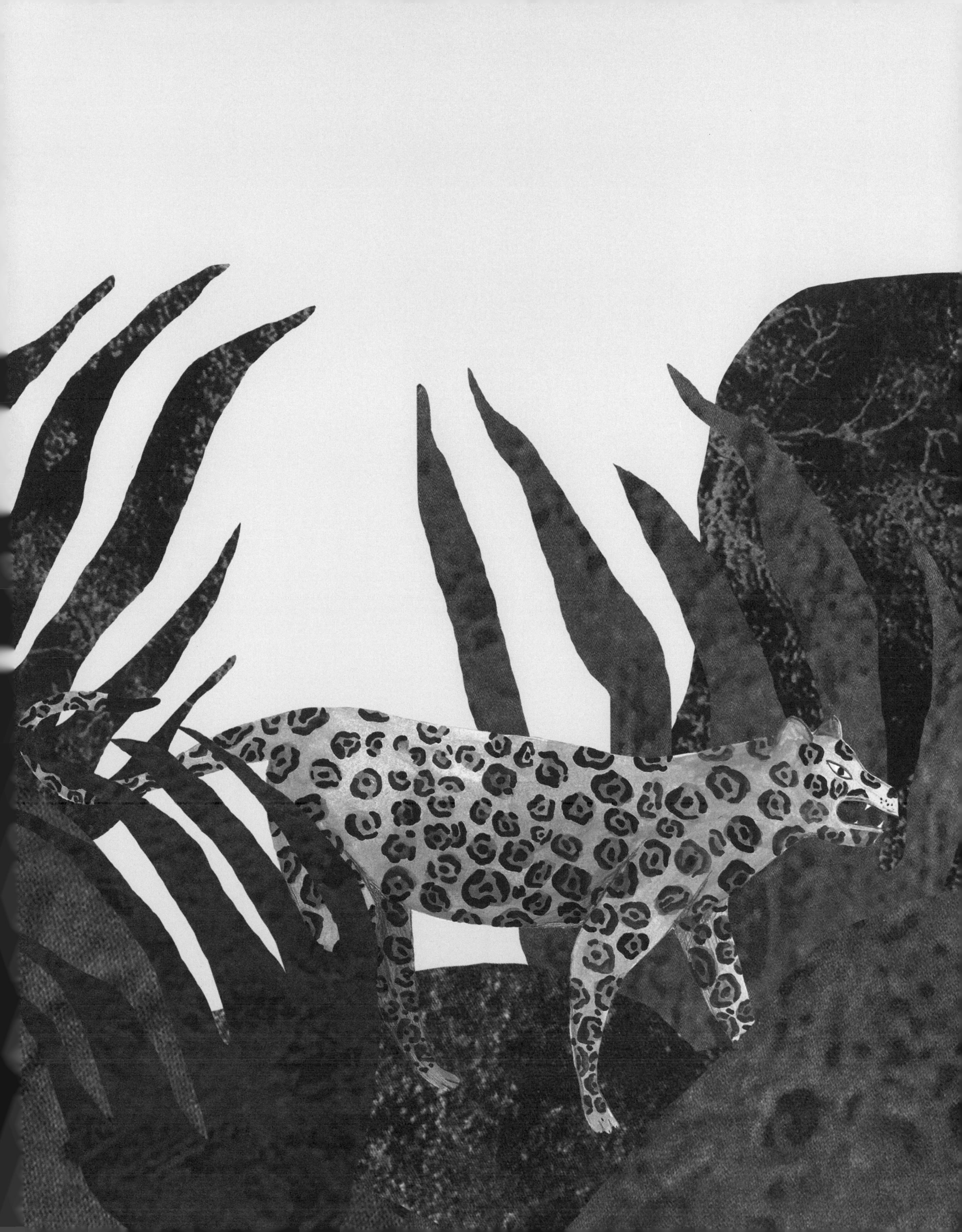

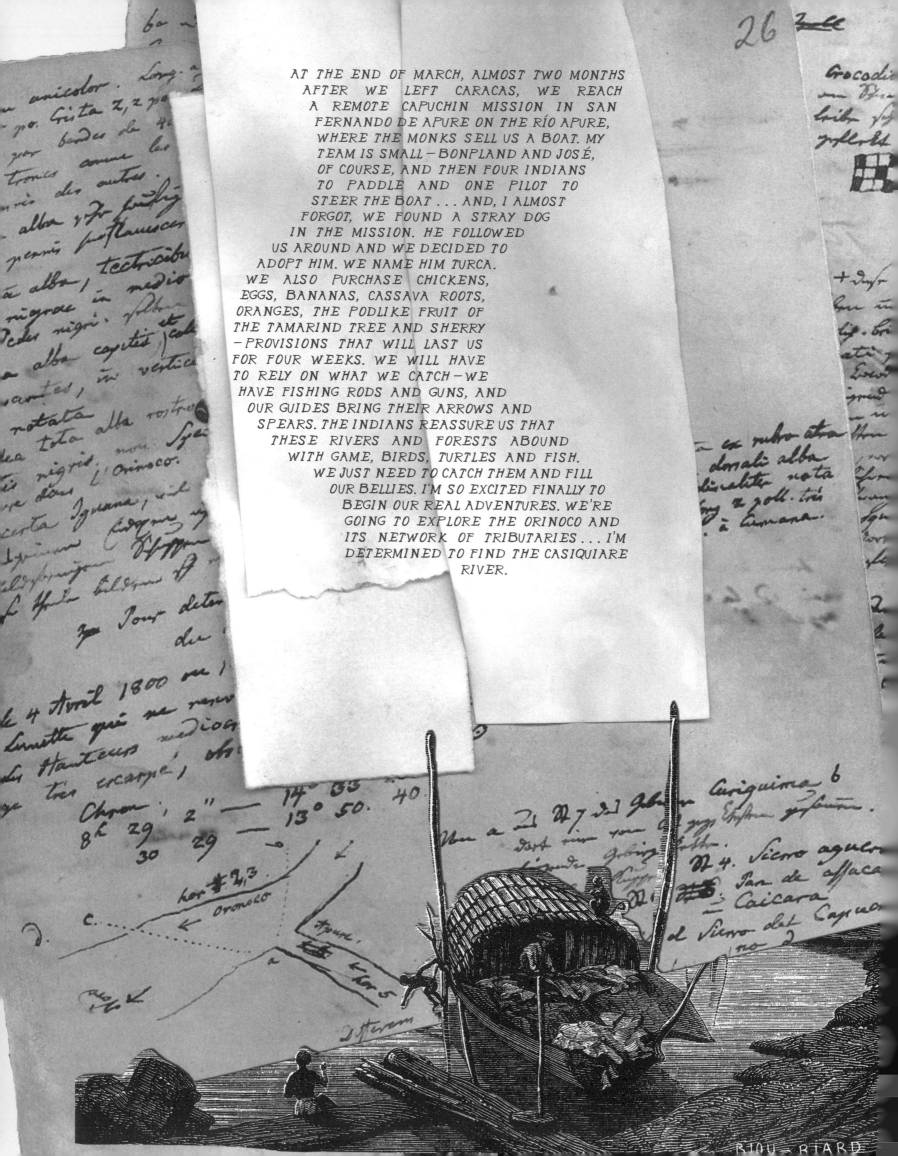

AT THE END OF MARCH, ALMOST TWO MONTHS
AFTER WE LEFT CARACAS, WE REACH
A REMOTE CAPUCHIN MISSION IN SAN
FERNANDO DE APURE ON THE RÍO APURE,
WHERE THE MONKS SELL US A BOAT. MY
TEAM IS SMALL — BONPLAND AND JOSÉ,
OF COURSE, AND THEN FOUR INDIANS
TO PADDLE AND ONE PILOT TO
STEER THE BOAT . . . AND, I ALMOST
FORGOT, WE FOUND A STRAY DOG
IN THE MISSION. HE FOLLOWED
US AROUND AND WE DECIDED TO
ADOPT HIM. WE NAME HIM TURCA.
WE ALSO PURCHASE CHICKENS,
EGGS, BANANAS, CASSAVA ROOTS,
ORANGES, THE PODLIKE FRUIT OF
THE TAMARIND TREE AND SHERRY
— PROVISIONS THAT WILL LAST US
FOR FOUR WEEKS. WE WILL HAVE
TO RELY ON WHAT WE CATCH — WE
HAVE FISHING RODS AND GUNS, AND
OUR GUIDES BRING THEIR ARROWS AND
SPEARS. THE INDIANS REASSURE US THAT
THESE RIVERS AND FORESTS ABOUND
WITH GAME, BIRDS, TURTLES AND FISH.
WE JUST NEED TO CATCH THEM AND FILL
OUR BELLIES. I'M SO EXCITED FINALLY TO
BEGIN OUR REAL ADVENTURES. WE'RE
GOING TO EXPLORE THE ORINOCO AND
ITS NETWORK OF TRIBUTARIES . . . I'M
DETERMINED TO FIND THE CASIQUIARE
RIVER.

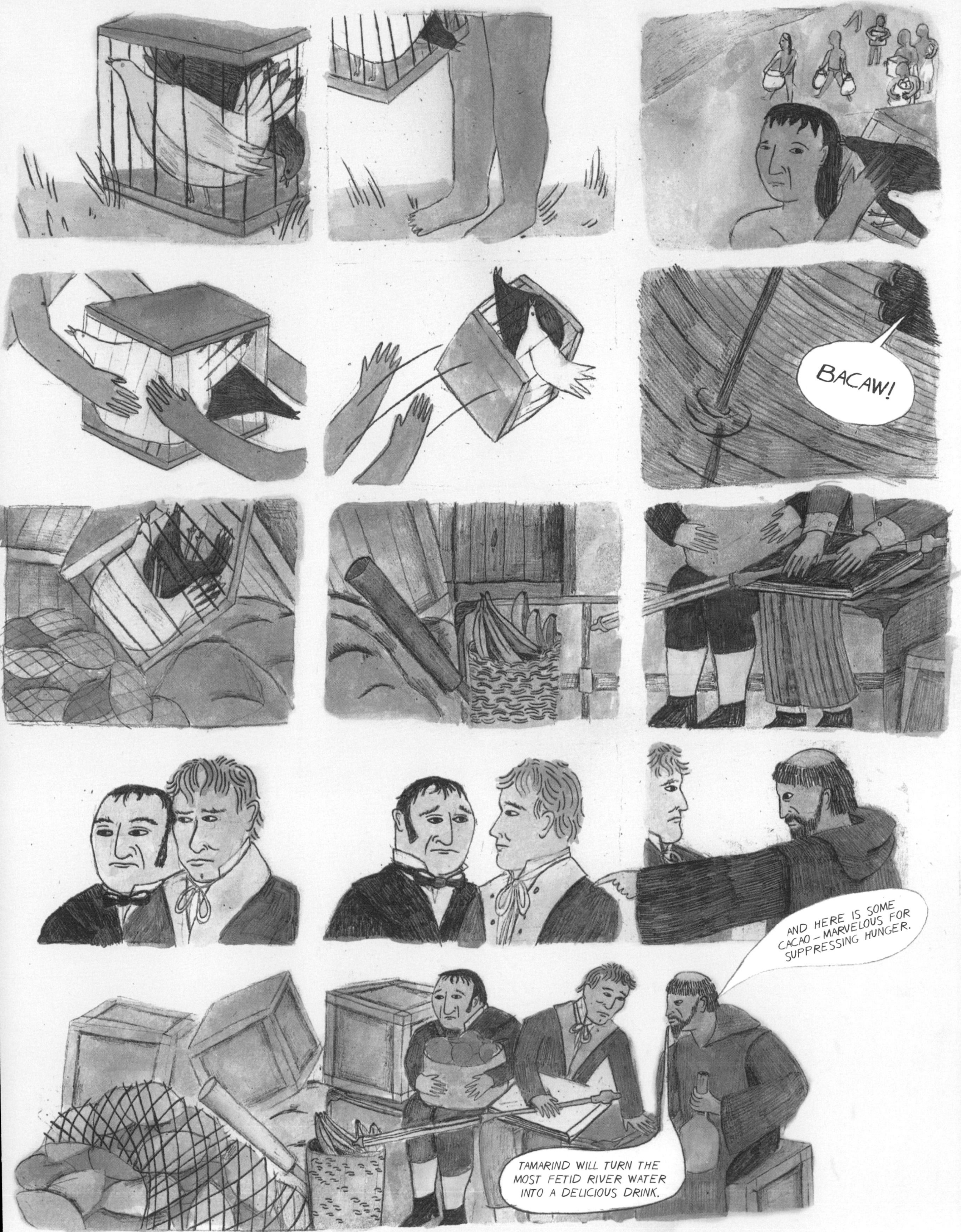
BACAW!
AND HERE IS SOME CACAO—MARVELOUS FOR SUPPRESSING HUNGER.
TAMARIND WILL TURN THE MOST FETID RIVER WATER INTO A DELICIOUS DRINK.

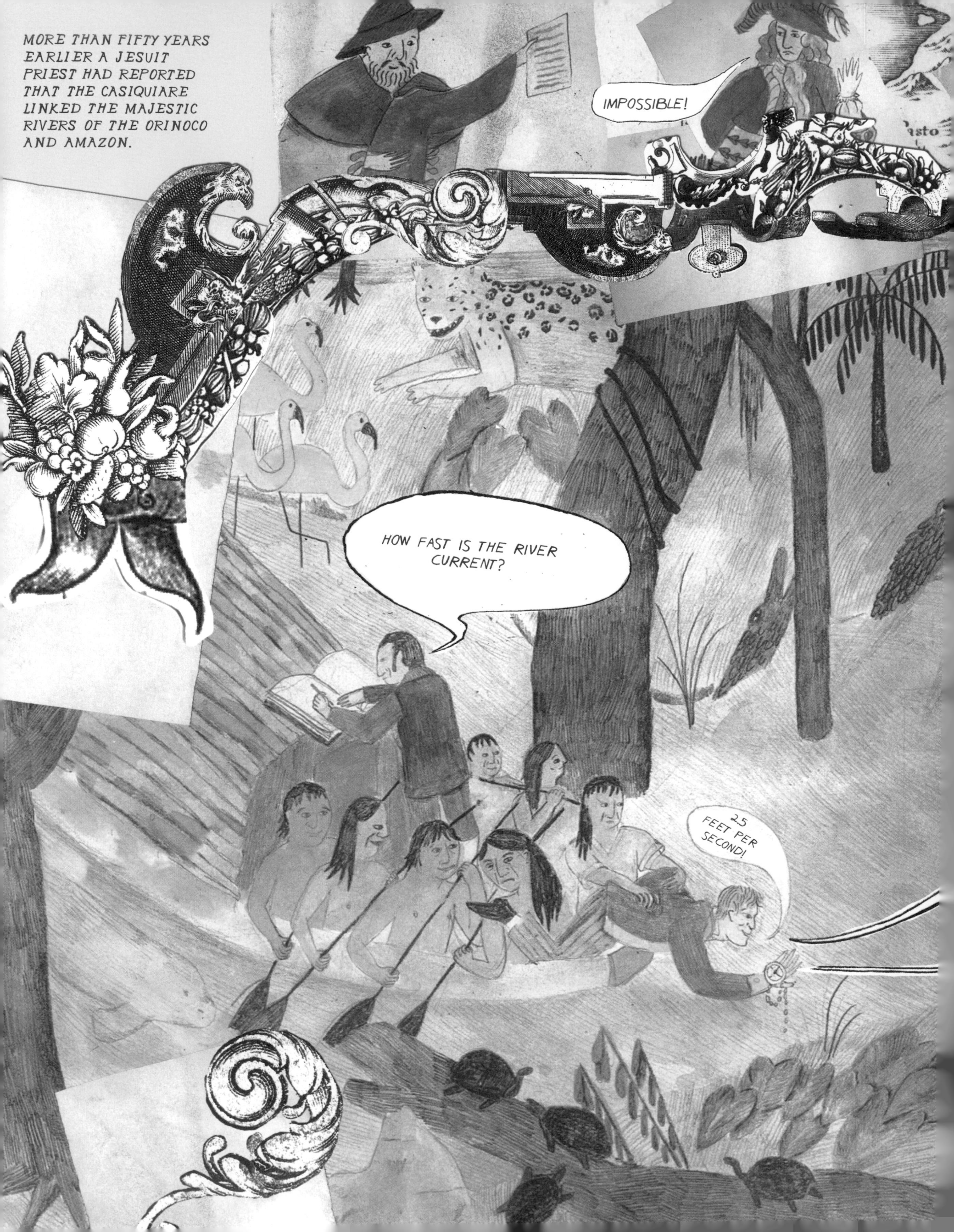
MORE THAN FIFTY YEARS EARLIER A JESUIT PRIEST HAD REPORTED THAT THE CASIQUIARE LINKED THE MAJESTIC RIVERS OF THE ORINOCO AND AMAZON.
IMPOSSIBLE!
HOW FAST IS THE RIVER CURRENT?
25 FEET PER SECOND!

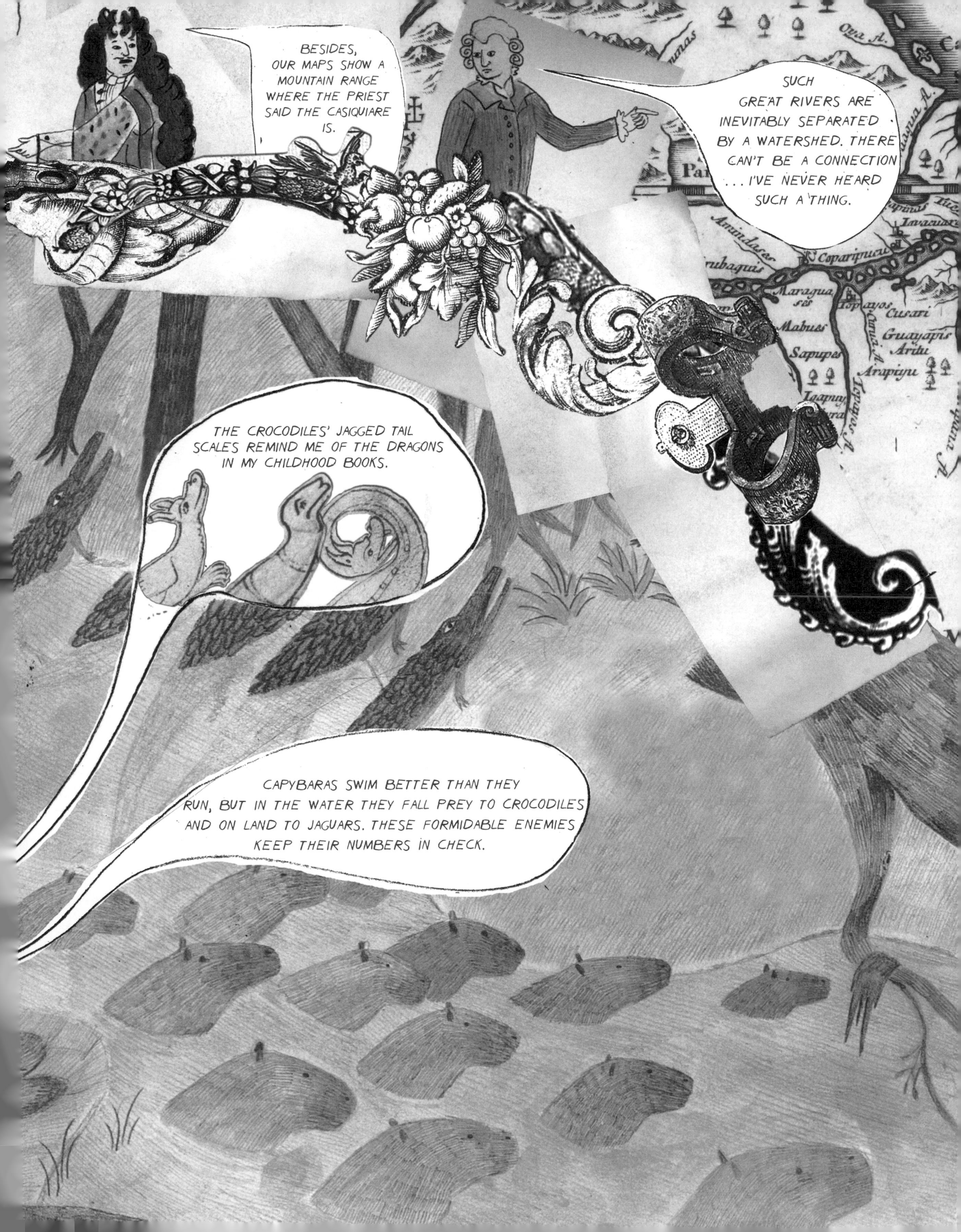
BESIDES, OUR MAPS SHOW A MOUNTAIN RANGE WHERE THE PRIEST SAID THE CASIQUIARE IS.
SUCH GREAT RIVERS ARE INEVITABLY SEPARATED BY A WATERSHED. THERE CAN'T BE A CONNECTION . . . I'VE NEVER HEARD SUCH A THING.
THE CROCODILES' JAGGED TAIL SCALES REMIND ME OF THE DRAGONS IN MY CHILDHOOD BOOKS.
CAPYBARAS SWIM BETTER THAN THEY RUN, BUT IN THE WATER THEY FALL PREY TO CROCODILES AND ON LAND TO JAGUARS. THESE FORMIDABLE ENEMIES KEEP THEIR NUMBERS IN CHECK.

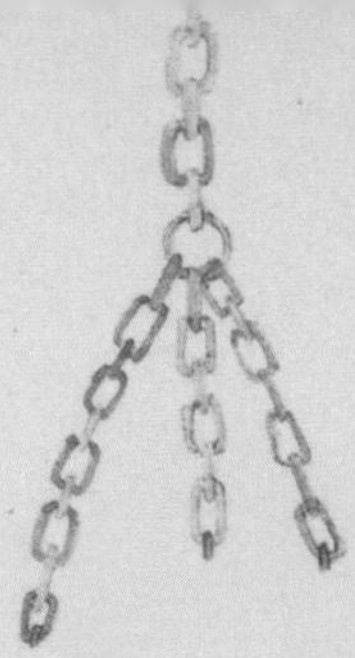

YOU MIGHT HAVE NOTICED THAT I MEASURE WHATEVER I CAN. IT'S THE REASON I CARRY SO MANY INSTRUMENTS. I ALWAYS MEASURE. BACK HOME I TOOK MY INSTRUMENTS OUTSIDE TO DETERMINE THE ELECTRICITY IN THE ATMOSPHERE DURING VIOLENT THUNDERSTORMS AND I CARRIED THEM UP THE ICY SLOPES OF THE SWISS ALPS. I MEASURED THE DRY HEAT OF THE LLANOS AND THE HUMIDITY OF THE RAINFOREST. LATER, I TOOK MAGNETIC MEASUREMENTS IN THE RUSSIAN ALTAI MOUNTAINS NEAR THE CHINESE BORDER, BUT MOST MEMORABLE OF ALL WAS THE DAY I DESCENDED TO THE BOTTOM OF THE THAMES. IT WAS MANY YEARS AFTER MY EXPEDITION. I WAS IN LONDON, WHERE I MET THE YOUNG ENGINEER ISAMBARD KINGDOM BRUNEL.

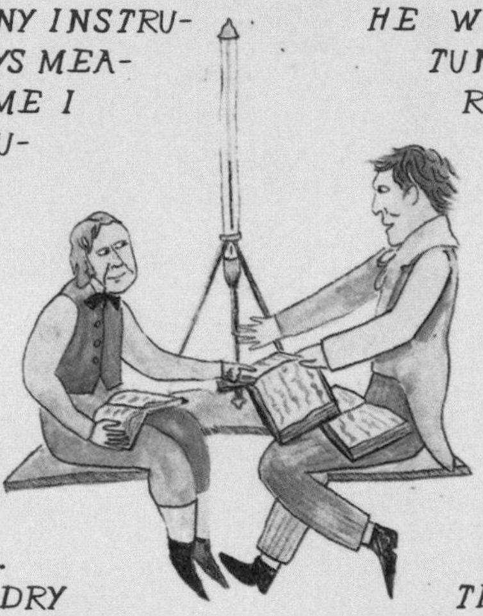

HE WAS BUILDING A TUNNEL UNDER THE RIVER. THE AUDACITY! BUT WATER KEPT SEEPING IN AND BRUNEL WANTED TO INSPECT THE CONSTRUCTION FROM THE OUTSIDE. HE KINDLY INVITED ME TO JOIN HIM. A HUGE DIVING BELL WAS LOWERED TO THE BOTTOM OF THE THAMES BY CRANE. WE SPENT 40 LONG MINUTES 36 FEET UNDER THE SURFACE. IT WAS EERILY DARK, AND WITH ONLY WATER ABOVE US, IT WAS NOT EXACTLY COMFORTABLE . . . BUT I COULD FINALLY COMPARE THE AIR PRESSURE DOWN THERE WITH MY OBSERVATIONS FROM THE ANDES. BUT SORRY, I'M DIGRESSING AGAIN . . .

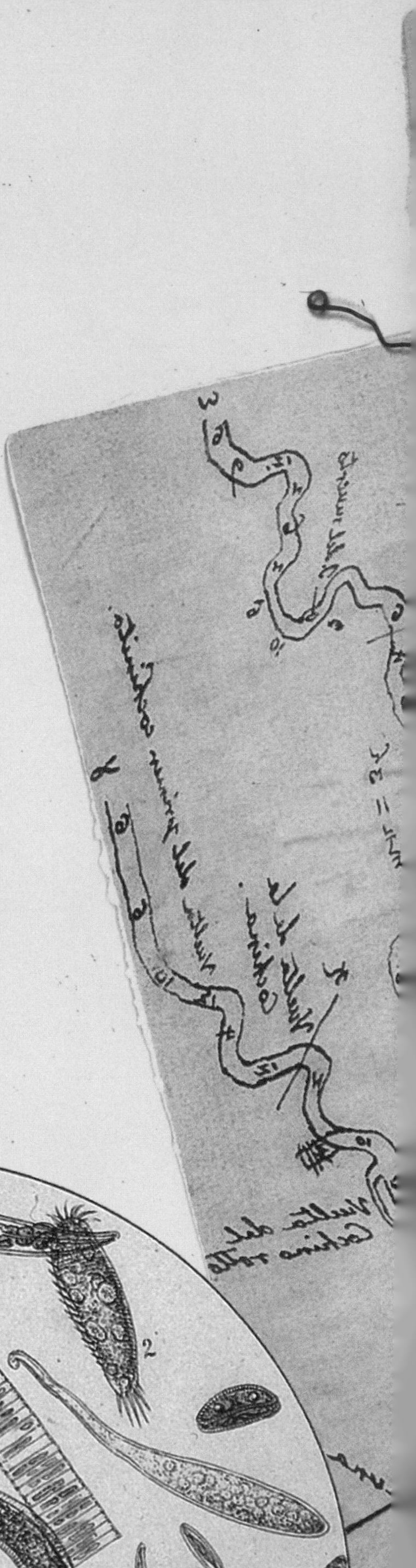

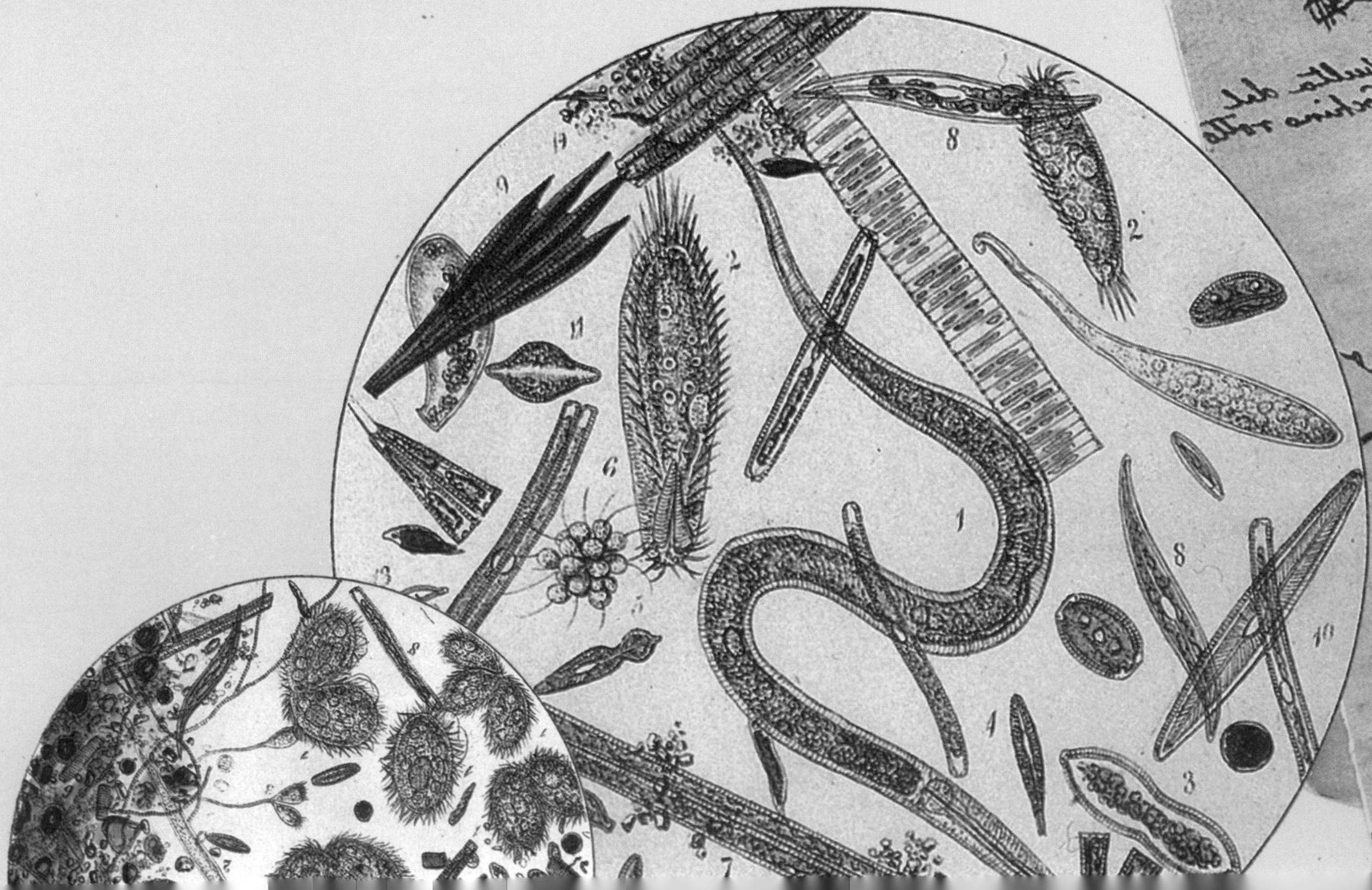

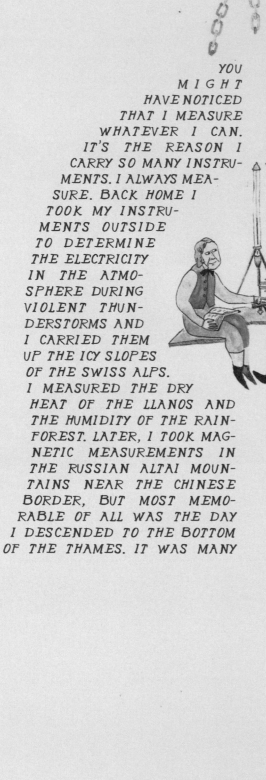

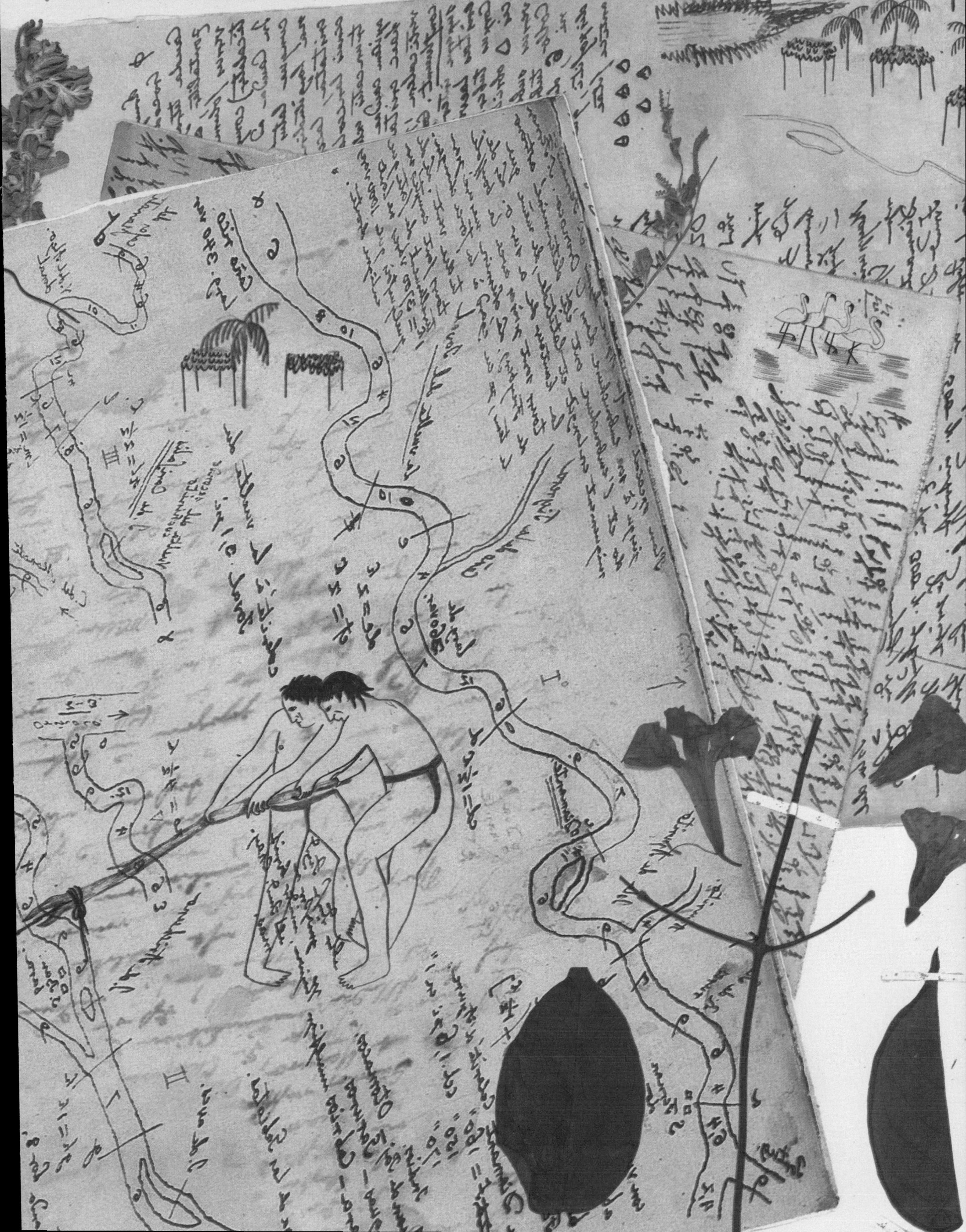

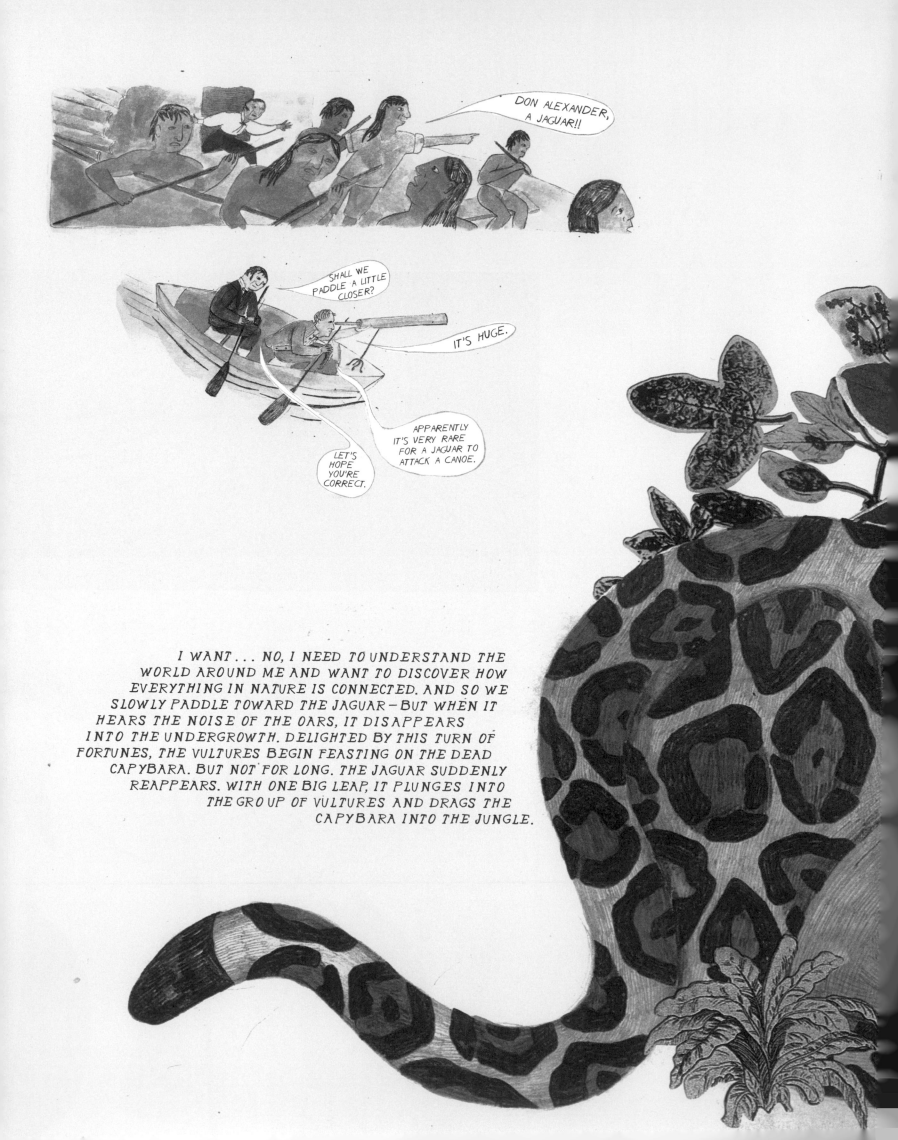

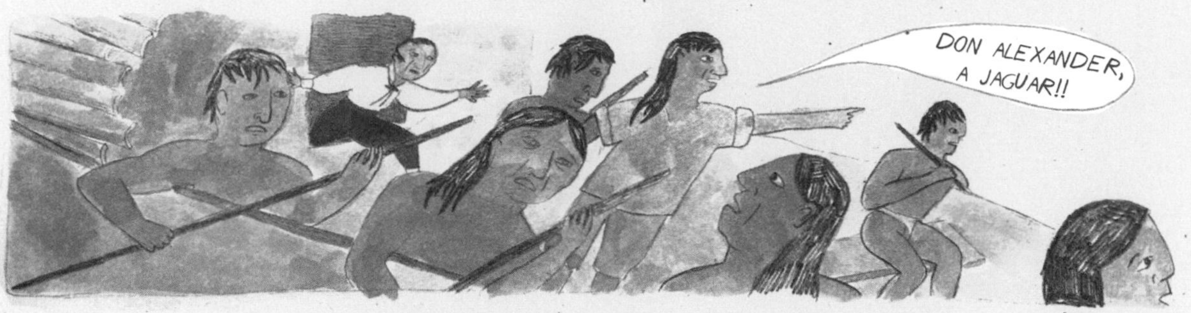
DON ALEXANDER, A JAGUAR!!

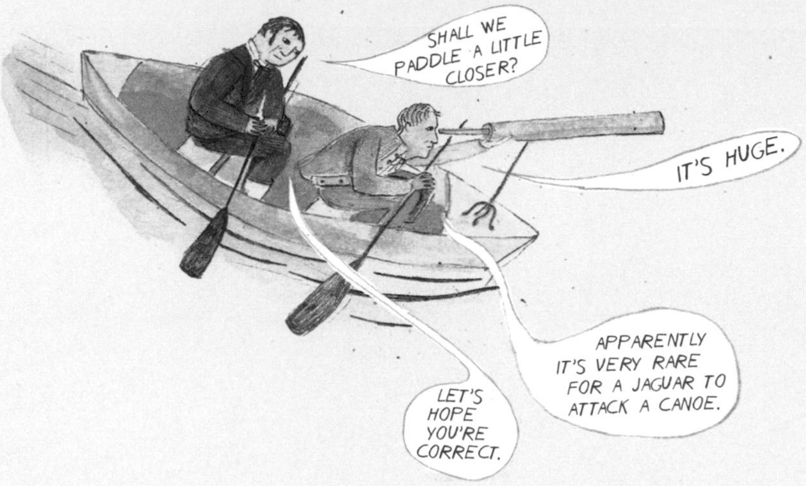
SHALL WE PADDLE A LITTLE CLOSER?
IT'S HUGE.
APPARENTLY IT'S VERY RARE FOR A JAGUAR TO ATTACK A CANOE.
LET'S HOPE YOU'RE CORRECT.

I WANT . . . NO, I NEED TO UNDERSTAND THE WORLD AROUND ME AND WANT TO DISCOVER HOW EVERYTHING IN NATURE IS CONNECTED. AND SO WE SLOWLY PADDLE TOWARD THE JAGUAR – BUT WHEN IT HEARS THE NOISE OF THE OARS, IT DISAPPEARS INTO THE UNDERGROWTH. DELIGHTED BY THIS TURN OF FORTUNES, THE VULTURES BEGIN FEASTING ON THE DEAD CAPYBARA. BUT NOT FOR LONG. THE JAGUAR SUDDENLY REAPPEARS. WITH ONE BIG LEAP, IT PLUNGES INTO THE GROUP OF VULTURES AND DRAGS THE CAPYBARA INTO THE JUNGLE.

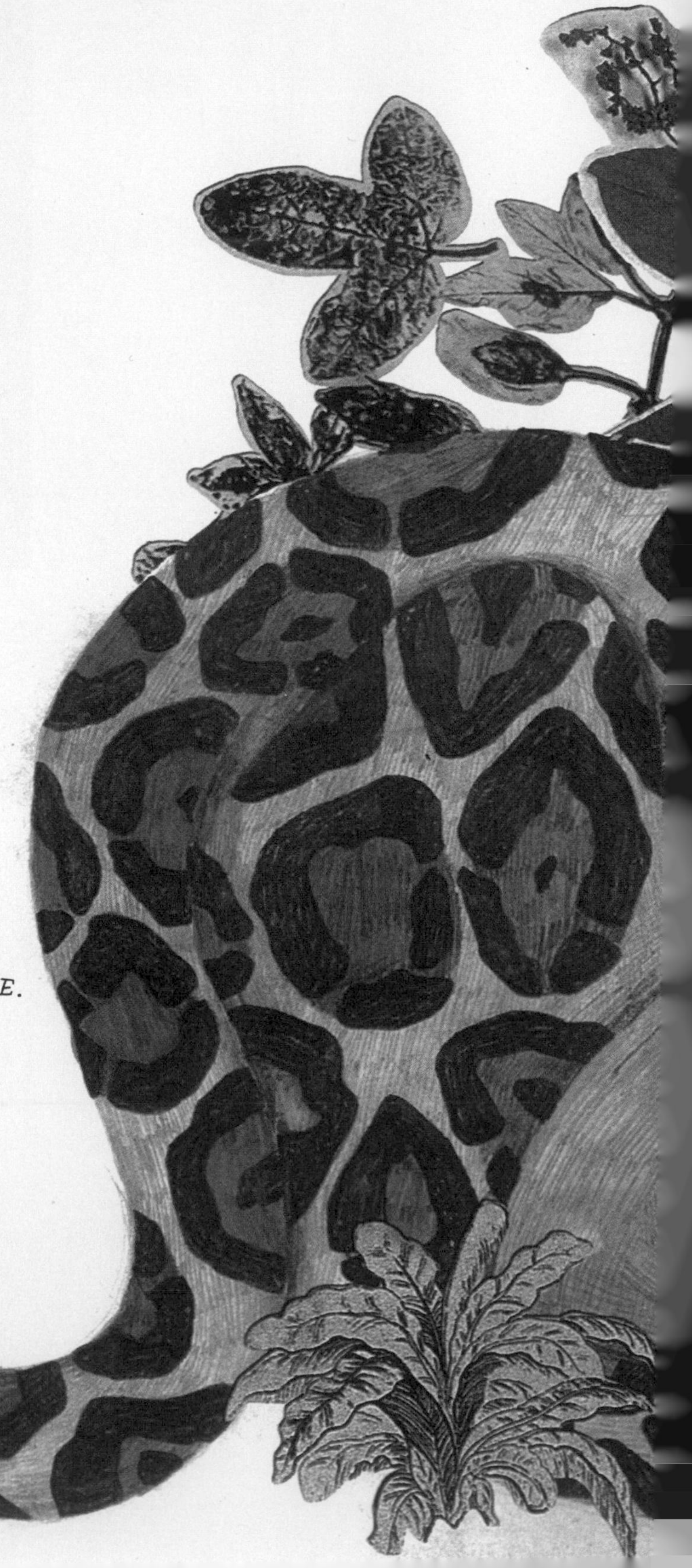
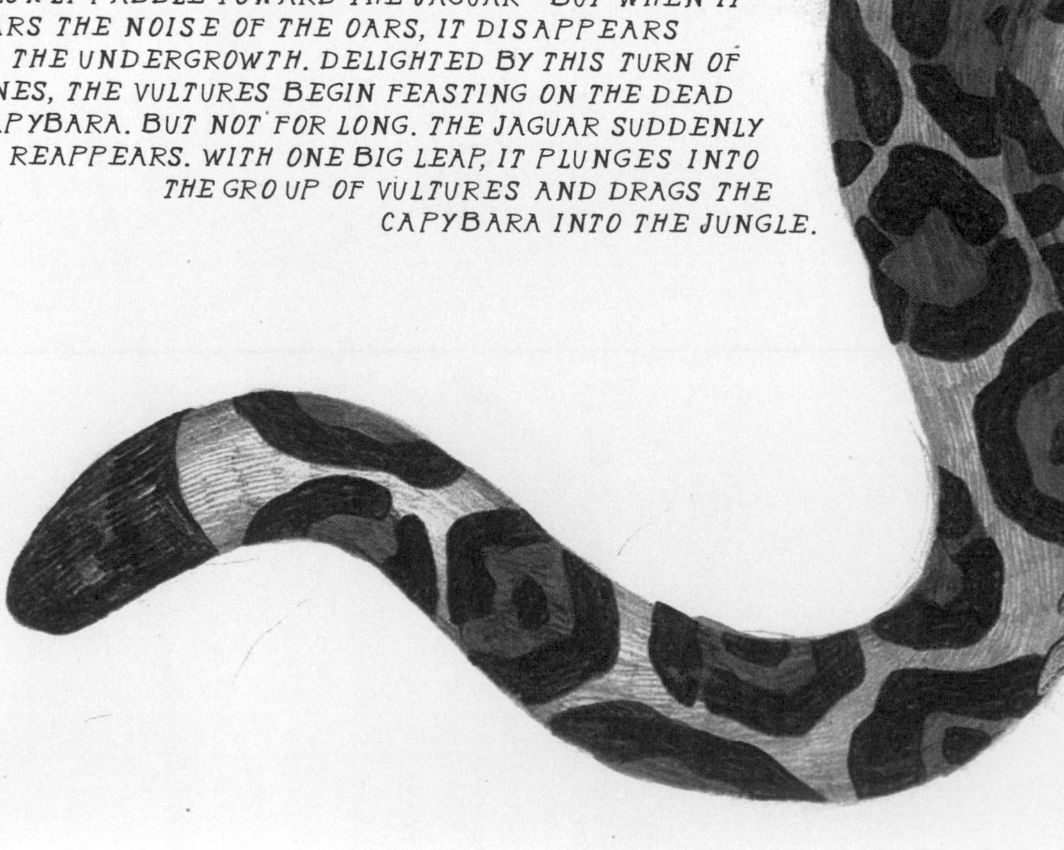

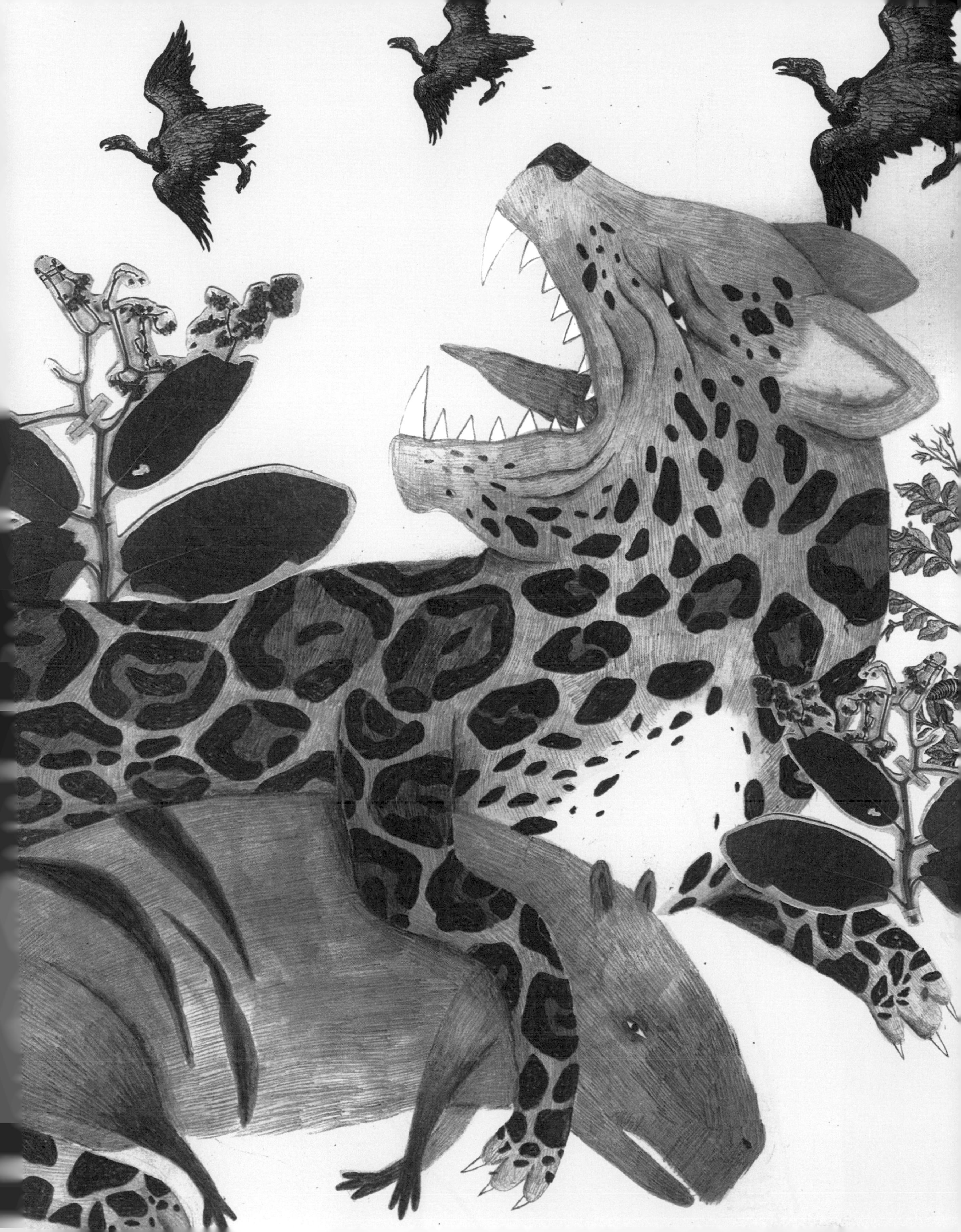

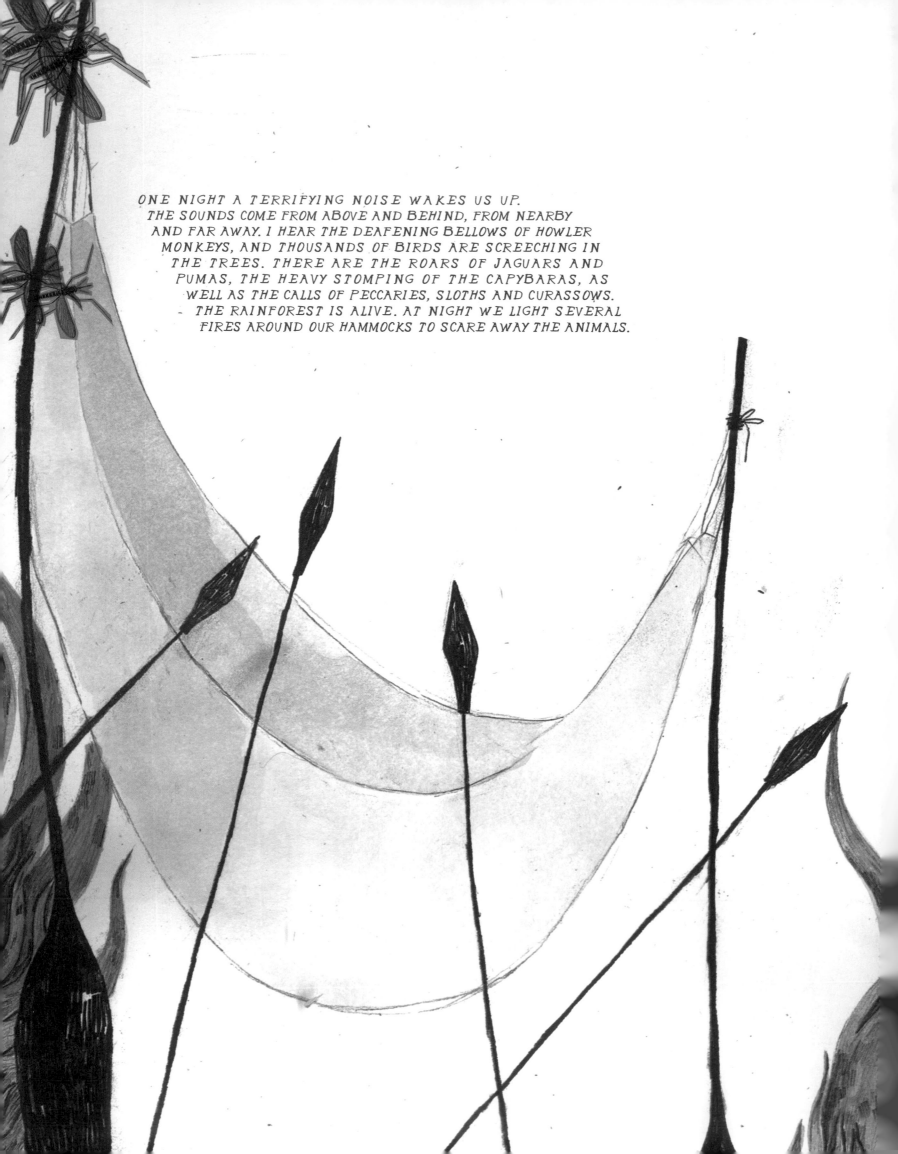

ONE NIGHT A TERRIFYING NOISE WAKES US UP.
THE SOUNDS COME FROM ABOVE AND BEHIND, FROM NEARBY
AND FAR AWAY. I HEAR THE DEAFENING BELLOWS OF HOWLER
MONKEYS, AND THOUSANDS OF BIRDS ARE SCREECHING IN
THE TREES. THERE ARE THE ROARS OF JAGUARS AND
PUMAS, THE HEAVY STOMPING OF THE CAPYBARAS, AS
WELL AS THE CALLS OF PECCARIES, SLOTHS AND CURASSOWS.
THE RAINFOREST IS ALIVE. AT NIGHT WE LIGHT SEVERAL
FIRES AROUND OUR HAMMOCKS TO SCARE AWAY THE ANIMALS.

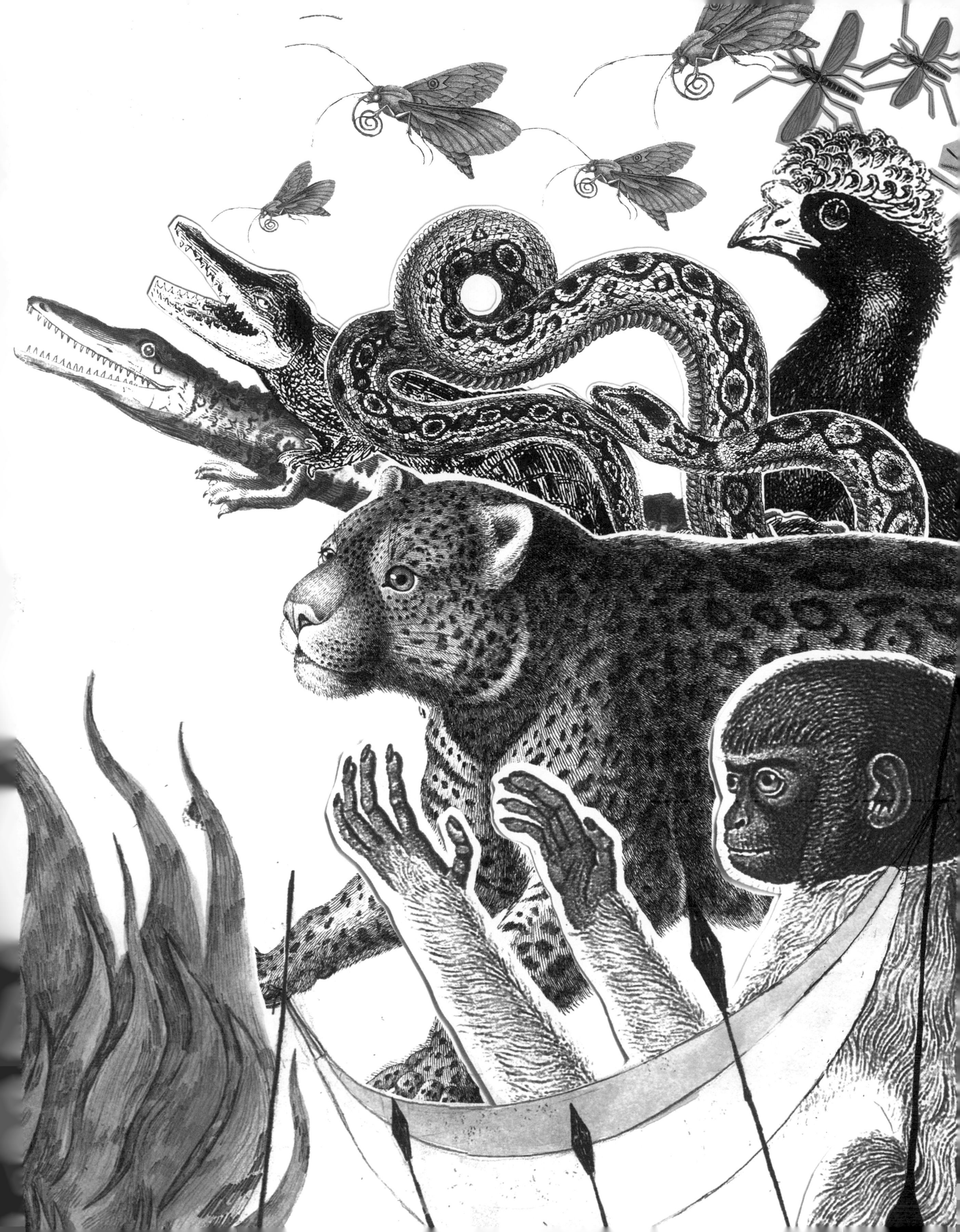

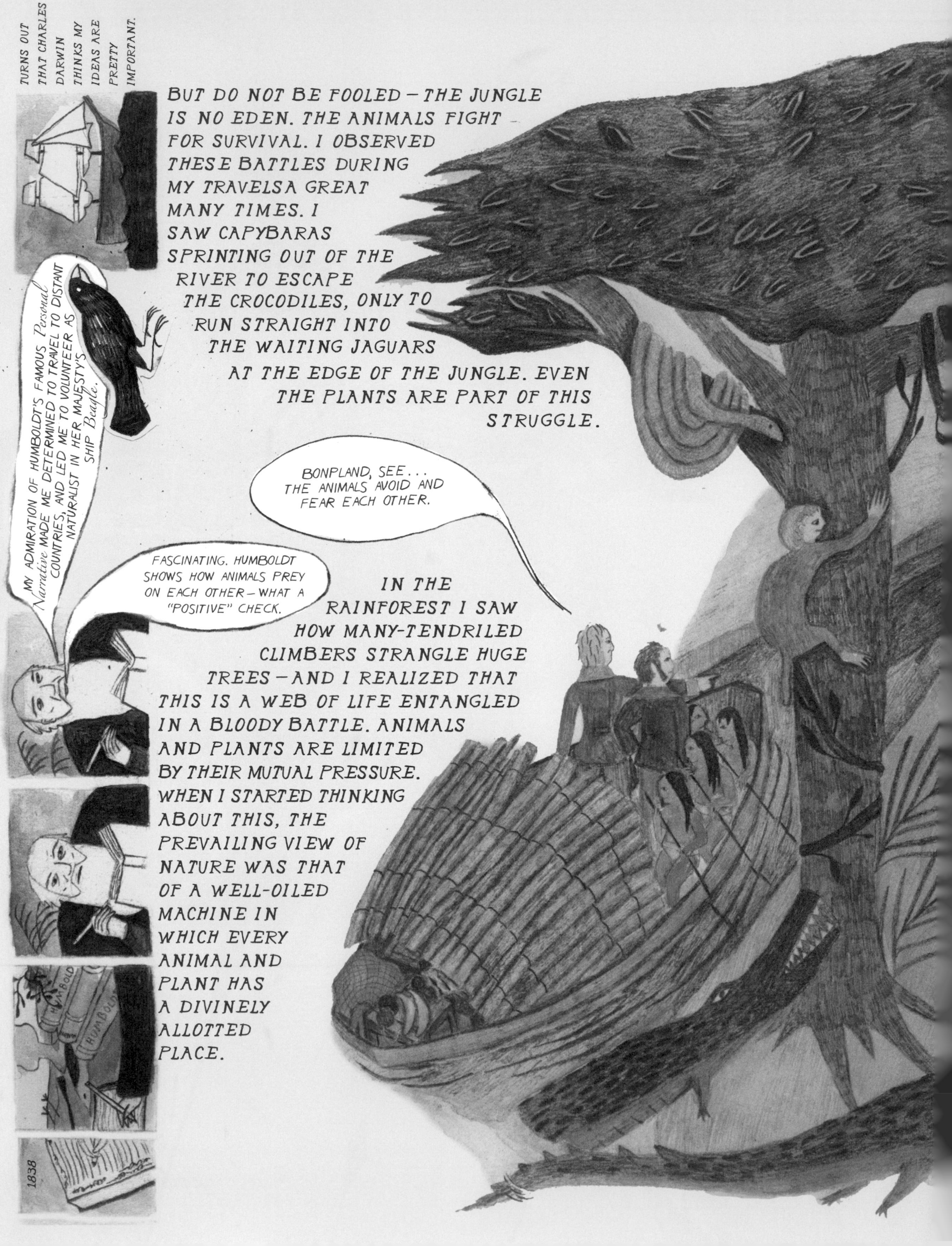
TURNS OUT THAT CHARLES DARWIN THINKS MY IDEAS ARE PRETTY IMPORTANT.
BUT DO NOT BE FOOLED – THE JUNGLE IS NO EDEN. THE ANIMALS FIGHT FOR SURVIVAL. I OBSERVED THESE BATTLES DURING MY TRAVELSA GREAT MANY TIMES. I SAW CAPYBARAS SPRINTING OUT OF THE RIVER TO ESCAPE THE CROCODILES, ONLY TO RUN STRAIGHT INTO THE WAITING JAGUARS AT THE EDGE OF THE JUNGLE. EVEN THE PLANTS ARE PART OF THIS STRUGGLE.
MY ADMIRATION OF HUMBOLDT'S FAMOUS *Personal Narrative* MADE ME DETERMINED TO TRAVEL TO DISTANT COUNTRIES, AND LED ME TO VOLUNTEER AS NATURALIST IN HER MAJESTY'S SHIP *Beagle*.
BONPLAND, SEE... THE ANIMALS AVOID AND FEAR EACH OTHER.
FASCINATING. HUMBOLDT SHOWS HOW ANIMALS PREY ON EACH OTHER – WHAT A "POSITIVE" CHECK.
IN THE RAINFOREST I SAW HOW MANY-TENDRILED CLIMBERS STRANGLE HUGE TREES – AND I REALIZED THAT THIS IS A WEB OF LIFE ENTANGLED IN A BLOODY BATTLE. ANIMALS AND PLANTS ARE LIMITED BY THEIR MUTUAL PRESSURE. WHEN I STARTED THINKING ABOUT THIS, THE PREVAILING VIEW OF NATURE WAS THAT OF A WELL-OILED MACHINE IN WHICH EVERY ANIMAL AND PLANT HAS A DIVINELY ALLOTTED PLACE.
HUMBOLDT
HUMBOLDT
1838

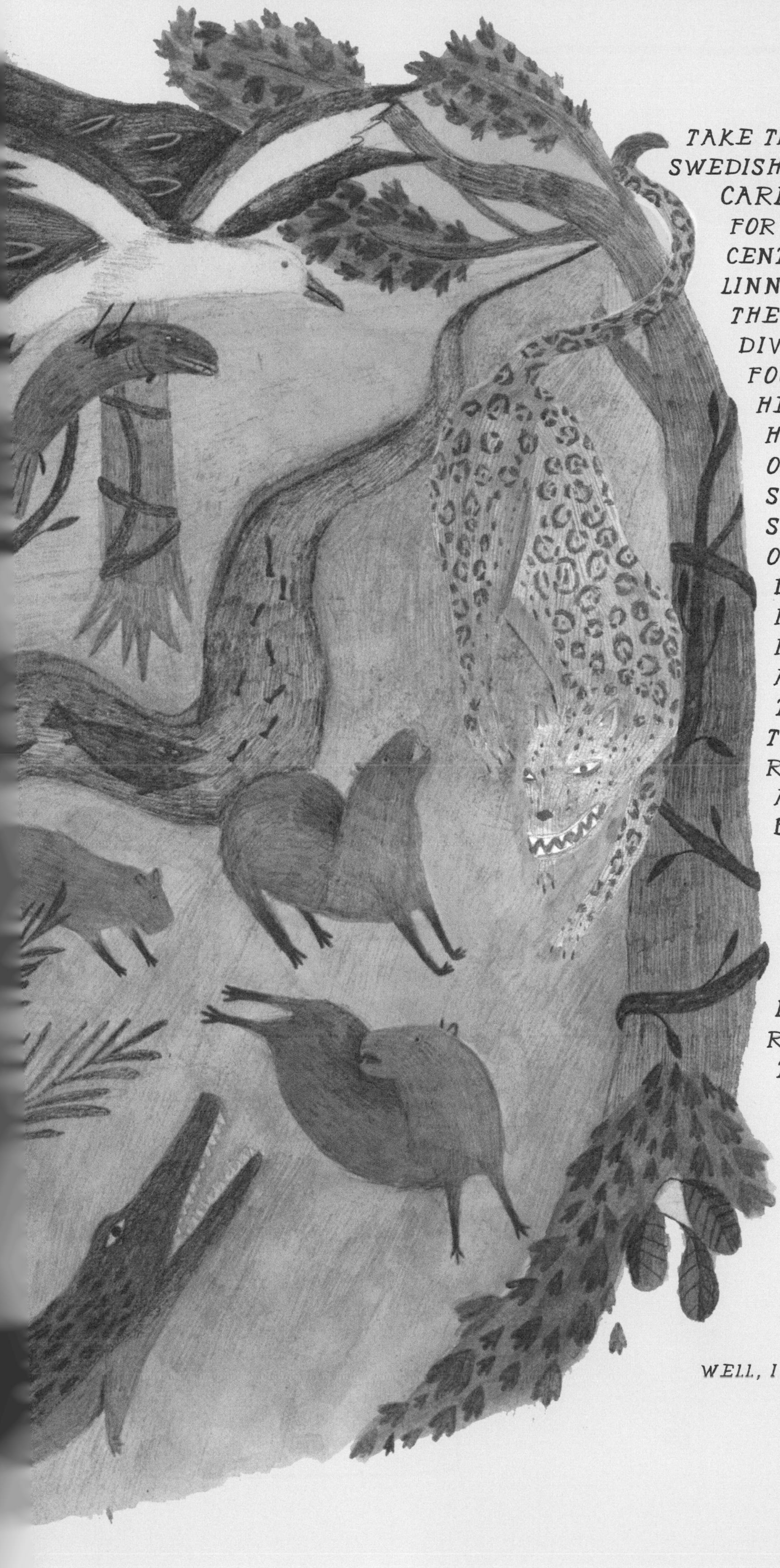

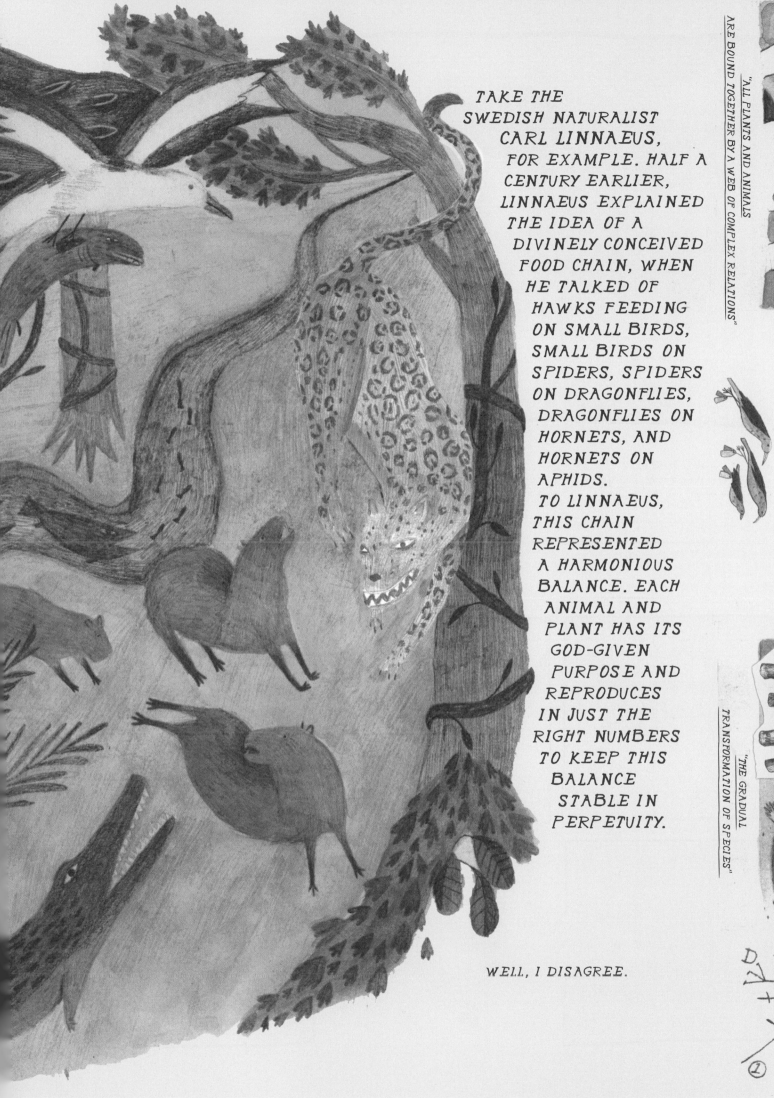

TAKE THE SWEDISH NATURALIST CARL LINNAEUS, FOR EXAMPLE. HALF A CENTURY EARLIER, LINNAEUS EXPLAINED THE IDEA OF A DIVINELY CONCEIVED FOOD CHAIN, WHEN HE TALKED OF HAWKS FEEDING ON SMALL BIRDS, SMALL BIRDS ON SPIDERS, SPIDERS ON DRAGONFLIES, DRAGONFLIES ON HORNETS, AND HORNETS ON APHIDS.

TO LINNAEUS, THIS CHAIN REPRESENTED A HARMONIOUS BALANCE. EACH ANIMAL AND PLANT HAS ITS GOD-GIVEN PURPOSE AND REPRODUCES IN JUST THE RIGHT NUMBERS TO KEEP THIS BALANCE STABLE IN PERPETUITY.

WELL, I DISAGREE.

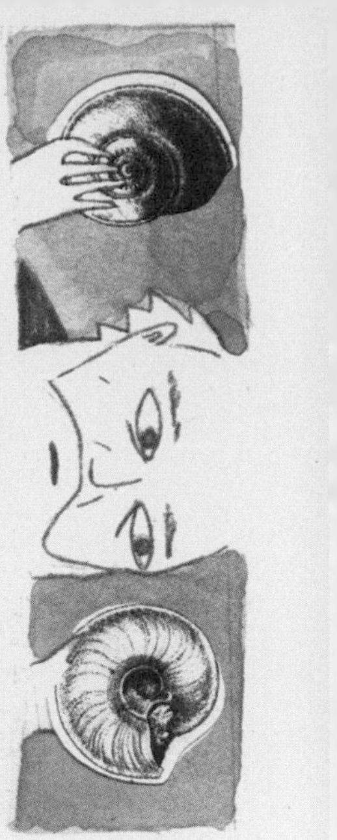

"ALL PLANTS AND ANIMALS ARE BOUND TOGETHER BY A WEB OF COMPLEX RELATIONS"

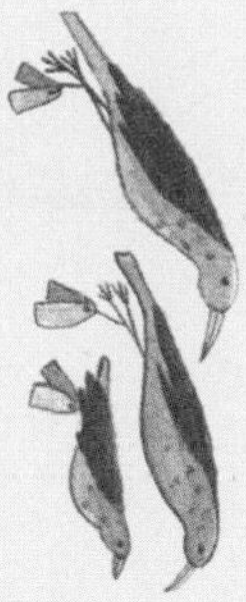

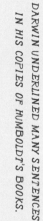

DARWIN UNDERLINED MANY SENTENCES IN HIS COPIES OF HUMBOLDT'S BOOKS.

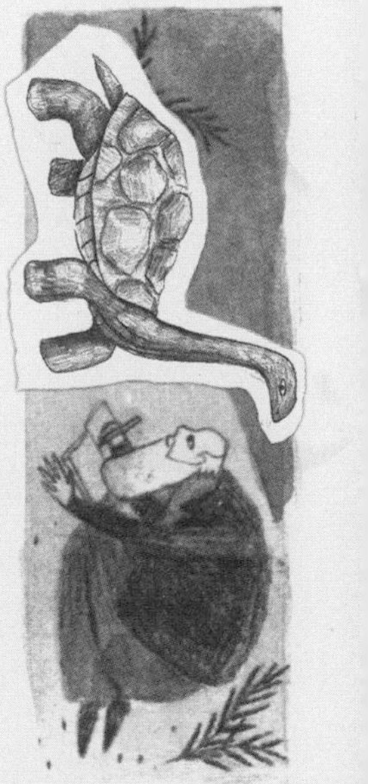

"THE GRADUAL TRANSFORMATION OF SPECIES"

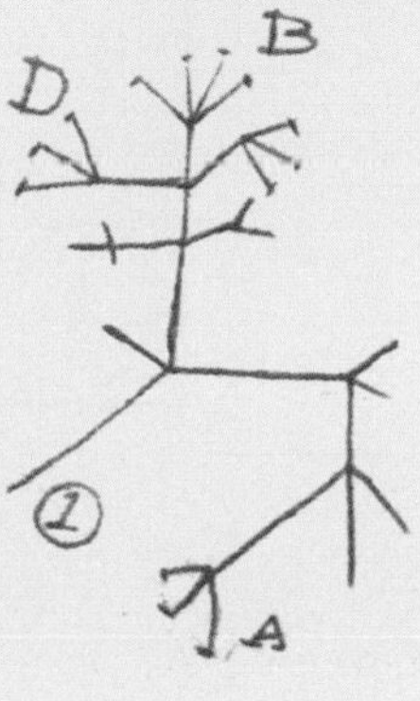

B
D
1
A

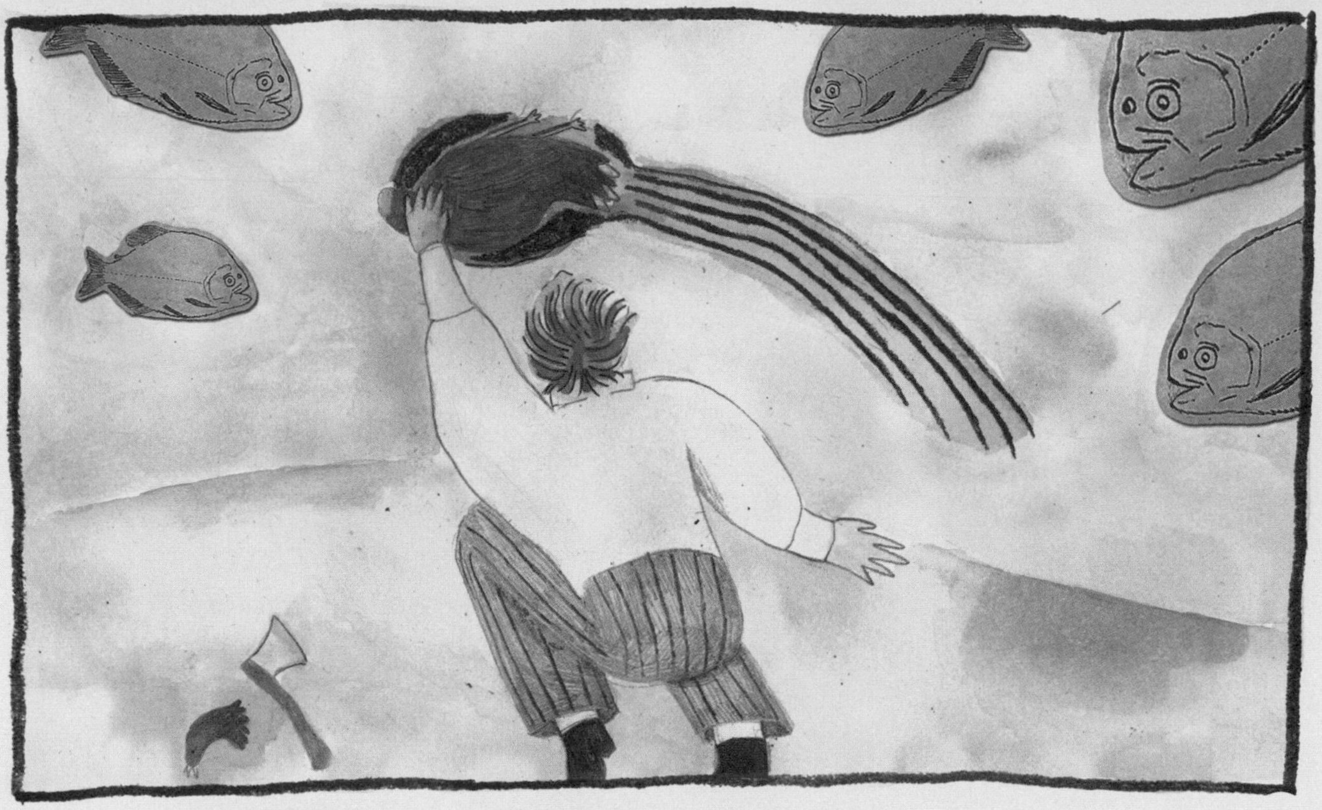

WE HAVE TO BE CAREFUL BECAUSE PIRANHA FIND HUMAN FLESH RATHER TASTY. OUR INDIAN GUIDES PROUDLY SHOW US THEIR MANY SCARS.

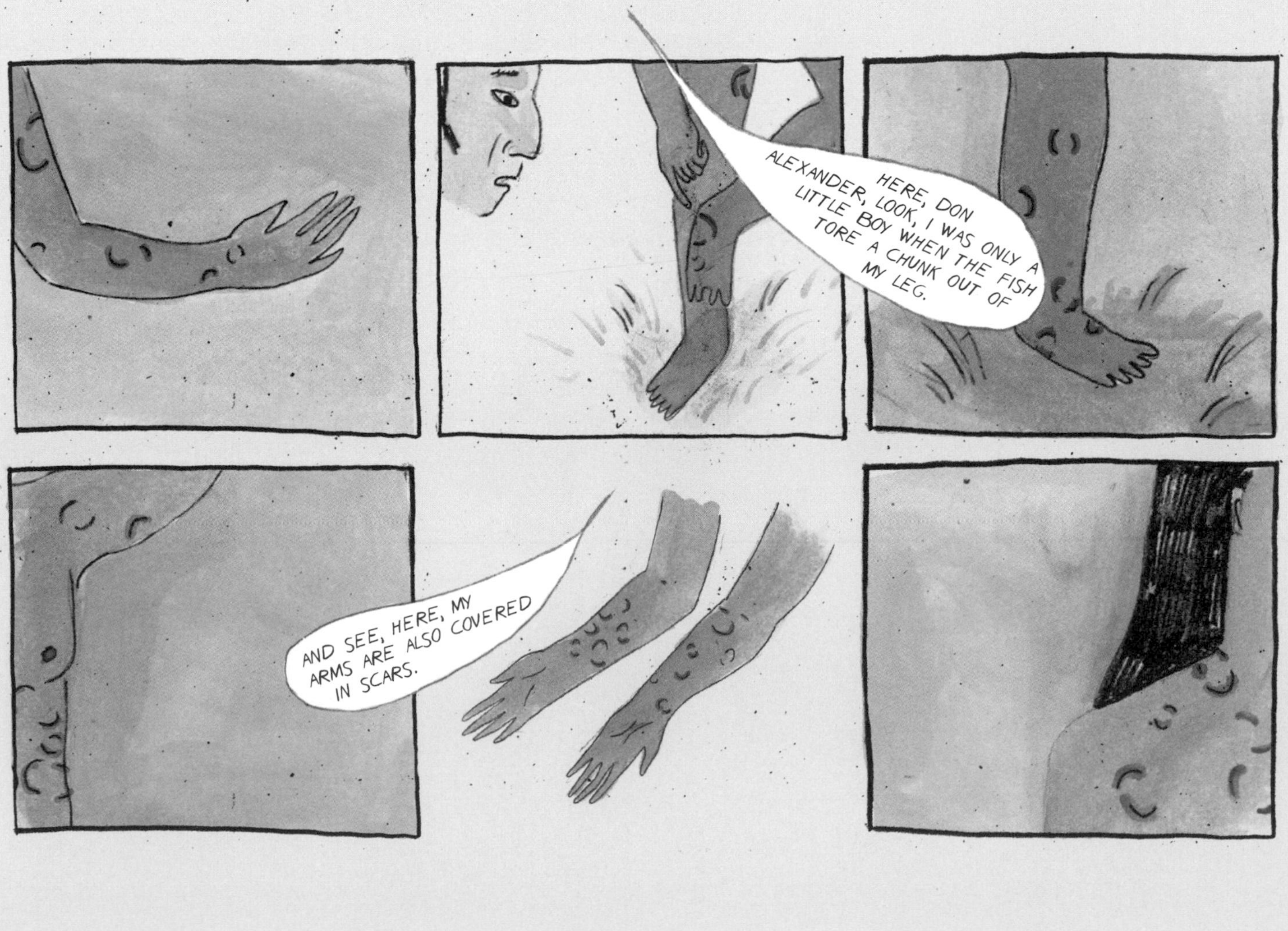
HERE, DON ALEXANDER, LOOK, I WAS ONLY A LITTLE BOY WHEN THE FISH TORE A CHUNK OUT OF MY LEG.
AND SEE, HERE, MY ARMS ARE ALSO COVERED IN SCARS.

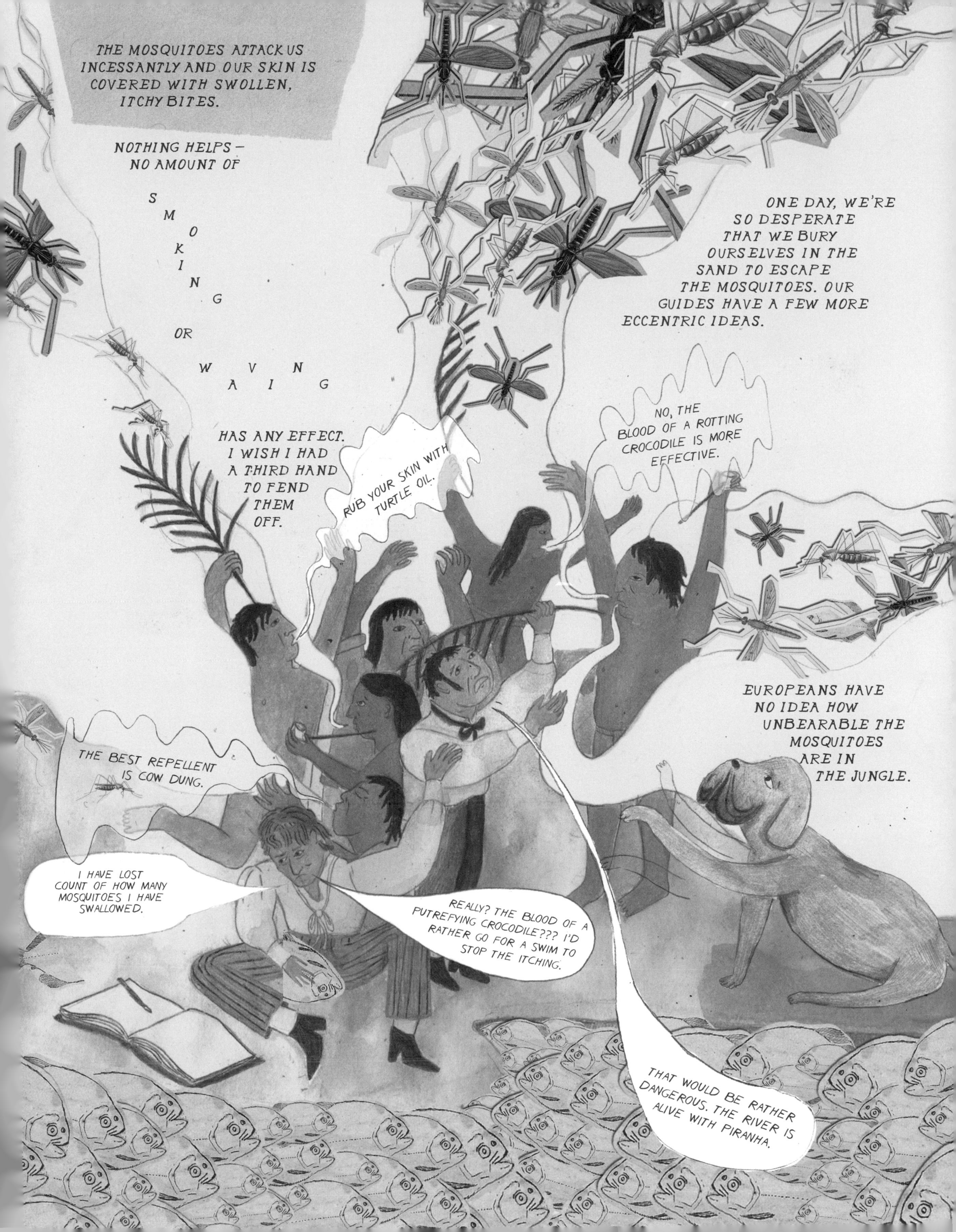
THE MOSQUITOES ATTACK US INCESSANTLY AND OUR SKIN IS COVERED WITH SWOLLEN, ITCHY BITES.
NOTHING HELPS — NO AMOUNT OF SMOKING OR WAVING HAS ANY EFFECT. I WISH I HAD A THIRD HAND TO FEND THEM OFF.
ONE DAY, WE'RE SO DESPERATE THAT WE BURY OURSELVES IN THE SAND TO ESCAPE THE MOSQUITOES. OUR GUIDES HAVE A FEW MORE ECCENTRIC IDEAS.
RUB YOUR SKIN WITH TURTLE OIL.
NO, THE BLOOD OF A ROTTING CROCODILE IS MORE EFFECTIVE.
THE BEST REPELLENT IS COW DUNG.
EUROPEANS HAVE NO IDEA HOW UNBEARABLE THE MOSQUITOES ARE IN THE JUNGLE.
I HAVE LOST COUNT OF HOW MANY MOSQUITOES I HAVE SWALLOWED.
REALLY? THE BLOOD OF A PUTREFYING CROCODILE??? I'D RATHER GO FOR A SWIM TO STOP THE ITCHING.
THAT WOULD BE RATHER DANGEROUS. THE RIVER IS ALIVE WITH PIRANHA.

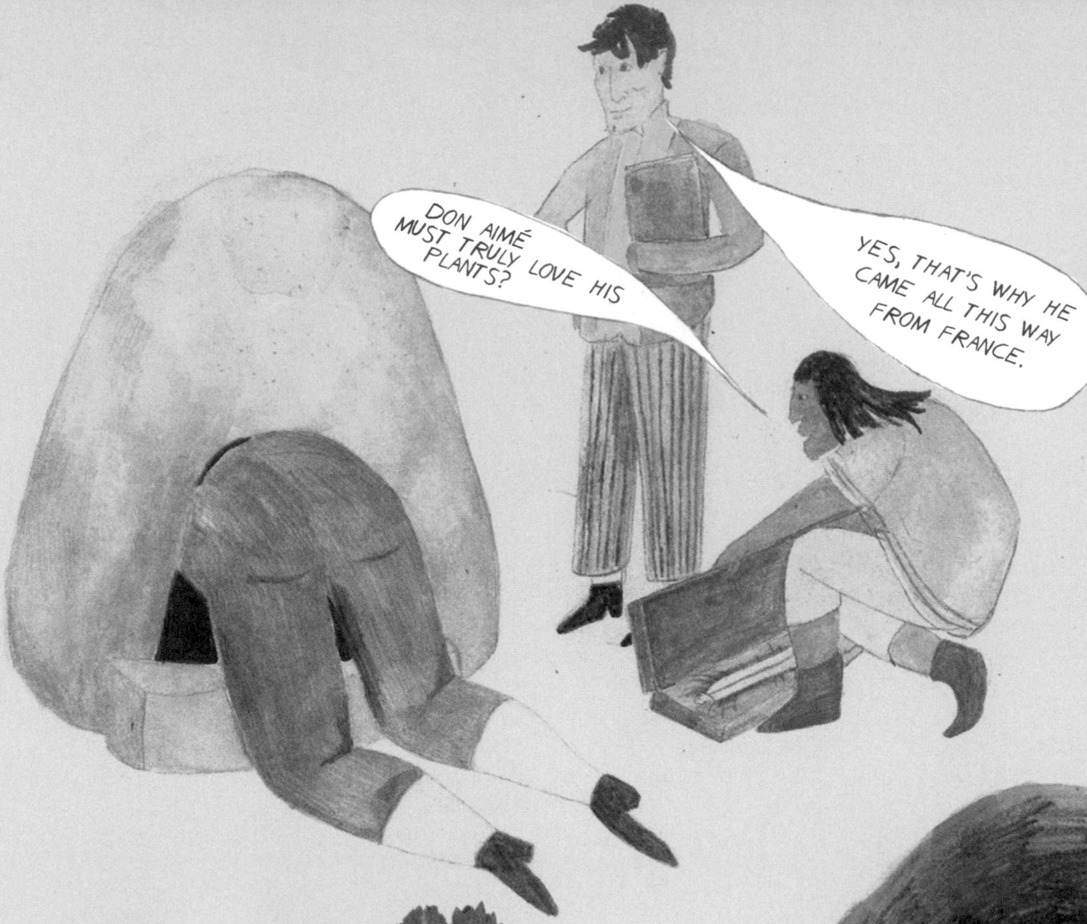
DON AIMÉ MUST TRULY LOVE HIS PLANTS?
YES, THAT'S WHY HE CAME ALL THIS WAY FROM FRANCE.

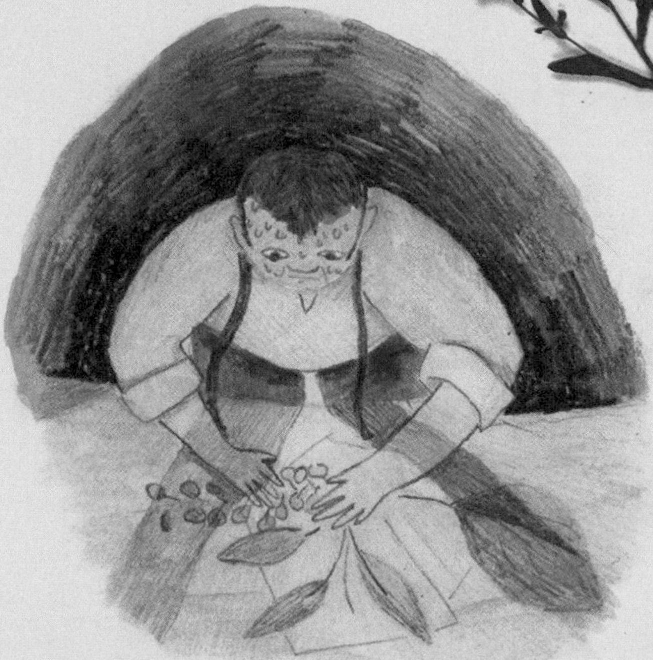

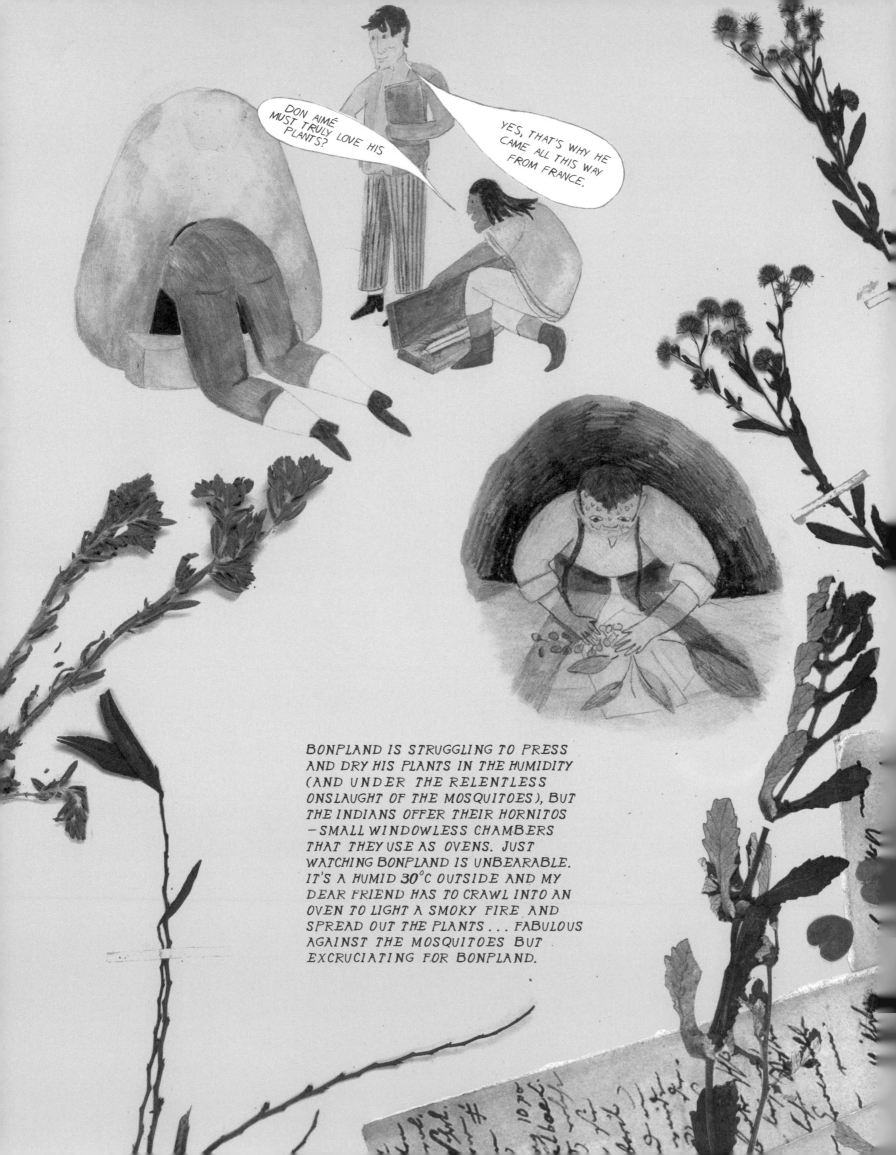

BONPLAND IS STRUGGLING TO PRESS AND DRY HIS PLANTS IN THE HUMIDITY (AND UNDER THE RELENTLESS ONSLAUGHT OF THE MOSQUITOES), BUT THE INDIANS OFFER THEIR HORNITOS – SMALL WINDOWLESS CHAMBERS THAT THEY USE AS OVENS. JUST WATCHING BONPLAND IS UNBEARABLE. IT'S A HUMID 30°C OUTSIDE AND MY DEAR FRIEND HAS TO CRAWL INTO AN OVEN TO LIGHT A SMOKY FIRE AND SPREAD OUT THE PLANTS . . . FABULOUS AGAINST THE MOSQUITOES BUT EXCRUCIATING FOR BONPLAND.

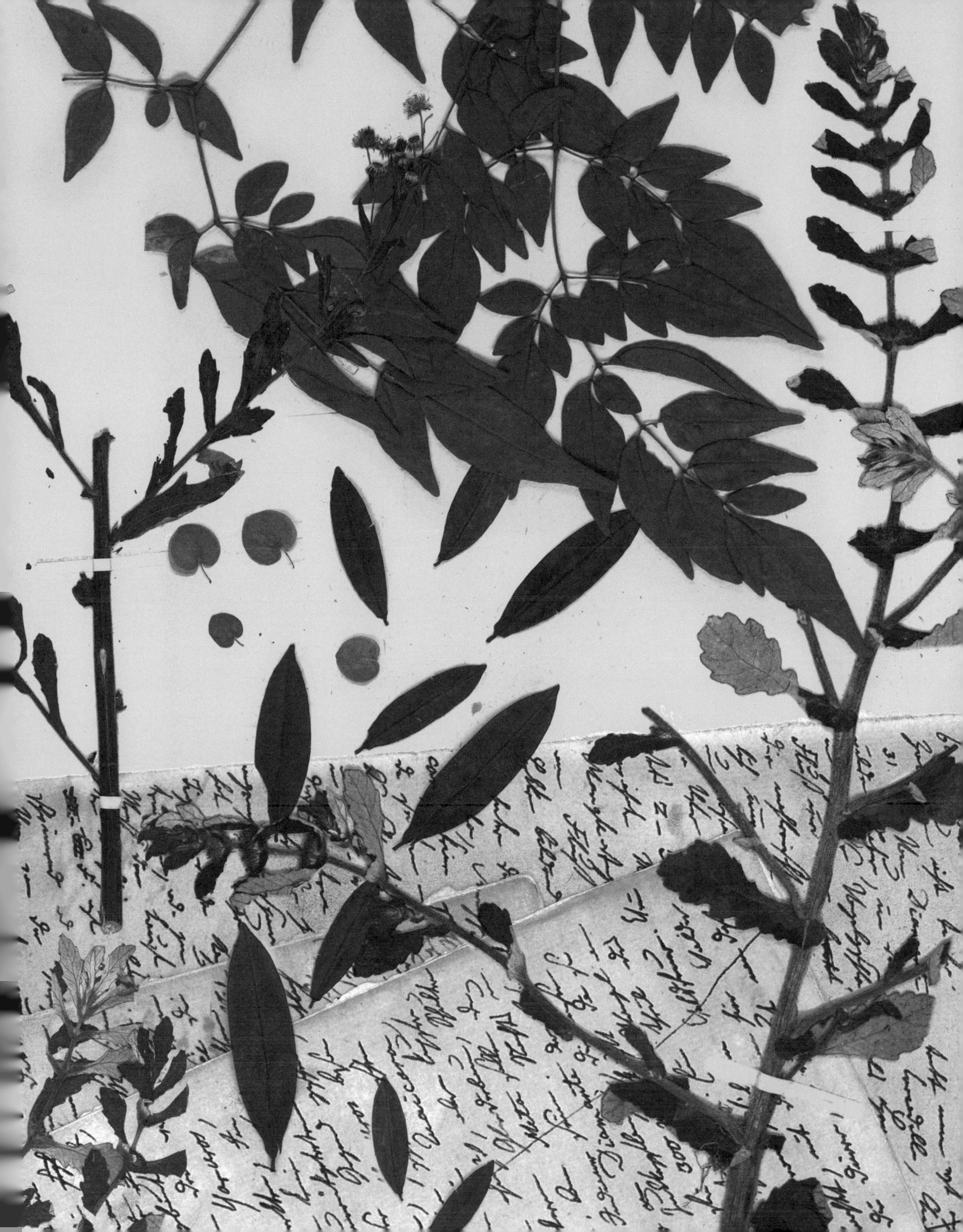

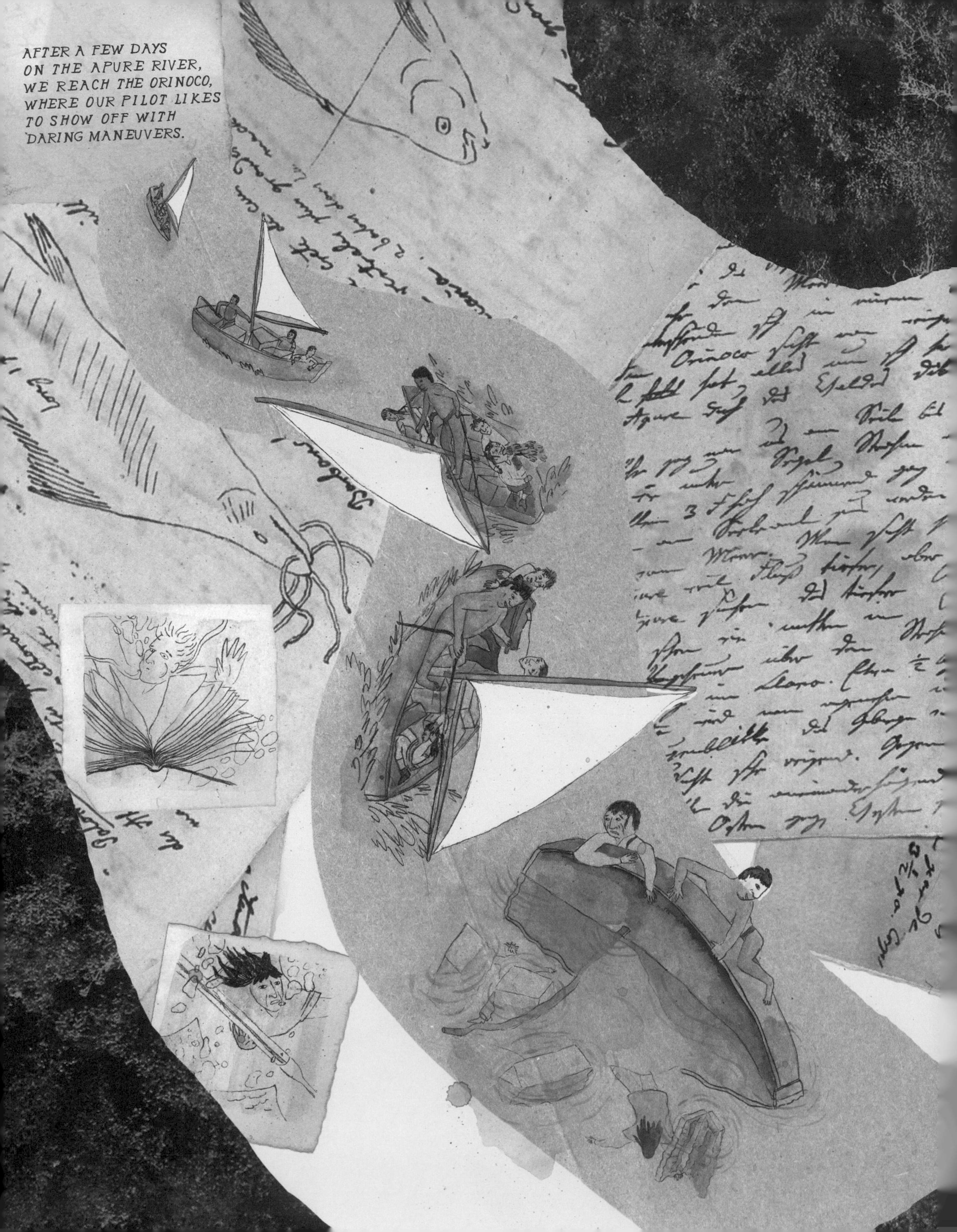
AFTER A FEW DAYS ON THE APURE RIVER, WE REACH THE ORINOCO, WHERE OUR PILOT LIKES TO SHOW OFF WITH DARING MANEUVERS.

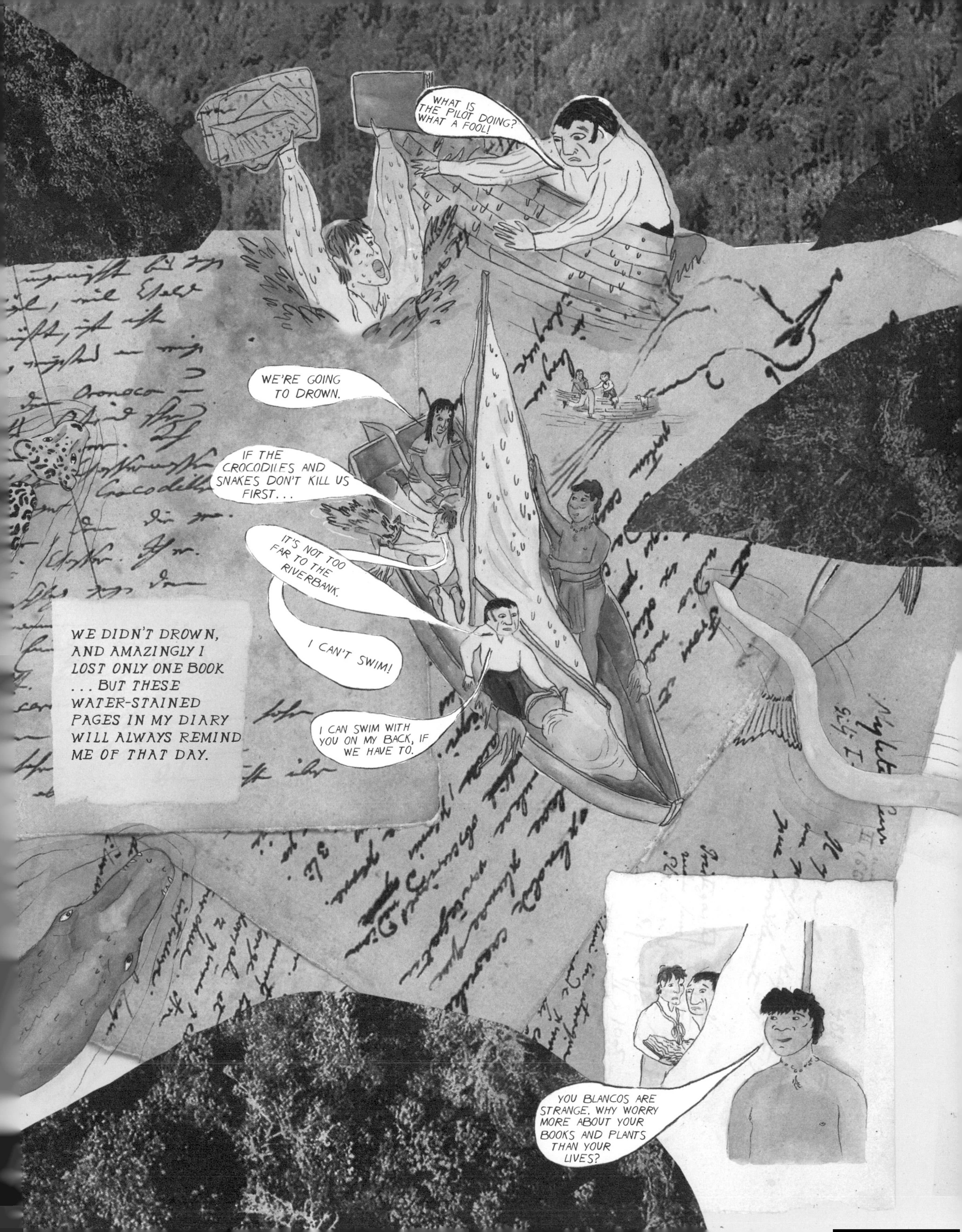
WHAT IS THE PILOT DOING? WHAT A FOOL!
WE'RE GOING TO DROWN.
IF THE CROCODILES AND SNAKES DON'T KILL US FIRST...
IT'S NOT TOO FAR TO THE RIVERBANK.
I CAN'T SWIM!
I CAN SWIM WITH YOU ON MY BACK, IF WE HAVE TO.
WE DIDN'T DROWN, AND AMAZINGLY I LOST ONLY ONE BOOK . . . BUT THESE WATER-STAINED PAGES IN MY DIARY WILL ALWAYS REMIND ME OF THAT DAY.
YOU BLANCOS ARE STRANGE. WHY WORRY MORE ABOUT YOUR BOOKS AND PLANTS THAN YOUR LIVES?

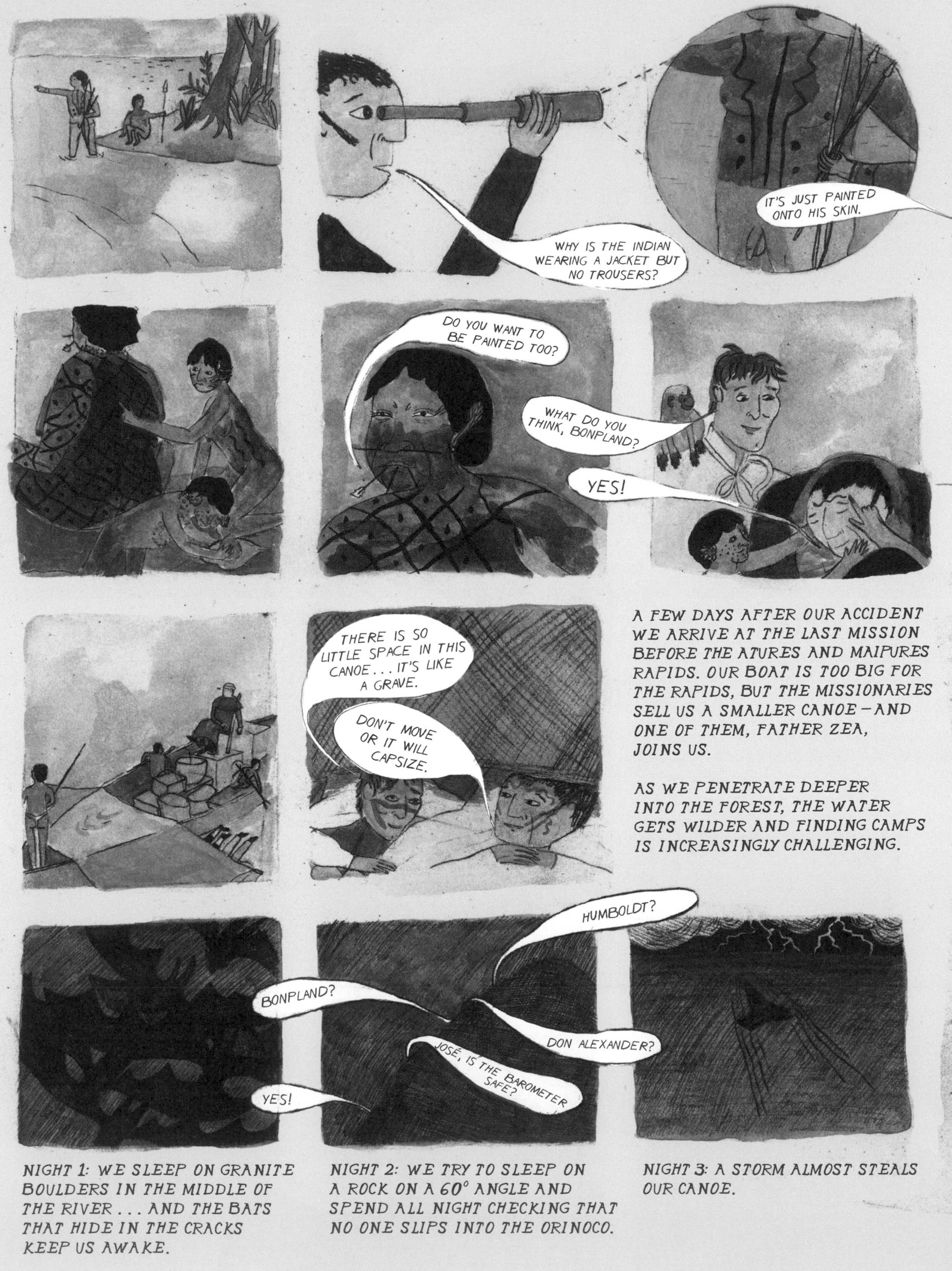

WHY IS THE INDIAN WEARING A JACKET BUT NO TROUSERS?
IT'S JUST PAINTED ONTO HIS SKIN.
DO YOU WANT TO BE PAINTED TOO?
WHAT DO YOU THINK, BONPLAND?
YES!
THERE IS SO LITTLE SPACE IN THIS CANOE . . . IT'S LIKE A GRAVE.
DON'T MOVE OR IT WILL CAPSIZE.
A FEW DAYS AFTER OUR ACCIDENT WE ARRIVE AT THE LAST MISSION BEFORE THE ATURES AND MAIPURES RAPIDS. OUR BOAT IS TOO BIG FOR THE RAPIDS, BUT THE MISSIONARIES SELL US A SMALLER CANOE – AND ONE OF THEM, FATHER ZEA, JOINS US.
AS WE PENETRATE DEEPER INTO THE FOREST, THE WATER GETS WILDER AND FINDING CAMPS IS INCREASINGLY CHALLENGING.
NIGHT 1: WE SLEEP ON GRANITE BOULDERS IN THE MIDDLE OF THE RIVER . . . AND THE BATS THAT HIDE IN THE CRACKS KEEP US AWAKE.
HUMBOLDT?
BONPLAND?
DON ALEXANDER?
JOSÉ, IS THE BAROMETER SAFE?
YES!
NIGHT 2: WE TRY TO SLEEP ON A ROCK ON A 60° ANGLE AND SPEND ALL NIGHT CHECKING THAT NO ONE SLIPS INTO THE ORINOCO.
NIGHT 3: A STORM ALMOST STEALS OUR CANOE.

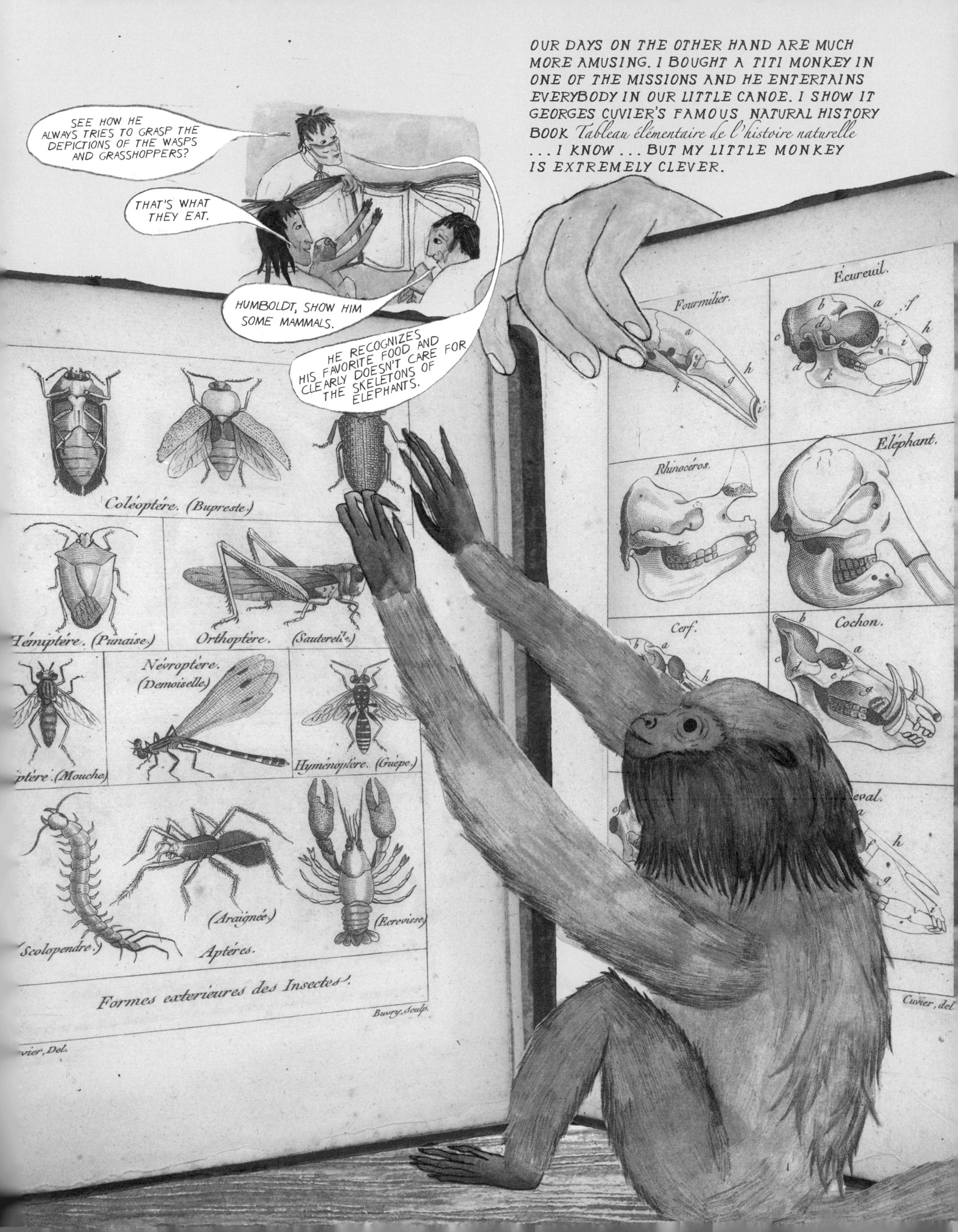
OUR DAYS ON THE OTHER HAND ARE MUCH MORE AMUSING. I BOUGHT A TITI MONKEY IN ONE OF THE MISSIONS AND HE ENTERTAINS EVERYBODY IN OUR LITTLE CANOE. I SHOW IT GEORGES CUVIER'S FAMOUS NATURAL HISTORY BOOK *Tableau élémentaire de l'histoire naturelle* . . . I KNOW . . . BUT MY LITTLE MONKEY IS EXTREMELY CLEVER.
SEE HOW HE ALWAYS TRIES TO GRASP THE DEPICTIONS OF THE WASPS AND GRASSHOPPERS?
THAT'S WHAT THEY EAT.
HUMBOLDT, SHOW HIM SOME MAMMALS.
HE RECOGNIZES HIS FAVORITE FOOD AND CLEARLY DOESN'T CARE FOR THE SKELETONS OF ELEPHANTS.
Coléoptère. (Bupreste.)
Hémiptère. (Punaise.)
Orthoptère. (Sauterelle.)
Névroptère. (Demoiselle.)
ptère. (Mouche.)
Hyménoptère. (Guêpe.)
(Scolopendre.)
(Araignée.)
(Ecrevisse.)
Aptères.
Formes exterieures des Insectes.
Bwory, Sculp.
vier, Del.
Fourmilier.
Écureuil.
Rhinocéros.
Eléphant.
Cerf.
Cochon.
Cuvier, del

IN MID-APRIL, WE REACH THE ATURES RAPIDS. HERE THE MIGHTY ORINOCO CUTS THROUGH A MOUNTAIN CHAIN IN A SERIES OF SMALL RIVER PASSAGES—A TREACHEROUS WHIRLING LABYRINTH. PASSING THE RAPIDS BY BOAT IS IMPOSSIBLE. EVERYTHING HAS TO BE CARRIED AROUND THE CASCADING WATERFALLS. AND THEN AN UNKNOWN LAND BEGINS. FATHER ZEA HAD WARNED THAT NO ONE WILL UNDERSTAND US HERE, NOR WILL WE UNDERSTAND THEM.

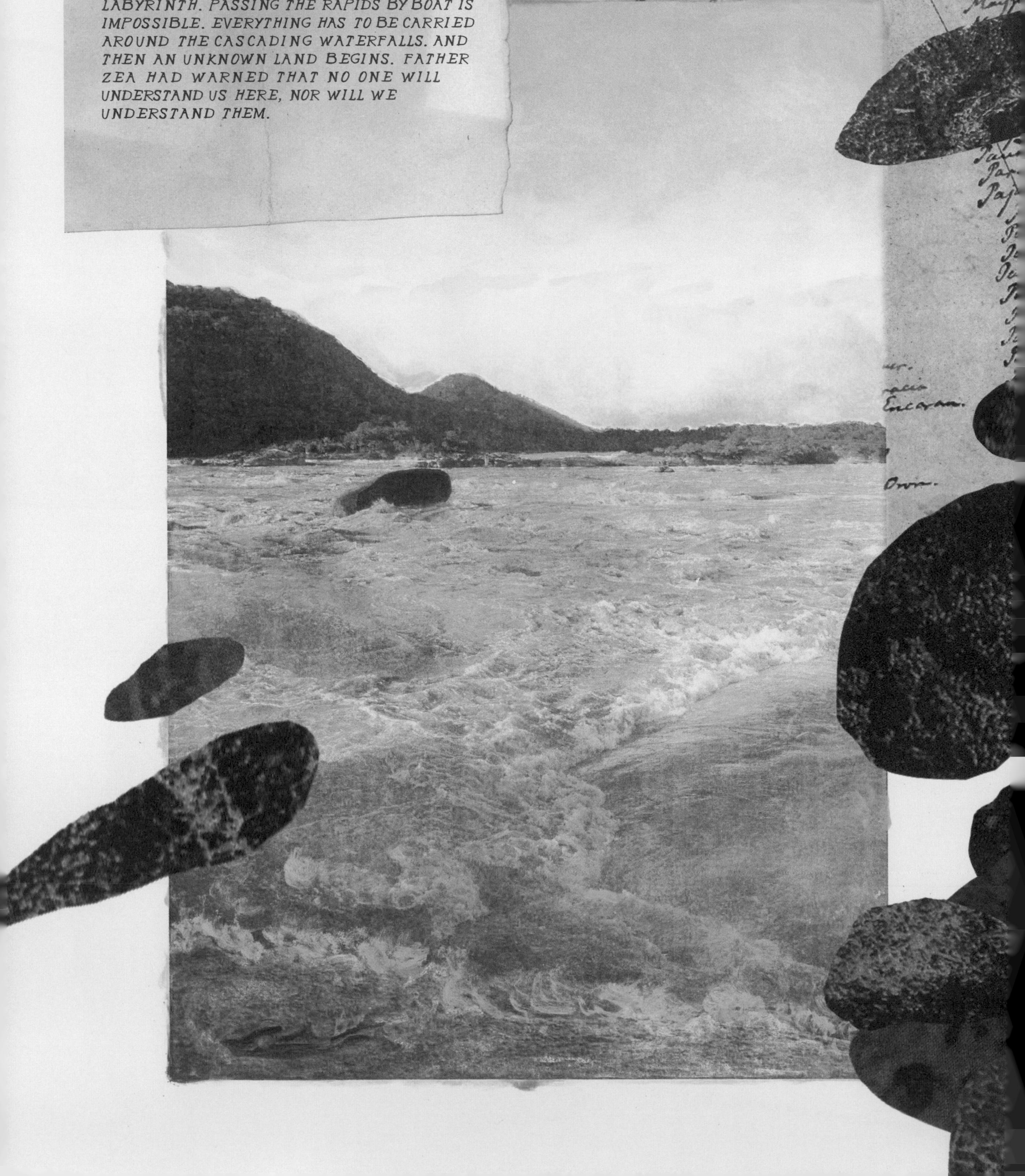

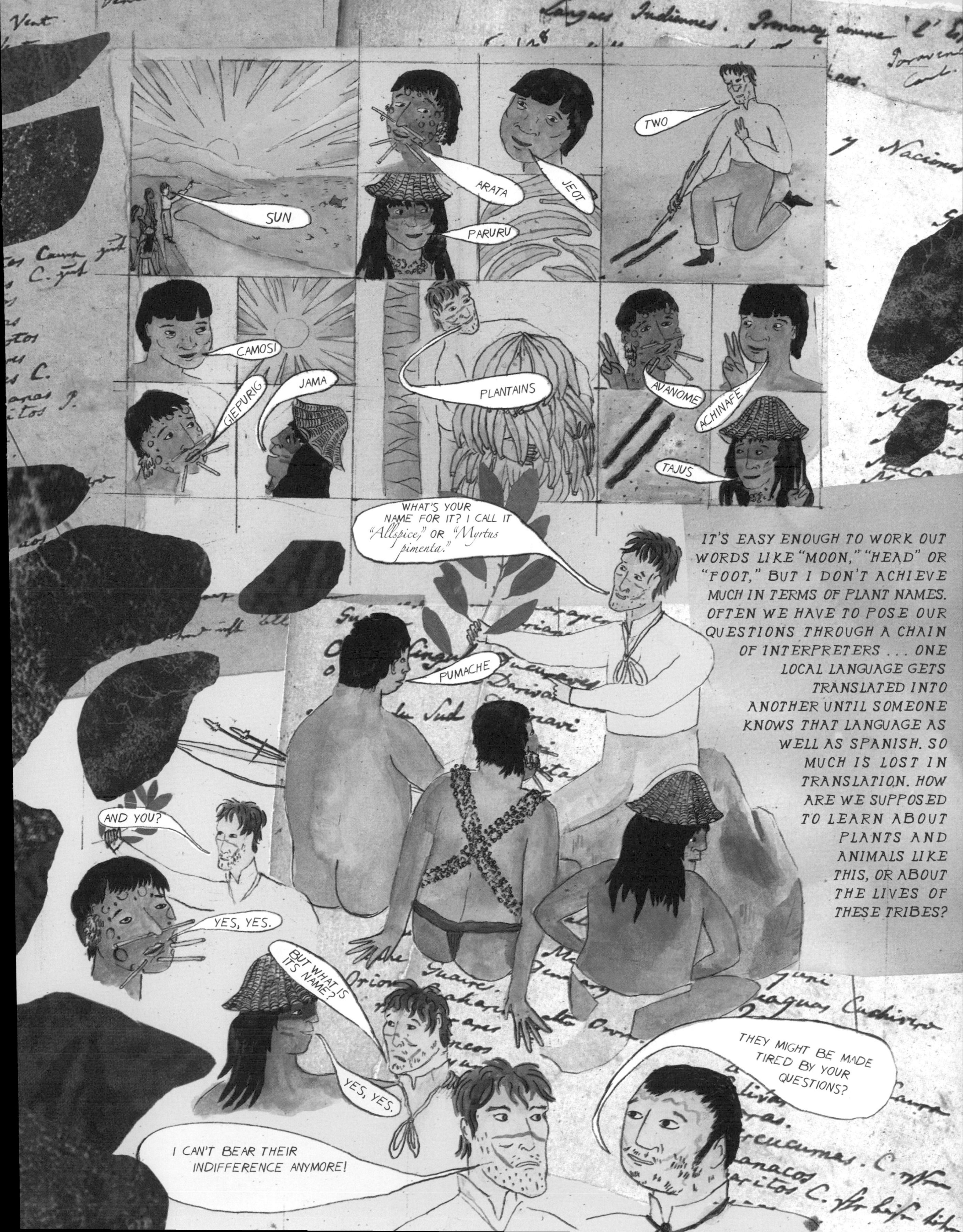
SUN
ARATA
PARURU
JEOT
TWO
CAMOSI
GIEPURIG
JAMA
PLANTAINS
AVANOME
ACHINAFE
TAJUS
WHAT'S YOUR NAME FOR IT? I CALL IT "Allspice," OR "Myrtus pimenta."
IT'S EASY ENOUGH TO WORK OUT WORDS LIKE "MOON," "HEAD" OR "FOOT," BUT I DON'T ACHIEVE MUCH IN TERMS OF PLANT NAMES. OFTEN WE HAVE TO POSE OUR QUESTIONS THROUGH A CHAIN OF INTERPRETERS . . . ONE LOCAL LANGUAGE GETS TRANSLATED INTO ANOTHER UNTIL SOMEONE KNOWS THAT LANGUAGE AS WELL AS SPANISH. SO MUCH IS LOST IN TRANSLATION. HOW ARE WE SUPPOSED TO LEARN ABOUT PLANTS AND ANIMALS LIKE THIS, OR ABOUT THE LIVES OF THESE TRIBES?
PUMACHE
AND YOU?
YES, YES.
BUT WHAT IS ITS NAME?
YES, YES.
THEY MIGHT BE MADE TIRED BY YOUR QUESTIONS?
I CAN'T BEAR THEIR INDIFFERENCE ANYMORE!

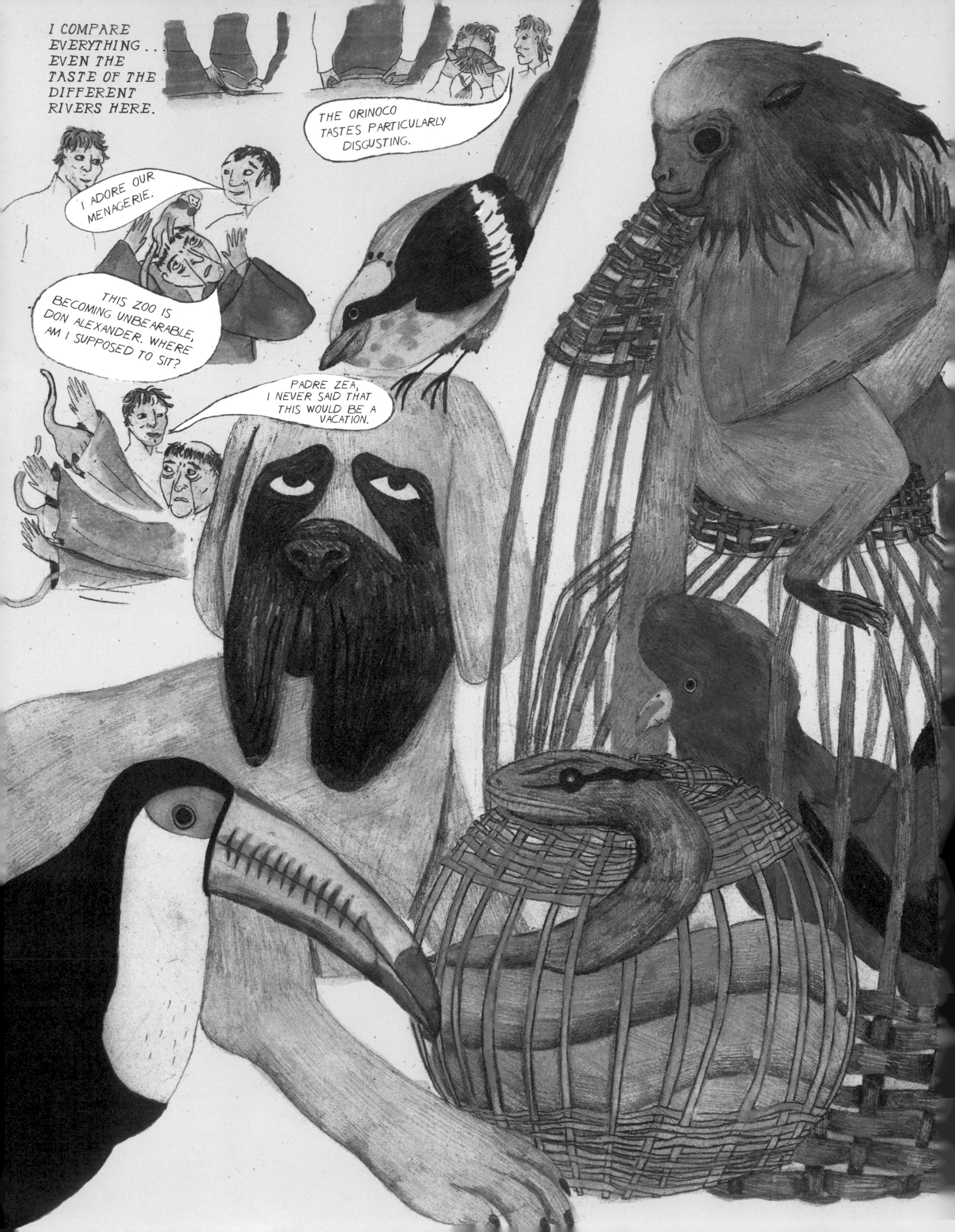
I COMPARE EVERYTHING . . . EVEN THE TASTE OF THE DIFFERENT RIVERS HERE.
THE ORINOCO TASTES PARTICULARLY DISGUSTING.
I ADORE OUR MENAGERIE.
THIS ZOO IS BECOMING UNBEARABLE, DON ALEXANDER. WHERE AM I SUPPOSED TO SIT?
PADRE ZEA, I NEVER SAID THAT THIS WOULD BE A VACATION.

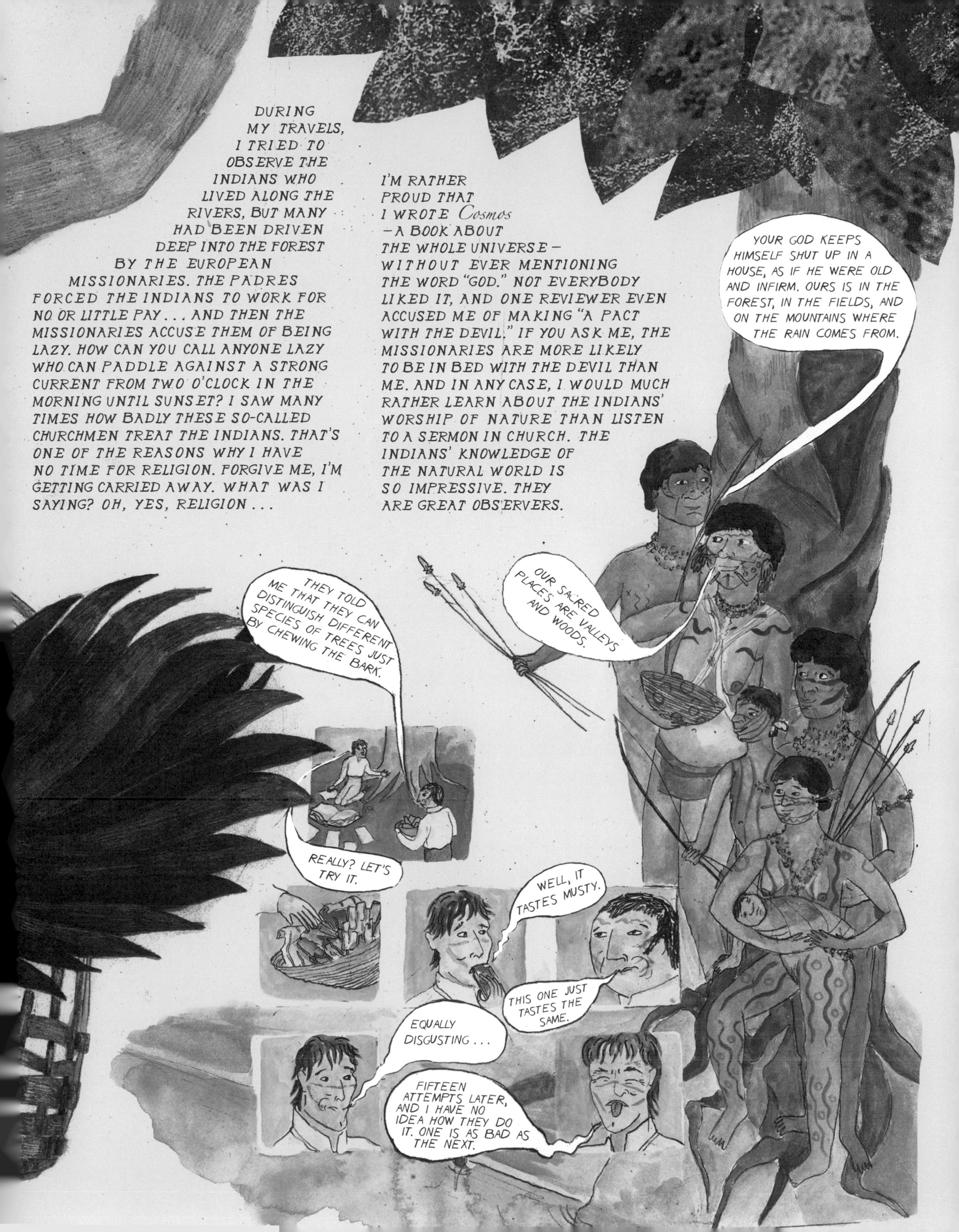
DURING MY TRAVELS, I TRIED TO OBSERVE THE INDIANS WHO LIVED ALONG THE RIVERS, BUT MANY HAD BEEN DRIVEN DEEP INTO THE FOREST BY THE EUROPEAN MISSIONARIES. THE PADRES FORCED THE INDIANS TO WORK FOR NO OR LITTLE PAY . . . AND THEN THE MISSIONARIES ACCUSE THEM OF BEING LAZY. HOW CAN YOU CALL ANYONE LAZY WHO CAN PADDLE AGAINST A STRONG CURRENT FROM TWO O'CLOCK IN THE MORNING UNTIL SUNSET? I SAW MANY TIMES HOW BADLY THESE SO-CALLED CHURCHMEN TREAT THE INDIANS. THAT'S ONE OF THE REASONS WHY I HAVE NO TIME FOR RELIGION. FORGIVE ME, I'M GETTING CARRIED AWAY. WHAT WAS I SAYING? OH, YES, RELIGION . . .
I'M RATHER PROUD THAT I WROTE *Cosmos* —A BOOK ABOUT THE WHOLE UNIVERSE— WITHOUT EVER MENTIONING THE WORD "GOD." NOT EVERYBODY LIKED IT, AND ONE REVIEWER EVEN ACCUSED ME OF MAKING "A PACT WITH THE DEVIL." IF YOU ASK ME, THE MISSIONARIES ARE MORE LIKELY TO BE IN BED WITH THE DEVIL THAN ME. AND IN ANY CASE, I WOULD MUCH RATHER LEARN ABOUT THE INDIANS' WORSHIP OF NATURE THAN LISTEN TO A SERMON IN CHURCH. THE INDIANS' KNOWLEDGE OF THE NATURAL WORLD IS SO IMPRESSIVE. THEY ARE GREAT OBSERVERS.
YOUR GOD KEEPS HIMSELF SHUT UP IN A HOUSE, AS IF HE WERE OLD AND INFIRM. OURS IS IN THE FOREST, IN THE FIELDS, AND ON THE MOUNTAINS WHERE THE RAIN COMES FROM.
OUR SACRED PLACES ARE VALLEYS AND WOODS.
THEY TOLD ME THAT THEY CAN DISTINGUISH DIFFERENT SPECIES OF TREES JUST BY CHEWING THE BARK.
REALLY? LET'S TRY IT.
WELL, IT TASTES MUSTY.
THIS ONE JUST TASTES THE SAME.
EQUALLY DISGUSTING . . .
FIFTEEN ATTEMPTS LATER, AND I HAVE NO IDEA HOW THEY DO IT. ONE IS AS BAD AS THE NEXT.

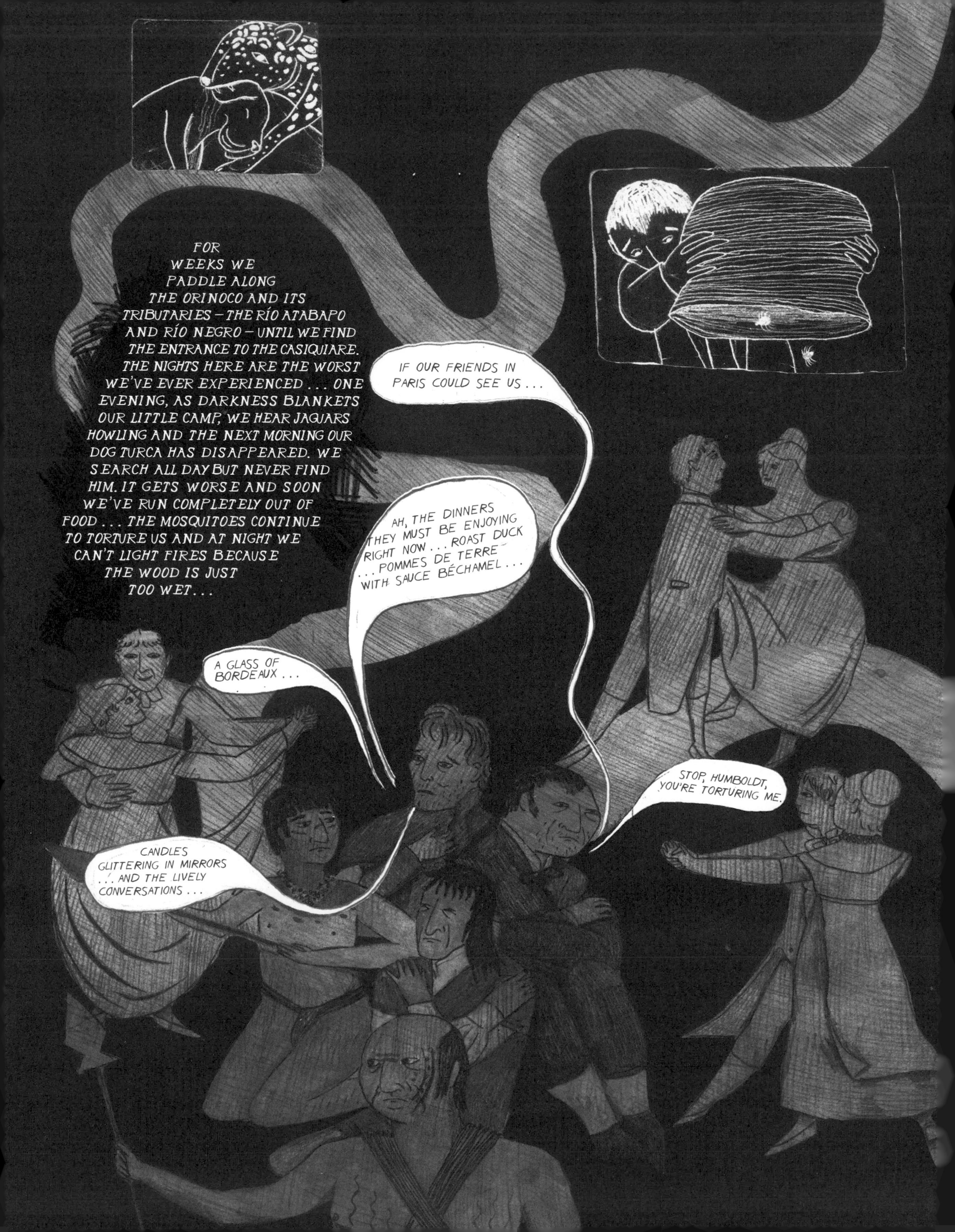
FOR WEEKS WE PADDLE ALONG THE ORINOCO AND ITS TRIBUTARIES – THE RÍO ATABAPO AND RÍO NEGRO – UNTIL WE FIND THE ENTRANCE TO THE CASIQUIARE. THE NIGHTS HERE ARE THE WORST WE'VE EVER EXPERIENCED . . . ONE EVENING, AS DARKNESS BLANKETS OUR LITTLE CAMP, WE HEAR JAGUARS HOWLING AND THE NEXT MORNING OUR DOG TURCA HAS DISAPPEARED. WE SEARCH ALL DAY BUT NEVER FIND HIM. IT GETS WORSE AND SOON WE'VE RUN COMPLETELY OUT OF FOOD . . . THE MOSQUITOES CONTINUE TO TORTURE US AND AT NIGHT WE CAN'T LIGHT FIRES BECAUSE THE WOOD IS JUST TOO WET . . .
IF OUR FRIENDS IN PARIS COULD SEE US . . .
AH, THE DINNERS THEY MUST BE ENJOYING RIGHT NOW . . . ROAST DUCK . . . POMMES DE TERRE WITH SAUCE BÉCHAMEL . . .
A GLASS OF BORDEAUX . . .
CANDLES GLITTERING IN MIRRORS . . . AND THE LIVELY CONVERSATIONS . . .
STOP, HUMBOLDT, YOU'RE TORTURING ME.

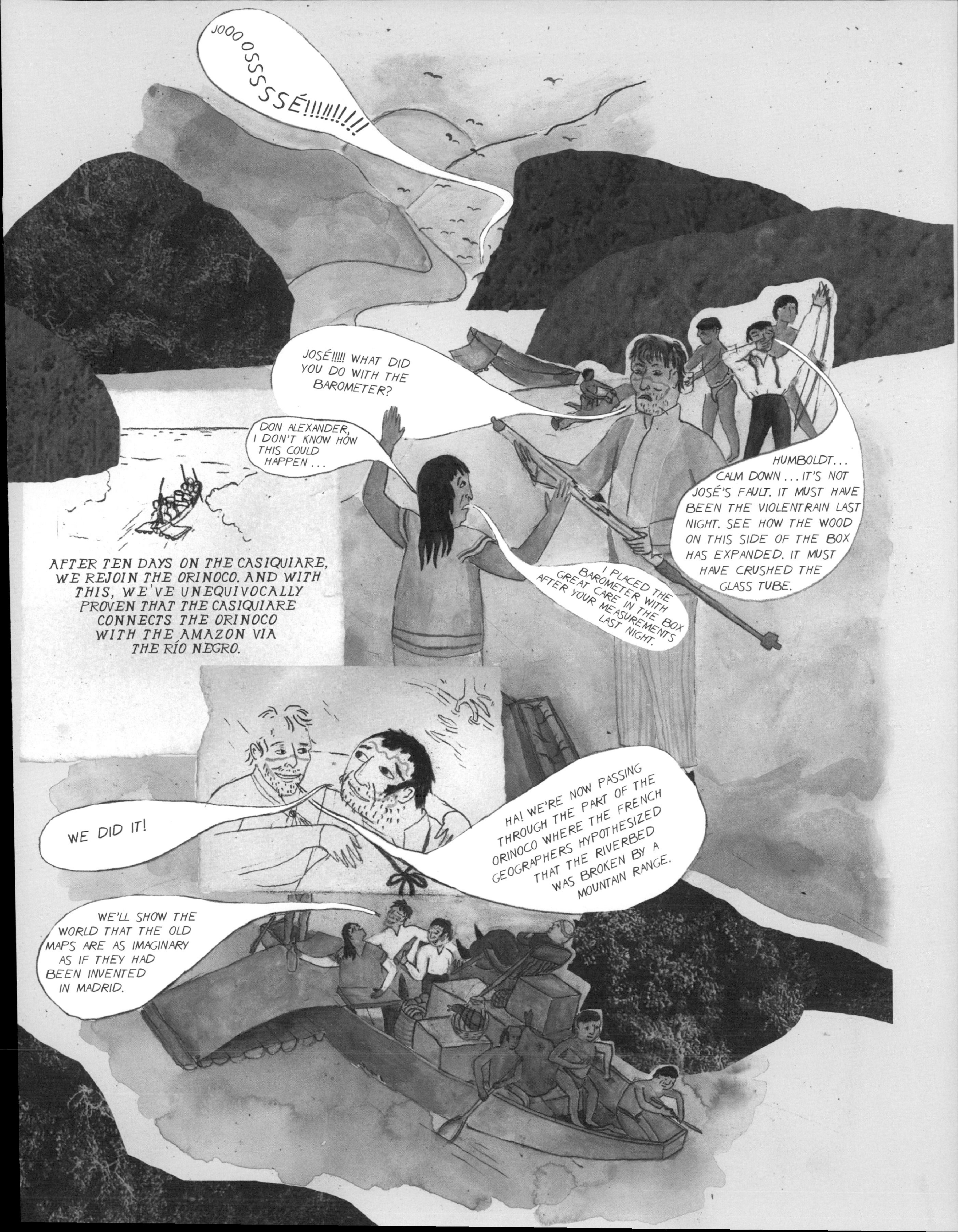
JOOO OSSSSSÉ!!!!!!!!!!
JOSÉ!!!!! WHAT DID YOU DO WITH THE BAROMETER?
DON ALEXANDER, I DON'T KNOW HOW THIS COULD HAPPEN . . .
HUMBOLDT . . . CALM DOWN . . . IT'S NOT JOSÉ'S FAULT. IT MUST HAVE BEEN THE VIOLENTRAIN LAST NIGHT. SEE HOW THE WOOD ON THIS SIDE OF THE BOX HAS EXPANDED. IT MUST HAVE CRUSHED THE GLASS TUBE.
I PLACED THE BAROMETER WITH GREAT CARE IN THE BOX AFTER YOUR MEASUREMENTS LAST NIGHT.
AFTER TEN DAYS ON THE CASIQUIARE, WE REJOIN THE ORINOCO. AND WITH THIS, WE'VE UNEQUIVOCALLY PROVEN THAT THE CASIQUIARE CONNECTS THE ORINOCO WITH THE AMAZON VIA THE RÍO NEGRO.
WE DID IT!
HA! WE'RE NOW PASSING THROUGH THE PART OF THE ORINOCO WHERE THE FRENCH GEOGRAPHERS HYPOTHESIZED THAT THE RIVERBED WAS BROKEN BY A MOUNTAIN RANGE.
WE'LL SHOW THE WORLD THAT THE OLD MAPS ARE AS IMAGINARY AS IF THEY HAD BEEN INVENTED IN MADRID.

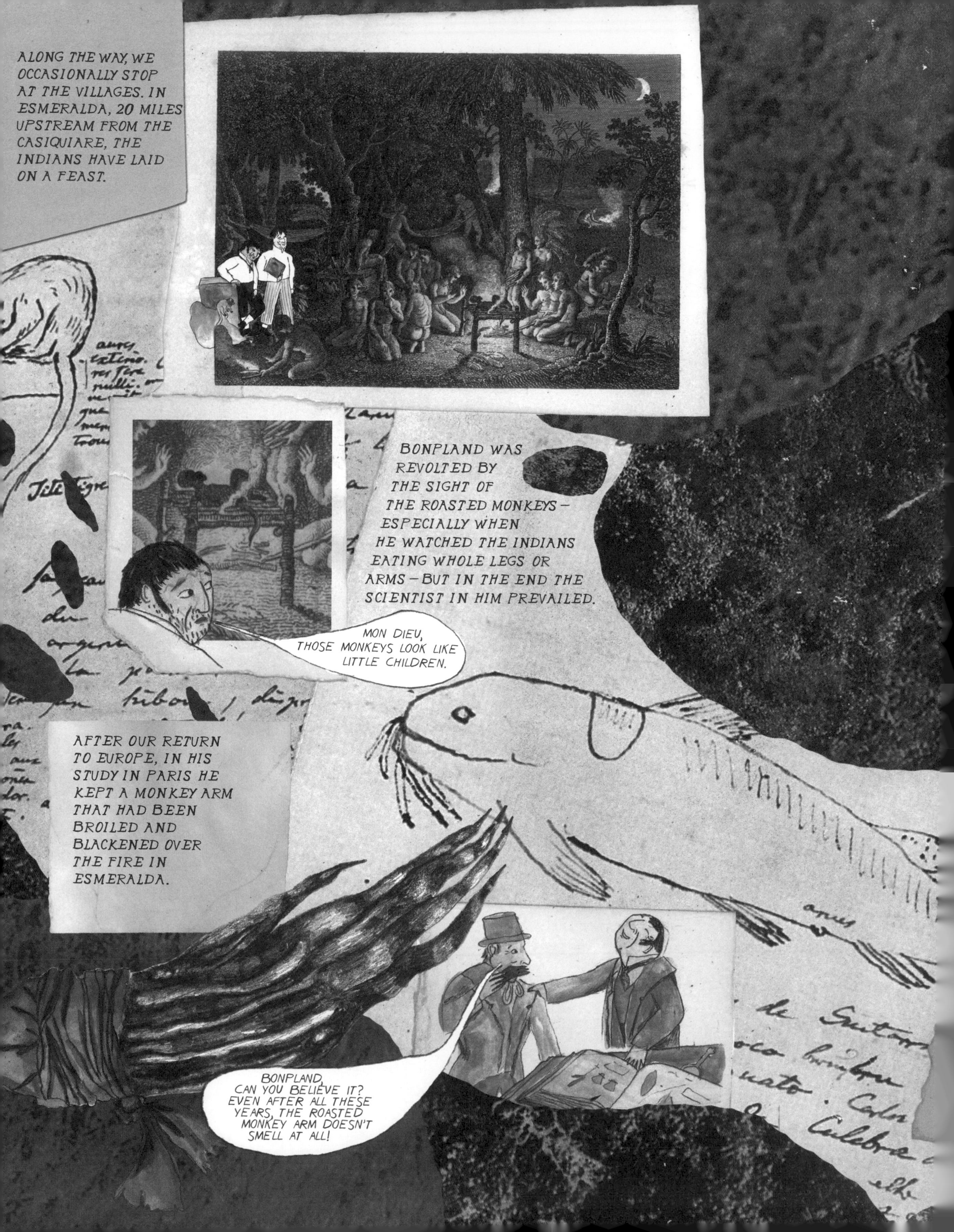
ALONG THE WAY, WE OCCASIONALLY STOP AT THE VILLAGES. IN ESMERALDA, 20 MILES UPSTREAM FROM THE CASIQUIARE, THE INDIANS HAVE LAID ON A FEAST.
BONPLAND WAS REVOLTED BY THE SIGHT OF THE ROASTED MONKEYS – ESPECIALLY WHEN HE WATCHED THE INDIANS EATING WHOLE LEGS OR ARMS – BUT IN THE END THE SCIENTIST IN HIM PREVAILED.
MON DIEU, THOSE MONKEYS LOOK LIKE LITTLE CHILDREN.
AFTER OUR RETURN TO EUROPE, IN HIS STUDY IN PARIS HE KEPT A MONKEY ARM THAT HAD BEEN BROILED AND BLACKENED OVER THE FIRE IN ESMERALDA.
BONPLAND, CAN YOU BELIEVE IT? EVEN AFTER ALL THESE YEARS, THE ROASTED MONKEY ARM DOESN'T SMELL AT ALL!

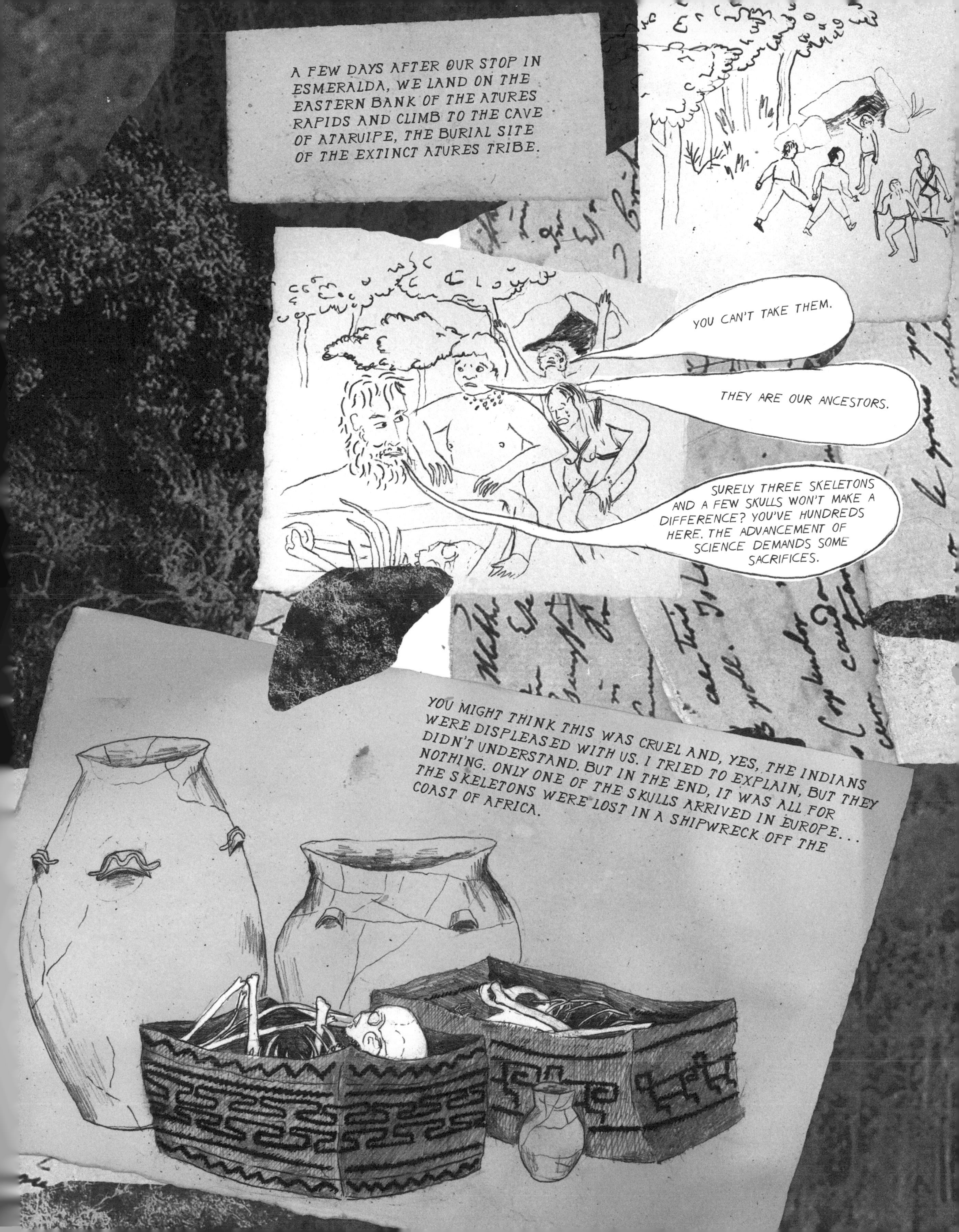
A FEW DAYS AFTER OUR STOP IN ESMERALDA, WE LAND ON THE EASTERN BANK OF THE ATURES RAPIDS AND CLIMB TO THE CAVE OF ATARUIPE, THE BURIAL SITE OF THE EXTINCT ATURES TRIBE.
YOU CAN'T TAKE THEM.
THEY ARE OUR ANCESTORS.
SURELY THREE SKELETONS AND A FEW SKULLS WON'T MAKE A DIFFERENCE? YOU'VE HUNDREDS HERE. THE ADVANCEMENT OF SCIENCE DEMANDS SOME SACRIFICES.
YOU MIGHT THINK THIS WAS CRUEL AND, YES, THE INDIANS WERE DISPLEASED WITH US. I TRIED TO EXPLAIN, BUT THEY DIDN'T UNDERSTAND. BUT IN THE END, IT WAS ALL FOR NOTHING. ONLY ONE OF THE SKULLS ARRIVED IN EUROPE... THE SKELETONS WERE LOST IN A SHIPWRECK OFF THE COAST OF AFRICA.

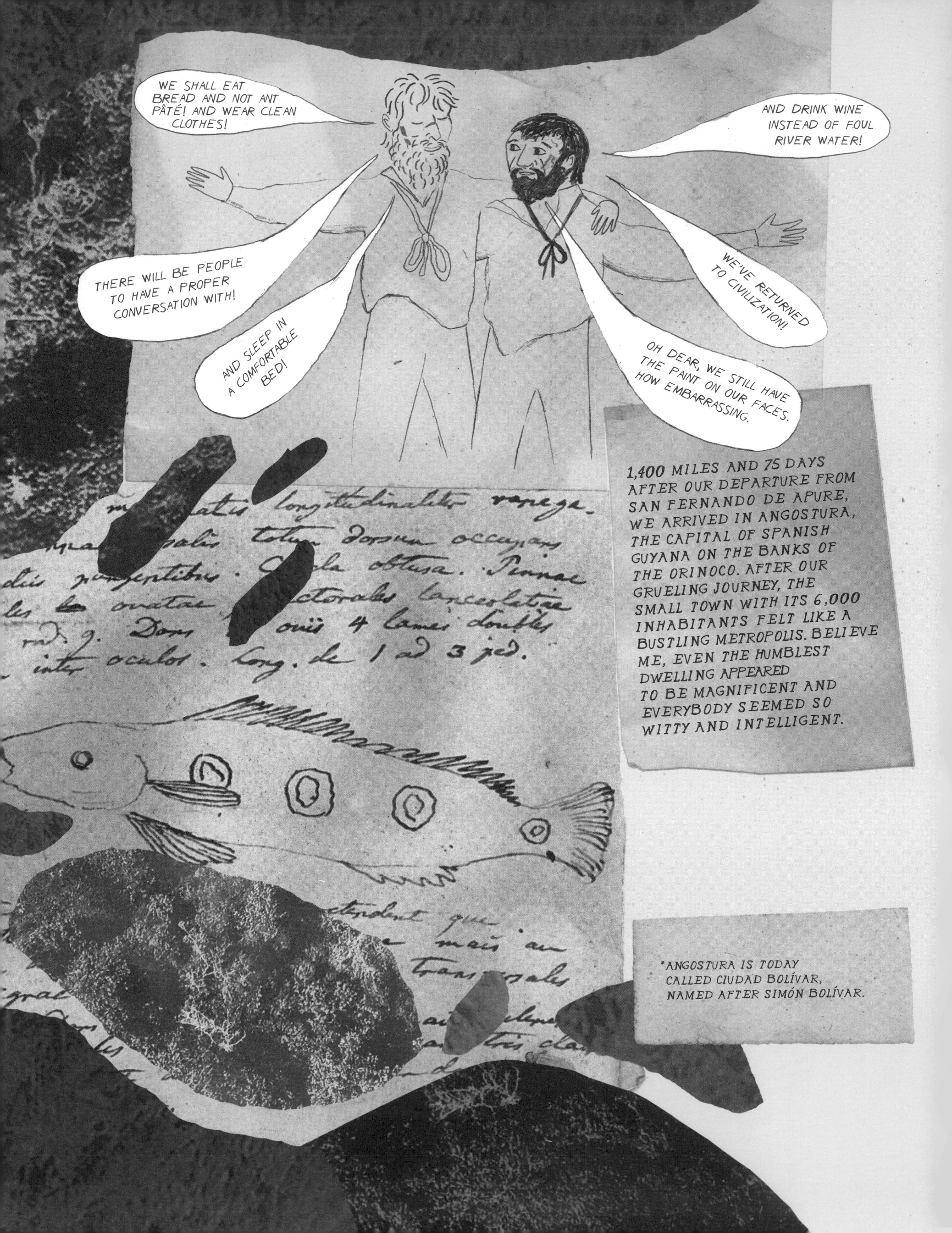
WE SHALL EAT BREAD AND NOT ANT PÂTÉ! AND WEAR CLEAN CLOTHES!
AND DRINK WINE INSTEAD OF FOUL RIVER WATER!
THERE WILL BE PEOPLE TO HAVE A PROPER CONVERSATION WITH!
WE'VE RETURNED TO CIVILIZATION!
AND SLEEP IN A COMFORTABLE BED!
OH DEAR, WE STILL HAVE THE PAINT ON OUR FACES. HOW EMBARRASSING.
1,400 MILES AND 75 DAYS AFTER OUR DEPARTURE FROM SAN FERNANDO DE APURE, WE ARRIVED IN ANGOSTURA, THE CAPITAL OF SPANISH GUYANA ON THE BANKS OF THE ORINOCO. AFTER OUR GRUELING JOURNEY, THE SMALL TOWN WITH ITS 6,000 INHABITANTS FELT LIKE A BUSTLING METROPOLIS. BELIEVE ME, EVEN THE HUMBLEST DWELLING APPEARED TO BE MAGNIFICENT AND EVERYBODY SEEMED SO WITTY AND INTELLIGENT.
*ANGOSTURA IS TODAY CALLED CIUDAD BOLÍVAR, NAMED AFTER SIMÓN BOLÍVAR.

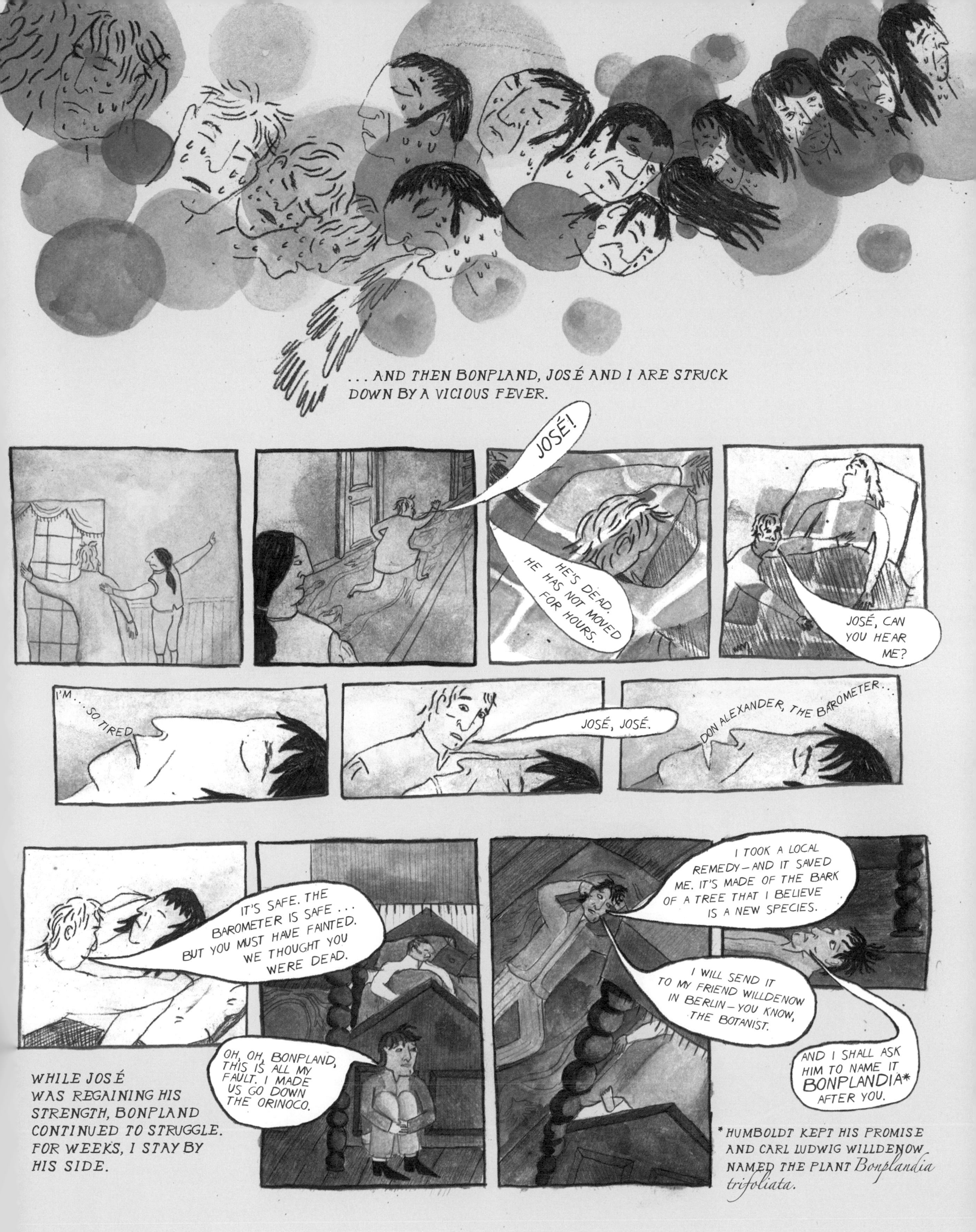
. . . AND THEN BONPLAND, JOSÉ AND I ARE STRUCK DOWN BY A VICIOUS FEVER.
JOSÉ!
HE'S DEAD. HE HAS NOT MOVED FOR HOURS.
JOSÉ, CAN YOU HEAR ME?
I'M . . . SO TIRED
JOSÉ, JOSÉ.
DON ALEXANDER, THE BAROMETER . . .
IT'S SAFE. THE BAROMETER IS SAFE . . . BUT YOU MUST HAVE FAINTED. WE THOUGHT YOU WERE DEAD.
WHILE JOSÉ WAS REGAINING HIS STRENGTH, BONPLAND CONTINUED TO STRUGGLE. FOR WEEKS, I STAY BY HIS SIDE.
OH, OH, BONPLAND, THIS IS ALL MY FAULT. I MADE US GO DOWN THE ORINOCO.
I TOOK A LOCAL REMEDY—AND IT SAVED ME. IT'S MADE OF THE BARK OF A TREE THAT I BELIEVE IS A NEW SPECIES.
I WILL SEND IT TO MY FRIEND WILLDENOW IN BERLIN—YOU KNOW, THE BOTANIST.
AND I SHALL ASK HIM TO NAME IT BONPLANDIA* AFTER YOU.

*HUMBOLDT KEPT HIS PROMISE AND CARL LUDWIG WILLDENOW NAMED THE PLANT *Bonplandia trifoliata*.

I WON'T BORE YOU WITH ALL THE DETAILS OF OUR JOURNEY FROM ANGOSTURA BACK TO CUMANÁ, BUT I SHALL TRY TO SUMMARIZE BRIEFLY . . . MOST IMPORTANT, BONPLAND SURVIVED THE FEVER – AND DESPITE HIS ILLNESS, HE ALWAYS REMAINED CHEERFUL.

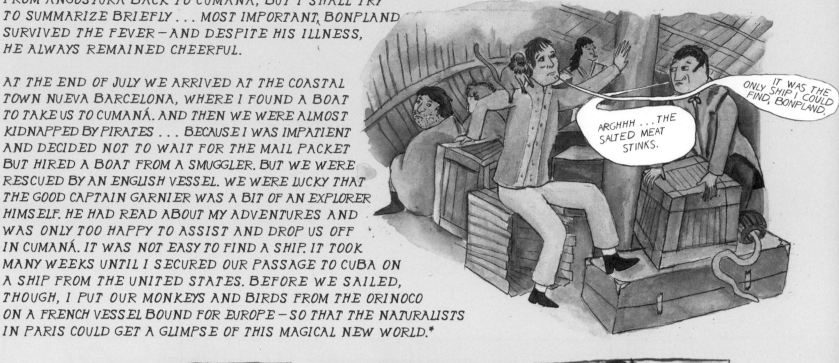

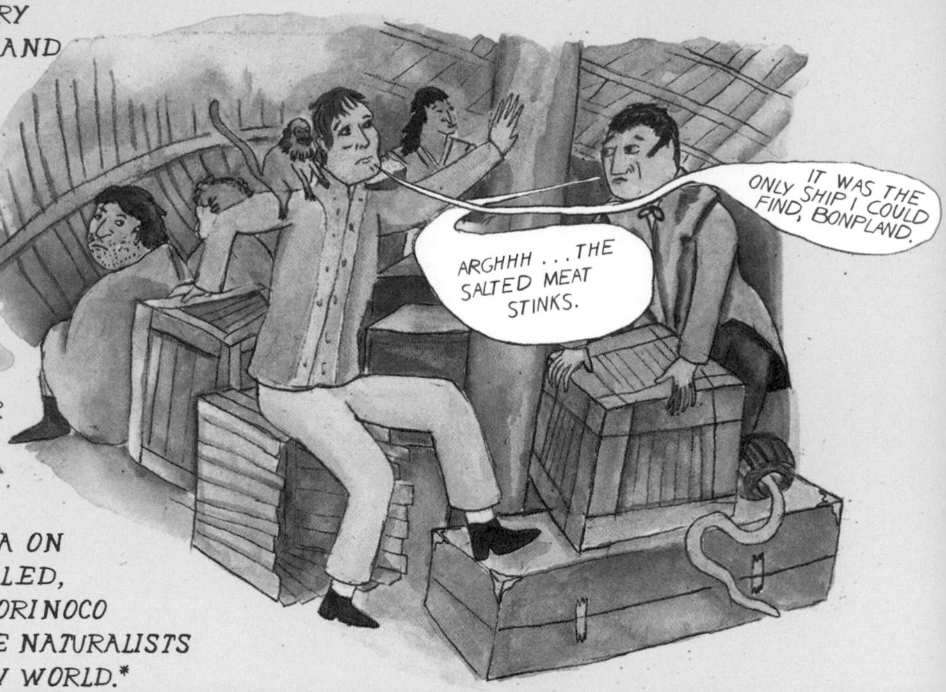
IT WAS THE ONLY SHIP I COULD FIND, BONPLAND.
ARGHHH . . . THE SALTED MEAT STINKS.

AT THE END OF JULY WE ARRIVED AT THE COASTAL TOWN NUEVA BARCELONA, WHERE I FOUND A BOAT TO TAKE US TO CUMANÁ. AND THEN WE WERE ALMOST KIDNAPPED BY PIRATES . . . BECAUSE I WAS IMPATIENT AND DECIDED NOT TO WAIT FOR THE MAIL PACKET BUT HIRED A BOAT FROM A SMUGGLER. BUT WE WERE RESCUED BY AN ENGLISH VESSEL. WE WERE LUCKY THAT THE GOOD CAPTAIN GARNIER WAS A BIT OF AN EXPLORER HIMSELF. HE HAD READ ABOUT MY ADVENTURES AND WAS ONLY TOO HAPPY TO ASSIST AND DROP US OFF IN CUMANÁ. IT WAS NOT EASY TO FIND A SHIP. IT TOOK MANY WEEKS UNTIL I SECURED OUR PASSAGE TO CUBA ON A SHIP FROM THE UNITED STATES. BEFORE WE SAILED, THOUGH, I PUT OUR MONKEYS AND BIRDS FROM THE ORINOCO ON A FRENCH VESSEL BOUND FOR EUROPE – SO THAT THE NATURALISTS IN PARIS COULD GET A GLIMPSE OF THIS MAGICAL NEW WORLD.*

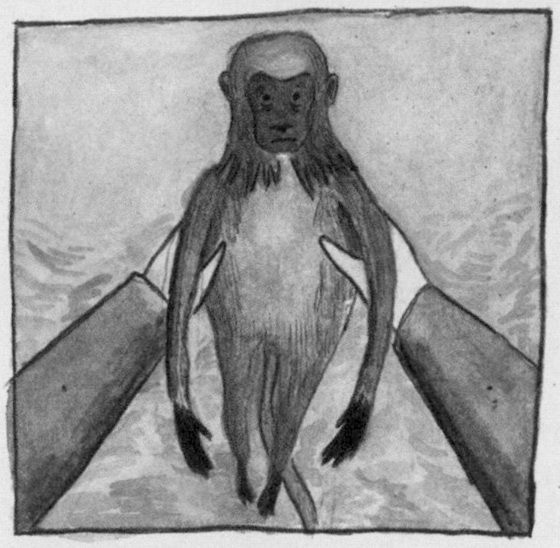

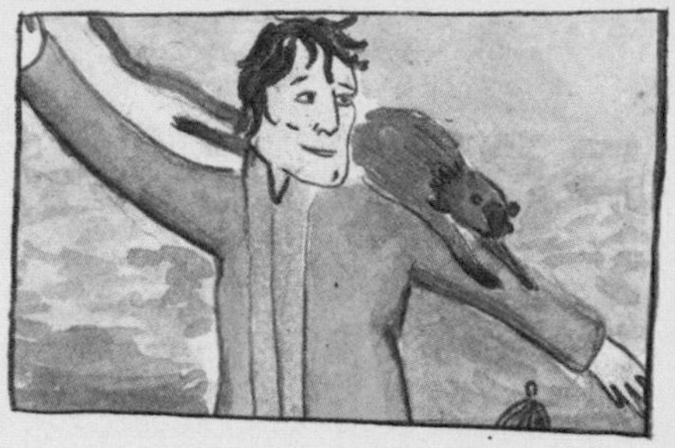

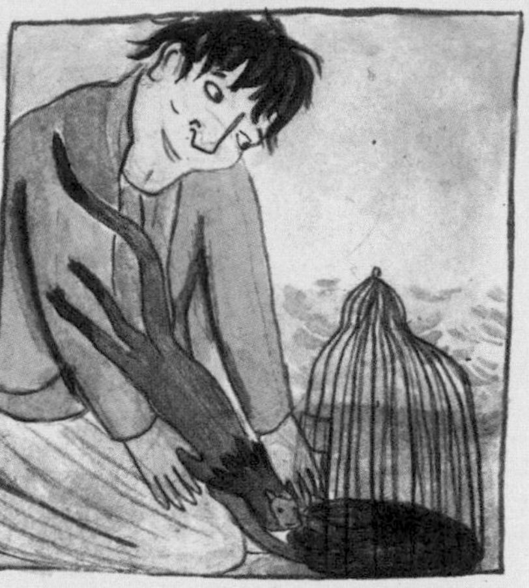

* SADLY, THE ANIMALS DID NOT SURVIVE THE LONG SEA VOYAGE, BUT THEIR SKINS MADE IT TO PARIS, WHERE THEY WERE KEPT AT THE NATURAL HISTORY MUSEUM.

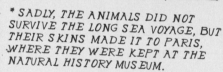

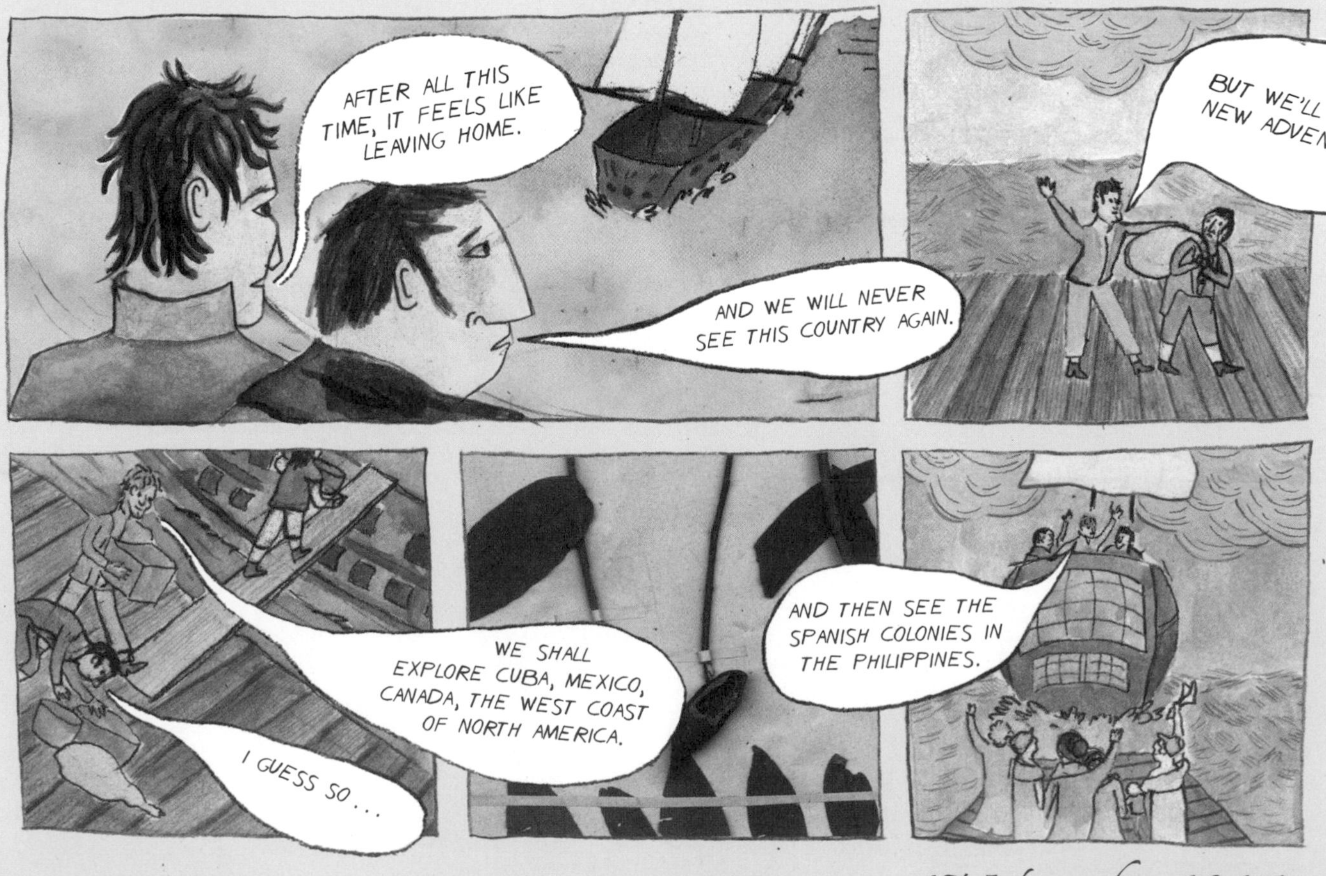
AFTER ALL THIS TIME, IT FEELS LIKE LEAVING HOME.
AND WE WILL NEVER SEE THIS COUNTRY AGAIN.
BUT WE'LL HAVE NEW ADVENTURES.
WE SHALL EXPLORE CUBA, MEXICO, CANADA, THE WEST COAST OF NORTH AMERICA.
I GUESS SO . . .
AND THEN SEE THE SPANISH COLONIES IN THE PHILIPPINES.

17 November 1800

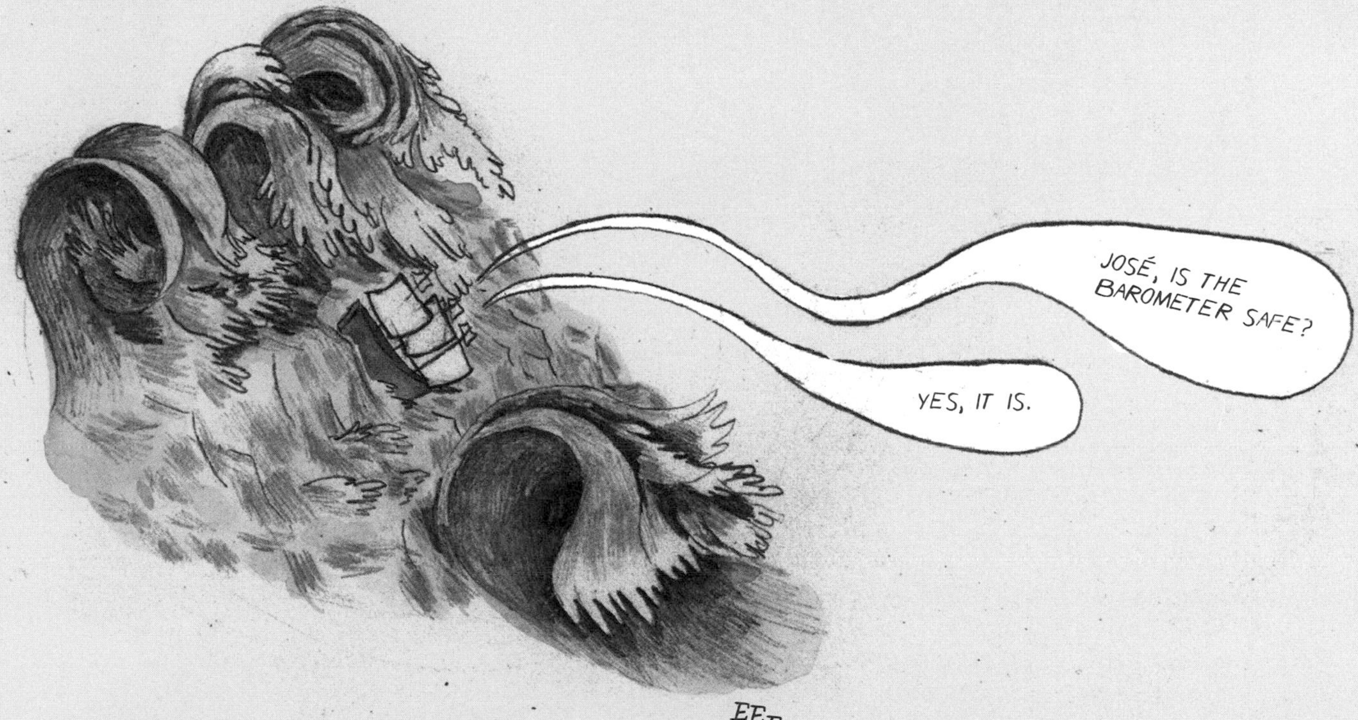
JOSÉ, IS THE BAROMETER SAFE?
YES, IT IS.

AND THEN THERE WAS A HUUUUUUUUUGGGGGGEEEEEEE SSTOOOOOOOOOOORRRMMMMM

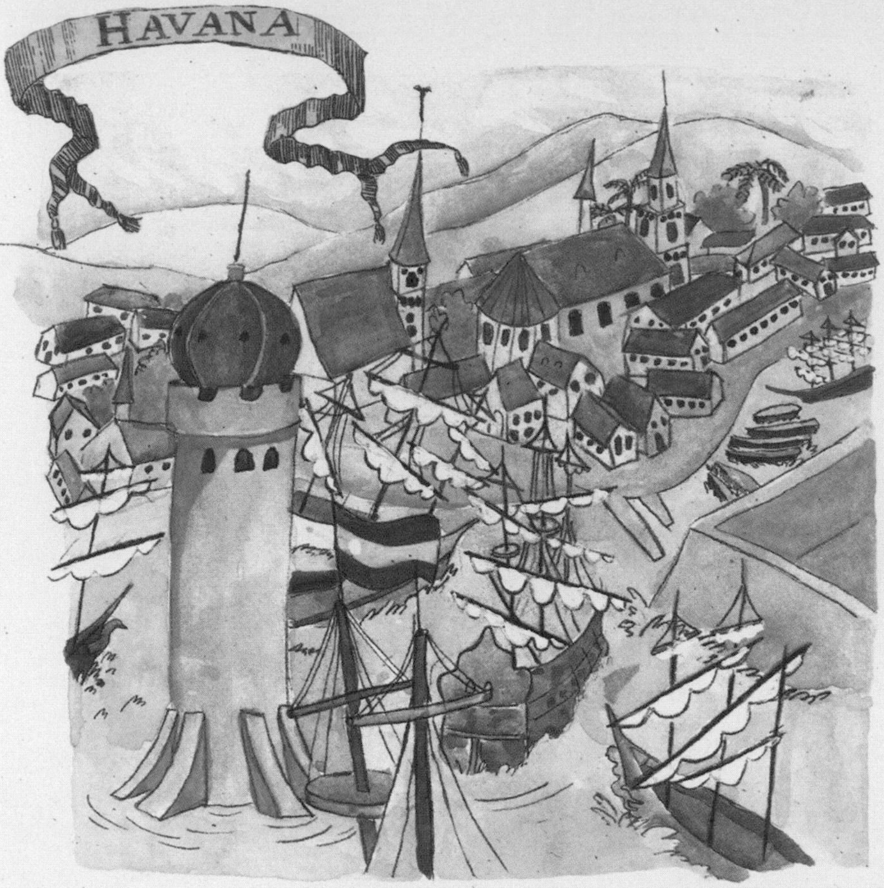
HAVANA

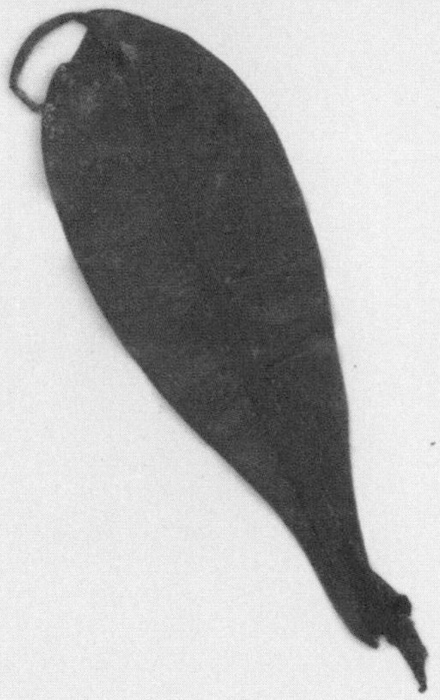

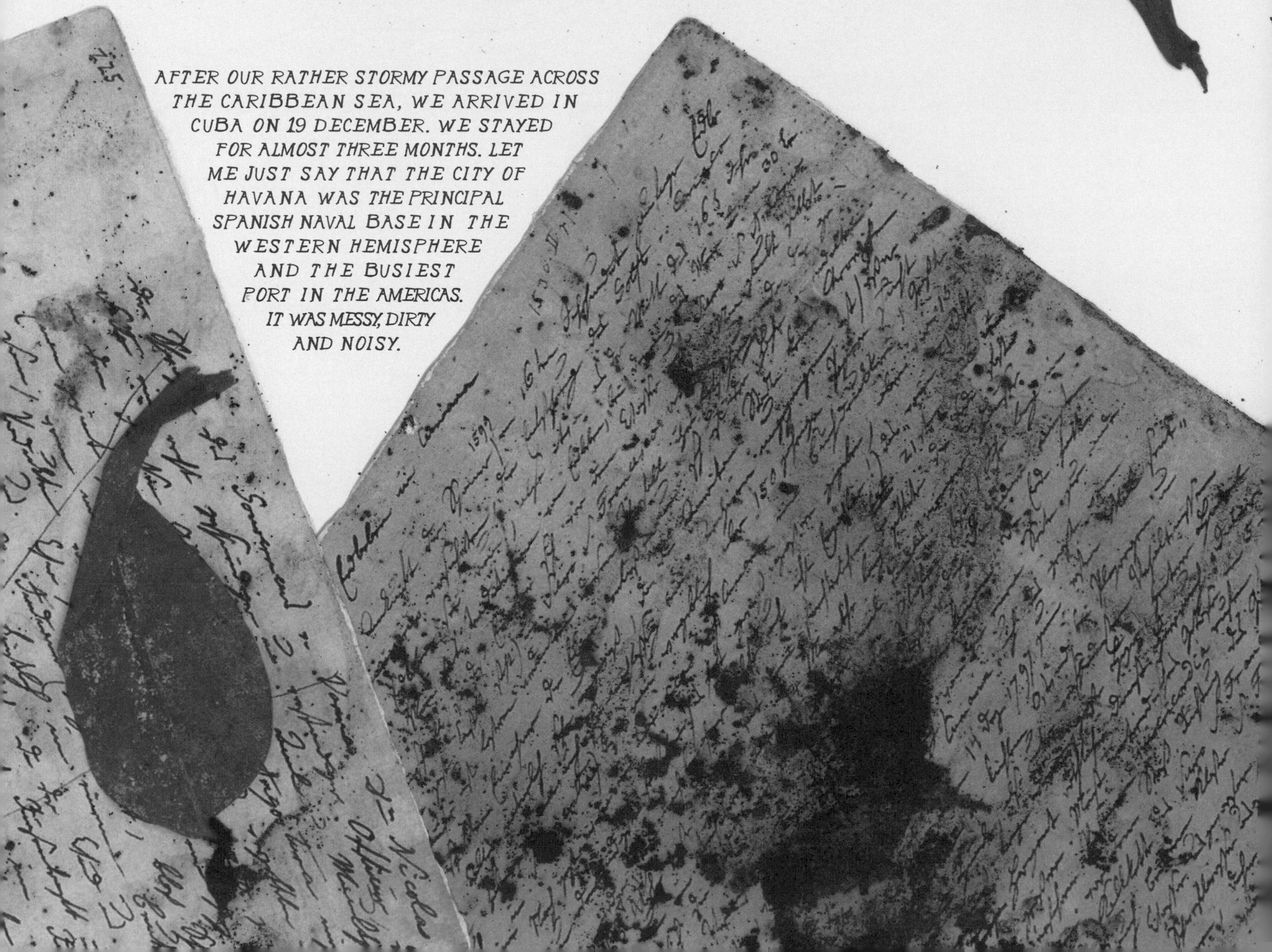

AFTER OUR RATHER STORMY PASSAGE ACROSS THE CARIBBEAN SEA, WE ARRIVED IN CUBA ON 19 DECEMBER. WE STAYED FOR ALMOST THREE MONTHS. LET ME JUST SAY THAT THE CITY OF HAVANA WAS THE PRINCIPAL SPANISH NAVAL BASE IN THE WESTERN HEMISPHERE AND THE BUSIEST PORT IN THE AMERICAS. IT WAS MESSY, DIRTY AND NOISY.

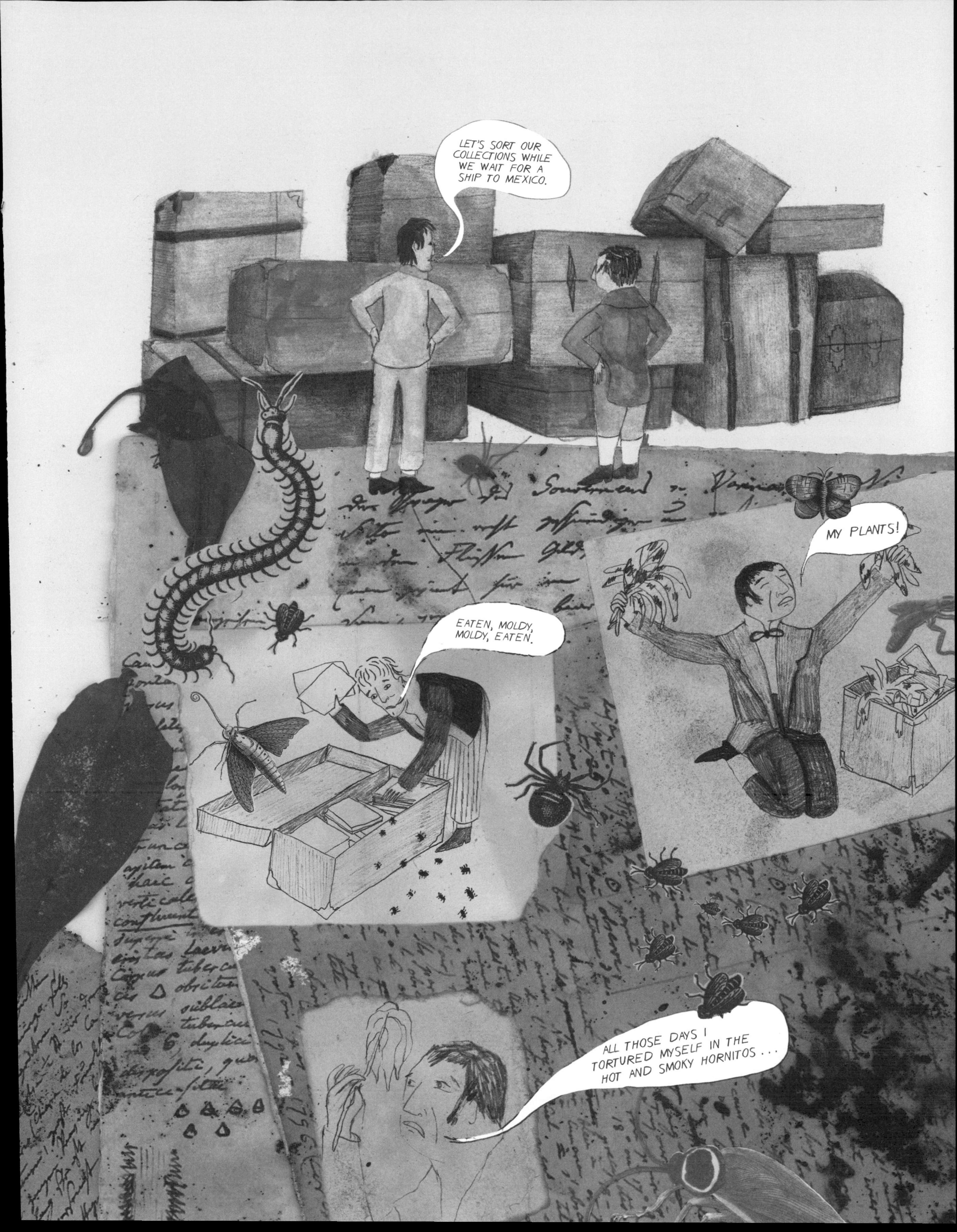
LET'S SORT OUR COLLECTIONS WHILE WE WAIT FOR A SHIP TO MEXICO.
MY PLANTS!
EATEN, MOLDY, MOLDY, EATEN.
ALL THOSE DAYS I TORTURED MYSELF IN THE HOT AND SMOKY HORNITOS . . .

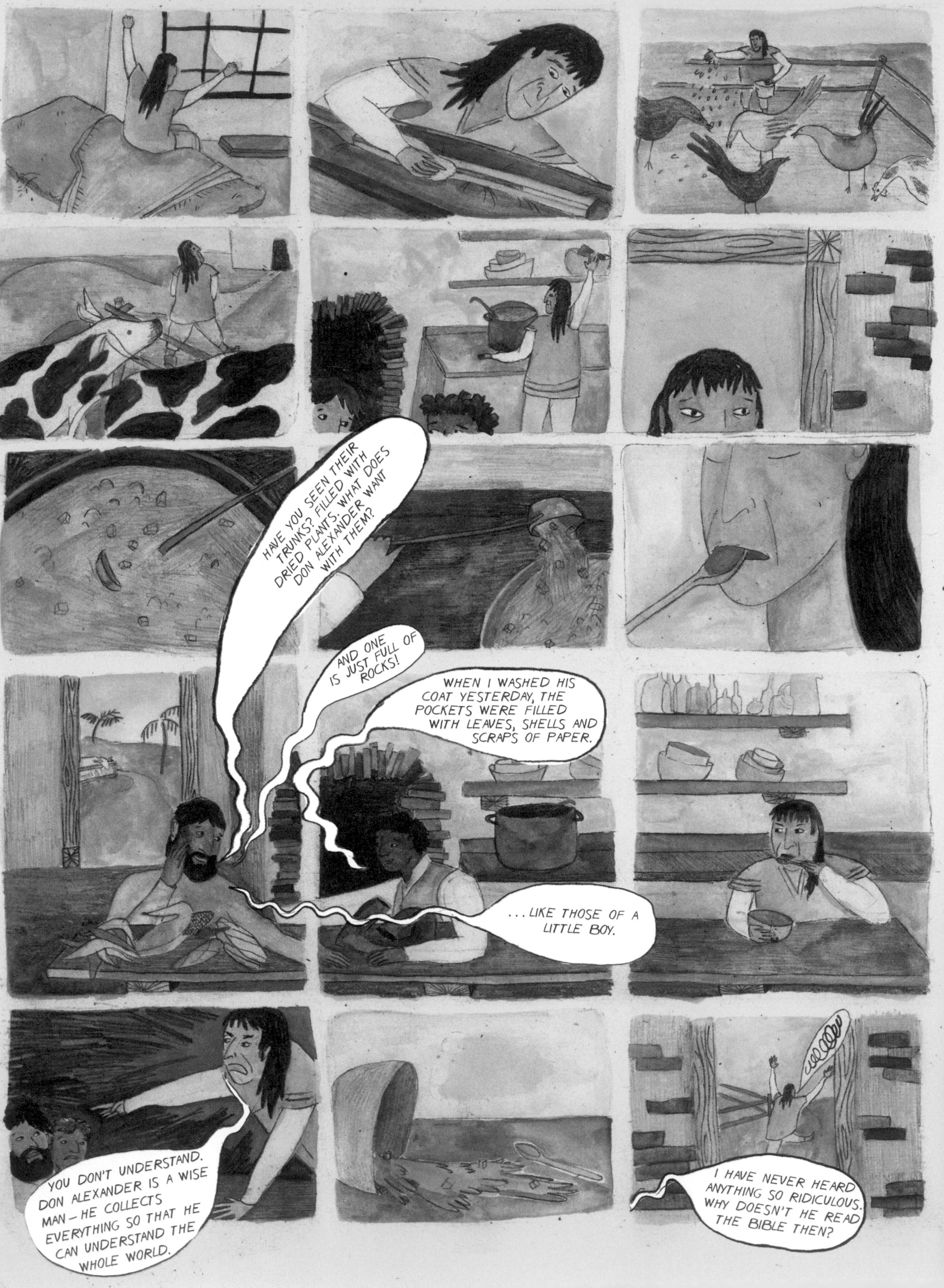
HAVE YOU SEEN THEIR TRUNKS? FILLED WITH DRIED PLANTS. WHAT DOES DON ALEXANDER WANT WITH THEM?
AND ONE IS JUST FULL OF ROCKS!
WHEN I WASHED HIS COAT YESTERDAY, THE POCKETS WERE FILLED WITH LEAVES, SHELLS AND SCRAPS OF PAPER.
...LIKE THOSE OF A LITTLE BOY.
YOU DON'T UNDERSTAND. DON ALEXANDER IS A WISE MAN—HE COLLECTS EVERYTHING SO THAT HE CAN UNDERSTAND THE WHOLE WORLD.
I HAVE NEVER HEARD ANYTHING SO RIDICULOUS. WHY DOESN'T HE READ THE BIBLE THEN?

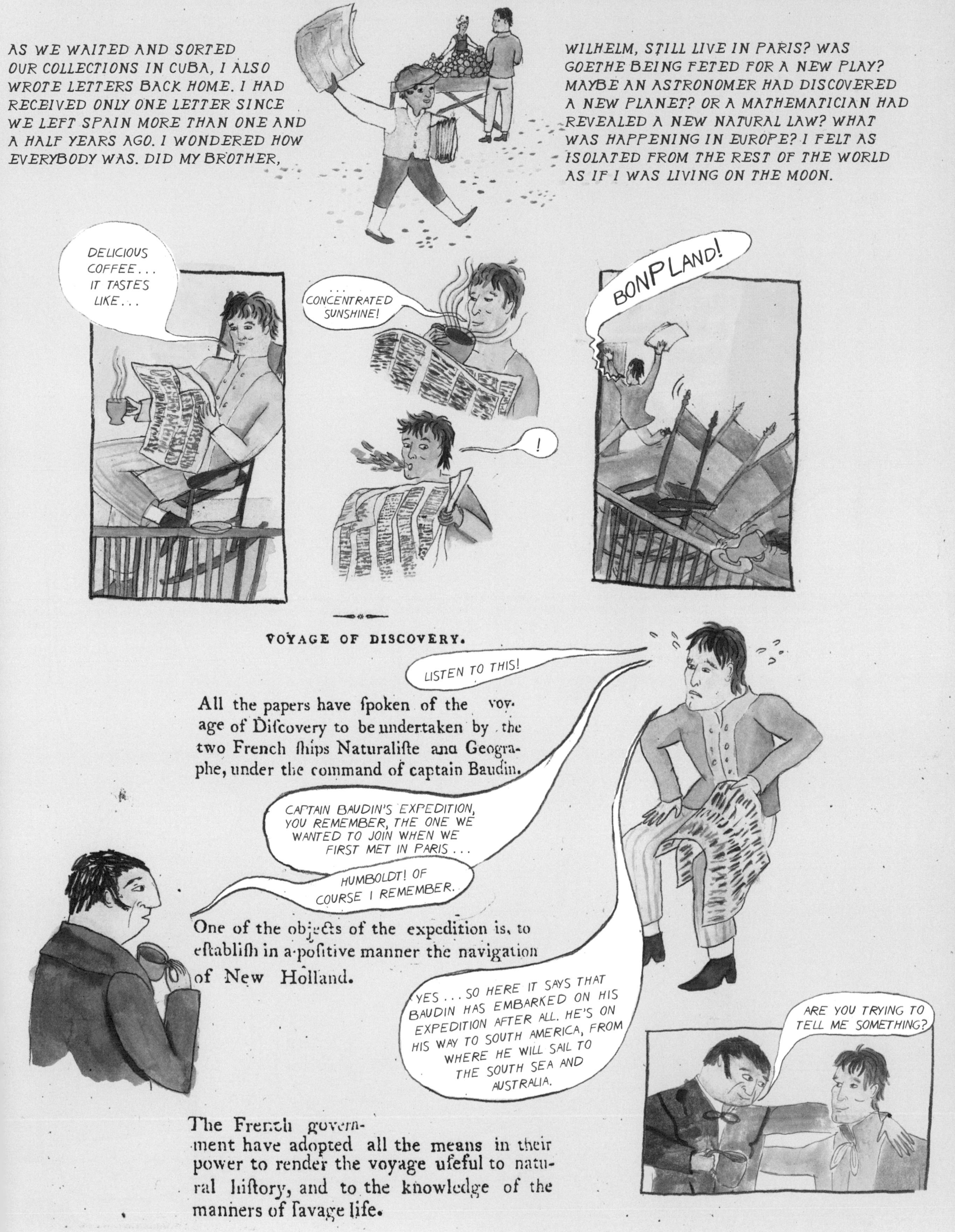
AS WE WAITED AND SORTED OUR COLLECTIONS IN CUBA, I ALSO WROTE LETTERS BACK HOME. I HAD RECEIVED ONLY ONE LETTER SINCE WE LEFT SPAIN MORE THAN ONE AND A HALF YEARS AGO. I WONDERED HOW EVERYBODY WAS. DID MY BROTHER,
WILHELM, STILL LIVE IN PARIS? WAS GOETHE BEING FETED FOR A NEW PLAY? MAYBE AN ASTRONOMER HAD DISCOVERED A NEW PLANET? OR A MATHEMATICIAN HAD REVEALED A NEW NATURAL LAW? WHAT WAS HAPPENING IN EUROPE? I FELT AS ISOLATED FROM THE REST OF THE WORLD AS IF I WAS LIVING ON THE MOON.
DELICIOUS COFFEE . . . IT TASTES LIKE . . .
. . . CONCENTRATED SUNSHINE!
!
BONPLAND!
VOYAGE OF DISCOVERY.
LISTEN TO THIS!
All the papers have ſpoken of the voyage of Diſcovery to be undertaken by the two French ſhips Naturaliſte ana Geographe, under the command of captain Baudin.
CAPTAIN BAUDIN'S EXPEDITION, YOU REMEMBER, THE ONE WE WANTED TO JOIN WHEN WE FIRST MET IN PARIS . . .
HUMBOLDT! OF COURSE I REMEMBER.
One of the objects of the expedition is, to eſtabliſh in a poſitive manner the navigation of New Holland.
YES . . . SO HERE IT SAYS THAT BAUDIN HAS EMBARKED ON HIS EXPEDITION AFTER ALL. HE'S ON HIS WAY TO SOUTH AMERICA, FROM WHERE HE WILL SAIL TO THE SOUTH SEA AND AUSTRALIA.
ARE YOU TRYING TO TELL ME SOMETHING?
The French government have adopted all the means in their power to render the voyage uſeful to natural hiſtory, and to the knowledge of the manners of ſavage life.

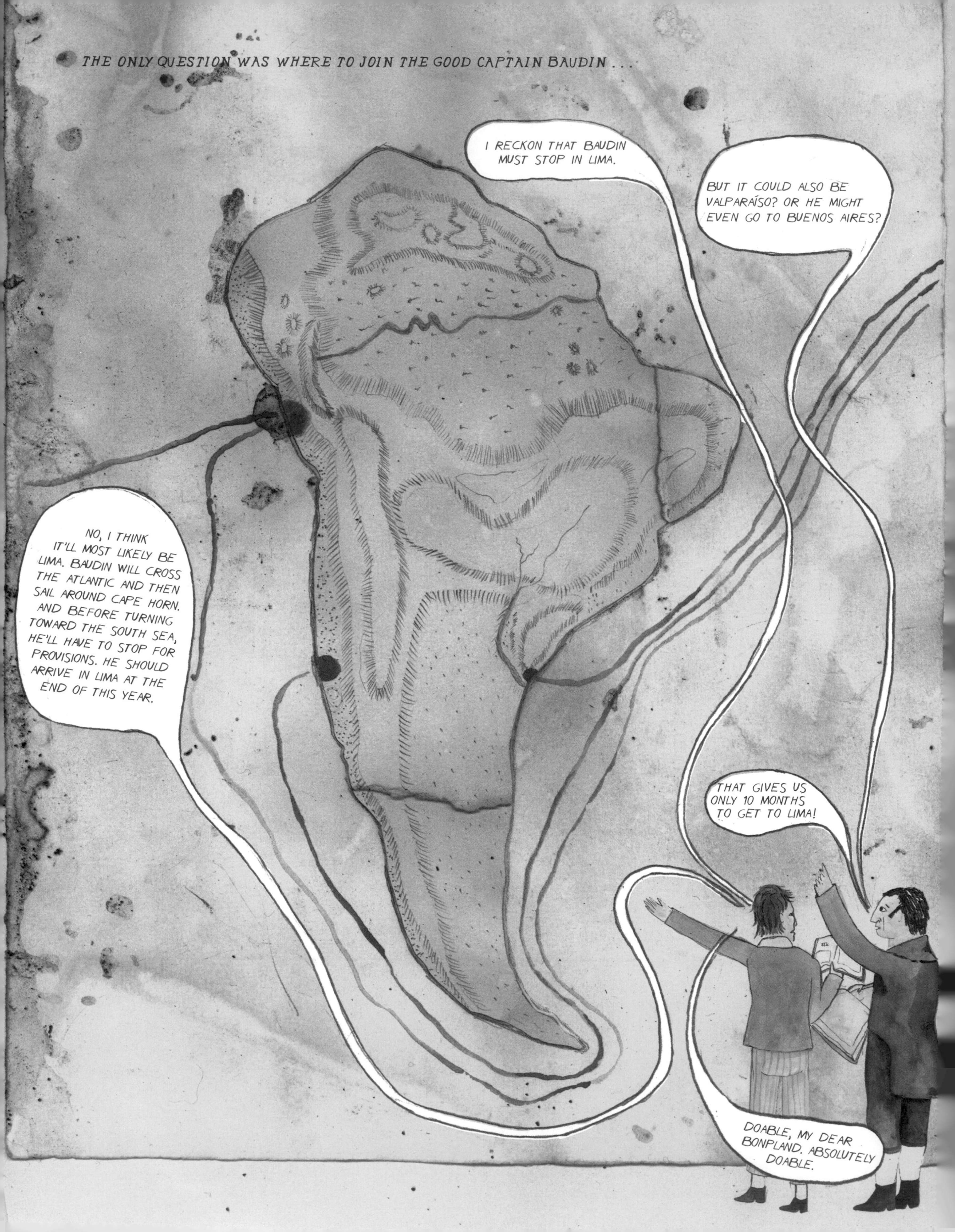
THE ONLY QUESTION WAS WHERE TO JOIN THE GOOD CAPTAIN BAUDIN . . .
I RECKON THAT BAUDIN MUST STOP IN LIMA.
BUT IT COULD ALSO BE VALPARAÍSO? OR HE MIGHT EVEN GO TO BUENOS AIRES?
NO, I THINK IT'LL MOST LIKELY BE LIMA. BAUDIN WILL CROSS THE ATLANTIC AND THEN SAIL AROUND CAPE HORN. AND BEFORE TURNING TOWARD THE SOUTH SEA, HE'LL HAVE TO STOP FOR PROVISIONS. HE SHOULD ARRIVE IN LIMA AT THE END OF THIS YEAR.
THAT GIVES US ONLY 10 MONTHS TO GET TO LIMA!
DOABLE, MY DEAR BONPLAND. ABSOLUTELY DOABLE.

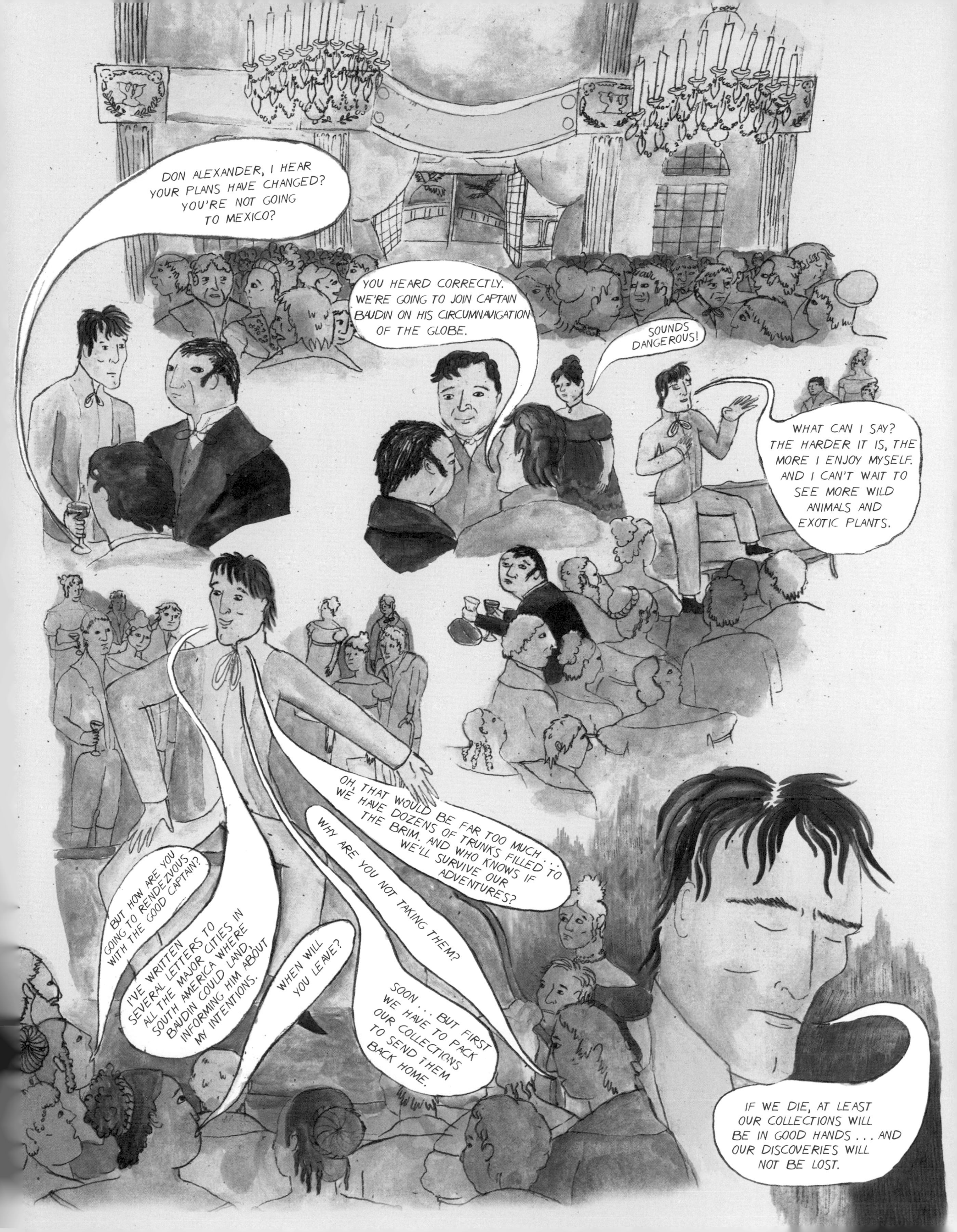
DON ALEXANDER, I HEAR YOUR PLANS HAVE CHANGED? YOU'RE NOT GOING TO MEXICO?
YOU HEARD CORRECTLY. WE'RE GOING TO JOIN CAPTAIN BAUDIN ON HIS CIRCUMNAVIGATION OF THE GLOBE.
SOUNDS DANGEROUS!
WHAT CAN I SAY? THE HARDER IT IS, THE MORE I ENJOY MYSELF. AND I CAN'T WAIT TO SEE MORE WILD ANIMALS AND EXOTIC PLANTS.
BUT HOW ARE YOU GOING TO RENDEZVOUS WITH THE GOOD CAPTAIN?
I'VE WRITTEN SEVERAL LETTERS TO ALL THE MAJOR CITIES IN SOUTH AMERICA WHERE BAUDIN COULD LAND, INFORMING HIM ABOUT MY INTENTIONS.
WHEN WILL YOU LEAVE?
SOON . . . BUT FIRST WE HAVE TO PACK OUR COLLECTIONS TO SEND THEM BACK HOME.
WHY ARE YOU NOT TAKING THEM?
OH, THAT WOULD BE FAR TOO MUCH . . . WE HAVE DOZENS OF TRUNKS FILLED TO THE BRIM. AND WHO KNOWS IF WE'LL SURVIVE OUR ADVENTURES?
IF WE DIE, AT LEAST OUR COLLECTIONS WILL BE IN GOOD HANDS . . . AND OUR DISCOVERIES WILL NOT BE LOST.

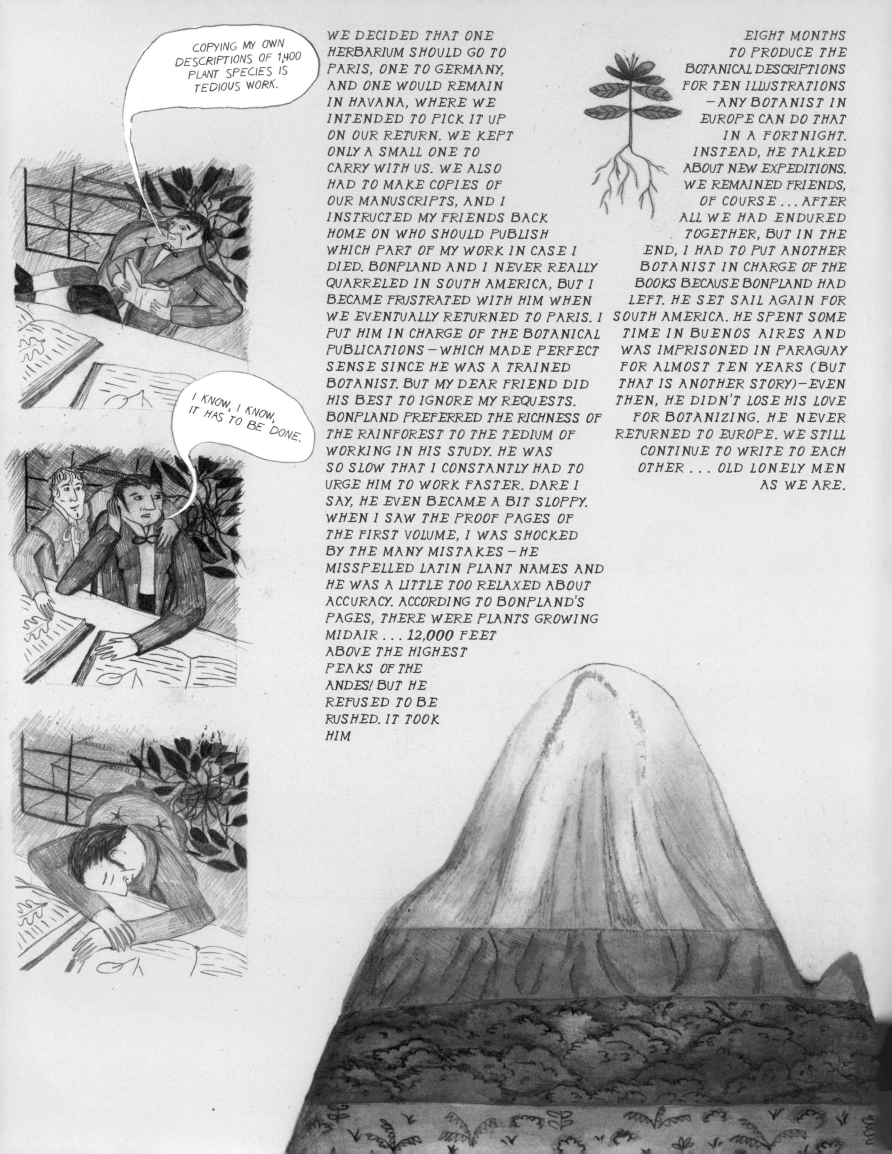

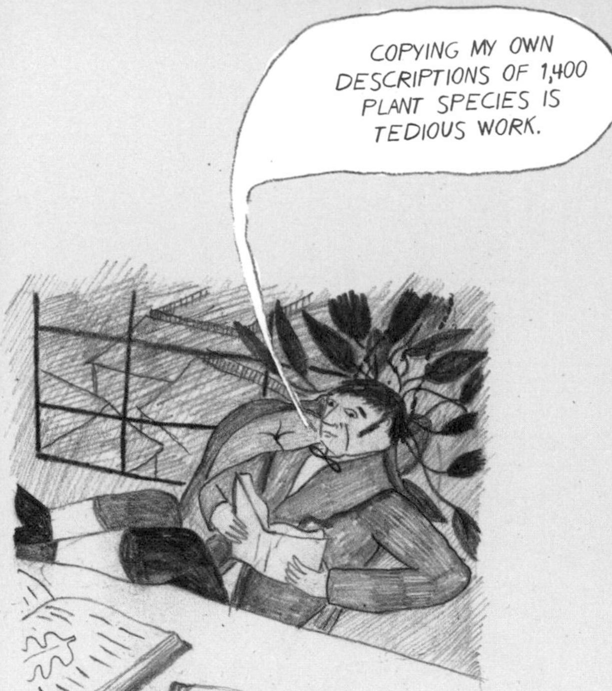
COPYING MY OWN DESCRIPTIONS OF 1,400 PLANT SPECIES IS TEDIOUS WORK.

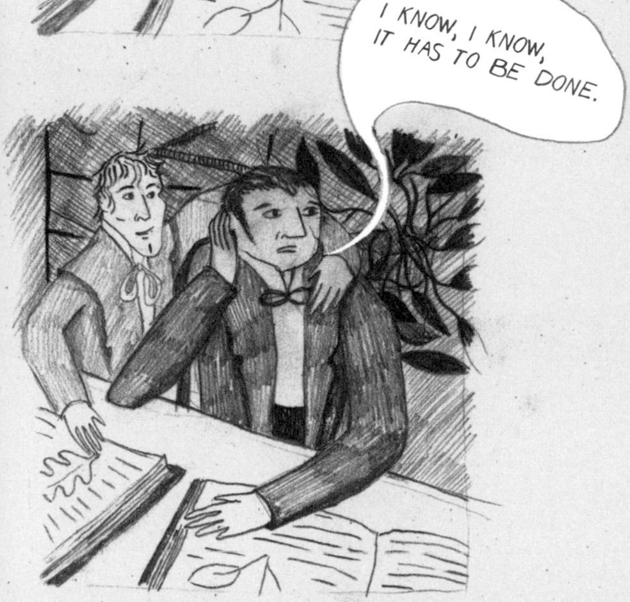
I KNOW, I KNOW, IT HAS TO BE DONE.

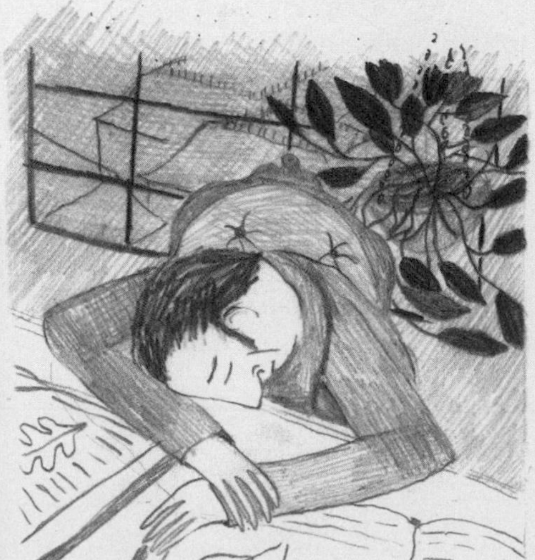

WE DECIDED THAT ONE HERBARIUM SHOULD GO TO PARIS, ONE TO GERMANY, AND ONE WOULD REMAIN IN HAVANA, WHERE WE INTENDED TO PICK IT UP ON OUR RETURN. WE KEPT ONLY A SMALL ONE TO CARRY WITH US. WE ALSO HAD TO MAKE COPIES OF OUR MANUSCRIPTS, AND I INSTRUCTED MY FRIENDS BACK HOME ON WHO SHOULD PUBLISH WHICH PART OF MY WORK IN CASE I DIED. BONPLAND AND I NEVER REALLY QUARRELED IN SOUTH AMERICA, BUT I BECAME FRUSTRATED WITH HIM WHEN WE EVENTUALLY RETURNED TO PARIS. I PUT HIM IN CHARGE OF THE BOTANICAL PUBLICATIONS—WHICH MADE PERFECT SENSE SINCE HE WAS A TRAINED BOTANIST. BUT MY DEAR FRIEND DID HIS BEST TO IGNORE MY REQUESTS. BONPLAND PREFERRED THE RICHNESS OF THE RAINFOREST TO THE TEDIUM OF WORKING IN HIS STUDY. HE WAS SO SLOW THAT I CONSTANTLY HAD TO URGE HIM TO WORK FASTER. DARE I SAY, HE EVEN BECAME A BIT SLOPPY. WHEN I SAW THE PROOF PAGES OF THE FIRST VOLUME, I WAS SHOCKED BY THE MANY MISTAKES—HE MISSPELLED LATIN PLANT NAMES AND HE WAS A LITTLE TOO RELAXED ABOUT ACCURACY. ACCORDING TO BONPLAND'S PAGES, THERE WERE PLANTS GROWING MIDAIR . . . 12,000 FEET ABOVE THE HIGHEST PEAKS OF THE ANDES! BUT HE REFUSED TO BE RUSHED. IT TOOK HIM

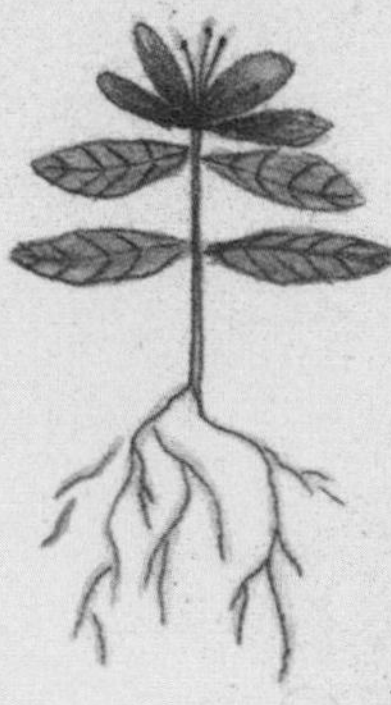

EIGHT MONTHS TO PRODUCE THE BOTANICAL DESCRIPTIONS FOR TEN ILLUSTRATIONS—ANY BOTANIST IN EUROPE CAN DO THAT IN A FORTNIGHT. INSTEAD, HE TALKED ABOUT NEW EXPEDITIONS. WE REMAINED FRIENDS, OF COURSE . . . AFTER ALL WE HAD ENDURED TOGETHER, BUT IN THE END, I HAD TO PUT ANOTHER BOTANIST IN CHARGE OF THE BOOKS BECAUSE BONPLAND HAD LEFT. HE SET SAIL AGAIN FOR SOUTH AMERICA. HE SPENT SOME TIME IN BUENOS AIRES AND WAS IMPRISONED IN PARAGUAY FOR ALMOST TEN YEARS (BUT THAT IS ANOTHER STORY)—EVEN THEN, HE DIDN'T LOSE HIS LOVE FOR BOTANIZING. HE NEVER RETURNED TO EUROPE. WE STILL CONTINUE TO WRITE TO EACH OTHER . . . OLD LONELY MEN AS WE ARE.

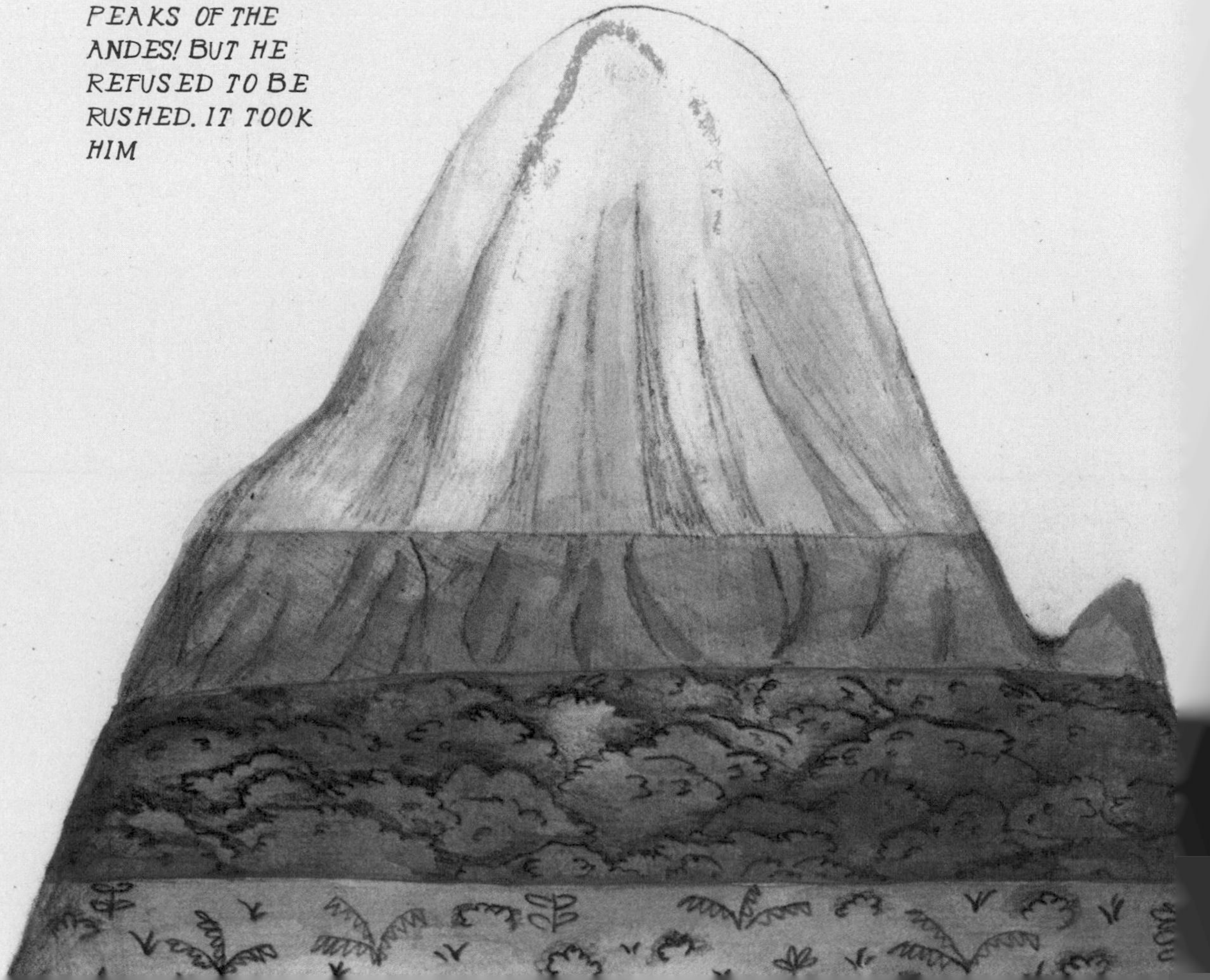

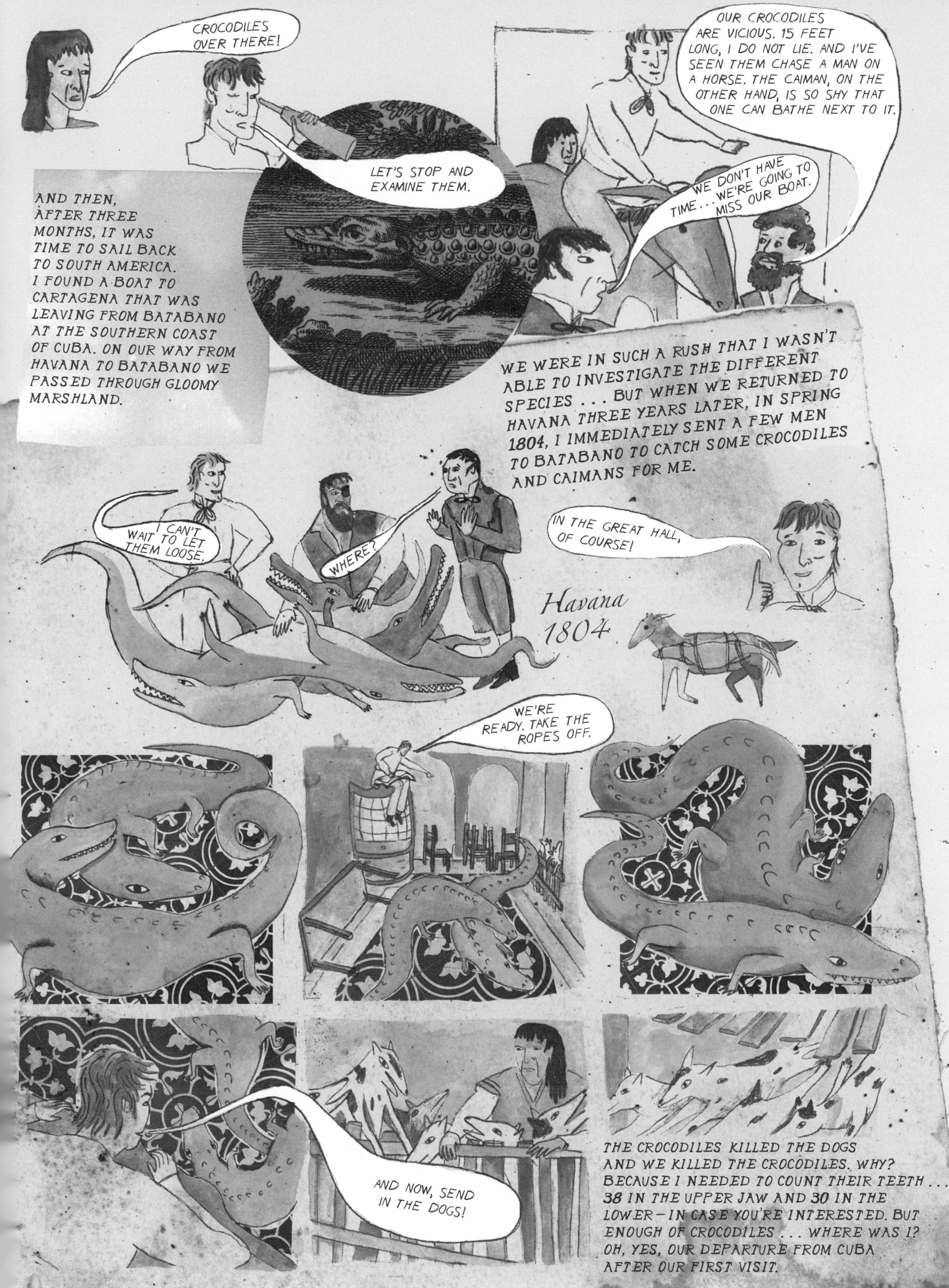
CROCODILES OVER THERE!
LET'S STOP AND EXAMINE THEM.
OUR CROCODILES ARE VICIOUS. 15 FEET LONG, I DO NOT LIE. AND I'VE SEEN THEM CHASE A MAN ON A HORSE. THE CAIMAN, ON THE OTHER HAND, IS SO SHY THAT ONE CAN BATHE NEXT TO IT.
WE DON'T HAVE TIME... WE'RE GOING TO MISS OUR BOAT.
AND THEN, AFTER THREE MONTHS, IT WAS TIME TO SAIL BACK TO SOUTH AMERICA. I FOUND A BOAT TO CARTAGENA THAT WAS LEAVING FROM BATABANO AT THE SOUTHERN COAST OF CUBA. ON OUR WAY FROM HAVANA TO BATABANO WE PASSED THROUGH GLOOMY MARSHLAND.
WE WERE IN SUCH A RUSH THAT I WASN'T ABLE TO INVESTIGATE THE DIFFERENT SPECIES . . . BUT WHEN WE RETURNED TO HAVANA THREE YEARS LATER, IN SPRING 1804, I IMMEDIATELY SENT A FEW MEN TO BATABANO TO CATCH SOME CROCODILES AND CAIMANS FOR ME.
I CAN'T WAIT TO LET THEM LOOSE.
WHERE?
IN THE GREAT HALL, OF COURSE!
Havana 1804
WE'RE READY. TAKE THE ROPES OFF.
AND NOW, SEND IN THE DOGS!
THE CROCODILES KILLED THE DOGS AND WE KILLED THE CROCODILES. WHY? BECAUSE I NEEDED TO COUNT THEIR TEETH . . . 38 IN THE UPPER JAW AND 30 IN THE LOWER – IN CASE YOU'RE INTERESTED. BUT ENOUGH OF CROCODILES . . . WHERE WAS I? OH, YES, OUR DEPARTURE FROM CUBA AFTER OUR FIRST VISIT.

WE LEFT CUBA ON 9 MARCH 1801 . . .

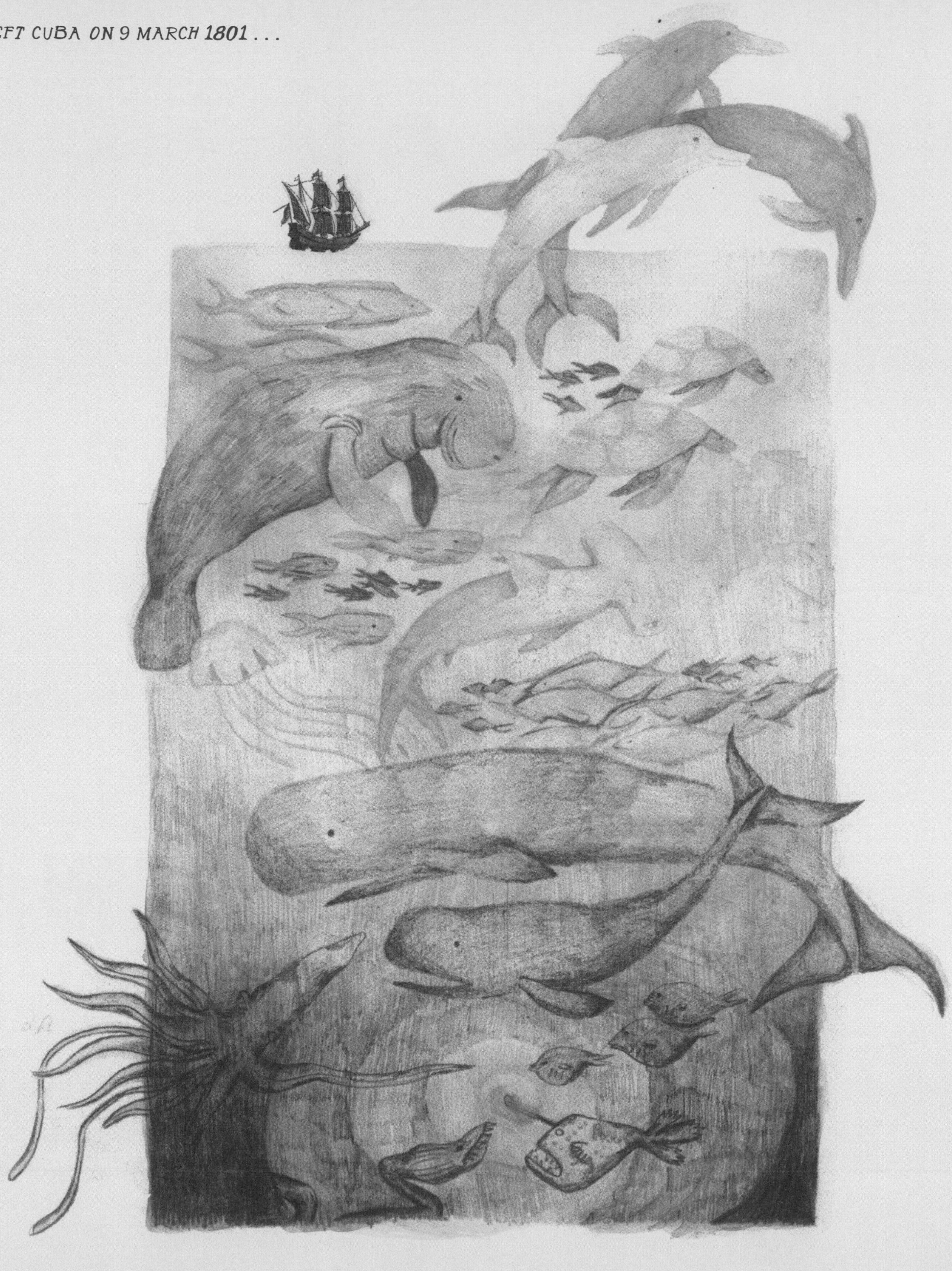

. . . AND AFTER 20 DAYS OF TERRIBLE WEATHER, WE ARRIVED IN CARTAGENA.

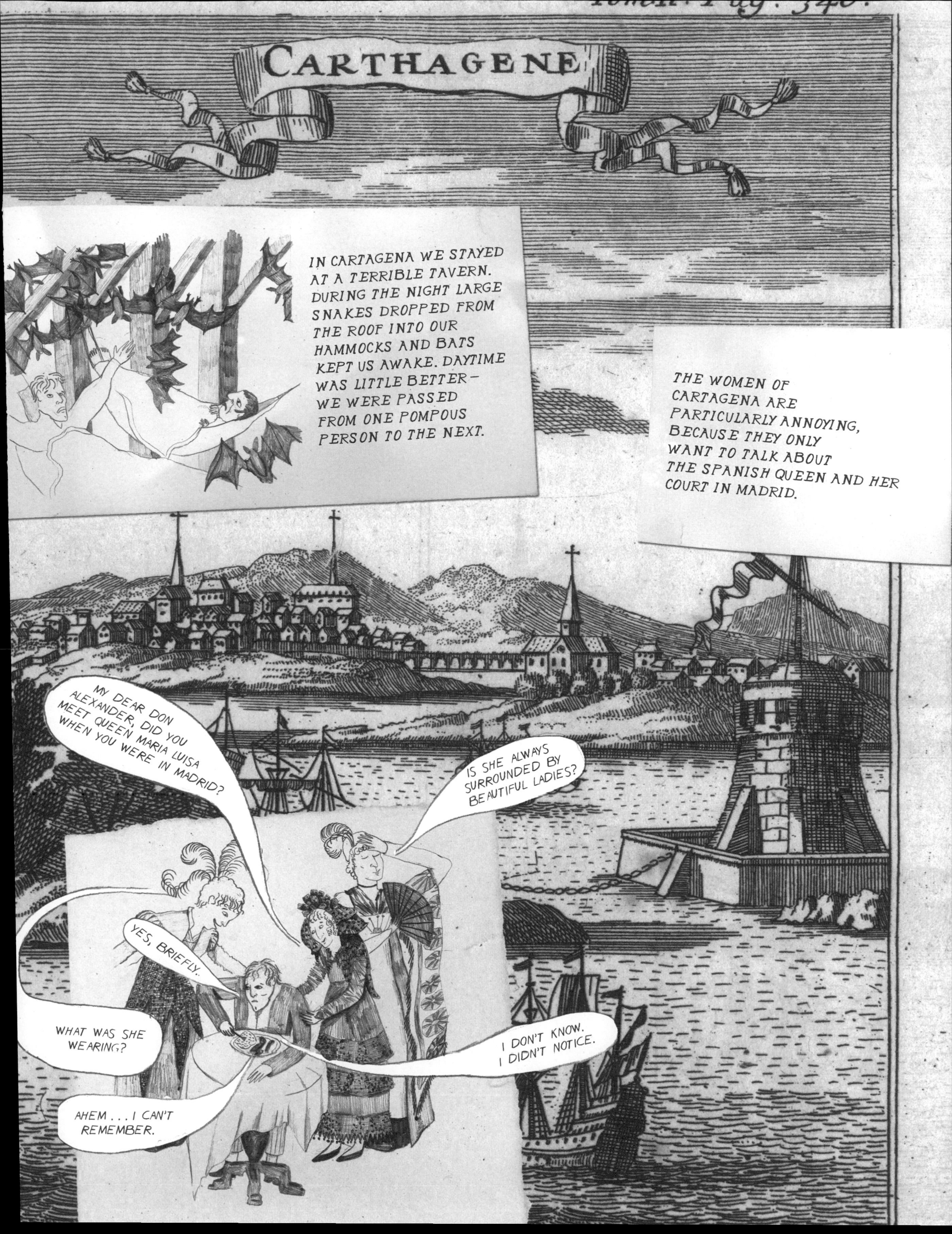
CARTHAGENE
IN CARTAGENA WE STAYED AT A TERRIBLE TAVERN. DURING THE NIGHT LARGE SNAKES DROPPED FROM THE ROOF INTO OUR HAMMOCKS AND BATS KEPT US AWAKE. DAYTIME WAS LITTLE BETTER— WE WERE PASSED FROM ONE POMPOUS PERSON TO THE NEXT.
THE WOMEN OF CARTAGENA ARE PARTICULARLY ANNOYING, BECAUSE THEY ONLY WANT TO TALK ABOUT THE SPANISH QUEEN AND HER COURT IN MADRID.
MY DEAR DON ALEXANDER, DID YOU MEET QUEEN MARIA LUISA WHEN YOU WERE IN MADRID?
YES, BRIEFLY.
IS SHE ALWAYS SURROUNDED BY BEAUTIFUL LADIES?
WHAT WAS SHE WEARING?
I DON'T KNOW. I DIDN'T NOTICE.
AHEM . . . I CAN'T REMEMBER.

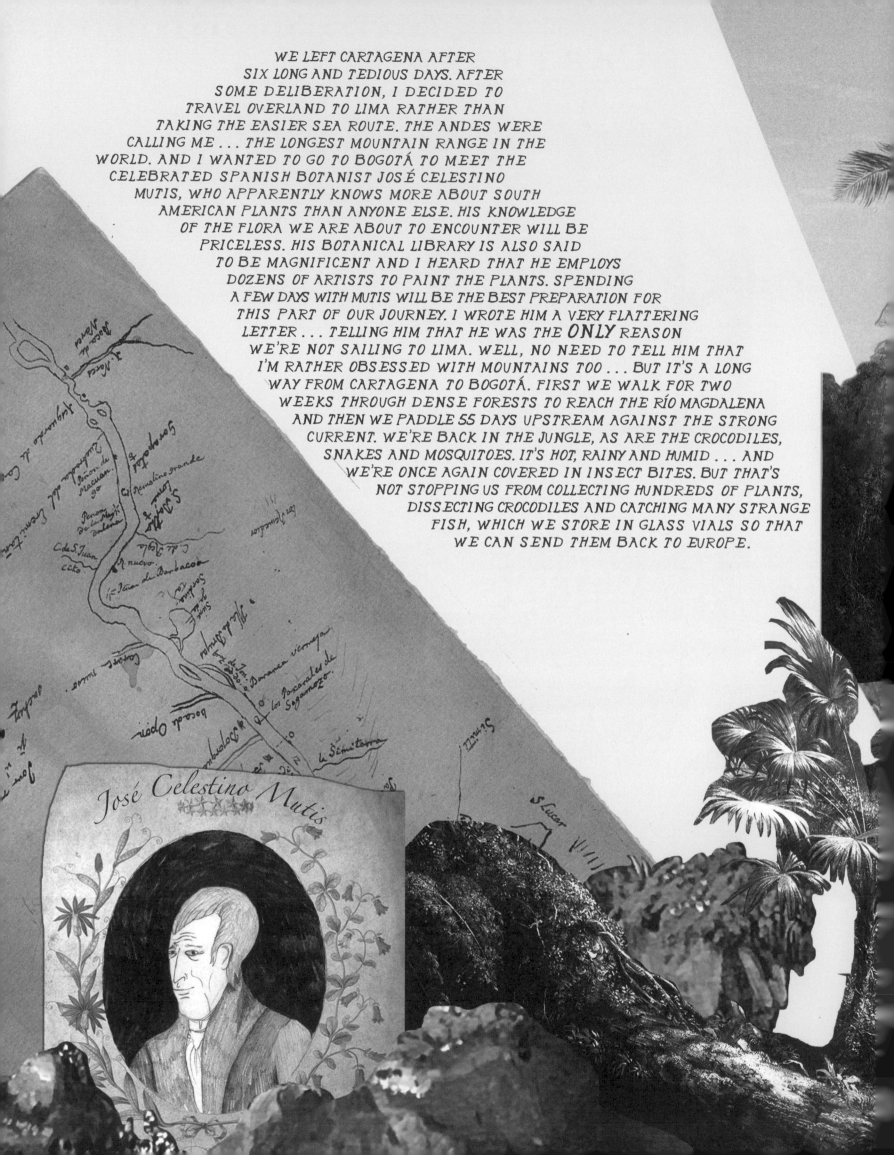

WE LEFT CARTAGENA AFTER
SIX LONG AND TEDIOUS DAYS. AFTER
SOME DELIBERATION, I DECIDED TO
TRAVEL OVERLAND TO LIMA RATHER THAN
TAKING THE EASIER SEA ROUTE. THE ANDES WERE
CALLING ME . . . THE LONGEST MOUNTAIN RANGE IN THE
WORLD. AND I WANTED TO GO TO BOGOTÁ TO MEET THE
CELEBRATED SPANISH BOTANIST JOSÉ CELESTINO
MUTIS, WHO APPARENTLY KNOWS MORE ABOUT SOUTH
AMERICAN PLANTS THAN ANYONE ELSE. HIS KNOWLEDGE
OF THE FLORA WE ARE ABOUT TO ENCOUNTER WILL BE
PRICELESS. HIS BOTANICAL LIBRARY IS ALSO SAID
TO BE MAGNIFICENT AND I HEARD THAT HE EMPLOYS
DOZENS OF ARTISTS TO PAINT THE PLANTS. SPENDING
A FEW DAYS WITH MUTIS WILL BE THE BEST PREPARATION FOR
THIS PART OF OUR JOURNEY. I WROTE HIM A VERY FLATTERING
LETTER . . . TELLING HIM THAT HE WAS THE ONLY REASON
WE'RE NOT SAILING TO LIMA. WELL, NO NEED TO TELL HIM THAT
I'M RATHER OBSESSED WITH MOUNTAINS TOO . . . BUT IT'S A LONG
WAY FROM CARTAGENA TO BOGOTÁ. FIRST WE WALK FOR TWO
WEEKS THROUGH DENSE FORESTS TO REACH THE RÍO MAGDALENA
AND THEN WE PADDLE 55 DAYS UPSTREAM AGAINST THE STRONG
CURRENT. WE'RE BACK IN THE JUNGLE, AS ARE THE CROCODILES,
SNAKES AND MOSQUITOES. IT'S HOT, RAINY AND HUMID . . . AND
WE'RE ONCE AGAIN COVERED IN INSECT BITES. BUT THAT'S
NOT STOPPING US FROM COLLECTING HUNDREDS OF PLANTS,
DISSECTING CROCODILES AND CATCHING MANY STRANGE
FISH, WHICH WE STORE IN GLASS VIALS SO THAT
WE CAN SEND THEM BACK TO EUROPE.

José Celestino Mutis

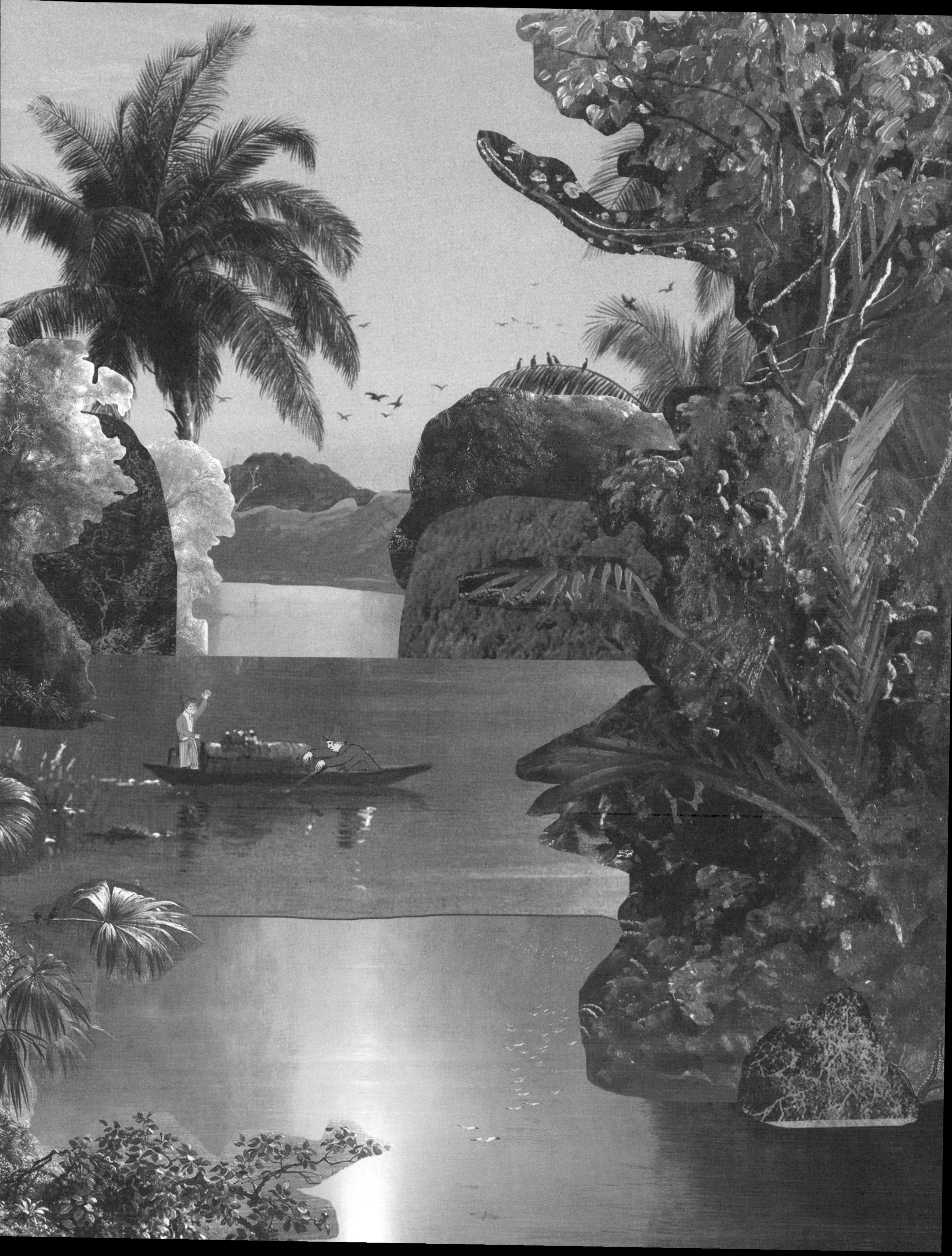

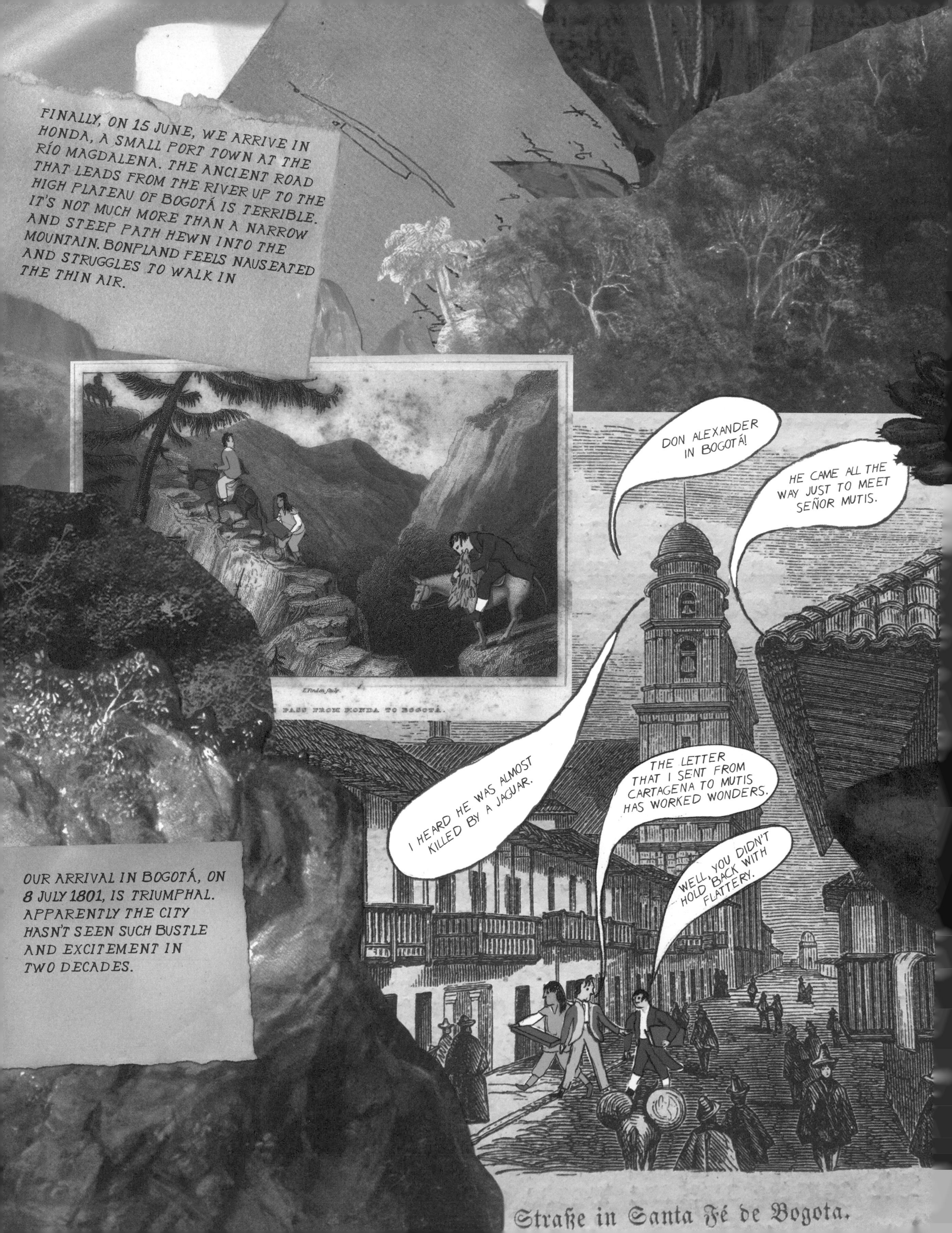
FINALLY, ON 15 JUNE, WE ARRIVE IN HONDA, A SMALL PORT TOWN AT THE RÍO MAGDALENA. THE ANCIENT ROAD THAT LEADS FROM THE RIVER UP TO THE HIGH PLATEAU OF BOGOTÁ IS TERRIBLE. IT'S NOT MUCH MORE THAN A NARROW AND STEEP PATH HEWN INTO THE MOUNTAIN. BONPLAND FEELS NAUSEATED AND STRUGGLES TO WALK IN THE THIN AIR.
PASS FROM HONDA TO BOGOTÁ.
DON ALEXANDER IN BOGOTÁ!
HE CAME ALL THE WAY JUST TO MEET SEÑOR MUTIS.
I HEARD HE WAS ALMOST KILLED BY A JAGUAR.
THE LETTER THAT I SENT FROM CARTAGENA TO MUTIS HAS WORKED WONDERS.
WELL, YOU DIDN'T HOLD BACK WITH FLATTERY.
OUR ARRIVAL IN BOGOTÁ, ON 8 JULY 1801, IS TRIUMPHAL. APPARENTLY THE CITY HASN'T SEEN SUCH BUSTLE AND EXCITEMENT IN TWO DECADES.
Straße in Santa Fé de Bogota.

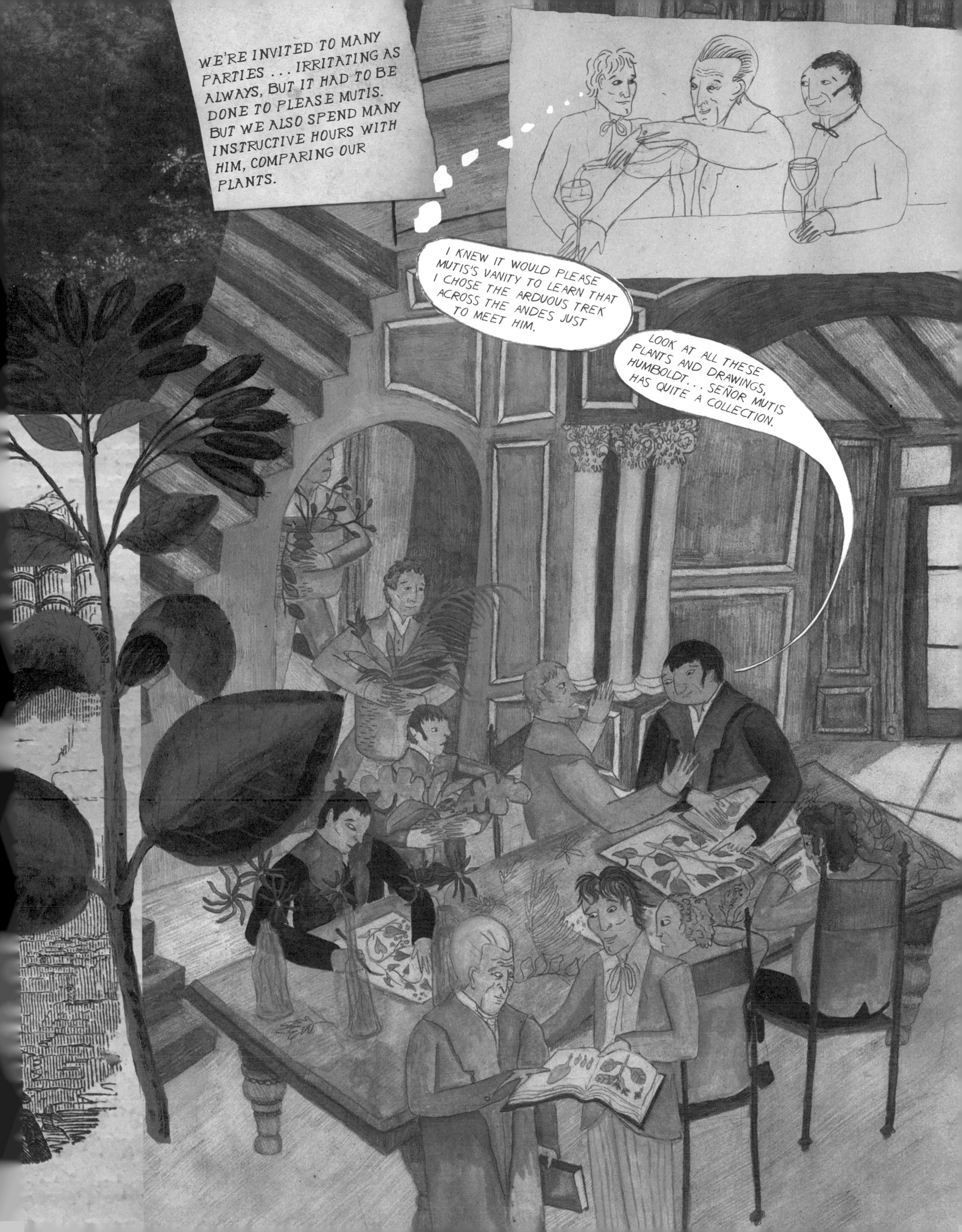
WE'RE INVITED TO MANY PARTIES . . . IRRITATING AS ALWAYS, BUT IT HAD TO BE DONE TO PLEASE MUTIS. BUT WE ALSO SPEND MANY INSTRUCTIVE HOURS WITH HIM, COMPARING OUR PLANTS.
I KNEW IT WOULD PLEASE MUTIS'S VANITY TO LEARN THAT I CHOSE THE ARDUOUS TREK ACROSS THE ANDES JUST TO MEET HIM.
LOOK AT ALL THESE PLANTS AND DRAWINGS, HUMBOLDT. . . SEÑOR MUTIS HAS QUITE A COLLECTION.

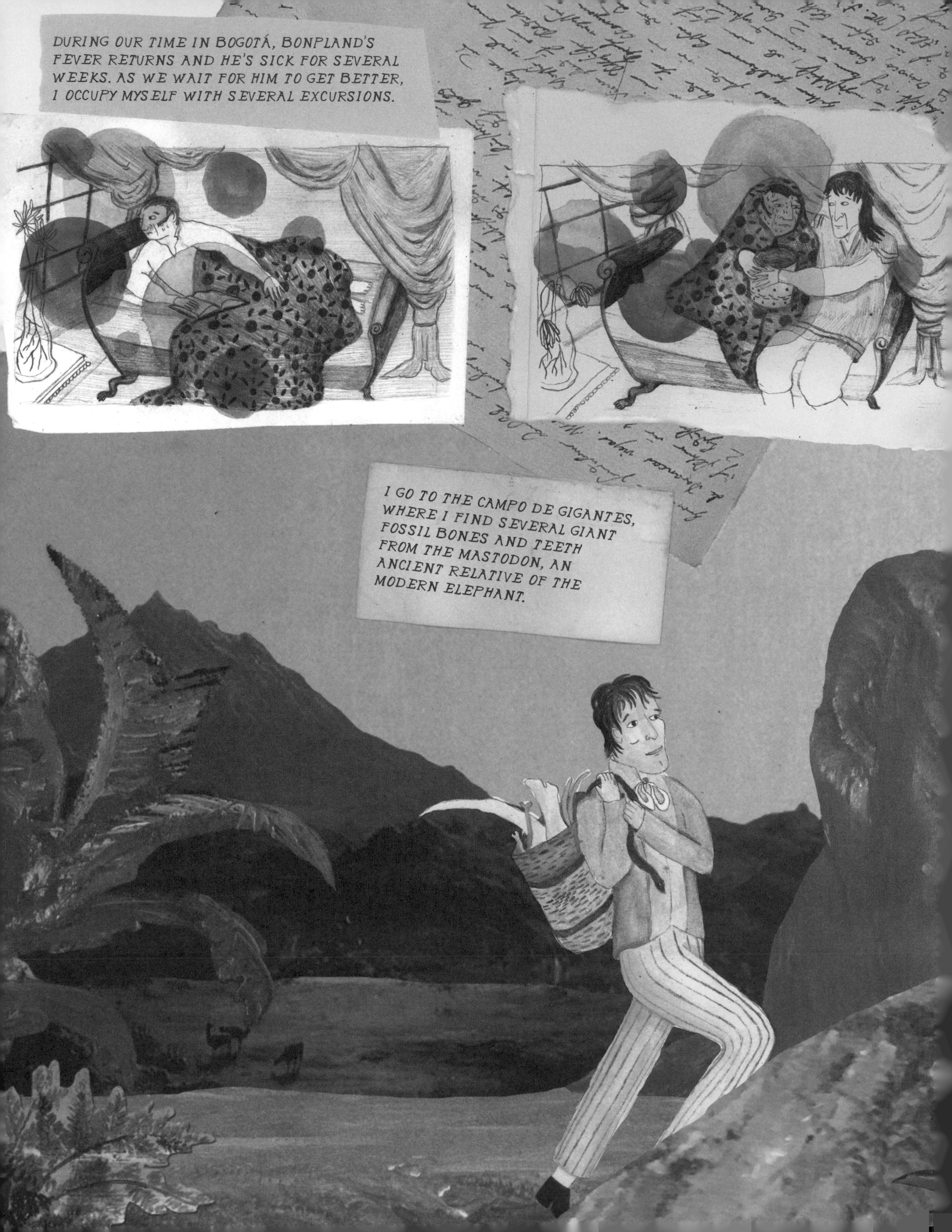
DURING OUR TIME IN BOGOTÁ, BONPLAND'S FEVER RETURNS AND HE'S SICK FOR SEVERAL WEEKS. AS WE WAIT FOR HIM TO GET BETTER, I OCCUPY MYSELF WITH SEVERAL EXCURSIONS.
I GO TO THE CAMPO DE GIGANTES, WHERE I FIND SEVERAL GIANT FOSSIL BONES AND TEETH FROM THE MASTODON, AN ANCIENT RELATIVE OF THE MODERN ELEPHANT.

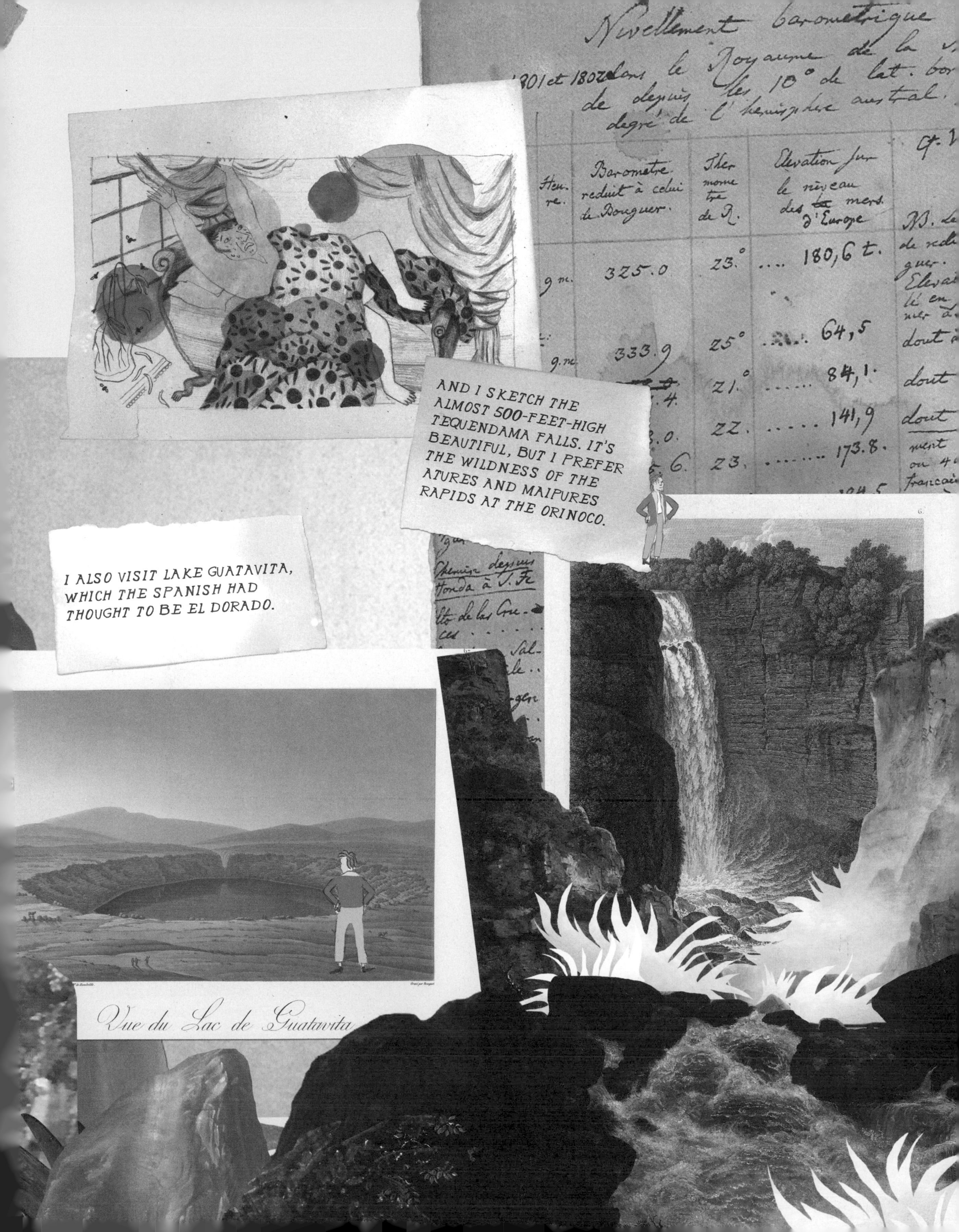
Nivellement barometrique
AND I SKETCH THE ALMOST 500-FEET-HIGH TEQUENDAMA FALLS. IT'S BEAUTIFUL, BUT I PREFER THE WILDNESS OF THE ATURES AND MAIPURES RAPIDS AT THE ORINOCO.
I ALSO VISIT LAKE GUATAVITA, WHICH THE SPANISH HAD THOUGHT TO BE EL DORADO.
Vue du Lac de Guatavita

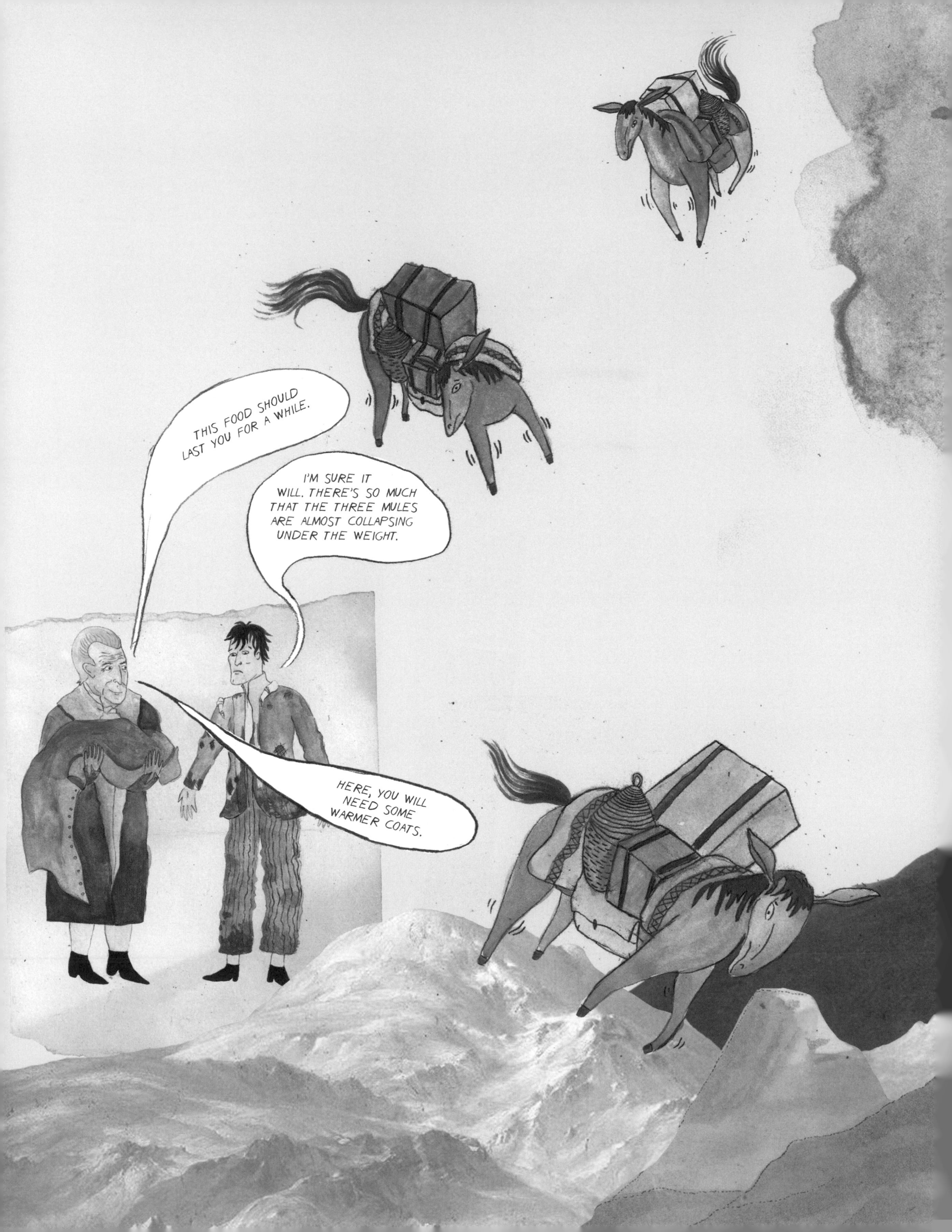
THIS FOOD SHOULD LAST YOU FOR A WHILE.
I'M SURE IT WILL. THERE'S SO MUCH THAT THE THREE MULES ARE ALMOST COLLAPSING UNDER THE WEIGHT.
HERE, YOU WILL NEED SOME WARMER COATS.

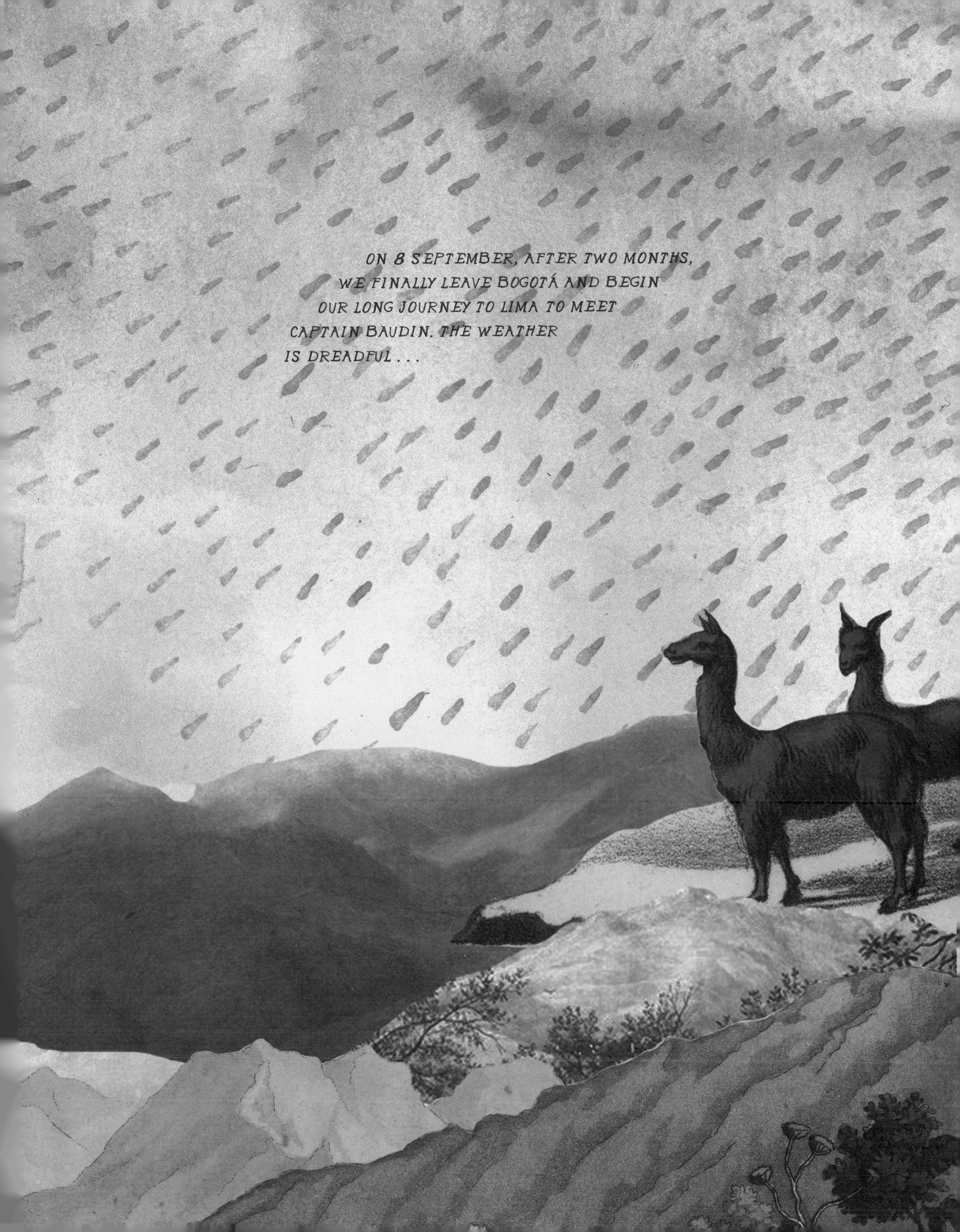
ON 8 SEPTEMBER, AFTER TWO MONTHS, WE FINALLY LEAVE BOGOTÁ AND BEGIN OUR LONG JOURNEY TO LIMA TO MEET CAPTAIN BAUDIN. THE WEATHER IS DREADFUL . . .

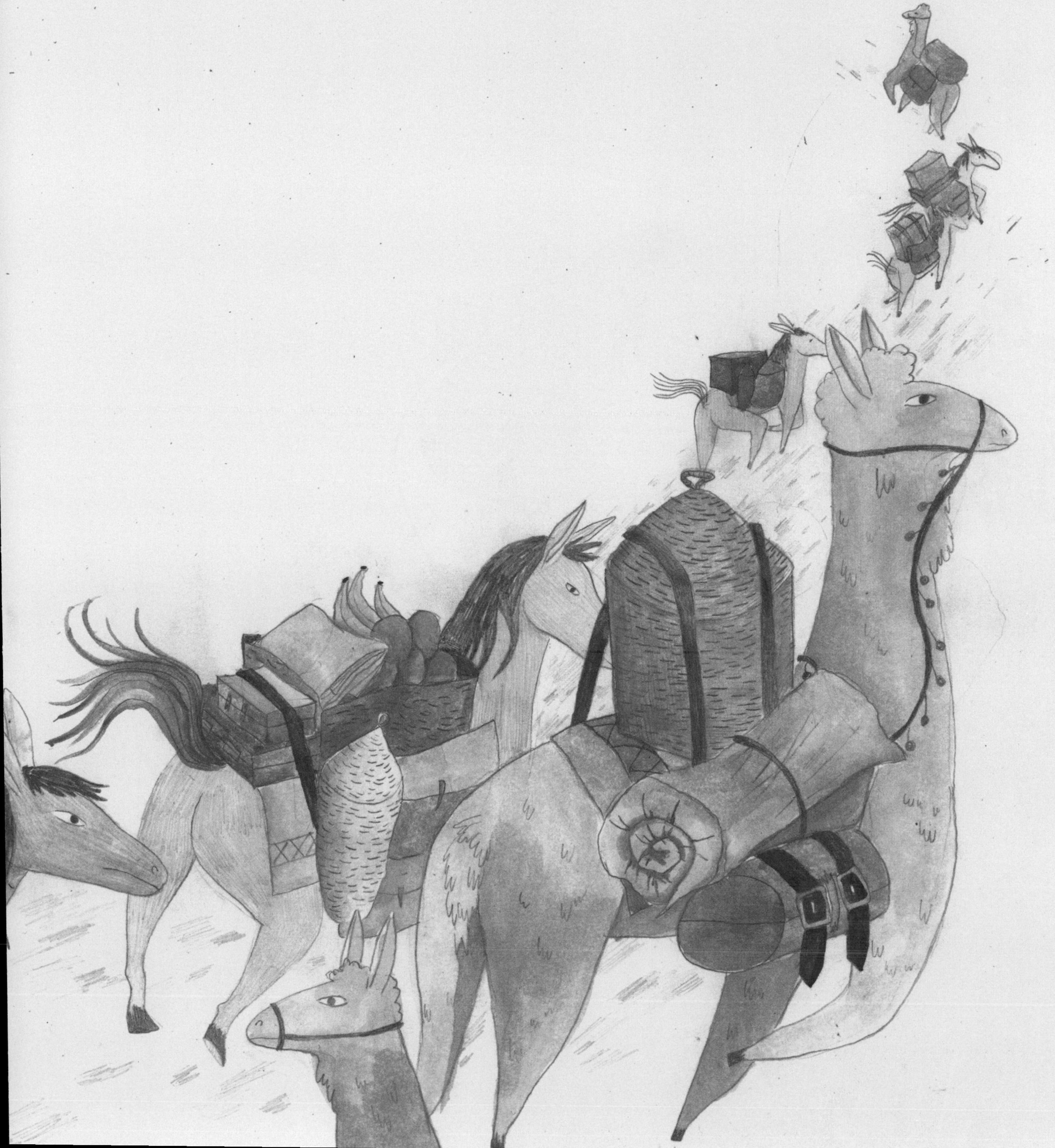

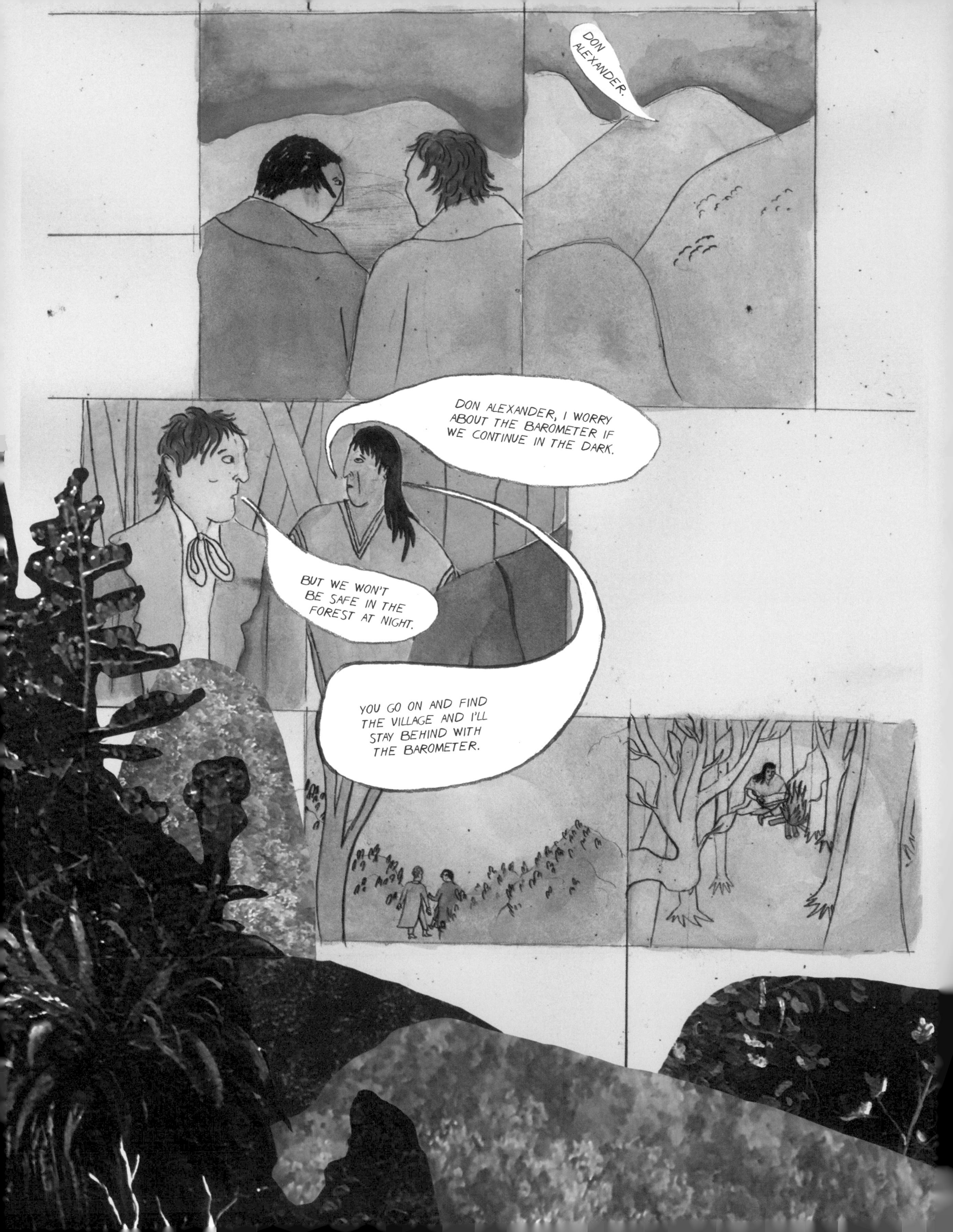
DON ALEXANDER.
DON ALEXANDER, I WORRY ABOUT THE BAROMETER IF WE CONTINUE IN THE DARK.
BUT WE WON'T BE SAFE IN THE FOREST AT NIGHT.
YOU GO ON AND FIND THE VILLAGE AND I'LL STAY BEHIND WITH THE BAROMETER.

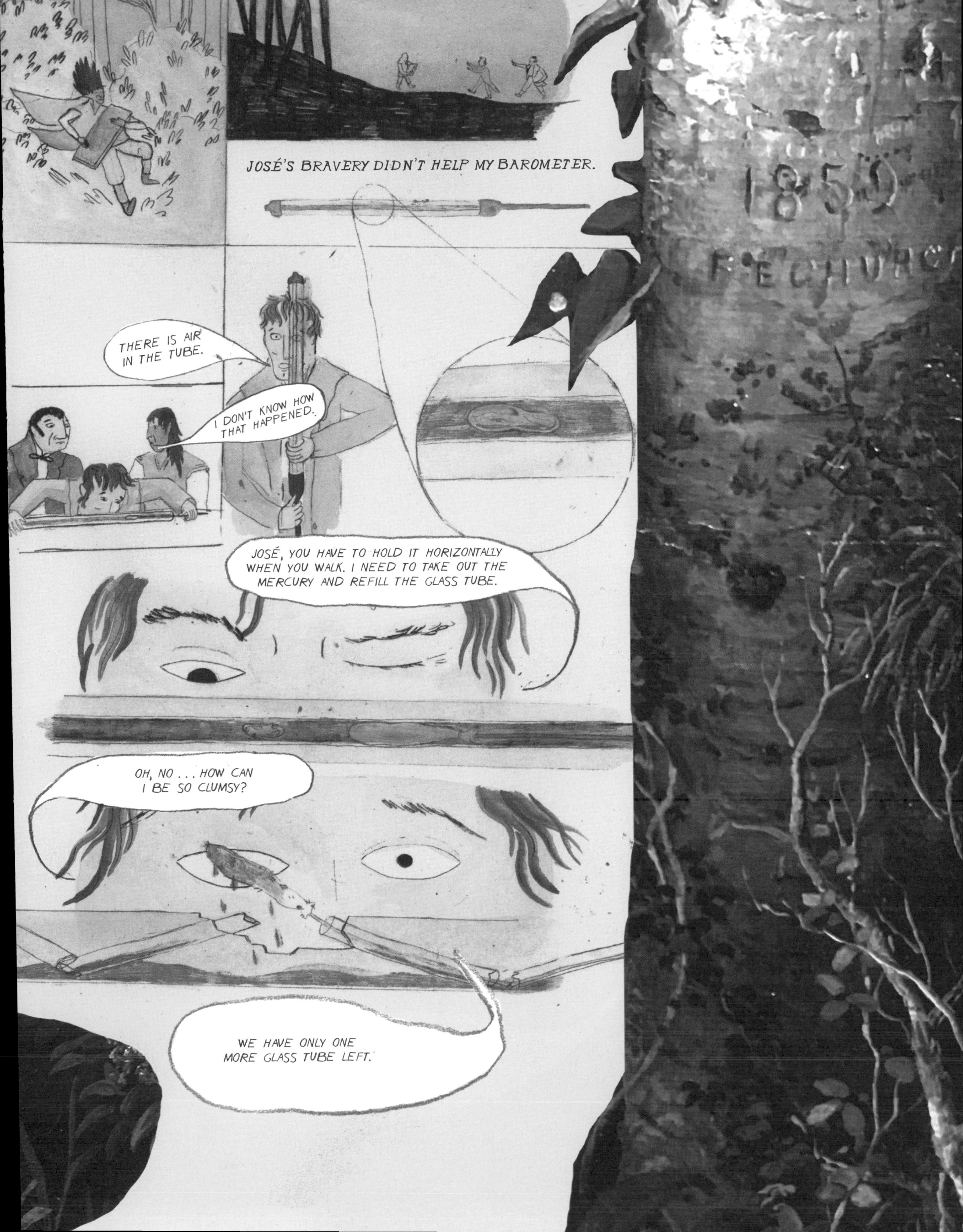
JOSÉ'S BRAVERY DIDN'T HELP MY BAROMETER.
THERE IS AIR IN THE TUBE.
I DON'T KNOW HOW THAT HAPPENED.
JOSÉ, YOU HAVE TO HOLD IT HORIZONTALLY WHEN YOU WALK. I NEED TO TAKE OUT THE MERCURY AND REFILL THE GLASS TUBE.
OH, NO . . . HOW CAN I BE SO CLUMSY?
WE HAVE ONLY ONE MORE GLASS TUBE LEFT.

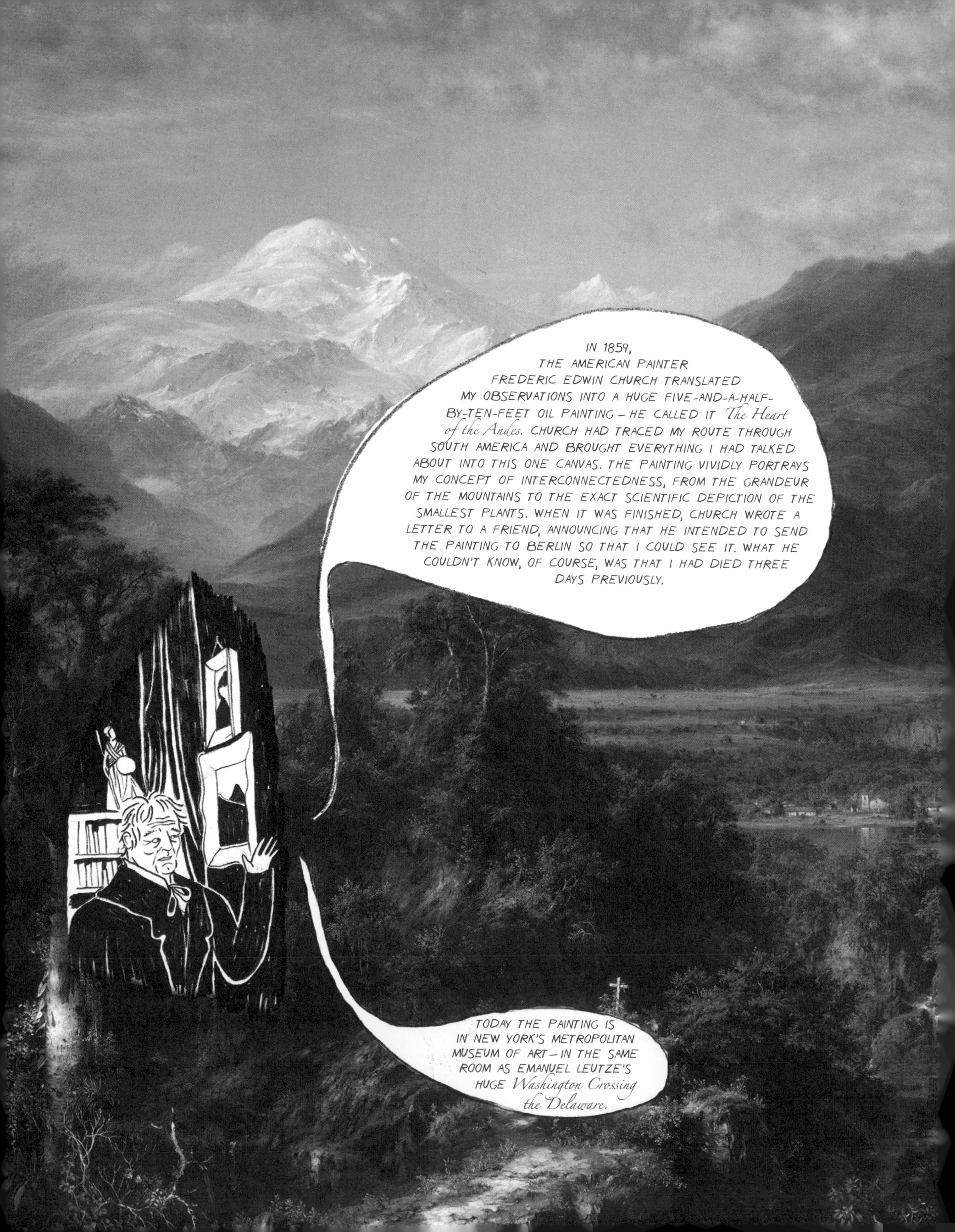
IN 1859, THE AMERICAN PAINTER FREDERIC EDWIN CHURCH TRANSLATED MY OBSERVATIONS INTO A HUGE FIVE-AND-A-HALF-BY-TEN-FEET OIL PAINTING – HE CALLED IT *The Heart of the Andes.* CHURCH HAD TRACED MY ROUTE THROUGH SOUTH AMERICA AND BROUGHT EVERYTHING I HAD TALKED ABOUT INTO THIS ONE CANVAS. THE PAINTING VIVIDLY PORTRAYS MY CONCEPT OF INTERCONNECTEDNESS, FROM THE GRANDEUR OF THE MOUNTAINS TO THE EXACT SCIENTIFIC DEPICTION OF THE SMALLEST PLANTS. WHEN IT WAS FINISHED, CHURCH WROTE A LETTER TO A FRIEND, ANNOUNCING THAT HE INTENDED TO SEND THE PAINTING TO BERLIN SO THAT I COULD SEE IT. WHAT HE COULDN'T KNOW, OF COURSE, WAS THAT I HAD DIED THREE DAYS PREVIOUSLY.
TODAY THE PAINTING IS IN NEW YORK'S METROPOLITAN MUSEUM OF ART – IN THE SAME ROOM AS EMANUEL LEUTZE'S HUGE *Washington Crossing the Delaware.*

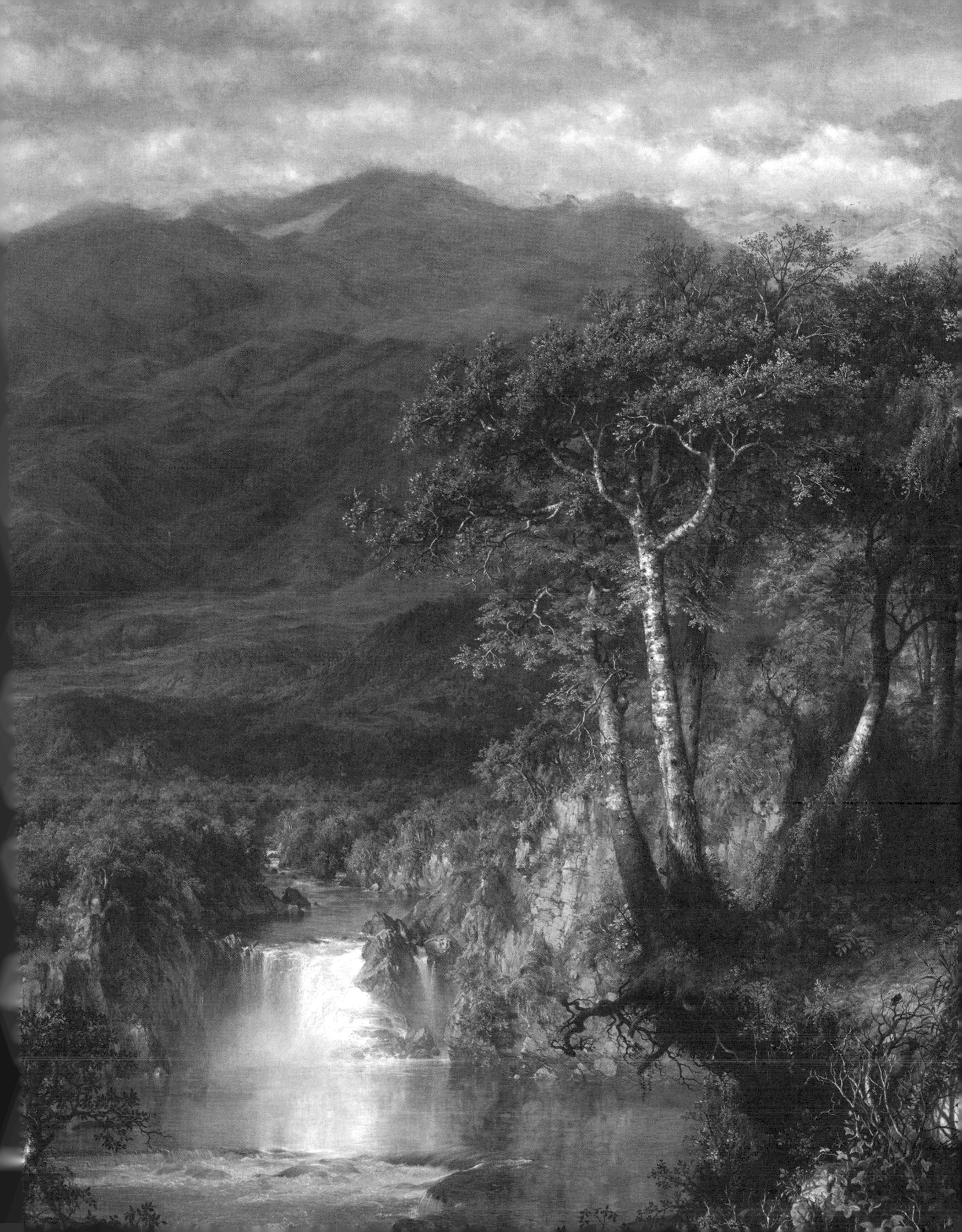

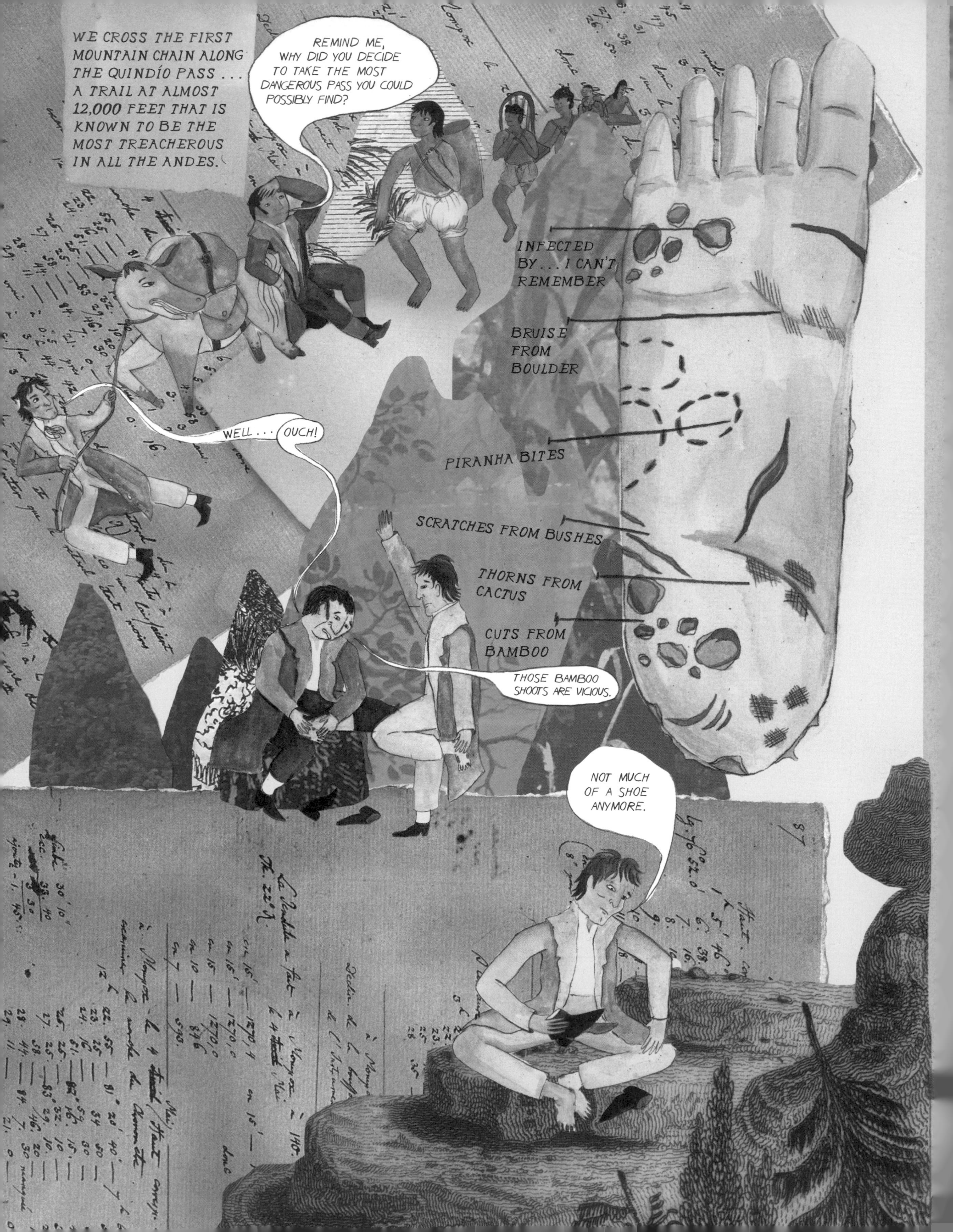
WE CROSS THE FIRST MOUNTAIN CHAIN ALONG THE QUINDÍO PASS . . . A TRAIL AT ALMOST 12,000 FEET THAT IS KNOWN TO BE THE MOST TREACHEROUS IN ALL THE ANDES.
REMIND ME, WHY DID YOU DECIDE TO TAKE THE MOST DANGEROUS PASS YOU COULD POSSIBLY FIND?
WELL . . .
OUCH!
INFECTED BY . . . I CAN'T REMEMBER
BRUISE FROM BOULDER
PIRANHA BITES
SCRATCHES FROM BUSHES
THORNS FROM CACTUS
CUTS FROM BAMBOO
THOSE BAMBOO SHOOTS ARE VICIOUS.
NOT MUCH OF A SHOE ANYMORE.

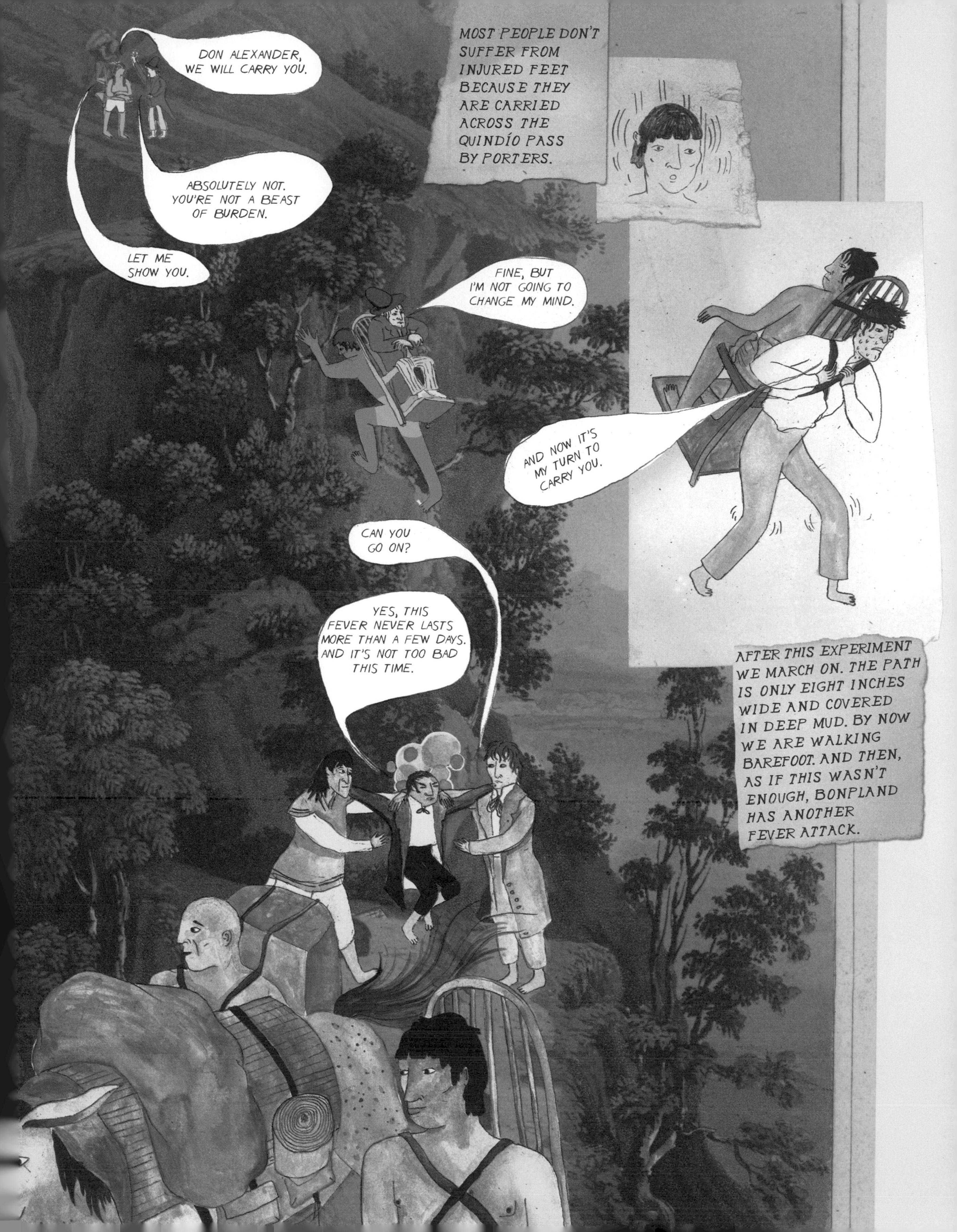
DON ALEXANDER, WE WILL CARRY YOU.
ABSOLUTELY NOT. YOU'RE NOT A BEAST OF BURDEN.
LET ME SHOW YOU.
MOST PEOPLE DON'T SUFFER FROM INJURED FEET BECAUSE THEY ARE CARRIED ACROSS THE QUINDÍO PASS BY PORTERS.
FINE, BUT I'M NOT GOING TO CHANGE MY MIND.
AND NOW IT'S MY TURN TO CARRY YOU.
CAN YOU GO ON?
YES, THIS FEVER NEVER LASTS MORE THAN A FEW DAYS. AND IT'S NOT TOO BAD THIS TIME.
AFTER THIS EXPERIMENT WE MARCH ON. THE PATH IS ONLY EIGHT INCHES WIDE AND COVERED IN DEEP MUD. BY NOW WE ARE WALKING BAREFOOT. AND THEN, AS IF THIS WASN'T ENOUGH, BONPLAND HAS ANOTHER FEVER ATTACK.

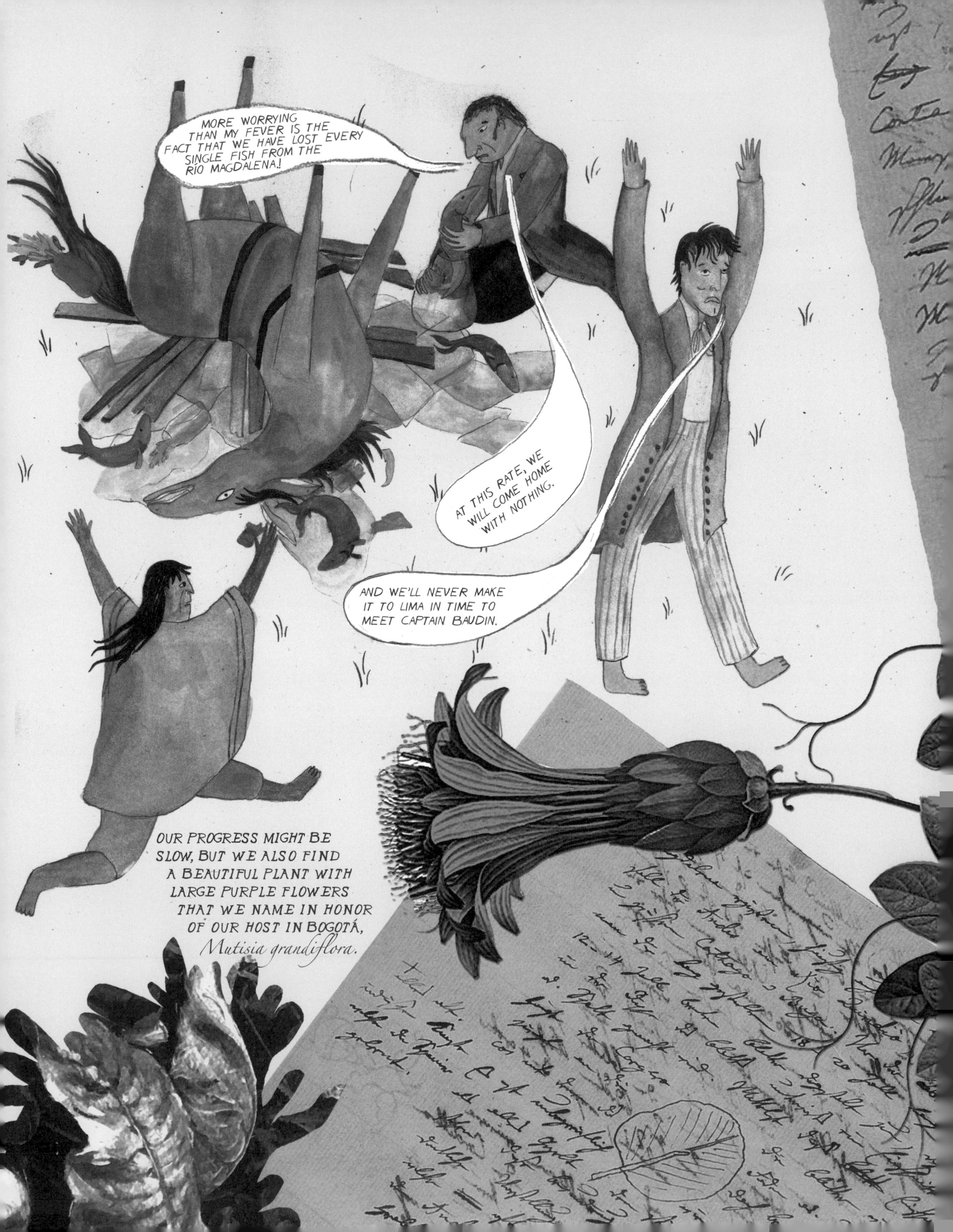
MORE WORRYING THAN MY FEVER IS THE FACT THAT WE HAVE LOST EVERY SINGLE FISH FROM THE RIO MAGDALENA!
AT THIS RATE, WE WILL COME HOME WITH NOTHING.
AND WE'LL NEVER MAKE IT TO LIMA IN TIME TO MEET CAPTAIN BAUDIN.
OUR PROGRESS MIGHT BE SLOW, BUT WE ALSO FIND A BEAUTIFUL PLANT WITH LARGE PURPLE FLOWERS THAT WE NAME IN HONOR OF OUR HOST IN BOGOTÁ, *Mutisia grandiflora*.

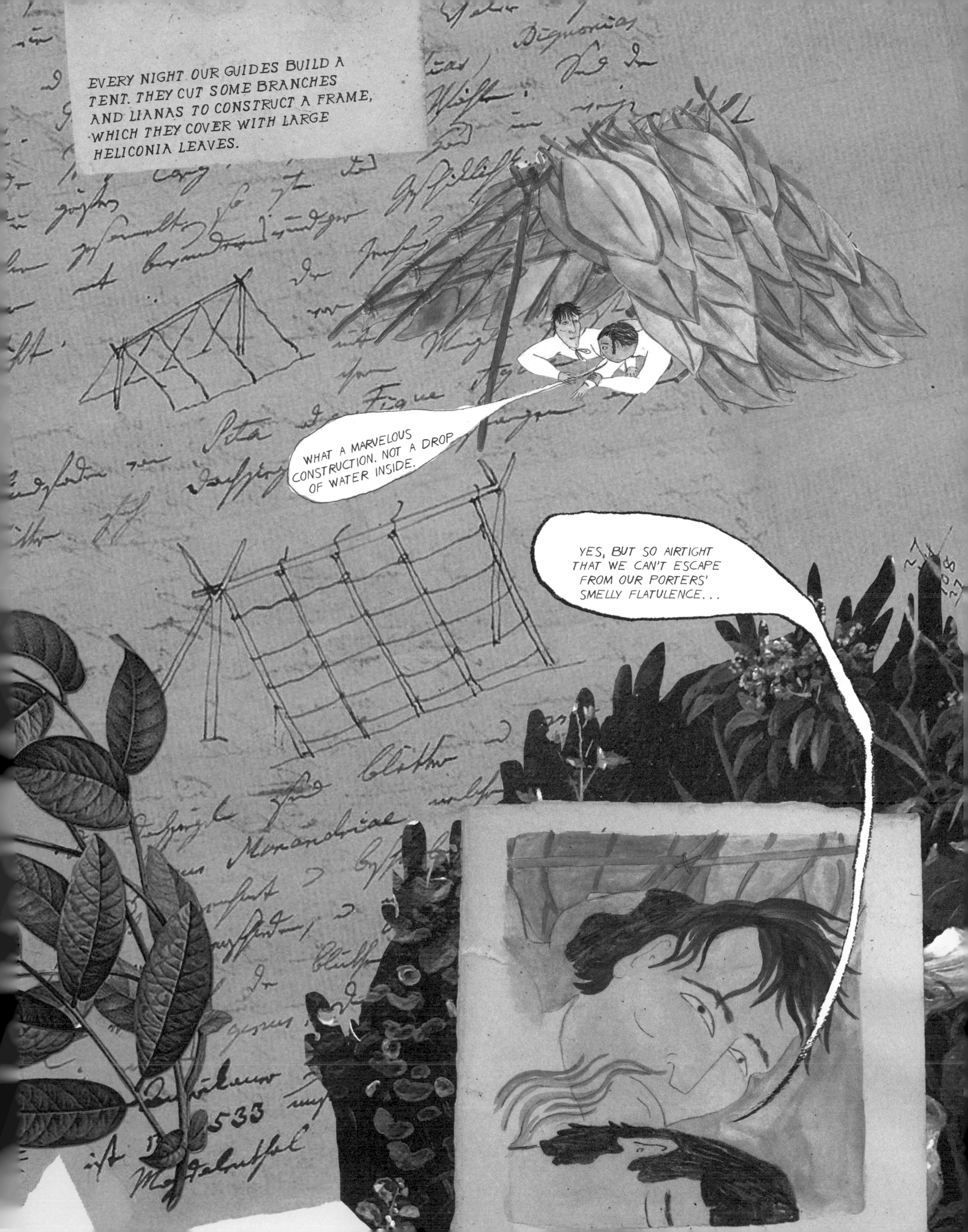
EVERY NIGHT OUR GUIDES BUILD A TENT. THEY CUT SOME BRANCHES AND LIANAS TO CONSTRUCT A FRAME, WHICH THEY COVER WITH LARGE HELICONIA LEAVES.
WHAT A MARVELOUS CONSTRUCTION. NOT A DROP OF WATER INSIDE.
YES, BUT SO AIRTIGHT THAT WE CAN'T ESCAPE FROM OUR PORTERS' SMELLY FLATULENCE...

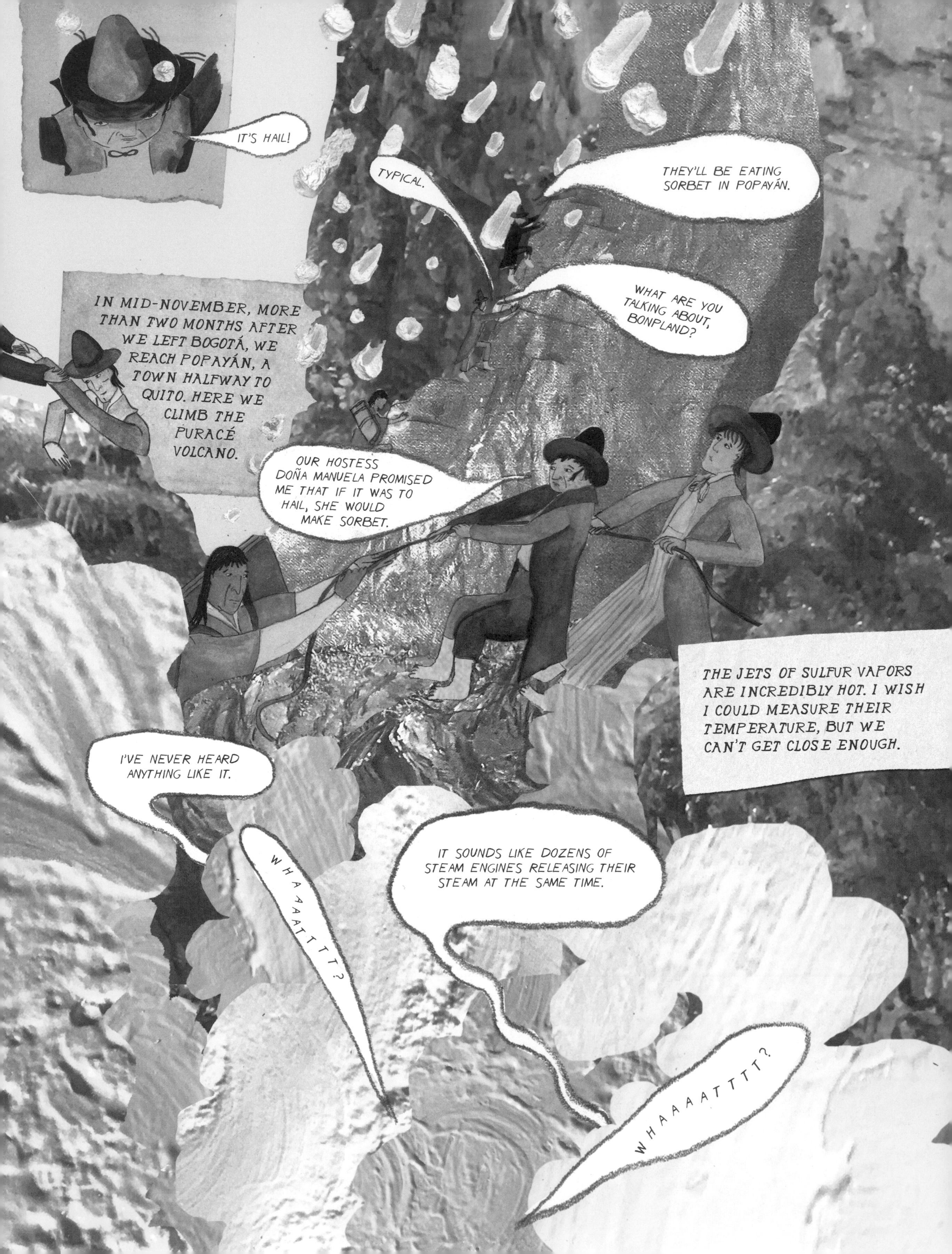
IT'S HAIL!
TYPICAL.
THEY'LL BE EATING SORBET IN POPAYÁN.
IN MID-NOVEMBER, MORE THAN TWO MONTHS AFTER WE LEFT BOGOTÁ, WE REACH POPAYÁN, A TOWN HALFWAY TO QUITO. HERE WE CLIMB THE PURACÉ VOLCANO.
WHAT ARE YOU TALKING ABOUT, BONPLAND?
OUR HOSTESS DOÑA MANUELA PROMISED ME THAT IF IT WAS TO HAIL, SHE WOULD MAKE SORBET.
THE JETS OF SULFUR VAPORS ARE INCREDIBLY HOT. I WISH I COULD MEASURE THEIR TEMPERATURE, BUT WE CAN'T GET CLOSE ENOUGH.
I'VE NEVER HEARD ANYTHING LIKE IT.
WHAAATTTT?
IT SOUNDS LIKE DOZENS OF STEAM ENGINES RELEASING THEIR STEAM AT THE SAME TIME.
WHAAAATTTT?

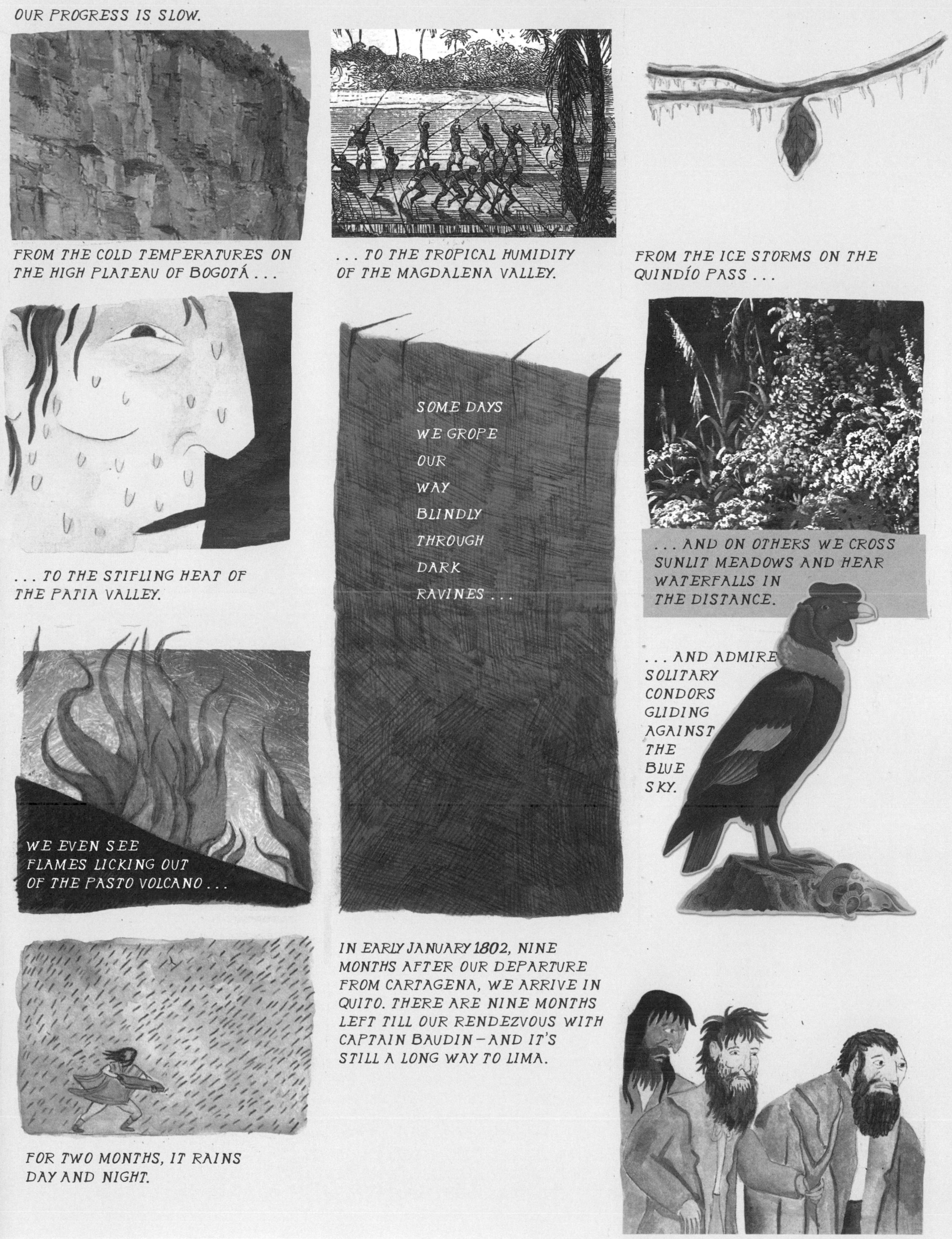
OUR PROGRESS IS SLOW.
FROM THE COLD TEMPERATURES ON THE HIGH PLATEAU OF BOGOTÁ . . .
. . . TO THE TROPICAL HUMIDITY OF THE MAGDALENA VALLEY.
FROM THE ICE STORMS ON THE QUINDÍO PASS . . .
. . . TO THE STIFLING HEAT OF THE PATIA VALLEY.
SOME DAYS WE GROPE OUR WAY BLINDLY THROUGH DARK RAVINES . . .
. . . AND ON OTHERS WE CROSS SUNLIT MEADOWS AND HEAR WATERFALLS IN THE DISTANCE.
. . . AND ADMIRE SOLITARY CONDORS GLIDING AGAINST THE BLUE SKY.
WE EVEN SEE FLAMES LICKING OUT OF THE PASTO VOLCANO . . .
FOR TWO MONTHS, IT RAINS DAY AND NIGHT.
IN EARLY JANUARY 1802, NINE MONTHS AFTER OUR DEPARTURE FROM CARTAGENA, WE ARRIVE IN QUITO. THERE ARE NINE MONTHS LEFT TILL OUR RENDEZVOUS WITH CAPTAIN BAUDIN—AND IT'S STILL A LONG WAY TO LIMA.

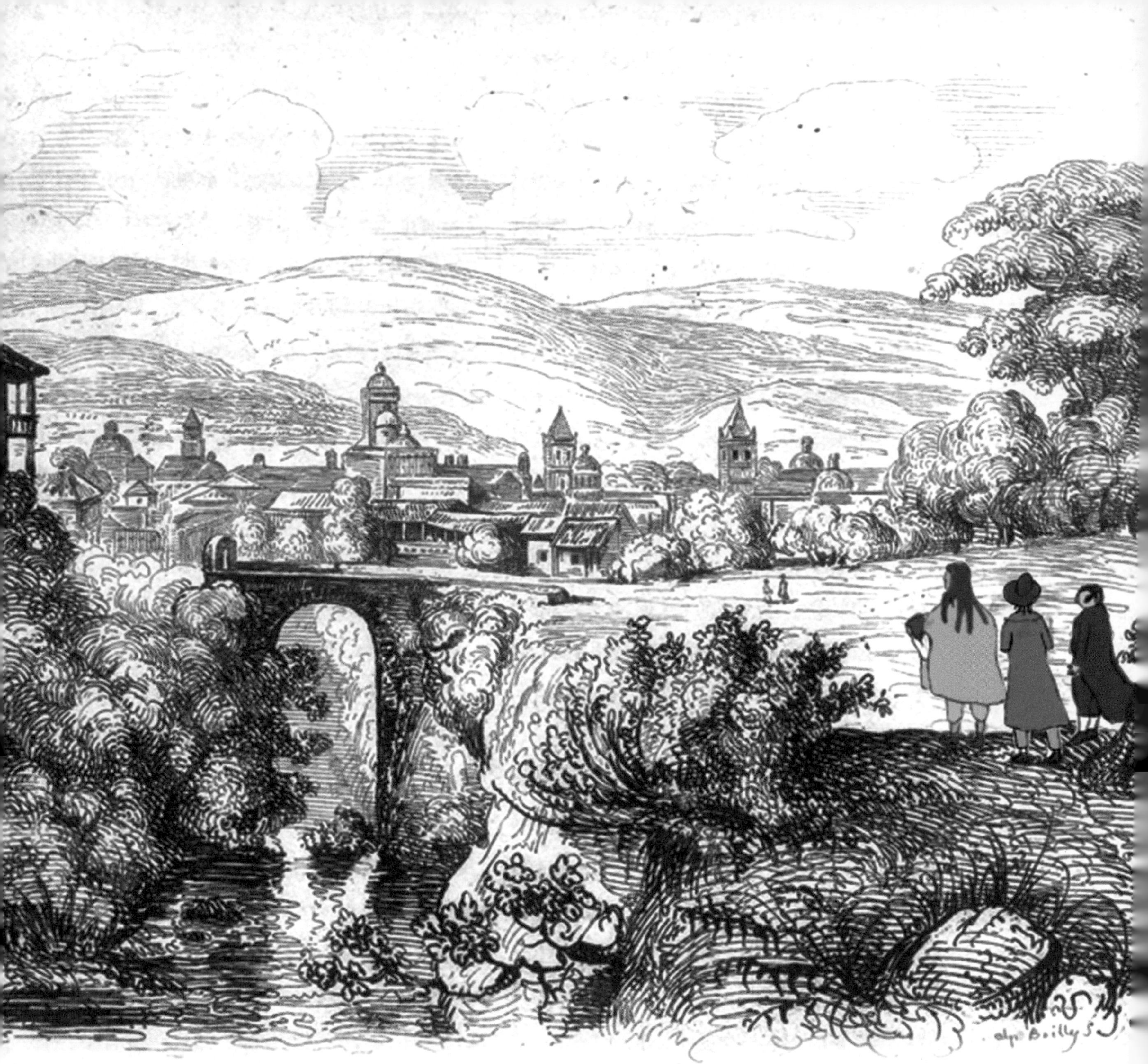

QUITO IS BEAUTIFUL BUT EXUDES THE MIGHT OF THE CATHOLIC CHURCH. NO OTHER CITY IN SOUTH AMERICA HAS SO MANY MAGNIFICENT MONASTERIES AND CHURCHES. THE PROVINCIAL GOVERNOR, THE MARQUÉS DE AGUIRRE Y MONTÚFAR, FOUND A WONDERFUL HOUSE FOR US (AND LENDS ME SOME MONEY). AND MUCH THOUGH I LOVE OUR ADVENTURES, I HAVE TO ADMIT THAT I'M ALSO VERY MUCH ENJOYING SLEEPING IN A BED AGAIN. THE WEATHER IS NOT SO SPLENDID. SINCE THE GREAT EARTHQUAKE OF 1797 IN RIOBAMBA, A LITTLE MORE THAN 100 MILES SOUTH, QUITO'S SKIES ARE MOSTLY GRAY, AND I'M TOLD THAT TEMPERATURES HAVE DROPPED SIGNIFICANTLY. THE TREMORS CONTINUE . . . BUT THE PEOPLE OF QUITO HAVE GOTTEN USED TO LIVING NEXT TO THIS SLEEPING BEAST.

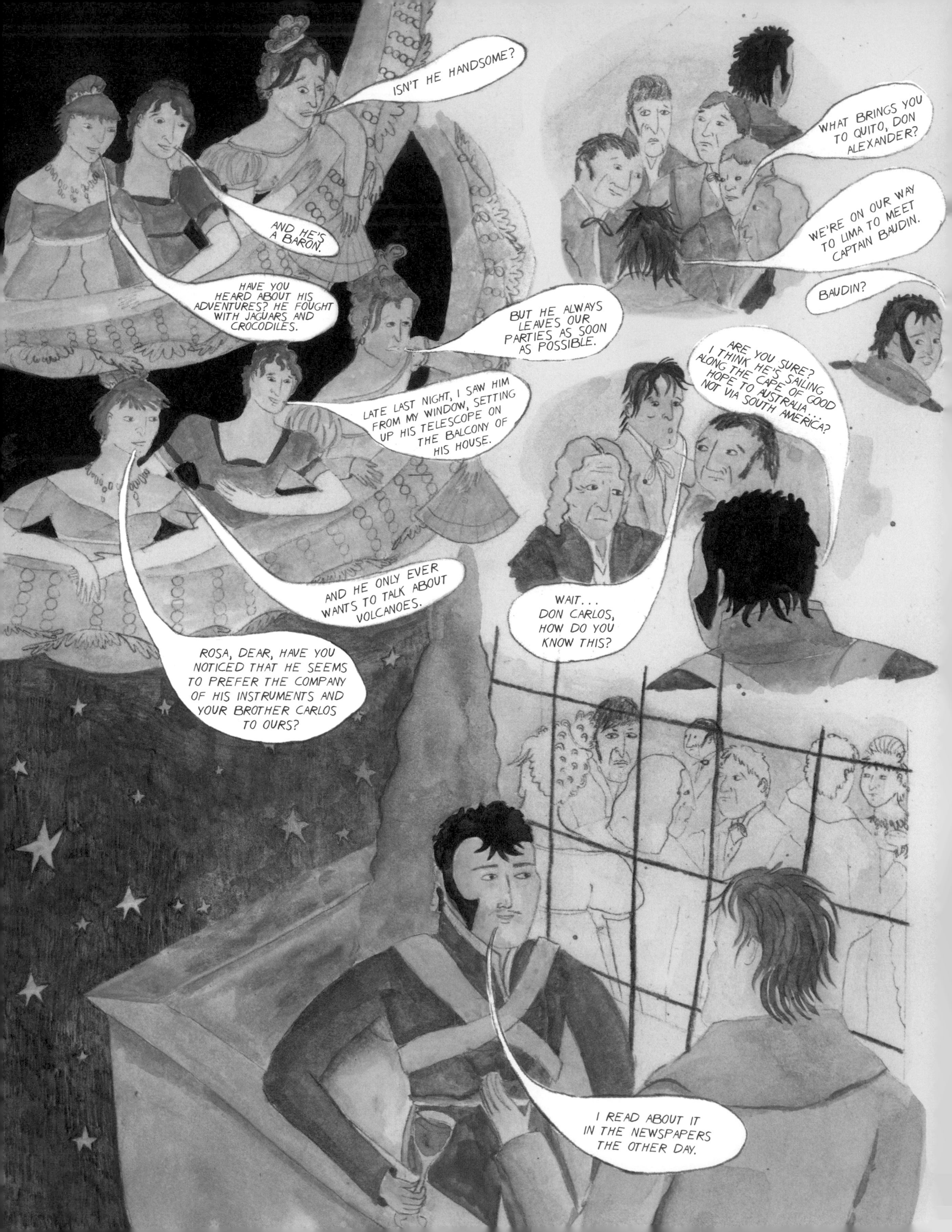
ISN'T HE HANDSOME?
AND HE'S A BARON.
HAVE YOU HEARD ABOUT HIS ADVENTURES? HE FOUGHT WITH JAGUARS AND CROCODILES.
BUT HE ALWAYS LEAVES OUR PARTIES AS SOON AS POSSIBLE.
LATE LAST NIGHT, I SAW HIM FROM MY WINDOW, SETTING UP HIS TELESCOPE ON THE BALCONY OF HIS HOUSE.
AND HE ONLY EVER WANTS TO TALK ABOUT VOLCANOES.
ROSA, DEAR, HAVE YOU NOTICED THAT HE SEEMS TO PREFER THE COMPANY OF HIS INSTRUMENTS AND YOUR BROTHER CARLOS TO OURS?
WHAT BRINGS YOU TO QUITO, DON ALEXANDER?
WE'RE ON OUR WAY TO LIMA TO MEET CAPTAIN BAUDIN.
BAUDIN?
ARE YOU SURE? I THINK HE'S SAILING ALONG THE CAPE OF GOOD HOPE TO AUSTRALIA... NOT VIA SOUTH AMERICA?
WAIT... DON CARLOS, HOW DO YOU KNOW THIS?
I READ ABOUT IT IN THE NEWSPAPERS THE OTHER DAY.

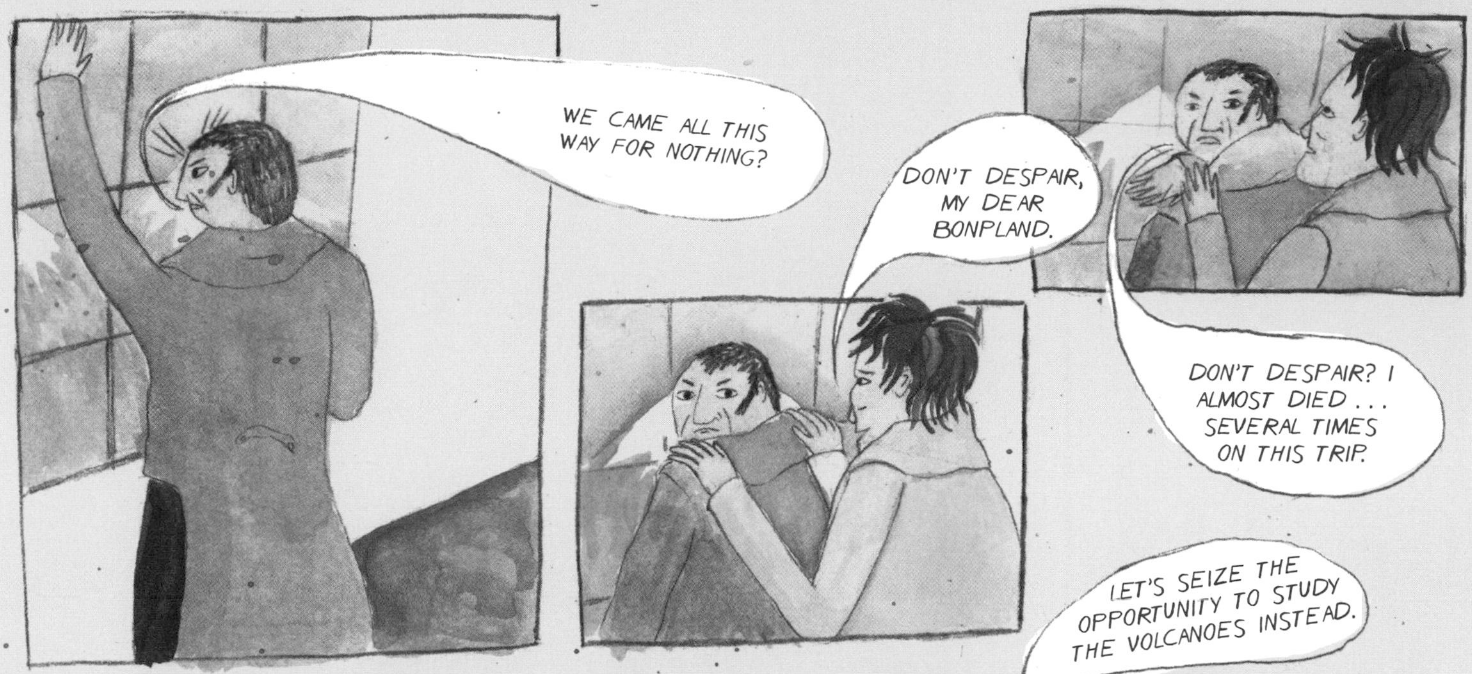
WE CAME ALL THIS WAY FOR NOTHING?
DON'T DESPAIR, MY DEAR BONPLAND.
DON'T DESPAIR? I ALMOST DIED . . . SEVERAL TIMES ON THIS TRIP.

YOU MIGHT WONDER WHY I'M SO KEEN ON VOLCANOES. I THINK THEY ARE ALL CONNECTED . . . THEY OCCUR IN CLUSTERS OR LONG CHAINS – AND SOMETIMES ACROSS HUGE DISTANCES. I SUSPECT THAT THEY MIGHT BE LINKED SUBTERRANEOUSLY, LIKE A GIGANTIC FURNACE DEEP INSIDE OUR PLANET. VOLCANIC ERUPTIONS, EARTHQUAKES AND TSUNAMIS OFTEN HAPPEN AT THE SAME TIME. AND WHERE BETTER TO INVESTIGATE ALL THIS THAN IN QUITO? STRETCHING OUT SOUTH FROM HERE ARE TWO PARALLEL MOUNTAIN CHAINS MADE UP OF VOLCANOES, A DOUBLE RIDGE . . . ALMOST LIKE AN AVENUE. I WANT TO CLIMB THEM ALL. BUT BEFORE I TAKE YOU TO THE VOLCANOES, LET ME BRIEFLY INTRODUCE MY NEW FRIEND AND SON OF THE PROVINCIAL GOVERNOR, CARLOS MONTÚFAR. HE'S TWENTY-TWO AND KEEN TO JOIN OUR ADVENTURES . . . AND VERY HANDSOME, I MIGHT ADD.

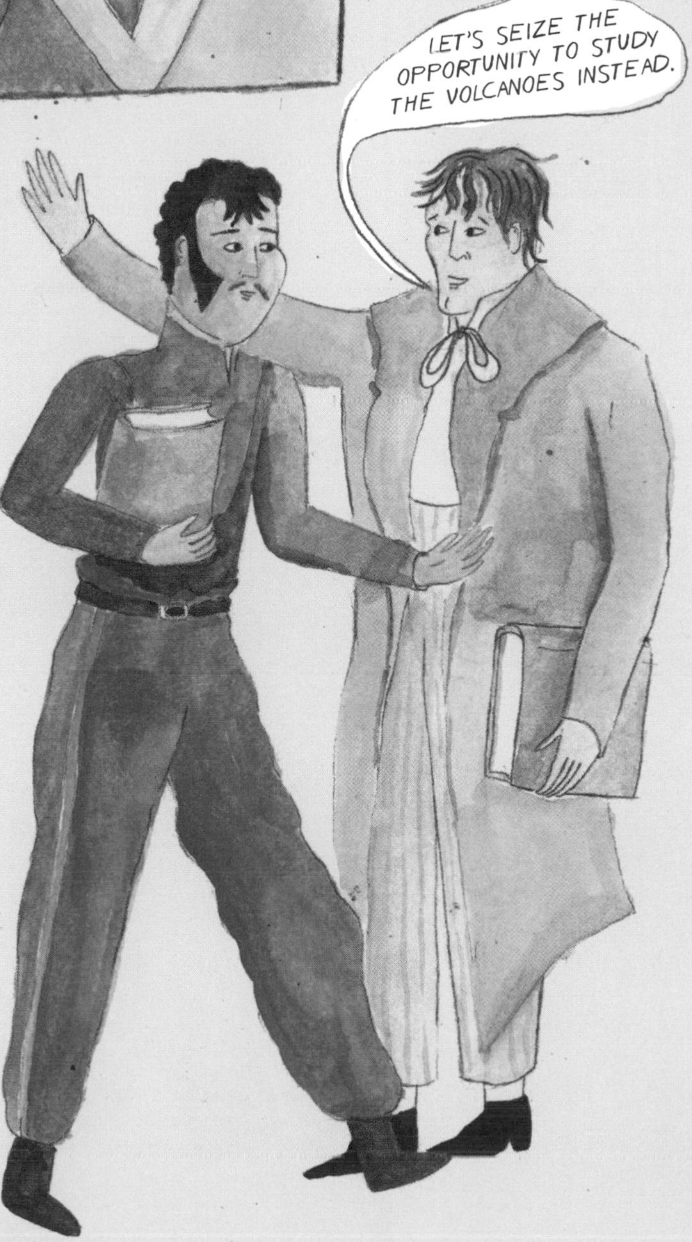
LET'S SEIZE THE OPPORTUNITY TO STUDY THE VOLCANOES INSTEAD.

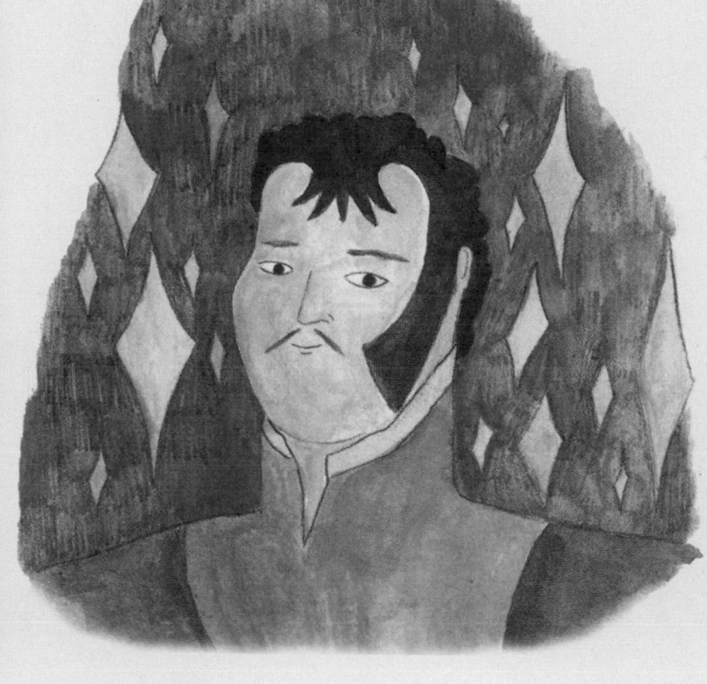

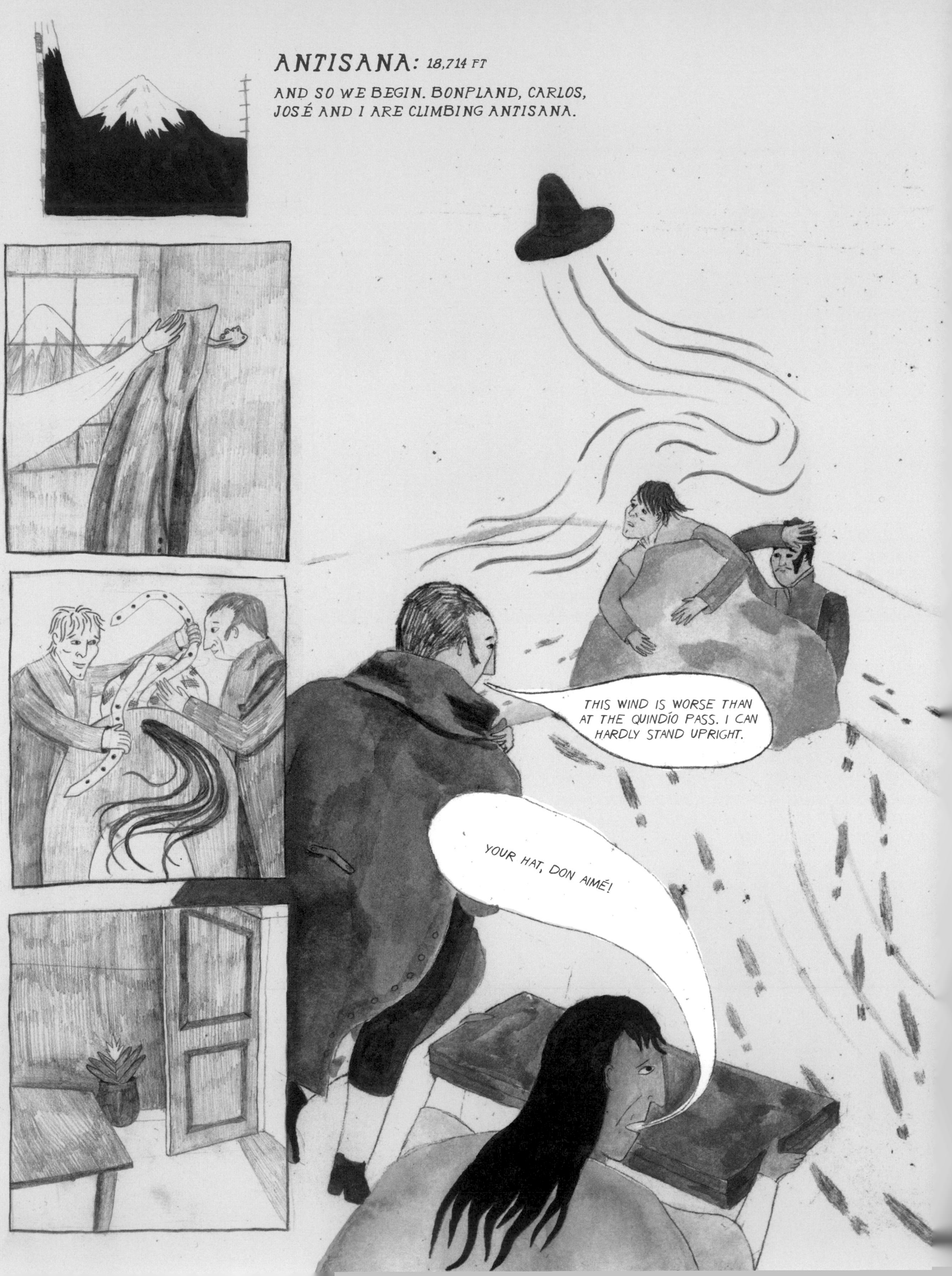
ANTISANA: 18,714 FT
AND SO WE BEGIN. BONPLAND, CARLOS, JOSÉ AND I ARE CLIMBING ANTISANA.
THIS WIND IS WORSE THAN AT THE QUINDÍO PASS. I CAN HARDLY STAND UPRIGHT.
YOUR HAT, DON AIMÉ!

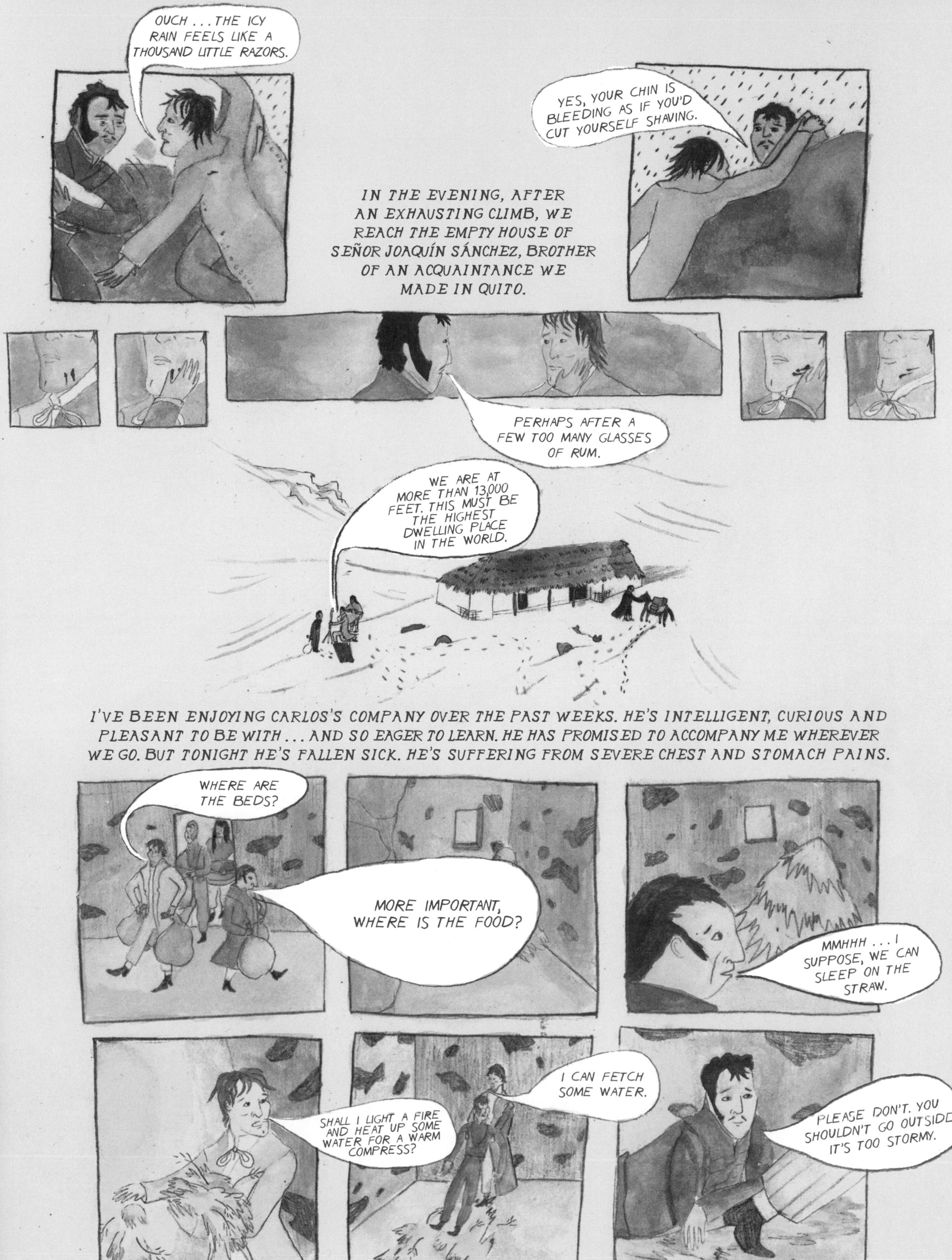
OUCH . . . THE ICY RAIN FEELS LIKE A THOUSAND LITTLE RAZORS.
YES, YOUR CHIN IS BLEEDING AS IF YOU'D CUT YOURSELF SHAVING.
IN THE EVENING, AFTER AN EXHAUSTING CLIMB, WE REACH THE EMPTY HOUSE OF SEÑOR JOAQUÍN SÁNCHEZ, BROTHER OF AN ACQUAINTANCE WE MADE IN QUITO.
PERHAPS AFTER A FEW TOO MANY GLASSES OF RUM.
WE ARE AT MORE THAN 13,000 FEET. THIS MUST BE THE HIGHEST DWELLING PLACE IN THE WORLD.
I'VE BEEN ENJOYING CARLOS'S COMPANY OVER THE PAST WEEKS. HE'S INTELLIGENT, CURIOUS AND PLEASANT TO BE WITH . . . AND SO EAGER TO LEARN. HE HAS PROMISED TO ACCOMPANY ME WHEREVER WE GO. BUT TONIGHT HE'S FALLEN SICK. HE'S SUFFERING FROM SEVERE CHEST AND STOMACH PAINS.
WHERE ARE THE BEDS?
MORE IMPORTANT, WHERE IS THE FOOD?
MMHHH . . . I SUPPOSE, WE CAN SLEEP ON THE STRAW.
SHALL I LIGHT A FIRE AND HEAT UP SOME WATER FOR A WARM COMPRESS?
I CAN FETCH SOME WATER.
PLEASE DON'T. YOU SHOULDN'T GO OUTSIDE, IT'S TOO STORMY.

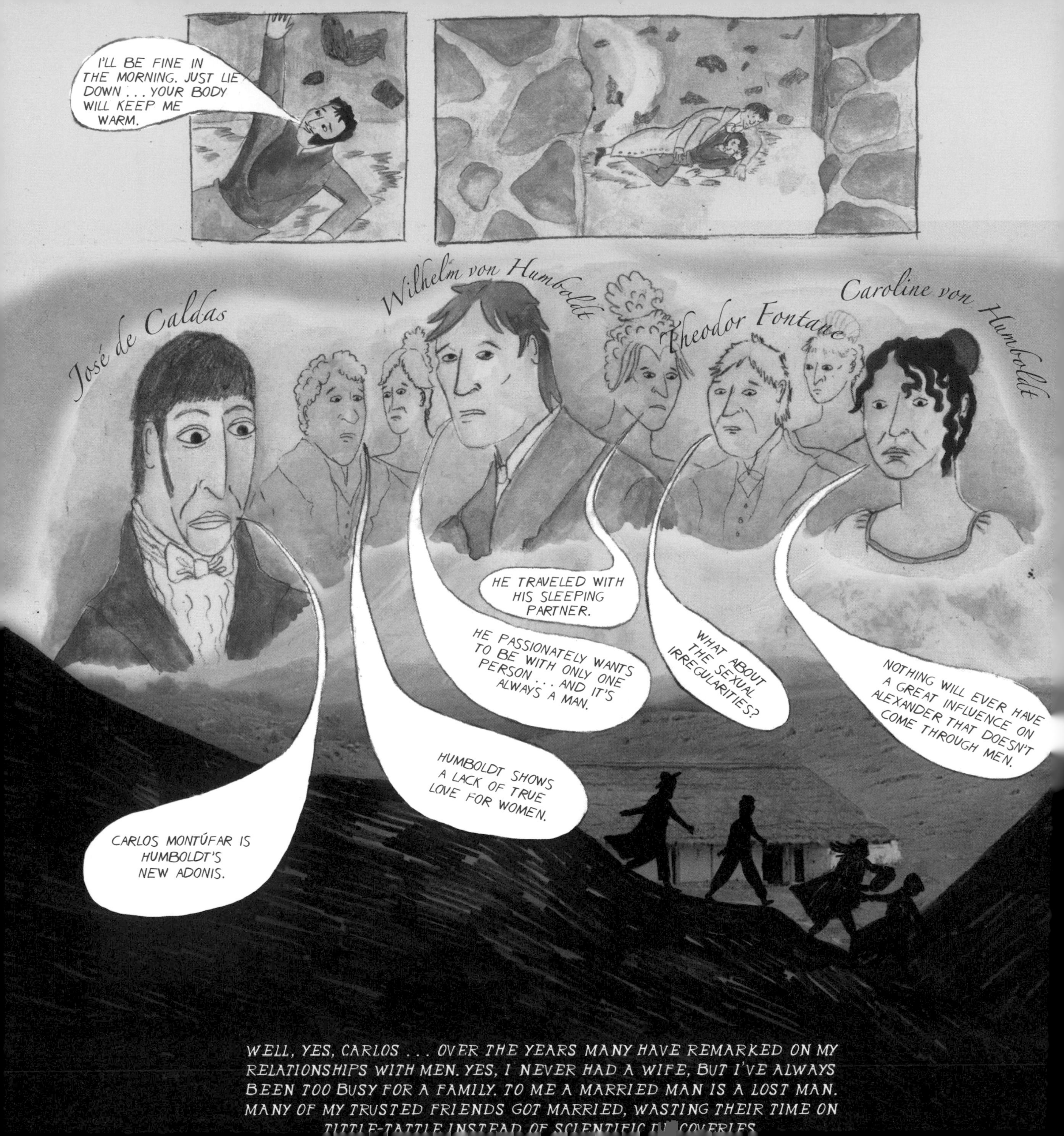
I'LL BE FINE IN THE MORNING. JUST LIE DOWN . . . YOUR BODY WILL KEEP ME WARM.
José de Caldas
Wilhelm von Humboldt
Theodor Fontane
Caroline von Humboldt
CARLOS MONTÚFAR IS HUMBOLDT'S NEW ADONIS.
HUMBOLDT SHOWS A LACK OF TRUE LOVE FOR WOMEN.
HE PASSIONATELY WANTS TO BE WITH ONLY ONE PERSON . . . AND IT'S ALWAYS A MAN.
HE TRAVELED WITH HIS SLEEPING PARTNER.
WHAT ABOUT THE SEXUAL IRREGULARITIES?
NOTHING WILL EVER HAVE A GREAT INFLUENCE ON ALEXANDER THAT DOESN'T COME THROUGH MEN.
WELL, YES, CARLOS . . . OVER THE YEARS MANY HAVE REMARKED ON MY RELATIONSHIPS WITH MEN. YES, I NEVER HAD A WIFE, BUT I'VE ALWAYS BEEN TOO BUSY FOR A FAMILY. TO ME A MARRIED MAN IS A LOST MAN. MANY OF MY TRUSTED FRIENDS GOT MARRIED, WASTING THEIR TIME ON TITTLE-TATTLE INSTEAD OF SCIENTIFIC

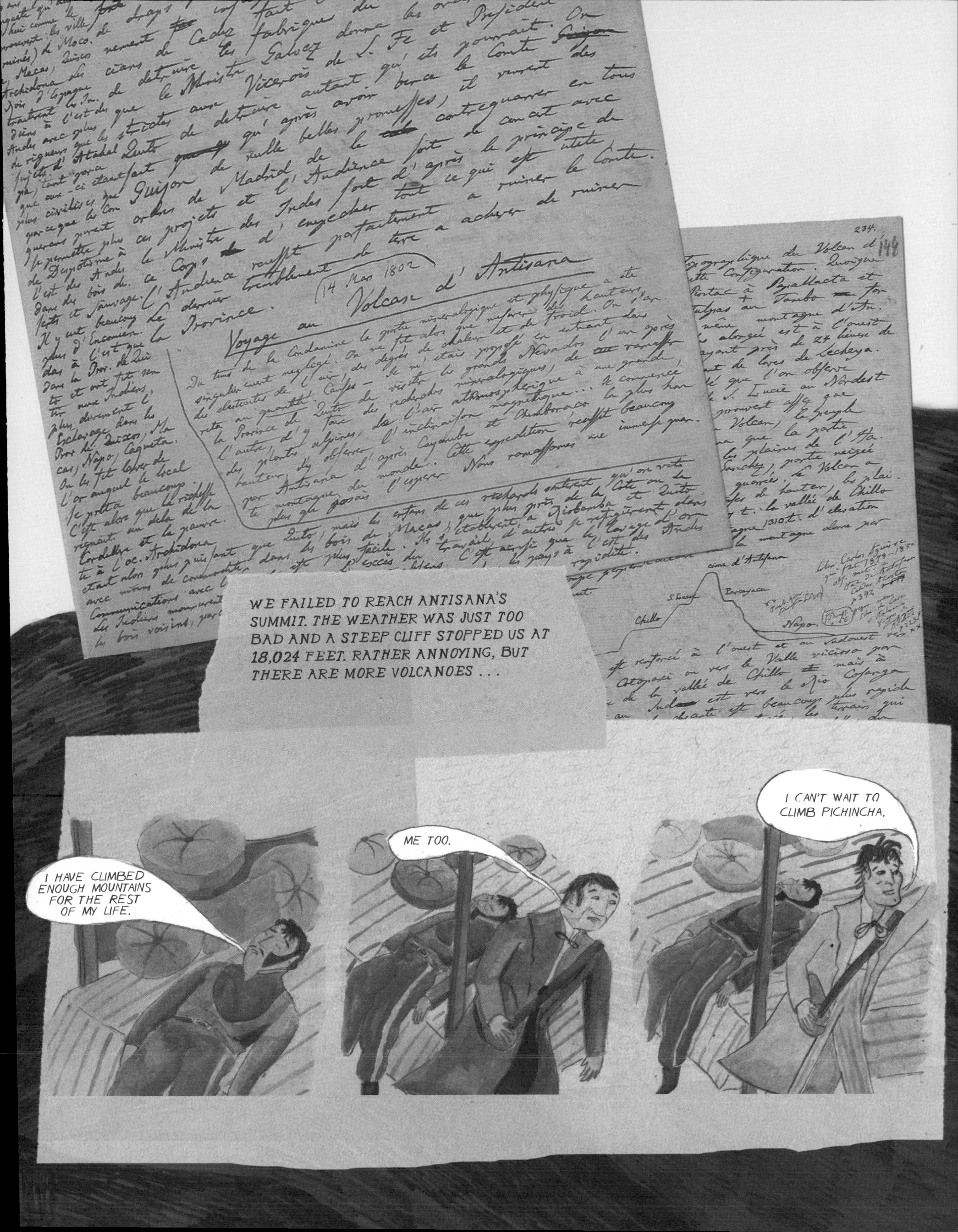
Voyage au Volcan d'Antisana
14 Mai 1802
WE FAILED TO REACH ANTISANA'S SUMMIT. THE WEATHER WAS JUST TOO BAD AND A STEEP CLIFF STOPPED US AT 18,024 FEET. RATHER ANNOYING, BUT THERE ARE MORE VOLCANOES . . .
I HAVE CLIMBED ENOUGH MOUNTAINS FOR THE REST OF MY LIFE.
ME TOO.
I CAN'T WAIT TO CLIMB PICHINCHA.

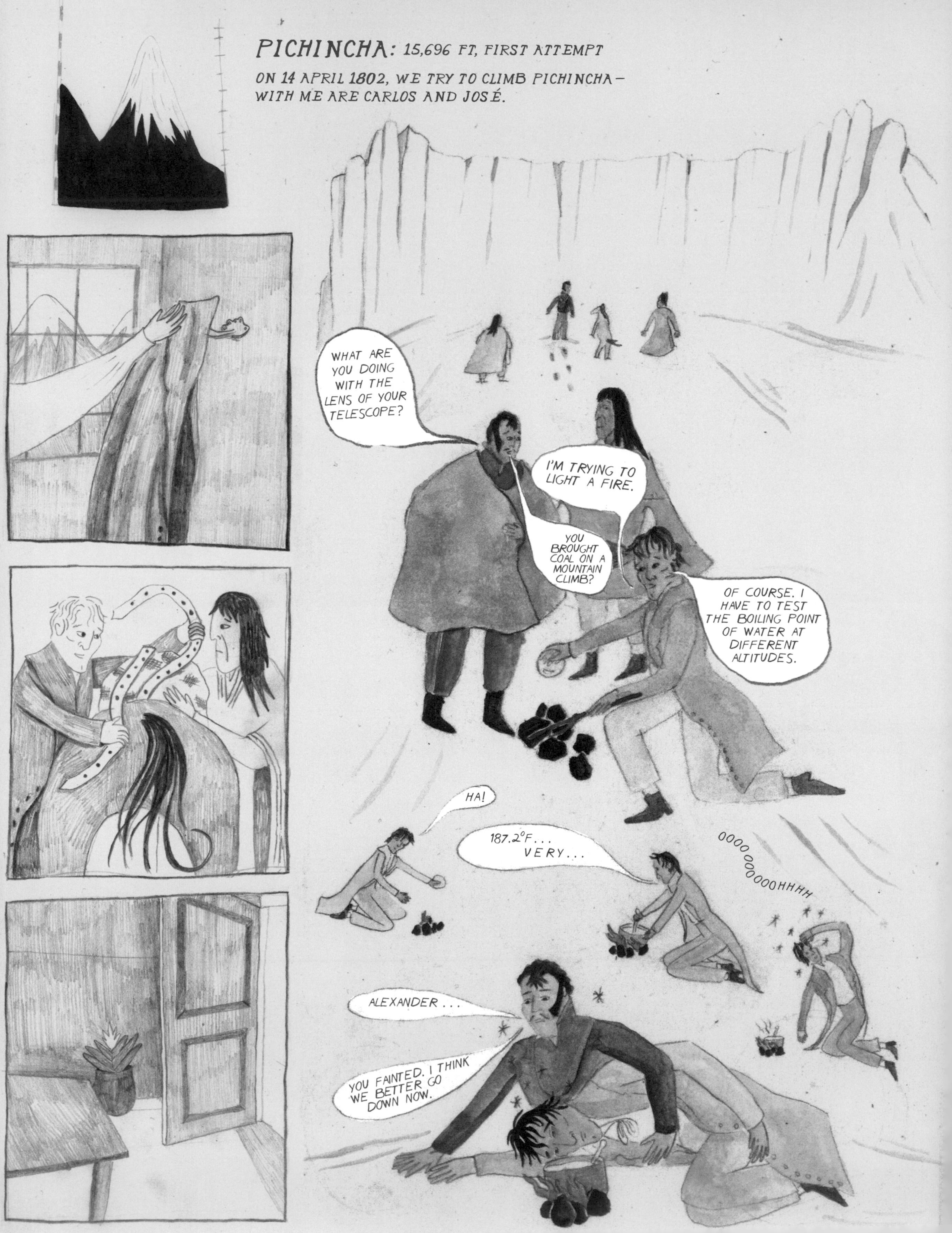
PICHINCHA: 15,696 FT, FIRST ATTEMPT
ON 14 APRIL 1802, WE TRY TO CLIMB PICHINCHA— WITH ME ARE CARLOS AND JOSÉ.
WHAT ARE YOU DOING WITH THE LENS OF YOUR TELESCOPE?
I'M TRYING TO LIGHT A FIRE.
YOU BROUGHT COAL ON A MOUNTAIN CLIMB?
OF COURSE. I HAVE TO TEST THE BOILING POINT OF WATER AT DIFFERENT ALTITUDES.
HA!
187.2°F... VERY...
OOOOOOOOOOOHHHH
ALEXANDER...
YOU FAINTED. I THINK WE BETTER GO DOWN NOW.

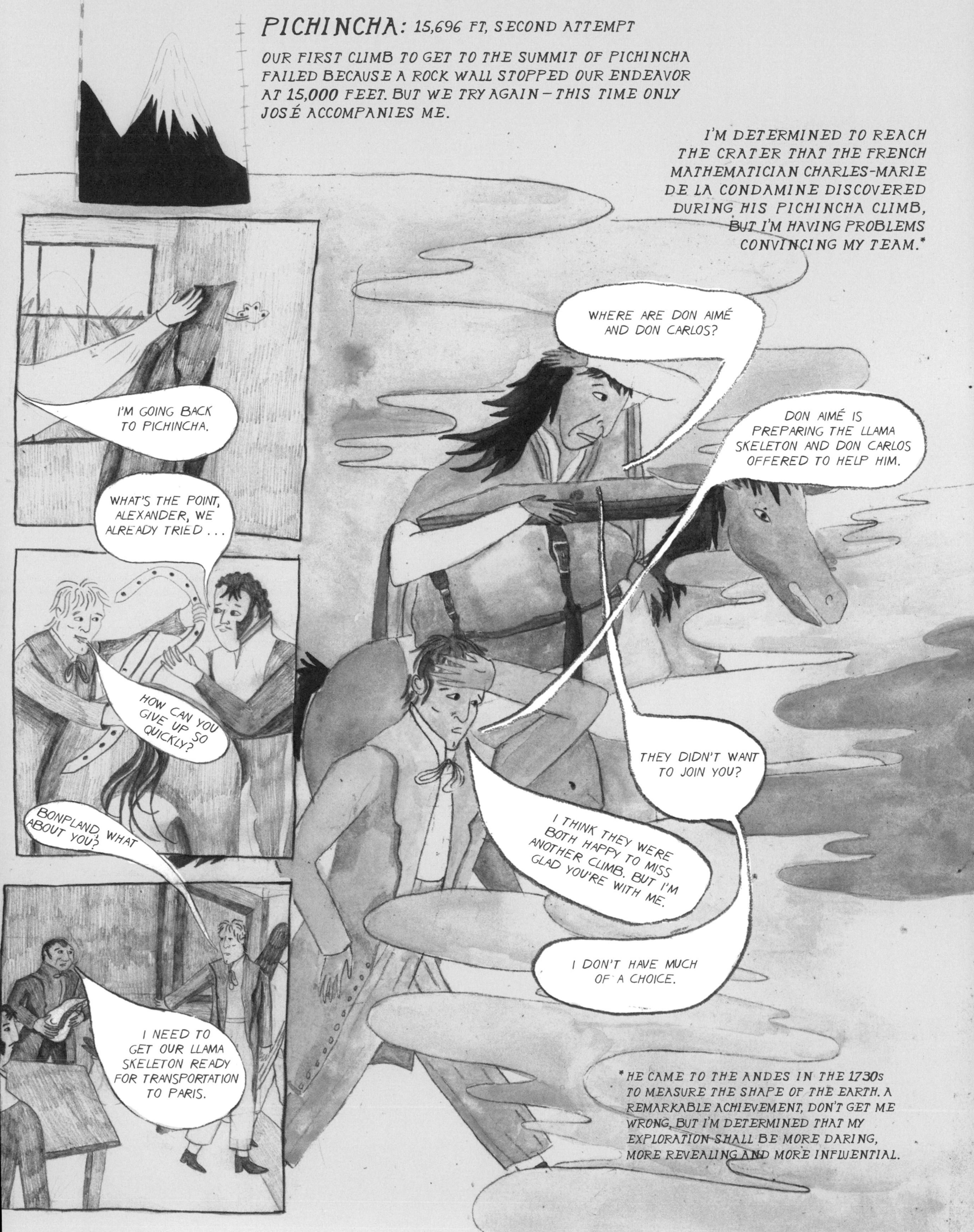
PICHINCHA: 15,696 FT, SECOND ATTEMPT
OUR FIRST CLIMB TO GET TO THE SUMMIT OF PICHINCHA FAILED BECAUSE A ROCK WALL STOPPED OUR ENDEAVOR AT 15,000 FEET. BUT WE TRY AGAIN – THIS TIME ONLY JOSÉ ACCOMPANIES ME.
I'M DETERMINED TO REACH THE CRATER THAT THE FRENCH MATHEMATICIAN CHARLES-MARIE DE LA CONDAMINE DISCOVERED DURING HIS PICHINCHA CLIMB, BUT I'M HAVING PROBLEMS CONVINCING MY TEAM.*
I'M GOING BACK TO PICHINCHA.
WHAT'S THE POINT, ALEXANDER, WE ALREADY TRIED . . .
HOW CAN YOU GIVE UP SO QUICKLY?
BONPLAND, WHAT ABOUT YOU?
I NEED TO GET OUR LLAMA SKELETON READY FOR TRANSPORTATION TO PARIS.
WHERE ARE DON AIMÉ AND DON CARLOS?
DON AIMÉ IS PREPARING THE LLAMA SKELETON AND DON CARLOS OFFERED TO HELP HIM.
THEY DIDN'T WANT TO JOIN YOU?
I THINK THEY WERE BOTH HAPPY TO MISS ANOTHER CLIMB. BUT I'M GLAD YOU'RE WITH ME.
I DON'T HAVE MUCH OF A CHOICE.
*HE CAME TO THE ANDES IN THE 1730s TO MEASURE THE SHAPE OF THE EARTH. A REMARKABLE ACHIEVEMENT, DON'T GET ME WRONG, BUT I'M DETERMINED THAT MY EXPLORATION SHALL BE MORE DARING, MORE REVEALING AND MORE INFLUENTIAL.

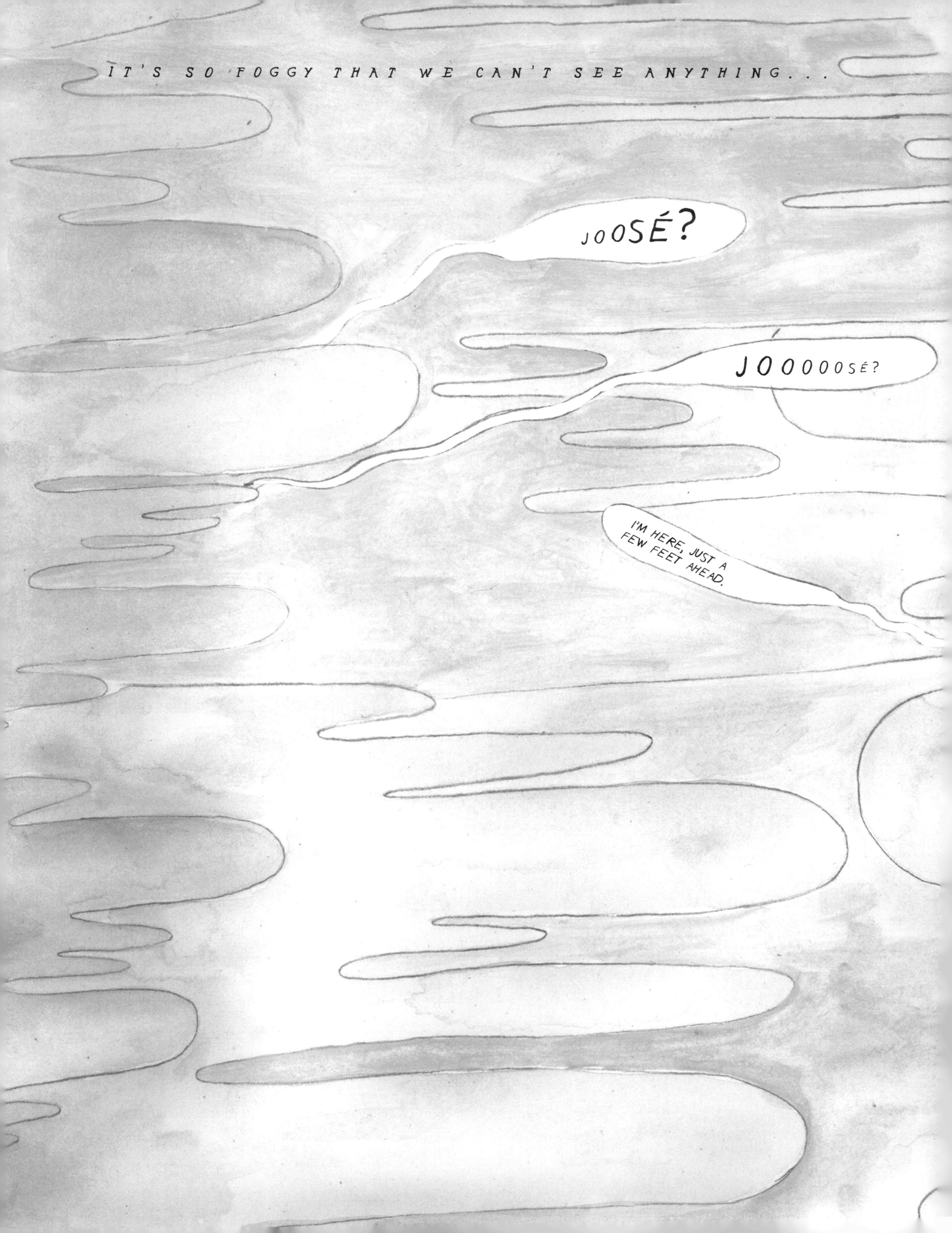
IT'S SO FOGGY THAT WE CAN'T SEE ANYTHING...
JOOSÉ?
JOOOOOOSÉ?
I'M HERE, JUST A FEW FEET AHEAD.

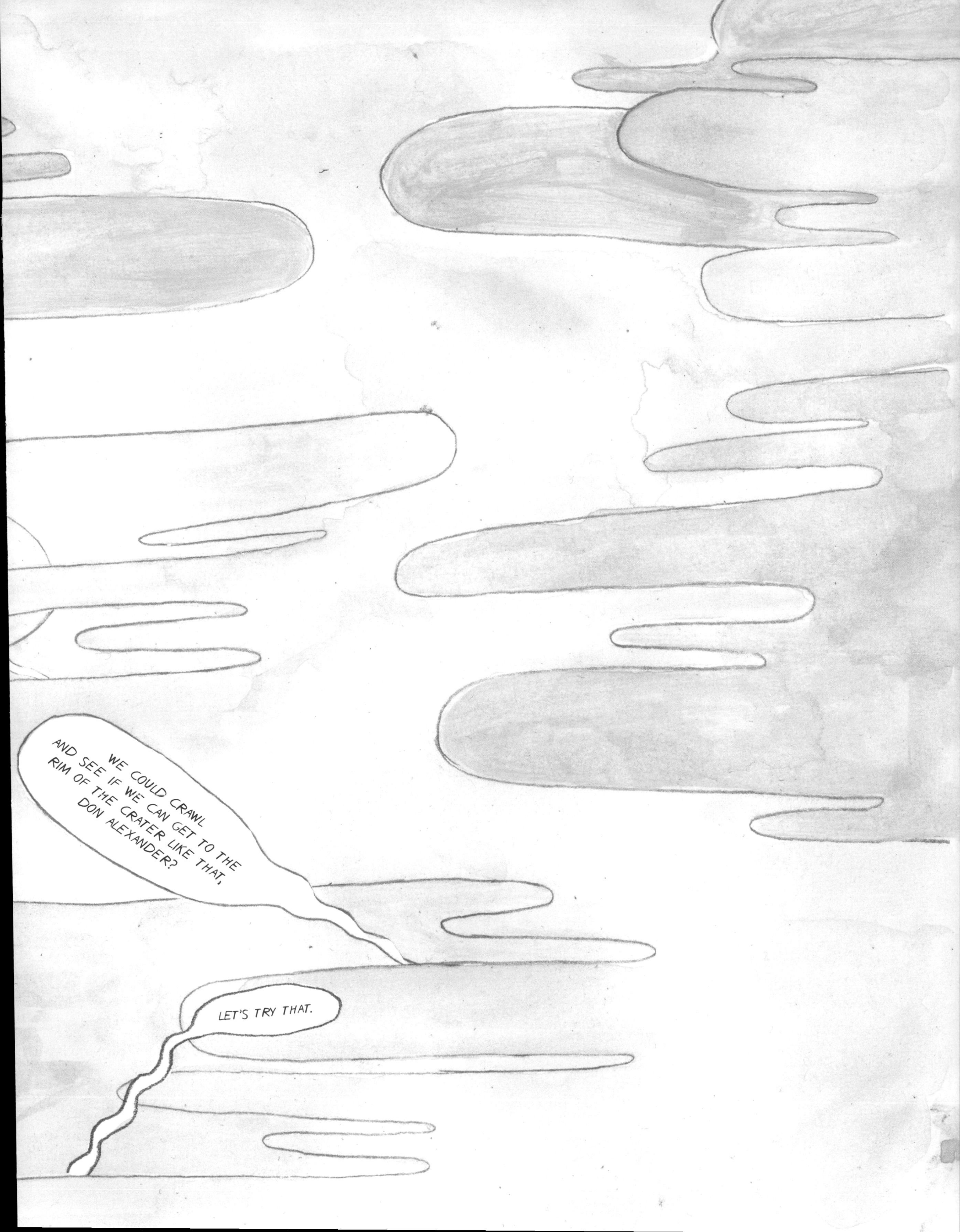
WE COULD CRAWL AND SEE IF WE CAN GET TO THE RIM OF THE CRATER LIKE THAT, DON ALEXANDER?
LET'S TRY THAT.

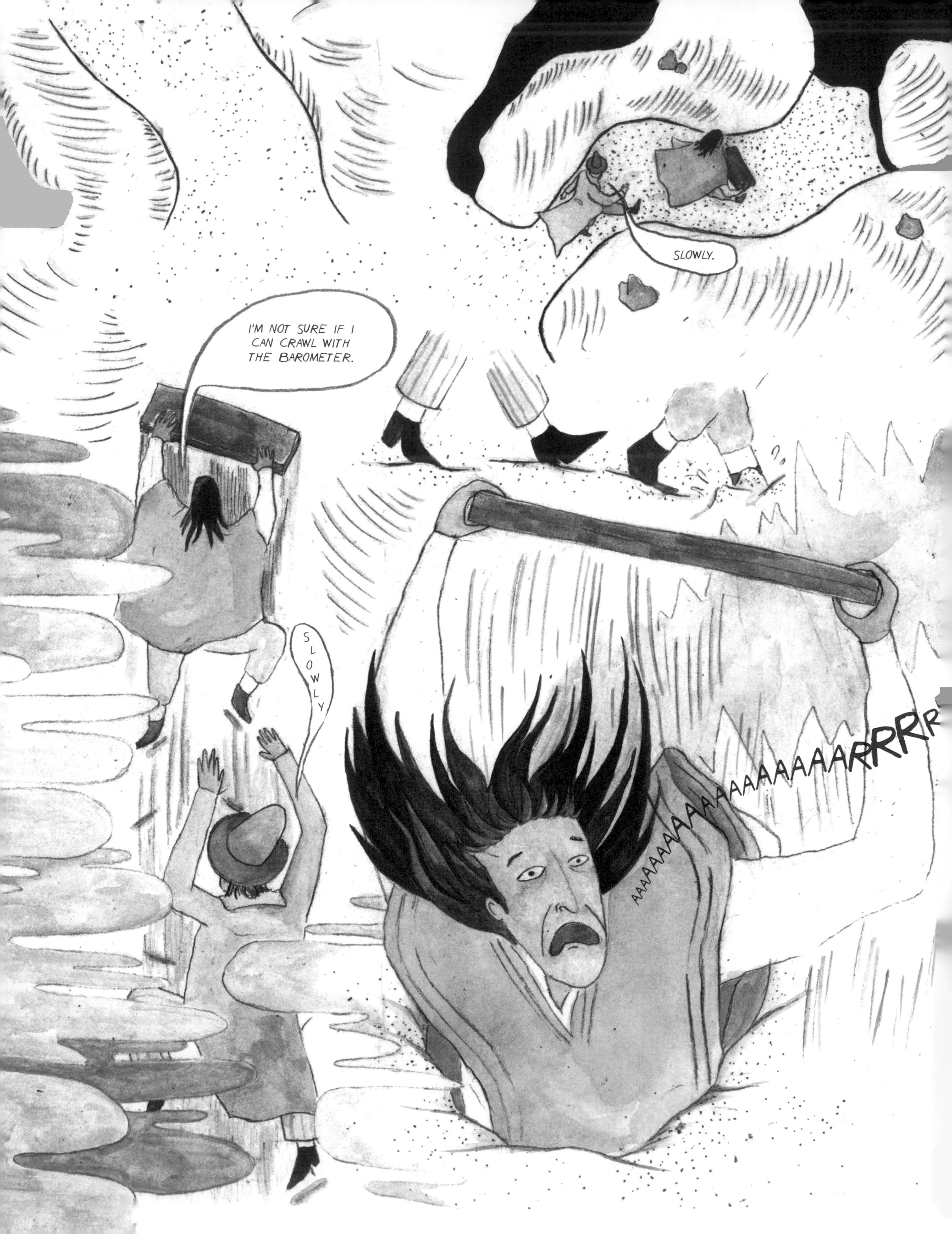
SLOWLY.
I'M NOT SURE IF I CAN CRAWL WITH THE BAROMETER.
SLOWLY
AAAAAAAAAAAAAAAAAAAAAARRRR

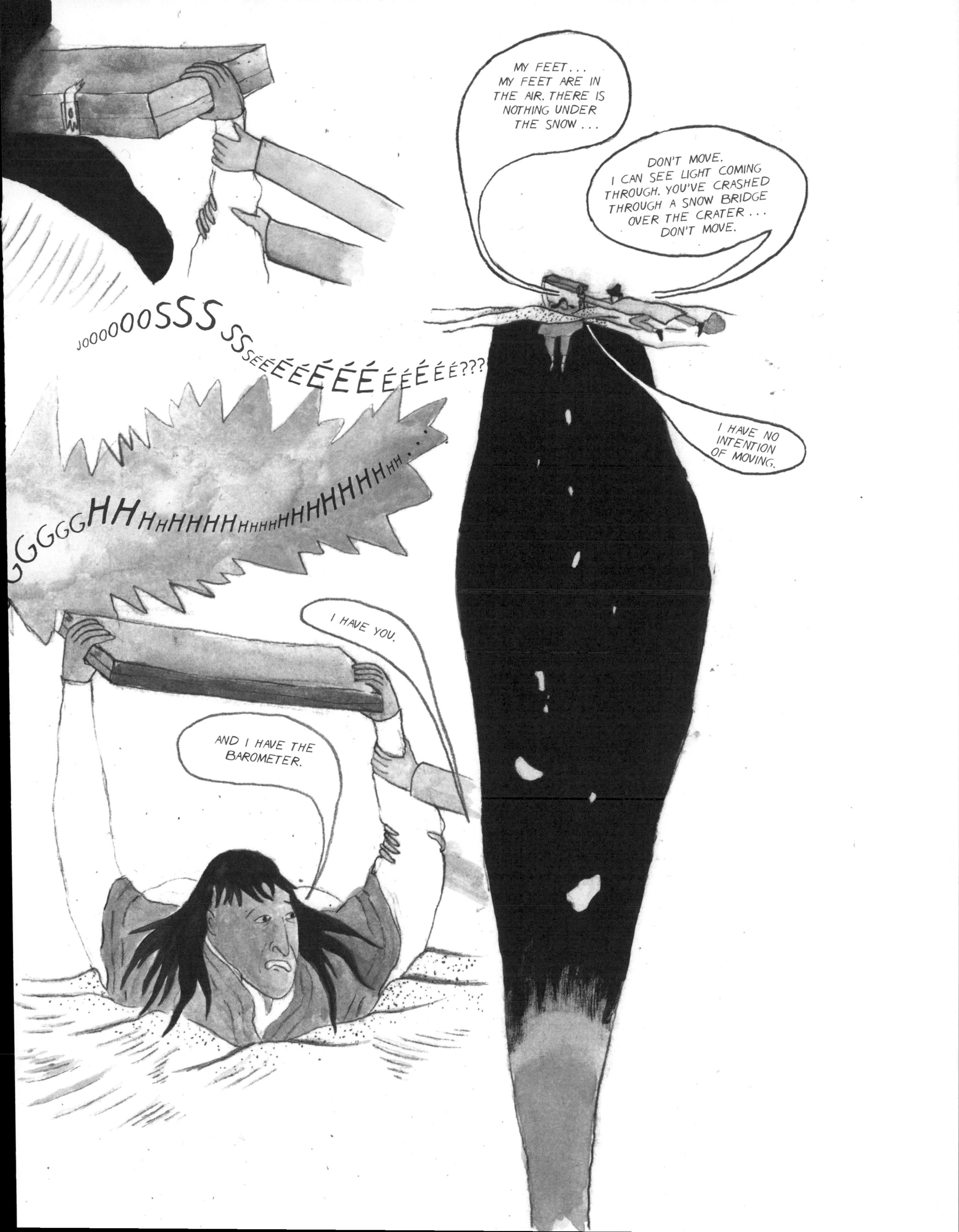
MY FEET... MY FEET ARE IN THE AIR. THERE IS NOTHING UNDER THE SNOW...
DON'T MOVE. I CAN SEE LIGHT COMING THROUGH. YOU'VE CRASHED THROUGH A SNOW BRIDGE OVER THE CRATER... DON'T MOVE.
JOOOOOOOSSS SSSÉÉÉÉÉÉÉÉÉÉÉÉÉ???
I HAVE NO INTENTION OF MOVING.
GGGGGHHHHHHHHHHHHHHHHHHHHHHHH...
I HAVE YOU.
AND I HAVE THE BAROMETER.

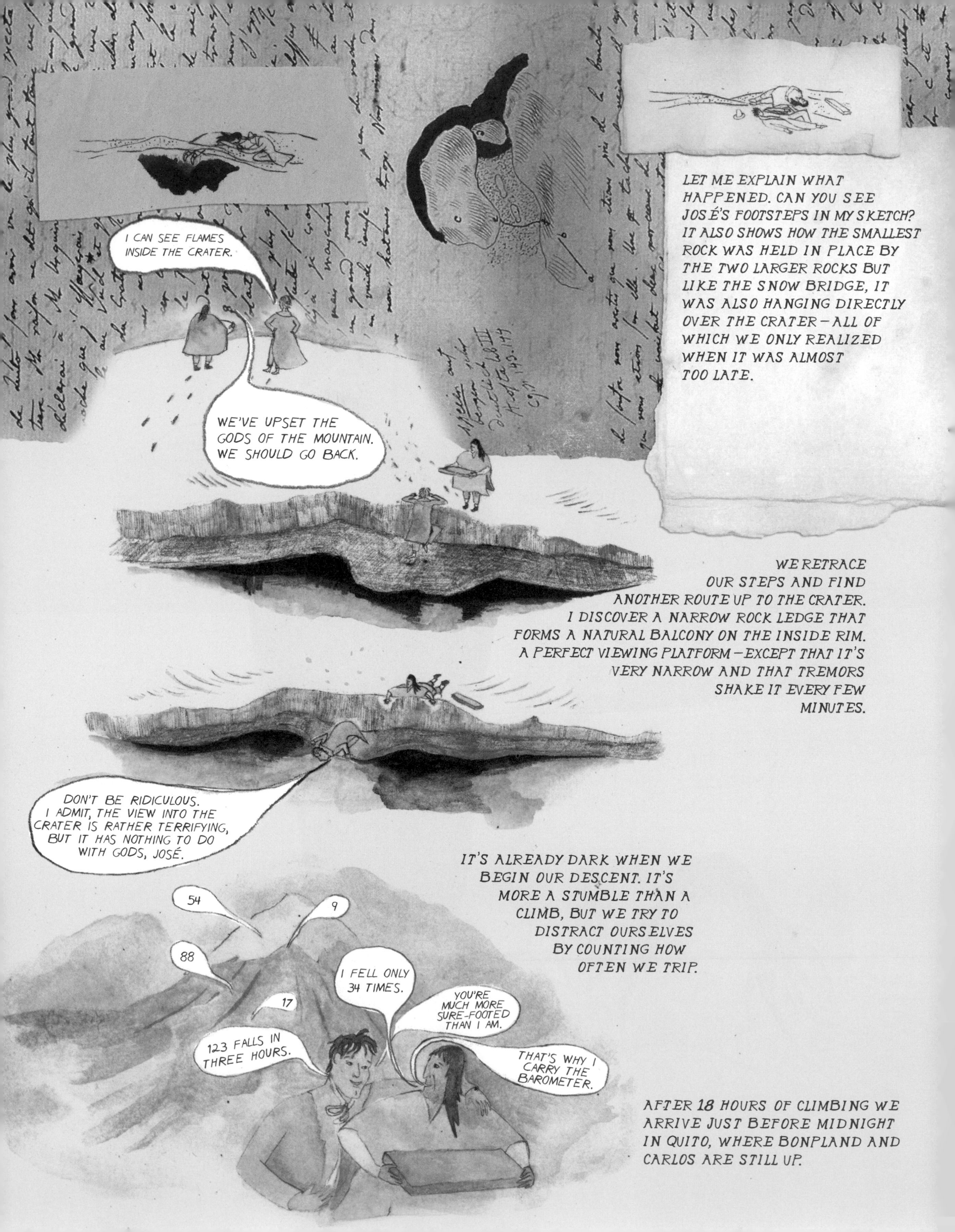
I CAN SEE FLAMES INSIDE THE CRATER.
WE'VE UPSET THE GODS OF THE MOUNTAIN. WE SHOULD GO BACK.
LET ME EXPLAIN WHAT HAPPENED. CAN YOU SEE JOSÉ'S FOOTSTEPS IN MY SKETCH? IT ALSO SHOWS HOW THE SMALLEST ROCK WAS HELD IN PLACE BY THE TWO LARGER ROCKS BUT LIKE THE SNOW BRIDGE, IT WAS ALSO HANGING DIRECTLY OVER THE CRATER—ALL OF WHICH WE ONLY REALIZED WHEN IT WAS ALMOST TOO LATE.
WE RETRACE OUR STEPS AND FIND ANOTHER ROUTE UP TO THE CRATER. I DISCOVER A NARROW ROCK LEDGE THAT FORMS A NATURAL BALCONY ON THE INSIDE RIM. A PERFECT VIEWING PLATFORM—EXCEPT THAT IT'S VERY NARROW AND THAT TREMORS SHAKE IT EVERY FEW MINUTES.
DON'T BE RIDICULOUS. I ADMIT, THE VIEW INTO THE CRATER IS RATHER TERRIFYING, BUT IT HAS NOTHING TO DO WITH GODS, JOSÉ.
IT'S ALREADY DARK WHEN WE BEGIN OUR DESCENT. IT'S MORE A STUMBLE THAN A CLIMB, BUT WE TRY TO DISTRACT OURSELVES BY COUNTING HOW OFTEN WE TRIP.
54
9
88
17
I FELL ONLY 34 TIMES.
YOU'RE MUCH MORE SURE-FOOTED THAN I AM.
123 FALLS IN THREE HOURS.
THAT'S WHY I CARRY THE BAROMETER.
AFTER 18 HOURS OF CLIMBING WE ARRIVE JUST BEFORE MIDNIGHT IN QUITO, WHERE BONPLAND AND CARLOS ARE STILL UP.

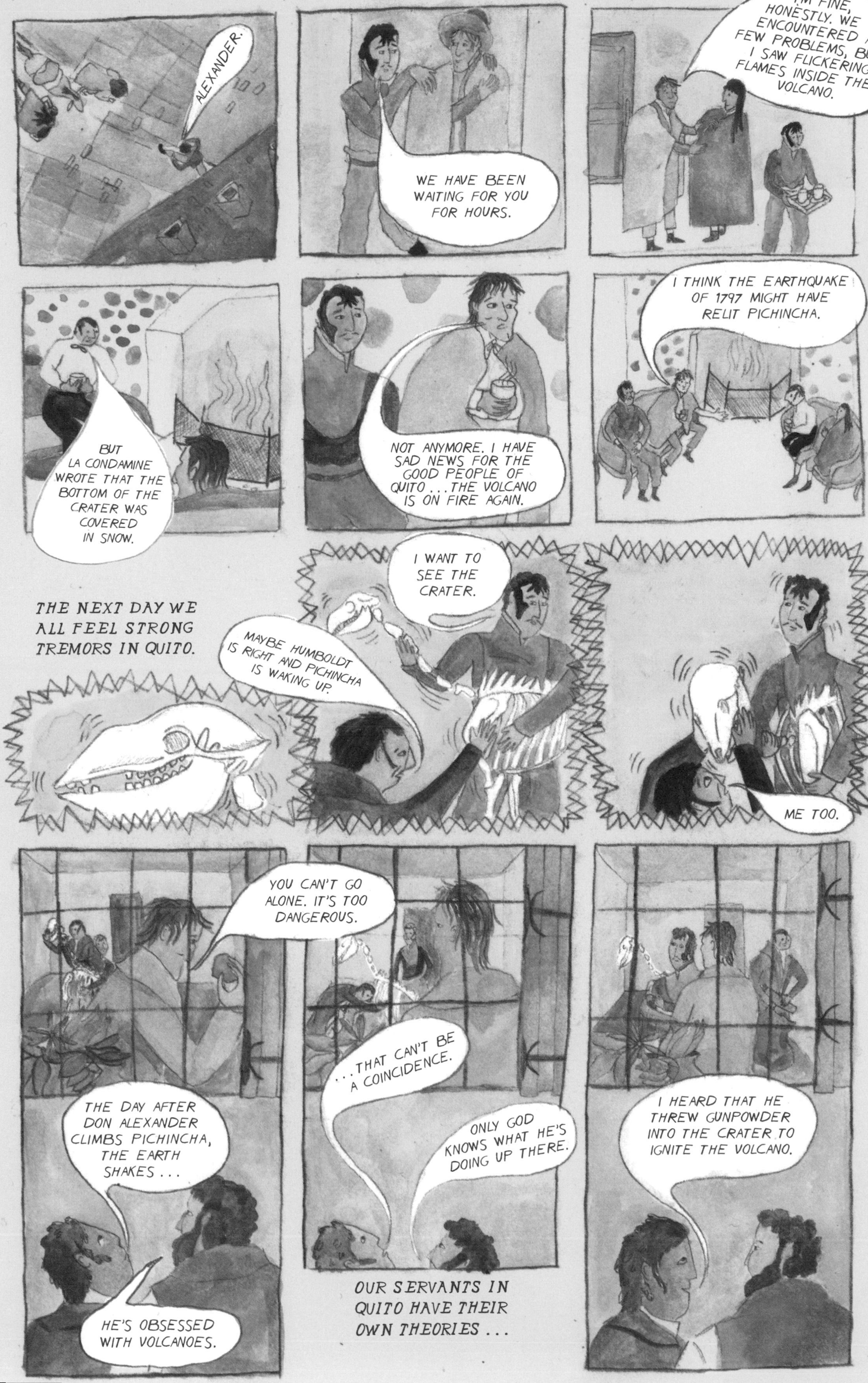
ALEXANDER.
WE HAVE BEEN WAITING FOR YOU FOR HOURS.
I'M FINE, HONESTLY. WE ENCOUNTERED A FEW PROBLEMS, BUT I SAW FLICKERING FLAMES INSIDE THE VOLCANO.
BUT LA CONDAMINE WROTE THAT THE BOTTOM OF THE CRATER WAS COVERED IN SNOW.
NOT ANYMORE. I HAVE SAD NEWS FOR THE GOOD PEOPLE OF QUITO . . . THE VOLCANO IS ON FIRE AGAIN.
I THINK THE EARTHQUAKE OF 1797 MIGHT HAVE RELIT PICHINCHA.
THE NEXT DAY WE ALL FEEL STRONG TREMORS IN QUITO.
I WANT TO SEE THE CRATER.
MAYBE HUMBOLDT IS RIGHT AND PICHINCHA IS WAKING UP.
ME TOO.
YOU CAN'T GO ALONE. IT'S TOO DANGEROUS.
THE DAY AFTER DON ALEXANDER CLIMBS PICHINCHA, THE EARTH SHAKES . . .
HE'S OBSESSED WITH VOLCANOES.
. . . THAT CAN'T BE A COINCIDENCE.
ONLY GOD KNOWS WHAT HE'S DOING UP THERE.
OUR SERVANTS IN QUITO HAVE THEIR OWN THEORIES . . .
I HEARD THAT HE THREW GUNPOWDER INTO THE CRATER TO IGNITE THE VOLCANO.

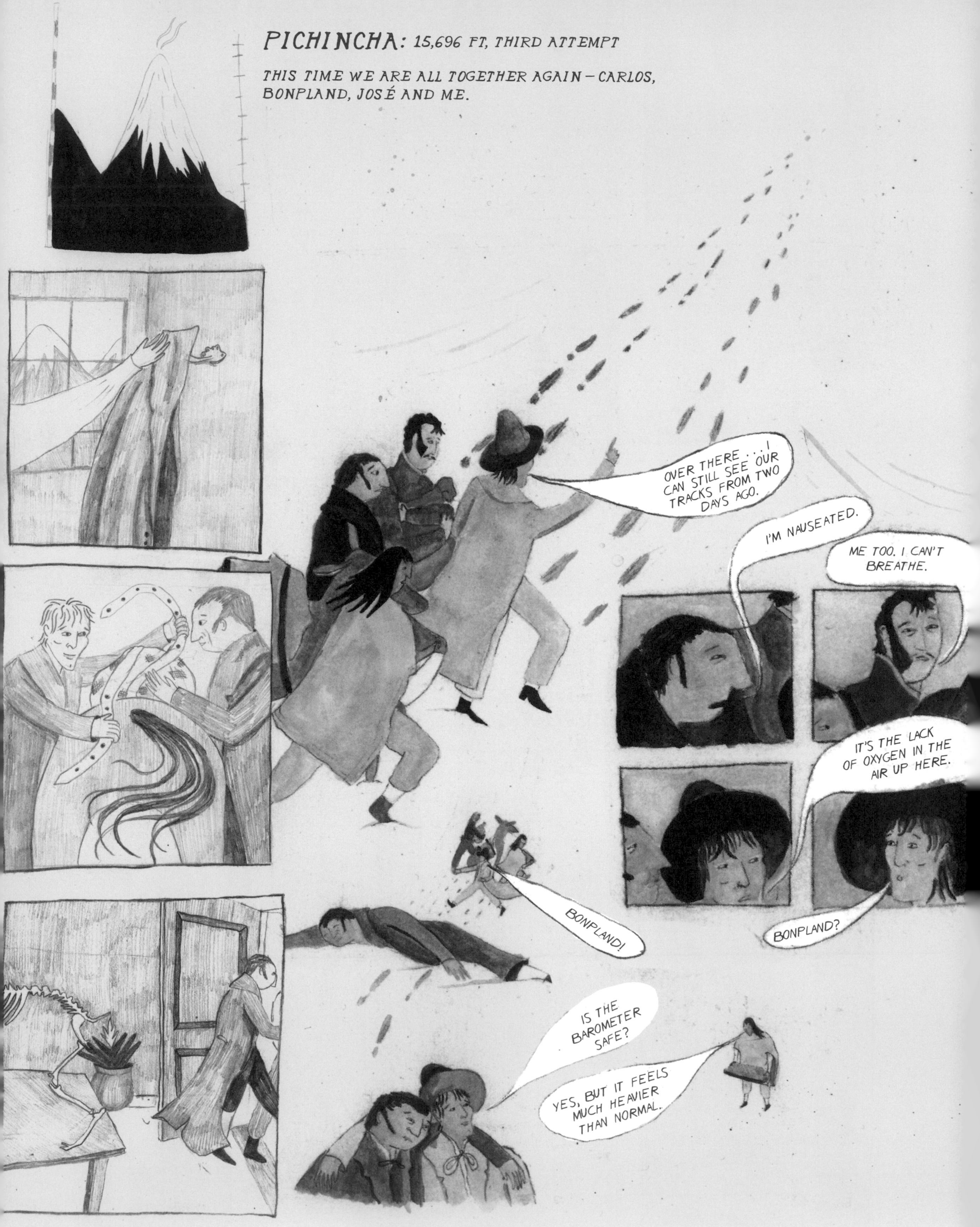
PICHINCHA: 15,696 FT, THIRD ATTEMPT
THIS TIME WE ARE ALL TOGETHER AGAIN – CARLOS, BONPLAND, JOSÉ AND ME.
OVER THERE . . . I CAN STILL SEE OUR TRACKS FROM TWO DAYS AGO.
I'M NAUSEATED.
ME TOO. I CAN'T BREATHE.
IT'S THE LACK OF OXYGEN IN THE AIR UP HERE.
BONPLAND!
BONPLAND?
IS THE BAROMETER SAFE?
YES, BUT IT FEELS MUCH HEAVIER THAN NORMAL.

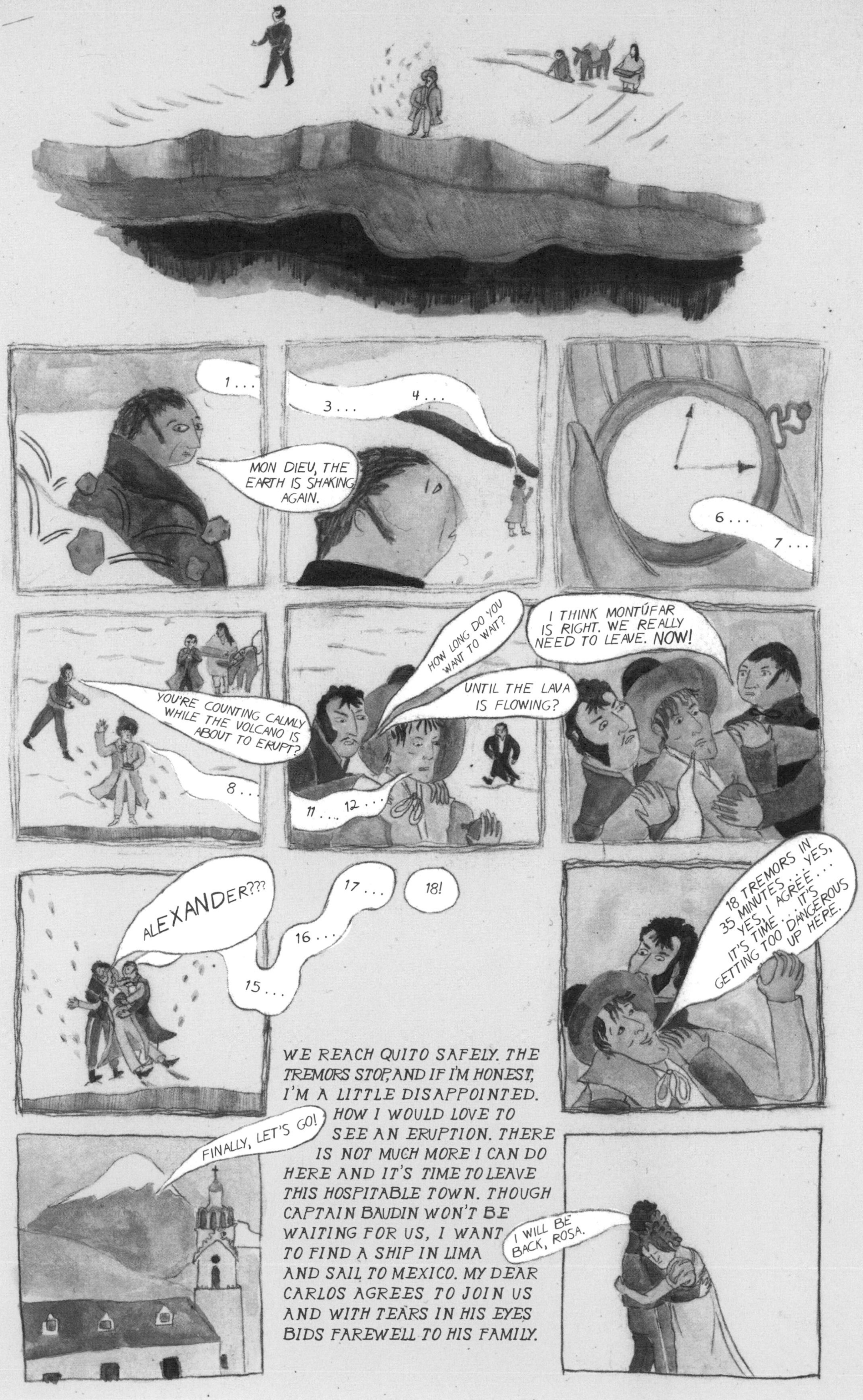
1 . . .
3 . . .
4 . . .
MON DIEU, THE EARTH IS SHAKING AGAIN.
6 . . .
7 . . .
YOU'RE COUNTING CALMLY WHILE THE VOLCANO IS ABOUT TO ERUPT?
8 . . .
HOW LONG DO YOU WANT TO WAIT?
UNTIL THE LAVA IS FLOWING?
11 . . . 12 . . .
I THINK MONTÚFAR IS RIGHT. WE REALLY NEED TO LEAVE. NOW!
ALEXANDER???
15 . . .
16 . . .
17 . . .
18!
18 TREMORS IN 35 MINUTES . . . YES, YES, I AGREE . . . IT'S TIME . . . IT'S GETTING TOO DANGEROUS UP HERE.
WE REACH QUITO SAFELY. THE TREMORS STOP, AND IF I'M HONEST, I'M A LITTLE DISAPPOINTED. HOW I WOULD LOVE TO SEE AN ERUPTION. THERE IS NOT MUCH MORE I CAN DO HERE AND IT'S TIME TO LEAVE THIS HOSPITABLE TOWN. THOUGH CAPTAIN BAUDIN WON'T BE WAITING FOR US, I WANT TO FIND A SHIP IN LIMA AND SAIL TO MEXICO. MY DEAR CARLOS AGREES TO JOIN US AND WITH TEARS IN HIS EYES BIDS FAREWELL TO HIS FAMILY.
FINALLY, LET'S GO!
I WILL BE BACK, ROSA.

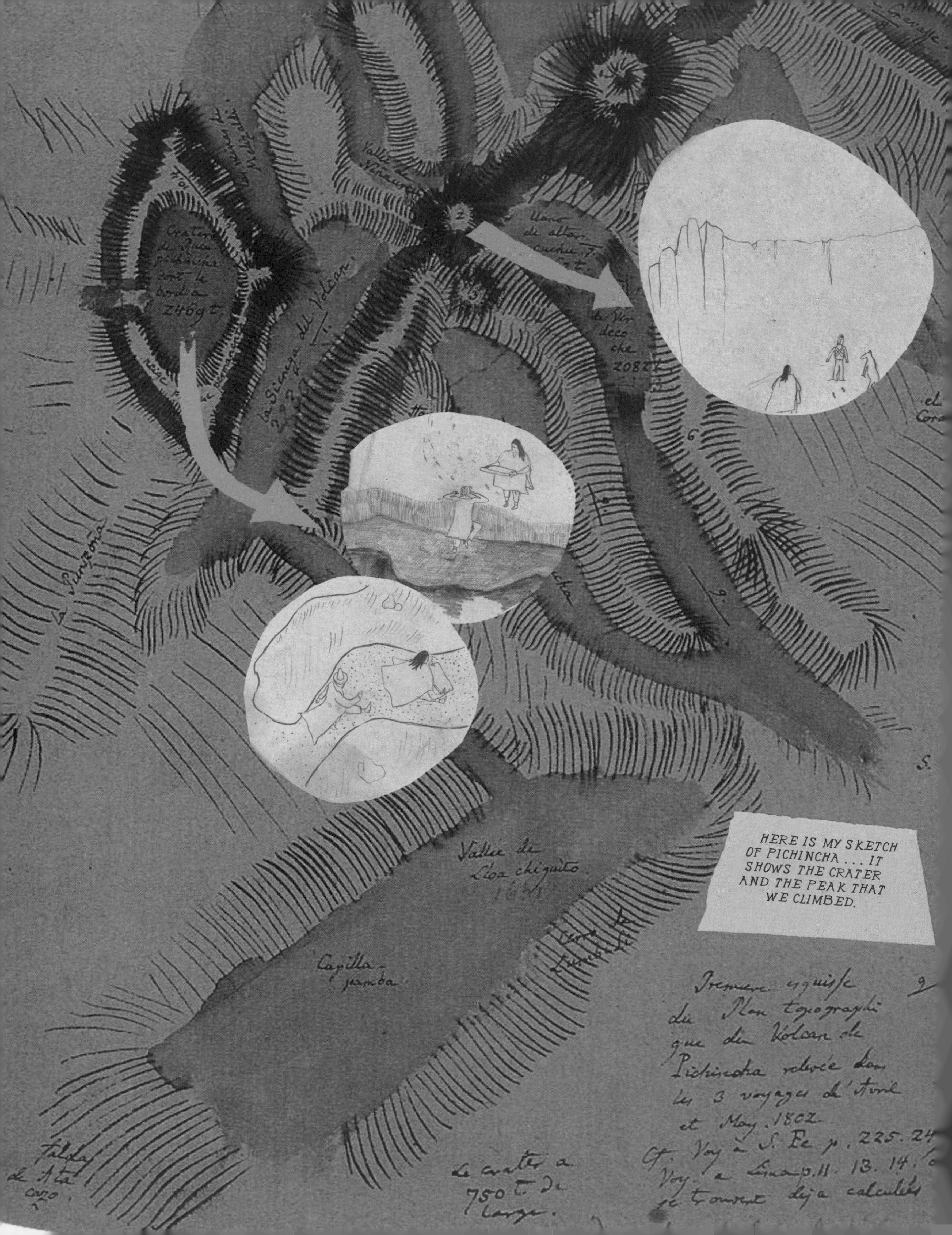
HERE IS MY SKETCH OF PICHINCHA . . . IT SHOWS THE CRATER AND THE PEAK THAT WE CLIMBED.
Vallée de Lloa chiquito
Capilla-pamba
la Sienega del Volcan
Falda de Atacazo
Le cratère a 750 t. de large.

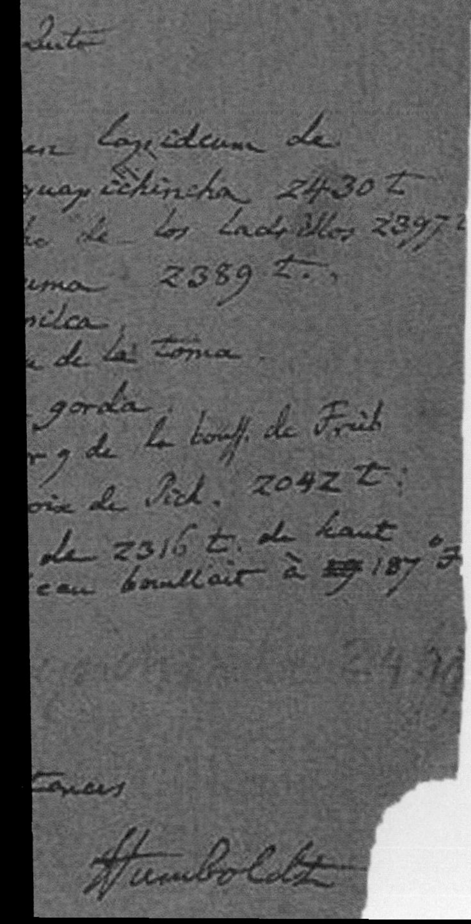

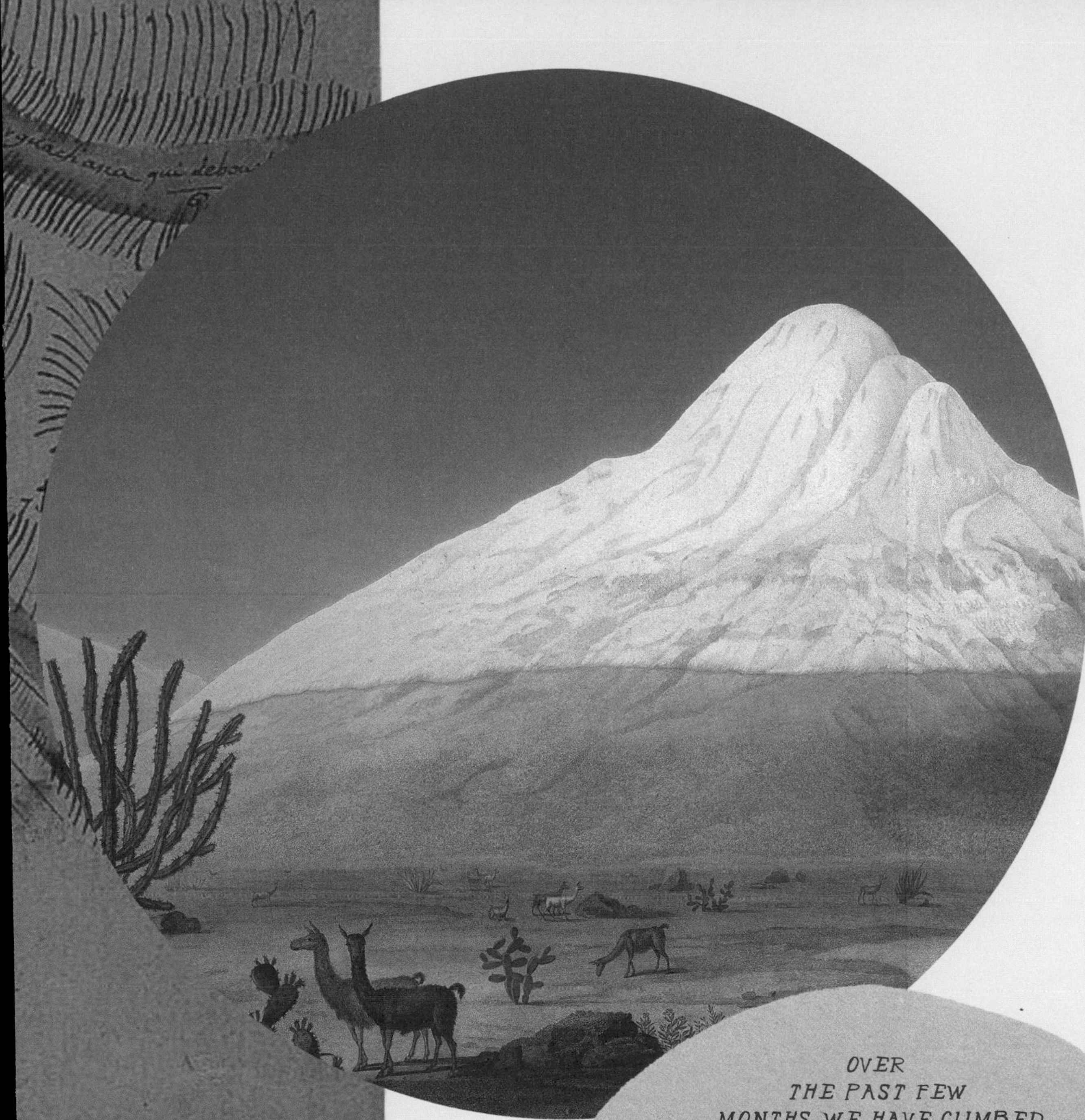

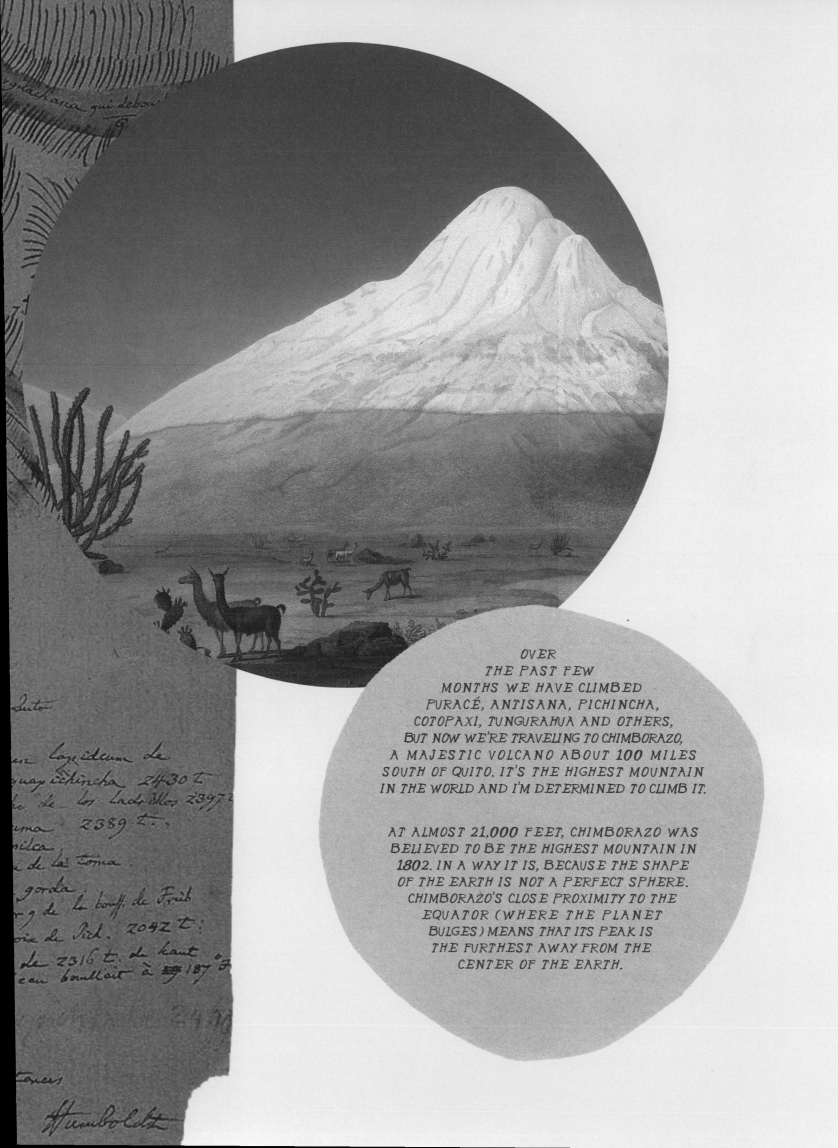

OVER THE PAST FEW MONTHS WE HAVE CLIMBED PURACÉ, ANTISANA, PICHINCHA, COTOPAXI, TUNGURAHUA AND OTHERS, BUT NOW WE'RE TRAVELING TO CHIMBORAZO, A MAJESTIC VOLCANO ABOUT 100 MILES SOUTH OF QUITO. IT'S THE HIGHEST MOUNTAIN IN THE WORLD AND I'M DETERMINED TO CLIMB IT.

AT ALMOST 21,000 FEET, CHIMBORAZO WAS BELIEVED TO BE THE HIGHEST MOUNTAIN IN 1802. IN A WAY IT IS, BECAUSE THE SHAPE OF THE EARTH IS NOT A PERFECT SPHERE. CHIMBORAZO'S CLOSE PROXIMITY TO THE EQUATOR (WHERE THE PLANET BULGES) MEANS THAT ITS PEAK IS THE FURTHEST AWAY FROM THE CENTER OF THE EARTH.

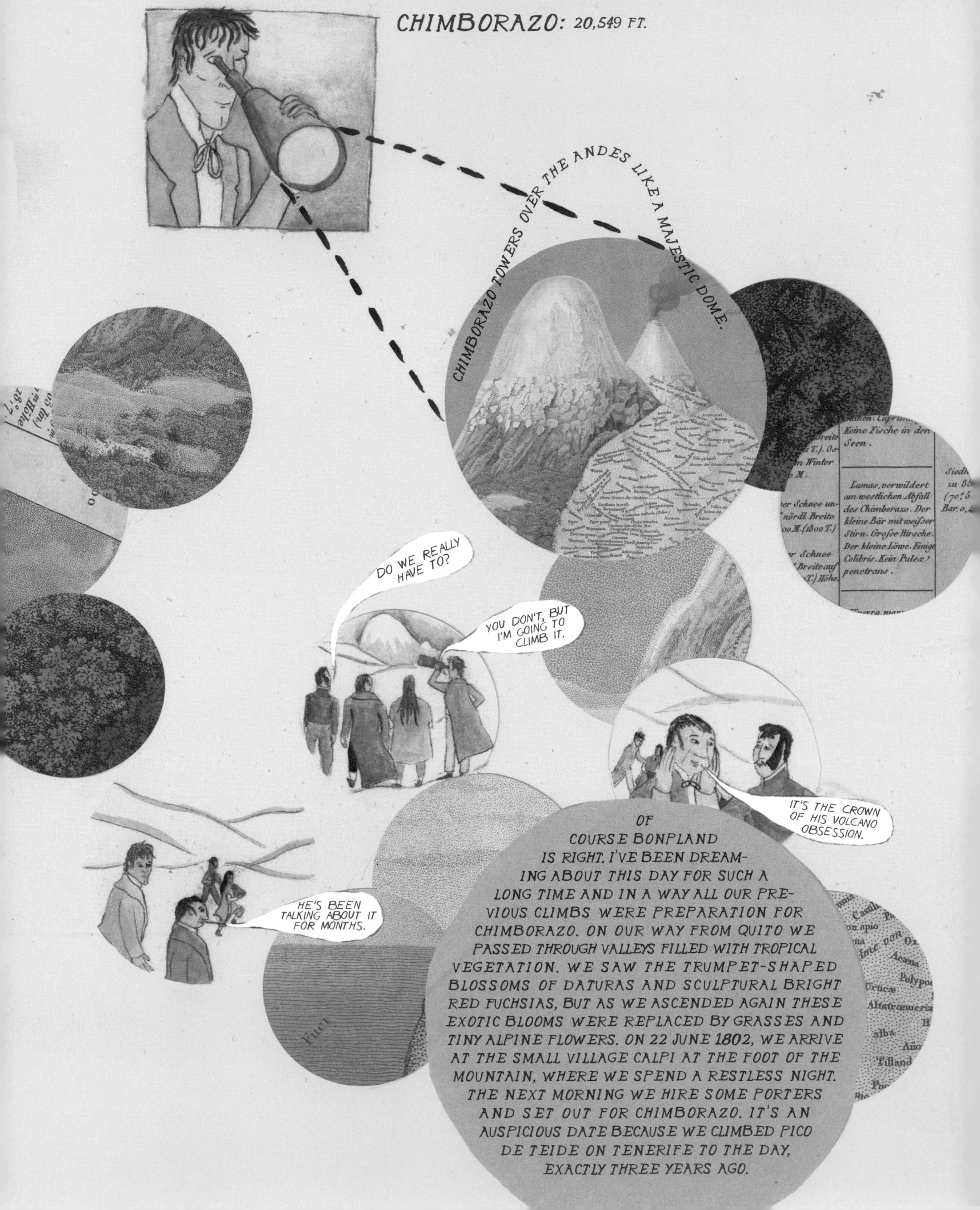
CHIMBORAZO: 20,549 FT.
CHIMBORAZO TOWERS OVER THE ANDES LIKE A MAJESTIC DOME.
Lamas, verwildert am westlichen Abfall des Chimborazo. Der kleine Bär mit weisser Stirn. Grosse Hirsche. Der kleine Löwe. Einige Colibris. Kein Pulex penetrans.
DO WE REALLY HAVE TO?
YOU DON'T, BUT I'M GOING TO CLIMB IT.
IT'S THE CROWN OF HIS VOLCANO OBSESSION.
HE'S BEEN TALKING ABOUT IT FOR MONTHS.
OF COURSE BONPLAND IS RIGHT. I'VE BEEN DREAMING ABOUT THIS DAY FOR SUCH A LONG TIME AND IN A WAY ALL OUR PREVIOUS CLIMBS WERE PREPARATION FOR CHIMBORAZO. ON OUR WAY FROM QUITO WE PASSED THROUGH VALLEYS FILLED WITH TROPICAL VEGETATION. WE SAW THE TRUMPET-SHAPED BLOSSOMS OF DATURAS AND SCULPTURAL BRIGHT RED FUCHSIAS, BUT AS WE ASCENDED AGAIN THESE EXOTIC BLOOMS WERE REPLACED BY GRASSES AND TINY ALPINE FLOWERS. ON 22 JUNE 1802, WE ARRIVE AT THE SMALL VILLAGE CALPI AT THE FOOT OF THE MOUNTAIN, WHERE WE SPEND A RESTLESS NIGHT. THE NEXT MORNING WE HIRE SOME PORTERS AND SET OUT FOR CHIMBORAZO. IT'S AN AUSPICIOUS DATE BECAUSE WE CLIMBED PICO DE TEIDE ON TENERIFE TO THE DAY, EXACTLY THREE YEARS AGO.

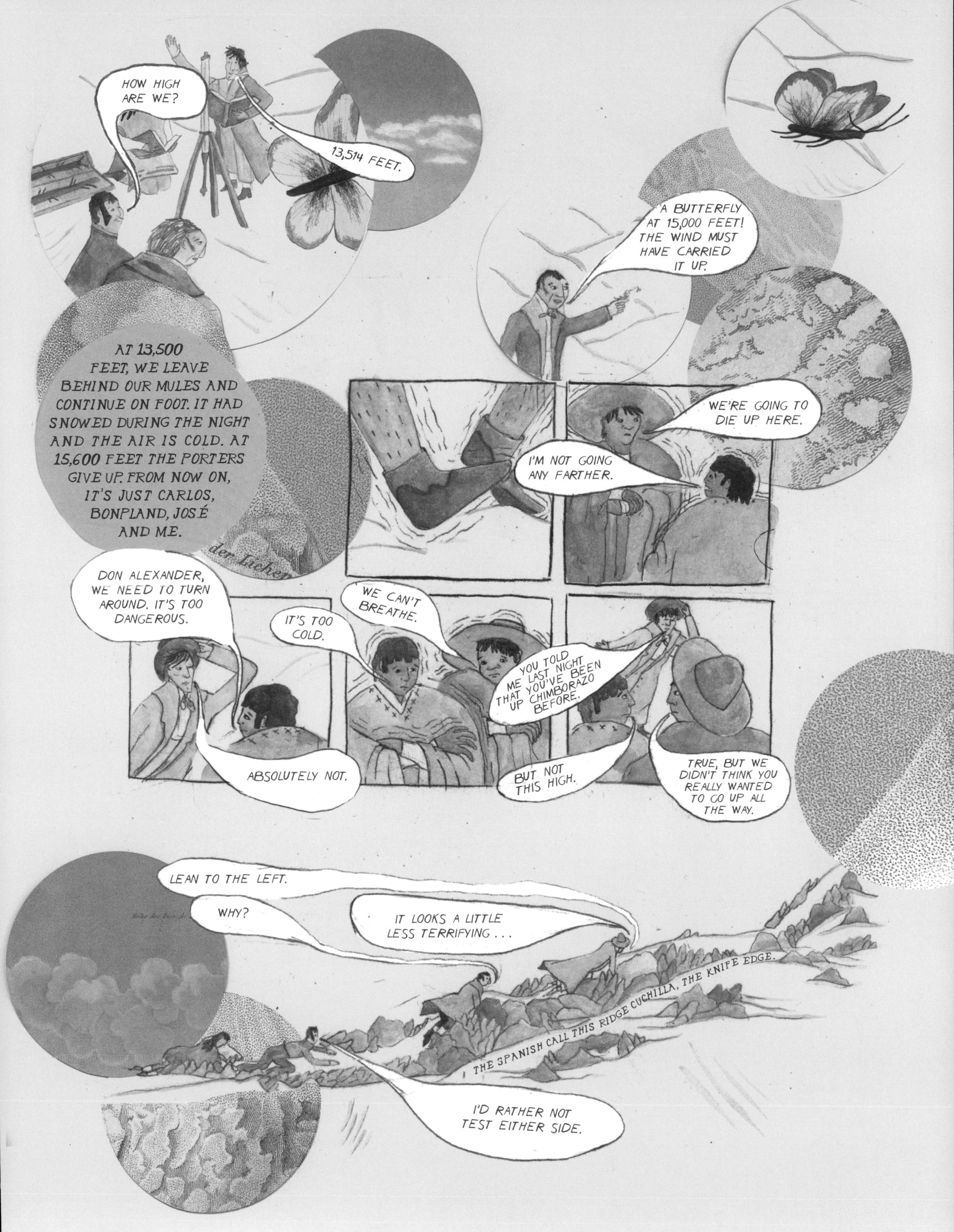

HOW HIGH ARE WE?
13,514 FEET.
A BUTTERFLY AT 15,000 FEET! THE WIND MUST HAVE CARRIED IT UP.
AT 13,500 FEET, WE LEAVE BEHIND OUR MULES AND CONTINUE ON FOOT. IT HAD SNOWED DURING THE NIGHT AND THE AIR IS COLD. AT 15,600 FEET THE PORTERS GIVE UP. FROM NOW ON, IT'S JUST CARLOS, BONPLAND, JOSÉ AND ME.
WE'RE GOING TO DIE UP HERE.
I'M NOT GOING ANY FARTHER.
DON ALEXANDER, WE NEED TO TURN AROUND. IT'S TOO DANGEROUS.
ABSOLUTELY NOT.
IT'S TOO COLD.
WE CAN'T BREATHE.
YOU TOLD ME LAST NIGHT THAT YOU'VE BEEN UP CHIMBORAZO BEFORE.
BUT NOT THIS HIGH.
TRUE, BUT WE DIDN'T THINK YOU REALLY WANTED TO GO UP ALL THE WAY.
LEAN TO THE LEFT.
WHY?
IT LOOKS A LITTLE LESS TERRIFYING . . .
THE SPANISH CALL THIS RIDGE CUCHILLA, THE KNIFE EDGE.
I'D RATHER NOT TEST EITHER SIDE.

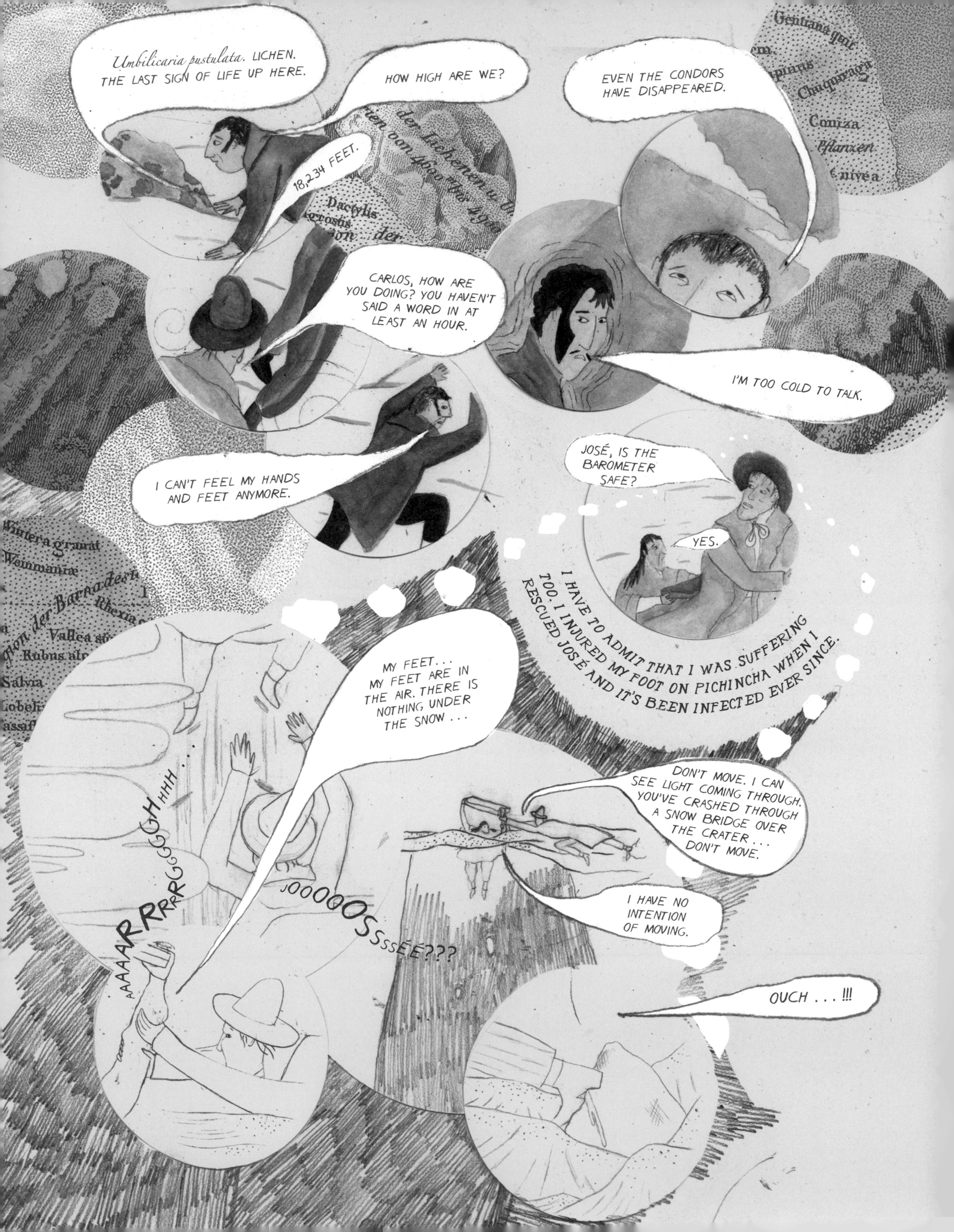
Umbilicaria pustulata. LICHEN. THE LAST SIGN OF LIFE UP HERE.
HOW HIGH ARE WE?
18,234 FEET.
EVEN THE CONDORS HAVE DISAPPEARED.
CARLOS, HOW ARE YOU DOING? YOU HAVEN'T SAID A WORD IN AT LEAST AN HOUR.
I'M TOO COLD TO TALK.
I CAN'T FEEL MY HANDS AND FEET ANYMORE.
JOSÉ, IS THE BAROMETER SAFE?
YES.
I HAVE TO ADMIT THAT I WAS SUFFERING TOO. I INJURED MY FOOT ON PICHINCHA WHEN I RESCUED JOSÉ AND IT'S BEEN INFECTED EVER SINCE.
MY FEET... MY FEET ARE IN THE AIR. THERE IS NOTHING UNDER THE SNOW...
AAAAARRRRRGGGGGHHHH...
JOOOOOSSSSÉÉ???
DON'T MOVE. I CAN SEE LIGHT COMING THROUGH. YOU'VE CRASHED THROUGH A SNOW BRIDGE OVER THE CRATER... DON'T MOVE.
I HAVE NO INTENTION OF MOVING.
OUCH...!!!

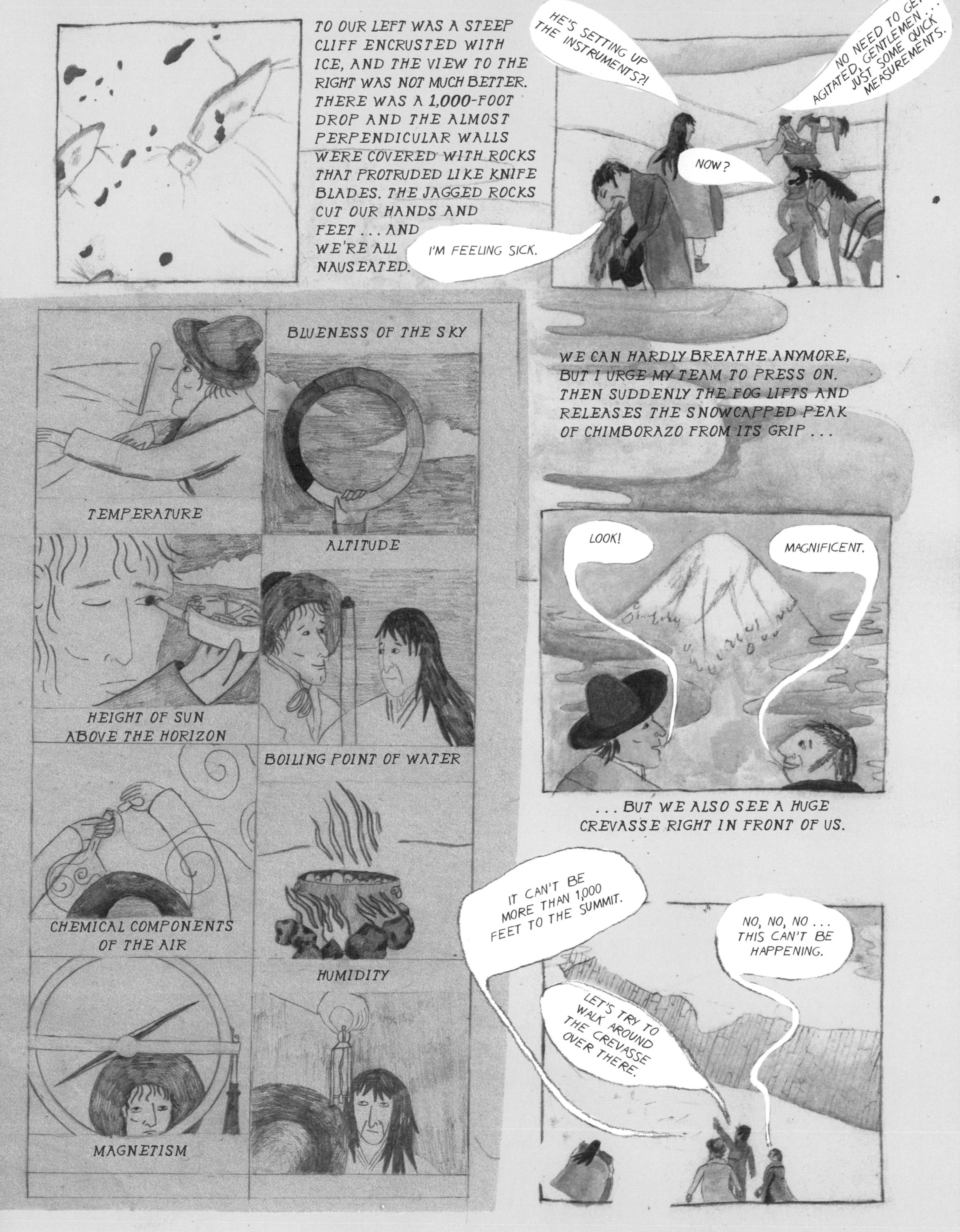
TO OUR LEFT WAS A STEEP CLIFF ENCRUSTED WITH ICE, AND THE VIEW TO THE RIGHT WAS NOT MUCH BETTER. THERE WAS A 1,000-FOOT DROP AND THE ALMOST PERPENDICULAR WALLS WERE COVERED WITH ROCKS THAT PROTRUDED LIKE KNIFE BLADES. THE JAGGED ROCKS CUT OUR HANDS AND FEET . . . AND WE'RE ALL NAUSEATED.
HE'S SETTING UP THE INSTRUMENTS?!
NO NEED TO GET AGITATED, GENTLEMEN . . . JUST SOME QUICK MEASUREMENTS.
NOW?
I'M FEELING SICK.
TEMPERATURE
BLUENESS OF THE SKY
ALTITUDE
HEIGHT OF SUN ABOVE THE HORIZON
BOILING POINT OF WATER
CHEMICAL COMPONENTS OF THE AIR
HUMIDITY
MAGNETISM
WE CAN HARDLY BREATHE ANYMORE, BUT I URGE MY TEAM TO PRESS ON. THEN SUDDENLY THE FOG LIFTS AND RELEASES THE SNOWCAPPED PEAK OF CHIMBORAZO FROM ITS GRIP . . .
LOOK!
MAGNIFICENT.
. . . BUT WE ALSO SEE A HUGE CREVASSE RIGHT IN FRONT OF US.
IT CAN'T BE MORE THAN 1,000 FEET TO THE SUMMIT.
NO, NO, NO . . . THIS CAN'T BE HAPPENING.
LET'S TRY TO WALK AROUND THE CREVASSE OVER THERE.

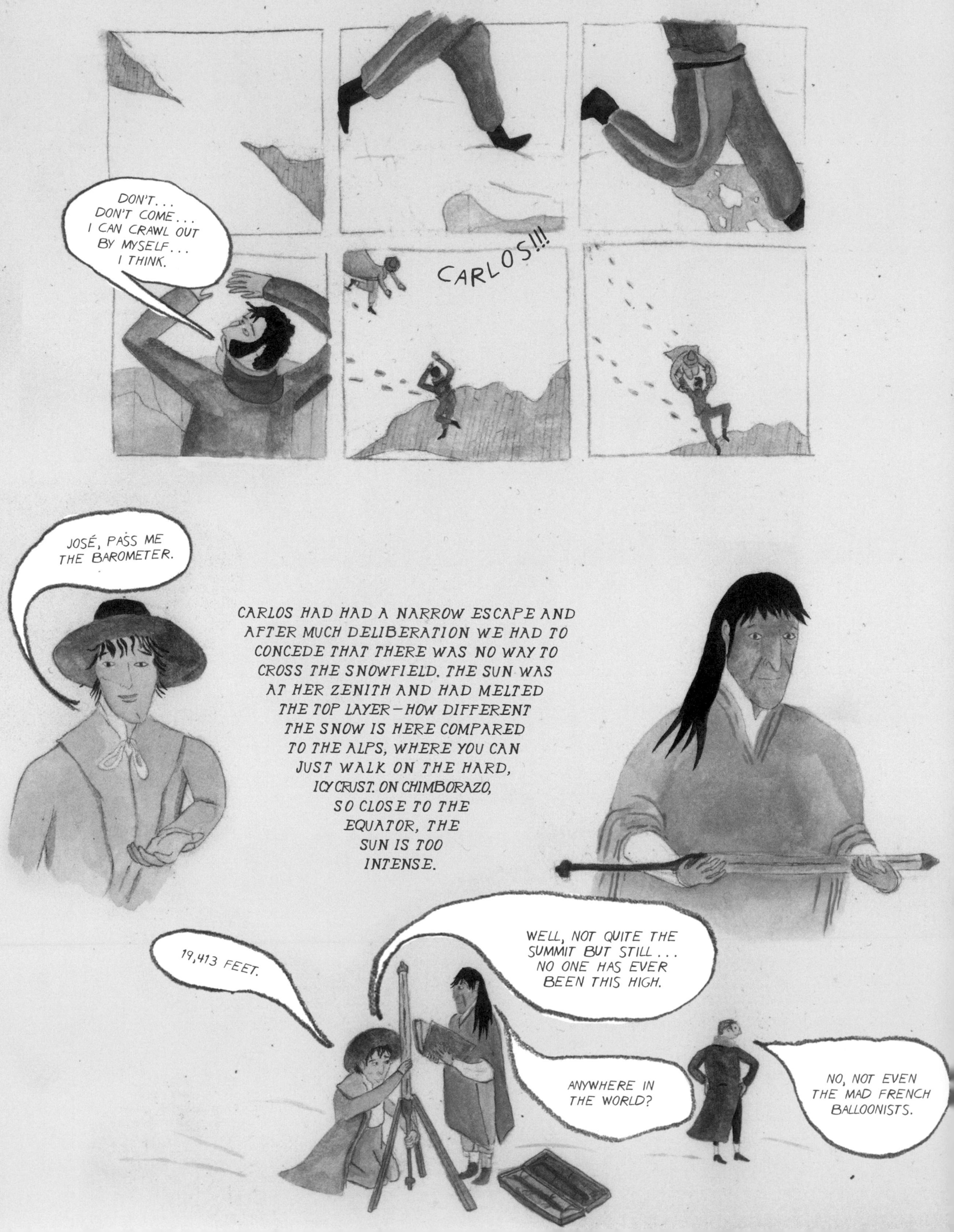
DON'T... DON'T COME... I CAN CRAWL OUT BY MYSELF... I THINK.
CARLOS!!!
JOSÉ, PASS ME THE BAROMETER.
CARLOS HAD HAD A NARROW ESCAPE AND AFTER MUCH DELIBERATION WE HAD TO CONCEDE THAT THERE WAS NO WAY TO CROSS THE SNOWFIELD. THE SUN WAS AT HER ZENITH AND HAD MELTED THE TOP LAYER—HOW DIFFERENT THE SNOW IS HERE COMPARED TO THE ALPS, WHERE YOU CAN JUST WALK ON THE HARD, ICY CRUST. ON CHIMBORAZO, SO CLOSE TO THE EQUATOR, THE SUN IS TOO INTENSE.
19,413 FEET.
WELL, NOT QUITE THE SUMMIT BUT STILL... NO ONE HAS EVER BEEN THIS HIGH.
ANYWHERE IN THE WORLD?
NO, NOT EVEN THE MAD FRENCH BALLOONISTS.

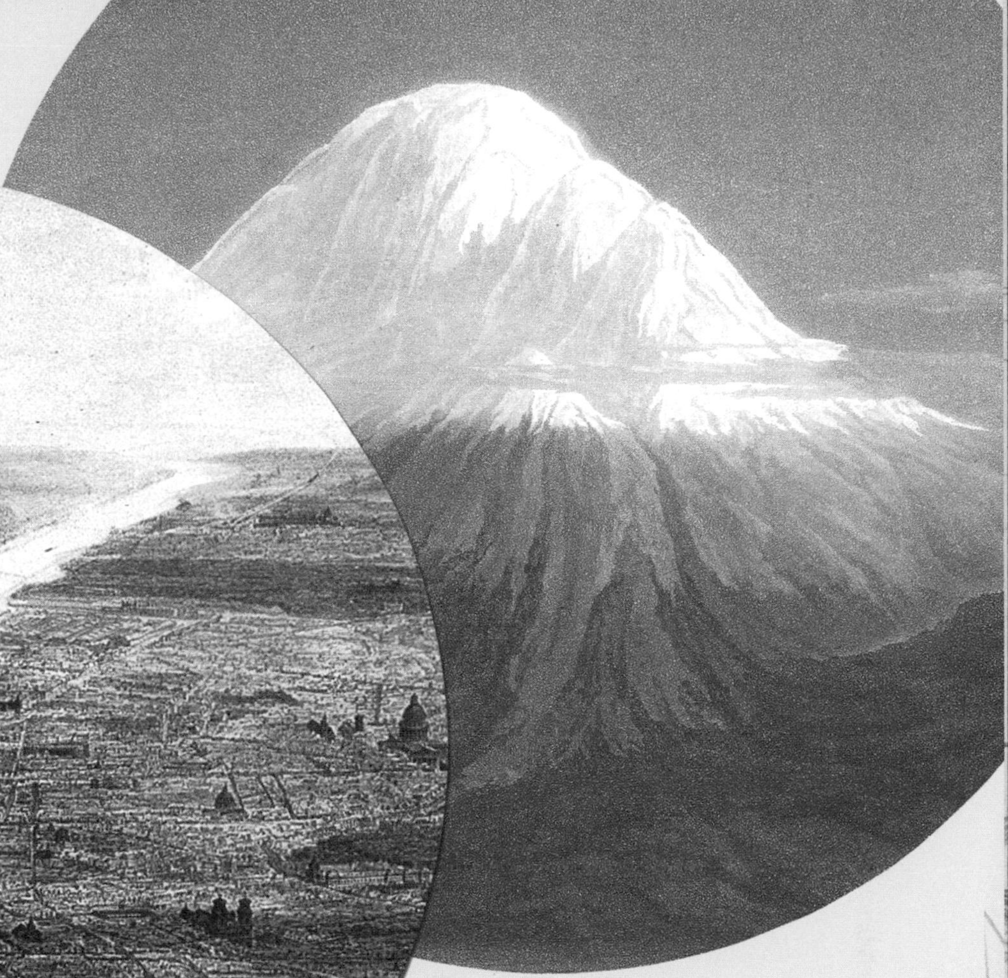

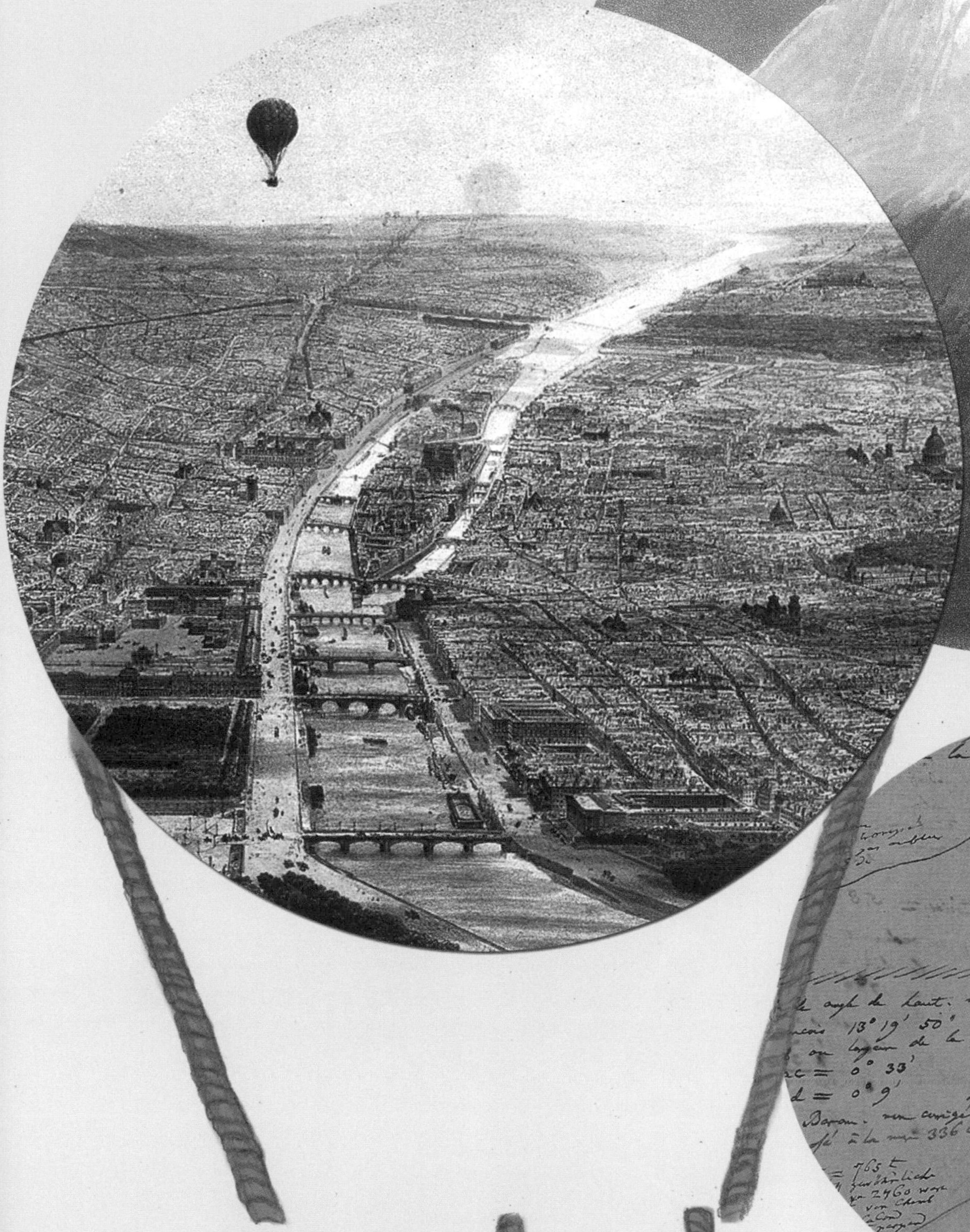

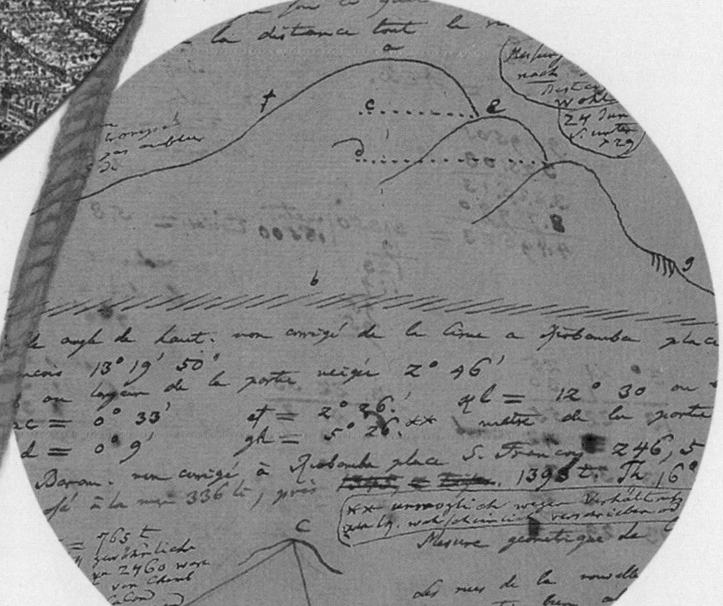

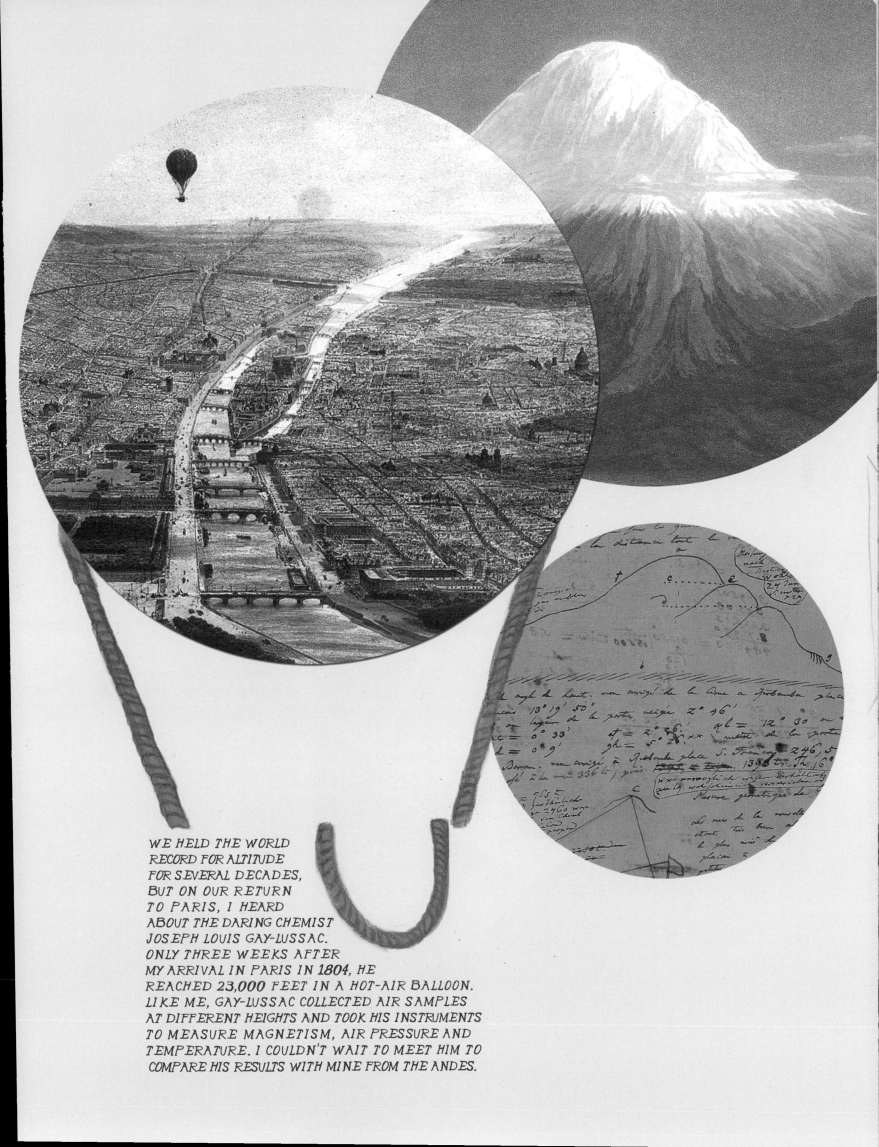

WE HELD THE WORLD RECORD FOR ALTITUDE FOR SEVERAL DECADES, BUT ON OUR RETURN TO PARIS, I HEARD ABOUT THE DARING CHEMIST JOSEPH LOUIS GAY-LUSSAC. ONLY THREE WEEKS AFTER MY ARRIVAL IN PARIS IN 1804, HE REACHED 23,000 FEET IN A HOT-AIR BALLOON. LIKE ME, GAY-LUSSAC COLLECTED AIR SAMPLES AT DIFFERENT HEIGHTS AND TOOK HIS INSTRUMENTS TO MEASURE MAGNETISM, AIR PRESSURE AND TEMPERATURE. I COULDN'T WAIT TO MEET HIM TO COMPARE HIS RESULTS WITH MINE FROM THE ANDES.

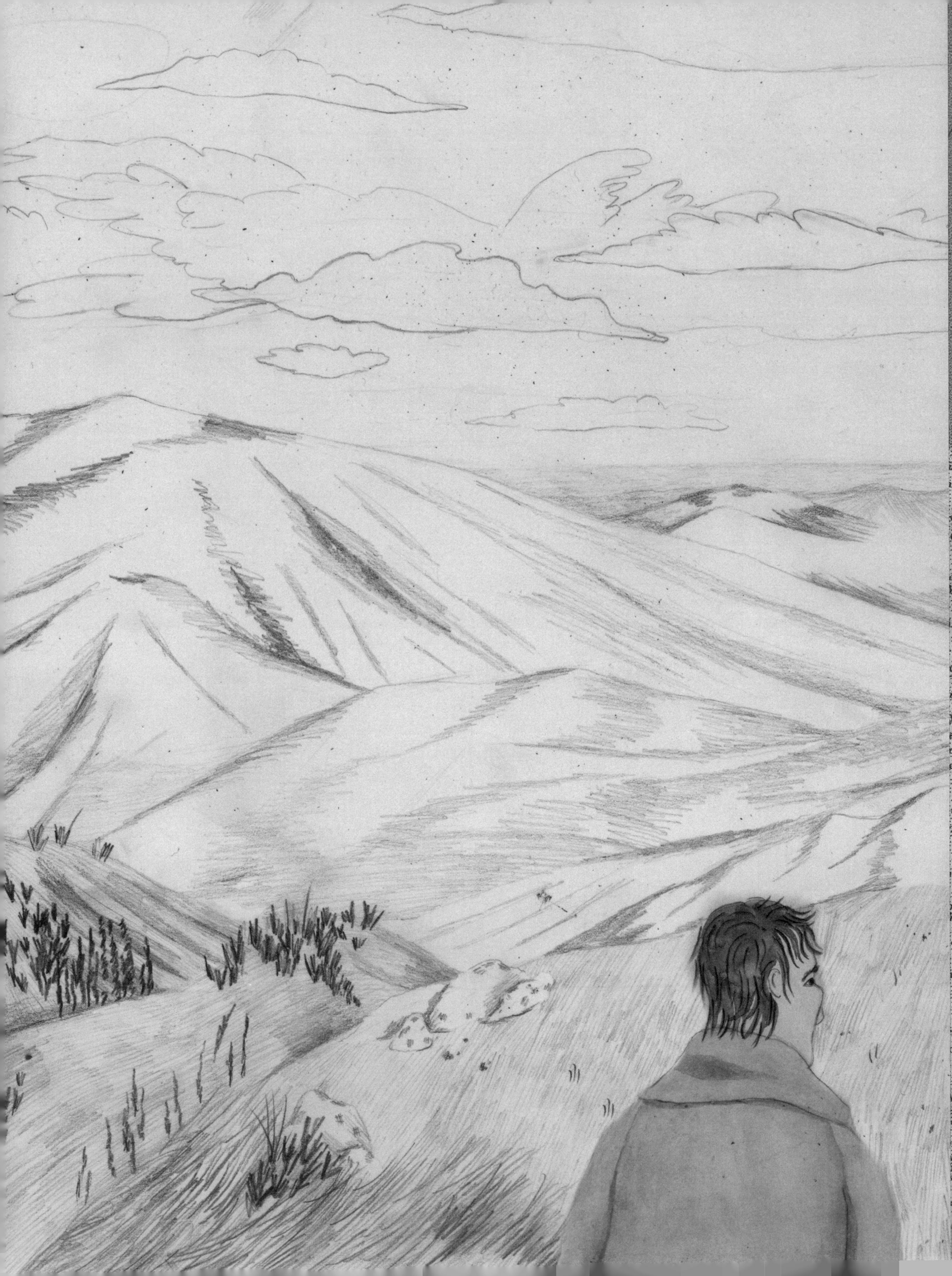

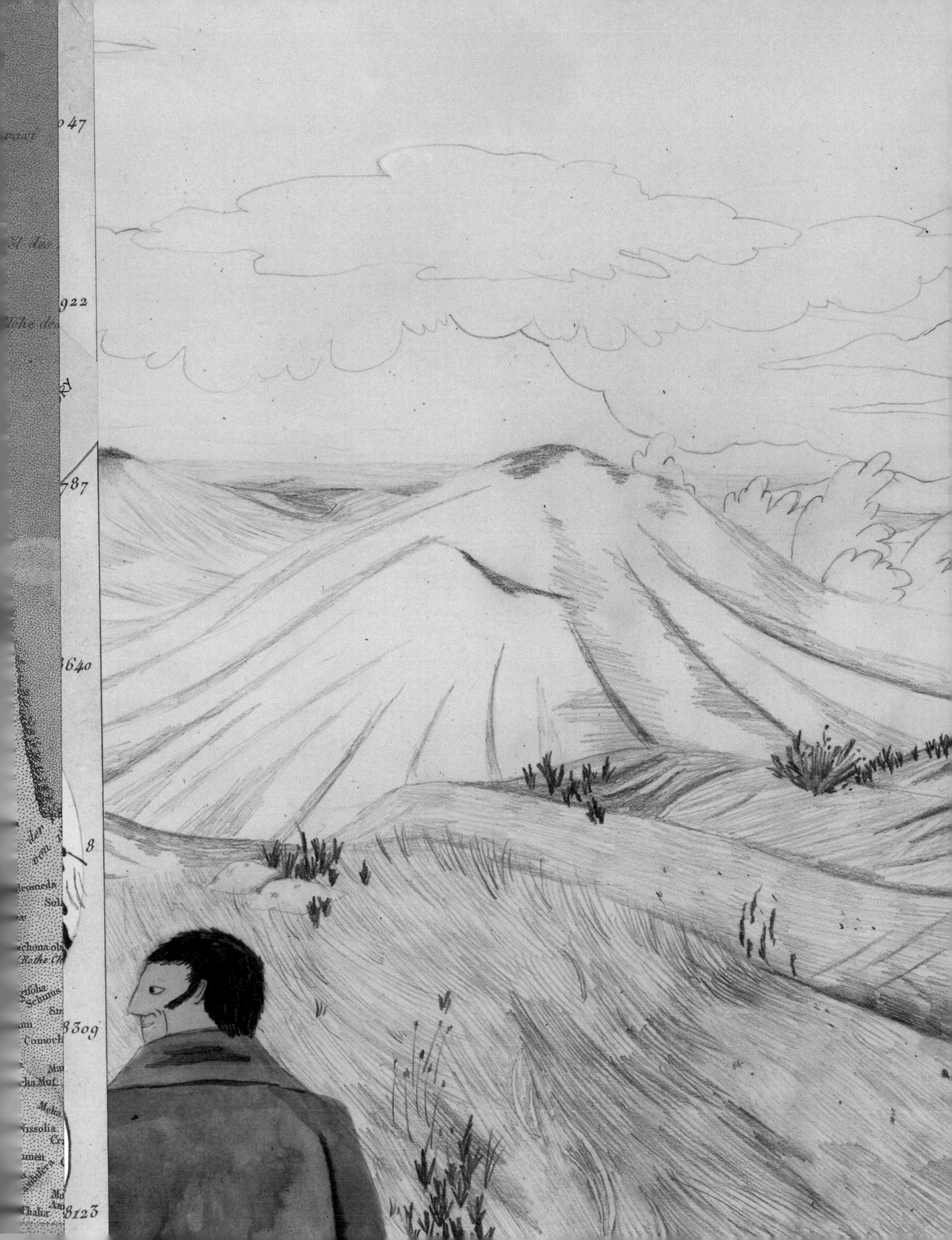

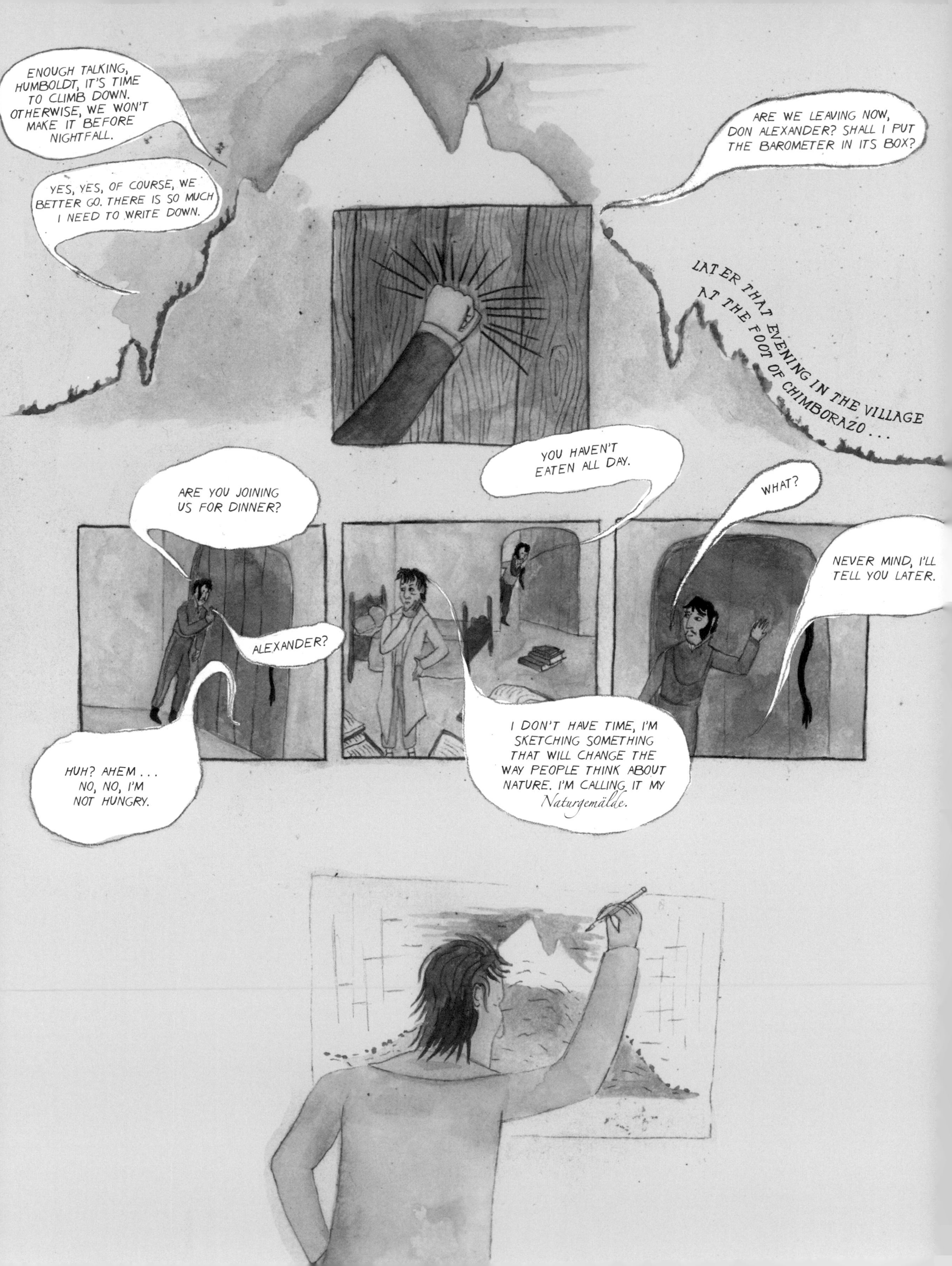
ENOUGH TALKING, HUMBOLDT, IT'S TIME TO CLIMB DOWN. OTHERWISE, WE WON'T MAKE IT BEFORE NIGHTFALL.
YES, YES, OF COURSE, WE BETTER GO. THERE IS SO MUCH I NEED TO WRITE DOWN.
ARE WE LEAVING NOW, DON ALEXANDER? SHALL I PUT THE BAROMETER IN ITS BOX?
LATER THAT EVENING IN THE VILLAGE AT THE FOOT OF CHIMBORAZO . . .
ARE YOU JOINING US FOR DINNER?
ALEXANDER?
HUH? AHEM . . . NO, NO, I'M NOT HUNGRY.
YOU HAVEN'T EATEN ALL DAY.
I DON'T HAVE TIME, I'M SKETCHING SOMETHING THAT WILL CHANGE THE WAY PEOPLE THINK ABOUT NATURE. I'M CALLING IT MY *Naturgemälde.*
WHAT?
NEVER MIND, I'LL TELL YOU LATER.

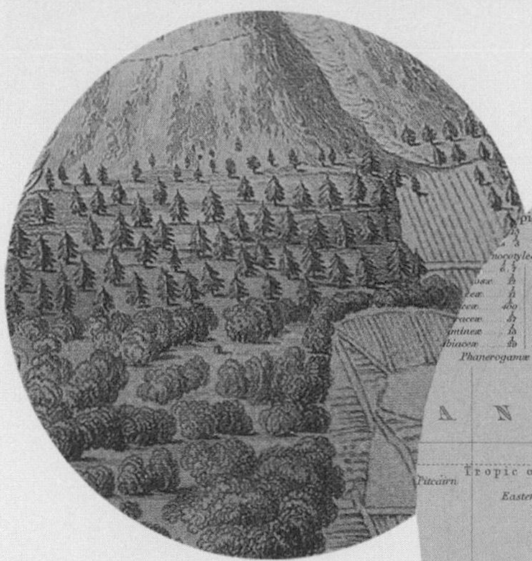

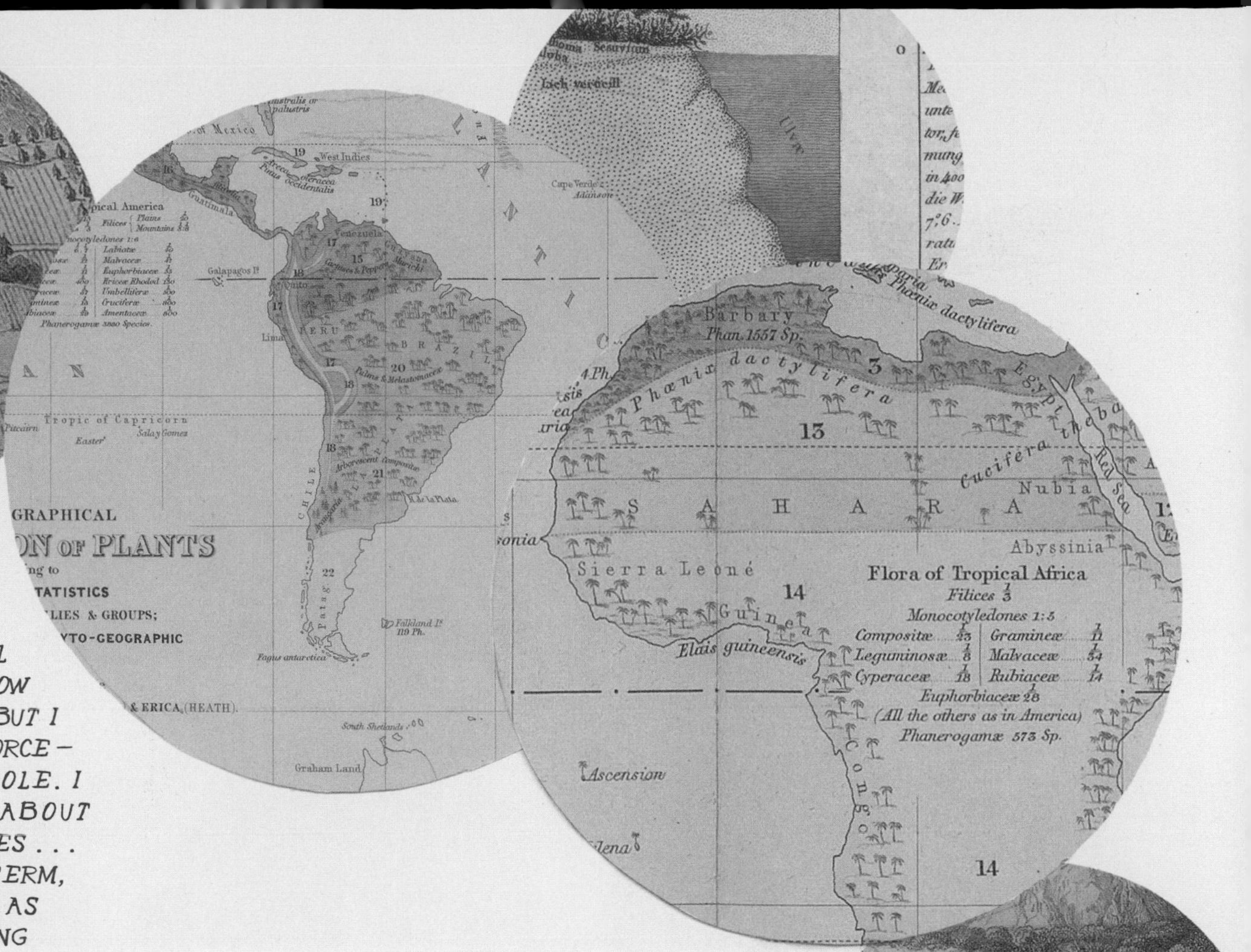
ON OF PLANTS
Flora of Tropical Africa
S A H A R A
Sierra Leoné
Abyssinia
Nubia
Barbary
Phœnix dactylifera
Ascension
Tropic of Capricorn

OTHERS MIGHT LOOK AT THE NATURAL WORLD THROUGH THE NARROW LENS OF CLASSIFICATION, BUT I SEE NATURE AS A GLOBAL FORCE—AN INTERCONNECTED WHOLE. I WAS THE FIRST TO TALK ABOUT GLOBAL VEGETATION ZONES . . . WELL, I DIDN'T USE THAT TERM, BUT I DESCRIBED THEM AS LONG BANDS THAT SLUNG ACROSS THE GLOBE.

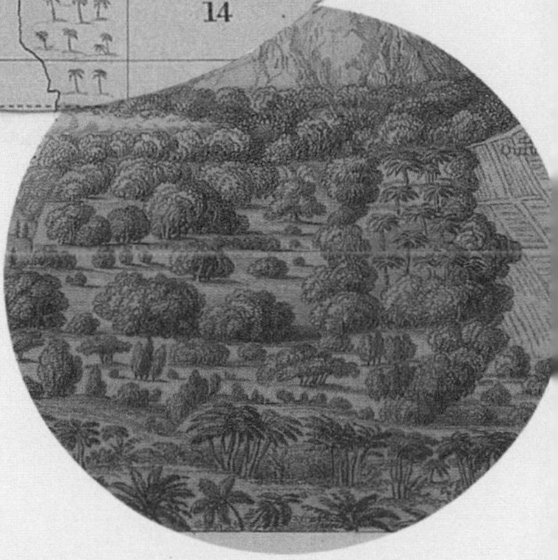

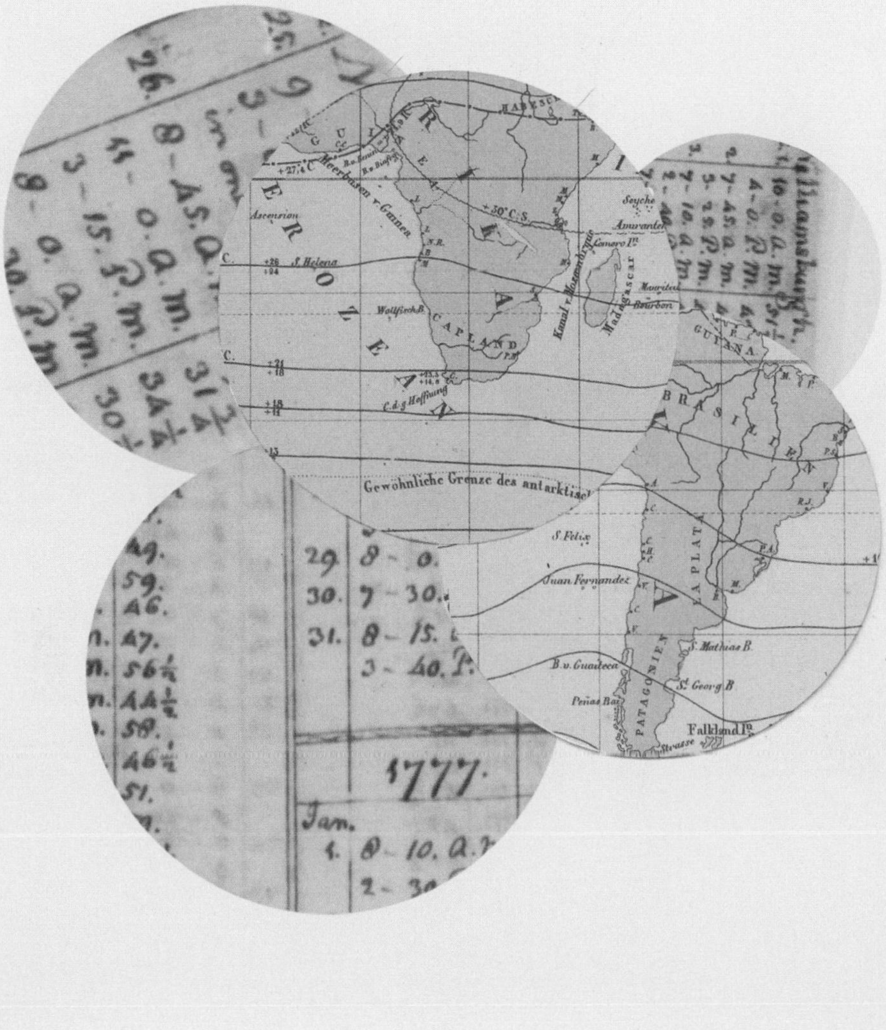
CAPLAND
Gewöhnliche Grenze des antarktis
Juan Fernandez
Falkland Iᵈ
1777.

I ALSO INVENTED ISOTHERMS, THE WAVY LINES THAT YOU SEE ON WEATHER MAPS. INSTEAD OF THE CONFUSING LONG TABLES OF TEMPERATURES EVERYBODY ELSE USED, I REVEALED A NEW WORLD OF PATTERNS THAT HUGGED THE EARTH IN WAVY BELTS. WHERE OTHERS THINK LOCALLY, I THINK GLOBALLY.

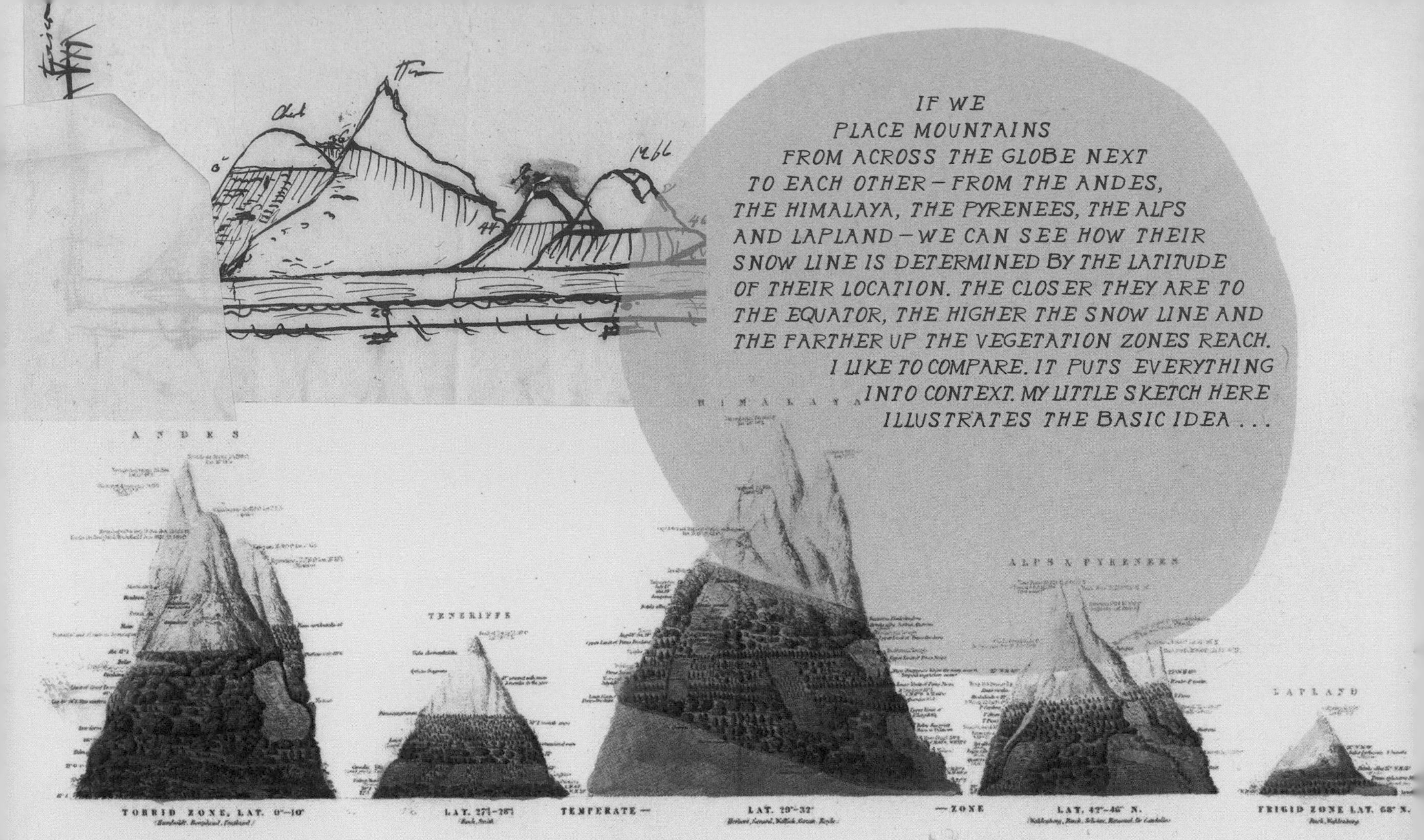
IF WE PLACE MOUNTAINS FROM ACROSS THE GLOBE NEXT TO EACH OTHER – FROM THE ANDES, THE HIMALAYA, THE PYRENEES, THE ALPS AND LAPLAND – WE CAN SEE HOW THEIR SNOW LINE IS DETERMINED BY THE LATITUDE OF THEIR LOCATION. THE CLOSER THEY ARE TO THE EQUATOR, THE HIGHER THE SNOW LINE AND THE FARTHER UP THE VEGETATION ZONES REACH. I LIKE TO COMPARE. IT PUTS EVERYTHING INTO CONTEXT. MY LITTLE SKETCH HERE ILLUSTRATES THE BASIC IDEA . . .
ANDES
TENERIFFE
HIMALAYA
ALPS & PYRENEES
LAPLAND
TORRID ZONE
TEMPERATE —
— ZONE
FRIGID ZONE

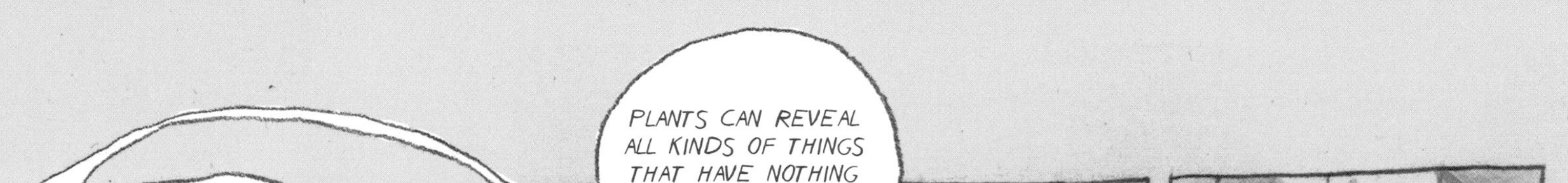
I READ PLANTS LIKE OTHERS READ BOOKS.
WHAT'S THAT SUPPOSED TO MEAN?
PLANTS CAN REVEAL ALL KINDS OF THINGS THAT HAVE NOTHING TO DO WITH THE KIND OF BOTANY YOU LEARNED.
SUCH AS?
THE MIGRATION OF THE HUMAN RACE . . . DON'T LOOK AT ME LIKE THIS, BONPLAND, IT'S SIMPLE . . . CROPS, VEGETABLES, FRUITS AND GRAINS HAVE FOLLOWED OUR FOOTPATHS FOR THOUSANDS OF YEARS.
I SUPPOSE . . .
OR TAKE POLITICS AND ECONOMICS . . . ALL SHAPED BY PLANTS. EMPIRES HAVE BEEN BUILT ON TEA, SUGAR AND TOBACCO.

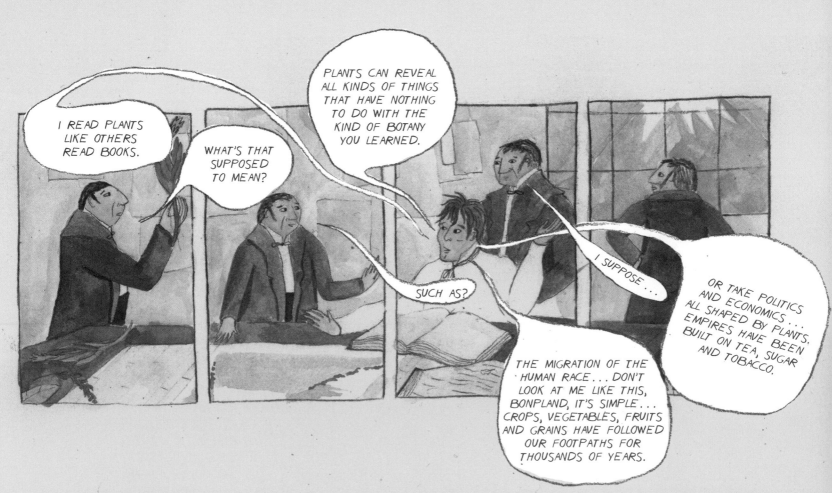

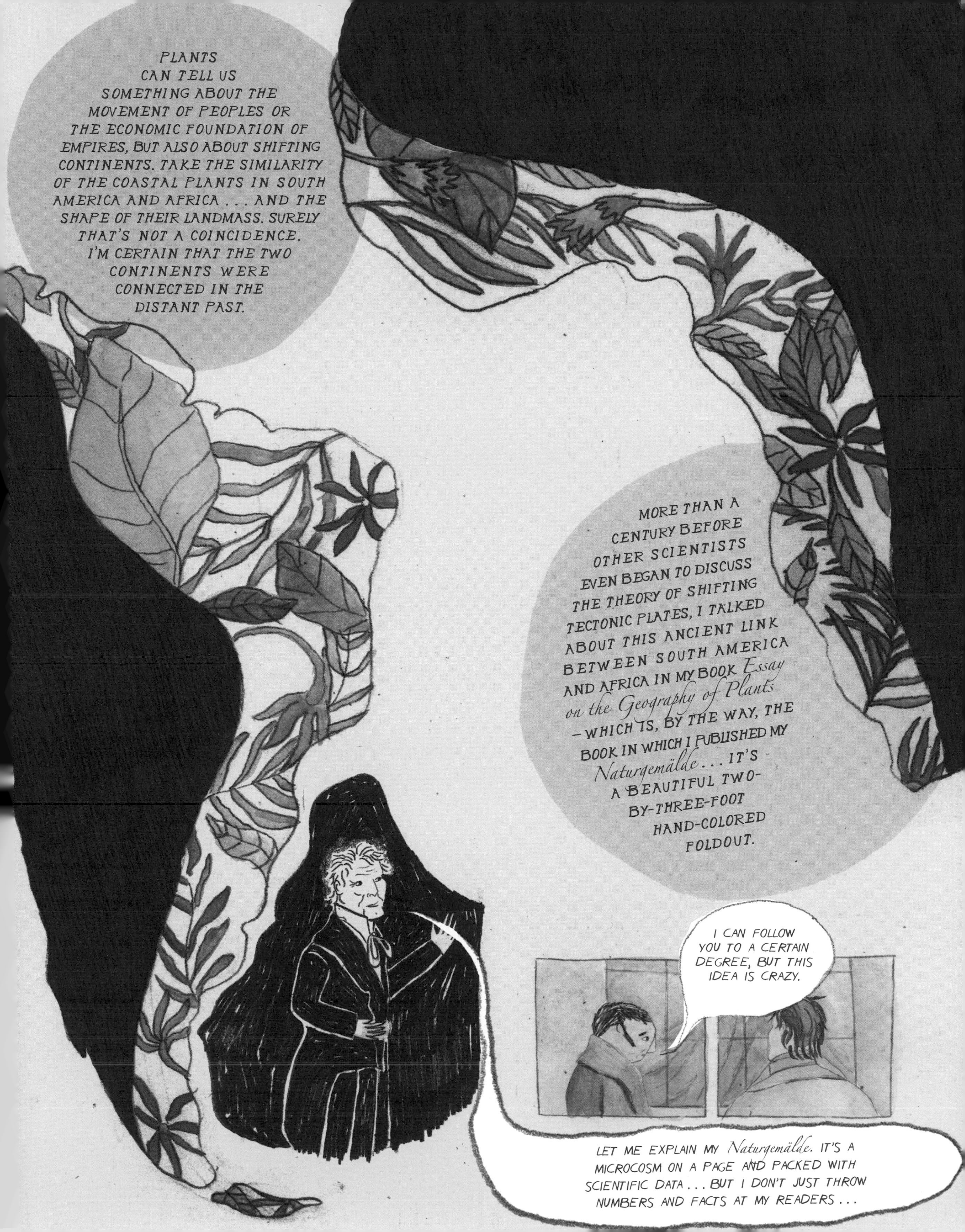
PLANTS CAN TELL US SOMETHING ABOUT THE MOVEMENT OF PEOPLES OR THE ECONOMIC FOUNDATION OF EMPIRES, BUT ALSO ABOUT SHIFTING CONTINENTS. TAKE THE SIMILARITY OF THE COASTAL PLANTS IN SOUTH AMERICA AND AFRICA . . . AND THE SHAPE OF THEIR LANDMASS. SURELY THAT'S NOT A COINCIDENCE. I'M CERTAIN THAT THE TWO CONTINENTS WERE CONNECTED IN THE DISTANT PAST.
MORE THAN A CENTURY BEFORE OTHER SCIENTISTS EVEN BEGAN TO DISCUSS THE THEORY OF SHIFTING TECTONIC PLATES, I TALKED ABOUT THIS ANCIENT LINK BETWEEN SOUTH AMERICA AND AFRICA IN MY BOOK *Essay on the Geography of Plants* —WHICH IS, BY THE WAY, THE BOOK IN WHICH I PUBLISHED MY *Naturgemälde* . . . IT'S A BEAUTIFUL TWO-BY-THREE-FOOT HAND-COLORED FOLDOUT.
I CAN FOLLOW YOU TO A CERTAIN DEGREE, BUT THIS IDEA IS CRAZY.
LET ME EXPLAIN MY *Naturgemälde*. IT'S A MICROCOSM ON A PAGE AND PACKED WITH SCIENTIFIC DATA . . . BUT I DON'T JUST THROW NUMBERS AND FACTS AT MY READERS . . .

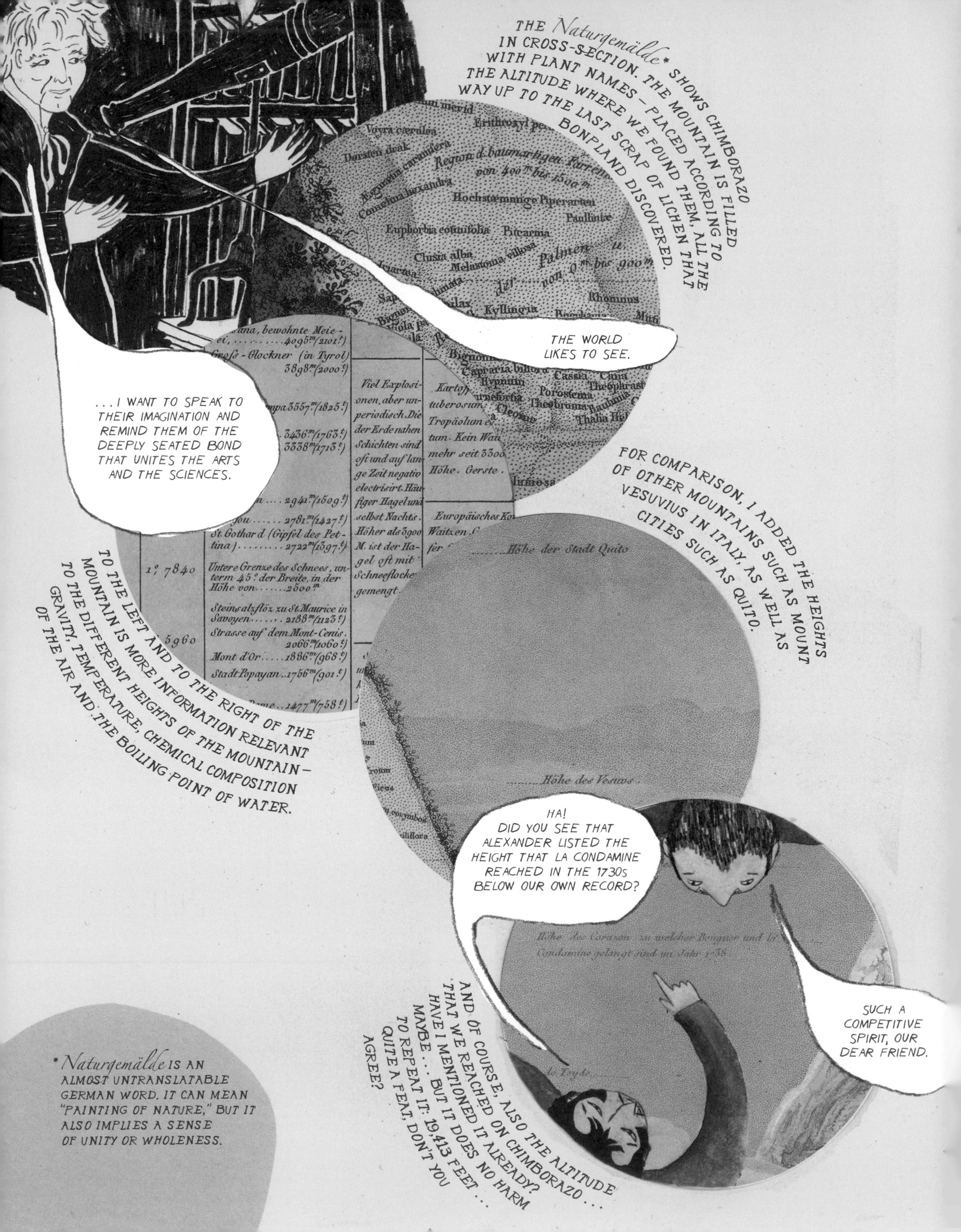
THE *Naturgemälde** SHOWS CHIMBORAZO IN CROSS-SECTION. THE MOUNTAIN IS FILLED WITH PLANT NAMES – PLACED ACCORDING TO THE ALTITUDE WHERE WE FOUND THEM, ALL THE WAY UP TO THE LAST SCRAP OF LICHEN THAT BONPLAND DISCOVERED.
THE WORLD LIKES TO SEE.
...I WANT TO SPEAK TO THEIR IMAGINATION AND REMIND THEM OF THE DEEPLY SEATED BOND THAT UNITES THE ARTS AND THE SCIENCES.
FOR COMPARISON, I ADDED THE HEIGHTS OF OTHER MOUNTAINS SUCH AS MOUNT VESUVIUS IN ITALY, AS WELL AS CITIES SUCH AS QUITO.
TO THE LEFT AND TO THE RIGHT OF THE MOUNTAIN IS MORE INFORMATION RELEVANT TO THE DIFFERENT HEIGHTS OF THE MOUNTAIN – GRAVITY, TEMPERATURE, CHEMICAL COMPOSITION OF THE AIR AND THE BOILING POINT OF WATER.
Höhe der Stadt Quito
Höhe des Vesuvs
HA! DID YOU SEE THAT ALEXANDER LISTED THE HEIGHT THAT LA CONDAMINE REACHED IN THE 1730S BELOW OUR OWN RECORD?
AND OF COURSE, ALSO THE ALTITUDE THAT WE REACHED ON CHIMBORAZO... HAVE I MENTIONED IT ALREADY? MAYBE... BUT IT DOES NO HARM TO REPEAT IT: 19,413 FEET... QUITE A FEAT, DON'T YOU AGREE?
SUCH A COMPETITIVE SPIRIT, OUR DEAR FRIEND.
**Naturgemälde* IS AN ALMOST UNTRANSLATABLE GERMAN WORD. IT CAN MEAN "PAINTING OF NATURE," BUT IT ALSO IMPLIES A SENSE OF UNITY OR WHOLENESS.

IT'S TIME TO LEAVE. WE STILL HAVE ANOTHER *800* MILES TO LIMA AHEAD OF US.

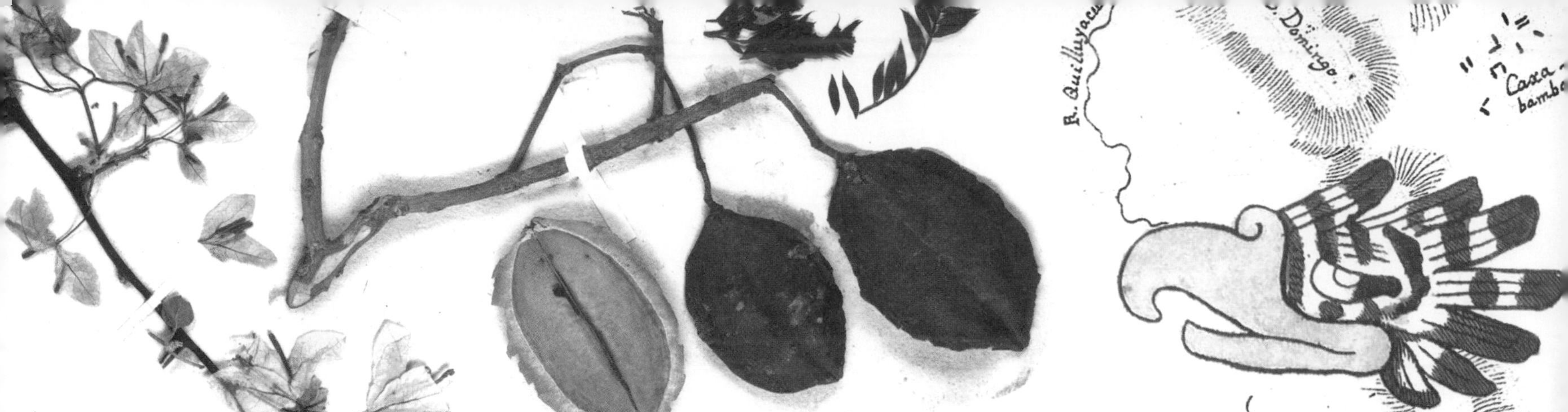

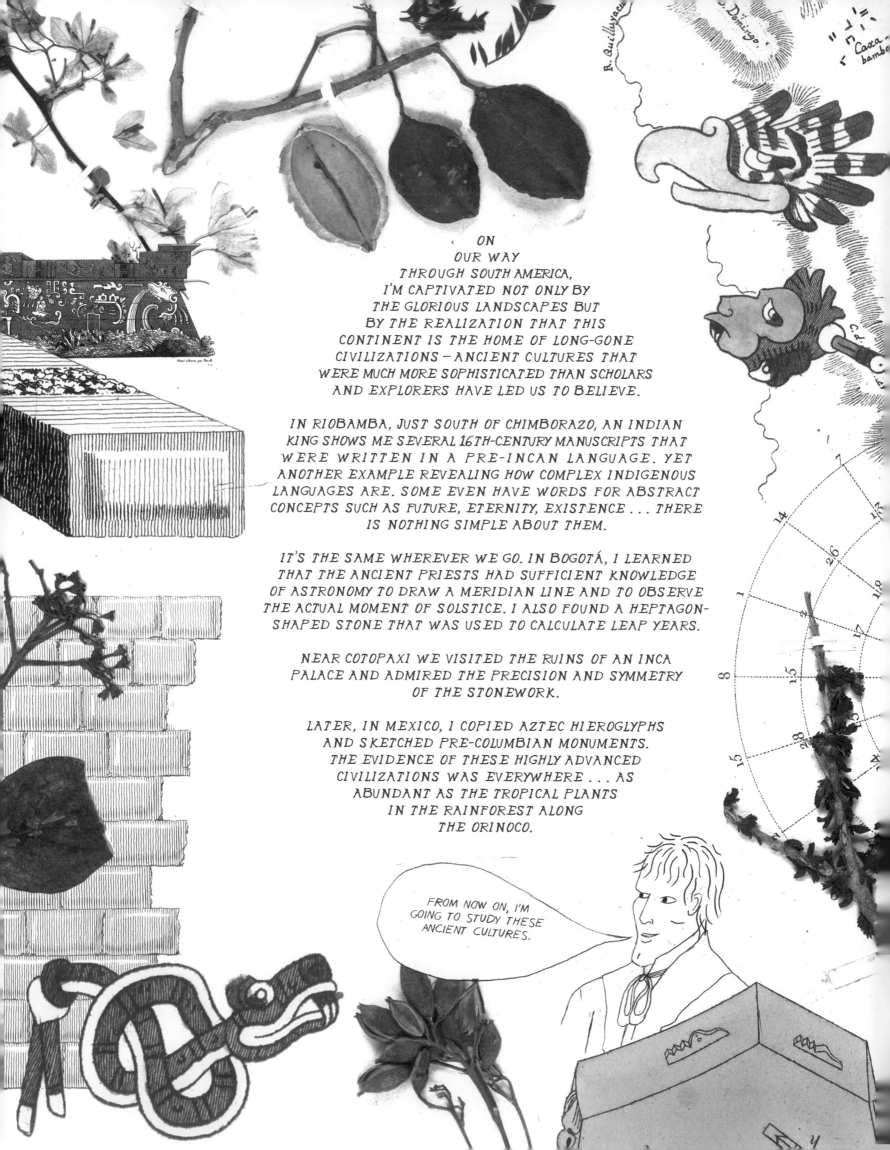

ON
OUR WAY
THROUGH SOUTH AMERICA,
I'M CAPTIVATED NOT ONLY BY
THE GLORIOUS LANDSCAPES BUT
BY THE REALIZATION THAT THIS
CONTINENT IS THE HOME OF LONG-GONE
CIVILIZATIONS – ANCIENT CULTURES THAT
WERE MUCH MORE SOPHISTICATED THAN SCHOLARS
AND EXPLORERS HAVE LED US TO BELIEVE.

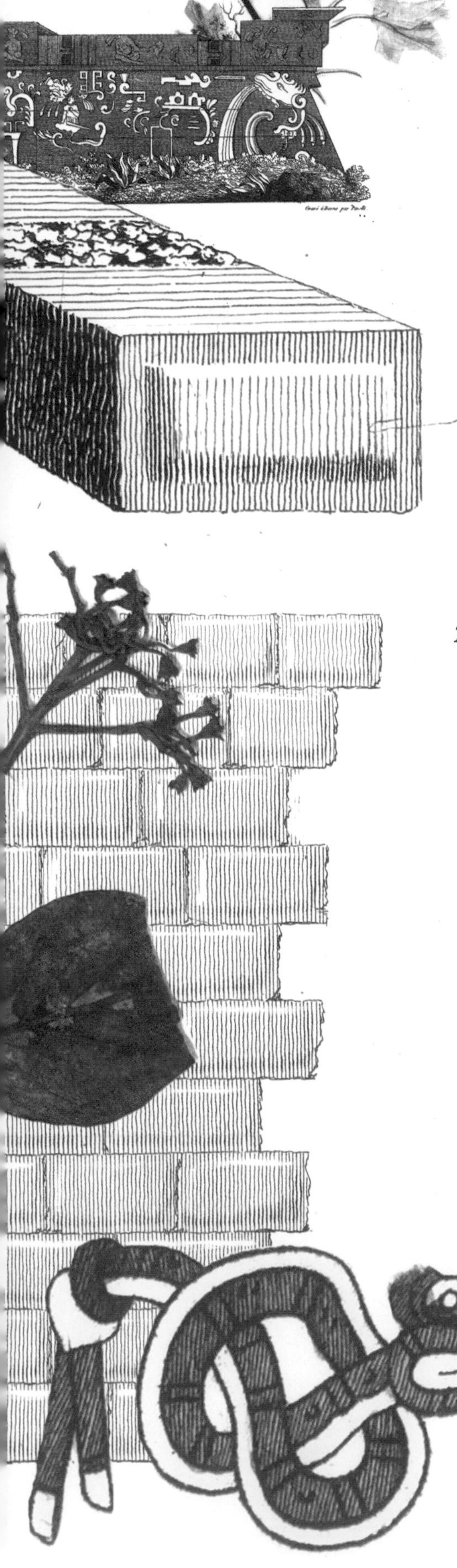

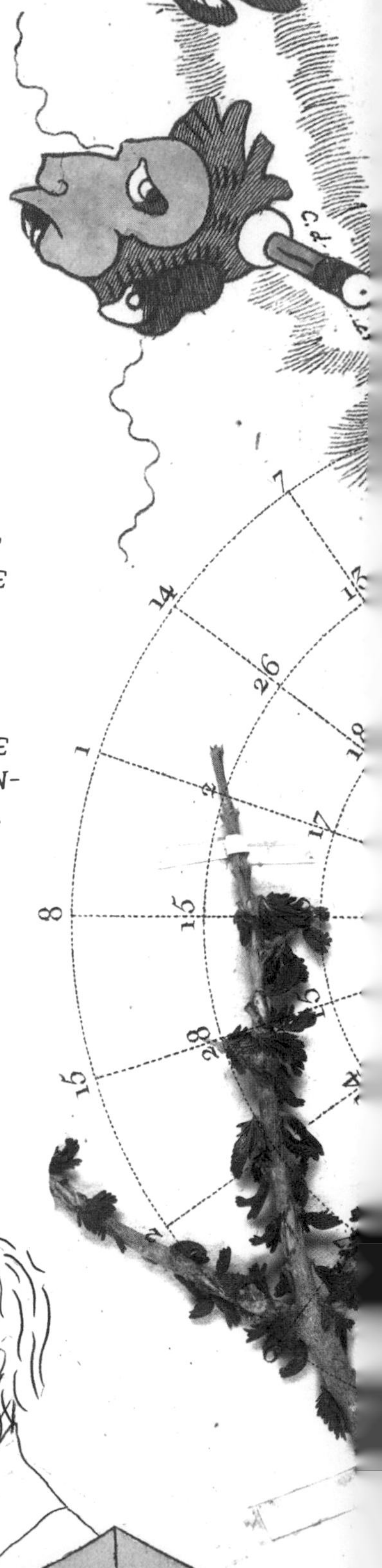

IN RIOBAMBA, JUST SOUTH OF CHIMBORAZO, AN INDIAN KING SHOWS ME SEVERAL 16TH-CENTURY MANUSCRIPTS THAT WERE WRITTEN IN A PRE-INCAN LANGUAGE. YET ANOTHER EXAMPLE REVEALING HOW COMPLEX INDIGENOUS LANGUAGES ARE. SOME EVEN HAVE WORDS FOR ABSTRACT CONCEPTS SUCH AS FUTURE, ETERNITY, EXISTENCE . . . THERE IS NOTHING SIMPLE ABOUT THEM.

IT'S THE SAME WHEREVER WE GO. IN BOGOTÁ, I LEARNED THAT THE ANCIENT PRIESTS HAD SUFFICIENT KNOWLEDGE OF ASTRONOMY TO DRAW A MERIDIAN LINE AND TO OBSERVE THE ACTUAL MOMENT OF SOLSTICE. I ALSO FOUND A HEPTAGON-SHAPED STONE THAT WAS USED TO CALCULATE LEAP YEARS.

NEAR COTOPAXI WE VISITED THE RUINS OF AN INCA PALACE AND ADMIRED THE PRECISION AND SYMMETRY OF THE STONEWORK.

LATER, IN MEXICO, I COPIED AZTEC HIEROGLYPHS AND SKETCHED PRE-COLUMBIAN MONUMENTS. THE EVIDENCE OF THESE HIGHLY ADVANCED CIVILIZATIONS WAS EVERYWHERE . . . AS ABUNDANT AS THE TROPICAL PLANTS IN THE RAINFOREST ALONG THE ORINOCO.

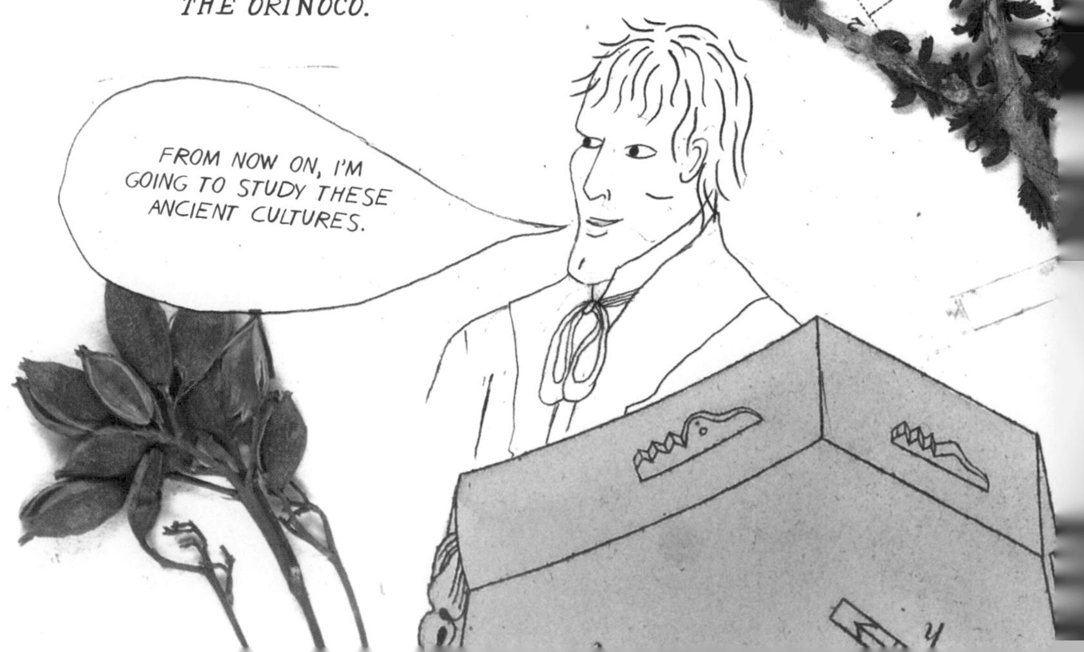
FROM NOW ON, I'M GOING TO STUDY THESE ANCIENT CULTURES.

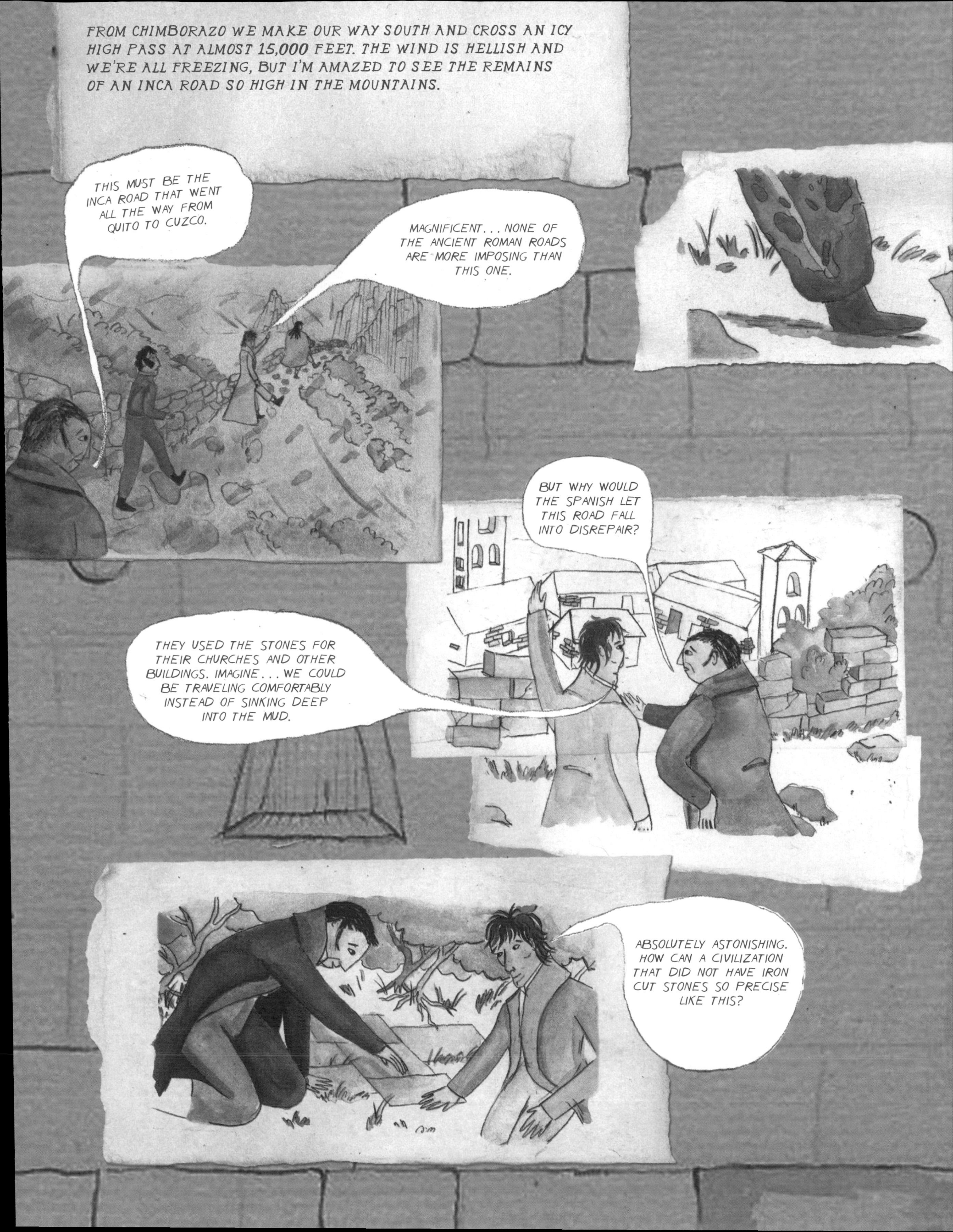
FROM CHIMBORAZO WE MAKE OUR WAY SOUTH AND CROSS AN ICY HIGH PASS AT ALMOST 15,000 FEET. THE WIND IS HELLISH AND WE'RE ALL FREEZING, BUT I'M AMAZED TO SEE THE REMAINS OF AN INCA ROAD SO HIGH IN THE MOUNTAINS.
THIS MUST BE THE INCA ROAD THAT WENT ALL THE WAY FROM QUITO TO CUZCO.
MAGNIFICENT. . . NONE OF THE ANCIENT ROMAN ROADS ARE MORE IMPOSING THAN THIS ONE.
BUT WHY WOULD THE SPANISH LET THIS ROAD FALL INTO DISREPAIR?
THEY USED THE STONES FOR THEIR CHURCHES AND OTHER BUILDINGS. IMAGINE . . . WE COULD BE TRAVELING COMFORTABLY INSTEAD OF SINKING DEEP INTO THE MUD.
ABSOLUTELY ASTONISHING. HOW CAN A CIVILIZATION THAT DID NOT HAVE IRON CUT STONES SO PRECISE LIKE THIS?

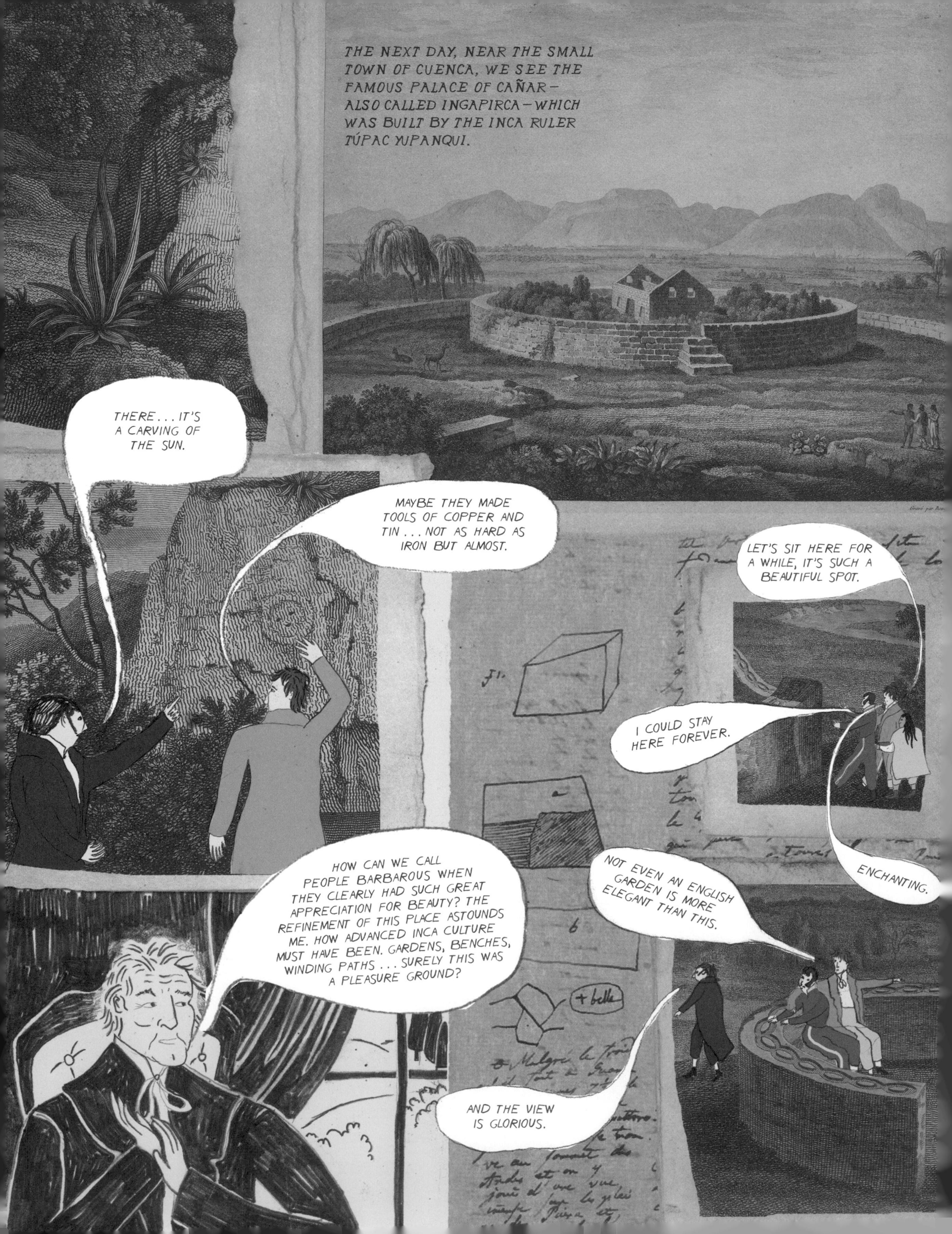
THE NEXT DAY, NEAR THE SMALL TOWN OF CUENCA, WE SEE THE FAMOUS PALACE OF CAÑAR—ALSO CALLED INGAPIRCA—WHICH WAS BUILT BY THE INCA RULER TÚPAC YUPANQUI.
THERE... IT'S A CARVING OF THE SUN.
MAYBE THEY MADE TOOLS OF COPPER AND TIN... NOT AS HARD AS IRON BUT ALMOST.
LET'S SIT HERE FOR A WHILE, IT'S SUCH A BEAUTIFUL SPOT.
I COULD STAY HERE FOREVER.
ENCHANTING.
HOW CAN WE CALL PEOPLE BARBAROUS WHEN THEY CLEARLY HAD SUCH GREAT APPRECIATION FOR BEAUTY? THE REFINEMENT OF THIS PLACE ASTOUNDS ME. HOW ADVANCED INCA CULTURE MUST HAVE BEEN. GARDENS, BENCHES, WINDING PATHS... SURELY THIS WAS A PLEASURE GROUND?
NOT EVEN AN ENGLISH GARDEN IS MORE ELEGANT THAN THIS.
AND THE VIEW IS GLORIOUS.
+ belle

WE
CONTINUE
SOUTH AND
THREE WEEKS LATER
WE REACH THE CINCHONA
FORESTS OF LOJA. THE BARK OF
THE CINCHONA TREE CONTAINS QUININE,
WHICH THE INDIANS HAVE USED FOR CENTURIES
TO TREAT FEVERS. THE ONLY TROUBLE IS THAT
ONCE THE BARK IS HARVESTED THE TREE DIES.
BY THE TIME WE ARRIVED IN LOJA, THE SPANISH
HAD DESTROYED HUGE SWATHS OF THE FOREST. THREE
DECADES AFTER OUR VISIT, SIMÓN BOLÍVAR ISSUED A
VISIONARY DECREE TO PROTECT THE FORESTS OF COLOMBIA.
MAYBE HE HAD READ THE WARNINGS IN MY BOOKS OR MAYBE
HE HAD SEEN THE DEVASTATION WITH HIS OWN EYES,
BUT WHATEVER THE REASONS, BOLÍVAR WAS THE FIRST TO
ENSHRINE MY IDEAS INTO LAW. OVER TIME OTHERS ALSO
BEGAN TO THINK ABOUT THE PROTECTION OF FORESTS. HENRY
DAVID THOREAU WAS ONE OF THEM. HAVE YOU HEARD OF HIM?
OH, YES, OF COURSE, AT LEAST IF YOU'RE FROM THE UNITED
STATES. THOREAU INSISTED THAT EVERY TOWN SHOULD HAVE
A PROTECTED FOREST OF SEVERAL HUNDRED ACRES. THE MAN
HAD CLEARLY READ AND LIKED MY BOOKS. AND THEN THERE
WAS GEORGE PERKINS MARSH (HE EVEN CALLED ME THE
GREAT APOSTLE OF NATURE!!!). IN 1864, ONLY FIVE YEARS
AFTER MY DEATH, MARSH PUBLISHED *Man and*
Nature—A BOOK IN WHICH HE TOOK MY EARLY
WARNINGS ABOUT DEFORESTATION TO THEIR
FULL CONCLUSION.

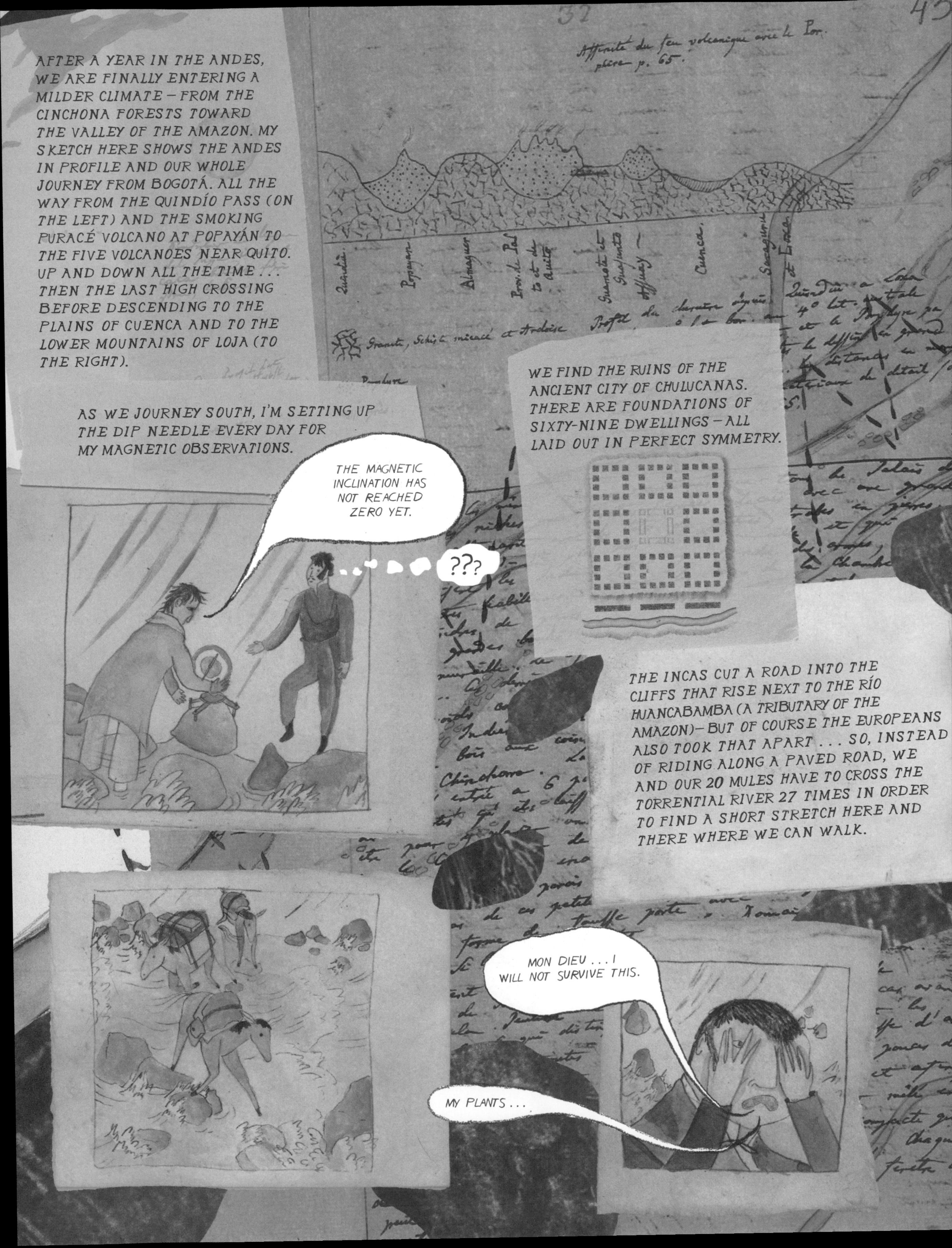
AFTER A YEAR IN THE ANDES, WE ARE FINALLY ENTERING A MILDER CLIMATE – FROM THE CINCHONA FORESTS TOWARD THE VALLEY OF THE AMAZON. MY SKETCH HERE SHOWS THE ANDES IN PROFILE AND OUR WHOLE JOURNEY FROM BOGOTÁ. ALL THE WAY FROM THE QUINDÍO PASS (ON THE LEFT) AND THE SMOKING PURACÉ VOLCANO AT POPAYÁN TO THE FIVE VOLCANOES NEAR QUITO. UP AND DOWN ALL THE TIME . . . THEN THE LAST HIGH CROSSING BEFORE DESCENDING TO THE PLAINS OF CUENCA AND TO THE LOWER MOUNTAINS OF LOJA (TO THE RIGHT).
Quindiu
Popayan
Almaguer
Cuenca
Loxa
AS WE JOURNEY SOUTH, I'M SETTING UP THE DIP NEEDLE EVERY DAY FOR MY MAGNETIC OBSERVATIONS.
THE MAGNETIC INCLINATION HAS NOT REACHED ZERO YET.
???
WE FIND THE RUINS OF THE ANCIENT CITY OF CHULUCANAS. THERE ARE FOUNDATIONS OF SIXTY-NINE DWELLINGS – ALL LAID OUT IN PERFECT SYMMETRY.
THE INCAS CUT A ROAD INTO THE CLIFFS THAT RISE NEXT TO THE RÍO HUANCABAMBA (A TRIBUTARY OF THE AMAZON) – BUT OF COURSE THE EUROPEANS ALSO TOOK THAT APART . . . SO, INSTEAD OF RIDING ALONG A PAVED ROAD, WE AND OUR 20 MULES HAVE TO CROSS THE TORRENTIAL RIVER 27 TIMES IN ORDER TO FIND A SHORT STRETCH HERE AND THERE WHERE WE CAN WALK.
MON DIEU . . . I WILL NOT SURVIVE THIS.
MY PLANTS . . .

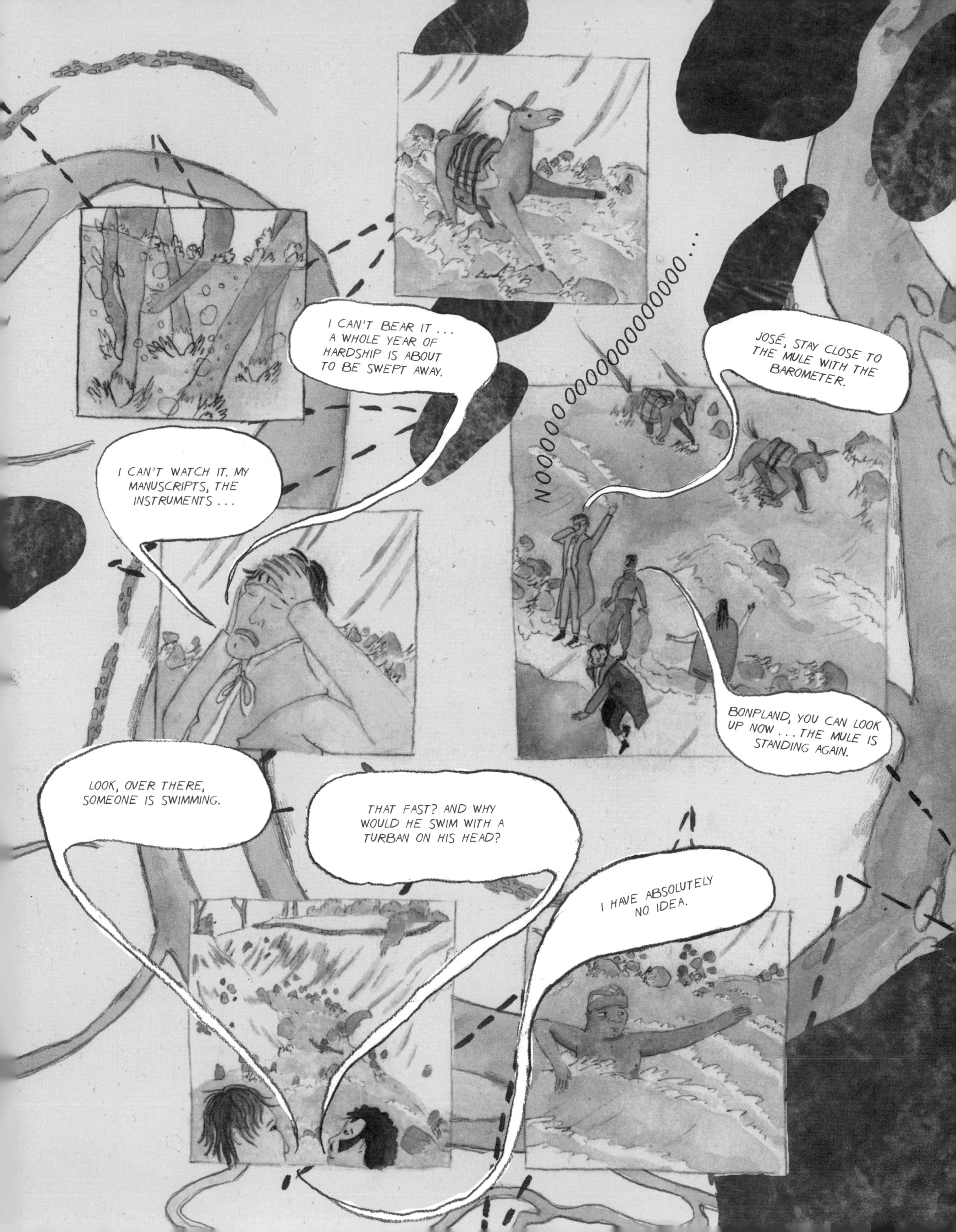
I CAN'T BEAR IT . . . A WHOLE YEAR OF HARDSHIP IS ABOUT TO BE SWEPT AWAY.
I CAN'T WATCH IT. MY MANUSCRIPTS, THE INSTRUMENTS . . .
NOOOOOOOOOOOOOOOOOOOOOO . . .
JOSÉ, STAY CLOSE TO THE MULE WITH THE BAROMETER.
BONPLAND, YOU CAN LOOK UP NOW . . . THE MULE IS STANDING AGAIN.
LOOK, OVER THERE, SOMEONE IS SWIMMING.
THAT FAST? AND WHY WOULD HE SWIM WITH A TURBAN ON HIS HEAD?
I HAVE ABSOLUTELY NO IDEA.

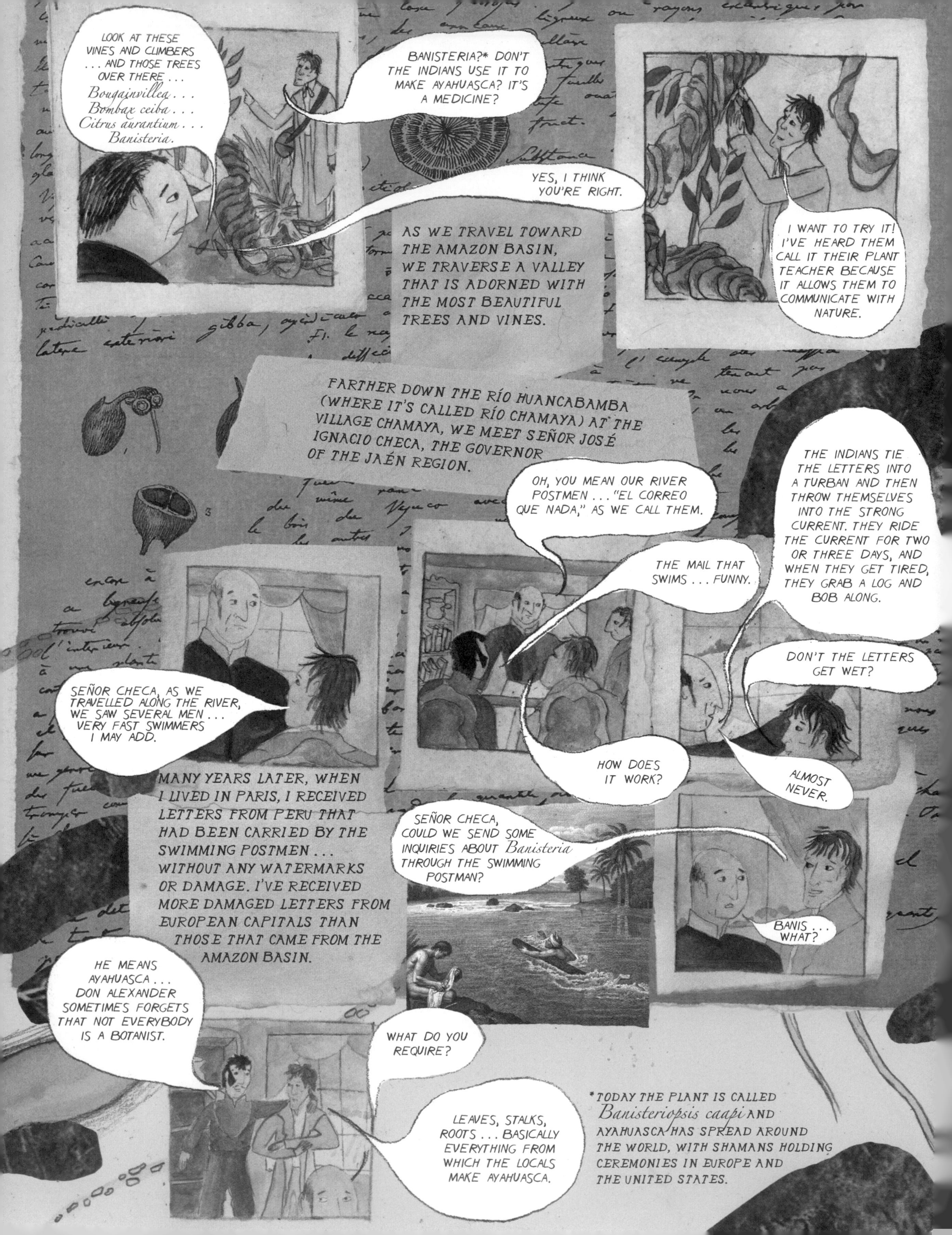

LOOK AT THESE VINES AND CLIMBERS . . . AND THOSE TREES OVER THERE . . . *Bougainvillea* . . . *Bombax ceiba* . . . *Citrus aurantium* . . . *Banisteria*.
BANISTERIA?* DON'T THE INDIANS USE IT TO MAKE AYAHUASCA? IT'S A MEDICINE?
YES, I THINK YOU'RE RIGHT.
I WANT TO TRY IT! I'VE HEARD THEM CALL IT THEIR PLANT TEACHER BECAUSE IT ALLOWS THEM TO COMMUNICATE WITH NATURE.
AS WE TRAVEL TOWARD THE AMAZON BASIN, WE TRAVERSE A VALLEY THAT IS ADORNED WITH THE MOST BEAUTIFUL TREES AND VINES.
FARTHER DOWN THE RÍO HUANCABAMBA (WHERE IT'S CALLED RÍO CHAMAYA) AT THE VILLAGE CHAMAYA, WE MEET SEÑOR JOSÉ IGNACIO CHECA, THE GOVERNOR OF THE JAÉN REGION.
SEÑOR CHECA, AS WE TRAVELLED ALONG THE RIVER, WE SAW SEVERAL MEN . . . VERY FAST SWIMMERS I MAY ADD.
OH, YOU MEAN OUR RIVER POSTMEN . . . "EL CORREO QUE NADA," AS WE CALL THEM.
THE MAIL THAT SWIMS . . . FUNNY.
HOW DOES IT WORK?
THE INDIANS TIE THE LETTERS INTO A TURBAN AND THEN THROW THEMSELVES INTO THE STRONG CURRENT. THEY RIDE THE CURRENT FOR TWO OR THREE DAYS, AND WHEN THEY GET TIRED, THEY GRAB A LOG AND BOB ALONG.
DON'T THE LETTERS GET WET?
ALMOST NEVER.
MANY YEARS LATER, WHEN I LIVED IN PARIS, I RECEIVED LETTERS FROM PERU THAT HAD BEEN CARRIED BY THE SWIMMING POSTMEN . . . WITHOUT ANY WATERMARKS OR DAMAGE. I'VE RECEIVED MORE DAMAGED LETTERS FROM EUROPEAN CAPITALS THAN THOSE THAT CAME FROM THE AMAZON BASIN.
SEÑOR CHECA, COULD WE SEND SOME INQUIRIES ABOUT *Banisteria* THROUGH THE SWIMMING POSTMAN?
BANIS . . . WHAT?
HE MEANS AYAHUASCA . . . DON ALEXANDER SOMETIMES FORGETS THAT NOT EVERYBODY IS A BOTANIST.
WHAT DO YOU REQUIRE?
LEAVES, STALKS, ROOTS . . . BASICALLY EVERYTHING FROM WHICH THE LOCALS MAKE AYAHUASCA.
*TODAY THE PLANT IS CALLED *Banisteriopsis caapi* AND AYAHUASCA HAS SPREAD AROUND THE WORLD, WITH SHAMANS HOLDING CEREMONIES IN EUROPE AND THE UNITED STATES.

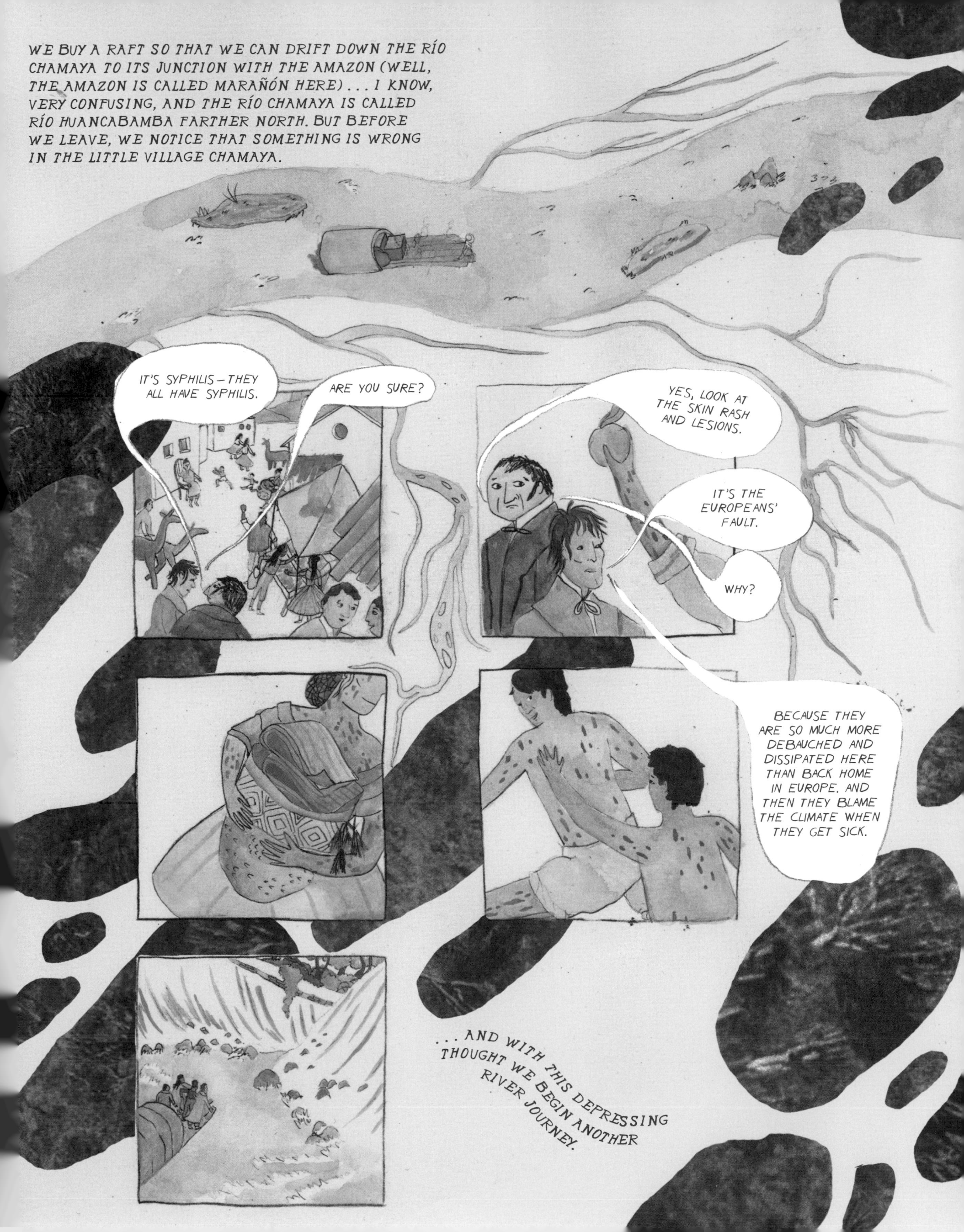
WE BUY A RAFT SO THAT WE CAN DRIFT DOWN THE RÍO CHAMAYA TO ITS JUNCTION WITH THE AMAZON (WELL, THE AMAZON IS CALLED MARAÑÓN HERE) . . . I KNOW, VERY CONFUSING, AND THE RÍO CHAMAYA IS CALLED RÍO HUANCABAMBA FARTHER NORTH. BUT BEFORE WE LEAVE, WE NOTICE THAT SOMETHING IS WRONG IN THE LITTLE VILLAGE CHAMAYA.
IT'S SYPHILIS—THEY ALL HAVE SYPHILIS.
ARE YOU SURE?
YES, LOOK AT THE SKIN RASH AND LESIONS.
IT'S THE EUROPEANS' FAULT.
WHY?
BECAUSE THEY ARE SO MUCH MORE DEBAUCHED AND DISSIPATED HERE THAN BACK HOME IN EUROPE. AND THEN THEY BLAME THE CLIMATE WHEN THEY GET SICK.
. . . AND WITH THIS DEPRESSING THOUGHT WE BEGIN ANOTHER RIVER JOURNEY.

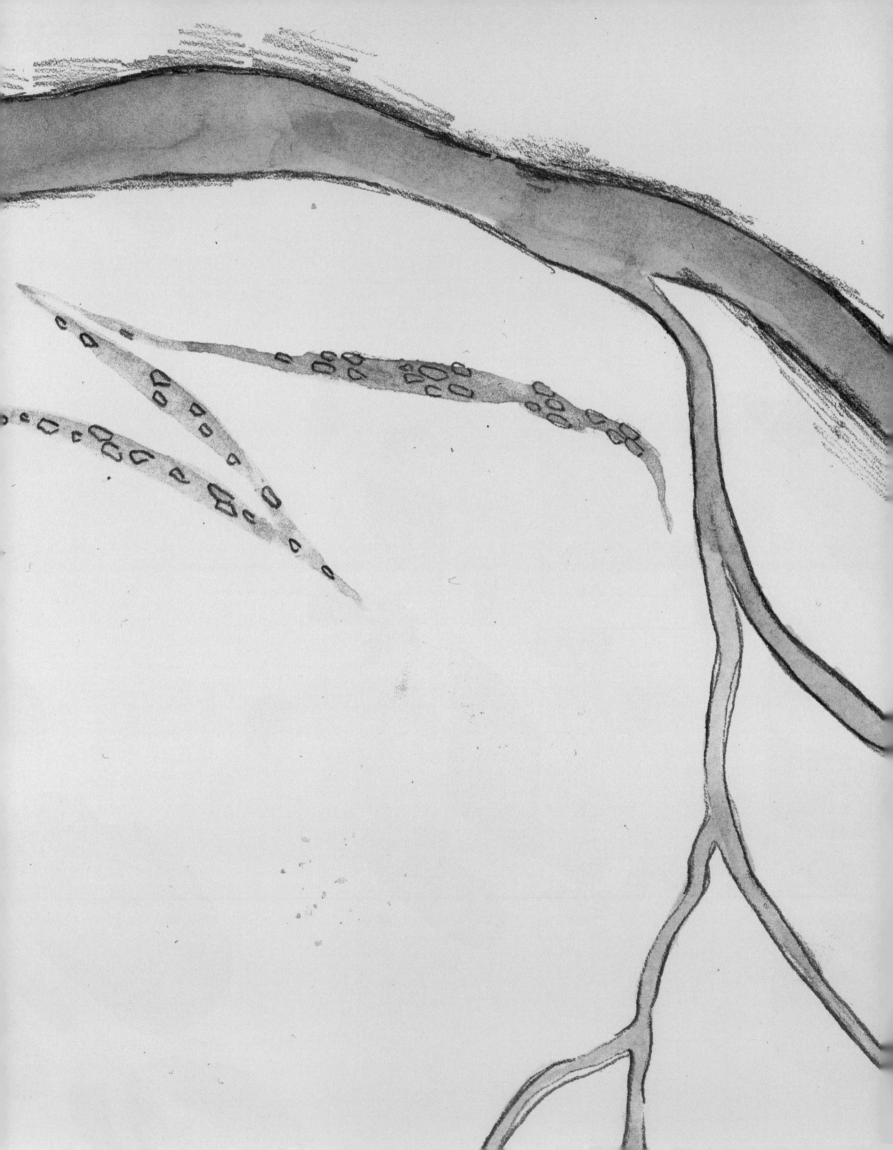

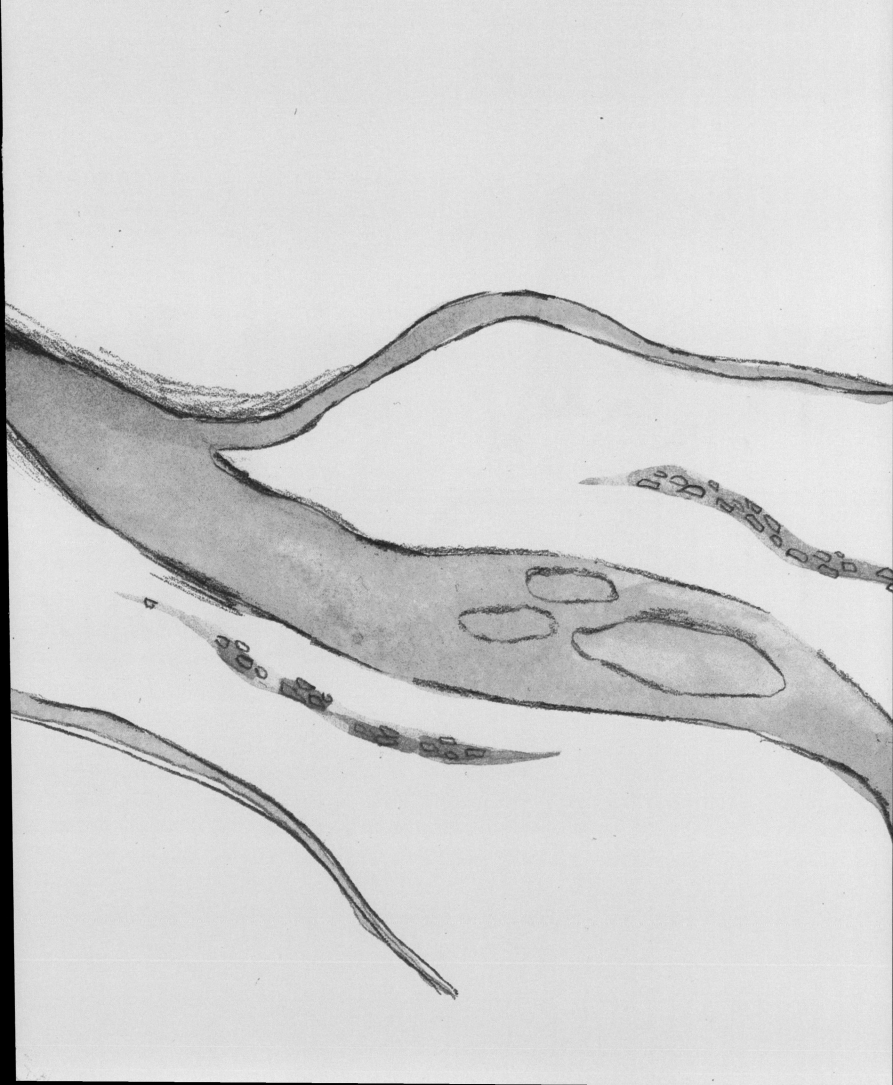

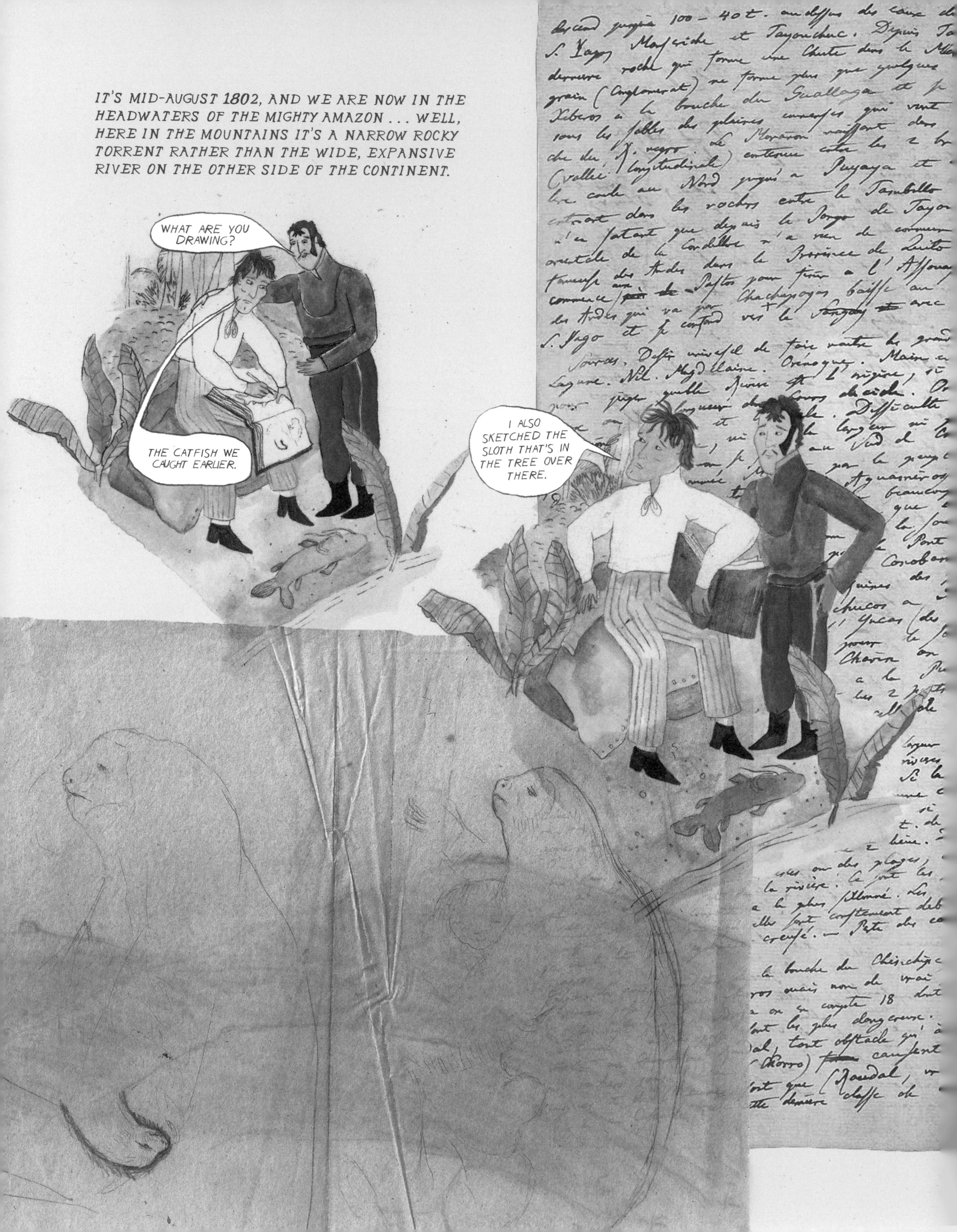
IT'S MID-AUGUST 1802, AND WE ARE NOW IN THE HEADWATERS OF THE MIGHTY AMAZON . . . WELL, HERE IN THE MOUNTAINS IT'S A NARROW ROCKY TORRENT RATHER THAN THE WIDE, EXPANSIVE RIVER ON THE OTHER SIDE OF THE CONTINENT.
WHAT ARE YOU DRAWING?
THE CATFISH WE CAUGHT EARLIER.
I ALSO SKETCHED THE SLOTH THAT'S IN THE TREE OVER THERE.

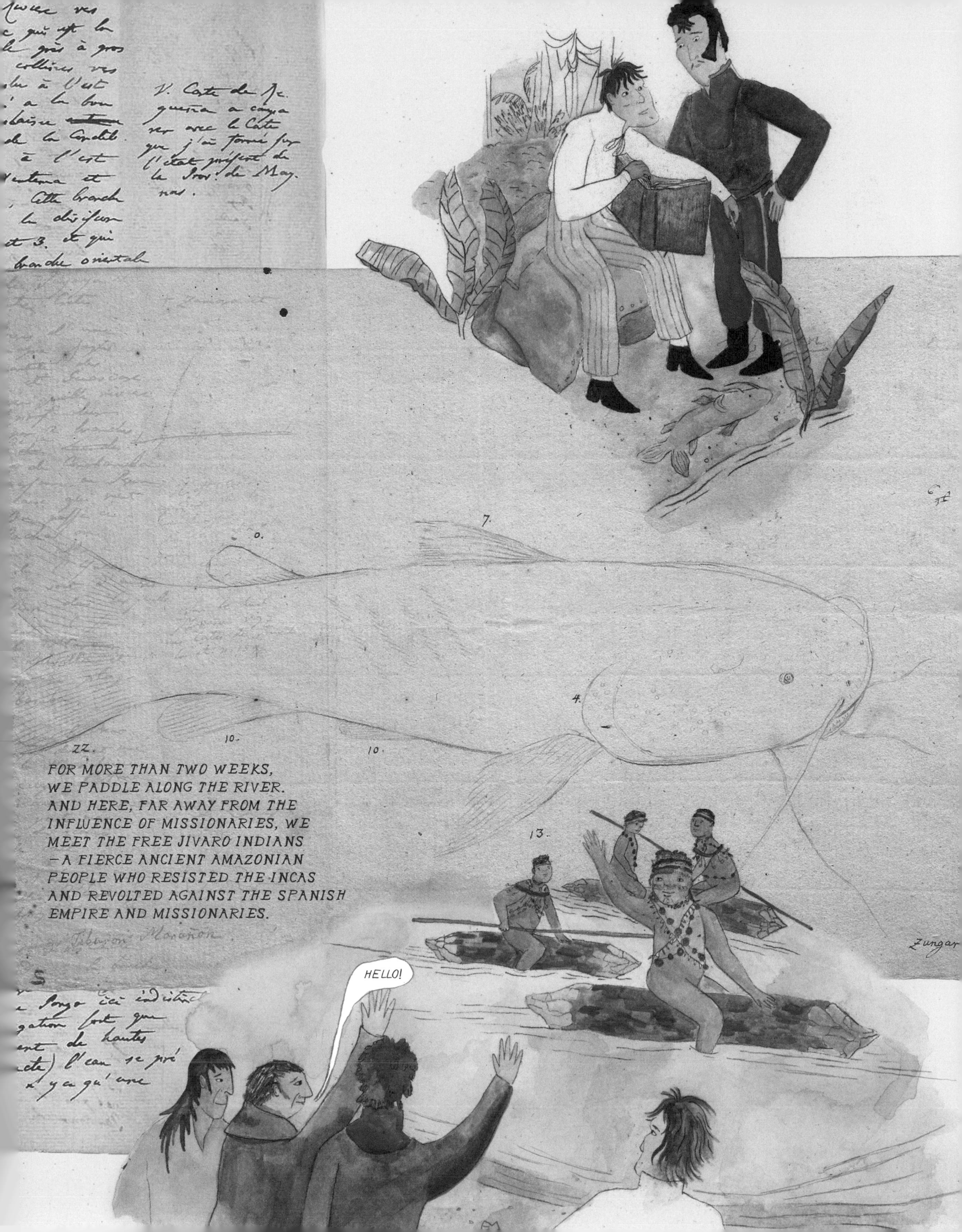
V. Carte de Jequeña a comparer avec la Carte que j'ai formé sur l'état présent de la Prov. de Maynas.
FOR MORE THAN TWO WEEKS, WE PADDLE ALONG THE RIVER. AND HERE, FAR AWAY FROM THE INFLUENCE OF MISSIONARIES, WE MEET THE FREE JIVARO INDIANS —A FIERCE ANCIENT AMAZONIAN PEOPLE WHO RESISTED THE INCAS AND REVOLTED AGAINST THE SPANISH EMPIRE AND MISSIONARIES.
Zungar
HELLO!

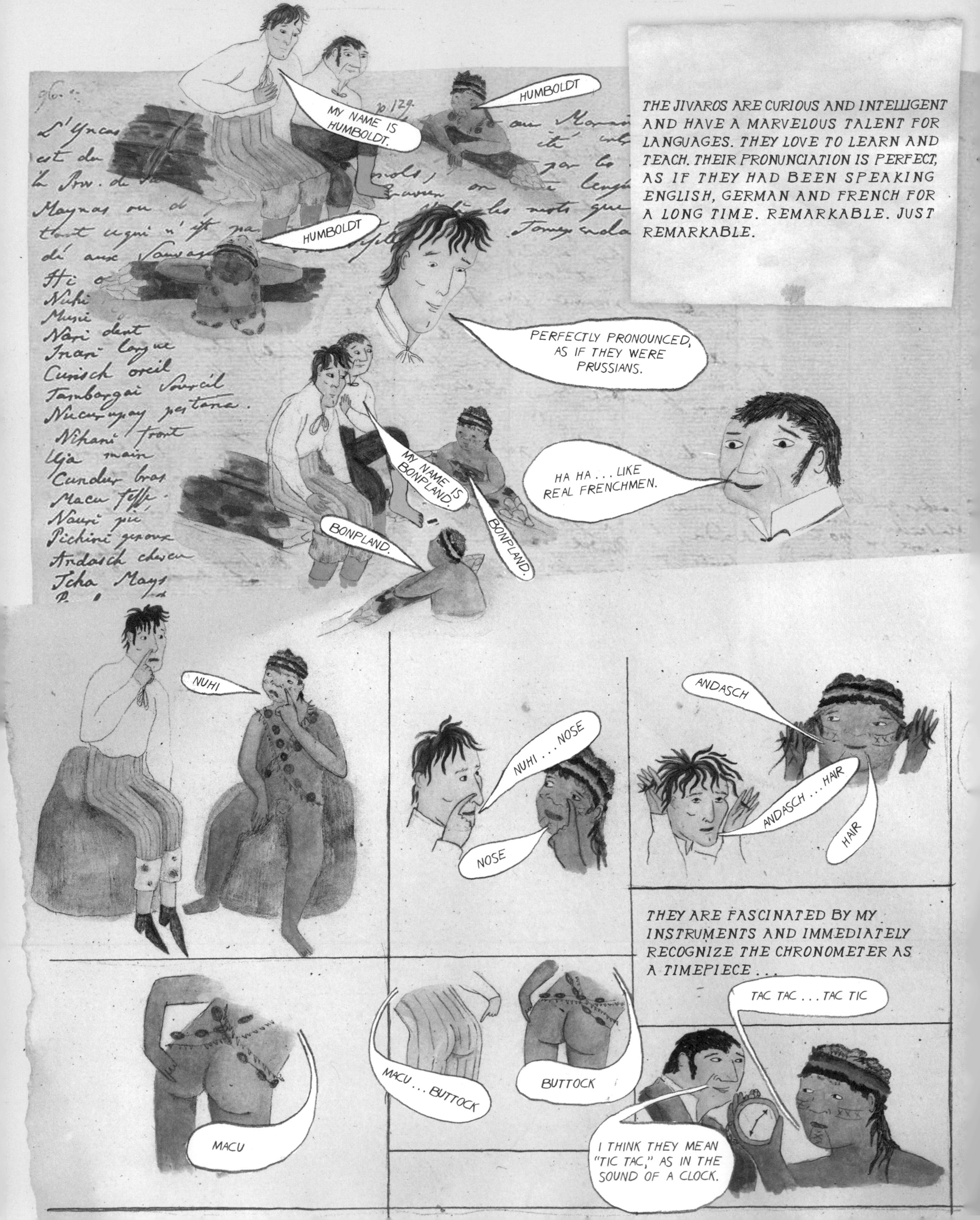
THE JIVAROS ARE CURIOUS AND INTELLIGENT AND HAVE A MARVELOUS TALENT FOR LANGUAGES. THEY LOVE TO LEARN AND TEACH. THEIR PRONUNCIATION IS PERFECT, AS IF THEY HAD BEEN SPEAKING ENGLISH, GERMAN AND FRENCH FOR A LONG TIME. REMARKABLE. JUST REMARKABLE.
MY NAME IS HUMBOLDT.
HUMBOLDT
HUMBOLDT
PERFECTLY PRONOUNCED, AS IF THEY WERE PRUSSIANS.
MY NAME IS BONPLAND.
BONPLAND.
BONPLAND.
HA HA . . . LIKE REAL FRENCHMEN.
NUHI
NUHI . . . NOSE
NOSE
ANDASCH
ANDASCH . . . HAIR
HAIR
MACU
MACU . . . BUTTOCK
BUTTOCK
THEY ARE FASCINATED BY MY INSTRUMENTS AND IMMEDIATELY RECOGNIZE THE CHRONOMETER AS A TIMEPIECE . . .
TAC TAC . . . TAC TIC
I THINK THEY MEAN "TIC TAC," AS IN THE SOUND OF A CLOCK.

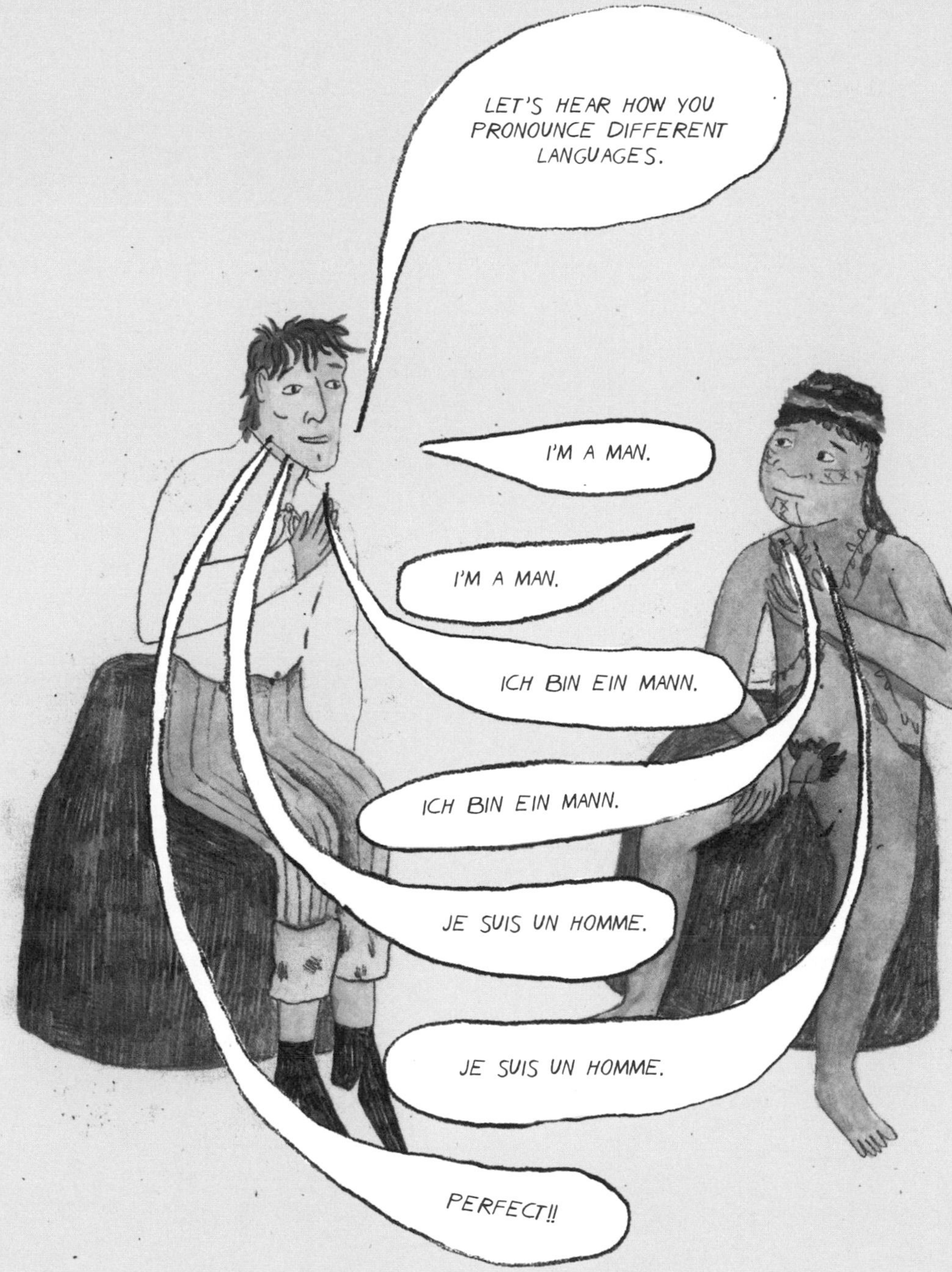
LET'S HEAR HOW YOU PRONOUNCE DIFFERENT LANGUAGES.
I'M A MAN.
I'M A MAN.
ICH BIN EIN MANN.
ICH BIN EIN MANN.
JE SUIS UN HOMME.
JE SUIS UN HOMME.
PERFECT!!

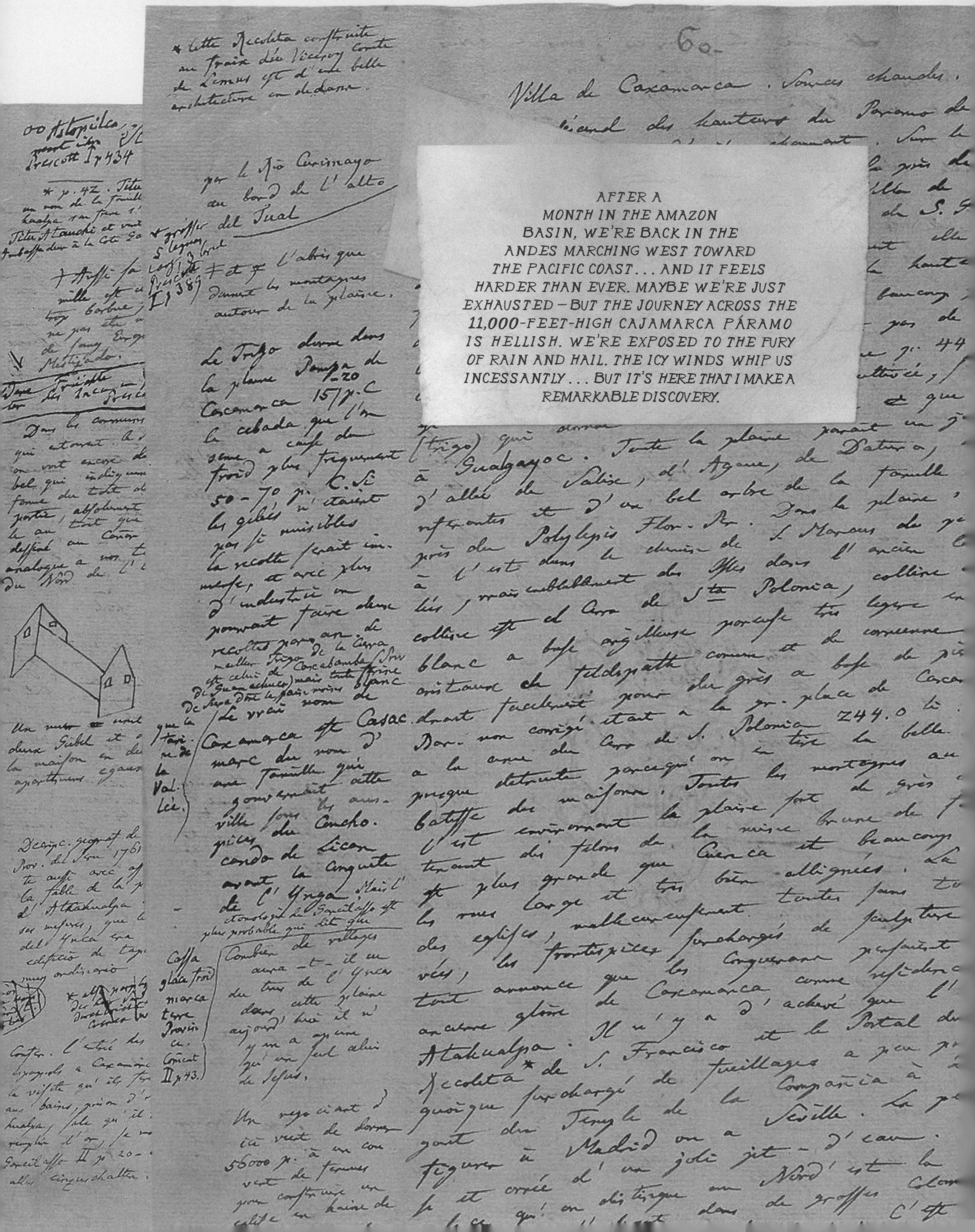
60
Villa de Caxamarca. Sources chaudes.

AFTER A MONTH IN THE AMAZON BASIN, WE'RE BACK IN THE ANDES MARCHING WEST TOWARD THE PACIFIC COAST . . . AND IT FEELS HARDER THAN EVER. MAYBE WE'RE JUST EXHAUSTED – BUT THE JOURNEY ACROSS THE 11,000-FEET-HIGH CAJAMARCA PÁRAMO IS HELLISH. WE'RE EXPOSED TO THE FURY OF RAIN AND HAIL. THE ICY WINDS WHIP US INCESSANTLY . . . BUT IT'S HERE THAT I MAKE A REMARKABLE DISCOVERY.

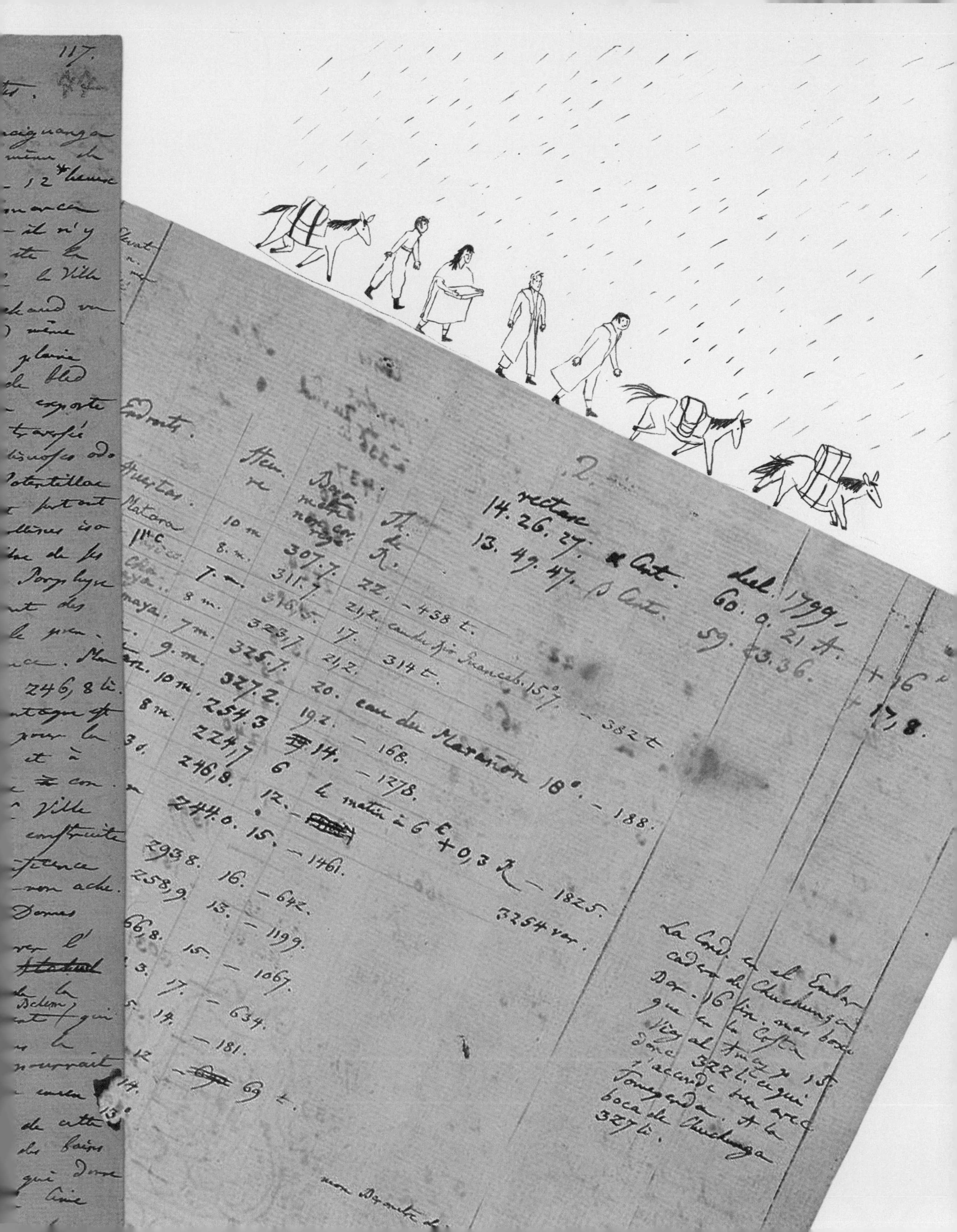

117.

14. 26. 27.
13. 49. 47.

del. 1799.
60. 0. 21.
59. 43. 36.

+ 16°
17,8

rector
Aut.
Cast.

Matara   10 m.
8 m. 307.7
7 m. 311.9   22.   — 438 t.
8 m.   21,2. cendre pie francese 157°   — 382 t
maya, 7 m. 328,7   17.   314 t.
9 m. 325.7   21,2.
10 m. 327.2   20.   eau du Marañon 18°.   — 188.
8 m. 254.3   192.   — 168.
30.   224,7   14.   — 1278.
246,8   6   le matin à 6   — 1825.
12.   + 0,3 R.
244.0. 15.   — 1461.
3254 var.
293 8.   16.   — 642.
258,9   13.   — 1199.
66,8   15.   — 1067.
3.   17.   — 634.
5.   14.   — 181.
12.
14.   69 t.
13.

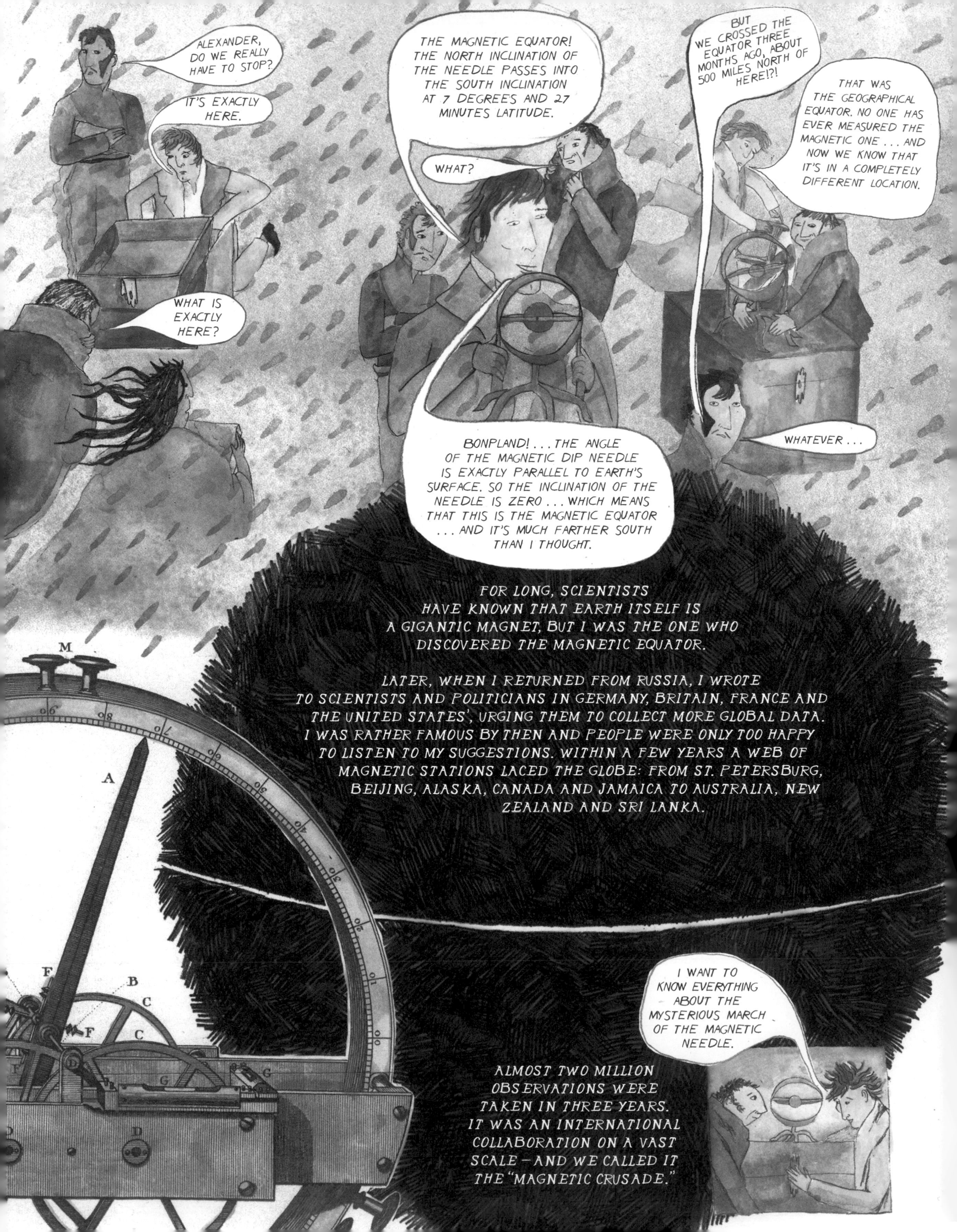
ALEXANDER, DO WE REALLY HAVE TO STOP?
IT'S EXACTLY HERE.
WHAT IS EXACTLY HERE?
THE MAGNETIC EQUATOR! THE NORTH INCLINATION OF THE NEEDLE PASSES INTO THE SOUTH INCLINATION AT 7 DEGREES AND 27 MINUTES LATITUDE.
WHAT?
BONPLAND! . . . THE ANGLE OF THE MAGNETIC DIP NEEDLE IS EXACTLY PARALLEL TO EARTH'S SURFACE. SO THE INCLINATION OF THE NEEDLE IS ZERO . . . WHICH MEANS THAT THIS IS THE MAGNETIC EQUATOR . . . AND IT'S MUCH FARTHER SOUTH THAN I THOUGHT.
BUT WE CROSSED THE EQUATOR THREE MONTHS AGO, ABOUT 500 MILES NORTH OF HERE!?!
THAT WAS THE GEOGRAPHICAL EQUATOR. NO ONE HAS EVER MEASURED THE MAGNETIC ONE . . . AND NOW WE KNOW THAT IT'S IN A COMPLETELY DIFFERENT LOCATION.
WHATEVER . . .
FOR LONG, SCIENTISTS HAVE KNOWN THAT EARTH ITSELF IS A GIGANTIC MAGNET, BUT I WAS THE ONE WHO DISCOVERED THE MAGNETIC EQUATOR.
LATER, WHEN I RETURNED FROM RUSSIA, I WROTE TO SCIENTISTS AND POLITICIANS IN GERMANY, BRITAIN, FRANCE AND THE UNITED STATES', URGING THEM TO COLLECT MORE GLOBAL DATA. I WAS RATHER FAMOUS BY THEN AND PEOPLE WERE ONLY TOO HAPPY TO LISTEN TO MY SUGGESTIONS. WITHIN A FEW YEARS A WEB OF MAGNETIC STATIONS LACED THE GLOBE: FROM ST. PETERSBURG, BEIJING, ALASKA, CANADA AND JAMAICA TO AUSTRALIA, NEW ZEALAND AND SRI LANKA.
I WANT TO KNOW EVERYTHING ABOUT THE MYSTERIOUS MARCH OF THE MAGNETIC NEEDLE.
ALMOST TWO MILLION OBSERVATIONS WERE TAKEN IN THREE YEARS. IT WAS AN INTERNATIONAL COLLABORATION ON A VAST SCALE – AND WE CALLED IT THE "MAGNETIC CRUSADE."

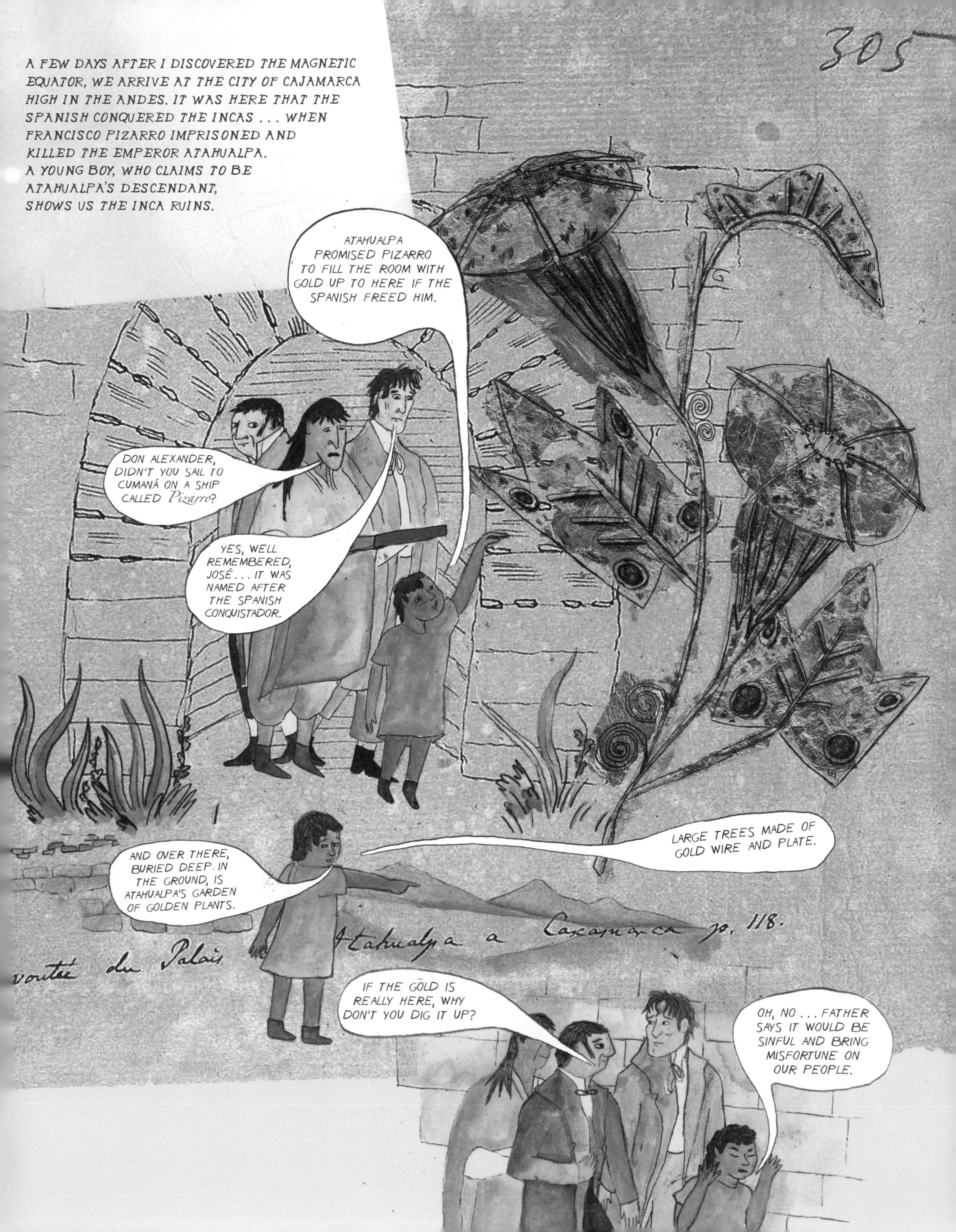
A FEW DAYS AFTER I DISCOVERED THE MAGNETIC EQUATOR, WE ARRIVE AT THE CITY OF CAJAMARCA HIGH IN THE ANDES. IT WAS HERE THAT THE SPANISH CONQUERED THE INCAS . . . WHEN FRANCISCO PIZARRO IMPRISONED AND KILLED THE EMPEROR ATAHUALPA.
A YOUNG BOY, WHO CLAIMS TO BE ATAHUALPA'S DESCENDANT, SHOWS US THE INCA RUINS.
ATAHUALPA PROMISED PIZARRO TO FILL THE ROOM WITH GOLD UP TO HERE IF THE SPANISH FREED HIM.
DON ALEXANDER, DIDN'T YOU SAIL TO CUMANÁ ON A SHIP CALLED *Pizarro*?
YES, WELL REMEMBERED, JOSÉ . . . IT WAS NAMED AFTER THE SPANISH CONQUISTADOR.
AND OVER THERE, BURIED DEEP IN THE GROUND, IS ATAHUALPA'S GARDEN OF GOLDEN PLANTS.
LARGE TREES MADE OF GOLD WIRE AND PLATE.
IF THE GOLD IS REALLY HERE, WHY DON'T YOU DIG IT UP?
OH, NO . . . FATHER SAYS IT WOULD BE SINFUL AND BRING MISFORTUNE ON OUR PEOPLE.

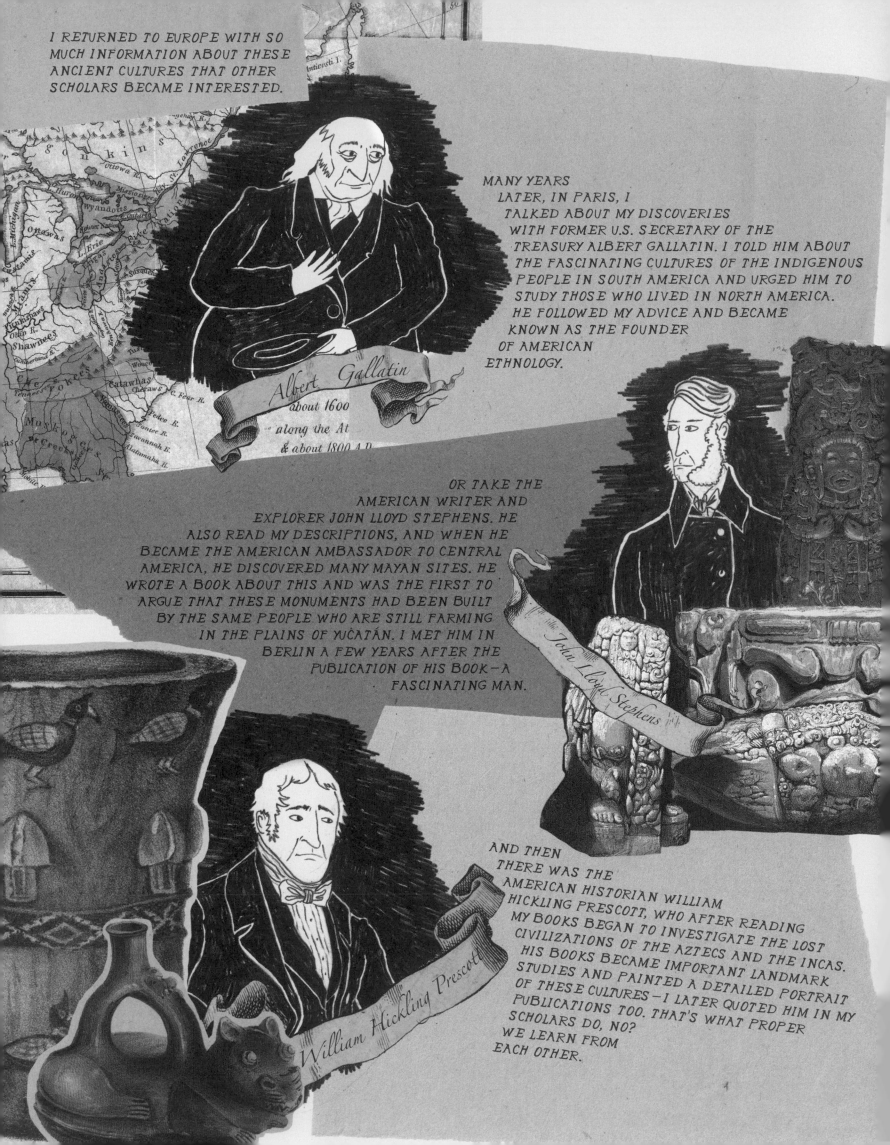

I RETURNED TO EUROPE WITH SO MUCH INFORMATION ABOUT THESE ANCIENT CULTURES THAT OTHER SCHOLARS BECAME INTERESTED.

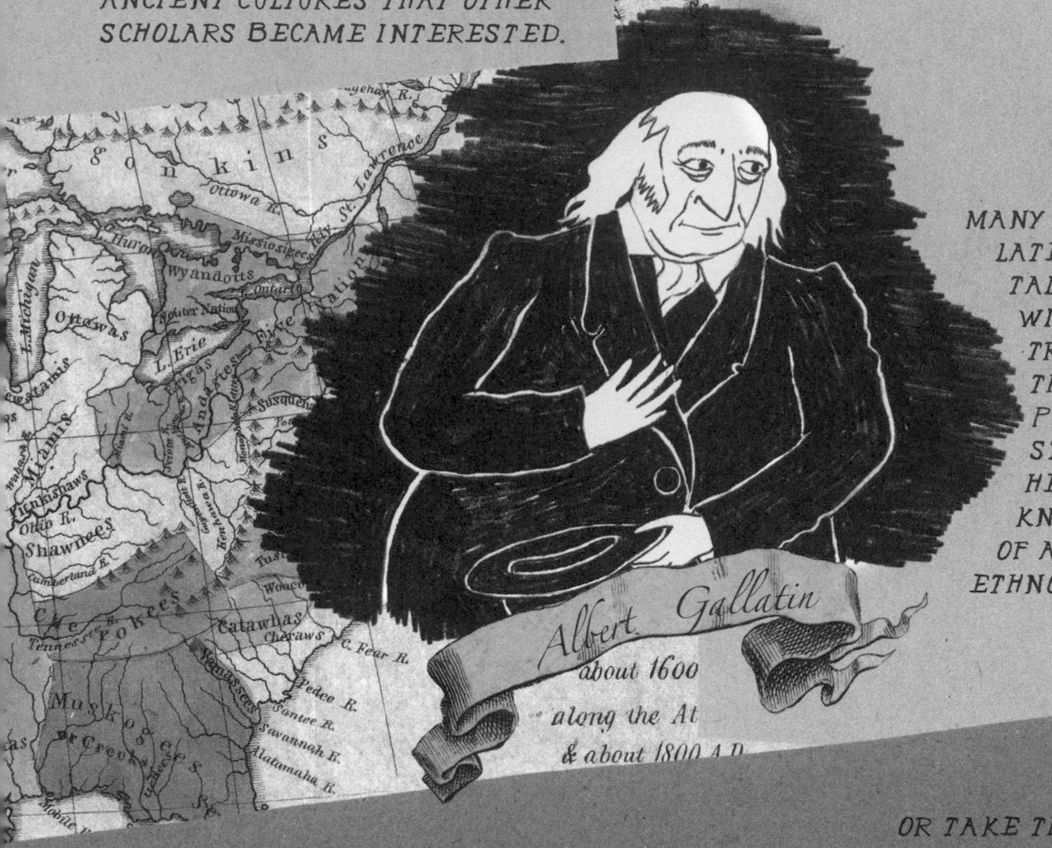
Albert Gallatin
about 1600

MANY YEARS LATER, IN PARIS, I TALKED ABOUT MY DISCOVERIES WITH FORMER U.S. SECRETARY OF THE TREASURY ALBERT GALLATIN. I TOLD HIM ABOUT THE FASCINATING CULTURES OF THE INDIGENOUS PEOPLE IN SOUTH AMERICA AND URGED HIM TO STUDY THOSE WHO LIVED IN NORTH AMERICA. HE FOLLOWED MY ADVICE AND BECAME KNOWN AS THE FOUNDER OF AMERICAN ETHNOLOGY.

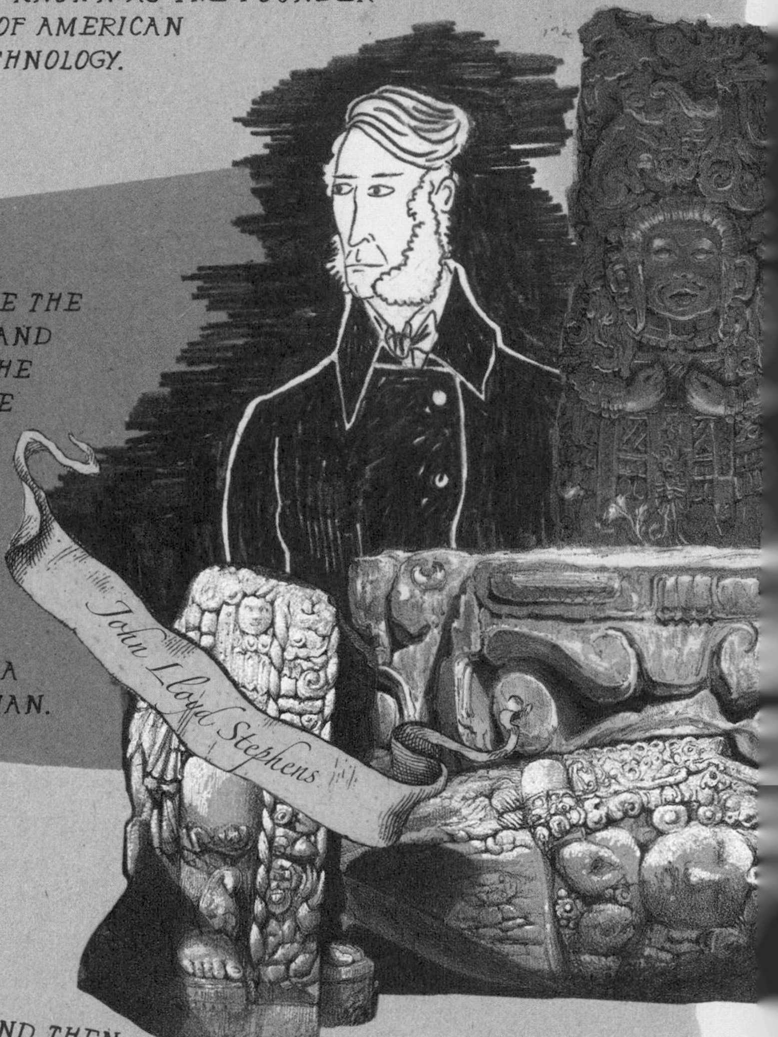
John Lloyd Stephens

OR TAKE THE AMERICAN WRITER AND EXPLORER JOHN LLOYD STEPHENS. HE ALSO READ MY DESCRIPTIONS, AND WHEN HE BECAME THE AMERICAN AMBASSADOR TO CENTRAL AMERICA, HE DISCOVERED MANY MAYAN SITES. HE WROTE A BOOK ABOUT THIS AND WAS THE FIRST TO ARGUE THAT THESE MONUMENTS HAD BEEN BUILT BY THE SAME PEOPLE WHO ARE STILL FARMING IN THE PLAINS OF YUCATÁN. I MET HIM IN BERLIN A FEW YEARS AFTER THE PUBLICATION OF HIS BOOK—A FASCINATING MAN.

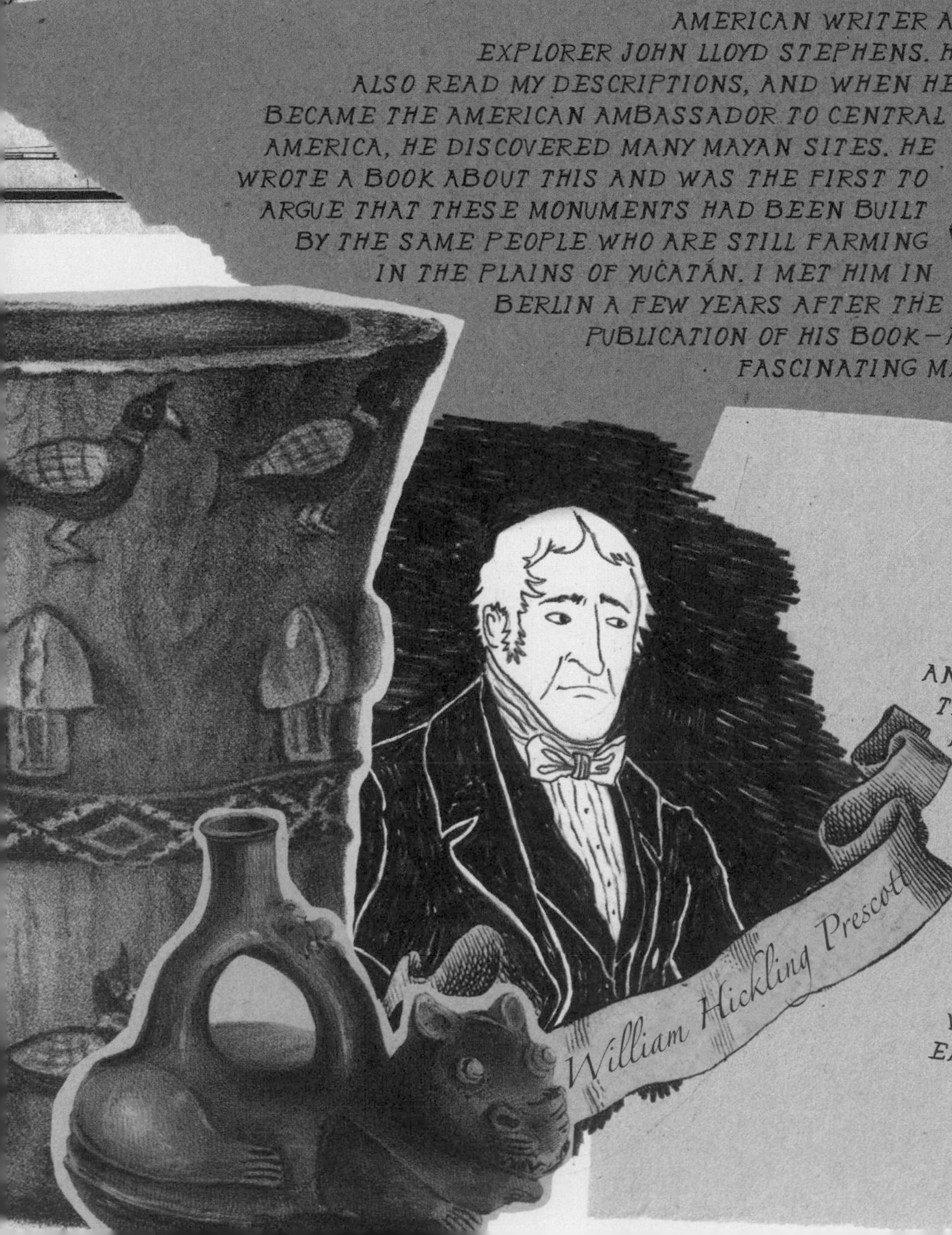
William Hickling Prescott

AND THEN THERE WAS THE AMERICAN HISTORIAN WILLIAM HICKLING PRESCOTT, WHO AFTER READING MY BOOKS BEGAN TO INVESTIGATE THE LOST CIVILIZATIONS OF THE AZTECS AND THE INCAS. HIS BOOKS BECAME IMPORTANT LANDMARK STUDIES AND PAINTED A DETAILED PORTRAIT OF THESE CULTURES—I LATER QUOTED HIM IN MY PUBLICATIONS TOO. THAT'S WHAT PROPER SCHOLARS DO, NO? WE LEARN FROM EACH OTHER.

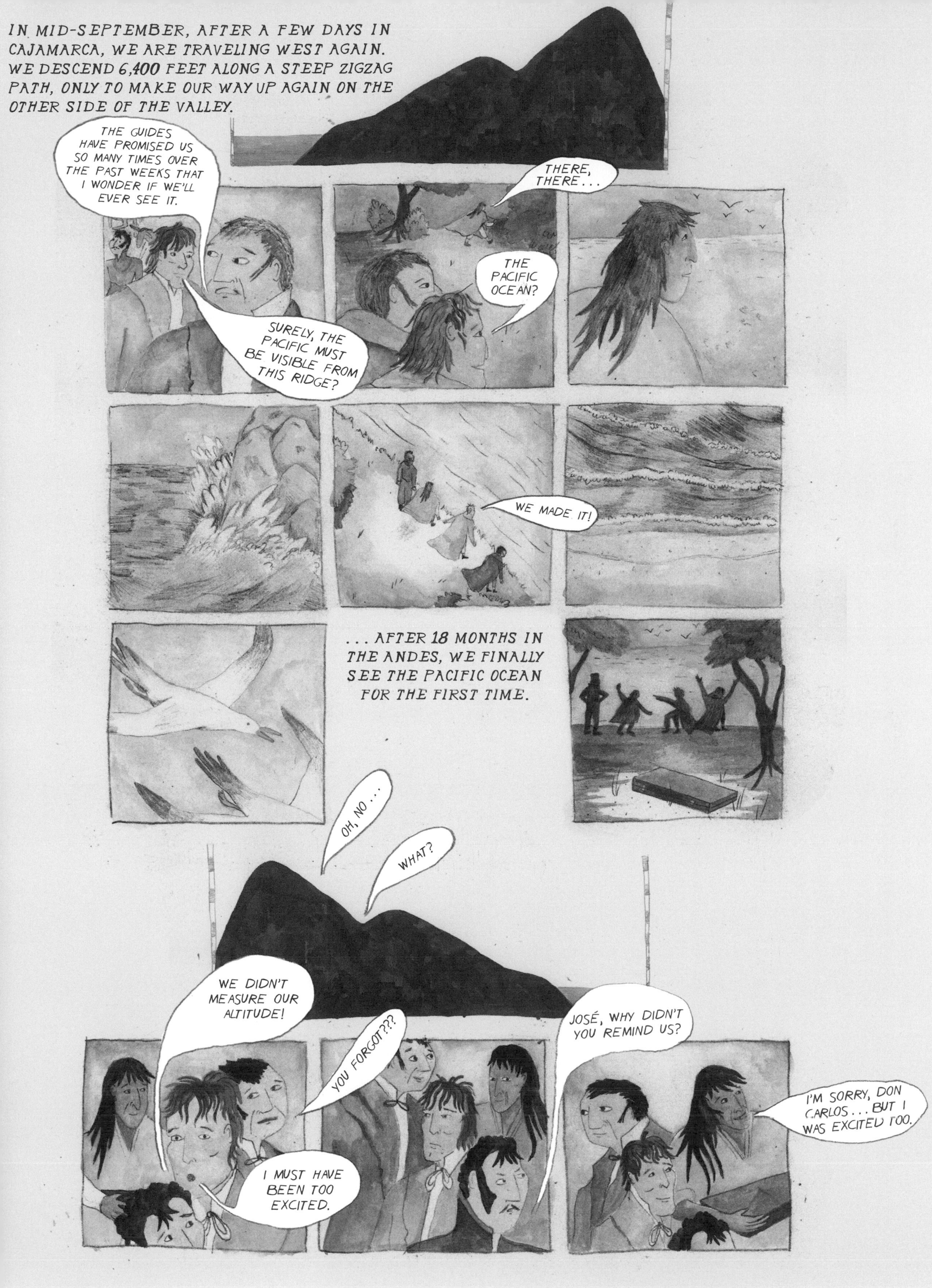
IN MID-SEPTEMBER, AFTER A FEW DAYS IN CAJAMARCA, WE ARE TRAVELING WEST AGAIN. WE DESCEND 6,400 FEET ALONG A STEEP ZIGZAG PATH, ONLY TO MAKE OUR WAY UP AGAIN ON THE OTHER SIDE OF THE VALLEY.
THE GUIDES HAVE PROMISED US SO MANY TIMES OVER THE PAST WEEKS THAT I WONDER IF WE'LL EVER SEE IT.
SURELY, THE PACIFIC MUST BE VISIBLE FROM THIS RIDGE?
THERE, THERE...
THE PACIFIC OCEAN?
WE MADE IT!
...AFTER 18 MONTHS IN THE ANDES, WE FINALLY SEE THE PACIFIC OCEAN FOR THE FIRST TIME.
OH, NO...
WHAT?
WE DIDN'T MEASURE OUR ALTITUDE!
YOU FORGOT???
I MUST HAVE BEEN TOO EXCITED.
JOSÉ, WHY DIDN'T YOU REMIND US?
I'M SORRY, DON CARLOS... BUT I WAS EXCITED TOO.

EVER SINCE I WAS A YOUNG BOY AND READ ABOUT

CAPTAIN COOK'S AND BOUGAINVILLE'S ADVENTURES,

I'VE LONGED TO SEE THE PACIFIC OCEAN.

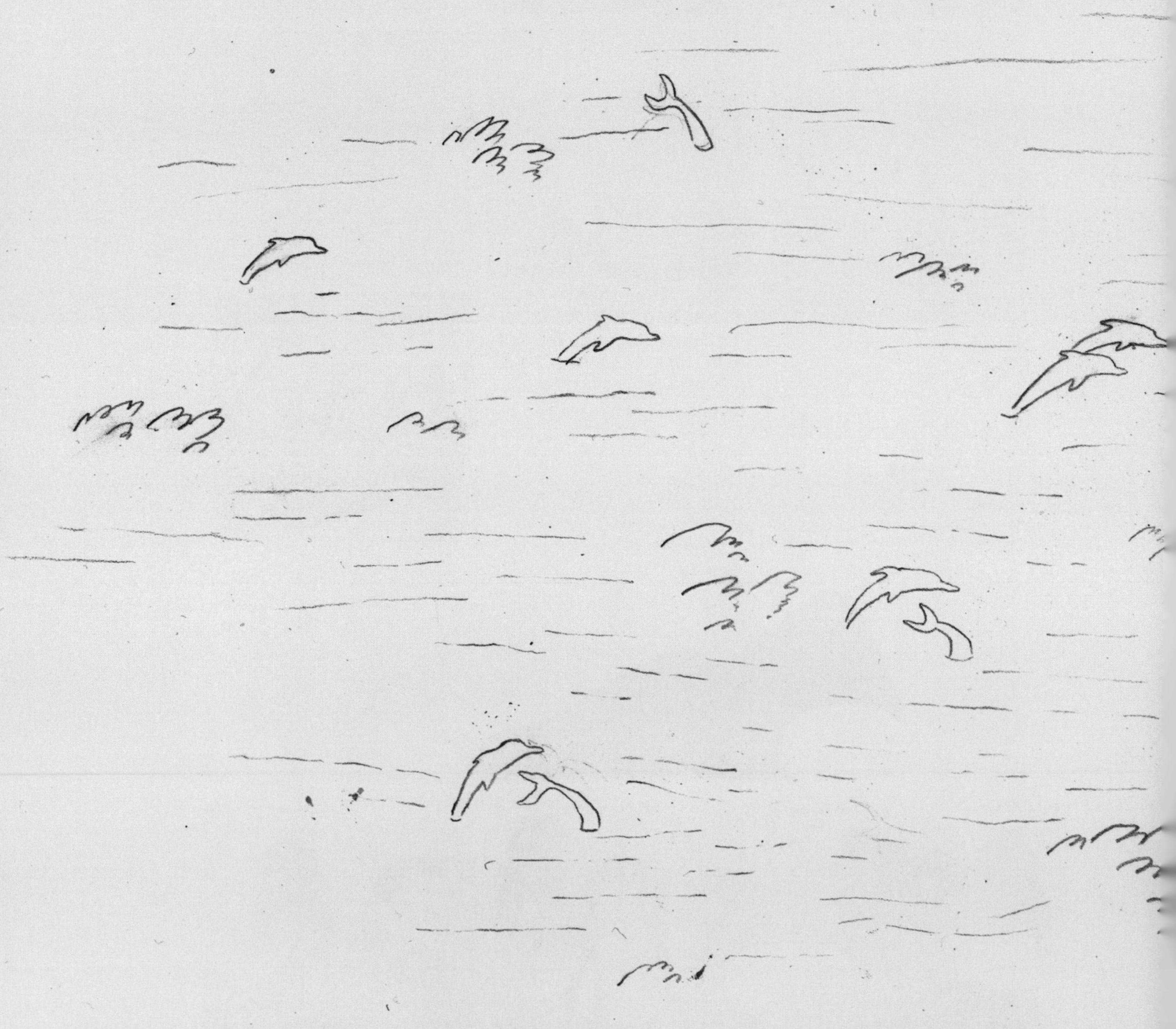

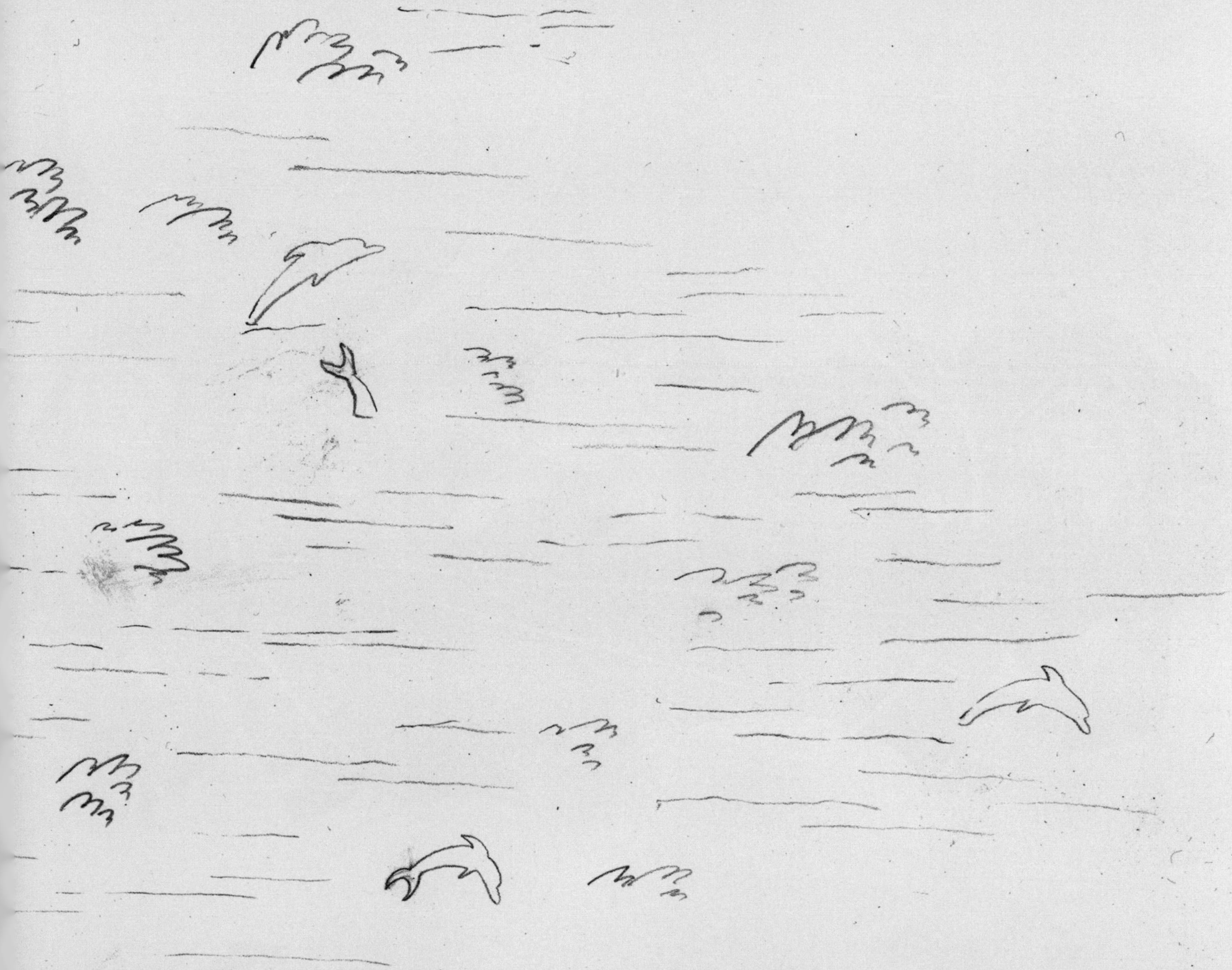

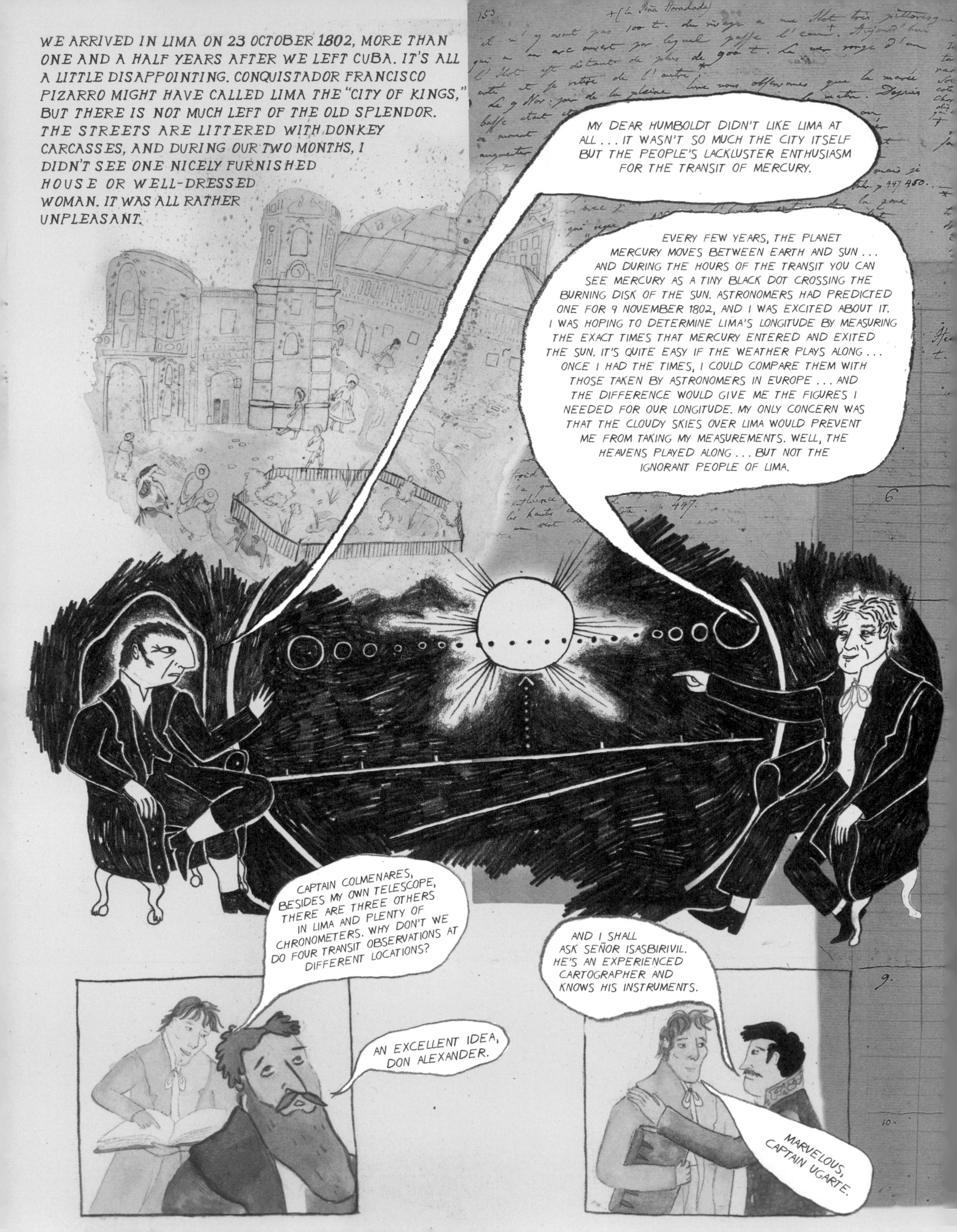
WE ARRIVED IN LIMA ON 23 OCTOBER 1802, MORE THAN ONE AND A HALF YEARS AFTER WE LEFT CUBA. IT'S ALL A LITTLE DISAPPOINTING. CONQUISTADOR FRANCISCO PIZARRO MIGHT HAVE CALLED LIMA THE "CITY OF KINGS," BUT THERE IS NOT MUCH LEFT OF THE OLD SPLENDOR. THE STREETS ARE LITTERED WITH DONKEY CARCASSES, AND DURING OUR TWO MONTHS, I DIDN'T SEE ONE NICELY FURNISHED HOUSE OR WELL-DRESSED WOMAN. IT WAS ALL RATHER UNPLEASANT.
MY DEAR HUMBOLDT DIDN'T LIKE LIMA AT ALL . . . IT WASN'T SO MUCH THE CITY ITSELF BUT THE PEOPLE'S LACKLUSTER ENTHUSIASM FOR THE TRANSIT OF MERCURY.
EVERY FEW YEARS, THE PLANET MERCURY MOVES BETWEEN EARTH AND SUN . . . AND DURING THE HOURS OF THE TRANSIT YOU CAN SEE MERCURY AS A TINY BLACK DOT CROSSING THE BURNING DISK OF THE SUN. ASTRONOMERS HAD PREDICTED ONE FOR 9 NOVEMBER 1802, AND I WAS EXCITED ABOUT IT. I WAS HOPING TO DETERMINE LIMA'S LONGITUDE BY MEASURING THE EXACT TIMES THAT MERCURY ENTERED AND EXITED THE SUN. IT'S QUITE EASY IF THE WEATHER PLAYS ALONG . . . ONCE I HAD THE TIMES, I COULD COMPARE THEM WITH THOSE TAKEN BY ASTRONOMERS IN EUROPE . . . AND THE DIFFERENCE WOULD GIVE ME THE FIGURES I NEEDED FOR OUR LONGITUDE. MY ONLY CONCERN WAS THAT THE CLOUDY SKIES OVER LIMA WOULD PREVENT ME FROM TAKING MY MEASUREMENTS. WELL, THE HEAVENS PLAYED ALONG . . . BUT NOT THE IGNORANT PEOPLE OF LIMA.
CAPTAIN COLMENARES, BESIDES MY OWN TELESCOPE, THERE ARE THREE OTHERS IN LIMA AND PLENTY OF CHRONOMETERS. WHY DON'T WE DO FOUR TRANSIT OBSERVATIONS AT DIFFERENT LOCATIONS?
AN EXCELLENT IDEA, DON ALEXANDER.
AND I SHALL ASK SEÑOR ISASBIRIVIL. HE'S AN EXPERIENCED CARTOGRAPHER AND KNOWS HIS INSTRUMENTS.
MARVELOUS, CAPTAIN UGARTE.

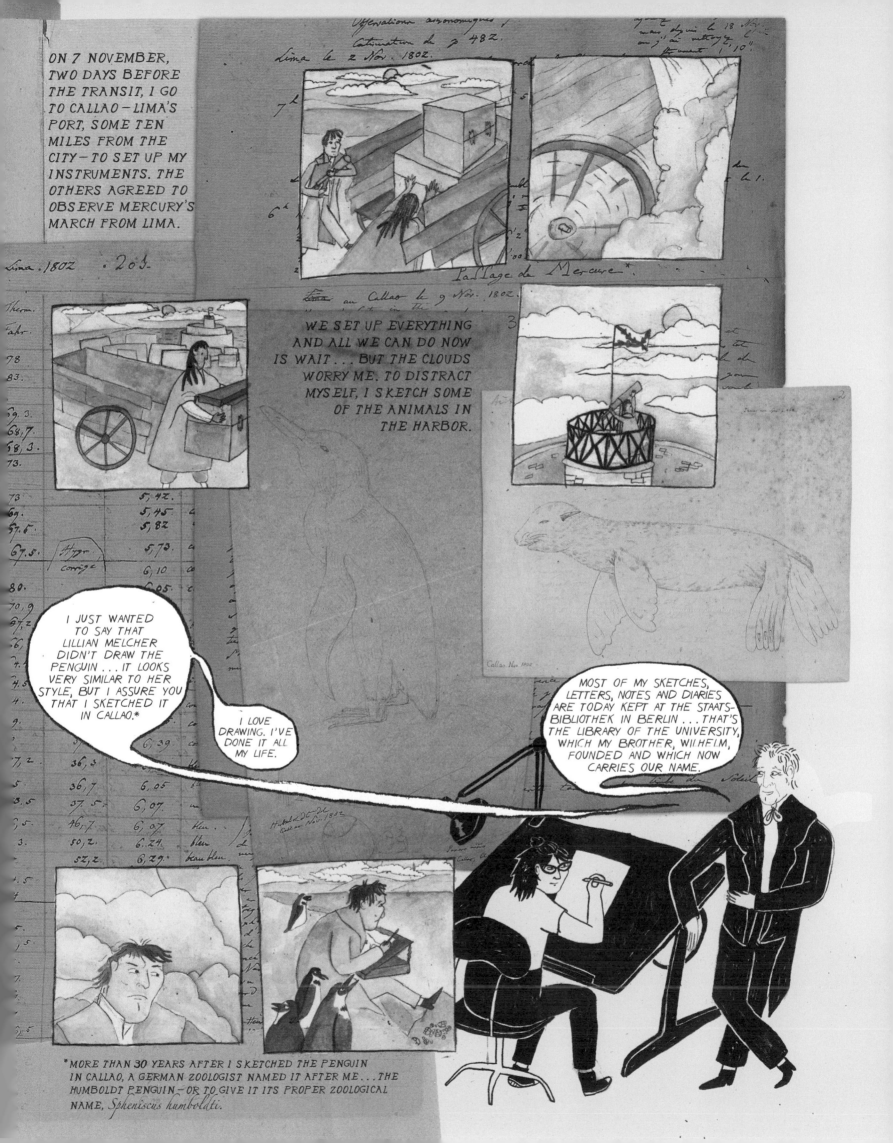

ON 7 NOVEMBER, TWO DAYS BEFORE THE TRANSIT, I GO TO CALLAO—LIMA'S PORT, SOME TEN MILES FROM THE CITY—TO SET UP MY INSTRUMENTS. THE OTHERS AGREED TO OBSERVE MERCURY'S MARCH FROM LIMA.

WE SET UP EVERYTHING AND ALL WE CAN DO NOW IS WAIT... BUT THE CLOUDS WORRY ME. TO DISTRACT MYSELF, I SKETCH SOME OF THE ANIMALS IN THE HARBOR.

I JUST WANTED TO SAY THAT LILLIAN MELCHER DIDN'T DRAW THE PENGUIN... IT LOOKS VERY SIMILAR TO HER STYLE, BUT I ASSURE YOU THAT I SKETCHED IT IN CALLAO.*

I LOVE DRAWING. I'VE DONE IT ALL MY LIFE.

MOST OF MY SKETCHES, LETTERS, NOTES AND DIARIES ARE TODAY KEPT AT THE STAATS-BIBLIOTHEK IN BERLIN... THAT'S THE LIBRARY OF THE UNIVERSITY, WHICH MY BROTHER, WILHELM, FOUNDED AND WHICH NOW CARRIES OUR NAME.

*MORE THAN 30 YEARS AFTER I SKETCHED THE PENGUIN IN CALLAO, A GERMAN ZOOLOGIST NAMED IT AFTER ME... THE HUMBOLDT PENGUIN—OR TO GIVE IT ITS PROPER ZOOLOGICAL NAME, Spheniscus humboldti.

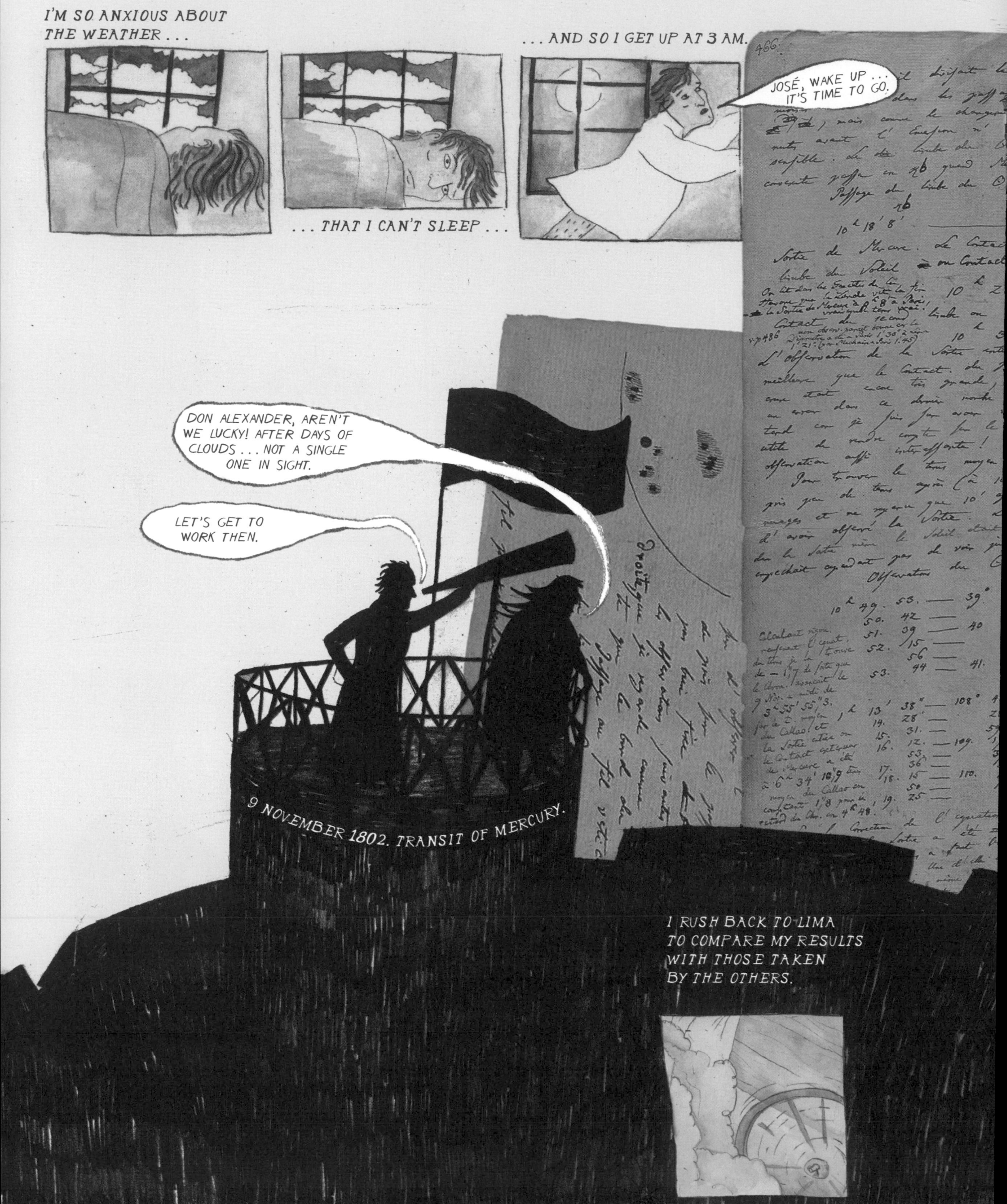
I'M SO ANXIOUS ABOUT THE WEATHER . . .
. . . THAT I CAN'T SLEEP . . .
. . . AND SO I GET UP AT 3 AM.
JOSÉ, WAKE UP . . . IT'S TIME TO GO.
DON ALEXANDER, AREN'T WE LUCKY! AFTER DAYS OF CLOUDS . . . NOT A SINGLE ONE IN SIGHT.
LET'S GET TO WORK THEN.
9 NOVEMBER 1802. TRANSIT OF MERCURY.
I RUSH BACK TO LIMA TO COMPARE MY RESULTS WITH THOSE TAKEN BY THE OTHERS.

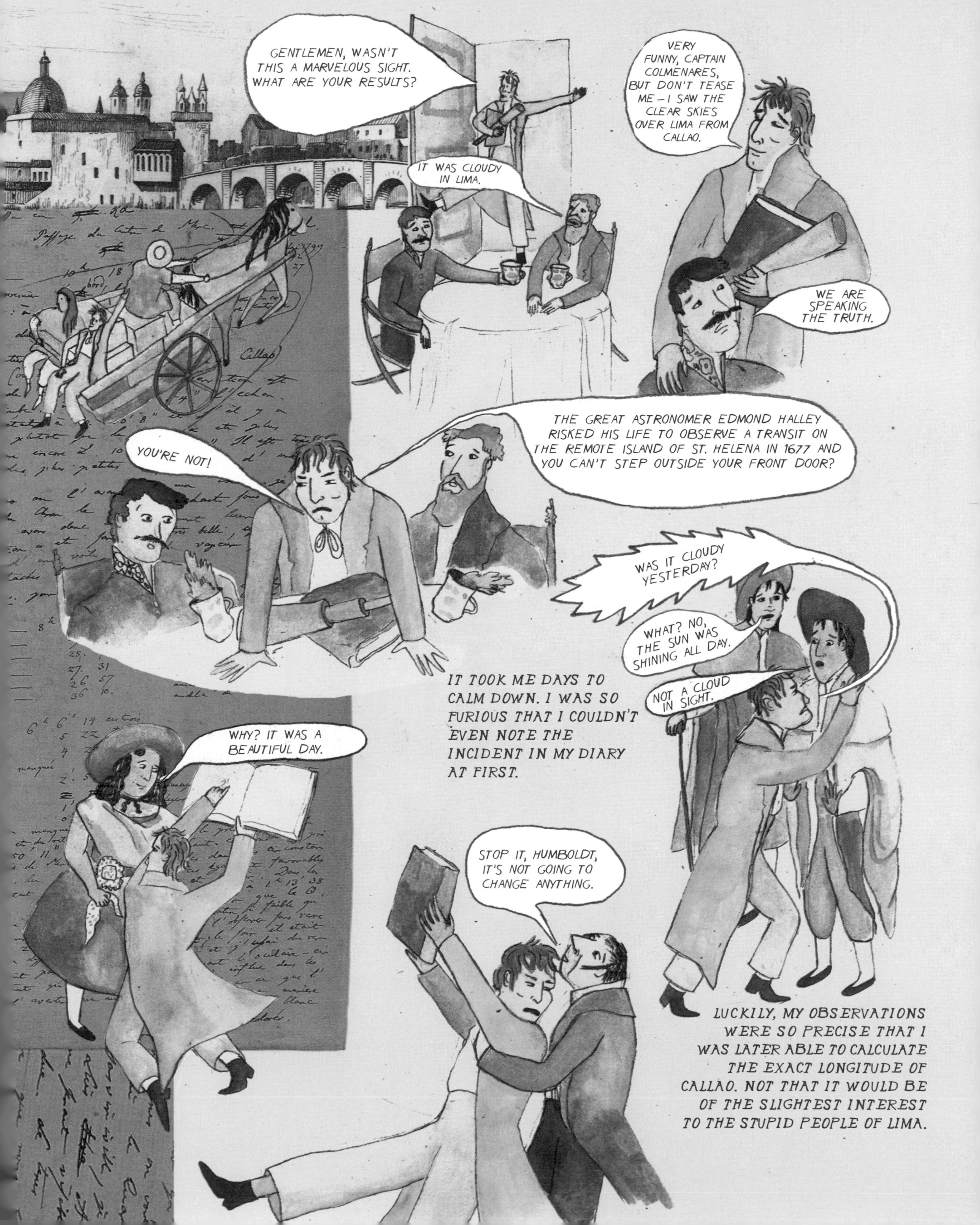
GENTLEMEN, WASN'T THIS A MARVELOUS SIGHT. WHAT ARE YOUR RESULTS?
IT WAS CLOUDY IN LIMA.
VERY FUNNY, CAPTAIN COLMENARES, BUT DON'T TEASE ME—I SAW THE CLEAR SKIES OVER LIMA FROM CALLAO.
WE ARE SPEAKING THE TRUTH.
YOU'RE NOT!
THE GREAT ASTRONOMER EDMOND HALLEY RISKED HIS LIFE TO OBSERVE A TRANSIT ON THE REMOTE ISLAND OF ST. HELENA IN 1677 AND YOU CAN'T STEP OUTSIDE YOUR FRONT DOOR?
WAS IT CLOUDY YESTERDAY?
WHAT? NO, THE SUN WAS SHINING ALL DAY.
NOT A CLOUD IN SIGHT.
IT TOOK ME DAYS TO CALM DOWN. I WAS SO FURIOUS THAT I COULDN'T EVEN NOTE THE INCIDENT IN MY DIARY AT FIRST.
WHY? IT WAS A BEAUTIFUL DAY.
STOP IT, HUMBOLDT, IT'S NOT GOING TO CHANGE ANYTHING.
LUCKILY, MY OBSERVATIONS WERE SO PRECISE THAT I WAS LATER ABLE TO CALCULATE THE EXACT LONGITUDE OF CALLAO. NOT THAT IT WOULD BE OF THE SLIGHTEST INTEREST TO THE STUPID PEOPLE OF LIMA.

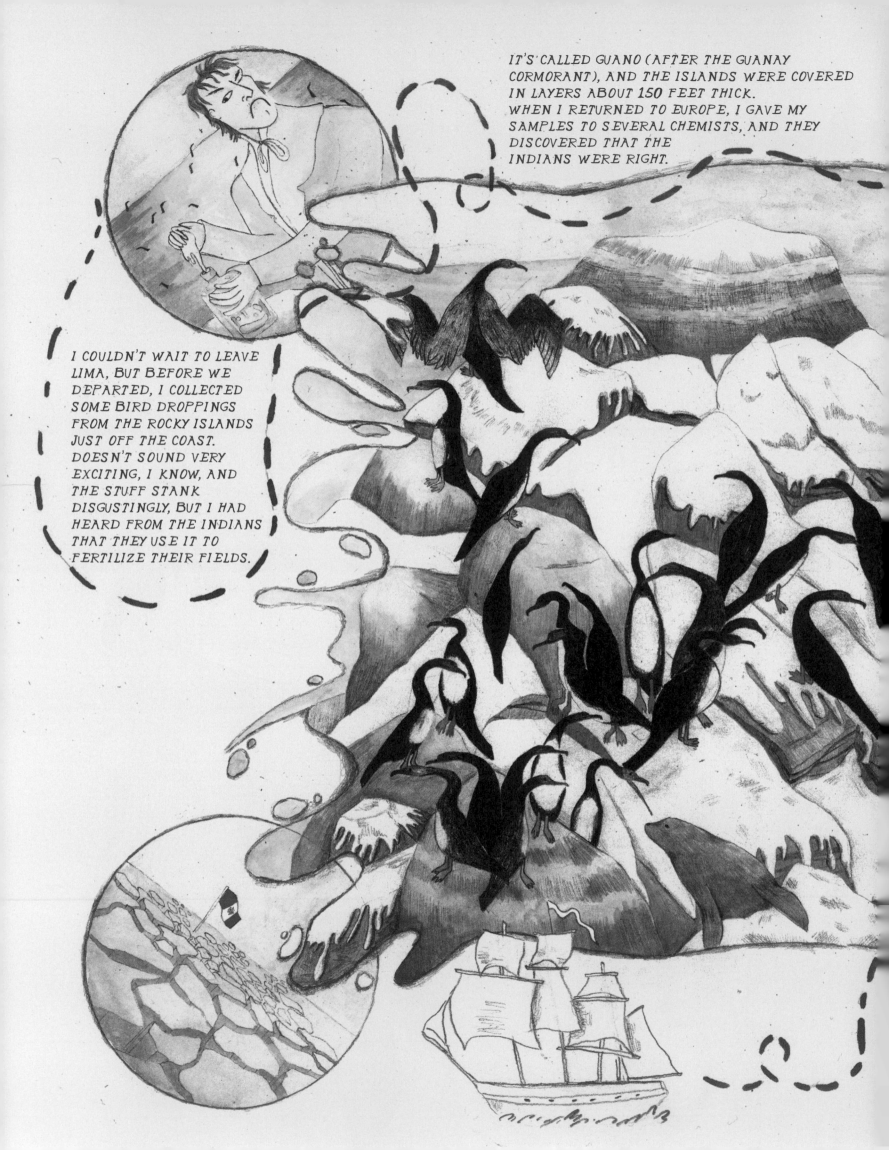

IT'S CALLED GUANO (AFTER THE GUANAY CORMORANT), AND THE ISLANDS WERE COVERED IN LAYERS ABOUT 150 FEET THICK. WHEN I RETURNED TO EUROPE, I GAVE MY SAMPLES TO SEVERAL CHEMISTS, AND THEY DISCOVERED THAT THE INDIANS WERE RIGHT.

I COULDN'T WAIT TO LEAVE LIMA, BUT BEFORE WE DEPARTED, I COLLECTED SOME BIRD DROPPINGS FROM THE ROCKY ISLANDS JUST OFF THE COAST. DOESN'T SOUND VERY EXCITING, I KNOW, AND THE STUFF STANK DISGUSTINGLY, BUT I HAD HEARD FROM THE INDIANS THAT THEY USE IT TO FERTILIZE THEIR FIELDS.

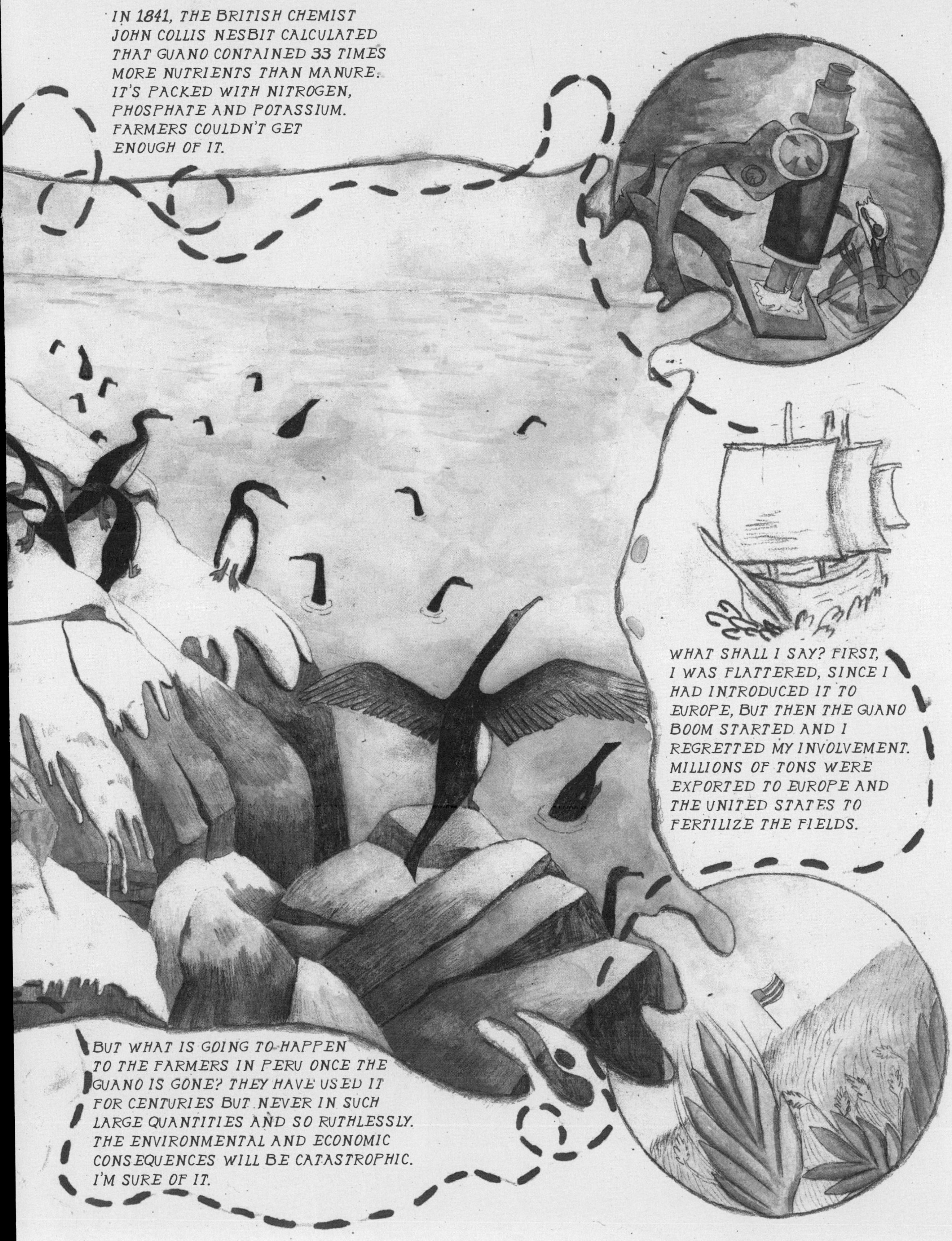
IN 1841, THE BRITISH CHEMIST JOHN COLLIS NESBIT CALCULATED THAT GUANO CONTAINED 33 TIMES MORE NUTRIENTS THAN MANURE. IT'S PACKED WITH NITROGEN, PHOSPHATE AND POTASSIUM. FARMERS COULDN'T GET ENOUGH OF IT.
WHAT SHALL I SAY? FIRST, I WAS FLATTERED, SINCE I HAD INTRODUCED IT TO EUROPE, BUT THEN THE GUANO BOOM STARTED AND I REGRETTED MY INVOLVEMENT. MILLIONS OF TONS WERE EXPORTED TO EUROPE AND THE UNITED STATES TO FERTILIZE THE FIELDS.
BUT WHAT IS GOING TO HAPPEN TO THE FARMERS IN PERU ONCE THE GUANO IS GONE? THEY HAVE USED IT FOR CENTURIES BUT NEVER IN SUCH LARGE QUANTITIES AND SO RUTHLESSLY. THE ENVIRONMENTAL AND ECONOMIC CONSEQUENCES WILL BE CATASTROPHIC. I'M SURE OF IT.

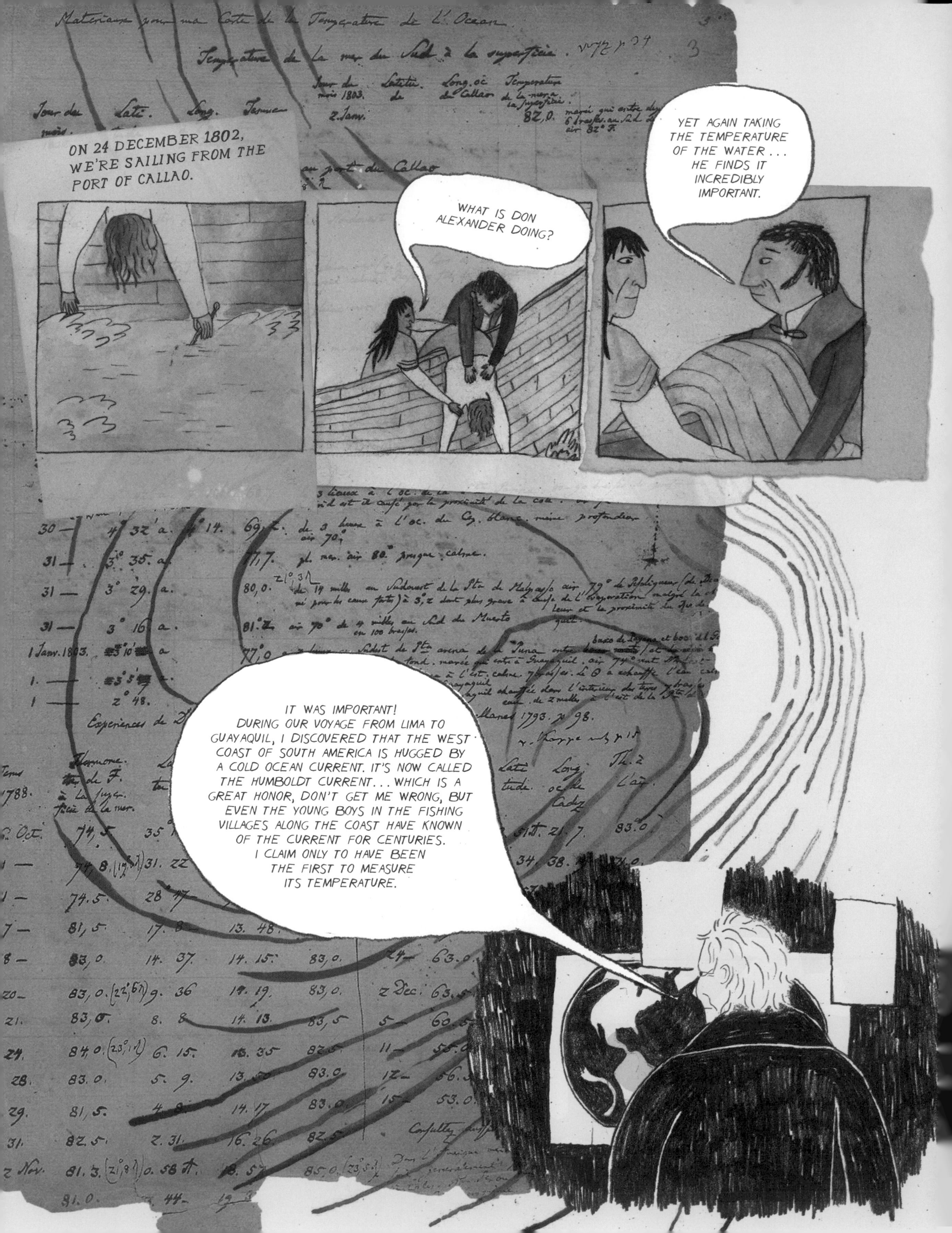
ON 24 DECEMBER 1802, WE'RE SAILING FROM THE PORT OF CALLAO.
WHAT IS DON ALEXANDER DOING?
YET AGAIN TAKING THE TEMPERATURE OF THE WATER . . . HE FINDS IT INCREDIBLY IMPORTANT.
IT WAS IMPORTANT! DURING OUR VOYAGE FROM LIMA TO GUAYAQUIL, I DISCOVERED THAT THE WEST COAST OF SOUTH AMERICA IS HUGGED BY A COLD OCEAN CURRENT. IT'S NOW CALLED THE HUMBOLDT CURRENT . . . WHICH IS A GREAT HONOR, DON'T GET ME WRONG, BUT EVEN THE YOUNG BOYS IN THE FISHING VILLAGES ALONG THE COAST HAVE KNOWN OF THE CURRENT FOR CENTURIES. I CLAIM ONLY TO HAVE BEEN THE FIRST TO MEASURE ITS TEMPERATURE.

WE ARRIVED IN GUAYAQUIL, A PORT TOWN
ON THE COAST OF ECUADOR, ON
4 JANUARY 1803.

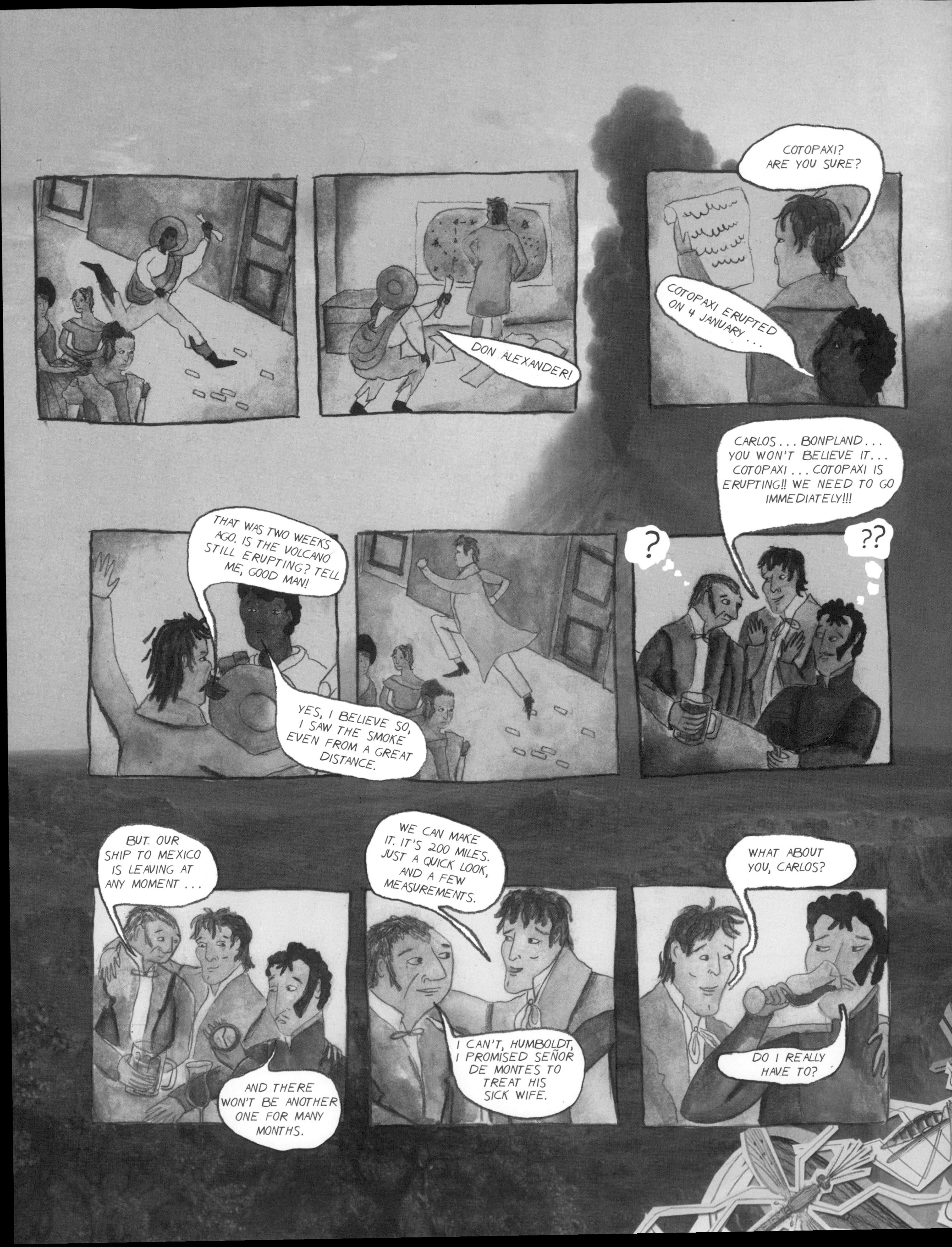

DON ALEXANDER!
COTOPAXI ERUPTED ON 4 JANUARY . . .
COTOPAXI? ARE YOU SURE?
THAT WAS TWO WEEKS AGO. IS THE VOLCANO STILL ERUPTING? TELL ME, GOOD MAN!
YES, I BELIEVE SO, I SAW THE SMOKE EVEN FROM A GREAT DISTANCE.
CARLOS . . . BONPLAND . . . YOU WON'T BELIEVE IT . . . COTOPAXI . . . COTOPAXI IS ERUPTING!! WE NEED TO GO IMMEDIATELY!!!
?
??
BUT OUR SHIP TO MEXICO IS LEAVING AT ANY MOMENT . . .
AND THERE WON'T BE ANOTHER ONE FOR MANY MONTHS.
WE CAN MAKE IT. IT'S 200 MILES. JUST A QUICK LOOK, AND A FEW MEASUREMENTS.
I CAN'T, HUMBOLDT, I PROMISED SEÑOR DE MONTES TO TREAT HIS SICK WIFE.
WHAT ABOUT YOU, CARLOS?
DO I REALLY HAVE TO?

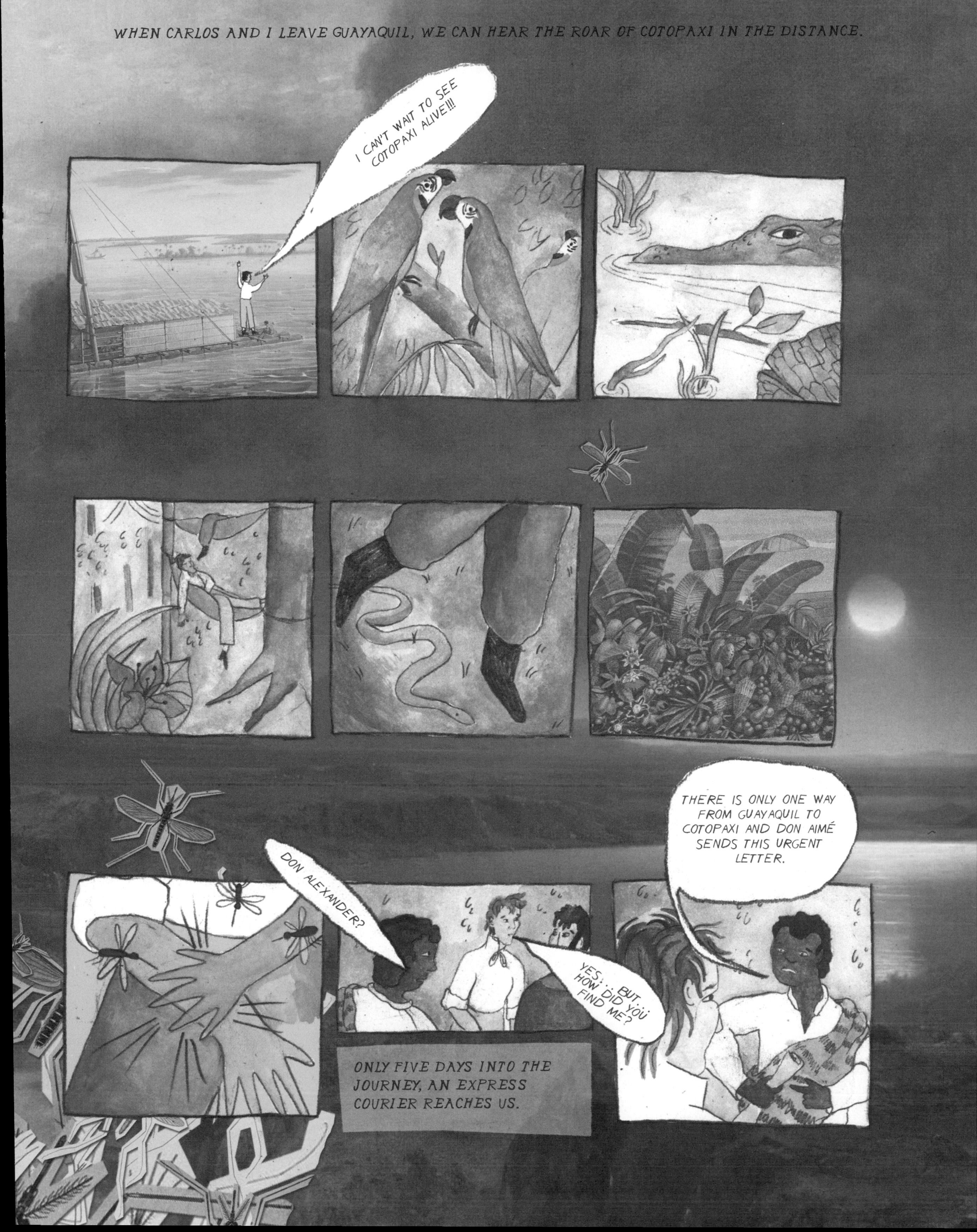
WHEN CARLOS AND I LEAVE GUAYAQUIL, WE CAN HEAR THE ROAR OF COTOPAXI IN THE DISTANCE.
I CAN'T WAIT TO SEE COTOPAXI ALIVE!!!
DON ALEXANDER?
YES... BUT... HOW DID YOU FIND ME?
ONLY FIVE DAYS INTO THE JOURNEY, AN EXPRESS COURIER REACHES US.
THERE IS ONLY ONE WAY FROM GUAYAQUIL TO COTOPAXI AND DON AIMÉ SENDS THIS URGENT LETTER.

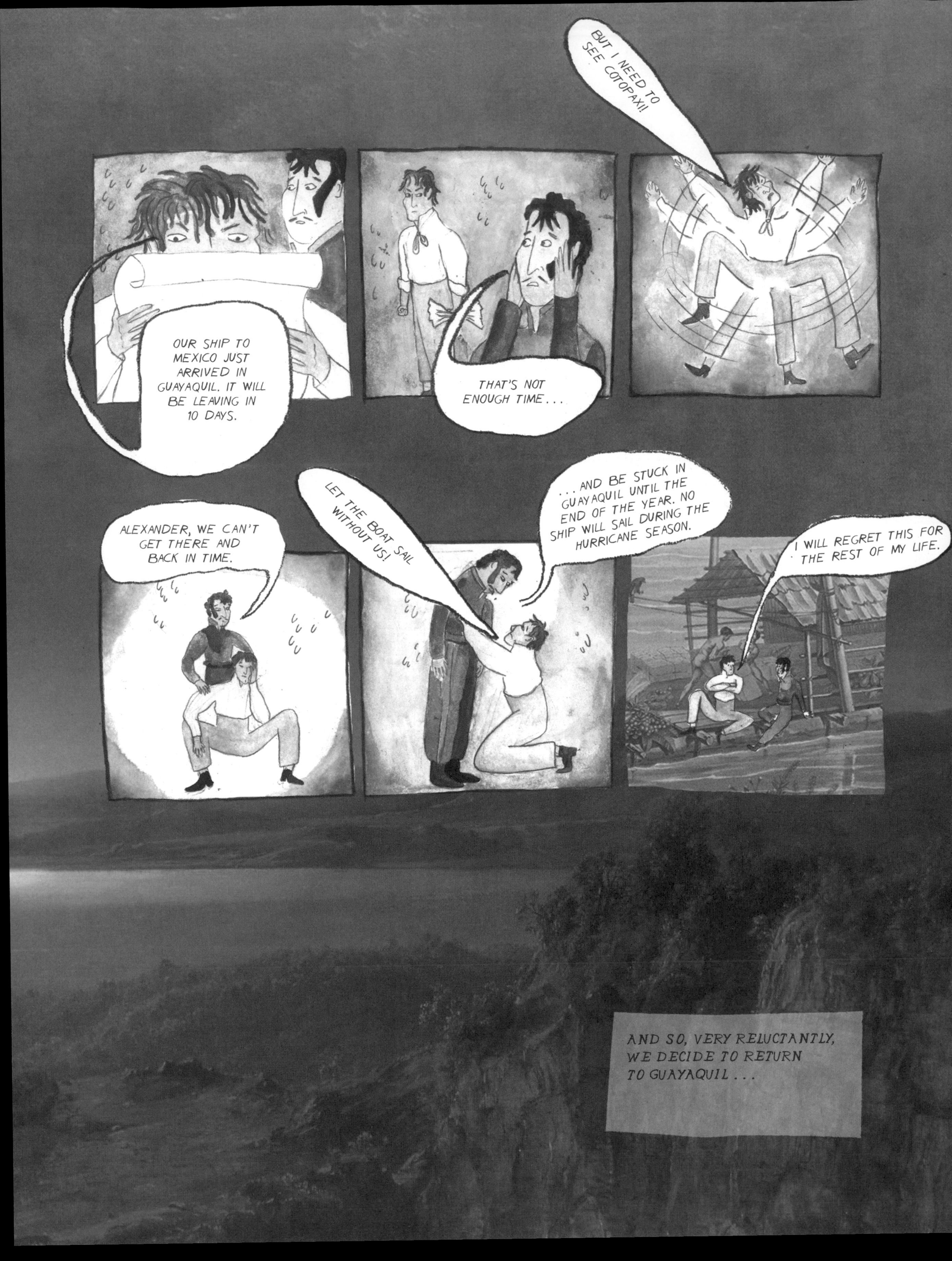
OUR SHIP TO MEXICO JUST ARRIVED IN GUAYAQUIL. IT WILL BE LEAVING IN 10 DAYS.
THAT'S NOT ENOUGH TIME . . .
BUT I NEED TO SEE COTOPAXI!
ALEXANDER, WE CAN'T GET THERE AND BACK IN TIME.
LET THE BOAT SAIL WITHOUT US!
. . . AND BE STUCK IN GUAYAQUIL UNTIL THE END OF THE YEAR. NO SHIP WILL SAIL DURING THE HURRICANE SEASON.
I WILL REGRET THIS FOR THE REST OF MY LIFE.
AND SO, VERY RELUCTANTLY, WE DECIDE TO RETURN TO GUAYAQUIL . . .

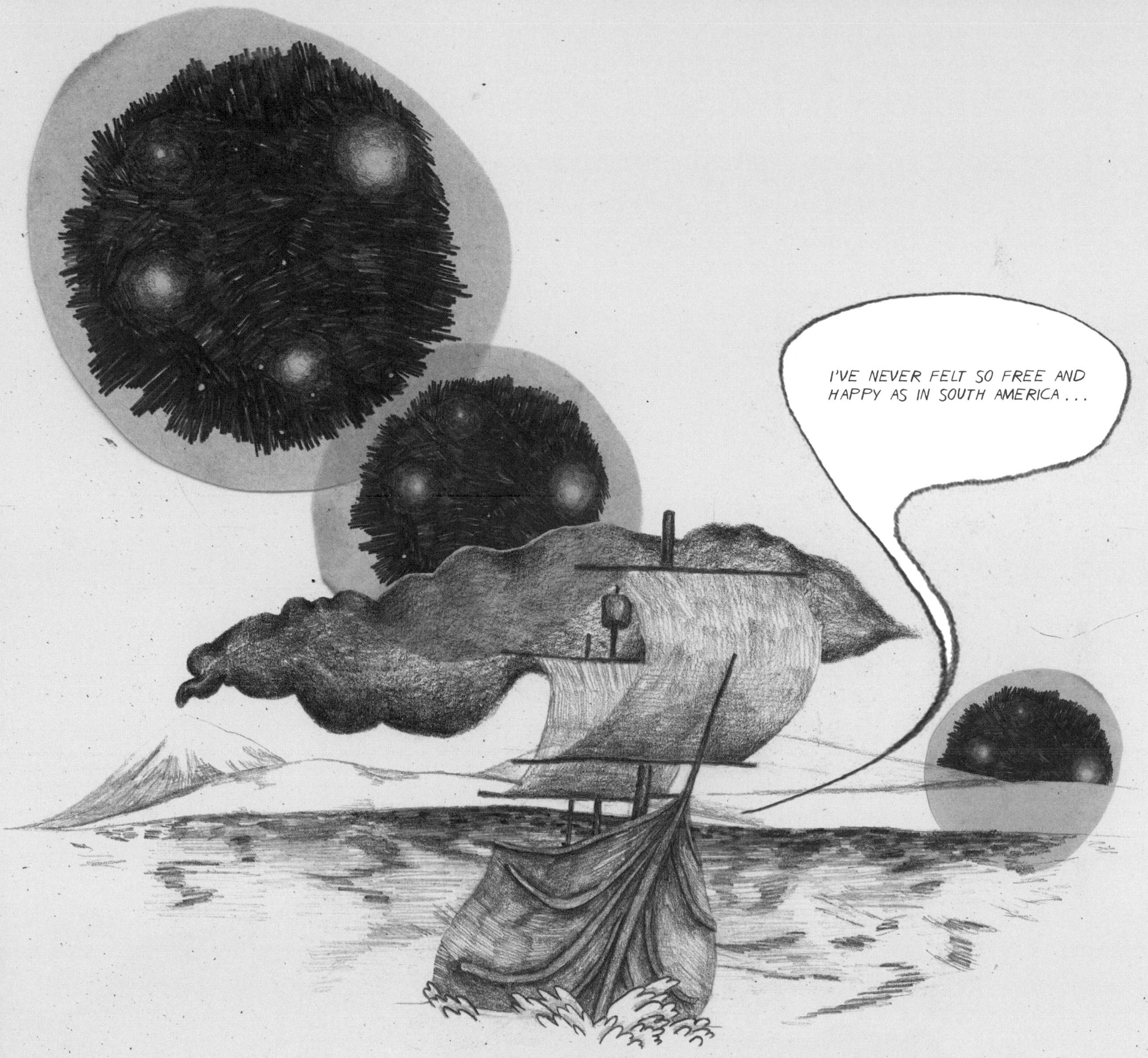
I'VE NEVER FELT SO FREE AND HAPPY AS IN SOUTH AMERICA...

WE SAIL ON 17 FEBRUARY 1803, AND NINE DAYS LATER WE CROSS THE EQUATOR ONE LAST TIME. THE STARS ALSO TELL US THAT WE'VE LEFT THE SOUTHERN HEMISPHERE... THE SOUTHERN CROSS SETS LOWER AND LOWER EVERY NIGHT.

ON 23 MARCH 1803, A LITTLE MORE THAN A MONTH AFTER WE HAD LEFT GUAYAQUIL, WE LANDED IN ACAPULCO . . . THEN WE MADE THE ARDUOUS TREK ACROSS THE RUGGED SIERRA MADRE DEL SUR TO MEXICO CITY.

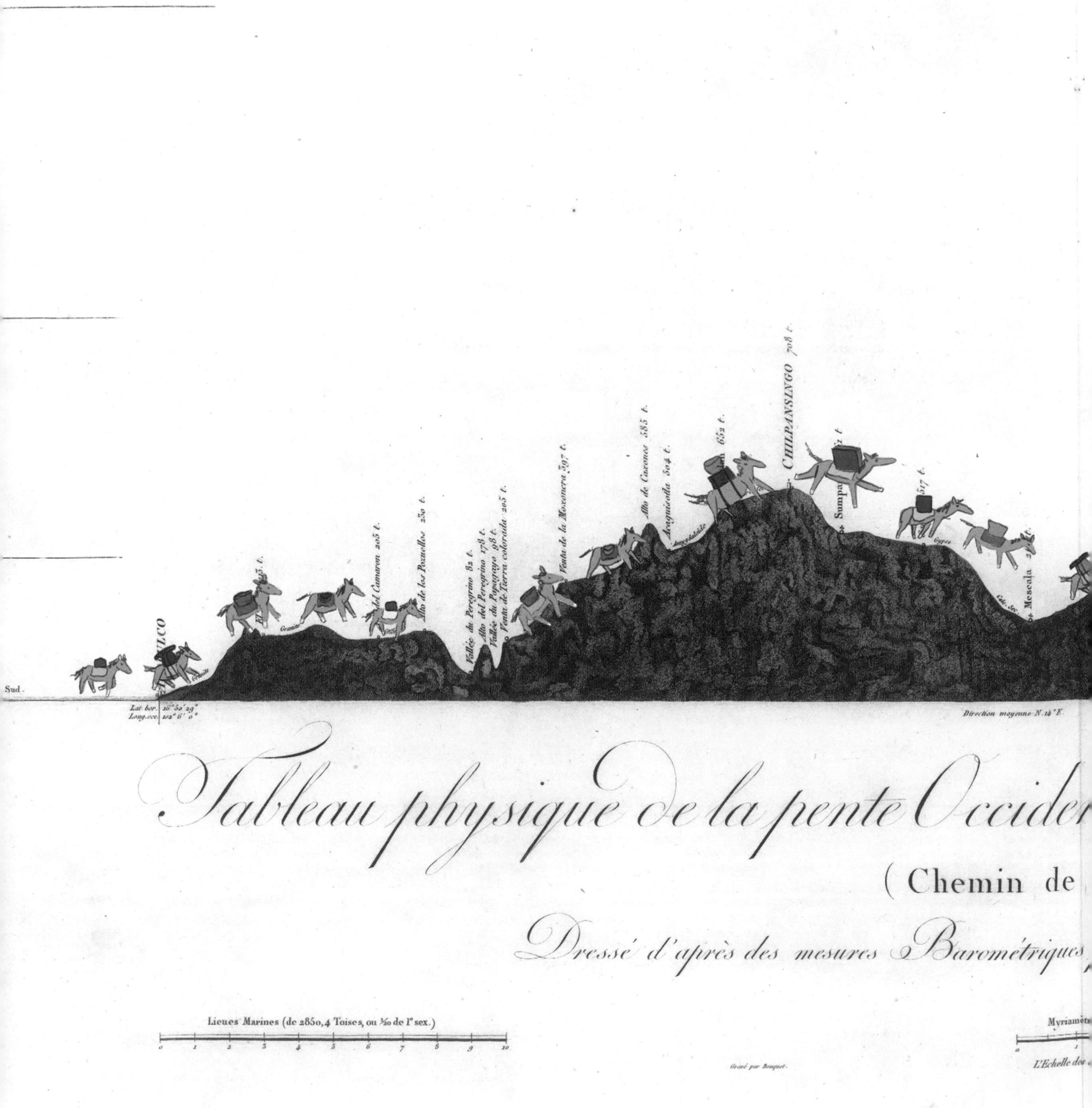

Sud.
Alto de los Pozuelos 250 t.
del Camaron 205 t.
Vallée du Peregrino 82 t.
Alto del Peregrino 178 t.
Vallée du Papagayo 98 t.
Venta de Tierra colorada 205 t.
Venta de la Moxonera 397 t.
Alto de Cacones 585 t.
Acaquisotla 504 t.
CHILPANSINGO 708 t.
Mescala
Lat. bor. 16° 50′ 29″
Long. occ. 102° 6′ 0″
Direction moyenne N. 14° E.
Tableau physique de la pente Occiden
(Chemin de
Dressé d'après des mesures Barométriques
Lieues Marines (de 2850,4 Toises, ou 1/20 de 1° sex.)
0 1 2 3 4 5 6 7 8 9 10
Gravé par Bouquet.

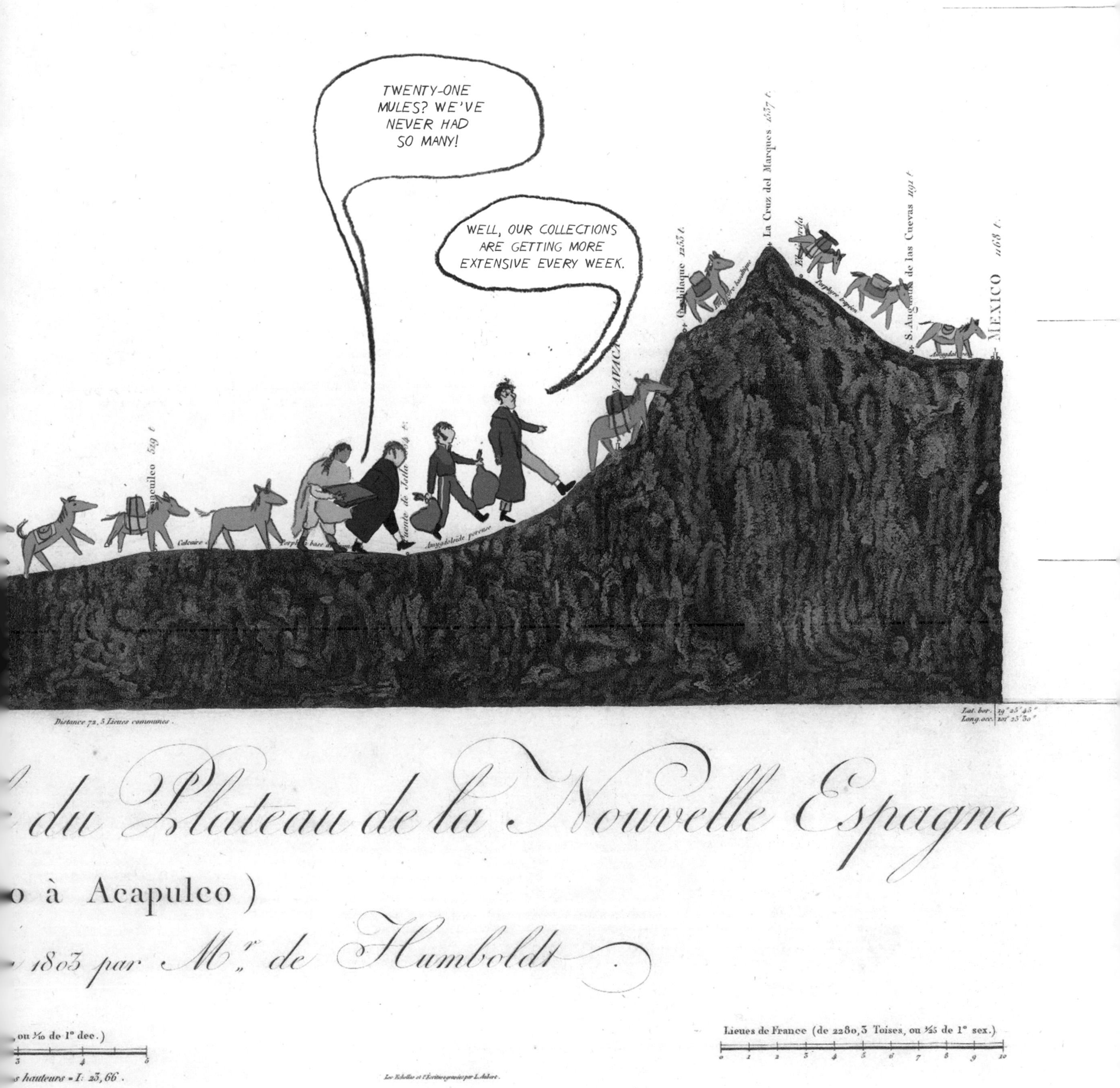
TWENTY-ONE MULES? WE'VE NEVER HAD SO MANY!
WELL, OUR COLLECTIONS ARE GETTING MORE EXTENSIVE EVERY WEEK.
La Cruz del Marques
MEXICO
Distance 72, 5 Lieues communes.
du Plateau de la Nouvelle Espagne
o à Acapulco)
1803 par Mr. de Humboldt
Lieues de France (de 2280,5 Toises, ou 1/25 de 1° sex.)

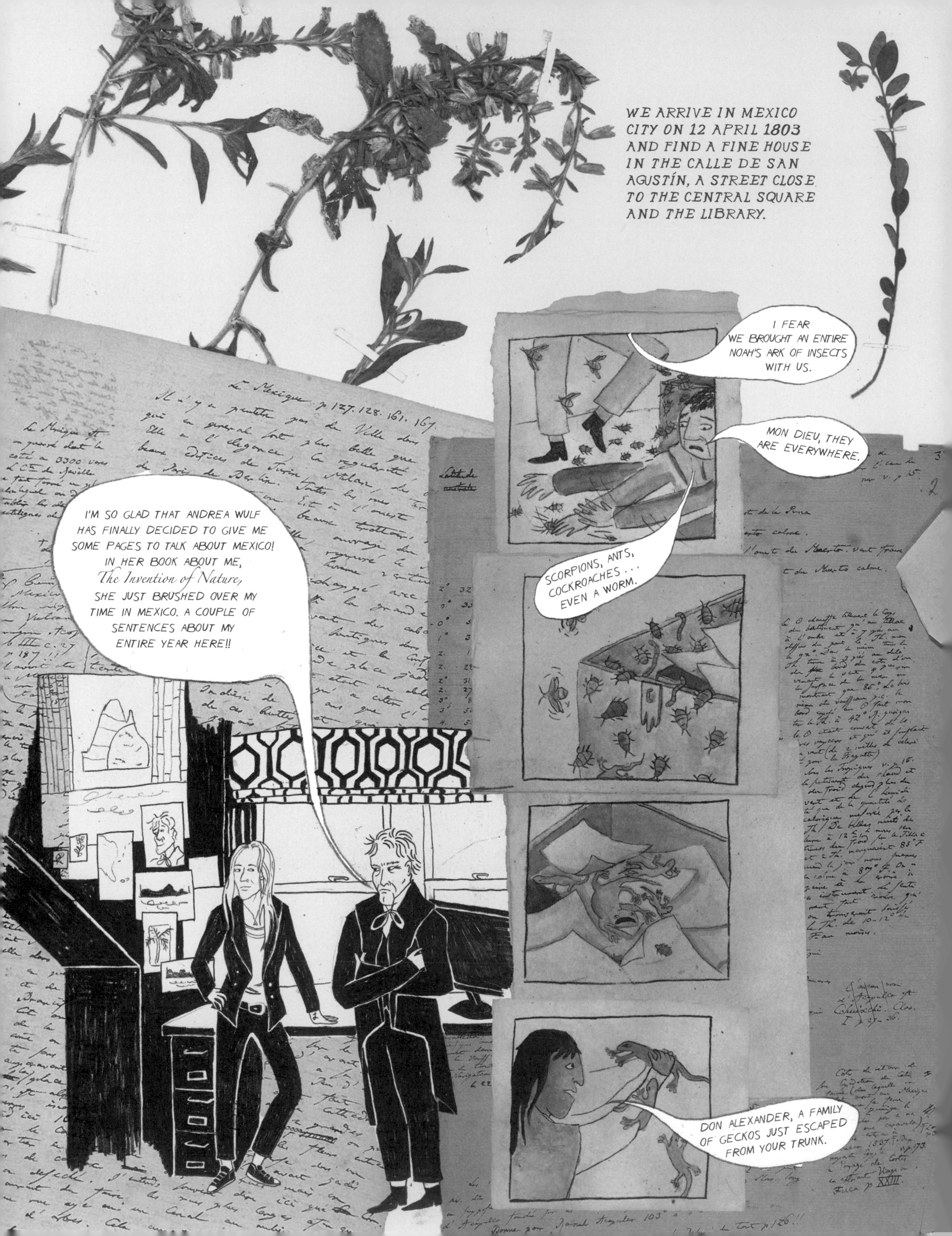
WE ARRIVE IN MEXICO CITY ON 12 APRIL 1803 AND FIND A FINE HOUSE IN THE CALLE DE SAN AGUSTÍN, A STREET CLOSE TO THE CENTRAL SQUARE AND THE LIBRARY.
I'M SO GLAD THAT ANDREA WULF HAS FINALLY DECIDED TO GIVE ME SOME PAGES TO TALK ABOUT MEXICO! IN HER BOOK ABOUT ME, *The Invention of Nature*, SHE JUST BRUSHED OVER MY TIME IN MEXICO. A COUPLE OF SENTENCES ABOUT MY ENTIRE YEAR HERE!!
I FEAR WE BROUGHT AN ENTIRE NOAH'S ARK OF INSECTS WITH US.
MON DIEU, THEY ARE EVERYWHERE.
SCORPIONS, ANTS, COCKROACHES . . . EVEN A WORM.
DON ALEXANDER, A FAMILY OF GECKOS JUST ESCAPED FROM YOUR TRUNK.

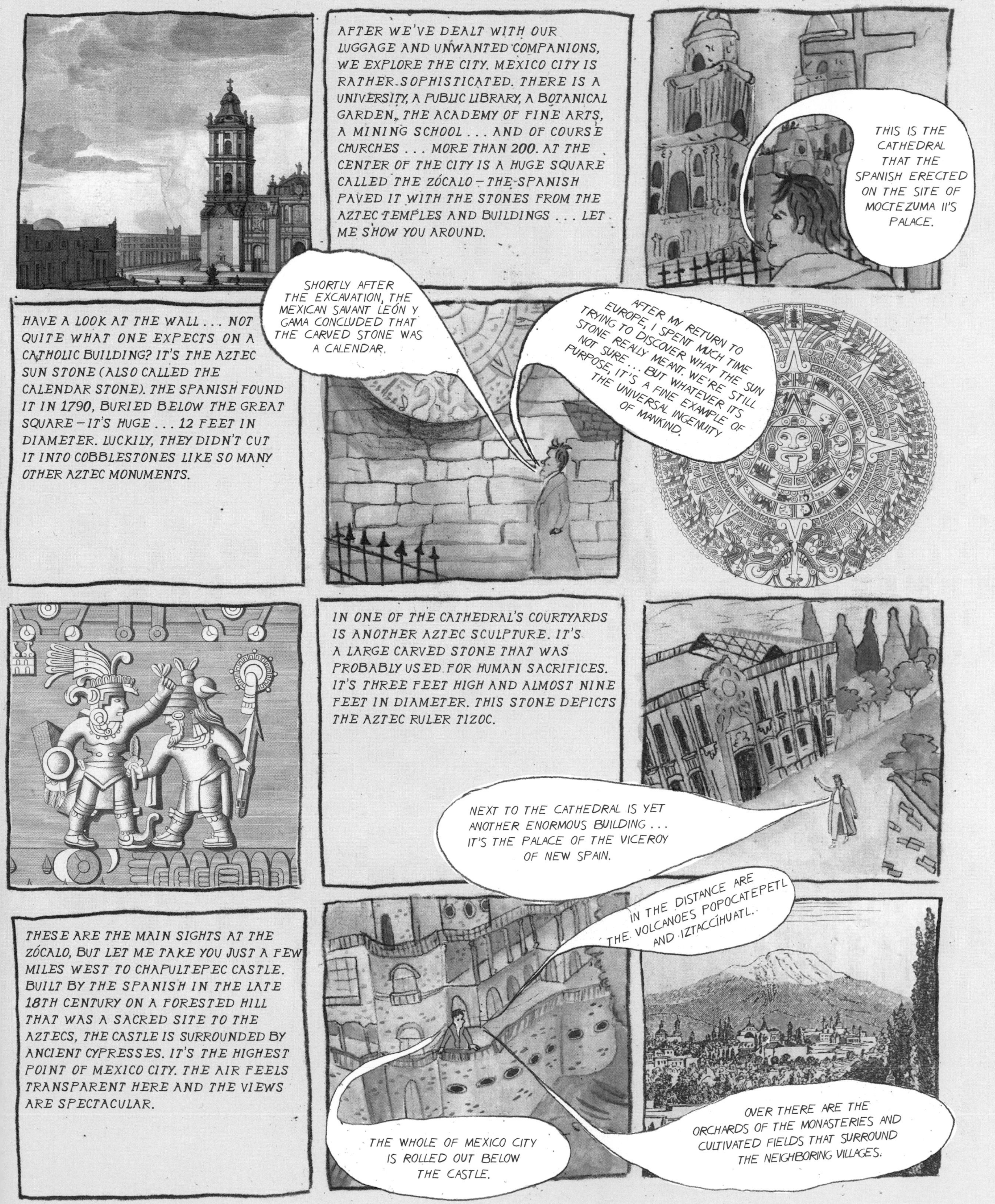
AFTER WE'VE DEALT WITH OUR LUGGAGE AND UNWANTED COMPANIONS, WE EXPLORE THE CITY. MEXICO CITY IS RATHER SOPHISTICATED. THERE IS A UNIVERSITY, A PUBLIC LIBRARY, A BOTANICAL GARDEN, THE ACADEMY OF FINE ARTS, A MINING SCHOOL . . . AND OF COURSE CHURCHES . . . MORE THAN 200. AT THE CENTER OF THE CITY IS A HUGE SQUARE CALLED THE ZÓCALO – THE SPANISH PAVED IT WITH THE STONES FROM THE AZTEC TEMPLES AND BUILDINGS . . . LET ME SHOW YOU AROUND.
THIS IS THE CATHEDRAL THAT THE SPANISH ERECTED ON THE SITE OF MOCTEZUMA II'S PALACE.
HAVE A LOOK AT THE WALL . . . NOT QUITE WHAT ONE EXPECTS ON A CATHOLIC BUILDING? IT'S THE AZTEC SUN STONE (ALSO CALLED THE CALENDAR STONE). THE SPANISH FOUND IT IN 1790, BURIED BELOW THE GREAT SQUARE – IT'S HUGE . . . 12 FEET IN DIAMETER. LUCKILY, THEY DIDN'T CUT IT INTO COBBLESTONES LIKE SO MANY OTHER AZTEC MONUMENTS.
SHORTLY AFTER THE EXCAVATION, THE MEXICAN SAVANT LEÓN Y GAMA CONCLUDED THAT THE CARVED STONE WAS A CALENDAR.
AFTER MY RETURN TO EUROPE, I SPENT MUCH TIME TRYING TO DISCOVER WHAT THE SUN STONE REALLY MEANT. WE'RE STILL NOT SURE . . . BUT WHATEVER ITS PURPOSE, IT'S A FINE EXAMPLE OF THE UNIVERSAL INGENUITY OF MANKIND.
IN ONE OF THE CATHEDRAL'S COURTYARDS IS ANOTHER AZTEC SCULPTURE. IT'S A LARGE CARVED STONE THAT WAS PROBABLY USED FOR HUMAN SACRIFICES. IT'S THREE FEET HIGH AND ALMOST NINE FEET IN DIAMETER. THIS STONE DEPICTS THE AZTEC RULER TIZOC.
NEXT TO THE CATHEDRAL IS YET ANOTHER ENORMOUS BUILDING . . . IT'S THE PALACE OF THE VICEROY OF NEW SPAIN.
THESE ARE THE MAIN SIGHTS AT THE ZÓCALO, BUT LET ME TAKE YOU JUST A FEW MILES WEST TO CHAPULTEPEC CASTLE. BUILT BY THE SPANISH IN THE LATE 18TH CENTURY ON A FORESTED HILL THAT WAS A SACRED SITE TO THE AZTECS, THE CASTLE IS SURROUNDED BY ANCIENT CYPRESSES. IT'S THE HIGHEST POINT OF MEXICO CITY. THE AIR FEELS TRANSPARENT HERE AND THE VIEWS ARE SPECTACULAR.
IN THE DISTANCE ARE THE VOLCANOES POPOCATEPETL AND IZTACCÍHUATL.
THE WHOLE OF MEXICO CITY IS ROLLED OUT BELOW THE CASTLE.
OVER THERE ARE THE ORCHARDS OF THE MONASTERIES AND CULTIVATED FIELDS THAT SURROUND THE NEIGHBORING VILLAGES.

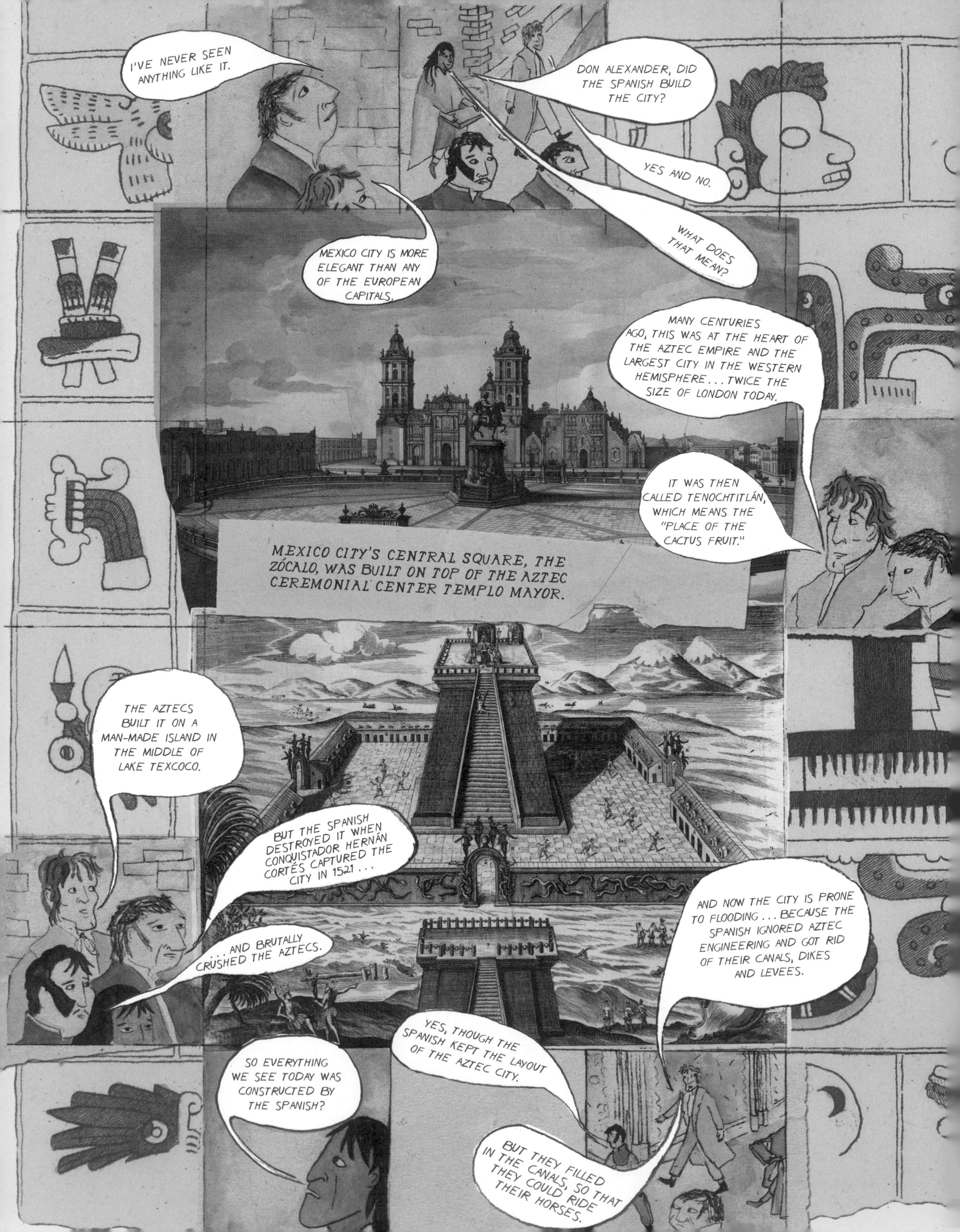
I'VE NEVER SEEN ANYTHING LIKE IT.
DON ALEXANDER, DID THE SPANISH BUILD THE CITY?
YES AND NO.
MEXICO CITY IS MORE ELEGANT THAN ANY OF THE EUROPEAN CAPITALS.
WHAT DOES THAT MEAN?
MANY CENTURIES AGO, THIS WAS AT THE HEART OF THE AZTEC EMPIRE AND THE LARGEST CITY IN THE WESTERN HEMISPHERE . . . TWICE THE SIZE OF LONDON TODAY.
IT WAS THEN CALLED TENOCHTITLÁN, WHICH MEANS THE "PLACE OF THE CACTUS FRUIT."
MEXICO CITY'S CENTRAL SQUARE, THE ZÓCALO, WAS BUILT ON TOP OF THE AZTEC CEREMONIAL CENTER TEMPLO MAYOR.
THE AZTECS BUILT IT ON A MAN-MADE ISLAND IN THE MIDDLE OF LAKE TEXCOCO.
BUT THE SPANISH DESTROYED IT WHEN CONQUISTADOR HERNÁN CORTÉS CAPTURED THE CITY IN 1521 . . .
. . . AND BRUTALLY CRUSHED THE AZTECS.
AND NOW THE CITY IS PRONE TO FLOODING . . . BECAUSE THE SPANISH IGNORED AZTEC ENGINEERING AND GOT RID OF THEIR CANALS, DIKES AND LEVEES.
SO EVERYTHING WE SEE TODAY WAS CONSTRUCTED BY THE SPANISH?
YES, THOUGH THE SPANISH KEPT THE LAYOUT OF THE AZTEC CITY.
BUT THEY FILLED IN THE CANALS, SO THAT THEY COULD RIDE THEIR HORSES.

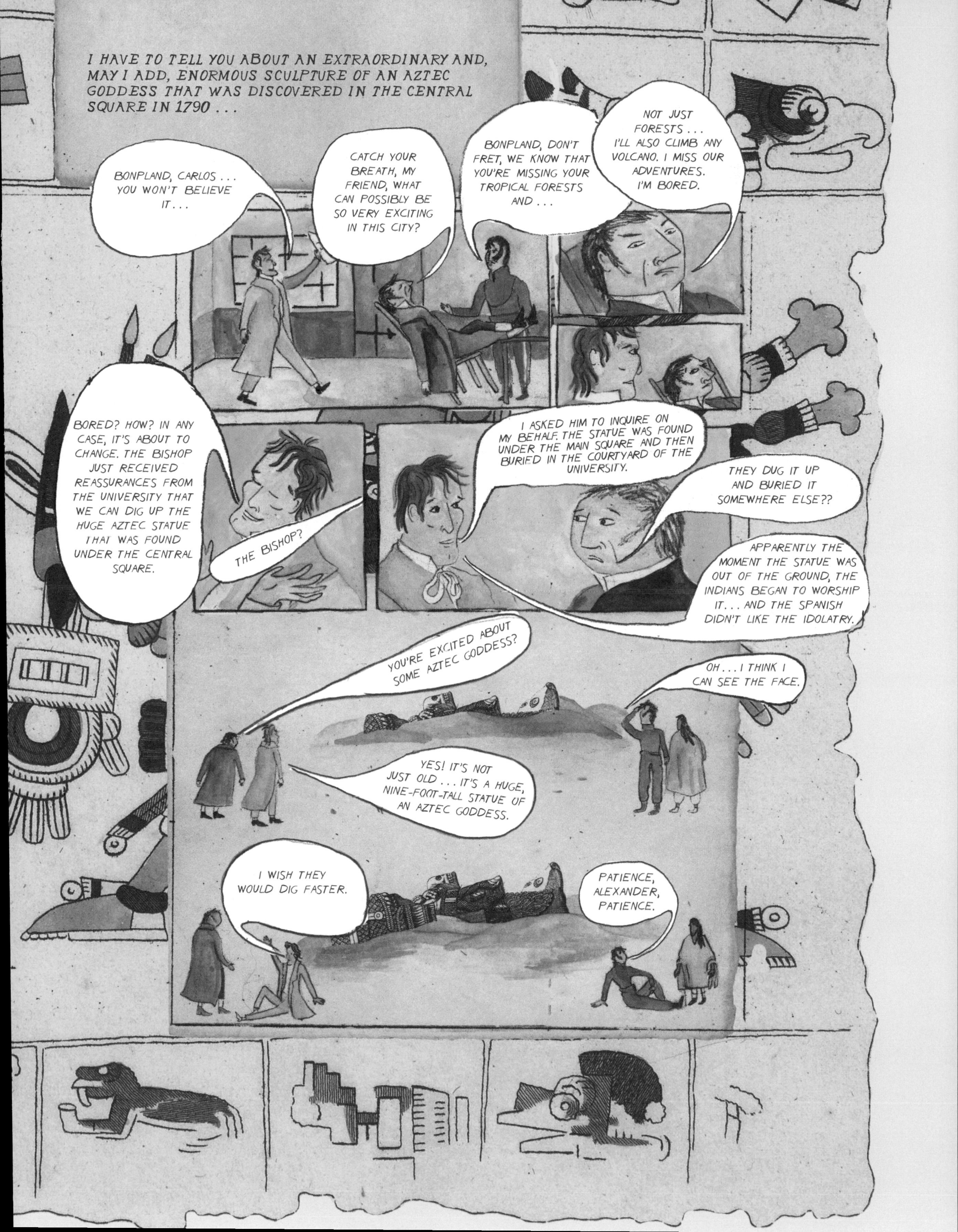
I HAVE TO TELL YOU ABOUT AN EXTRAORDINARY AND, MAY I ADD, ENORMOUS SCULPTURE OF AN AZTEC GODDESS THAT WAS DISCOVERED IN THE CENTRAL SQUARE IN 1790 . . .
BONPLAND, CARLOS . . . YOU WON'T BELIEVE IT . . .
CATCH YOUR BREATH, MY FRIEND, WHAT CAN POSSIBLY BE SO VERY EXCITING IN THIS CITY?
BONPLAND, DON'T FRET, WE KNOW THAT YOU'RE MISSING YOUR TROPICAL FORESTS AND . . .
NOT JUST FORESTS . . . I'LL ALSO CLIMB ANY VOLCANO. I MISS OUR ADVENTURES. I'M BORED.
BORED? HOW? IN ANY CASE, IT'S ABOUT TO CHANGE. THE BISHOP JUST RECEIVED REASSURANCES FROM THE UNIVERSITY THAT WE CAN DIG UP THE HUGE AZTEC STATUE THAT WAS FOUND UNDER THE CENTRAL SQUARE.
THE BISHOP?
I ASKED HIM TO INQUIRE ON MY BEHALF. THE STATUE WAS FOUND UNDER THE MAIN SQUARE AND THEN BURIED IN THE COURTYARD OF THE UNIVERSITY.
THEY DUG IT UP AND BURIED IT SOMEWHERE ELSE??
APPARENTLY THE MOMENT THE STATUE WAS OUT OF THE GROUND, THE INDIANS BEGAN TO WORSHIP IT . . . AND THE SPANISH DIDN'T LIKE THE IDOLATRY.
YOU'RE EXCITED ABOUT SOME AZTEC GODDESS?
OH . . . I THINK I CAN SEE THE FACE.
YES! IT'S NOT JUST OLD . . . IT'S A HUGE, NINE-FOOT-TALL STATUE OF AN AZTEC GODDESS.
I WISH THEY WOULD DIG FASTER.
PATIENCE, ALEXANDER, PATIENCE.

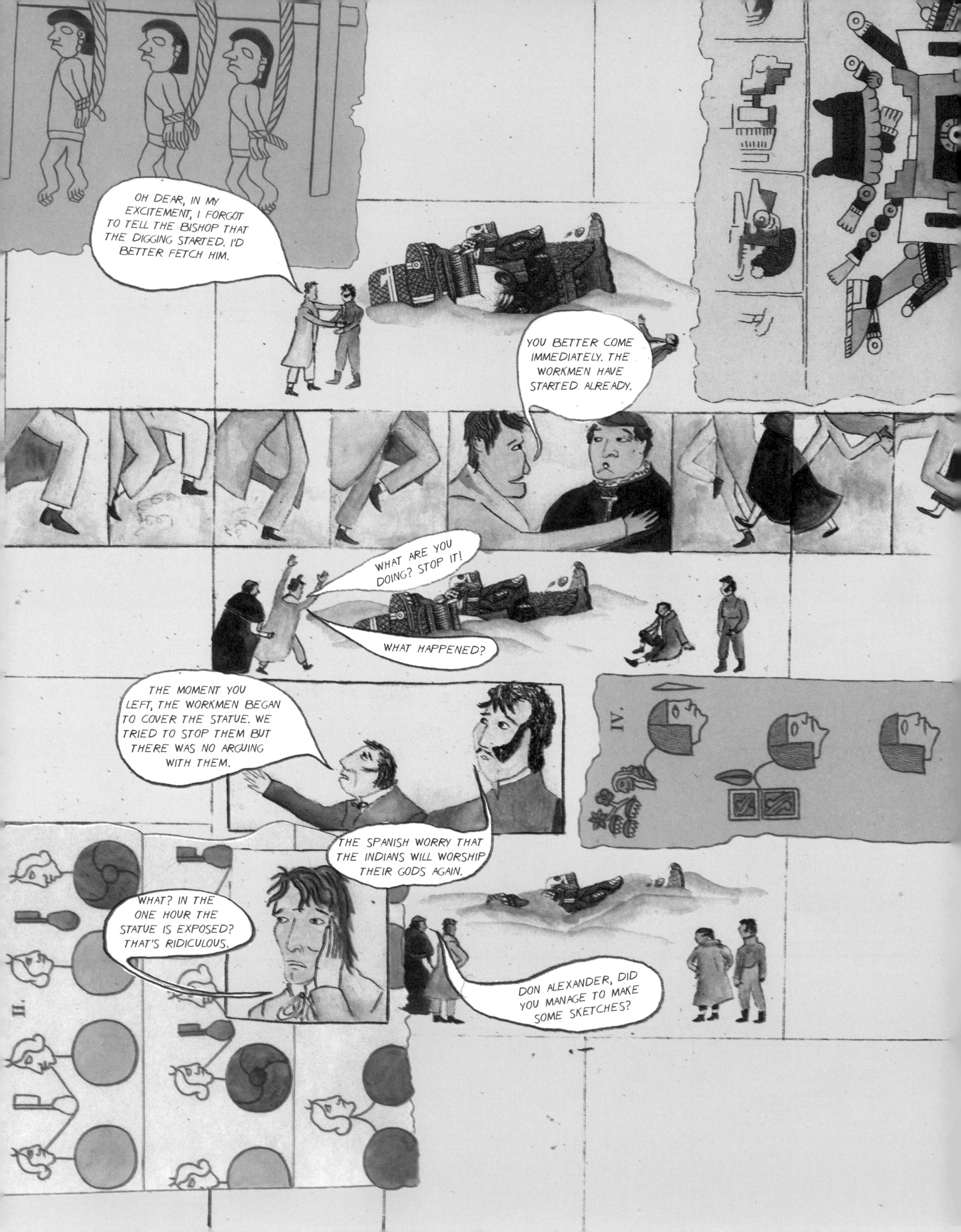
OH DEAR, IN MY EXCITEMENT, I FORGOT TO TELL THE BISHOP THAT THE DIGGING STARTED. I'D BETTER FETCH HIM.
YOU BETTER COME IMMEDIATELY. THE WORKMEN HAVE STARTED ALREADY.
WHAT ARE YOU DOING? STOP IT!
WHAT HAPPENED?
THE MOMENT YOU LEFT, THE WORKMEN BEGAN TO COVER THE STATUE. WE TRIED TO STOP THEM BUT THERE WAS NO ARGUING WITH THEM.
THE SPANISH WORRY THAT THE INDIANS WILL WORSHIP THEIR GODS AGAIN.
WHAT? IN THE ONE HOUR THE STATUE IS EXPOSED? THAT'S RIDICULOUS.
DON ALEXANDER, DID YOU MANAGE TO MAKE SOME SKETCHES?
IV.
II.

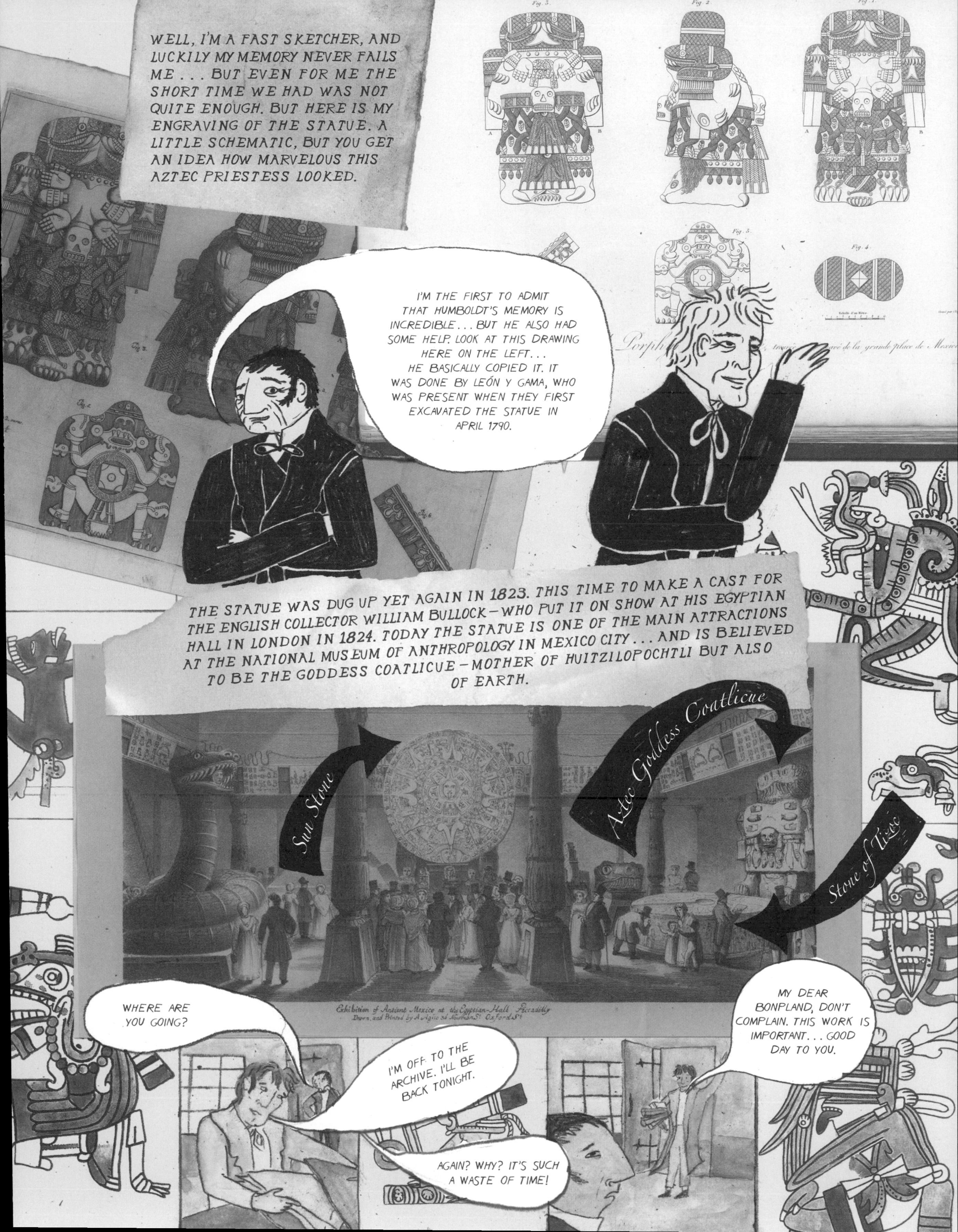
WELL, I'M A FAST SKETCHER, AND LUCKILY MY MEMORY NEVER FAILS ME . . . BUT EVEN FOR ME THE SHORT TIME WE HAD WAS NOT QUITE ENOUGH. BUT HERE IS MY ENGRAVING OF THE STATUE. A LITTLE SCHEMATIC, BUT YOU GET AN IDEA HOW MARVELOUS THIS AZTEC PRIESTESS LOOKED.
I'M THE FIRST TO ADMIT THAT HUMBOLDT'S MEMORY IS INCREDIBLE . . . BUT HE ALSO HAD SOME HELP. LOOK AT THIS DRAWING HERE ON THE LEFT . . . HE BASICALLY COPIED IT. IT WAS DONE BY LEÓN Y GAMA, WHO WAS PRESENT WHEN THEY FIRST EXCAVATED THE STATUE IN APRIL 1790.
THE STATUE WAS DUG UP YET AGAIN IN 1823. THIS TIME TO MAKE A CAST FOR THE ENGLISH COLLECTOR WILLIAM BULLOCK – WHO PUT IT ON SHOW AT HIS EGYPTIAN HALL IN LONDON IN 1824. TODAY THE STATUE IS ONE OF THE MAIN ATTRACTIONS AT THE NATIONAL MUSEUM OF ANTHROPOLOGY IN MEXICO CITY . . . AND IS BELIEVED TO BE THE GODDESS COATLICUE – MOTHER OF HUITZILOPOCHTLI BUT ALSO OF EARTH.
Sun Stone
Aztec Goddess Coatlicue
Stone of Tizoc
Exhibition of Ancient Mexico at the Egyptian-Hall Piccadilly
WHERE ARE YOU GOING?
I'M OFF TO THE ARCHIVE. I'LL BE BACK TONIGHT.
AGAIN? WHY? IT'S SUCH A WASTE OF TIME!
MY DEAR BONPLAND, DON'T COMPLAIN. THIS WORK IS IMPORTANT . . . GOOD DAY TO YOU.

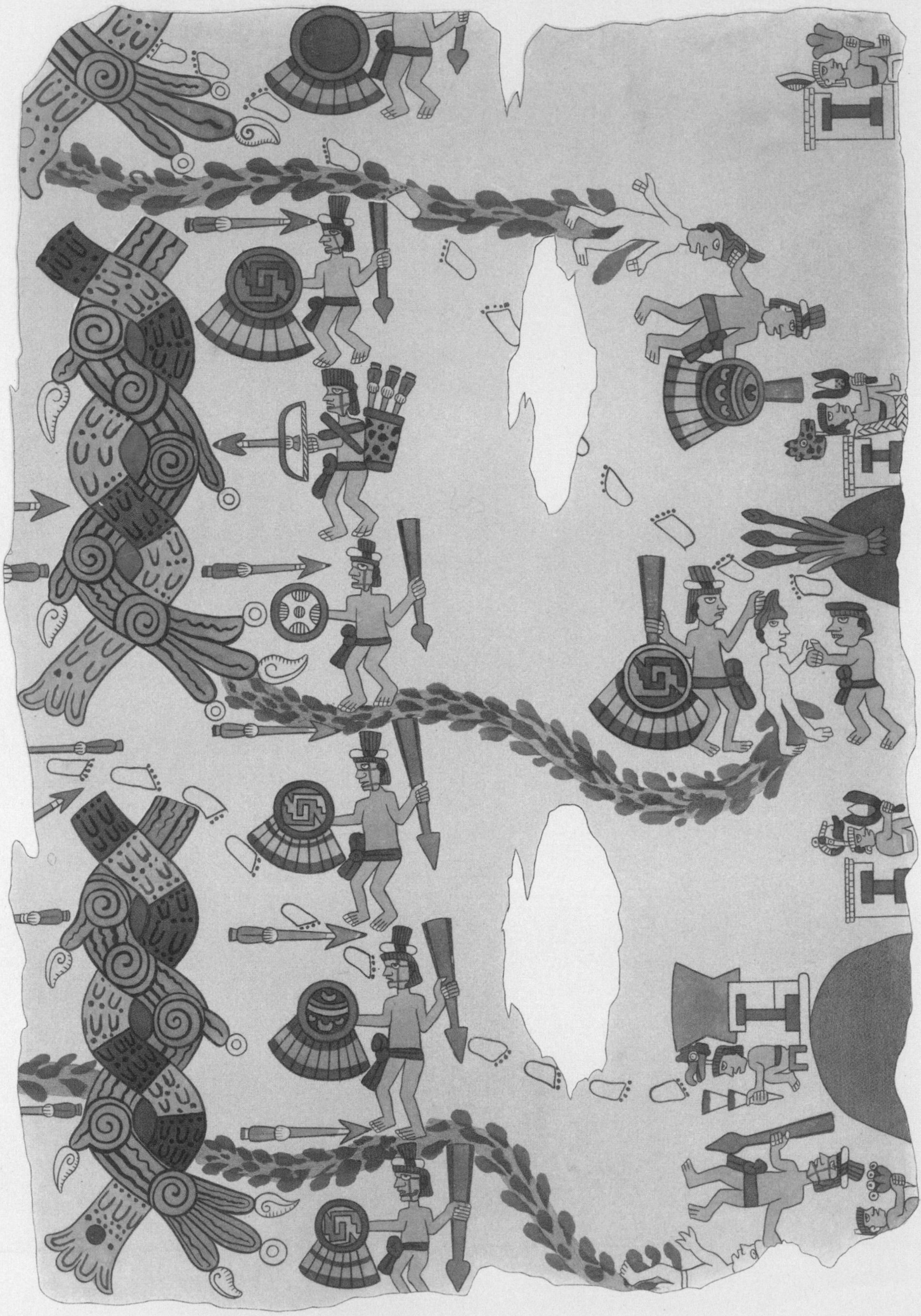

IN THE ARCHIVES IN MEXICO CITY . . .

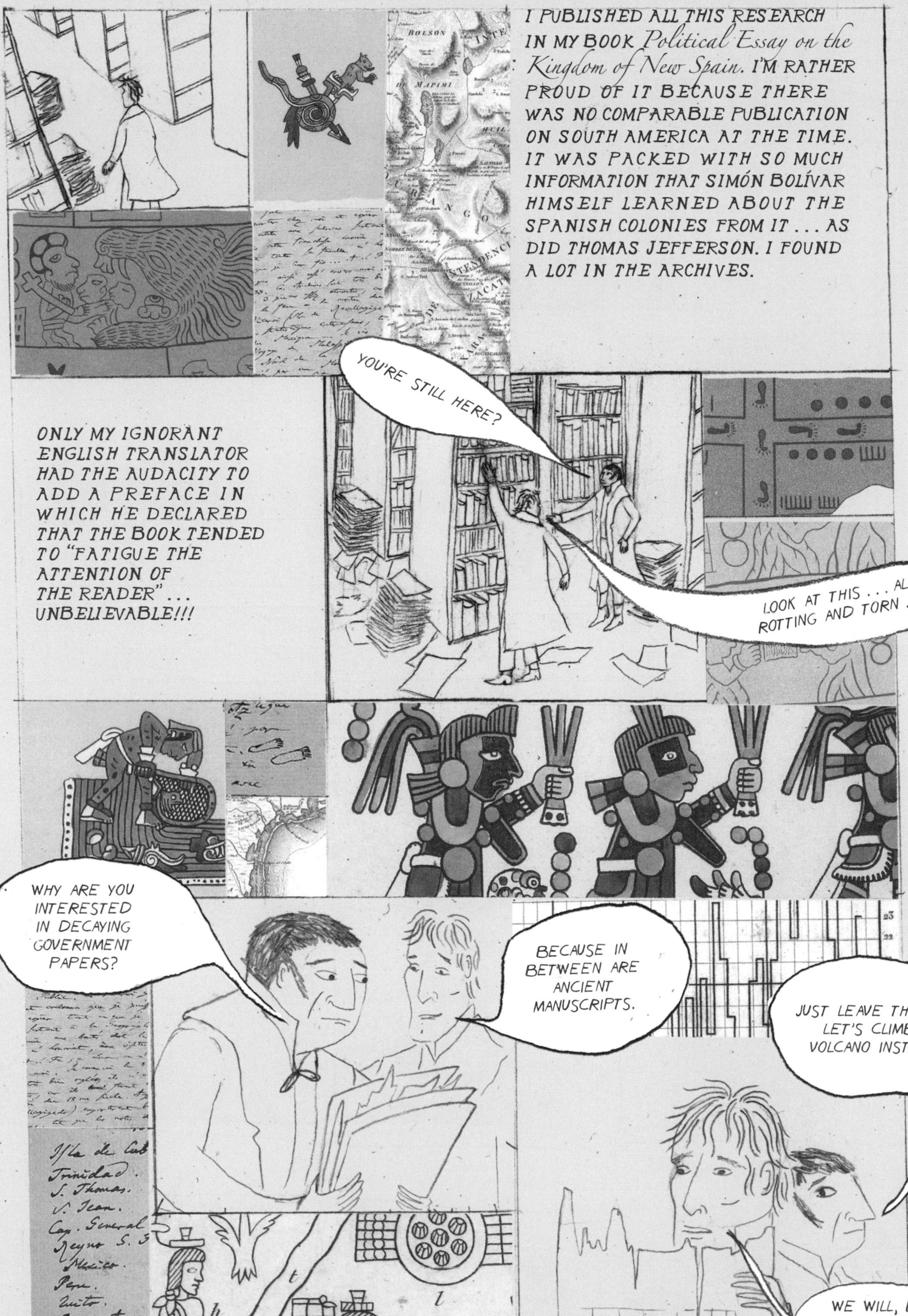
I PUBLISHED ALL THIS RESEARCH IN MY BOOK Political Essay on the Kingdom of New Spain. I'M RATHER PROUD OF IT BECAUSE THERE WAS NO COMPARABLE PUBLICATION ON SOUTH AMERICA AT THE TIME. IT WAS PACKED WITH SO MUCH INFORMATION THAT SIMÓN BOLÍVAR HIMSELF LEARNED ABOUT THE SPANISH COLONIES FROM IT . . . AS DID THOMAS JEFFERSON. I FOUND A LOT IN THE ARCHIVES.
ONLY MY IGNORANT ENGLISH TRANSLATOR HAD THE AUDACITY TO ADD A PREFACE IN WHICH HE DECLARED THAT THE BOOK TENDED TO "FATIGUE THE ATTENTION OF THE READER" . . . UNBELIEVABLE!!!
YOU'RE STILL HERE?
LOOK AT THIS . . . ALL ROTTING AND TORN . . .
WHY ARE YOU INTERESTED IN DECAYING GOVERNMENT PAPERS?
BECAUSE IN BETWEEN ARE ANCIENT MANUSCRIPTS.
JUST LEAVE THEM . . . LET'S CLIMB A VOLCANO INSTEAD!
WE WILL, BUT FIRST I NEED TO SORT THESE OUT AND RESCUE WHAT I CAN.

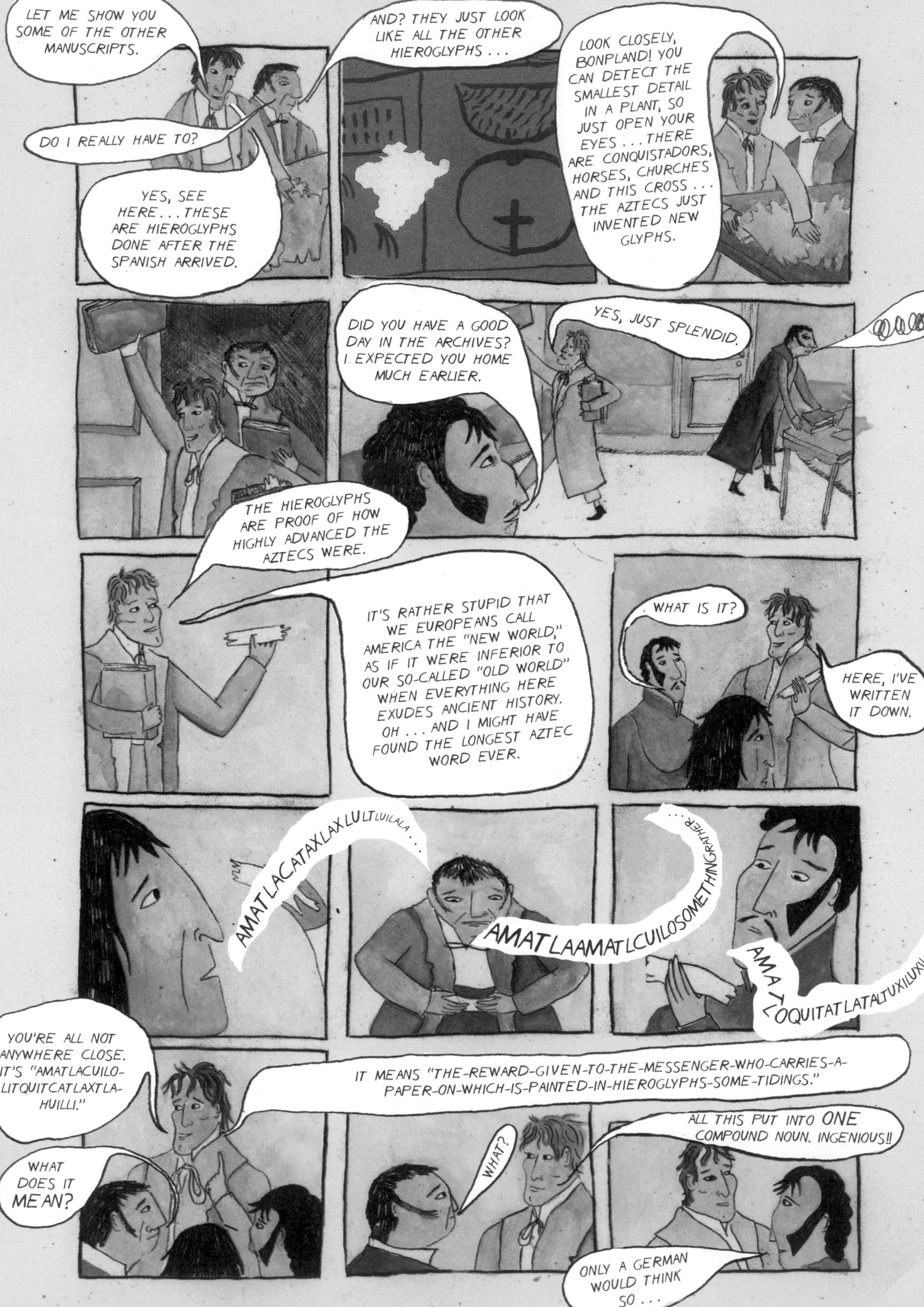
LET ME SHOW YOU SOME OF THE OTHER MANUSCRIPTS.
DO I REALLY HAVE TO?
YES, SEE HERE . . . THESE ARE HIEROGLYPHS DONE AFTER THE SPANISH ARRIVED.
AND? THEY JUST LOOK LIKE ALL THE OTHER HIEROGLYPHS . . .
LOOK CLOSELY, BONPLAND! YOU CAN DETECT THE SMALLEST DETAIL IN A PLANT, SO JUST OPEN YOUR EYES . . . THERE ARE CONQUISTADORS, HORSES, CHURCHES AND THIS CROSS . . . THE AZTECS JUST INVENTED NEW GLYPHS.
DID YOU HAVE A GOOD DAY IN THE ARCHIVES? I EXPECTED YOU HOME MUCH EARLIER.
YES, JUST SPLENDID.
THE HIEROGLYPHS ARE PROOF OF HOW HIGHLY ADVANCED THE AZTECS WERE.
IT'S RATHER STUPID THAT WE EUROPEANS CALL AMERICA THE "NEW WORLD," AS IF IT WERE INFERIOR TO OUR SO-CALLED "OLD WORLD" WHEN EVERYTHING HERE EXUDES ANCIENT HISTORY. OH . . . AND I MIGHT HAVE FOUND THE LONGEST AZTEC WORD EVER.
. . . WHAT IS IT?
HERE, I'VE WRITTEN IT DOWN.
AMATLACATAXLAXLULTLUILALA . . .
AMATLAAMATLCUILOSOMETHINGRATHER . . .
AMATLOQUITATLATALTUXILUXILWHATEVER . . .
YOU'RE ALL NOT ANYWHERE CLOSE. IT'S "AMATLACUILO-LITQUITCATLAXTLA-HUILLI."
WHAT DOES IT MEAN?
IT MEANS "THE-REWARD-GIVEN-TO-THE-MESSENGER-WHO-CARRIES-A-PAPER-ON-WHICH-IS-PAINTED-IN-HIEROGLYPHS-SOME-TIDINGS."
WHAT?
ALL THIS PUT INTO ONE COMPOUND NOUN. INGENIOUS!!
ONLY A GERMAN WOULD THINK SO . . .

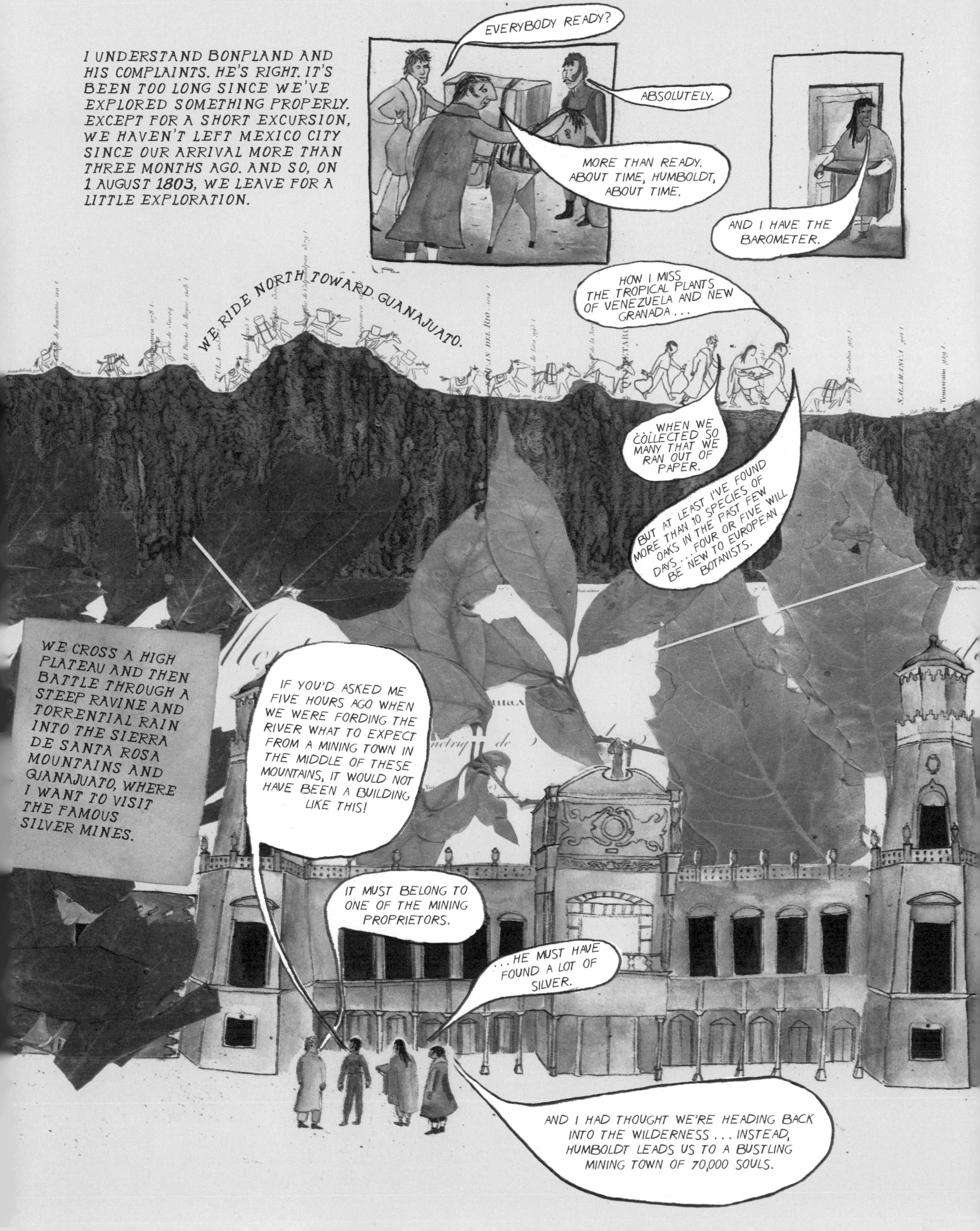
I UNDERSTAND BONPLAND AND HIS COMPLAINTS. HE'S RIGHT. IT'S BEEN TOO LONG SINCE WE'VE EXPLORED SOMETHING PROPERLY. EXCEPT FOR A SHORT EXCURSION, WE HAVEN'T LEFT MEXICO CITY SINCE OUR ARRIVAL MORE THAN THREE MONTHS AGO. AND SO, ON 1 AUGUST 1803, WE LEAVE FOR A LITTLE EXPLORATION.
EVERYBODY READY?
ABSOLUTELY.
MORE THAN READY. ABOUT TIME, HUMBOLDT, ABOUT TIME.
AND I HAVE THE BAROMETER.
WE RIDE NORTH TOWARD GUANAJUATO.
HOW I MISS THE TROPICAL PLANTS OF VENEZUELA AND NEW GRANADA . . .
WHEN WE COLLECTED SO MANY THAT WE RAN OUT OF PAPER.
BUT AT LEAST I'VE FOUND MORE THAN 10 SPECIES OF OAKS IN THE PAST FEW DAYS . . . FOUR OR FIVE WILL BE NEW TO EUROPEAN BOTANISTS.
WE CROSS A HIGH PLATEAU AND THEN BATTLE THROUGH A STEEP RAVINE AND TORRENTIAL RAIN INTO THE SIERRA DE SANTA ROSA MOUNTAINS AND GUANAJUATO, WHERE I WANT TO VISIT THE FAMOUS SILVER MINES.
IF YOU'D ASKED ME FIVE HOURS AGO WHEN WE WERE FORDING THE RIVER WHAT TO EXPECT FROM A MINING TOWN IN THE MIDDLE OF THESE MOUNTAINS, IT WOULD NOT HAVE BEEN A BUILDING LIKE THIS!
IT MUST BELONG TO ONE OF THE MINING PROPRIETORS.
. . . HE MUST HAVE FOUND A LOT OF SILVER.
AND I HAD THOUGHT WE'RE HEADING BACK INTO THE WILDERNESS . . . INSTEAD, HUMBOLDT LEADS US TO A BUSTLING MINING TOWN OF 70,000 SOULS.

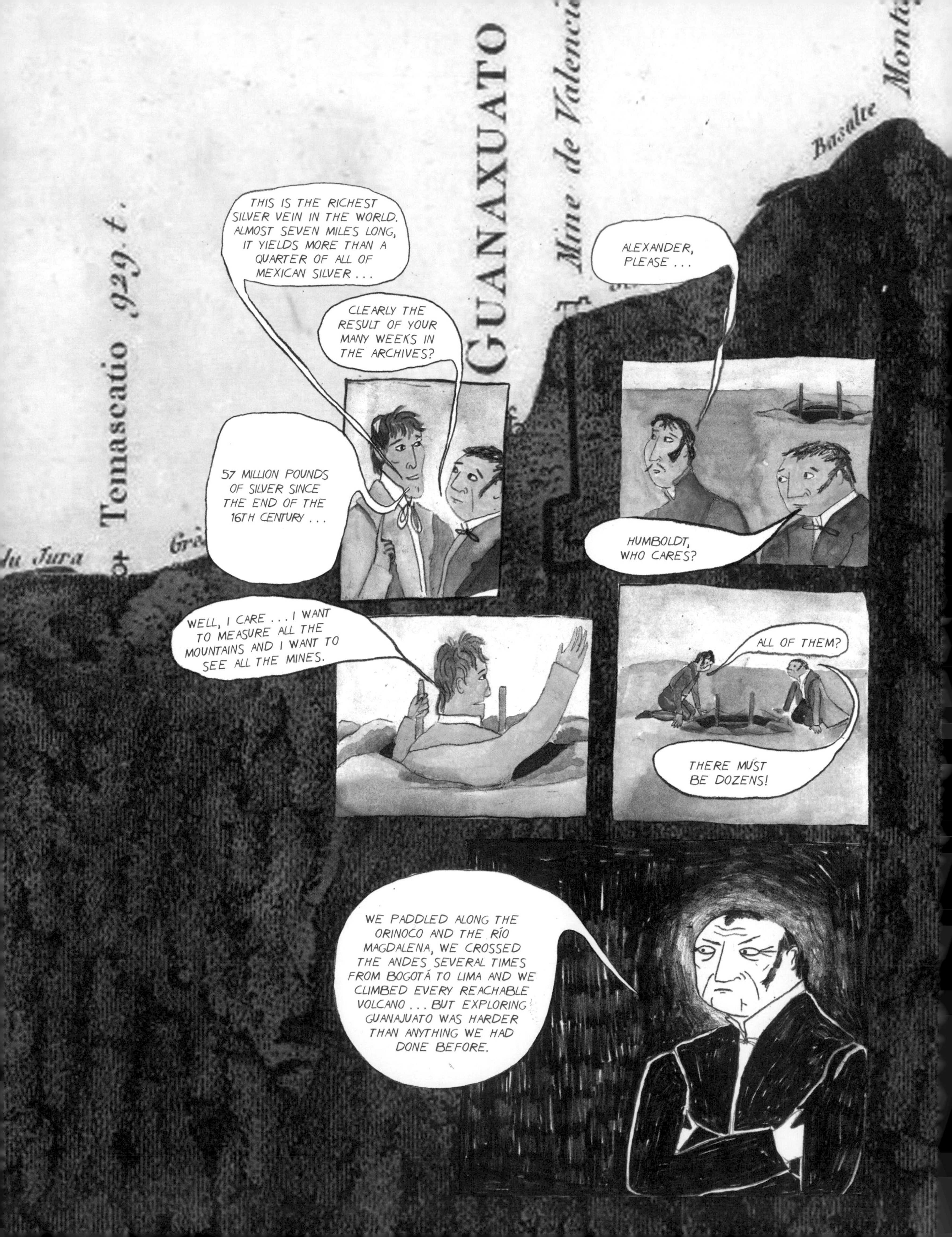
Temascatio 929. t.
GUANAXUATO
Mine de Valenci
Basalte
THIS IS THE RICHEST SILVER VEIN IN THE WORLD. ALMOST SEVEN MILES LONG, IT YIELDS MORE THAN A QUARTER OF ALL OF MEXICAN SILVER . . .
CLEARLY THE RESULT OF YOUR MANY WEEKS IN THE ARCHIVES?
57 MILLION POUNDS OF SILVER SINCE THE END OF THE 16TH CENTURY . . .
ALEXANDER, PLEASE . . .
HUMBOLDT, WHO CARES?
WELL, I CARE . . . I WANT TO MEASURE ALL THE MOUNTAINS AND I WANT TO SEE ALL THE MINES.
ALL OF THEM?
THERE MUST BE DOZENS!
WE PADDLED ALONG THE ORINOCO AND THE RÍO MAGDALENA, WE CROSSED THE ANDES SEVERAL TIMES FROM BOGOTÁ TO LIMA AND WE CLIMBED EVERY REACHABLE VOLCANO . . . BUT EXPLORING GUANAJUATO WAS HARDER THAN ANYTHING WE HAD DONE BEFORE.

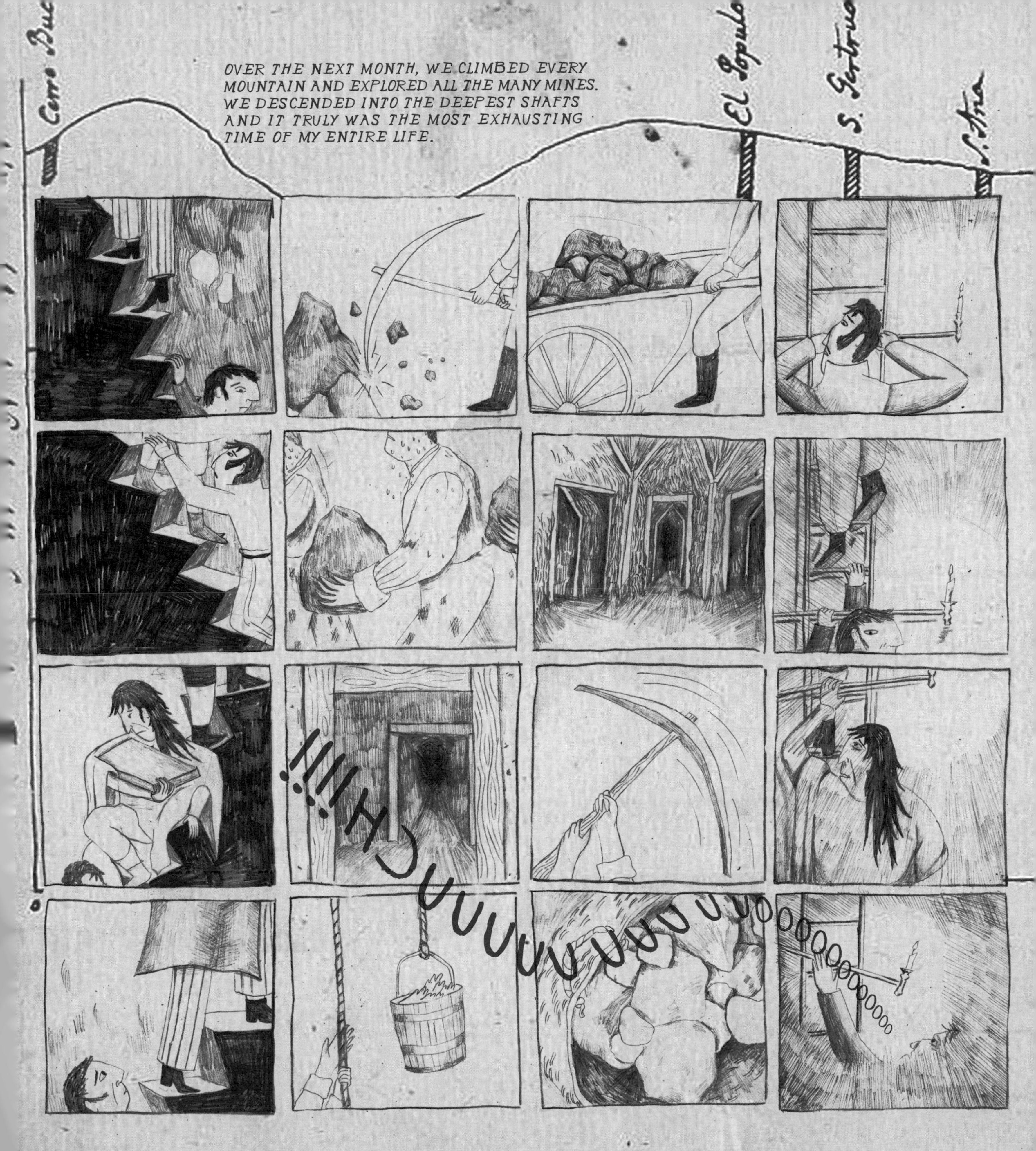
OVER THE NEXT MONTH, WE CLIMBED EVERY MOUNTAIN AND EXPLORED ALL THE MANY MINES. WE DESCENDED INTO THE DEEPEST SHAFTS AND IT TRULY WAS THE MOST EXHAUSTING TIME OF MY ENTIRE LIFE.
Cerro Bue
El Populo
S. Gertru
S. Ana
OOOOOOOOOOOOOOUUUUUUUUUUUUUUCH!!!!

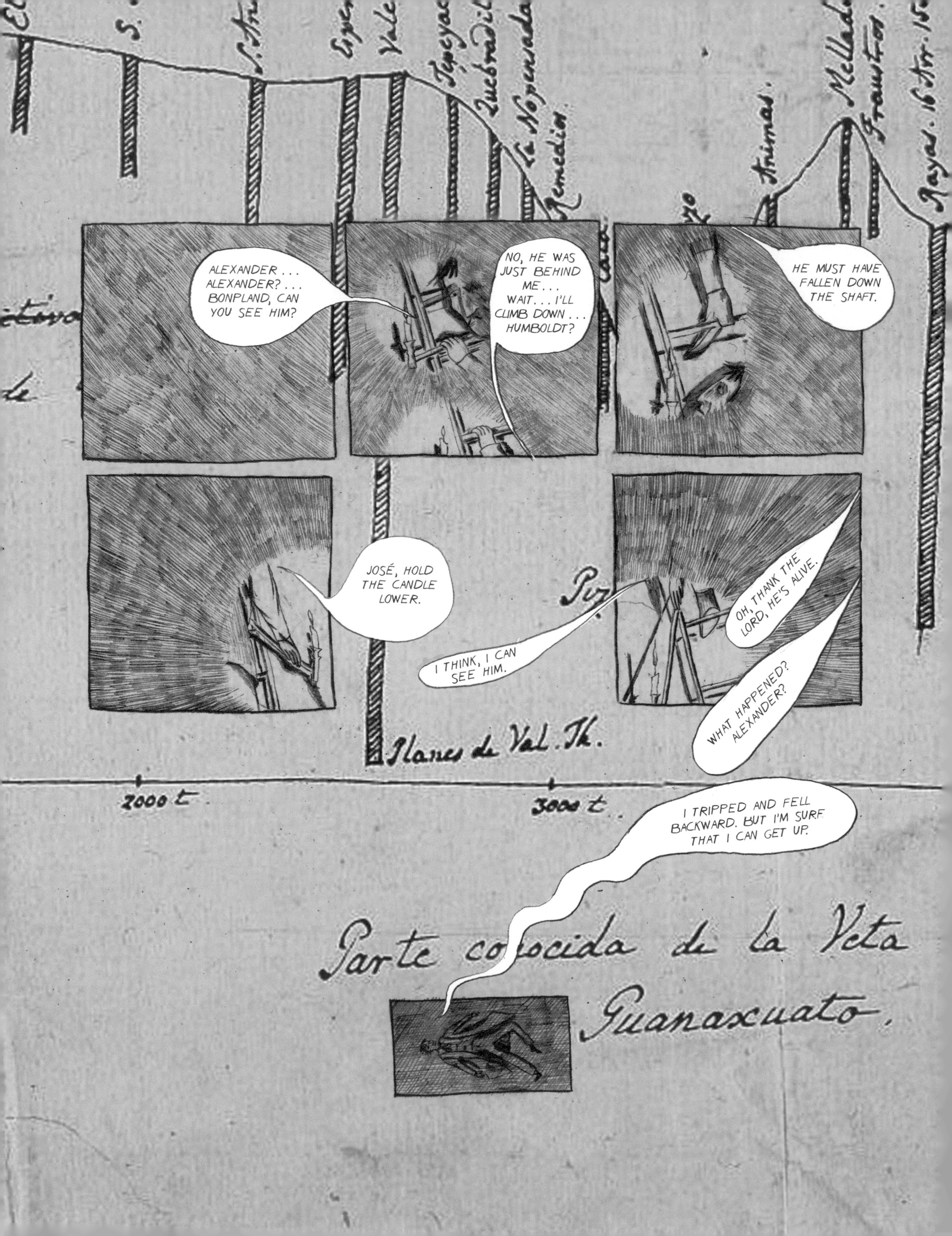
ALEXANDER . . . ALEXANDER? . . . BONPLAND, CAN YOU SEE HIM?
NO, HE WAS JUST BEHIND ME . . . WAIT . . . I'LL CLIMB DOWN . . . HUMBOLDT?
HE MUST HAVE FALLEN DOWN THE SHAFT.
JOSÉ, HOLD THE CANDLE LOWER.
I THINK, I CAN SEE HIM.
OH, THANK THE LORD, HE'S ALIVE.
WHAT HAPPENED? ALEXANDER?
I TRIPPED AND FELL BACKWARD. BUT I'M SURE THAT I CAN GET UP.
2000 t
3000 t
Guanaxuato.

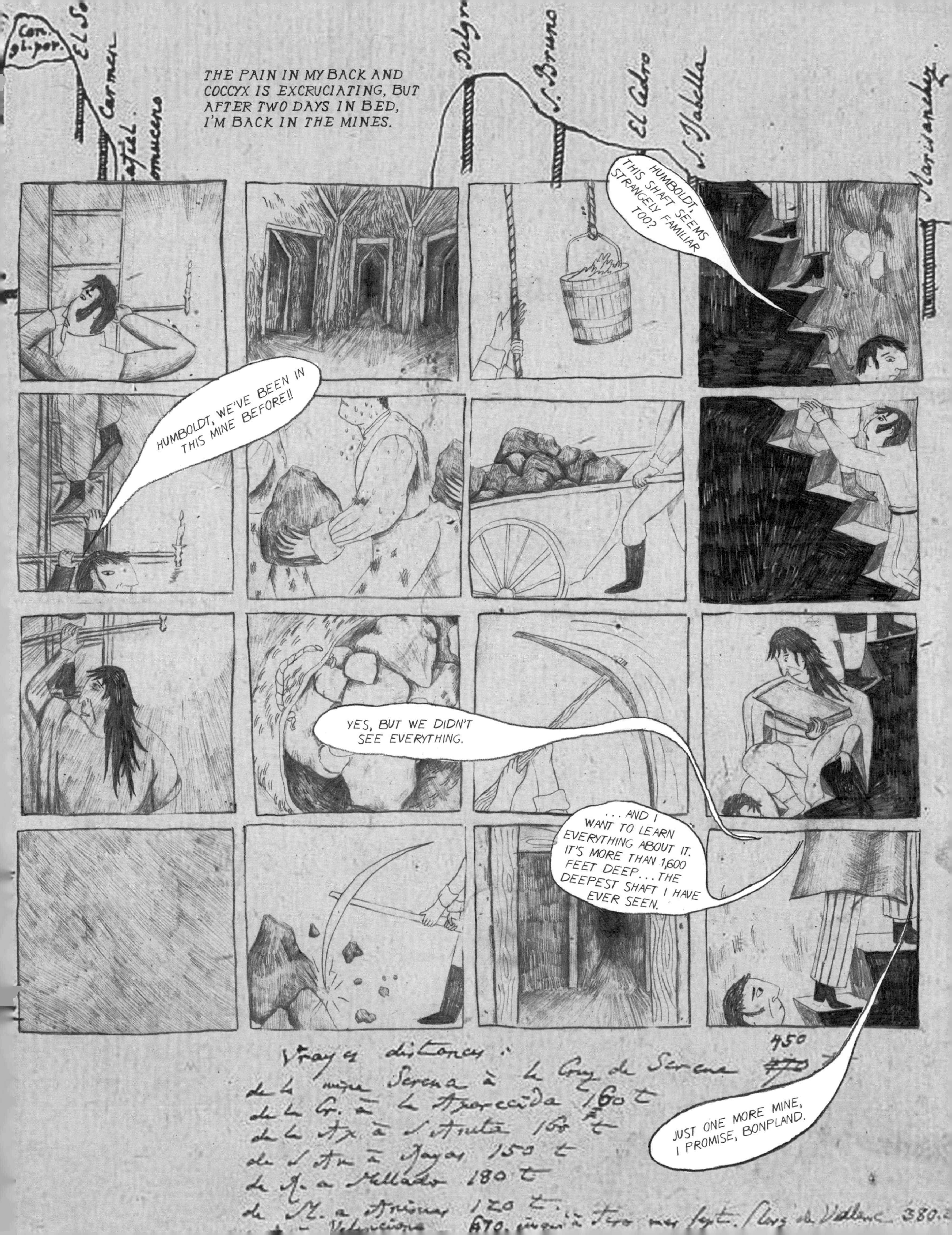
THE PAIN IN MY BACK AND COCCYX IS EXCRUCIATING, BUT AFTER TWO DAYS IN BED, I'M BACK IN THE MINES.
HUMBOLDT, THIS SHAFT SEEMS STRANGELY FAMILIAR TOO?
HUMBOLDT, WE'VE BEEN IN THIS MINE BEFORE!!
YES, BUT WE DIDN'T SEE EVERYTHING.
. . . AND I WANT TO LEARN EVERYTHING ABOUT IT. IT'S MORE THAN 1,600 FEET DEEP . . . THE DEEPEST SHAFT I HAVE EVER SEEN.
JUST ONE MORE MINE, I PROMISE, BONPLAND.
Carmen
El Cedro

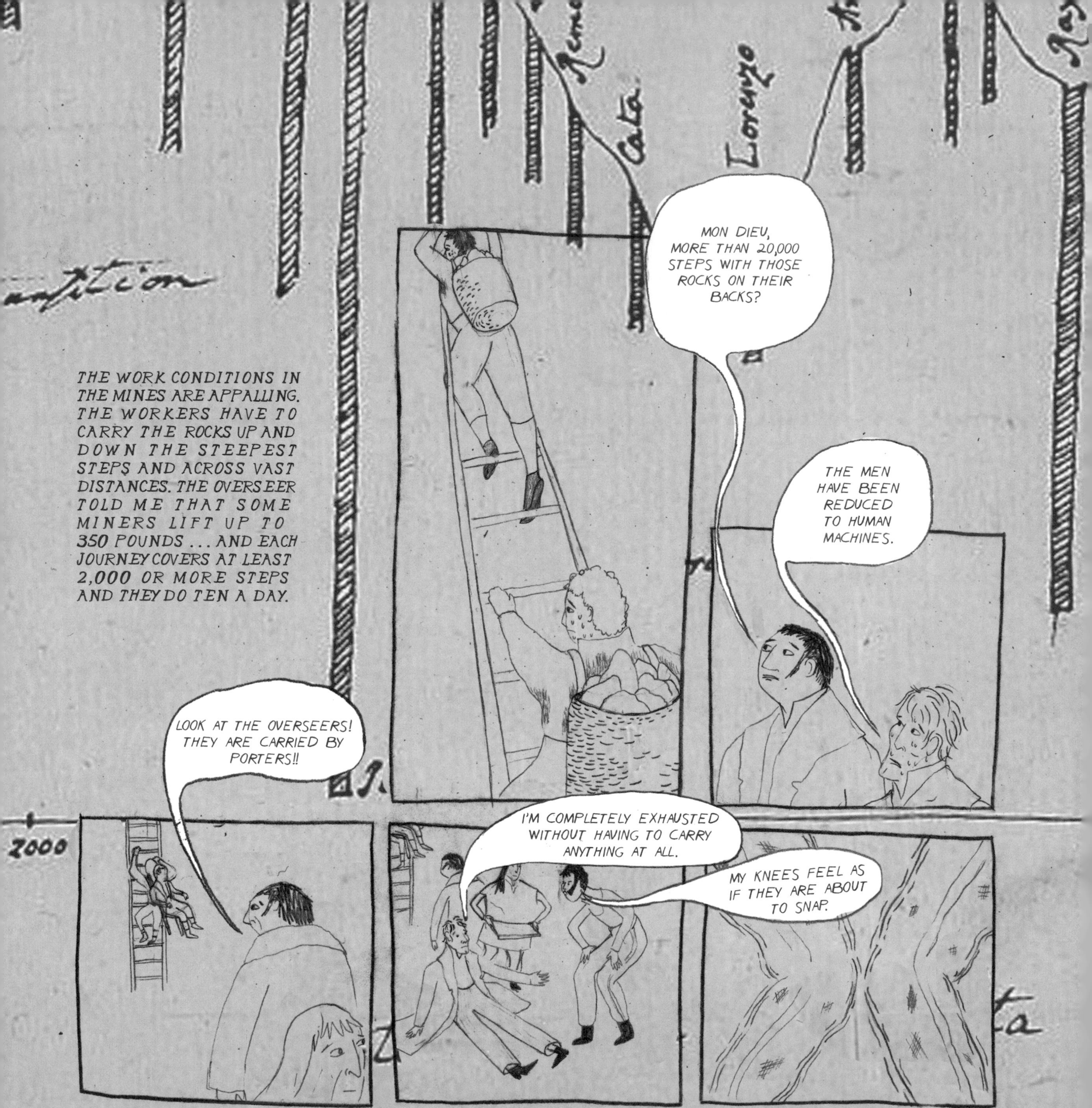

Cata.
Lorenzo
THE WORK CONDITIONS IN THE MINES ARE APPALLING. THE WORKERS HAVE TO CARRY THE ROCKS UP AND DOWN THE STEEPEST STEPS AND ACROSS VAST DISTANCES. THE OVERSEER TOLD ME THAT SOME MINERS LIFT UP TO 350 POUNDS ... AND EACH JOURNEY COVERS AT LEAST 2,000 OR MORE STEPS AND THEY DO TEN A DAY.
MON DIEU, MORE THAN 20,000 STEPS WITH THOSE ROCKS ON THEIR BACKS?
THE MEN HAVE BEEN REDUCED TO HUMAN MACHINES.
2000
LOOK AT THE OVERSEERS! THEY ARE CARRIED BY PORTERS!!
I'M COMPLETELY EXHAUSTED WITHOUT HAVING TO CARRY ANYTHING AT ALL.
MY KNEES FEEL AS IF THEY ARE ABOUT TO SNAP.

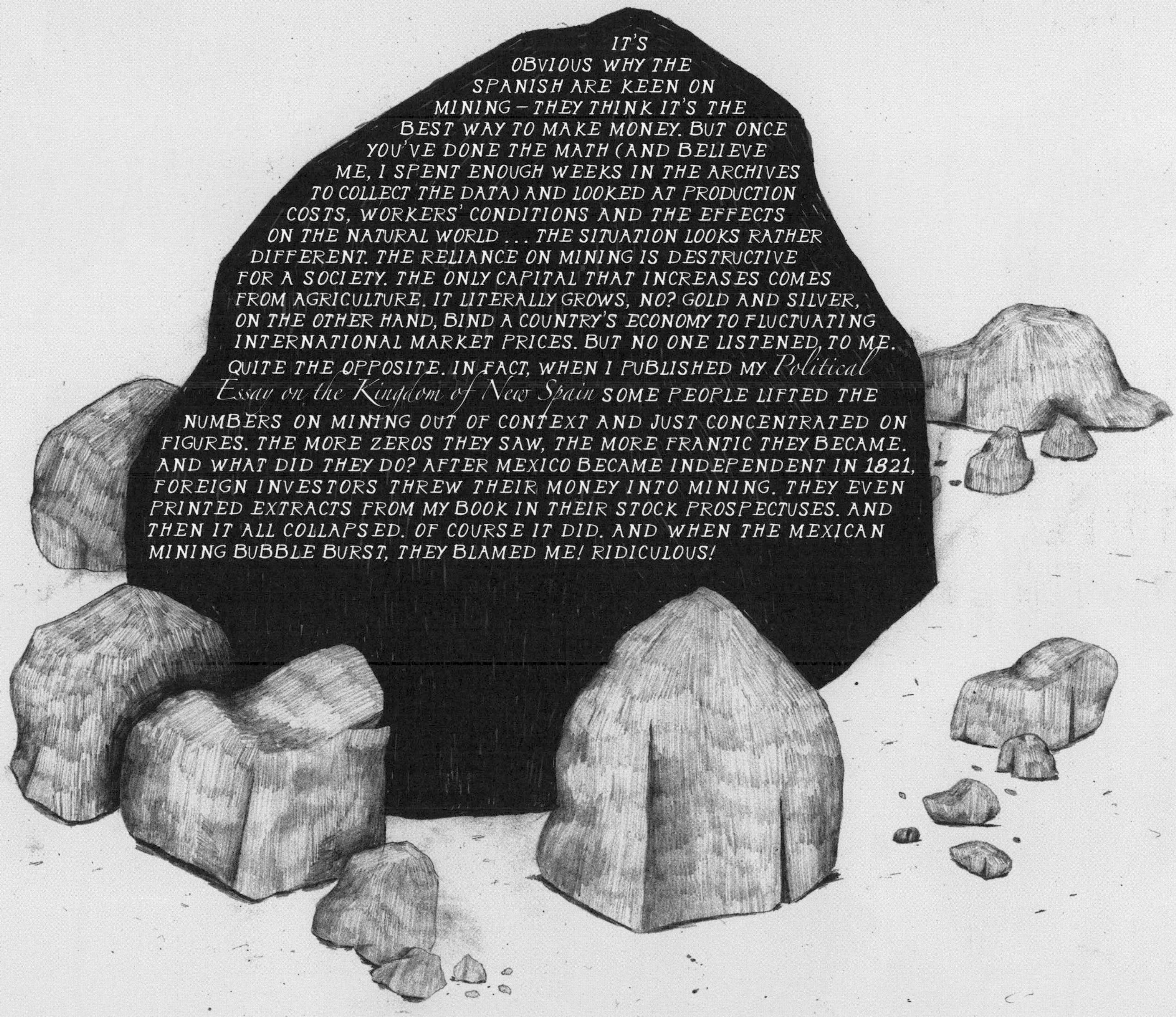
IT'S OBVIOUS WHY THE SPANISH ARE KEEN ON MINING – THEY THINK IT'S THE BEST WAY TO MAKE MONEY. BUT ONCE YOU'VE DONE THE MATH (AND BELIEVE ME, I SPENT ENOUGH WEEKS IN THE ARCHIVES TO COLLECT THE DATA) AND LOOKED AT PRODUCTION COSTS, WORKERS' CONDITIONS AND THE EFFECTS ON THE NATURAL WORLD . . . THE SITUATION LOOKS RATHER DIFFERENT. THE RELIANCE ON MINING IS DESTRUCTIVE FOR A SOCIETY. THE ONLY CAPITAL THAT INCREASES COMES FROM AGRICULTURE. IT LITERALLY GROWS, NO? GOLD AND SILVER, ON THE OTHER HAND, BIND A COUNTRY'S ECONOMY TO FLUCTUATING INTERNATIONAL MARKET PRICES. BUT NO ONE LISTENED TO ME. QUITE THE OPPOSITE. IN FACT, WHEN I PUBLISHED MY *Political Essay on the Kingdom of New Spain* SOME PEOPLE LIFTED THE NUMBERS ON MINING OUT OF CONTEXT AND JUST CONCENTRATED ON FIGURES. THE MORE ZEROS THEY SAW, THE MORE FRANTIC THEY BECAME. AND WHAT DID THEY DO? AFTER MEXICO BECAME INDEPENDENT IN 1821, FOREIGN INVESTORS THREW THEIR MONEY INTO MINING. THEY EVEN PRINTED EXTRACTS FROM MY BOOK IN THEIR STOCK PROSPECTUSES. AND THEN IT ALL COLLAPSED. OF COURSE IT DID. AND WHEN THE MEXICAN MINING BUBBLE BURST, THEY BLAMED ME! RIDICULOUS!

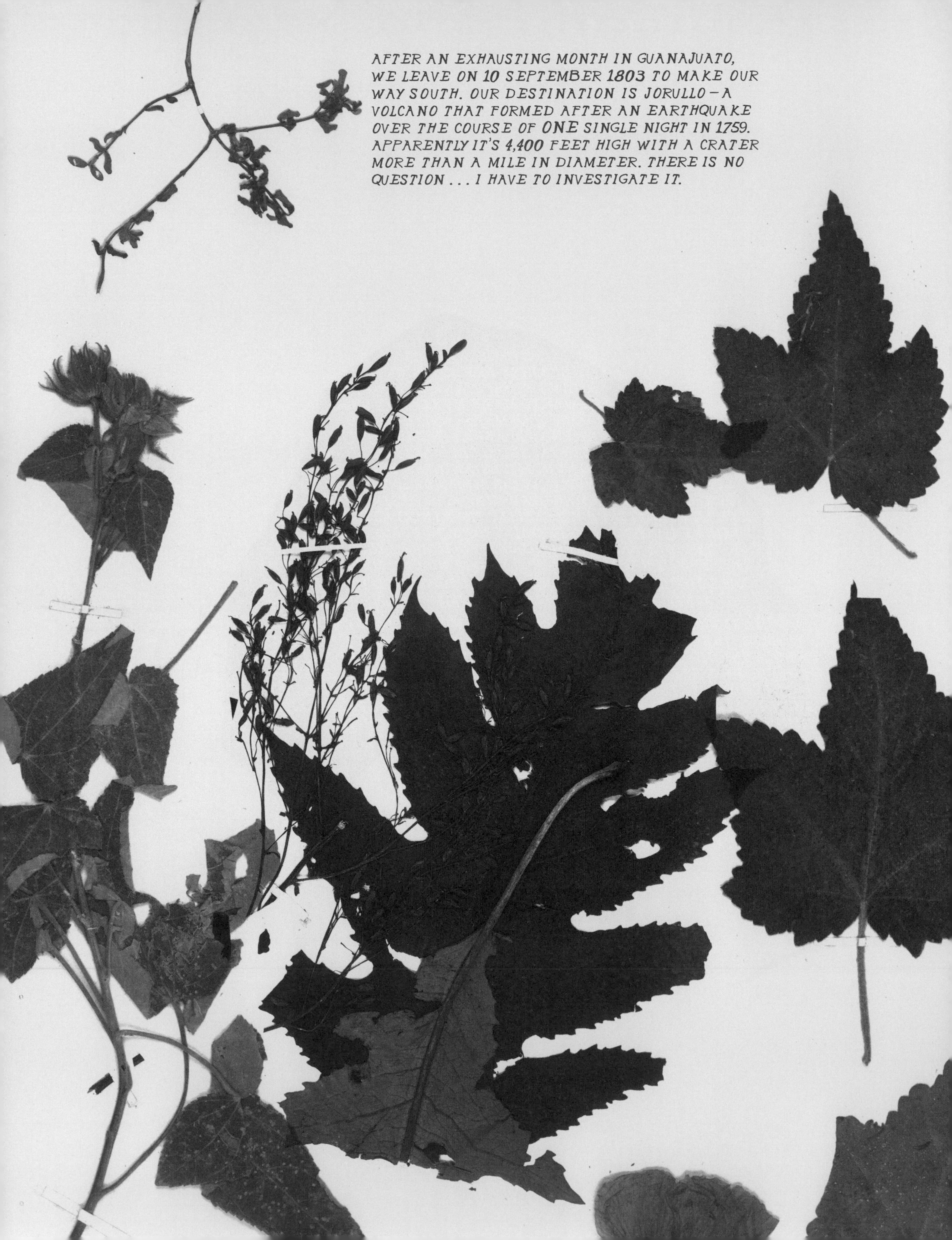
AFTER AN EXHAUSTING MONTH IN GUANAJUATO, WE LEAVE ON 10 SEPTEMBER 1803 TO MAKE OUR WAY SOUTH. OUR DESTINATION IS JORULLO – A VOLCANO THAT FORMED AFTER AN EARTHQUAKE OVER THE COURSE OF ONE SINGLE NIGHT IN 1759. APPARENTLY IT'S 4,400 FEET HIGH WITH A CRATER MORE THAN A MILE IN DIAMETER. THERE IS NO QUESTION . . . I HAVE TO INVESTIGATE IT.

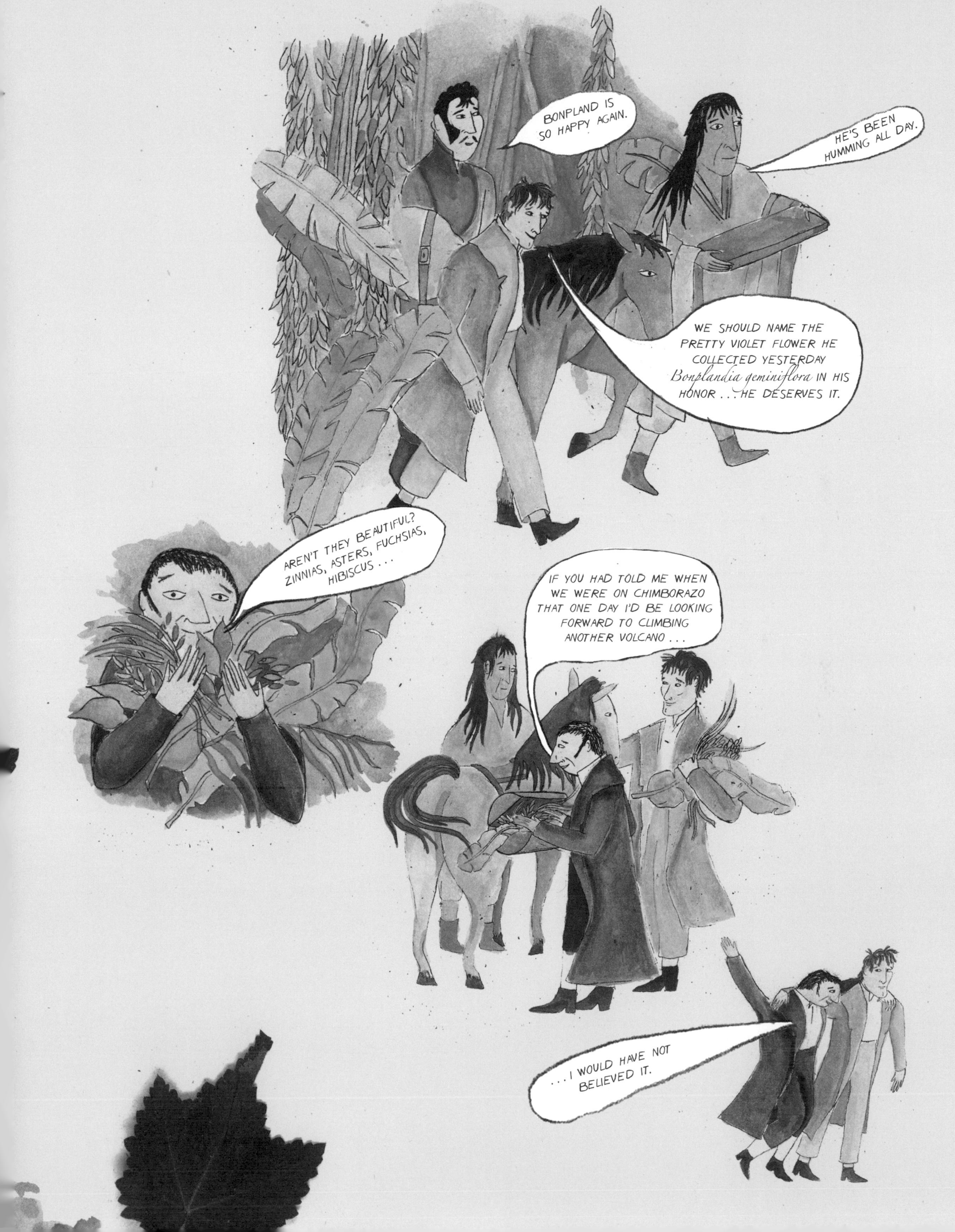
BONPLAND IS SO HAPPY AGAIN.
HE'S BEEN HUMMING ALL DAY.
WE SHOULD NAME THE PRETTY VIOLET FLOWER HE COLLECTED YESTERDAY *Bonplandia geminiflora* IN HIS HONOR . . . HE DESERVES IT.
AREN'T THEY BEAUTIFUL? ZINNIAS, ASTERS, FUCHSIAS, HIBISCUS . . .
IF YOU HAD TOLD ME WHEN WE WERE ON CHIMBORAZO THAT ONE DAY I'D BE LOOKING FORWARD TO CLIMBING ANOTHER VOLCANO . . .
. . . I WOULD HAVE NOT BELIEVED IT.

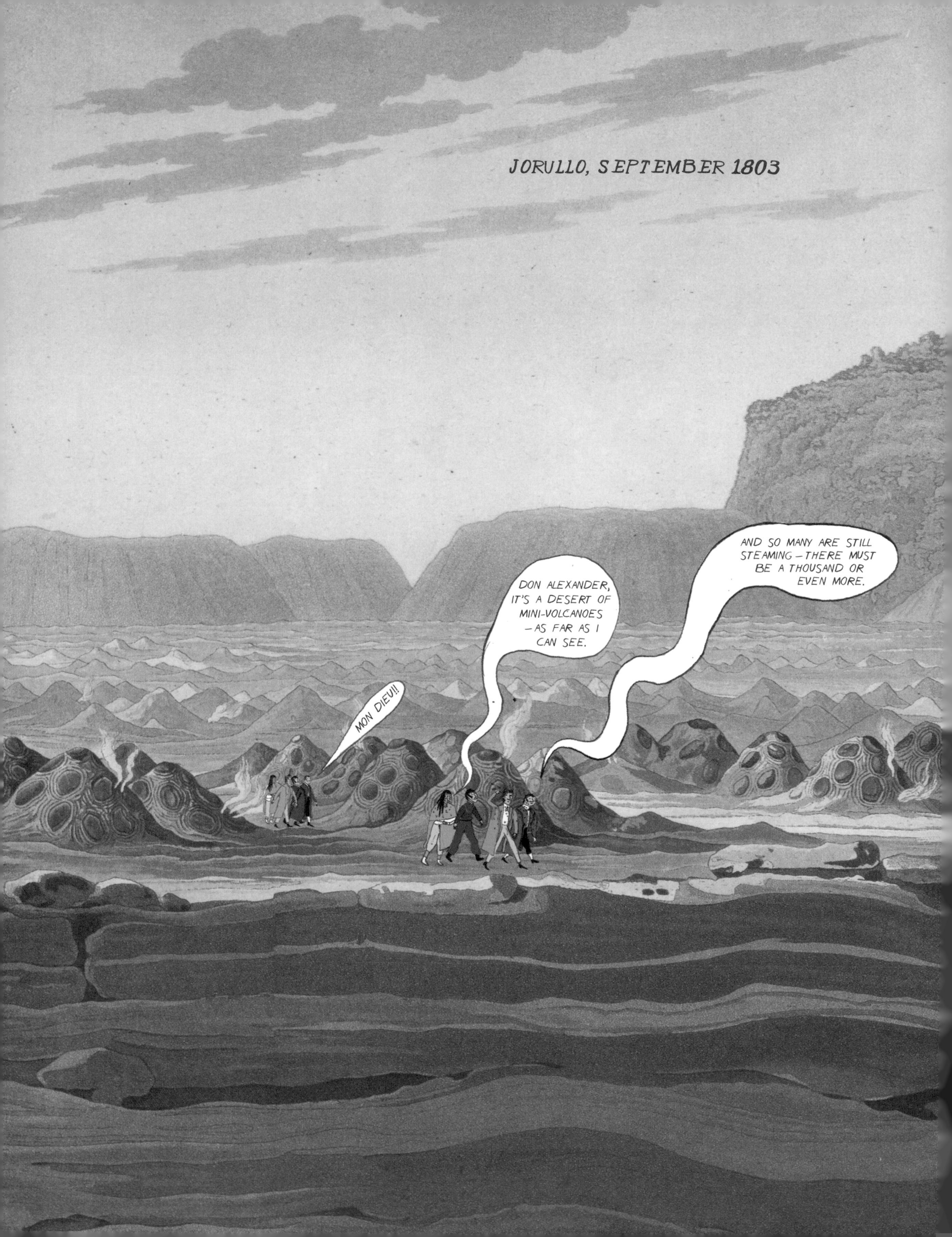
JORULLO, SEPTEMBER 1803
MON DIEU!!
DON ALEXANDER, IT'S A DESERT OF MINI-VOLCANOES —AS FAR AS I CAN SEE.
AND SO MANY ARE STILL STEAMING—THERE MUST BE A THOUSAND OR EVEN MORE.

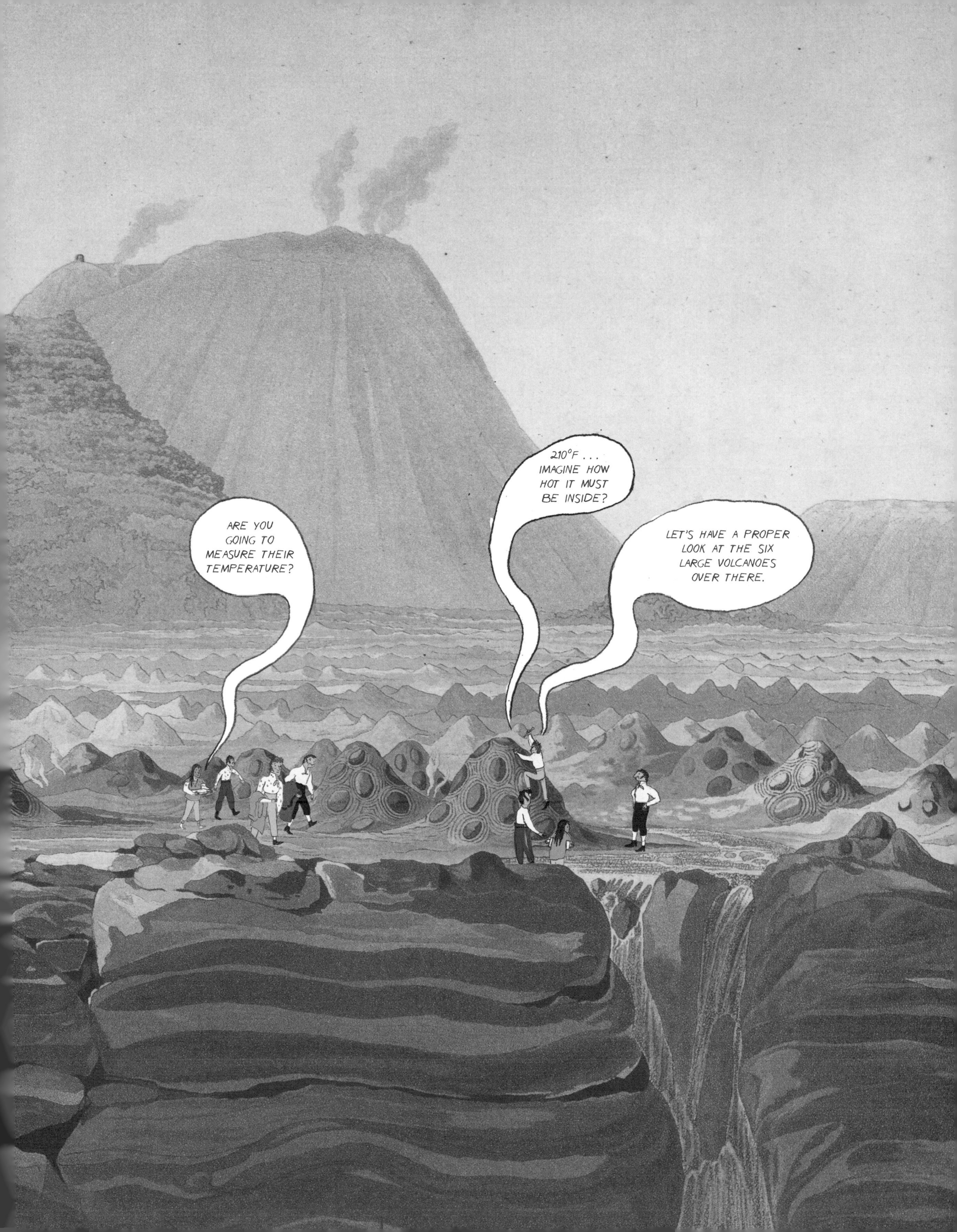
ARE YOU GOING TO MEASURE THEIR TEMPERATURE?
210°F . . . IMAGINE HOW HOT IT MUST BE INSIDE?
LET'S HAVE A PROPER LOOK AT THE SIX LARGE VOLCANOES OVER THERE.

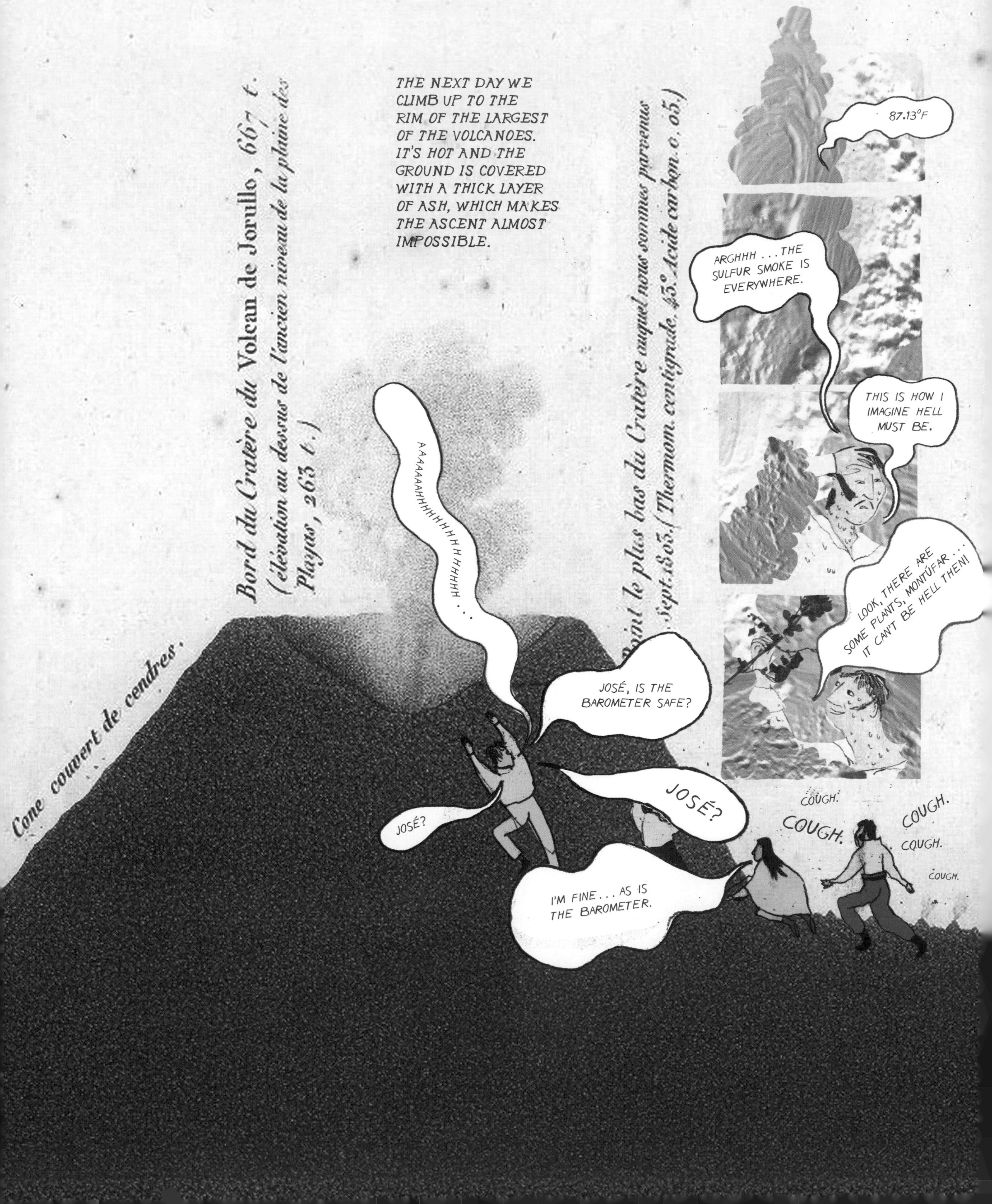
THE NEXT DAY WE CLIMB UP TO THE RIM OF THE LARGEST OF THE VOLCANOES. IT'S HOT AND THE GROUND IS COVERED WITH A THICK LAYER OF ASH, WHICH MAKES THE ASCENT ALMOST IMPOSSIBLE.
Cone couvert de cendres.
Bord du Cratère du Volcan de Jorullo, 667 t.
(élévation au dessus de l'ancien niveau de la plaine des Playas, 263 t.)
oint le plus bas du Cratère auquel nous sommes parvenus
Sept. 1803. (Thermom. centigrade. 45°. Acide carbon. 0.05.)
AAAAAAAHHHHHHHHHHHHHHHHH...
JOSÉ, IS THE BAROMETER SAFE?
JOSÉ?
JOSÉ?
I'M FINE... AS IS THE BAROMETER.
COUGH.
COUGH.
COUGH.
COUGH.
COUGH.
87.13°F
ARGHHH... THE SULFUR SMOKE IS EVERYWHERE.
THIS IS HOW I IMAGINE HELL MUST BE.
LOOK, THERE ARE SOME PLANTS, MONTÚFAR... IT CAN'T BE HELL THEN!

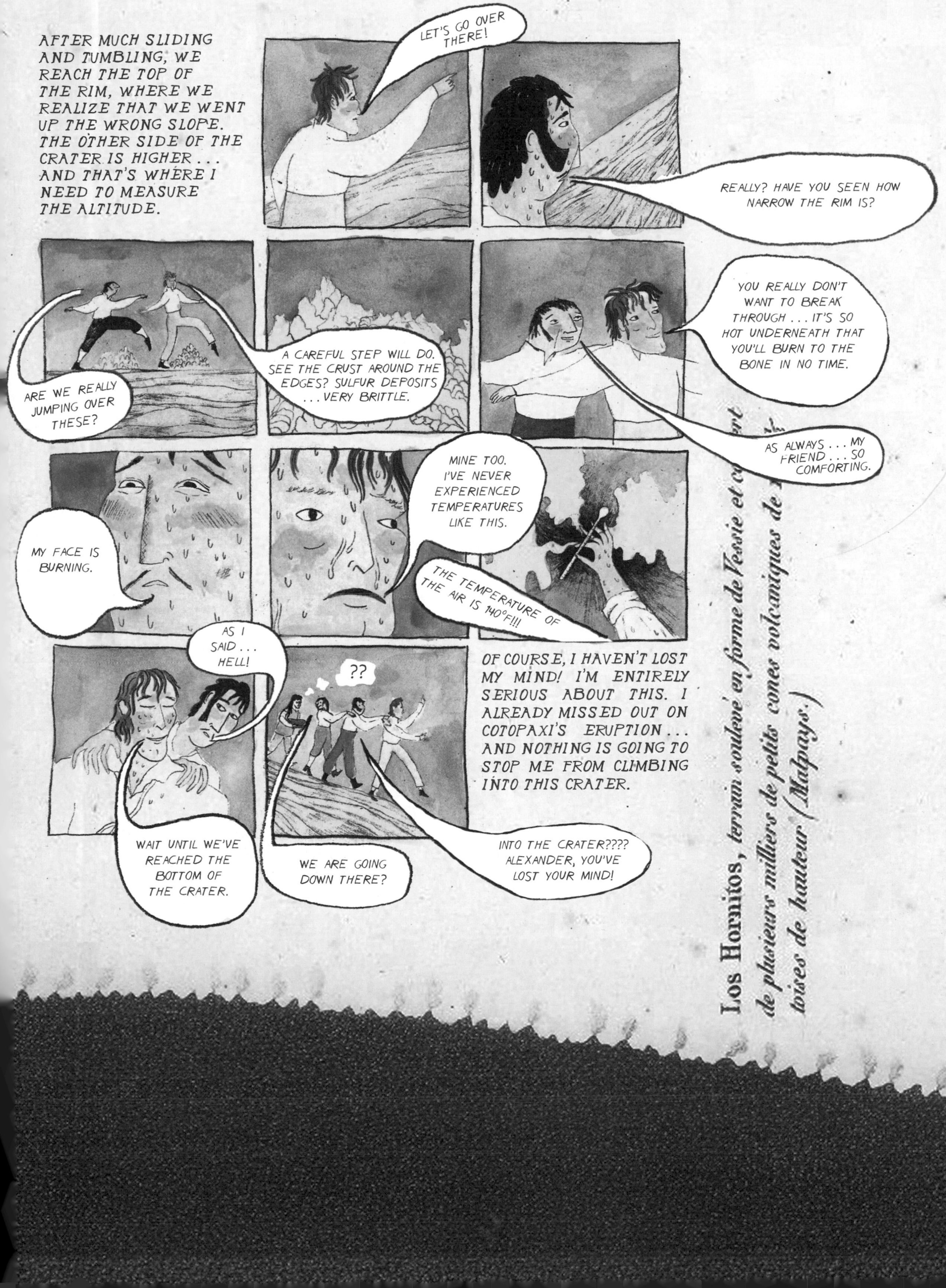

AFTER MUCH SLIDING AND TUMBLING, WE REACH THE TOP OF THE RIM, WHERE WE REALIZE THAT WE WENT UP THE WRONG SLOPE. THE OTHER SIDE OF THE CRATER IS HIGHER... AND THAT'S WHERE I NEED TO MEASURE THE ALTITUDE.

LET'S GO OVER THERE!

REALLY? HAVE YOU SEEN HOW NARROW THE RIM IS?

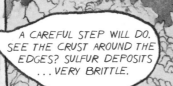

A CAREFUL STEP WILL DO. SEE THE CRUST AROUND THE EDGES? SULFUR DEPOSITS ...VERY BRITTLE.

ARE WE REALLY JUMPING OVER THESE?

YOU REALLY DON'T WANT TO BREAK THROUGH ...IT'S SO HOT UNDERNEATH THAT YOU'LL BURN TO THE BONE IN NO TIME.

AS ALWAYS ... MY FRIEND ... SO COMFORTING.

MY FACE IS BURNING.

MINE TOO. I'VE NEVER EXPERIENCED TEMPERATURES LIKE THIS.

THE TEMPERATURE OF THE AIR IS 140°F!!!

OF COURSE, I HAVEN'T LOST MY MIND! I'M ENTIRELY SERIOUS ABOUT THIS. I ALREADY MISSED OUT ON COTOPAXI'S ERUPTION... AND NOTHING IS GOING TO STOP ME FROM CLIMBING INTO THIS CRATER.

AS I SAID ... HELL!

WAIT UNTIL WE'VE REACHED THE BOTTOM OF THE CRATER.

??

WE ARE GOING DOWN THERE?

INTO THE CRATER???? ALEXANDER, YOU'VE LOST YOUR MIND!

Los Hornitos, *terrain soulevé en forme de l'essie et co... ... de plusieurs milliers de petits cones volcaniques de ... toises de hauteur. (Malpays.)*

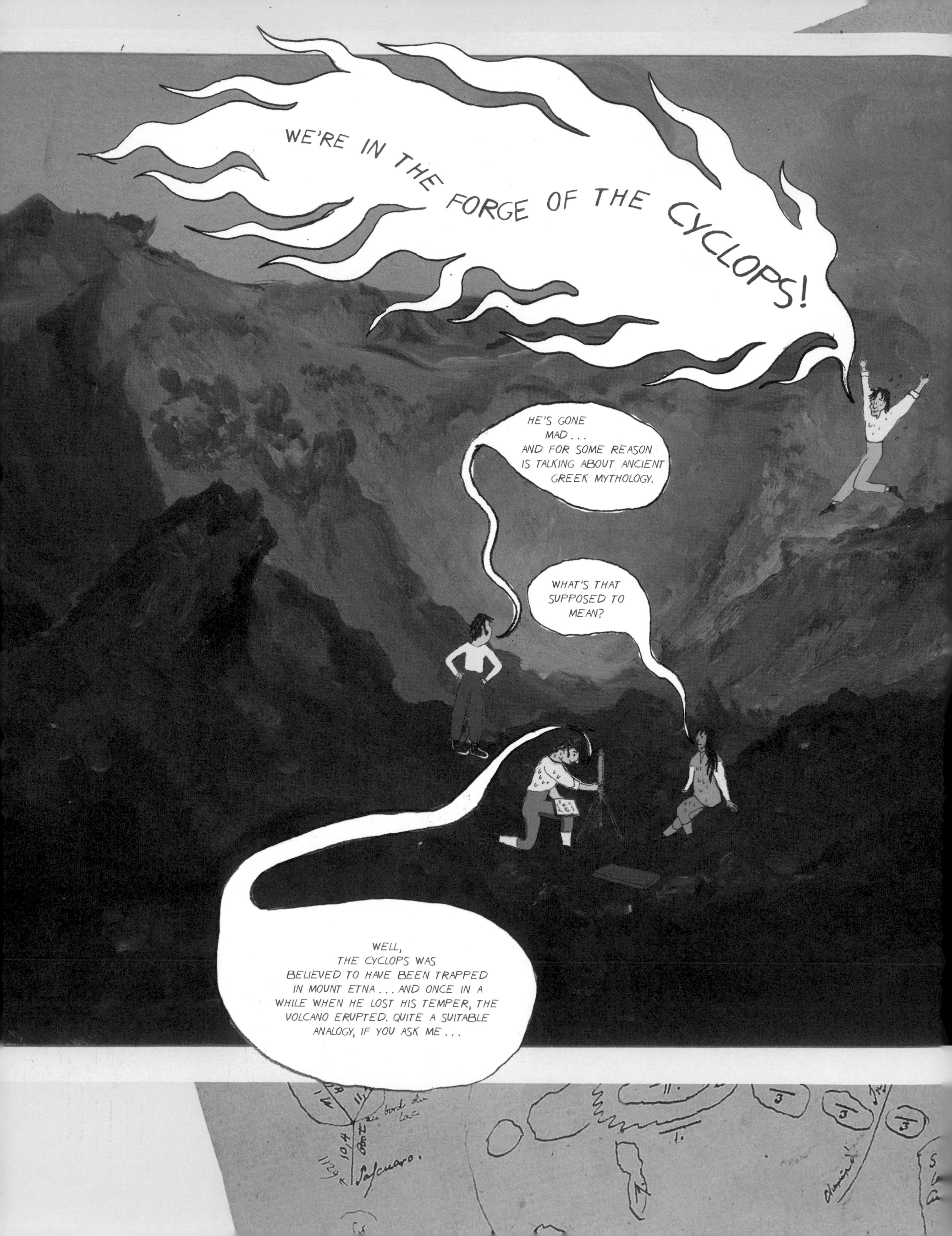
WE'RE IN THE FORGE OF THE CYCLOPS!
HE'S GONE MAD . . . AND FOR SOME REASON IS TALKING ABOUT ANCIENT GREEK MYTHOLOGY.
WHAT'S THAT SUPPOSED TO MEAN?
WELL, THE CYCLOPS WAS BELIEVED TO HAVE BEEN TRAPPED IN MOUNT ETNA . . . AND ONCE IN A WHILE WHEN HE LOST HIS TEMPER, THE VOLCANO ERUPTED. QUITE A SUITABLE ANALOGY, IF YOU ASK ME . . .

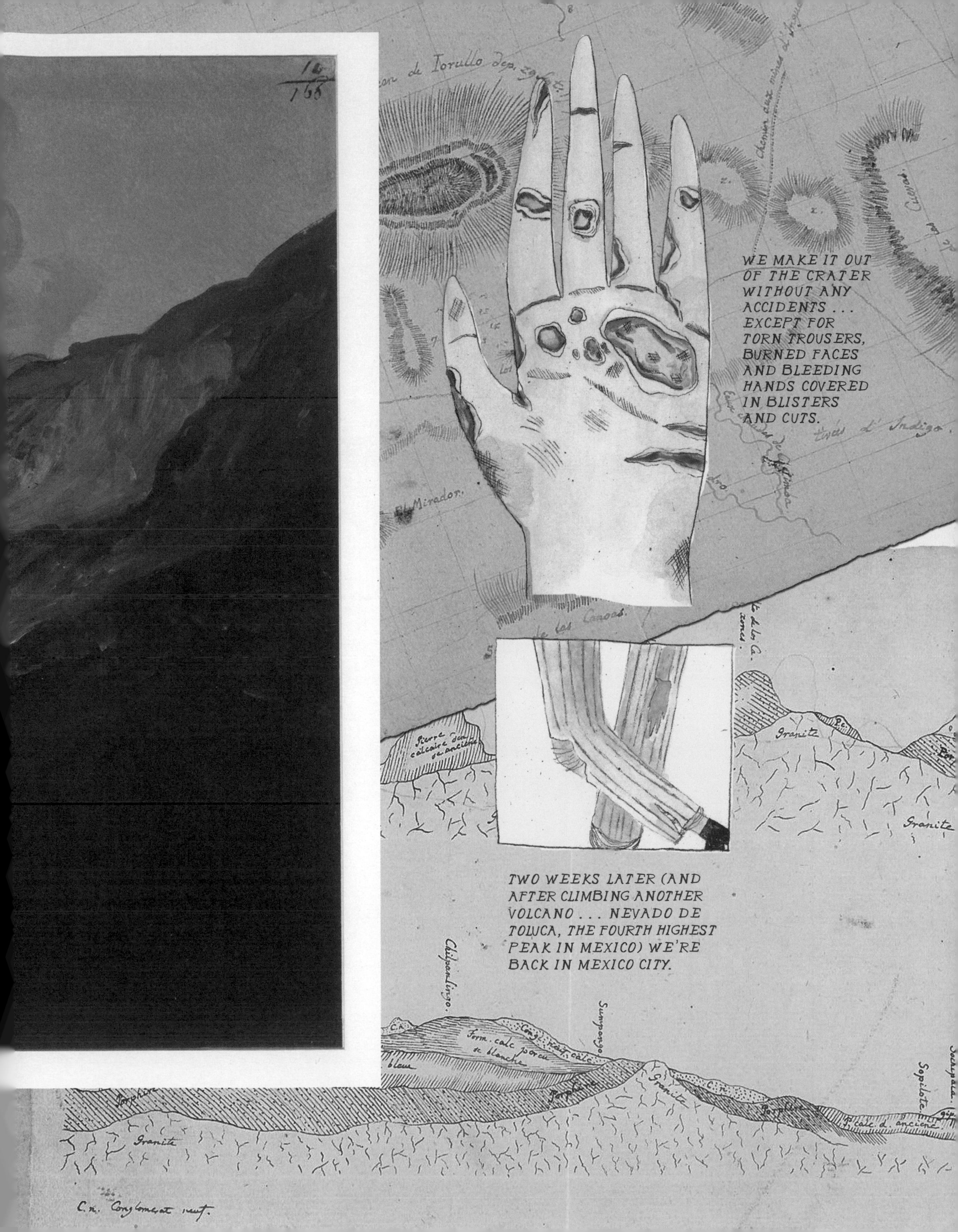
WE MAKE IT OUT OF THE CRATER WITHOUT ANY ACCIDENTS . . . EXCEPT FOR TORN TROUSERS, BURNED FACES AND BLEEDING HANDS COVERED IN BLISTERS AND CUTS.
TWO WEEKS LATER (AND AFTER CLIMBING ANOTHER VOLCANO . . . NEVADO DE TOLUCA, THE FOURTH HIGHEST PEAK IN MEXICO) WE'RE BACK IN MEXICO CITY.
El Mirador
Granite

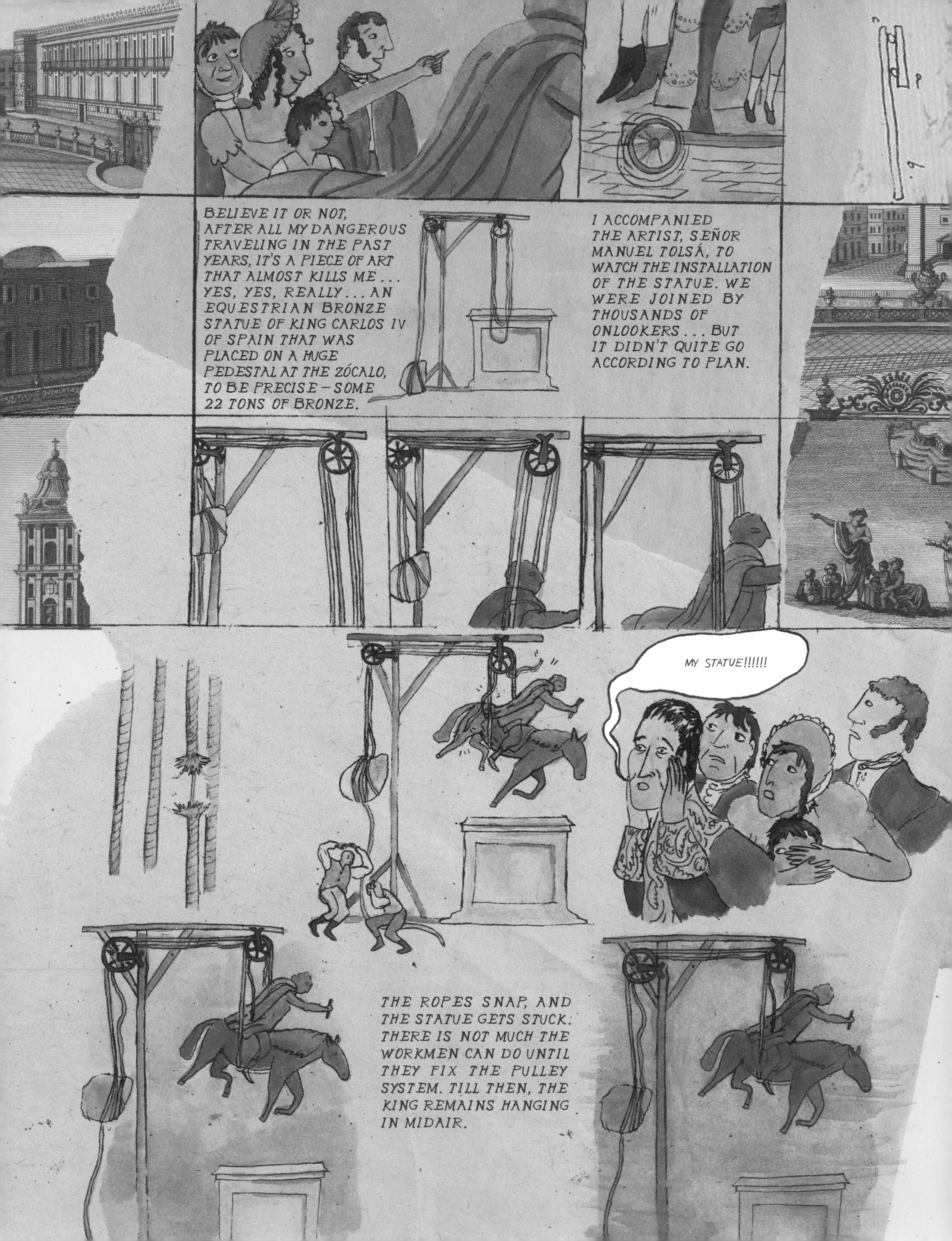
BELIEVE IT OR NOT, AFTER ALL MY DANGEROUS TRAVELING IN THE PAST YEARS, IT'S A PIECE OF ART THAT ALMOST KILLS ME . . . YES, YES, REALLY . . . AN EQUESTRIAN BRONZE STATUE OF KING CARLOS IV OF SPAIN THAT WAS PLACED ON A HUGE PEDESTAL AT THE ZÓCALO, TO BE PRECISE – SOME 22 TONS OF BRONZE.
I ACCOMPANIED THE ARTIST, SEÑOR MANUEL TOLSÁ, TO WATCH THE INSTALLATION OF THE STATUE. WE WERE JOINED BY THOUSANDS OF ONLOOKERS . . . BUT IT DIDN'T QUITE GO ACCORDING TO PLAN.
MY STATUE!!!!!!
THE ROPES SNAP, AND THE STATUE GETS STUCK. THERE IS NOT MUCH THE WORKMEN CAN DO UNTIL THEY FIX THE PULLEY SYSTEM. TILL THEN, THE KING REMAINS HANGING IN MIDAIR.

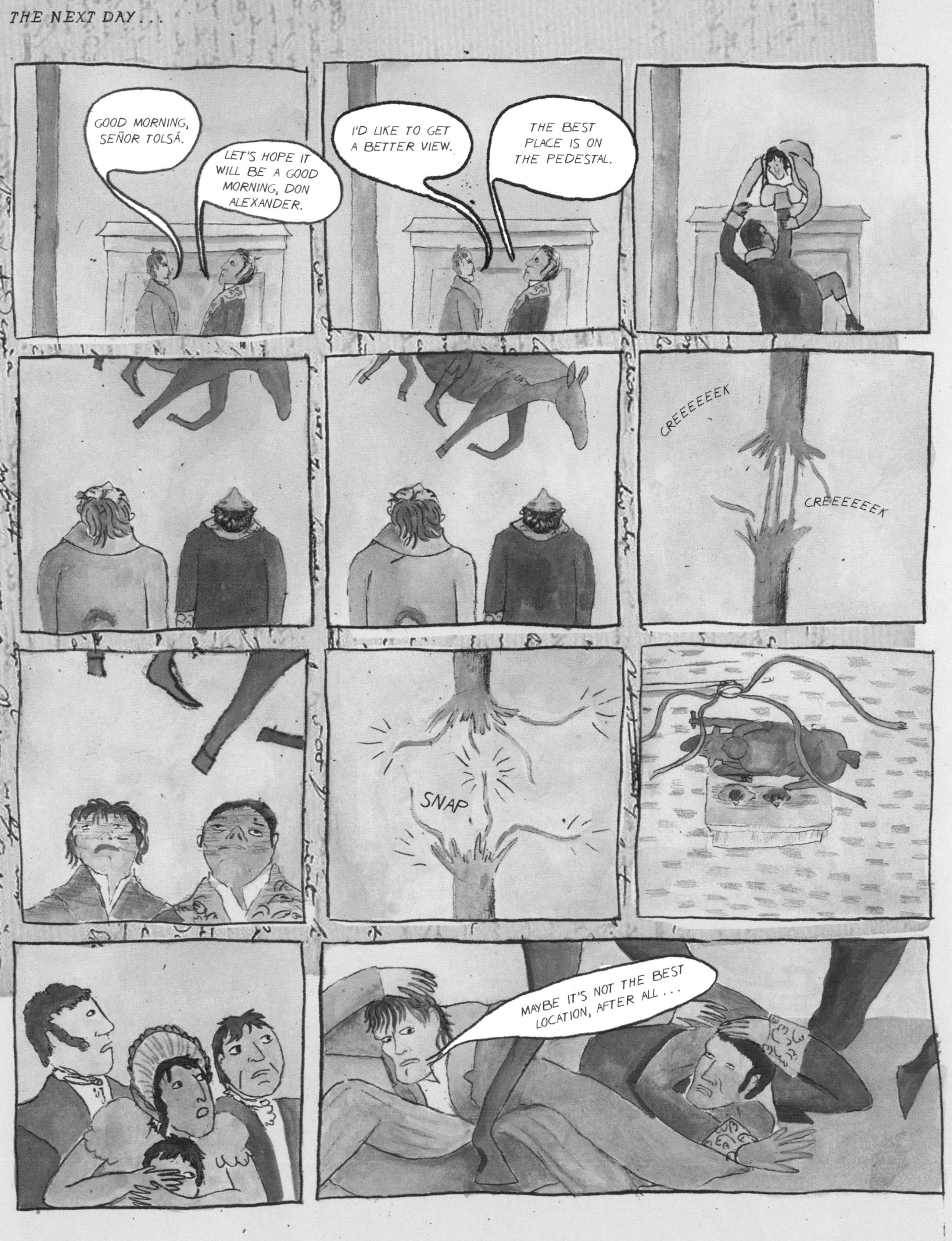
THE NEXT DAY...
GOOD MORNING, SEÑOR TOLSÁ.
LET'S HOPE IT WILL BE A GOOD MORNING, DON ALEXANDER.
I'D LIKE TO GET A BETTER VIEW.
THE BEST PLACE IS ON THE PEDESTAL.
CREEEEEEK
CREEEEEEK
SNAP
MAYBE IT'S NOT THE BEST LOCATION, AFTER ALL...

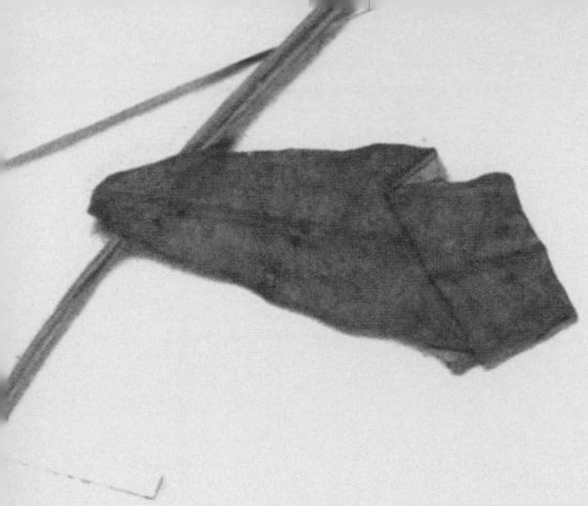

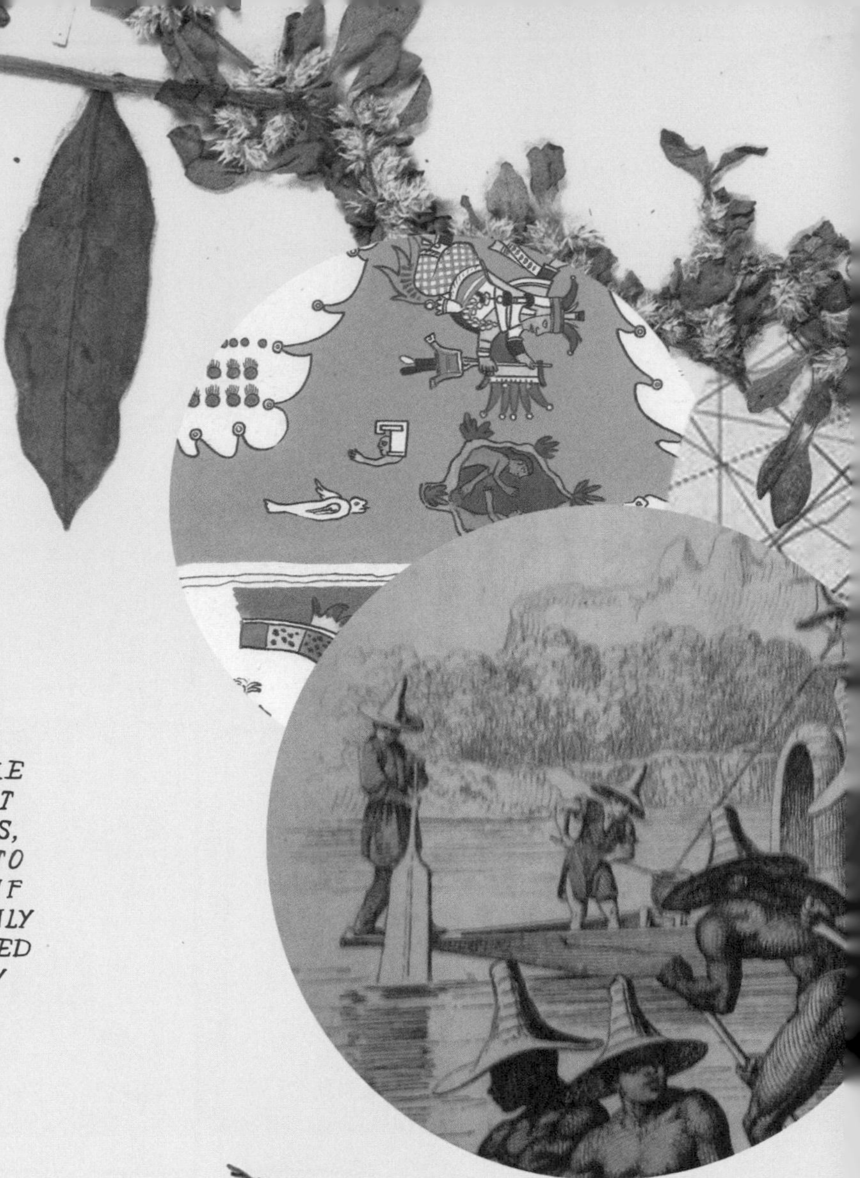

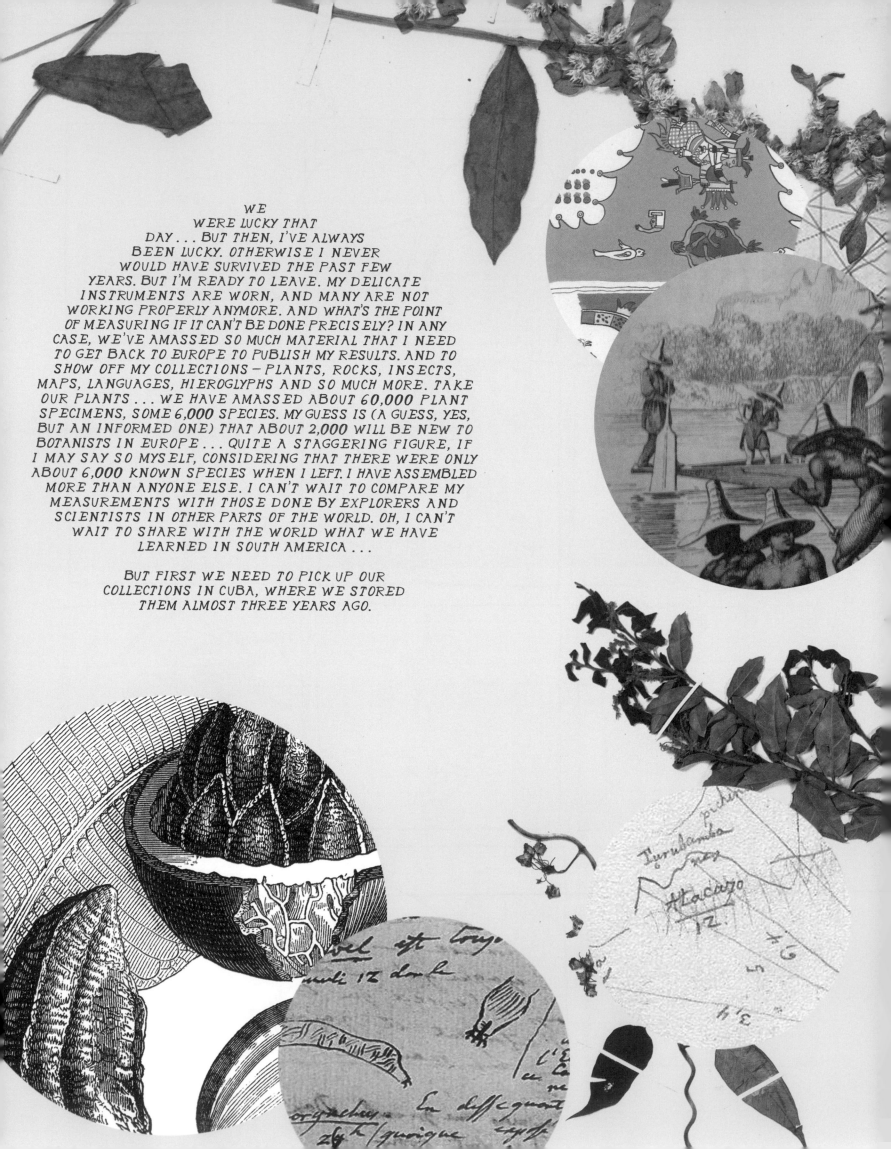

WE WERE LUCKY THAT DAY . . . BUT THEN, I'VE ALWAYS BEEN LUCKY. OTHERWISE I NEVER WOULD HAVE SURVIVED THE PAST FEW YEARS. BUT I'M READY TO LEAVE. MY DELICATE INSTRUMENTS ARE WORN, AND MANY ARE NOT WORKING PROPERLY ANYMORE. AND WHAT'S THE POINT OF MEASURING IF IT CAN'T BE DONE PRECISELY? IN ANY CASE, WE'VE AMASSED SO MUCH MATERIAL THAT I NEED TO GET BACK TO EUROPE TO PUBLISH MY RESULTS. AND TO SHOW OFF MY COLLECTIONS – PLANTS, ROCKS, INSECTS, MAPS, LANGUAGES, HIEROGLYPHS AND SO MUCH MORE. TAKE OUR PLANTS . . . WE HAVE AMASSED ABOUT **60,000** PLANT SPECIMENS, SOME **6,000** SPECIES. MY GUESS IS (A GUESS, YES, BUT AN INFORMED ONE) THAT ABOUT **2,000** WILL BE NEW TO BOTANISTS IN EUROPE . . . QUITE A STAGGERING FIGURE, IF I MAY SAY SO MYSELF, CONSIDERING THAT THERE WERE ONLY ABOUT **6,000** KNOWN SPECIES WHEN I LEFT. I HAVE ASSEMBLED MORE THAN ANYONE ELSE. I CAN'T WAIT TO COMPARE MY MEASUREMENTS WITH THOSE DONE BY EXPLORERS AND SCIENTISTS IN OTHER PARTS OF THE WORLD. OH, I CAN'T WAIT TO SHARE WITH THE WORLD WHAT WE HAVE LEARNED IN SOUTH AMERICA . . .

BUT FIRST WE NEED TO PICK UP OUR COLLECTIONS IN CUBA, WHERE WE STORED THEM ALMOST THREE YEARS AGO.

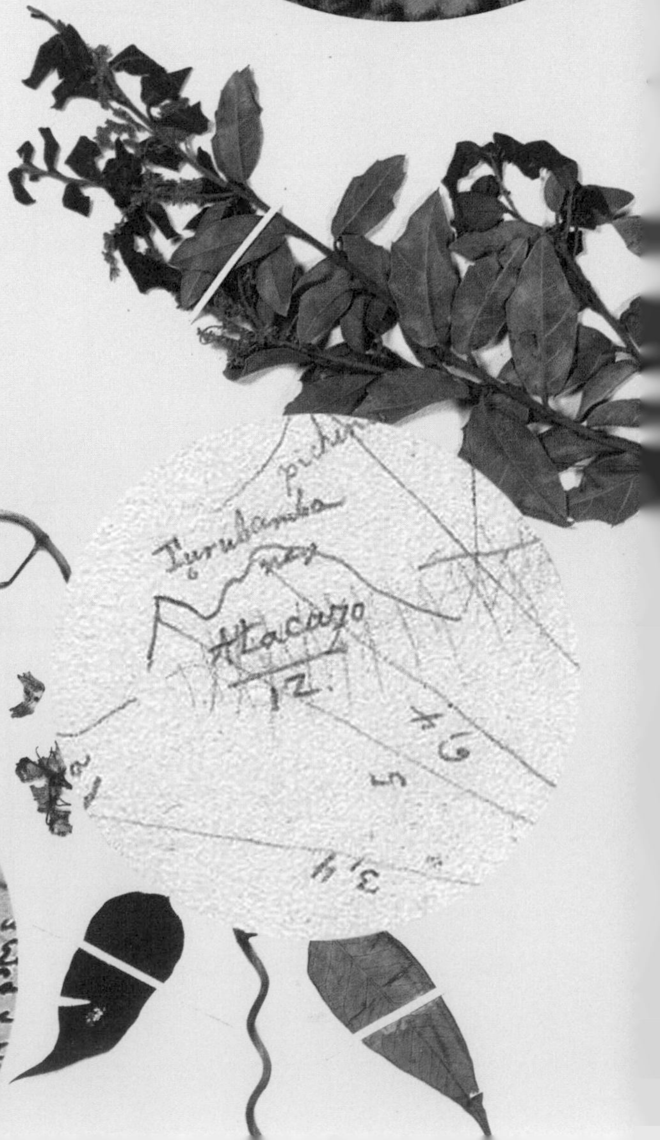

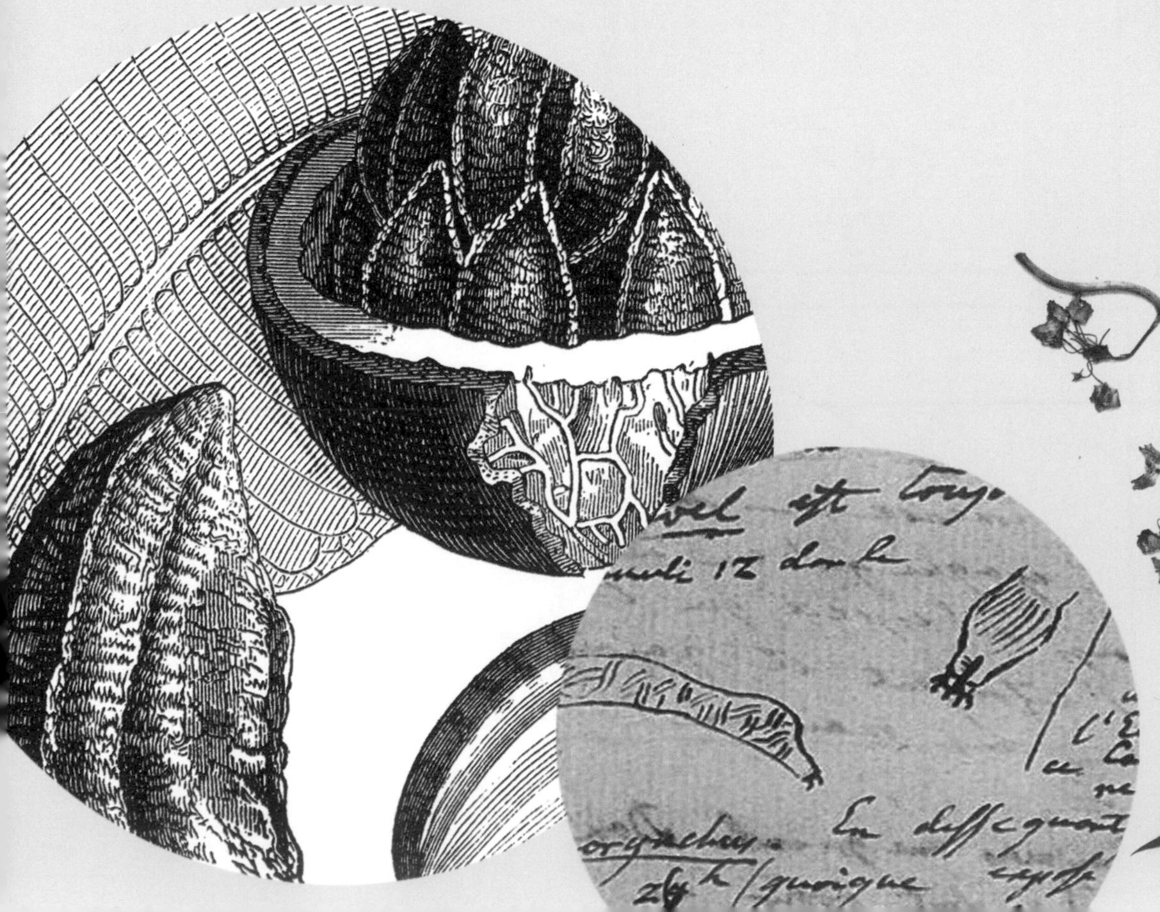

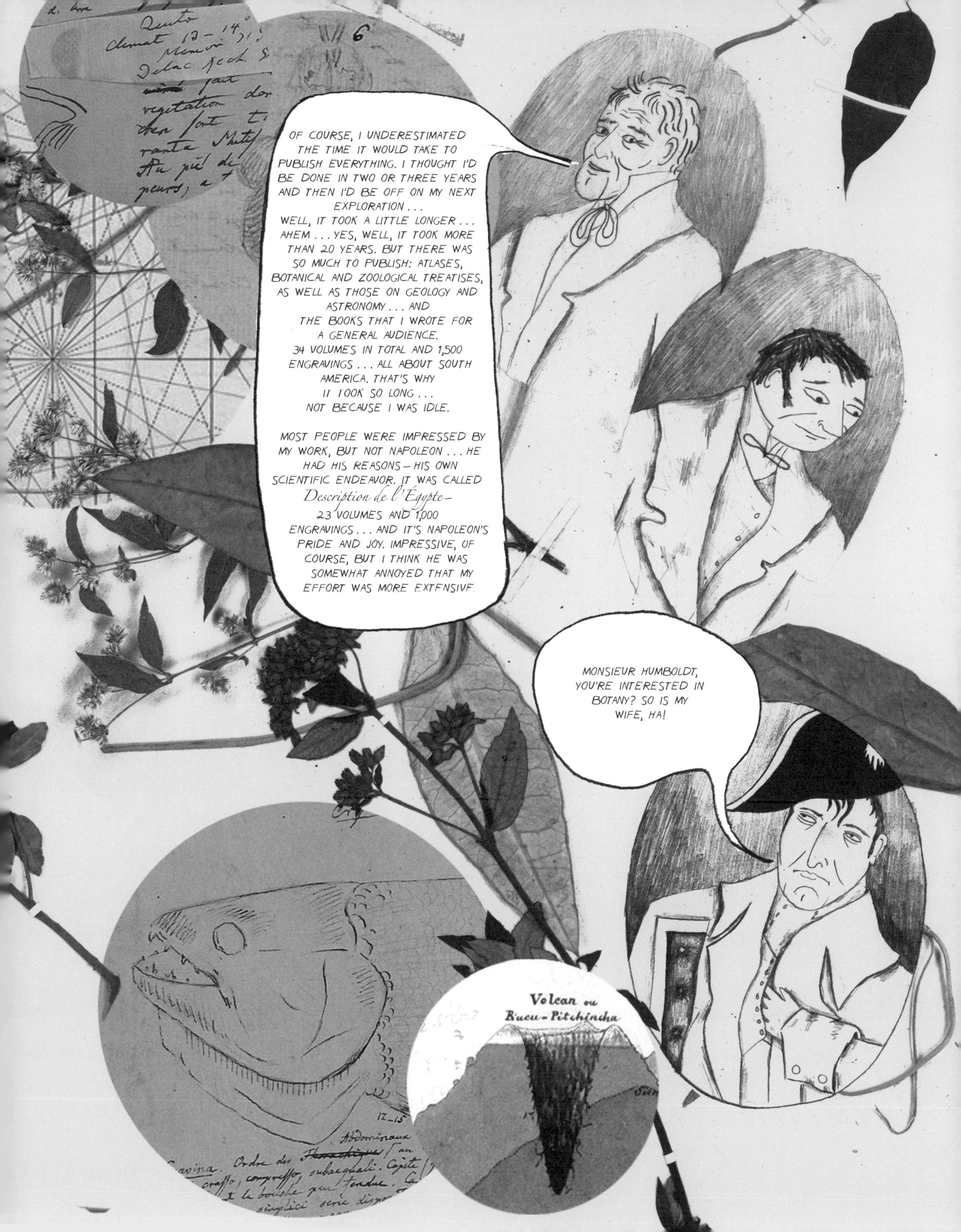
OF COURSE, I UNDERESTIMATED THE TIME IT WOULD TAKE TO PUBLISH EVERYTHING. I THOUGHT I'D BE DONE IN TWO OR THREE YEARS AND THEN I'D BE OFF ON MY NEXT EXPLORATION . . . WELL, IT TOOK A LITTLE LONGER . . . AHEM . . . YES, WELL, IT TOOK MORE THAN 20 YEARS. BUT THERE WAS SO MUCH TO PUBLISH: ATLASES, BOTANICAL AND ZOOLOGICAL TREATISES, AS WELL AS THOSE ON GEOLOGY AND ASTRONOMY . . . AND THE BOOKS THAT I WROTE FOR A GENERAL AUDIENCE. 34 VOLUMES IN TOTAL AND 1,500 ENGRAVINGS . . . ALL ABOUT SOUTH AMERICA. THAT'S WHY IT TOOK SO LONG . . . NOT BECAUSE I WAS IDLE.
MOST PEOPLE WERE IMPRESSED BY MY WORK, BUT NOT NAPOLEON . . . HE HAD HIS REASONS—HIS OWN SCIENTIFIC ENDEAVOR. IT WAS CALLED *Description de l'Égypte*—23 VOLUMES AND 1,000 ENGRAVINGS . . . AND IT'S NAPOLEON'S PRIDE AND JOY. IMPRESSIVE, OF COURSE, BUT I THINK HE WAS SOMEWHAT ANNOYED THAT MY EFFORT WAS MORE EXTENSIVE.
MONSIEUR HUMBOLDT, YOU'RE INTERESTED IN BOTANY? SO IS MY WIFE, HA!
Volcan ou Rucu-Pitchincha

ON 20 JANUARY 1804,
WE LEFT MEXICO CITY AND
TRAVELED TO VERACRUZ
ON THE GULF OF MEXICO.

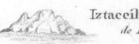

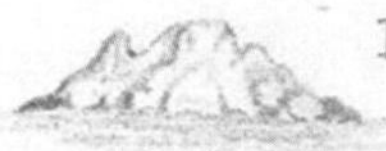
Iztaccíhuatl ou Sierra Nevada
de Puebla. 4786.m (2456 t.)

ON OUR WAY, I MEASURED THE MAJESTIC VOLCANOES POPOCATÉPETL AND IZTACCÍHUATL. WE TRIED TO CLIMB POPOCATÉPETL BUT DIDN'T GET MUCH BEYOND THE SNOW LINE. THERE WAS SO MUCH LOOSE SAND BENEATH THE SNOW THAT THE GROUND WAS IMPOSSIBLE TO TRAVERSE.

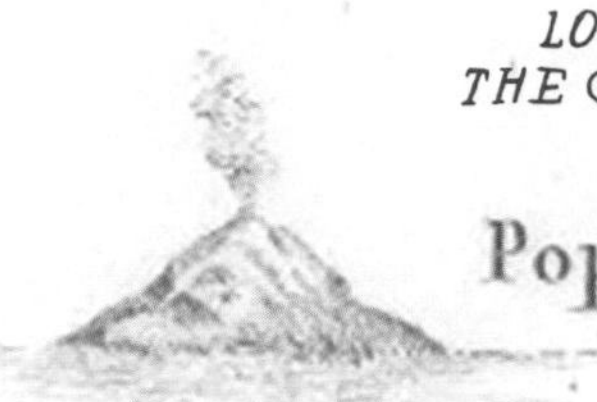
Popocatepetl ou Grand Volcan
de Puebla.. 5400.m (2771 t.)

WE ALSO VISITED THE RUINS OF CHOLULA— THE LARGEST PYRAMID IN THE WORLD.

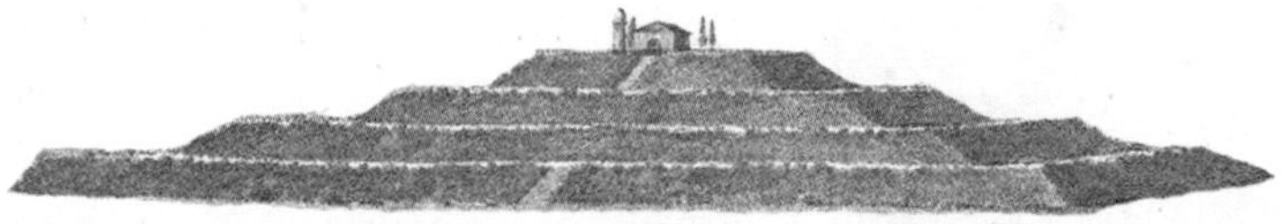

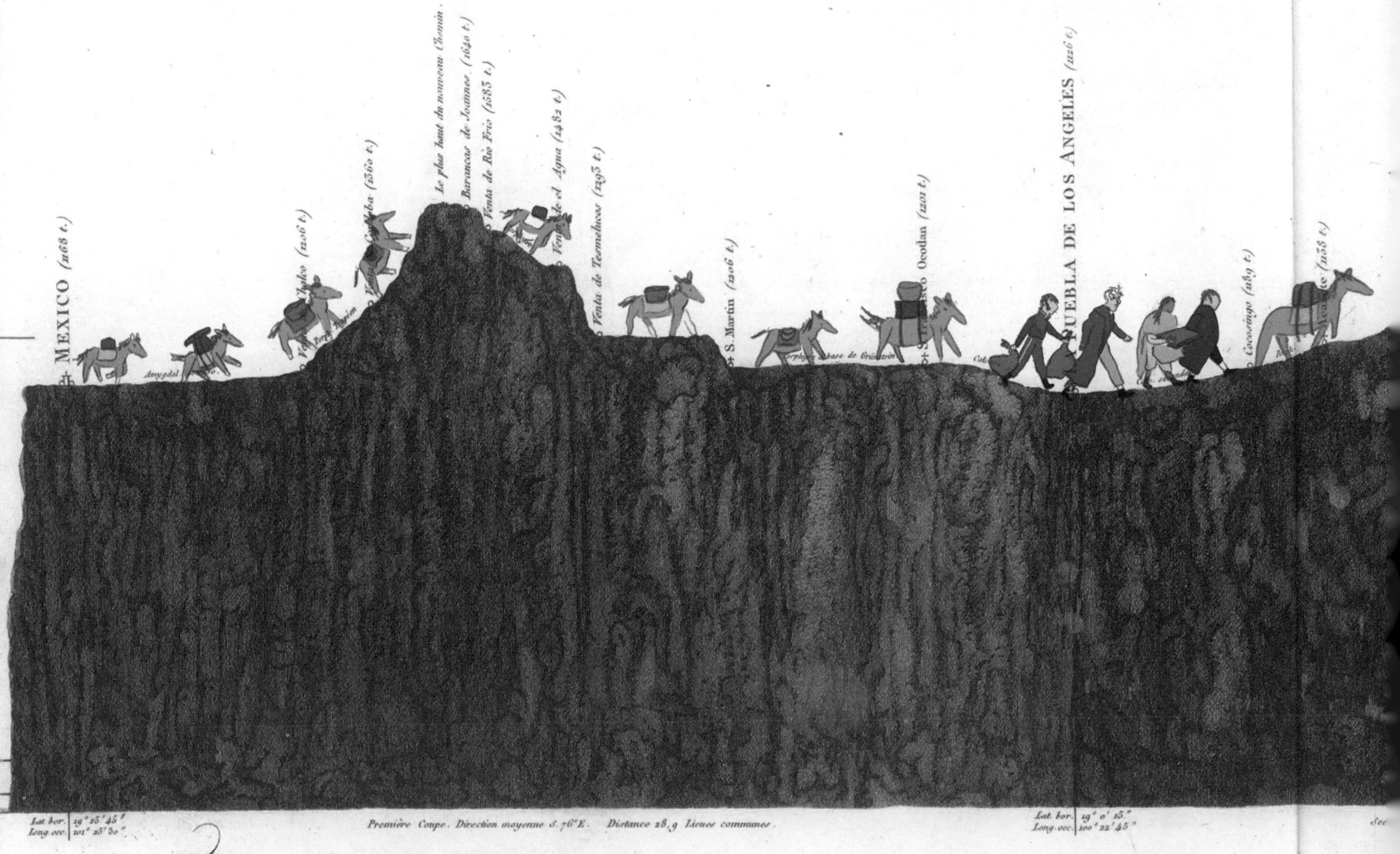
MEXICO (1168 t.)
Le plus haut du nouveau Chemin
Barancas de Joannes (1640 t.)
Venta de Rio Frio (1585 t.)
Venta de Teremelucos (1293 t.)
S. Martin (1206 t.)
Ocotlan (1201 t.)
PUEBLA DE LOS ANGELES (1126 t.)
Cocosingo (1189 t.)
Lat. bor. 19° 25' 45"
Long. occ. 101° 25' 30"
Première Coupe. Direction moyenne S. 76° E. Distance 28,9 Lieues communes.
Lat. bor. 19° 0' 15"
Long. occ. 100° 22' 45"

Tableau physique de la pente Orient

(Chemin de Mexico à V

Pic d'Orizava *ou* Citlaltépetl
5295 ᵐ (2717 t.)

WE MEASURED PIC D'ORIZABA,
THE HIGHEST MOUNTAIN IN MEXICO...

... AND I CLIMBED COFRE DE
PEROTE WITH CARLOS WHILE
BONPLAND WENT BOTANIZING.

Le Cofre de Perote *ou* Nauhcampatepetl
4089 ᵐ (2098 t.)

WE FINALLY LEFT
MEXICO ON 7 MARCH 1804,
ALMOST EXACTLY ONE YEAR
AFTER OUR ARRIVAL.

on moyenne N. 52° S.   Distance 27,2 Lieues communes.

Lat. bor. 19° 38' 30"
Long. occ. 99° 30' 0"

Troisième Coupe. Direction moyenne S. 65° E.   Distance 28,4 Lieues communes.

du Plateau de la Nouvelle Espa

z par Puebla et Xalapa.)

WE SAILED FROM VERACRUZ TO CUBA, WHERE WE ARRIVED ON 19 MARCH 1804. I DIDN'T LIKE IT VERY MUCH. WHY NOT, YOU ASK? IN CUBA, NO ONE TALKS ABOUT NATURE, THE SCIENCES OR THE ARTS. NO ONE IS INTERESTED IN DISCOVERIES OR ANCIENT CIVILIZATIONS. THE ONLY TOPICS DISCUSSED IN HAVANA ARE SUGAR, PROFITS AND PLANTATIONS. ALL CONVERSATIONS REVOLVE AROUND HOW THE SMALLEST NUMBER OF SLAVES CAN PRODUCE THE LARGEST AMOUNT OF SUGAR. THAT'S ALL THEY ARE INTERESTED IN.

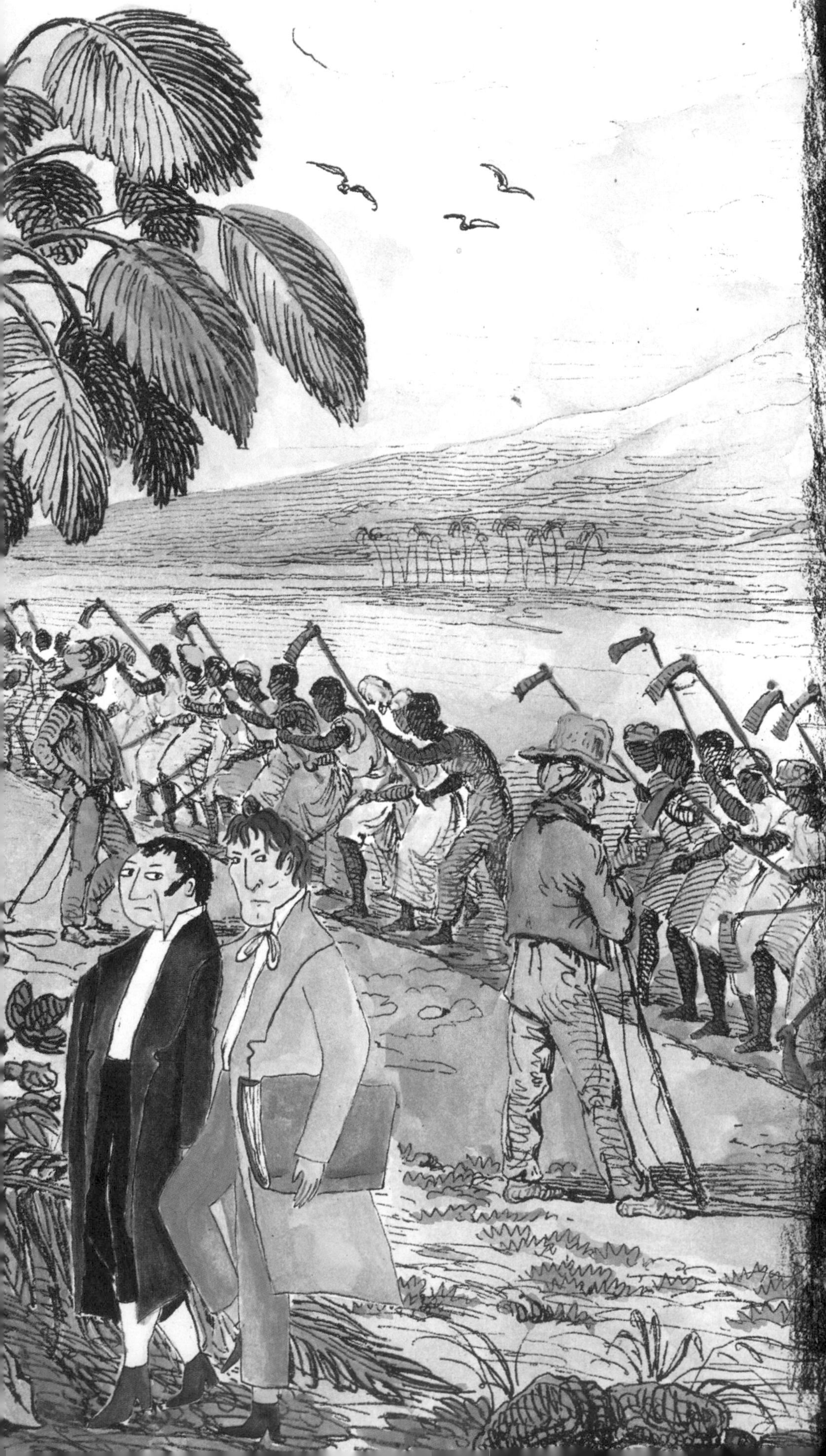

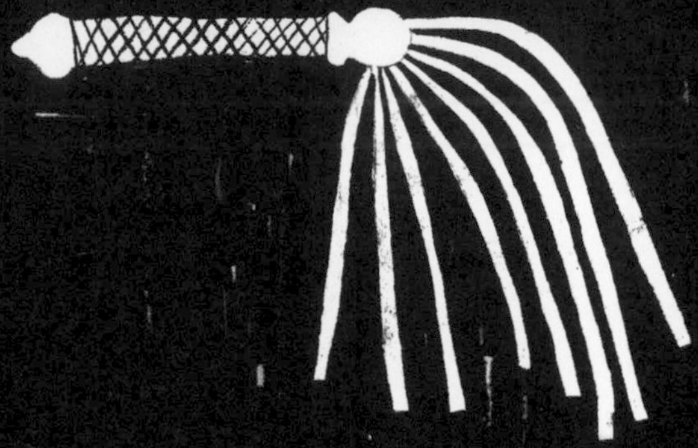

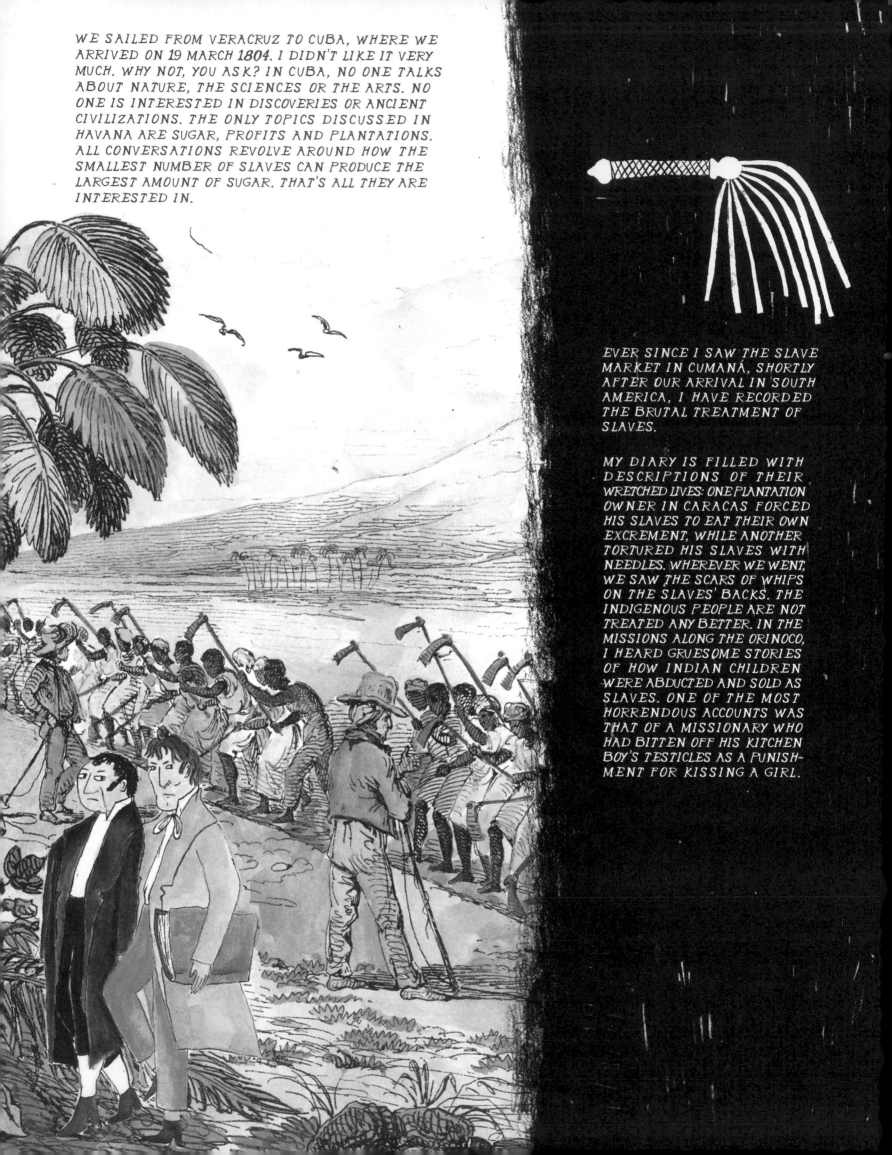

EVER SINCE I SAW THE SLAVE MARKET IN CUMANÁ, SHORTLY AFTER OUR ARRIVAL IN SOUTH AMERICA, I HAVE RECORDED THE BRUTAL TREATMENT OF SLAVES.

MY DIARY IS FILLED WITH DESCRIPTIONS OF THEIR WRETCHED LIVES: ONE PLANTATION OWNER IN CARACAS FORCED HIS SLAVES TO EAT THEIR OWN EXCREMENT, WHILE ANOTHER TORTURED HIS SLAVES WITH NEEDLES. WHEREVER WE WENT, WE SAW THE SCARS OF WHIPS ON THE SLAVES' BACKS. THE INDIGENOUS PEOPLE ARE NOT TREATED ANY BETTER. IN THE MISSIONS ALONG THE ORINOCO, I HEARD GRUESOME STORIES OF HOW INDIAN CHILDREN WERE ABDUCTED AND SOLD AS SLAVES. ONE OF THE MOST HORRENDOUS ACCOUNTS WAS THAT OF A MISSIONARY WHO HAD BITTEN OFF HIS KITCHEN BOY'S TESTICLES AS A PUNISHMENT FOR KISSING A GIRL.

EVERY DROP OF SUGARCANE JUICE COSTS BLOOD AND PAIN.

I EVEN WROTE A BOOK THAT ATTACKED SLAVERY—IT'S CALLED *Political Essay on the Island of Cuba,* BUT IT APPLIES TO ALL SLAVE-OWNING NATIONS.

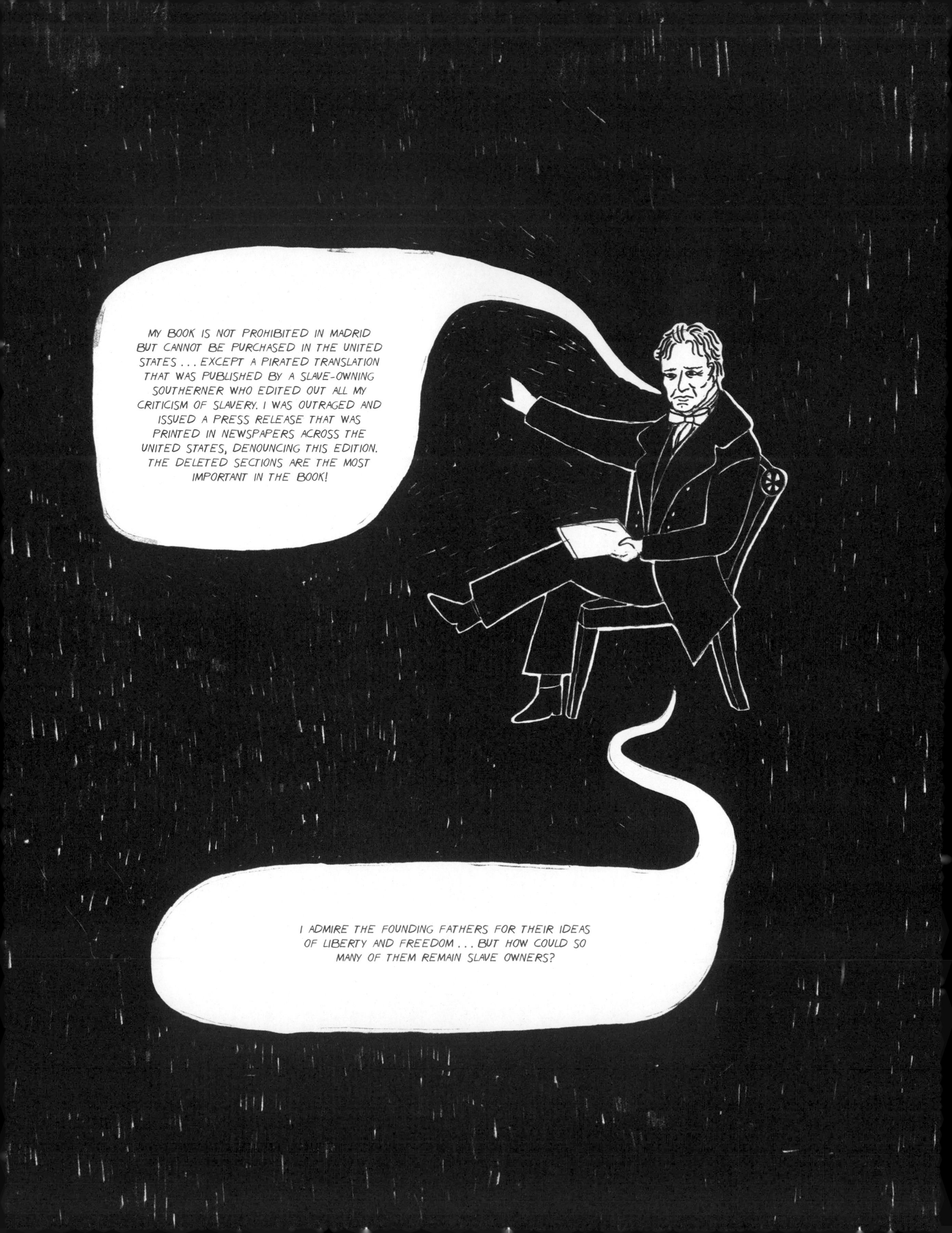
MY BOOK IS NOT PROHIBITED IN MADRID BUT CANNOT BE PURCHASED IN THE UNITED STATES . . . EXCEPT A PIRATED TRANSLATION THAT WAS PUBLISHED BY A SLAVE-OWNING SOUTHERNER WHO EDITED OUT ALL MY CRITICISM OF SLAVERY. I WAS OUTRAGED AND ISSUED A PRESS RELEASE THAT WAS PRINTED IN NEWSPAPERS ACROSS THE UNITED STATES, DENOUNCING THIS EDITION. THE DELETED SECTIONS ARE THE MOST IMPORTANT IN THE BOOK!
I ADMIRE THE FOUNDING FATHERS FOR THEIR IDEAS OF LIBERTY AND FREEDOM . . . BUT HOW COULD SO MANY OF THEM REMAIN SLAVE OWNERS?

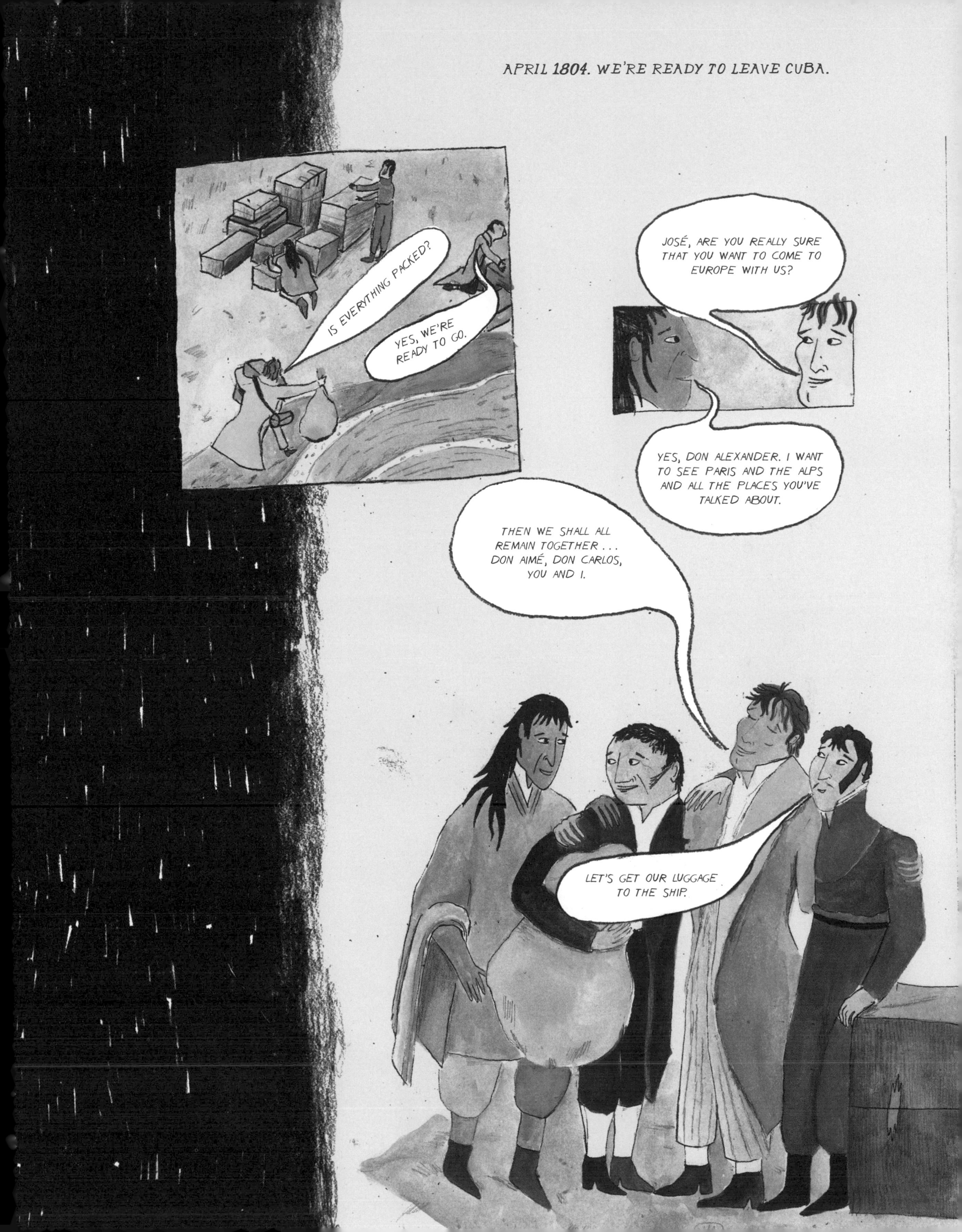
APRIL 1804. WE'RE READY TO LEAVE CUBA.
IS EVERYTHING PACKED?
YES, WE'RE READY TO GO.
JOSÉ, ARE YOU REALLY SURE THAT YOU WANT TO COME TO EUROPE WITH US?
YES, DON ALEXANDER. I WANT TO SEE PARIS AND THE ALPS AND ALL THE PLACES YOU'VE TALKED ABOUT.
THEN WE SHALL ALL REMAIN TOGETHER . . . DON AIMÉ, DON CARLOS, YOU AND I.
LET'S GET OUR LUGGAGE TO THE SHIP.

AFTER SOME DELAYS, WE ARE LEAVING HAVANA ON THE SPANISH FRIGATE *Concepción* ON 29 APRIL 1804 . . .

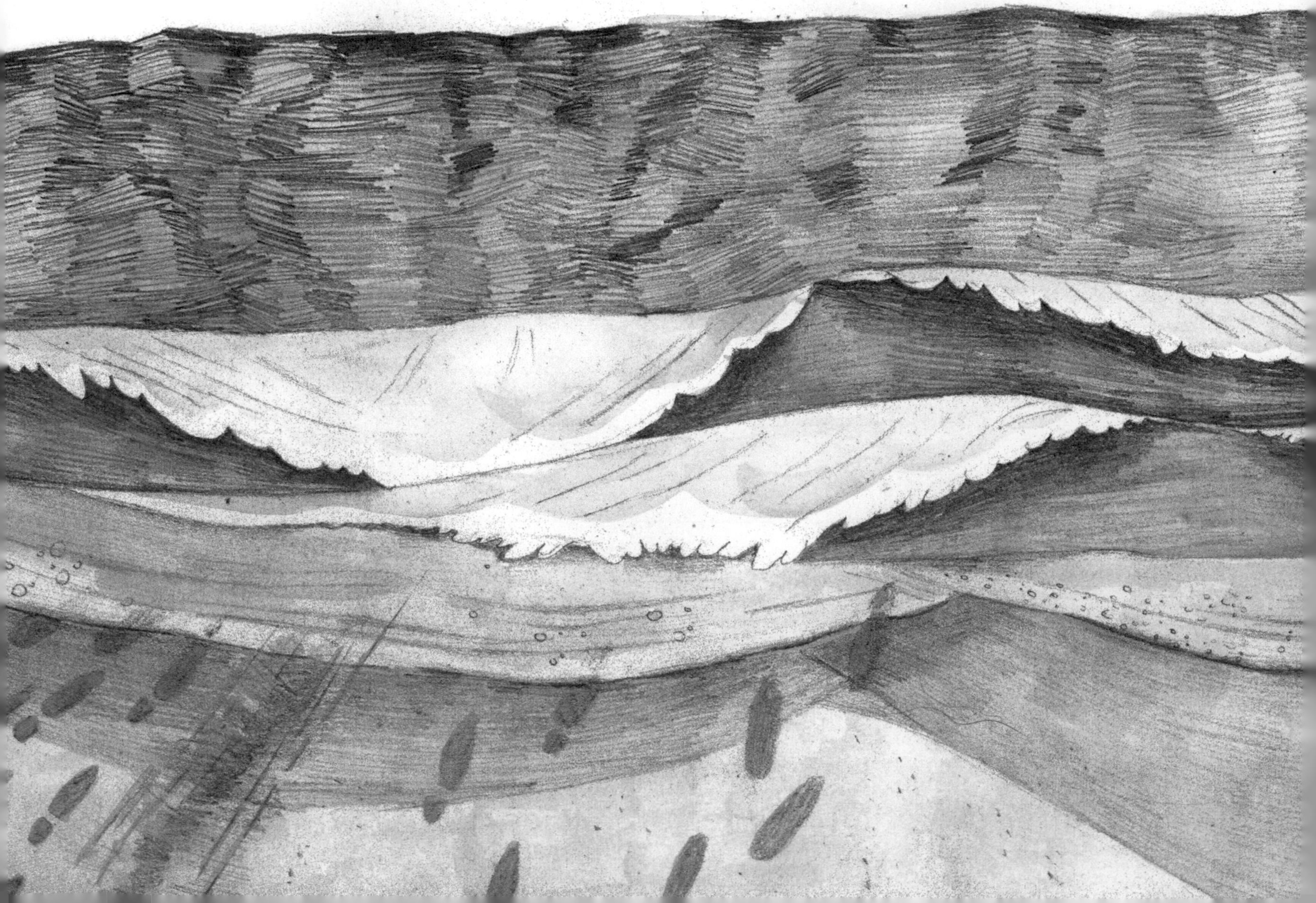

. . . BUT A WEEK LATER, WE'RE IN THE MIDST OF A HURRICANE.

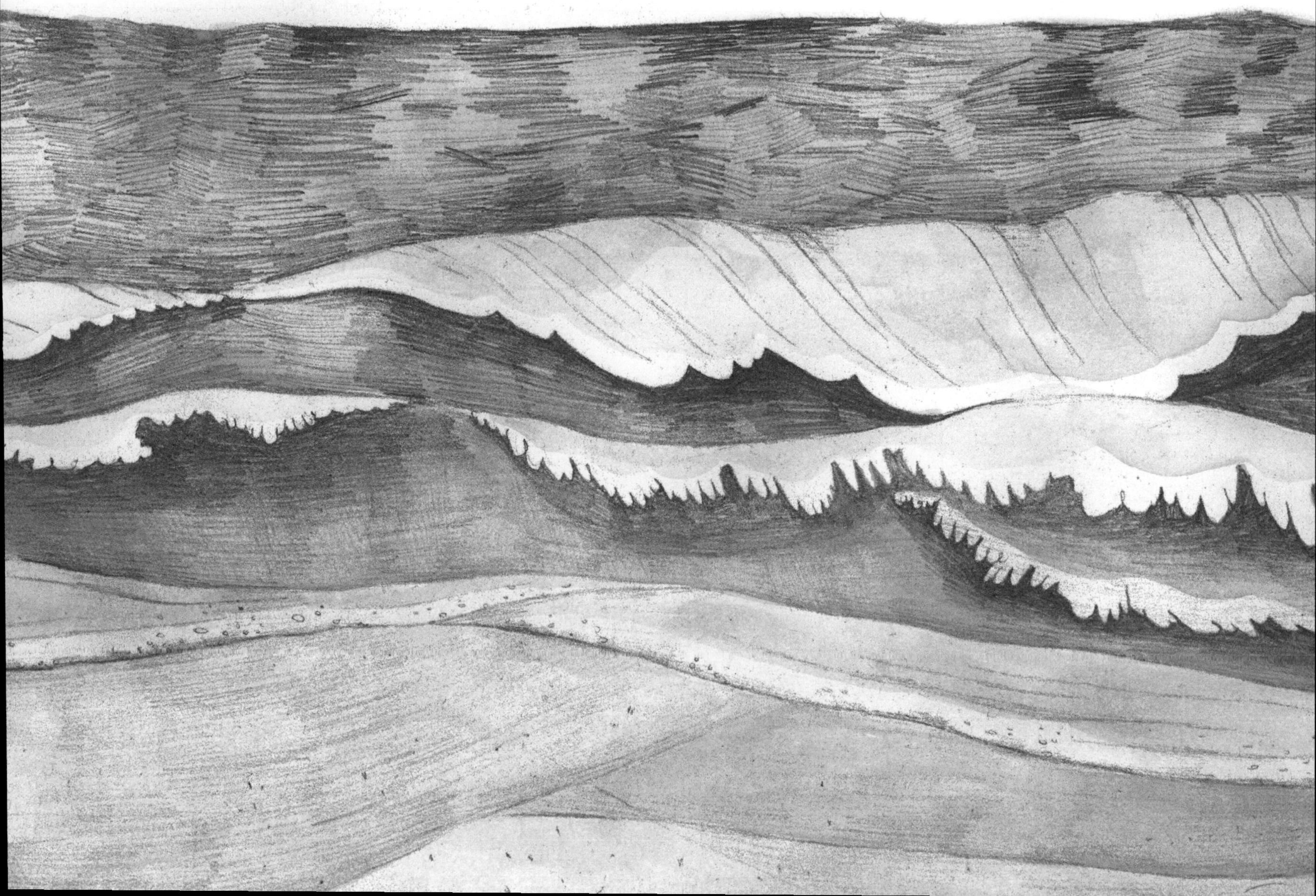

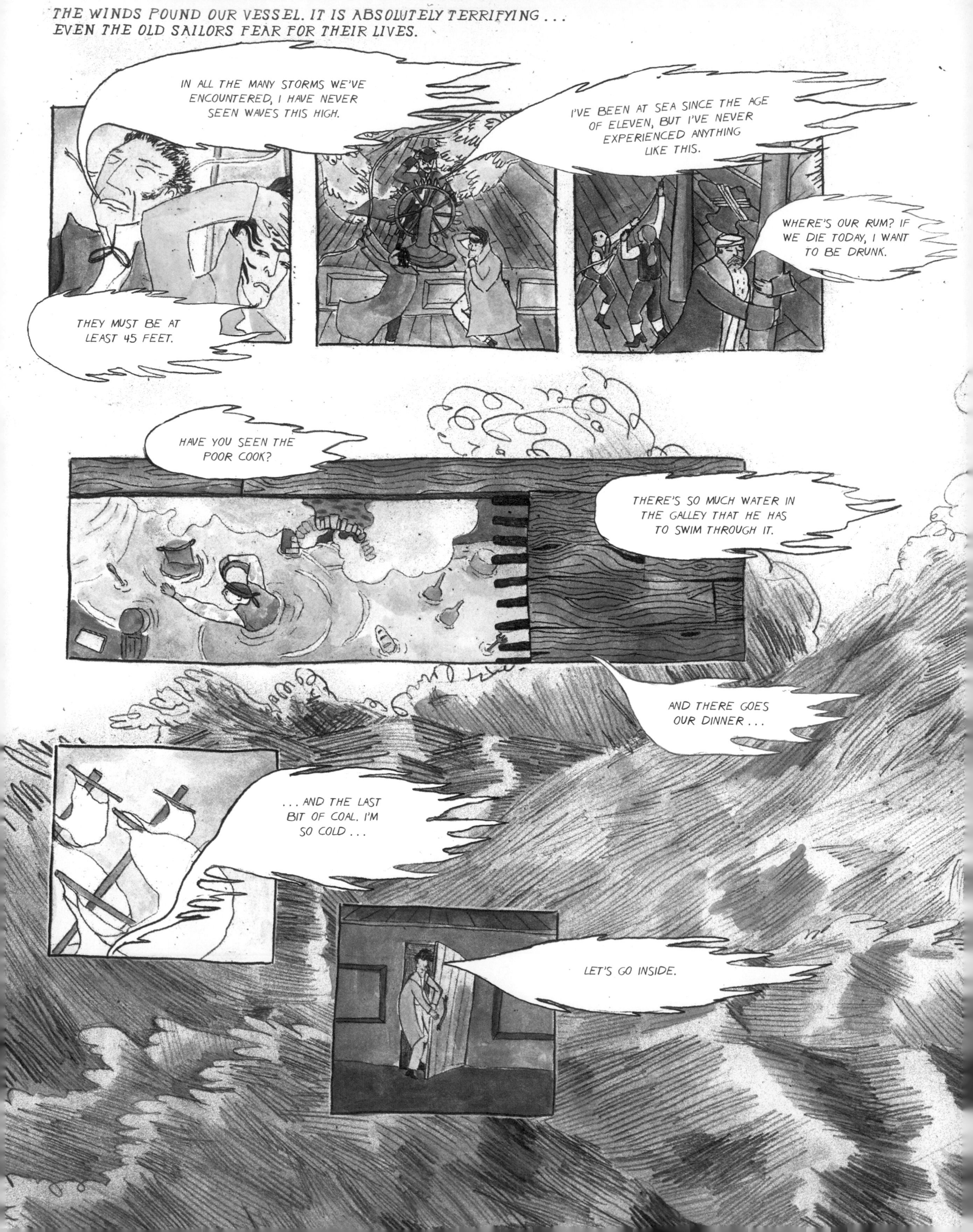
THE WINDS POUND OUR VESSEL. IT IS ABSOLUTELY TERRIFYING . . . EVEN THE OLD SAILORS FEAR FOR THEIR LIVES.
IN ALL THE MANY STORMS WE'VE ENCOUNTERED, I HAVE NEVER SEEN WAVES THIS HIGH.
THEY MUST BE AT LEAST 45 FEET.
I'VE BEEN AT SEA SINCE THE AGE OF ELEVEN, BUT I'VE NEVER EXPERIENCED ANYTHING LIKE THIS.
WHERE'S OUR RUM? IF WE DIE TODAY, I WANT TO BE DRUNK.
HAVE YOU SEEN THE POOR COOK?
THERE'S SO MUCH WATER IN THE GALLEY THAT HE HAS TO SWIM THROUGH IT.
AND THERE GOES OUR DINNER . . .
. . . AND THE LAST BIT OF COAL. I'M SO COLD . . .
LET'S GO INSIDE.

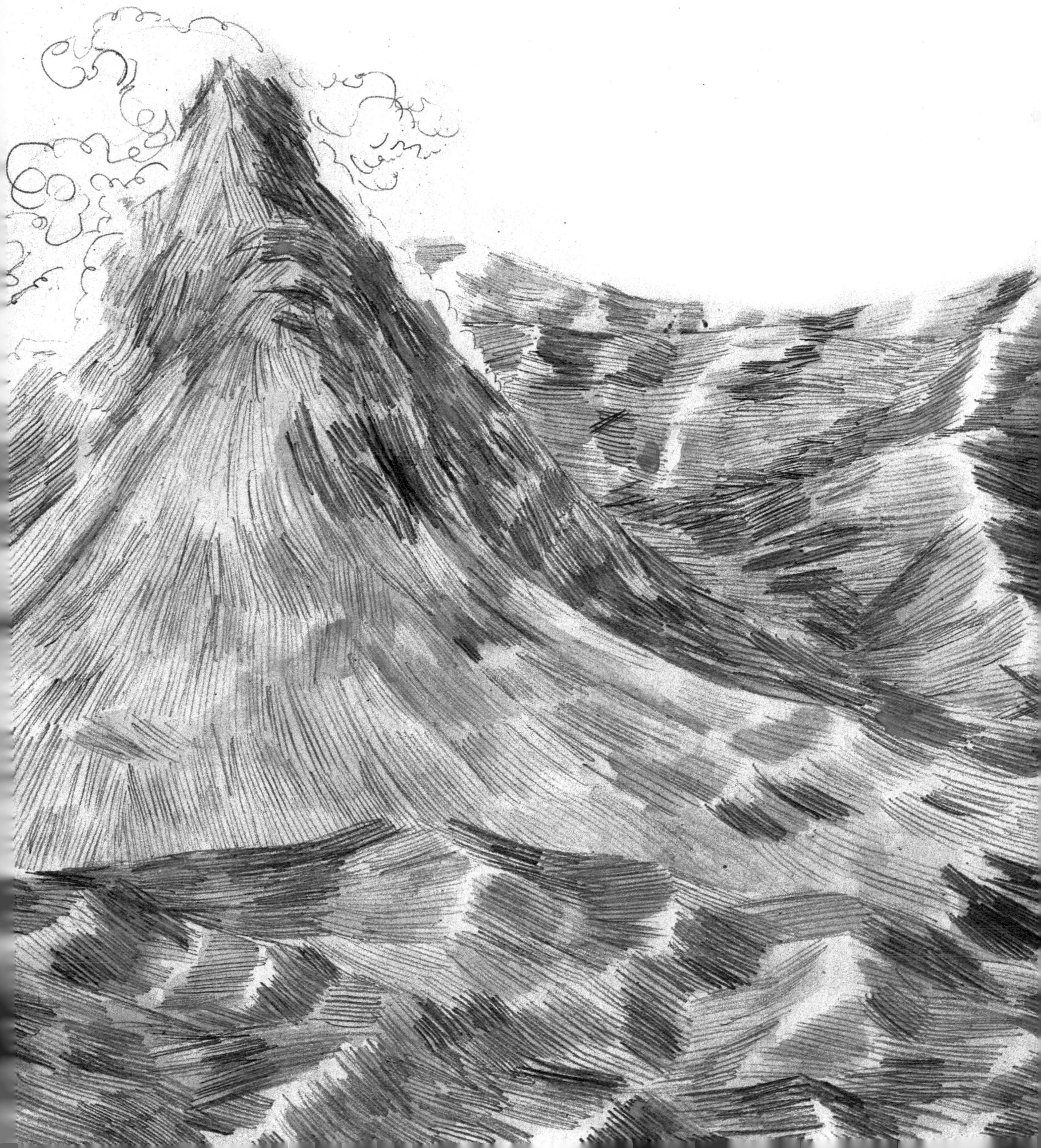

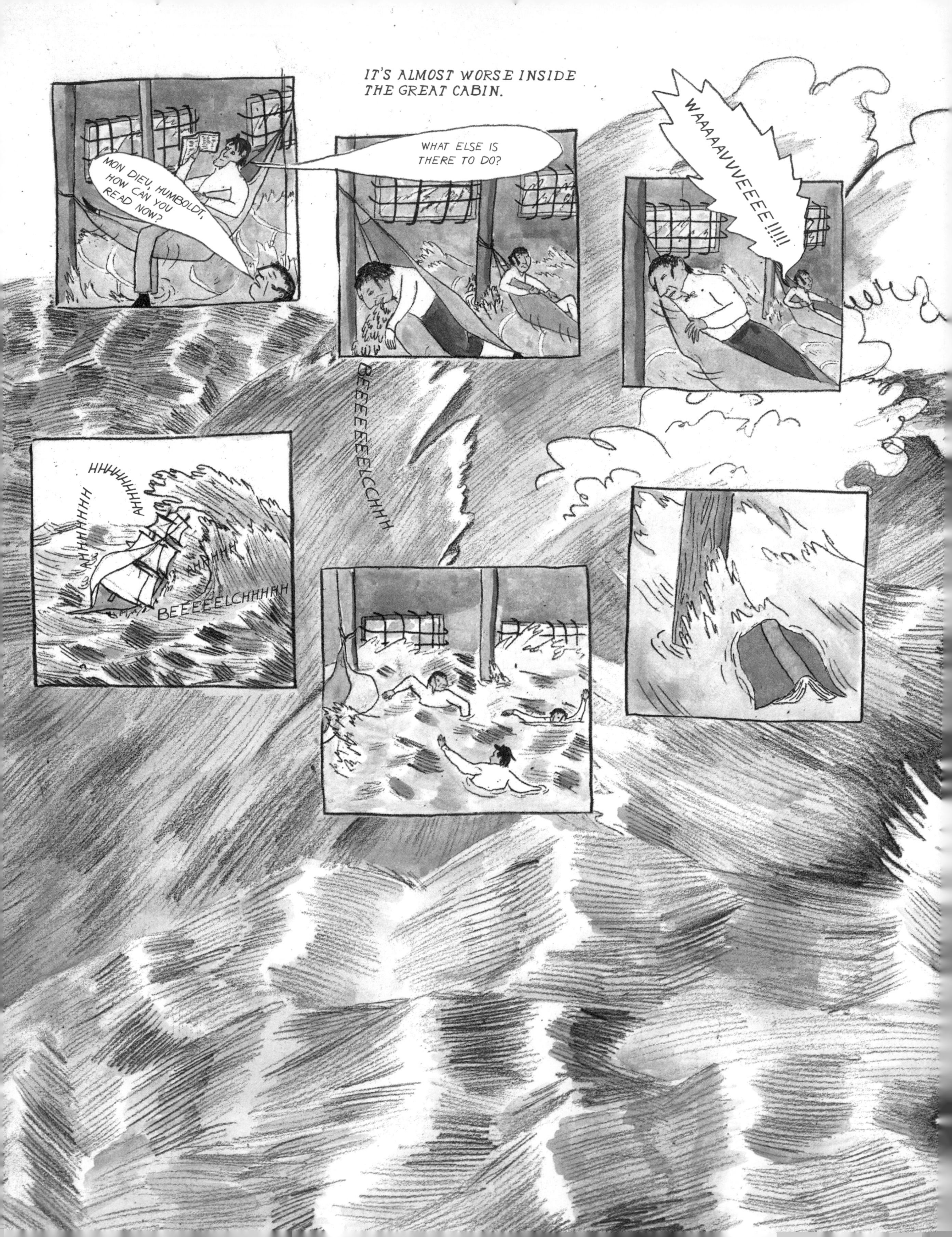
IT'S ALMOST WORSE INSIDE THE GREAT CABIN.
MON DIEU, HUMBOLDT, HOW CAN YOU READ NOW?
WHAT ELSE IS THERE TO DO?
WAAAAAVVVEEEE!!!!!
BEEEEEEEELCHHHH
HHHHHHHHHH AHHHH
AHHHHHHH
AHHHHH
BEEEEELCHHHHH

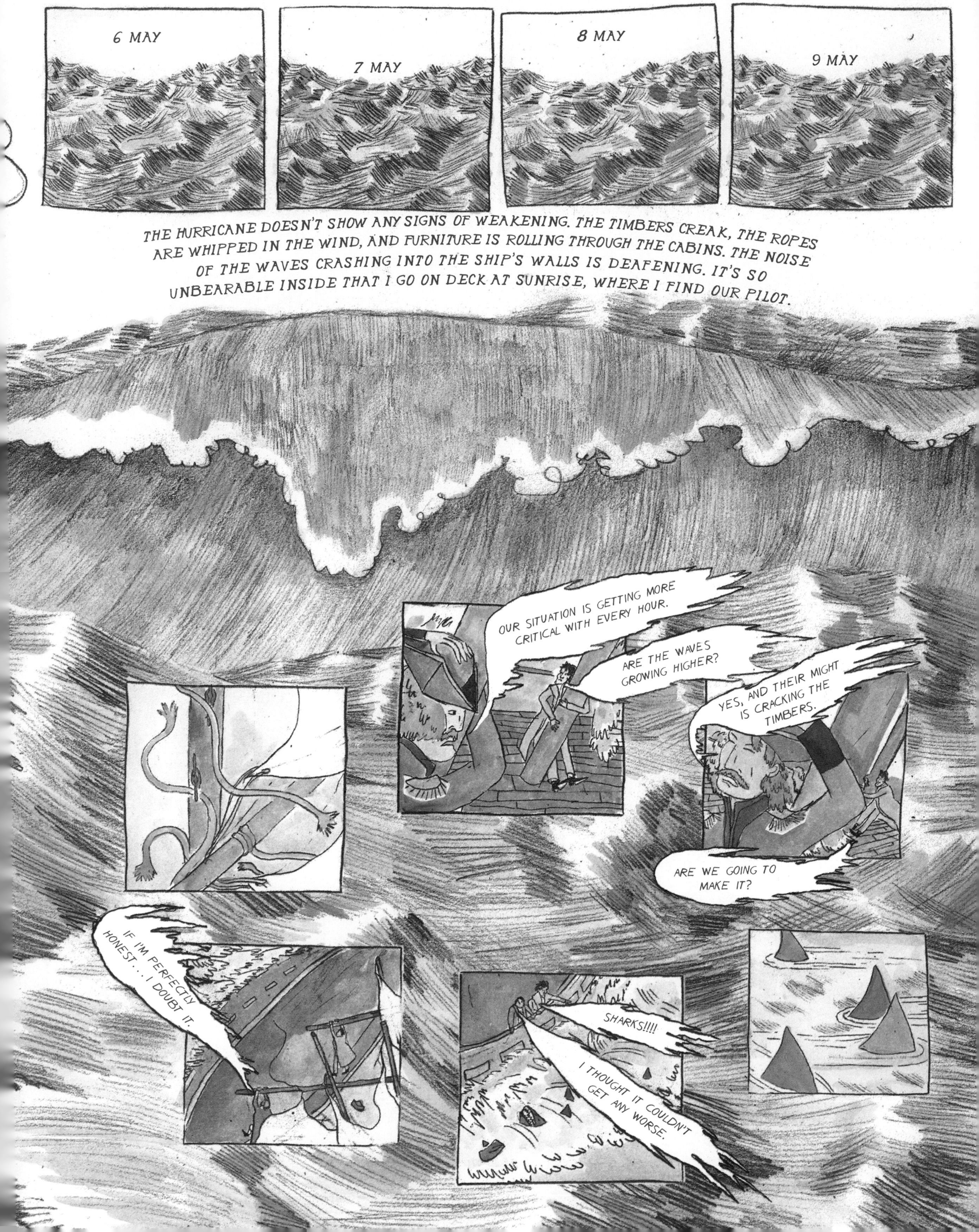
6 MAY
7 MAY
8 MAY
9 MAY
THE HURRICANE DOESN'T SHOW ANY SIGNS OF WEAKENING. THE TIMBERS CREAK, THE ROPES ARE WHIPPED IN THE WIND, AND FURNITURE IS ROLLING THROUGH THE CABINS. THE NOISE OF THE WAVES CRASHING INTO THE SHIP'S WALLS IS DEAFENING. IT'S SO UNBEARABLE INSIDE THAT I GO ON DECK AT SUNRISE, WHERE I FIND OUR PILOT.
OUR SITUATION IS GETTING MORE CRITICAL WITH EVERY HOUR.
ARE THE WAVES GROWING HIGHER?
YES, AND THEIR MIGHT IS CRACKING THE TIMBERS.
ARE WE GOING TO MAKE IT?
IF I'M PERFECTLY HONEST . . . I DOUBT IT.
SHARKS!!!!
I THOUGHT IT COULDN'T GET ANY WORSE.

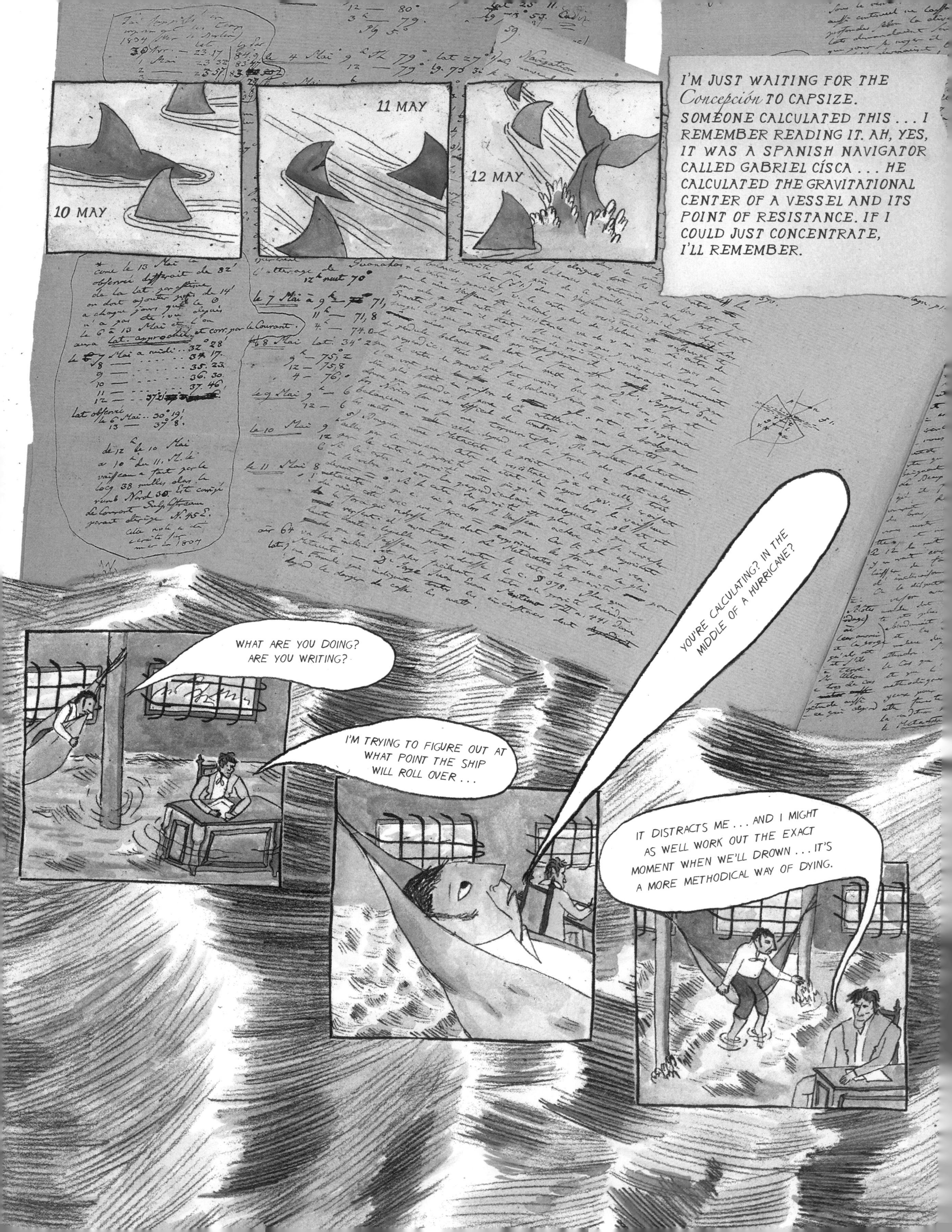
10 MAY
11 MAY
12 MAY
I'M JUST WAITING FOR THE *Concepción* TO CAPSIZE. SOMEONE CALCULATED THIS . . . I REMEMBER READING IT. AH, YES, IT WAS A SPANISH NAVIGATOR CALLED GABRIEL CÍSCA . . . HE CALCULATED THE GRAVITATIONAL CENTER OF A VESSEL AND ITS POINT OF RESISTANCE. IF I COULD JUST CONCENTRATE, I'LL REMEMBER.
WHAT ARE YOU DOING? ARE YOU WRITING?
I'M TRYING TO FIGURE OUT AT WHAT POINT THE SHIP WILL ROLL OVER . . .
YOU'RE CALCULATING? IN THE MIDDLE OF A HURRICANE?
IT DISTRACTS ME . . . AND I MIGHT AS WELL WORK OUT THE EXACT MOMENT WHEN WE'LL DROWN . . . IT'S A MORE METHODICAL WAY OF DYING.

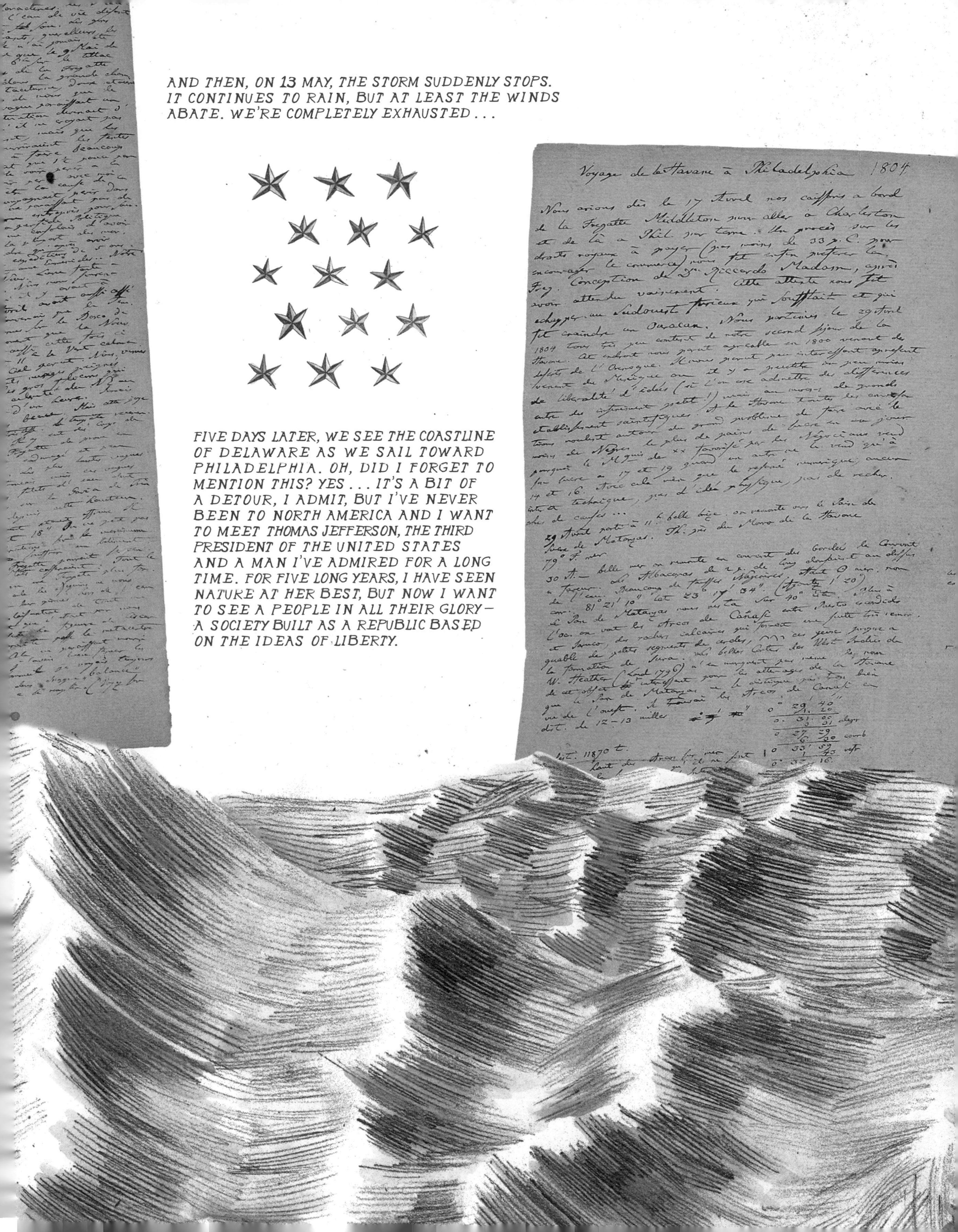

AND THEN, ON 13 MAY, THE STORM SUDDENLY STOPS. IT CONTINUES TO RAIN, BUT AT LEAST THE WINDS ABATE. WE'RE COMPLETELY EXHAUSTED . . .
Voyage de la Havane à Philadelphia 1804
FIVE DAYS LATER, WE SEE THE COASTLINE OF DELAWARE AS WE SAIL TOWARD PHILADELPHIA. OH, DID I FORGET TO MENTION THIS? YES . . . IT'S A BIT OF A DETOUR, I ADMIT, BUT I'VE NEVER BEEN TO NORTH AMERICA AND I WANT TO MEET THOMAS JEFFERSON, THE THIRD PRESIDENT OF THE UNITED STATES AND A MAN I'VE ADMIRED FOR A LONG TIME. FOR FIVE LONG YEARS, I HAVE SEEN NATURE AT HER BEST, BUT NOW I WANT TO SEE A PEOPLE IN ALL THEIR GLORY— A SOCIETY BUILT AS A REPUBLIC BASED ON THE IDEAS OF LIBERTY.

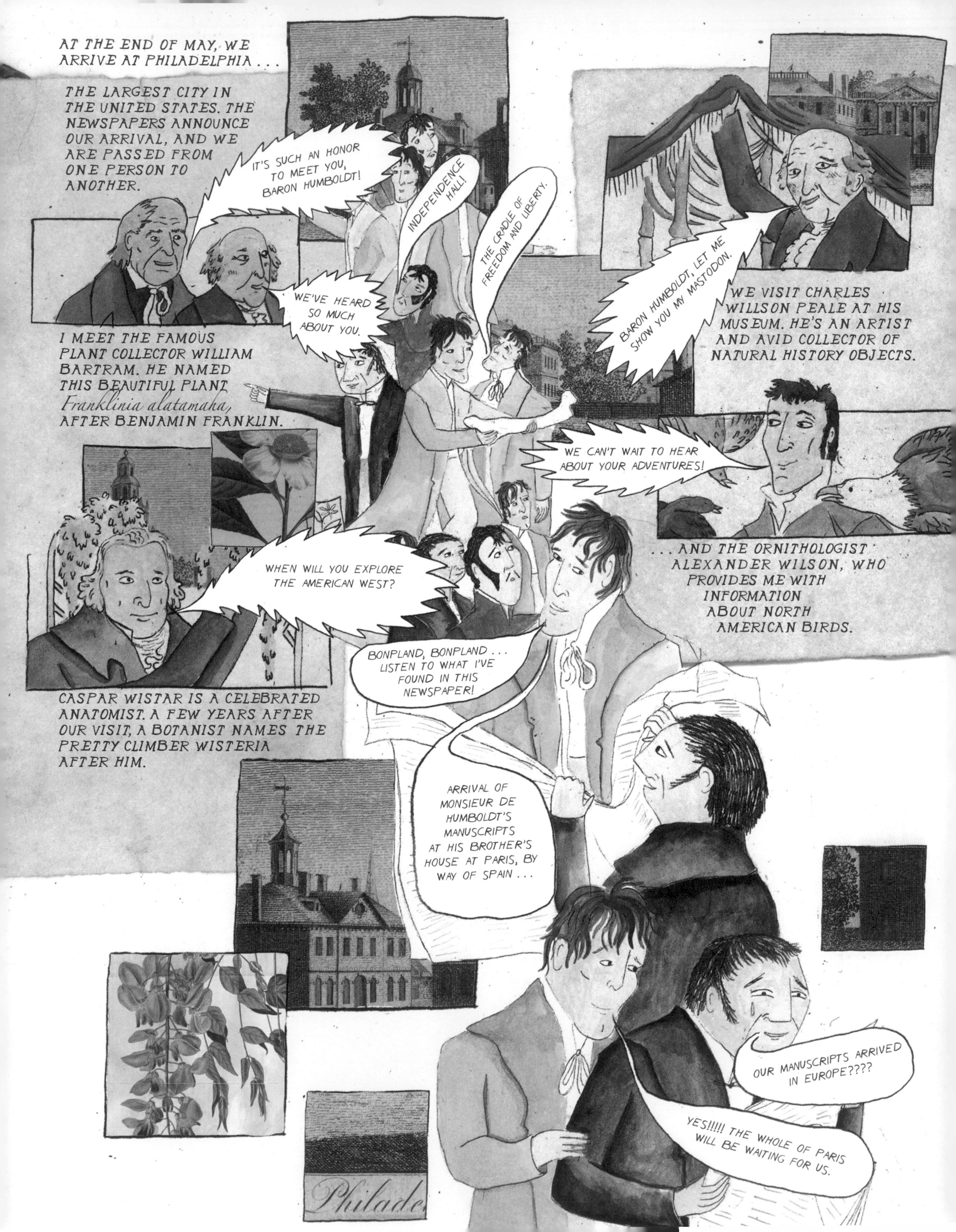
AT THE END OF MAY, WE ARRIVE AT PHILADELPHIA . . .
THE LARGEST CITY IN THE UNITED STATES. THE NEWSPAPERS ANNOUNCE OUR ARRIVAL, AND WE ARE PASSED FROM ONE PERSON TO ANOTHER.
IT'S SUCH AN HONOR TO MEET YOU, BARON HUMBOLDT!
INDEPENDENCE HALL!
THE CRADLE OF FREEDOM AND LIBERTY.
WE'VE HEARD SO MUCH ABOUT YOU.
I MEET THE FAMOUS PLANT COLLECTOR WILLIAM BARTRAM. HE NAMED THIS BEAUTIFUL PLANT *Franklinia alatamaha*, AFTER BENJAMIN FRANKLIN.
BARON HUMBOLDT, LET ME SHOW YOU MY MASTODON.
WE VISIT CHARLES WILLSON PEALE AT HIS MUSEUM. HE'S AN ARTIST AND AVID COLLECTOR OF NATURAL HISTORY OBJECTS.
WE CAN'T WAIT TO HEAR ABOUT YOUR ADVENTURES!
. . . AND THE ORNITHOLOGIST ALEXANDER WILSON, WHO PROVIDES ME WITH INFORMATION ABOUT NORTH AMERICAN BIRDS.
WHEN WILL YOU EXPLORE THE AMERICAN WEST?
CASPAR WISTAR IS A CELEBRATED ANATOMIST. A FEW YEARS AFTER OUR VISIT, A BOTANIST NAMES THE PRETTY CLIMBER WISTERIA AFTER HIM.
BONPLAND, BONPLAND . . . LISTEN TO WHAT I'VE FOUND IN THIS NEWSPAPER!
ARRIVAL OF MONSIEUR DE HUMBOLDT'S MANUSCRIPTS AT HIS BROTHER'S HOUSE AT PARIS, BY WAY OF SPAIN . . .
OUR MANUSCRIPTS ARRIVED IN EUROPE????
YES!!!!! THE WHOLE OF PARIS WILL BE WAITING FOR US.
Philade

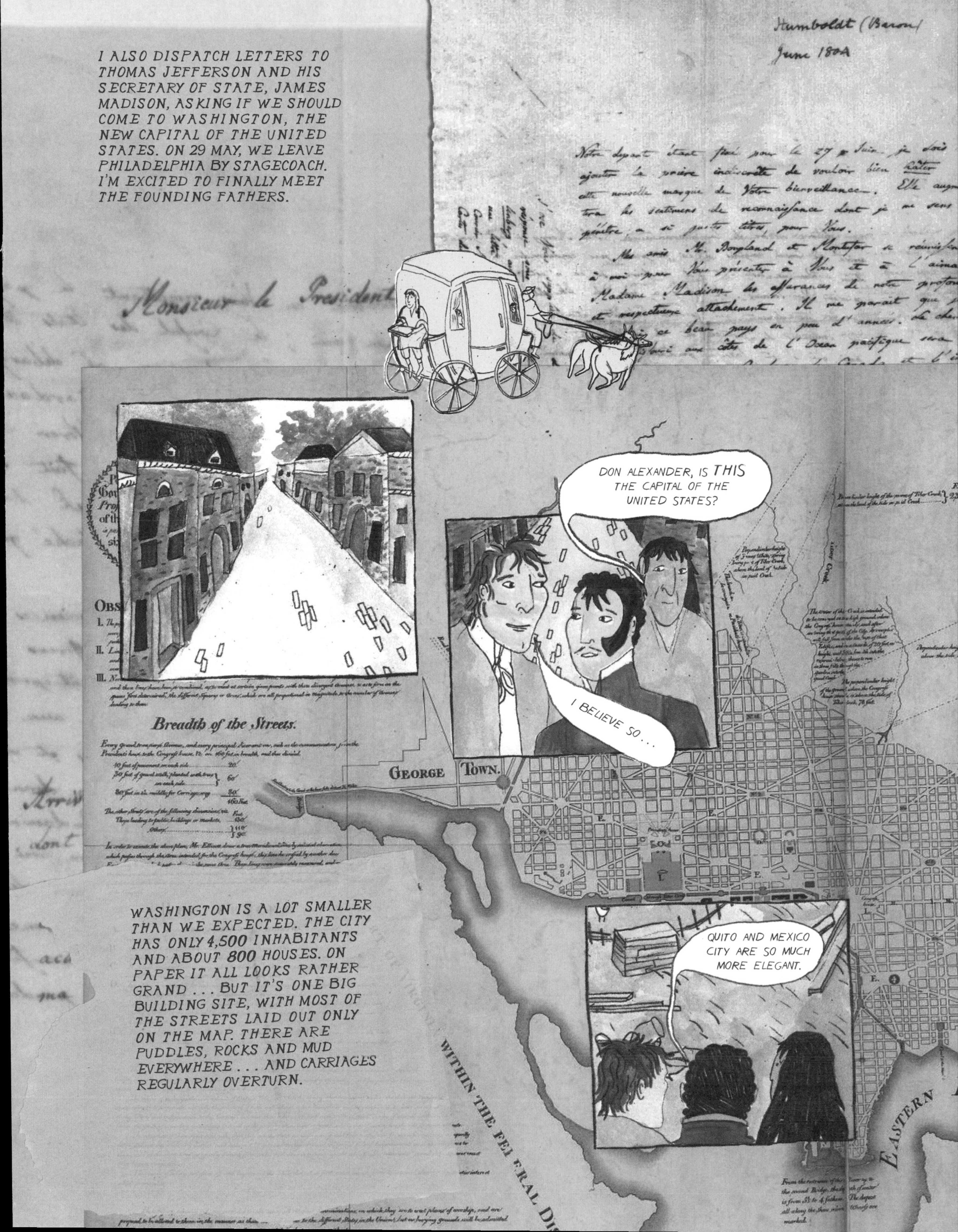
Humboldt (Baron)
June 1804
I ALSO DISPATCH LETTERS TO THOMAS JEFFERSON AND HIS SECRETARY OF STATE, JAMES MADISON, ASKING IF WE SHOULD COME TO WASHINGTON, THE NEW CAPITAL OF THE UNITED STATES. ON 29 MAY, WE LEAVE PHILADELPHIA BY STAGECOACH. I'M EXCITED TO FINALLY MEET THE FOUNDING FATHERS.
Monsieur le President
DON ALEXANDER, IS THIS THE CAPITAL OF THE UNITED STATES?
I BELIEVE SO . . .
Breadth of the Streets.
GEORGE TOWN.
WASHINGTON IS A LOT SMALLER THAN WE EXPECTED. THE CITY HAS ONLY 4,500 INHABITANTS AND ABOUT 800 HOUSES. ON PAPER IT ALL LOOKS RATHER GRAND . . . BUT IT'S ONE BIG BUILDING SITE, WITH MOST OF THE STREETS LAID OUT ONLY ON THE MAP. THERE ARE PUDDLES, ROCKS AND MUD EVERYWHERE . . . AND CARRIAGES REGULARLY OVERTURN.
QUITO AND MEXICO CITY ARE SO MUCH MORE ELEGANT.
WITHIN THE FEDERAL
EASTERN

EVEN THE PRESIDENT'S HOUSE IS NOT COMPLETED. IT'S ONLY HALF FURNISHED, AND INSTEAD OF GARDENS, THERE ARE WORKMEN'S SHEDS AND BRICK KILNS ON THE GROUNDS. BUT I COULDN'T CARE LESS . . . I'M THRILLED TO FINALLY MEET THOMAS JEFFERSON (THOUGH I'M A LITTLE IRRITATED TO SEE SLAVES WORKING EVERYWHERE).

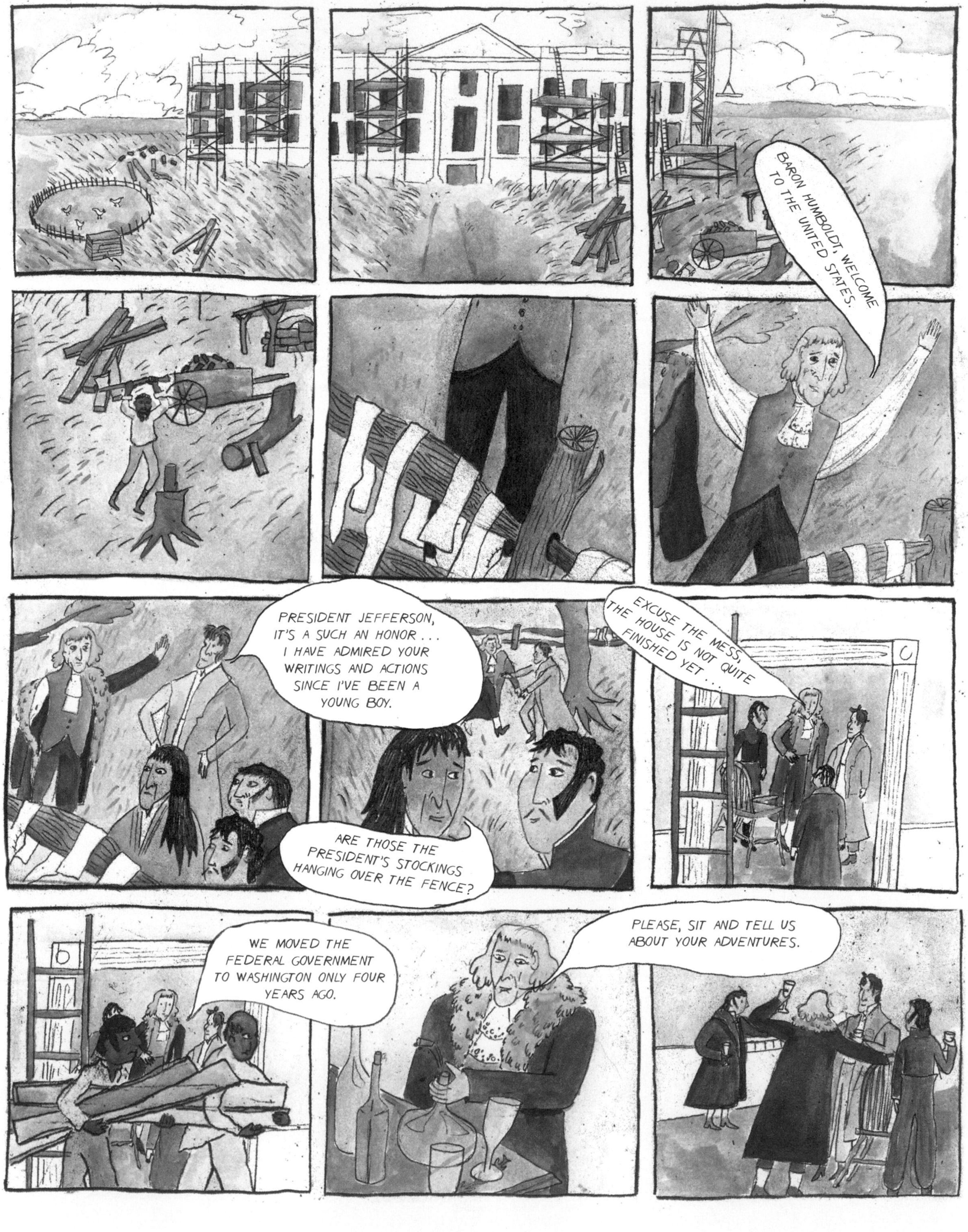
BARON HUMBOLDT, WELCOME TO THE UNITED STATES.
PRESIDENT JEFFERSON, IT'S A SUCH AN HONOR . . . I HAVE ADMIRED YOUR WRITINGS AND ACTIONS SINCE I'VE BEEN A YOUNG BOY.
ARE THOSE THE PRESIDENT'S STOCKINGS HANGING OVER THE FENCE?
EXCUSE THE MESS, THE HOUSE IS NOT QUITE FINISHED YET . . .
WE MOVED THE FEDERAL GOVERNMENT TO WASHINGTON ONLY FOUR YEARS AGO.
PLEASE, SIT AND TELL US ABOUT YOUR ADVENTURES.

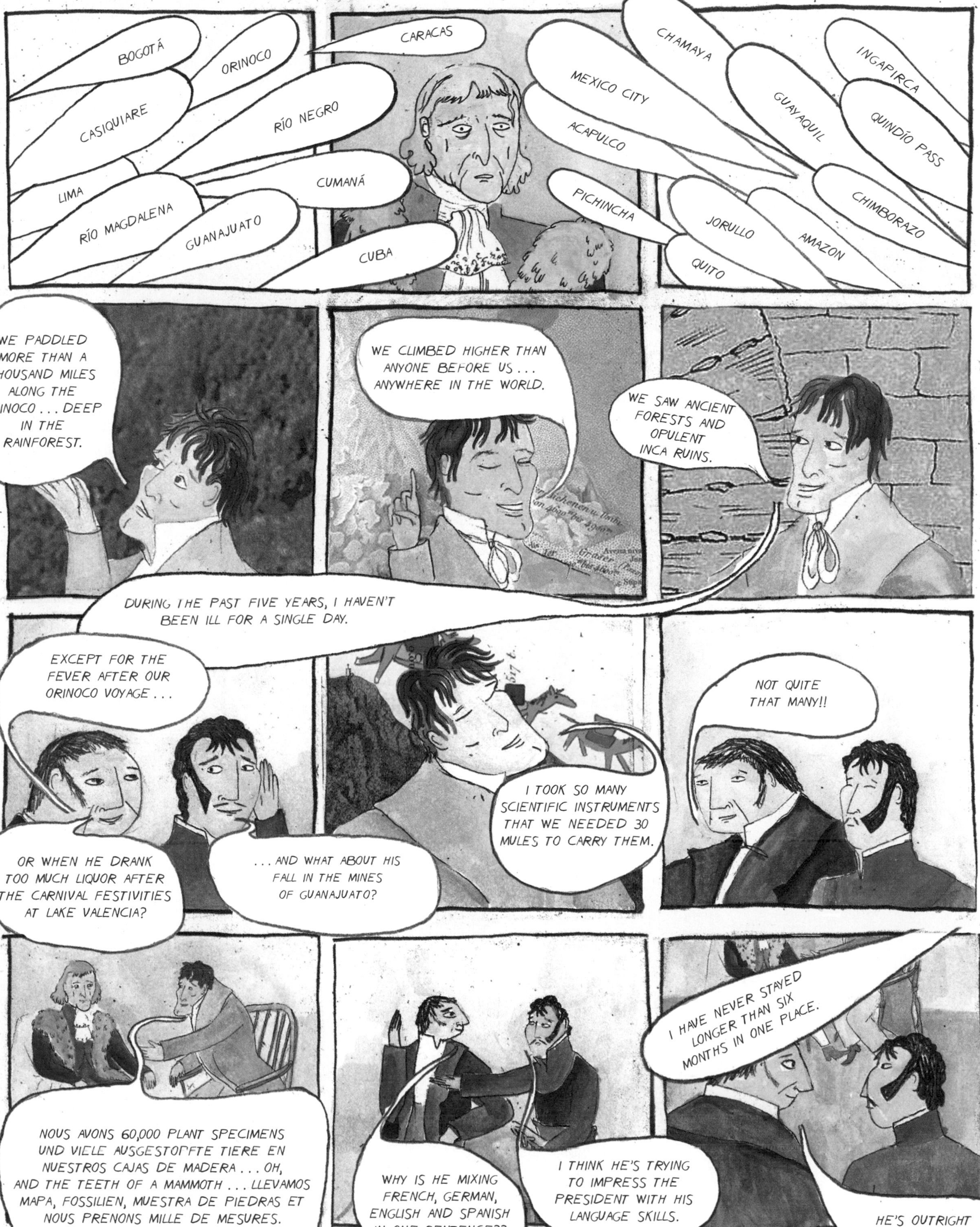
BOGOTÁ
ORINOCO
CASIQUIARE
RÍO NEGRO
LIMA
CUMANÁ
RÍO MAGDALENA
GUANAJUATO
CARACAS
CUBA
CHAMAYA
MEXICO CITY
ACAPULCO
PICHINCHA
GUAYAQUIL
JORULLO
QUITO
AMAZON
INGAPIRCA
QUINDÍO PASS
CHIMBORAZO
WE PADDLED MORE THAN A THOUSAND MILES ALONG THE ORINOCO . . . DEEP IN THE RAINFOREST.
WE CLIMBED HIGHER THAN ANYONE BEFORE US . . . ANYWHERE IN THE WORLD.
WE SAW ANCIENT FORESTS AND OPULENT INCA RUINS.
DURING THE PAST FIVE YEARS, I HAVEN'T BEEN ILL FOR A SINGLE DAY.
EXCEPT FOR THE FEVER AFTER OUR ORINOCO VOYAGE . . .
OR WHEN HE DRANK TOO MUCH LIQUOR AFTER THE CARNIVAL FESTIVITIES AT LAKE VALENCIA?
. . . AND WHAT ABOUT HIS FALL IN THE MINES OF GUANAJUATO?
I TOOK SO MANY SCIENTIFIC INSTRUMENTS THAT WE NEEDED 30 MULES TO CARRY THEM.
NOT QUITE THAT MANY!!
NOUS AVONS 60,000 PLANT SPECIMENS UND VIELE AUSGESTOPFTE TIERE EN NUESTROS CAJAS DE MADERA . . . OH, AND THE TEETH OF A MAMMOTH . . . LLEVAMOS MAPA, FOSSILIEN, MUESTRA DE PIEDRAS ET NOUS PRENONS MILLE DE MESURES.
WHY IS HE MIXING FRENCH, GERMAN, ENGLISH AND SPANISH IN ONE SENTENCE??
I THINK HE'S TRYING TO IMPRESS THE PRESIDENT WITH HIS LANGUAGE SKILLS.
I HAVE NEVER STAYED LONGER THAN SIX MONTHS IN ONE PLACE.
HE'S OUTRIGHT LYING NOW.

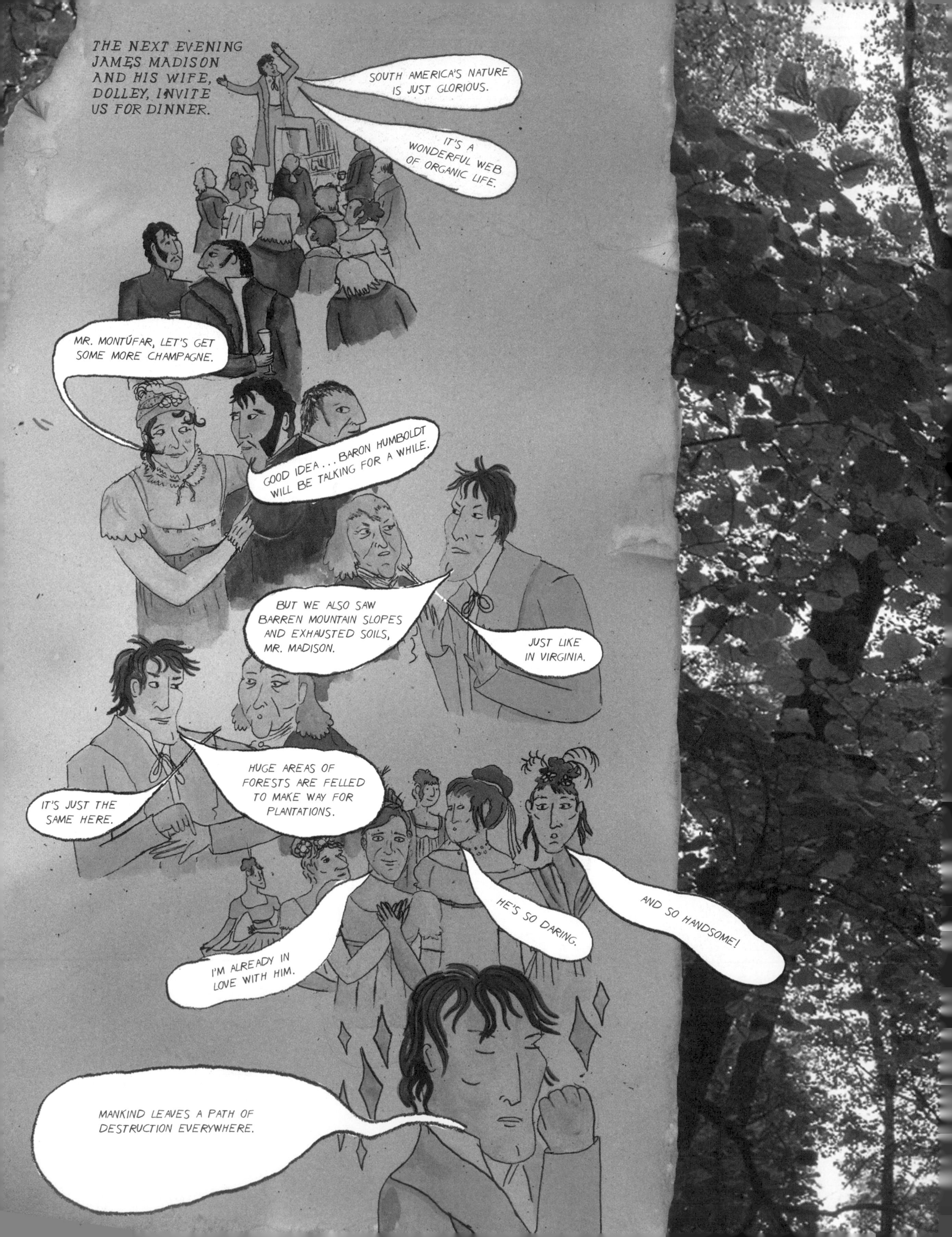
THE NEXT EVENING JAMES MADISON AND HIS WIFE, DOLLEY, INVITE US FOR DINNER.
SOUTH AMERICA'S NATURE IS JUST GLORIOUS.
IT'S A WONDERFUL WEB OF ORGANIC LIFE.
MR. MONTÚFAR, LET'S GET SOME MORE CHAMPAGNE.
GOOD IDEA . . . BARON HUMBOLDT WILL BE TALKING FOR A WHILE.
BUT WE ALSO SAW BARREN MOUNTAIN SLOPES AND EXHAUSTED SOILS, MR. MADISON.
JUST LIKE IN VIRGINIA.
HUGE AREAS OF FORESTS ARE FELLED TO MAKE WAY FOR PLANTATIONS.
IT'S JUST THE SAME HERE.
I'M ALREADY IN LOVE WITH HIM.
HE'S SO DARING.
AND SO HANDSOME!
MANKIND LEAVES A PATH OF DESTRUCTION EVERYWHERE.

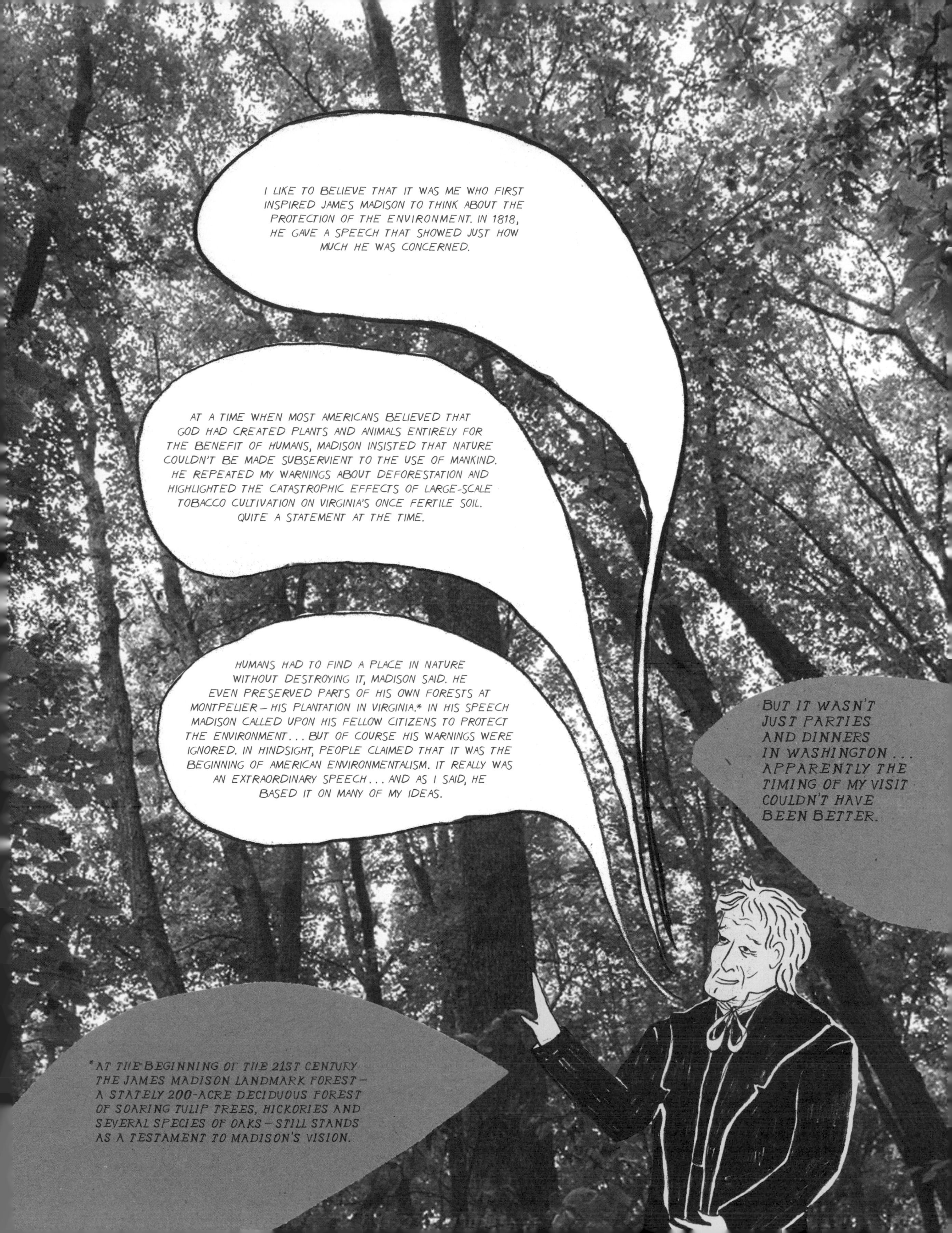
I LIKE TO BELIEVE THAT IT WAS ME WHO FIRST INSPIRED JAMES MADISON TO THINK ABOUT THE PROTECTION OF THE ENVIRONMENT. IN 1818, HE GAVE A SPEECH THAT SHOWED JUST HOW MUCH HE WAS CONCERNED.
AT A TIME WHEN MOST AMERICANS BELIEVED THAT GOD HAD CREATED PLANTS AND ANIMALS ENTIRELY FOR THE BENEFIT OF HUMANS, MADISON INSISTED THAT NATURE COULDN'T BE MADE SUBSERVIENT TO THE USE OF MANKIND. HE REPEATED MY WARNINGS ABOUT DEFORESTATION AND HIGHLIGHTED THE CATASTROPHIC EFFECTS OF LARGE-SCALE TOBACCO CULTIVATION ON VIRGINIA'S ONCE FERTILE SOIL. QUITE A STATEMENT AT THE TIME.
HUMANS HAD TO FIND A PLACE IN NATURE WITHOUT DESTROYING IT, MADISON SAID. HE EVEN PRESERVED PARTS OF HIS OWN FORESTS AT MONTPELIER – HIS PLANTATION IN VIRGINIA.* IN HIS SPEECH MADISON CALLED UPON HIS FELLOW CITIZENS TO PROTECT THE ENVIRONMENT . . . BUT OF COURSE HIS WARNINGS WERE IGNORED. IN HINDSIGHT, PEOPLE CLAIMED THAT IT WAS THE BEGINNING OF AMERICAN ENVIRONMENTALISM. IT REALLY WAS AN EXTRAORDINARY SPEECH . . . AND AS I SAID, HE BASED IT ON MANY OF MY IDEAS.
BUT IT WASN'T JUST PARTIES AND DINNERS IN WASHINGTON . . . APPARENTLY THE TIMING OF MY VISIT COULDN'T HAVE BEEN BETTER.
*AT THE BEGINNING OF THE 21ST CENTURY THE JAMES MADISON LANDMARK FOREST – A STATELY 200-ACRE DECIDUOUS FOREST OF SOARING TULIP TREES, HICKORIES AND SEVERAL SPECIES OF OAKS – STILL STANDS AS A TESTAMENT TO MADISON'S VISION.

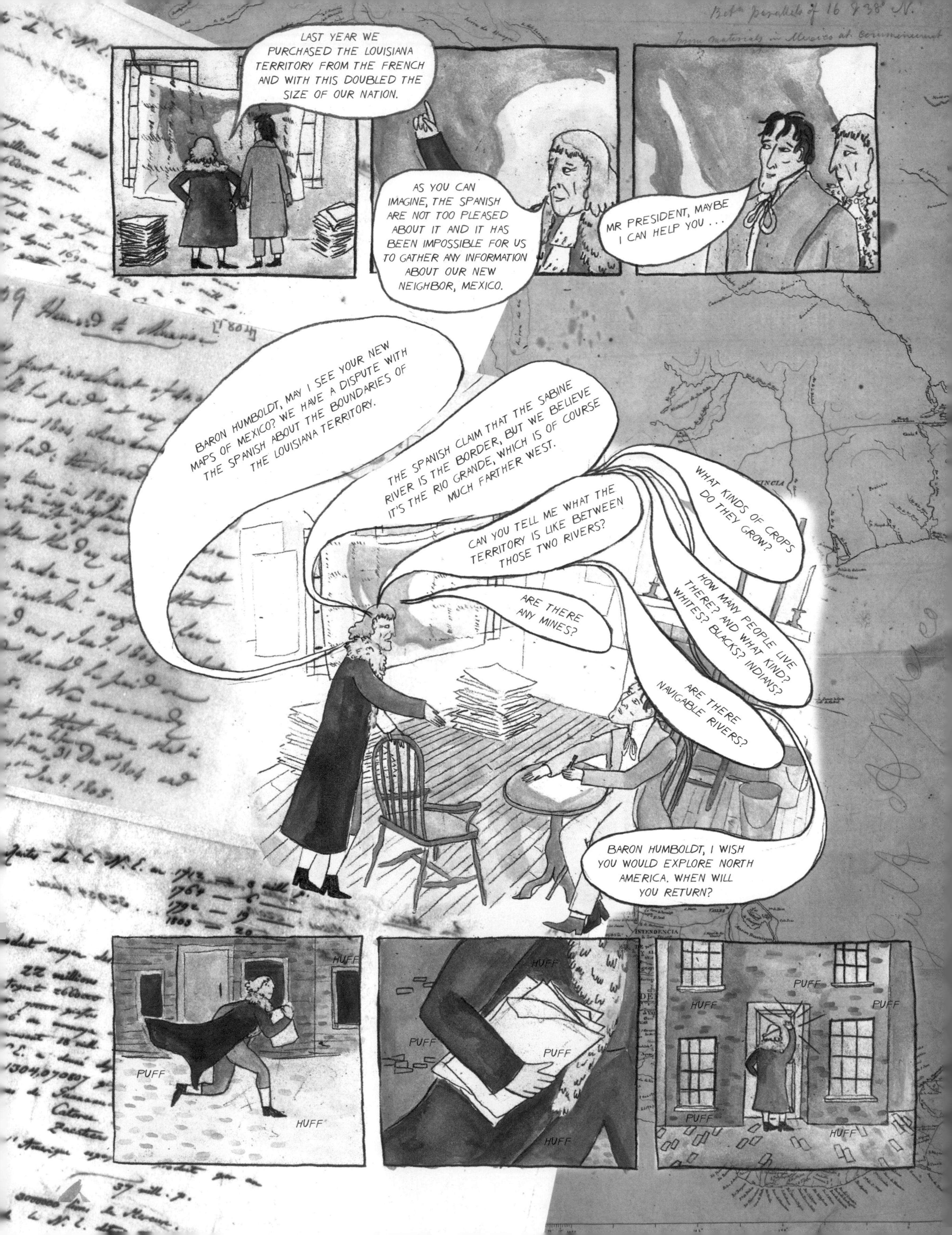
LAST YEAR WE PURCHASED THE LOUISIANA TERRITORY FROM THE FRENCH AND WITH THIS DOUBLED THE SIZE OF OUR NATION.
AS YOU CAN IMAGINE, THE SPANISH ARE NOT TOO PLEASED ABOUT IT AND IT HAS BEEN IMPOSSIBLE FOR US TO GATHER ANY INFORMATION ABOUT OUR NEW NEIGHBOR, MEXICO.
MR PRESIDENT, MAYBE I CAN HELP YOU . . .
BARON HUMBOLDT, MAY I SEE YOUR NEW MAPS OF MEXICO? WE HAVE A DISPUTE WITH THE SPANISH ABOUT THE BOUNDARIES OF THE LOUISIANA TERRITORY.
THE SPANISH CLAIM THAT THE SABINE RIVER IS THE BORDER, BUT WE BELIEVE IT'S THE RIO GRANDE, WHICH IS OF COURSE MUCH FARTHER WEST.
CAN YOU TELL ME WHAT THE TERRITORY IS LIKE BETWEEN THOSE TWO RIVERS?
WHAT KINDS OF CROPS DO THEY GROW?
ARE THERE ANY MINES?
HOW MANY PEOPLE LIVE THERE? AND WHAT KIND? WHITES? BLACKS? INDIANS?
ARE THERE NAVIGABLE RIVERS?
BARON HUMBOLDT, I WISH YOU WOULD EXPLORE NORTH AMERICA. WHEN WILL YOU RETURN?
HUFF
PUFF
HUFF
HUFF
PUFF
PUFF
HUFF
PUFF
HUFF
PUFF
PUFF
HUFF

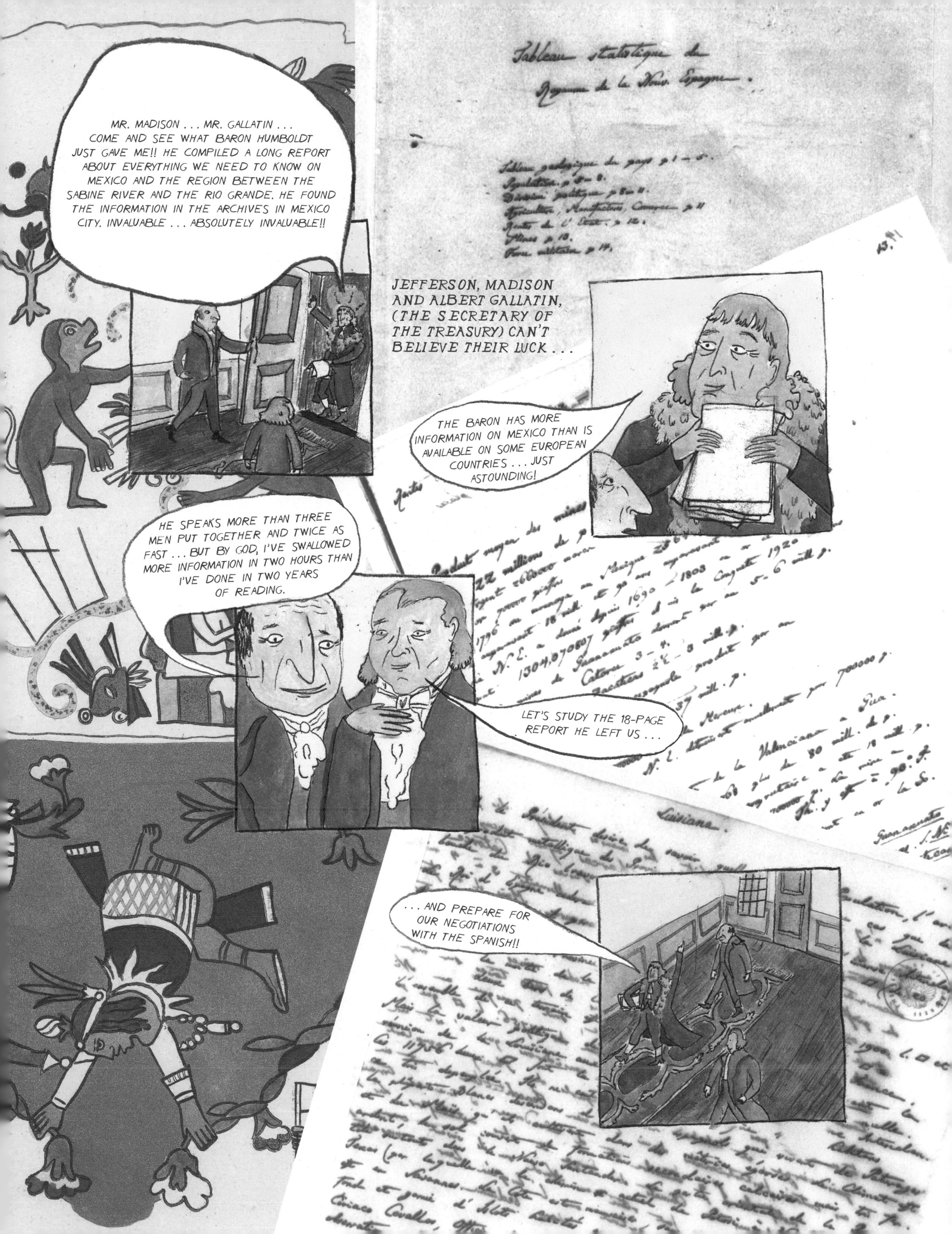
Tableau statistique du Royaume de la Nouv. Espagne.
MR. MADISON . . . MR. GALLATIN . . . COME AND SEE WHAT BARON HUMBOLDT JUST GAVE ME!! HE COMPILED A LONG REPORT ABOUT EVERYTHING WE NEED TO KNOW ON MEXICO AND THE REGION BETWEEN THE SABINE RIVER AND THE RIO GRANDE. HE FOUND THE INFORMATION IN THE ARCHIVES IN MEXICO CITY. INVALUABLE . . . ABSOLUTELY INVALUABLE!!
JEFFERSON, MADISON AND ALBERT GALLATIN, (THE SECRETARY OF THE TREASURY) CAN'T BELIEVE THEIR LUCK . . .
THE BARON HAS MORE INFORMATION ON MEXICO THAN IS AVAILABLE ON SOME EUROPEAN COUNTRIES . . . JUST ASTOUNDING!
HE SPEAKS MORE THAN THREE MEN PUT TOGETHER AND TWICE AS FAST . . . BUT BY GOD, I'VE SWALLOWED MORE INFORMATION IN TWO HOURS THAN I'VE DONE IN TWO YEARS OF READING.
LET'S STUDY THE 18-PAGE REPORT HE LEFT US . . .
. . . AND PREPARE FOR OUR NEGOTIATIONS WITH THE SPANISH!!

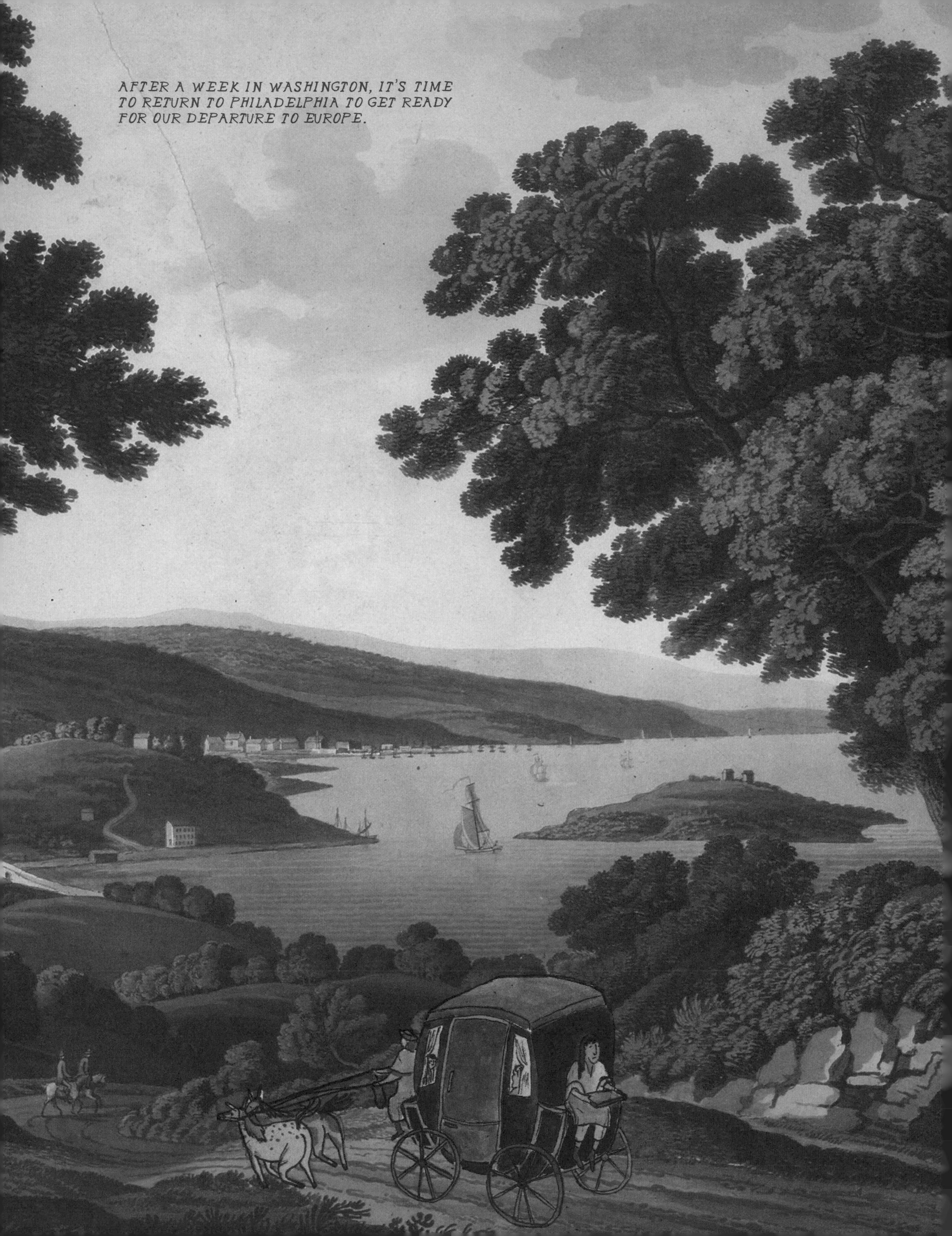
AFTER A WEEK IN WASHINGTON, IT'S TIME TO RETURN TO PHILADELPHIA TO GET READY FOR OUR DEPARTURE TO EUROPE.

WE LEAVE THE UNITED STATES ON A FRENCH FRIGATE
AT THE BEGINNING OF JULY *1804* . . . ALMOST EXACTLY
FIVE YEARS AFTER WE LEFT EUROPE.

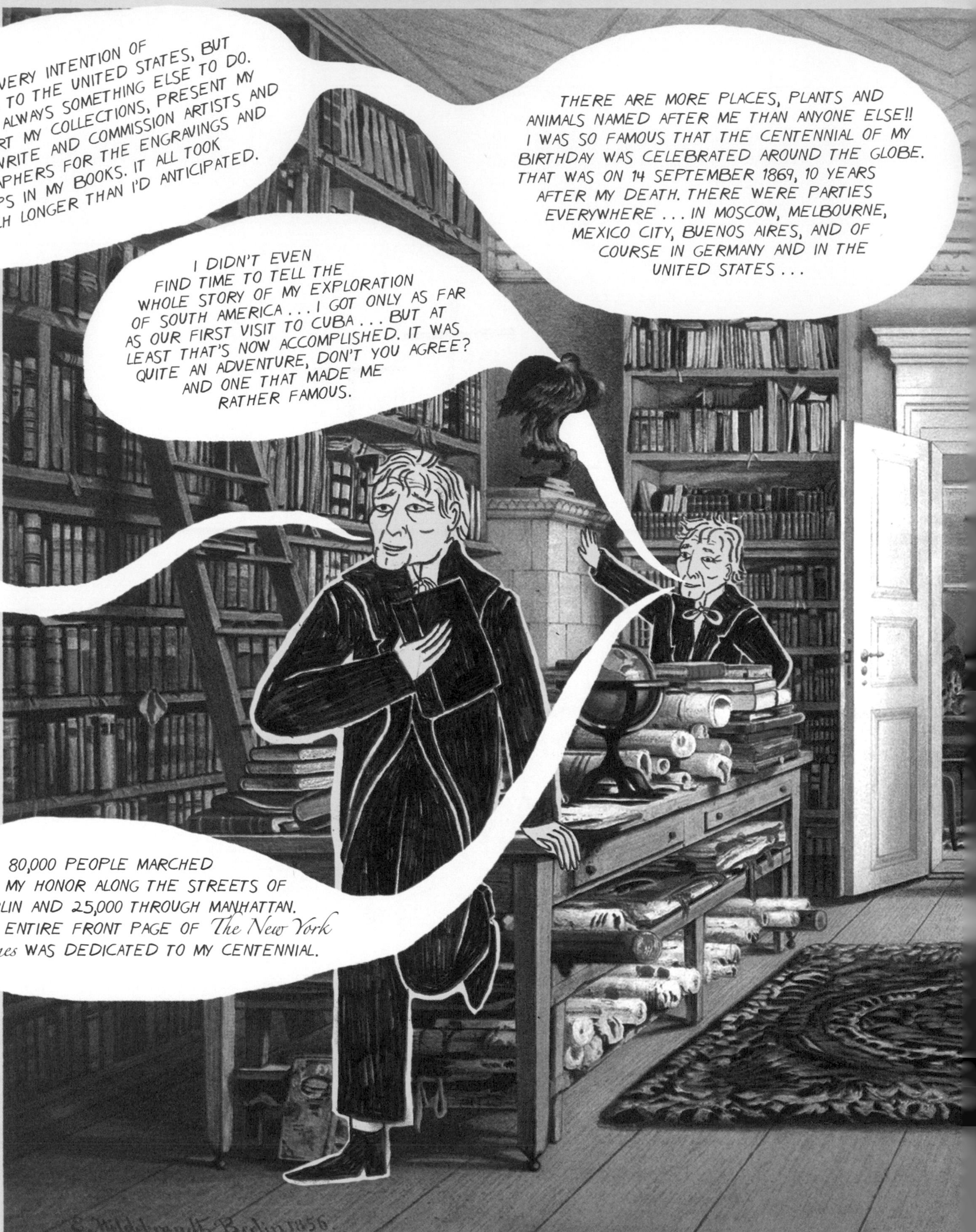
I HAD EVERY INTENTION OF RETURNING TO THE UNITED STATES, BUT THERE WAS ALWAYS SOMETHING ELSE TO DO. I HAD TO SORT MY COLLECTIONS, PRESENT MY FINDINGS, WRITE AND COMMISSION ARTISTS AND CARTOGRAPHERS FOR THE ENGRAVINGS AND MAPS IN MY BOOKS. IT ALL TOOK MUCH LONGER THAN I'D ANTICIPATED.
THERE ARE MORE PLACES, PLANTS AND ANIMALS NAMED AFTER ME THAN ANYONE ELSE!! I WAS SO FAMOUS THAT THE CENTENNIAL OF MY BIRTHDAY WAS CELEBRATED AROUND THE GLOBE. THAT WAS ON 14 SEPTEMBER 1869, 10 YEARS AFTER MY DEATH. THERE WERE PARTIES EVERYWHERE . . . IN MOSCOW, MELBOURNE, MEXICO CITY, BUENOS AIRES, AND OF COURSE IN GERMANY AND IN THE UNITED STATES . . .
I DIDN'T EVEN FIND TIME TO TELL THE WHOLE STORY OF MY EXPLORATION OF SOUTH AMERICA . . . I GOT ONLY AS FAR AS OUR FIRST VISIT TO CUBA . . . BUT AT LEAST THAT'S NOW ACCOMPLISHED. IT WAS QUITE AN ADVENTURE, DON'T YOU AGREE? AND ONE THAT MADE ME RATHER FAMOUS.
80,000 PEOPLE MARCHED IN MY HONOR ALONG THE STREETS OF BERLIN AND 25,000 THROUGH MANHATTAN. THE ENTIRE FRONT PAGE OF *The New York Times* WAS DEDICATED TO MY CENTENNIAL.
E. Hildebrandt Berlin 1856.

Berlin
1858

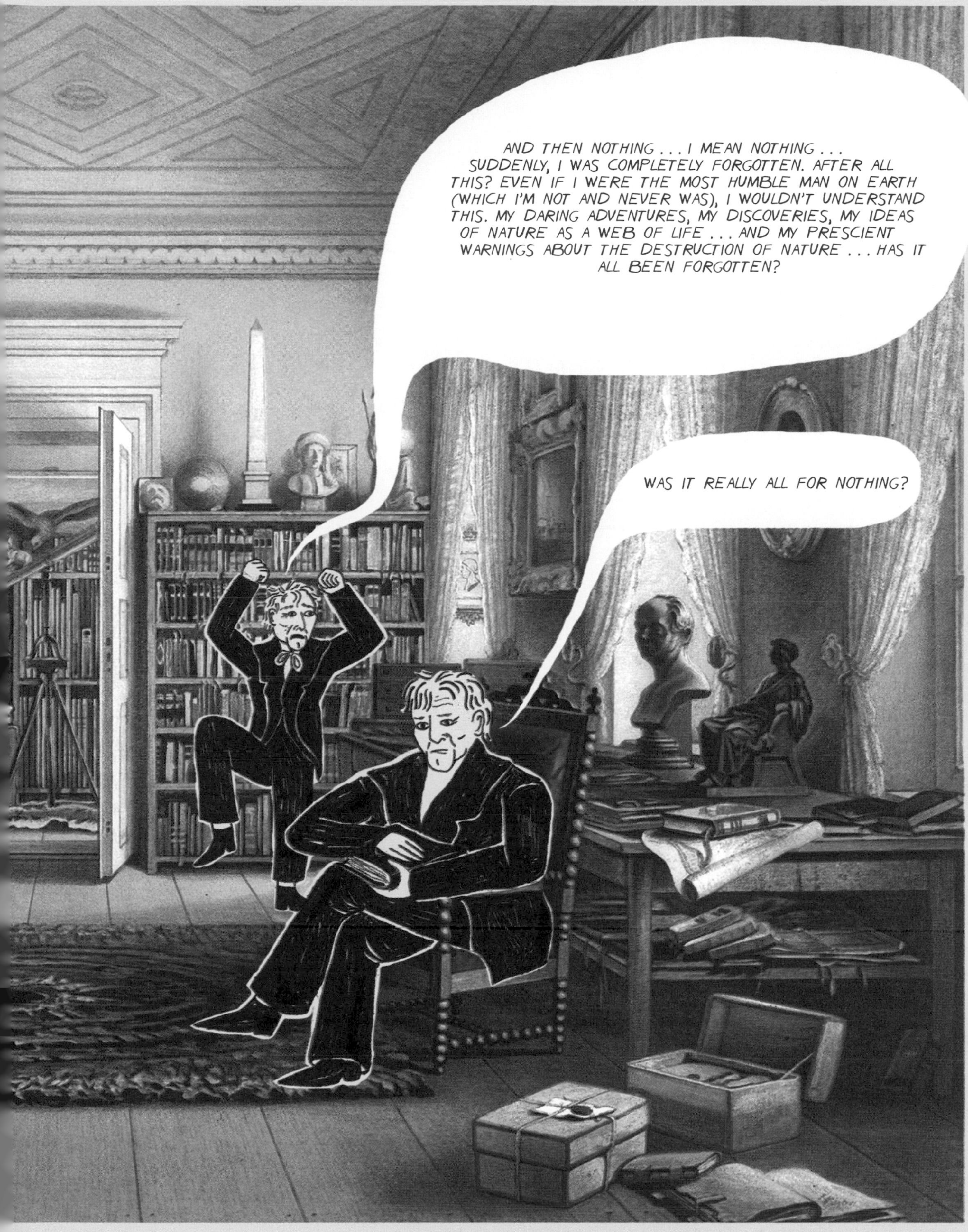
AND THEN NOTHING . . . I MEAN NOTHING . . . SUDDENLY, I WAS COMPLETELY FORGOTTEN. AFTER ALL THIS? EVEN IF I WERE THE MOST HUMBLE MAN ON EARTH (WHICH I'M NOT AND NEVER WAS), I WOULDN'T UNDERSTAND THIS. MY DARING ADVENTURES, MY DISCOVERIES, MY IDEAS OF NATURE AS A WEB OF LIFE . . . AND MY PRESCIENT WARNINGS ABOUT THE DESTRUCTION OF NATURE . . . HAS IT ALL BEEN FORGOTTEN?
WAS IT REALLY ALL FOR NOTHING?

AUTHORS' NOTE

The Adventures of Alexander von Humboldt IS A WORK OF GRAPHIC NONFICTION (FOR LACK OF A BETTER TERM). EVERYTHING THAT HAPPENS IN THIS STORY IS BASED ON ARCHIVAL RESEARCH, PRIMARY AND SECONDARY SOURCES. ONLY THE DIALOGUES ARE IMAGINED BUT BASED AS CLOSELY AS POSSIBLE ON HUMBOLDT'S OWN DESCRIPTIONS. THE SERVANTS IN QUITO, FOR EXAMPLE, GOSSIPED THAT HUMBOLDT IGNITED PICHINCHA BY THROWING GUNPOWDER INTO THE VOLCANO — THE SCENE AND DIALOGUE OUTSIDE THE WINDOW IS "INVENTED," BUT HUMBOLDT WROTE ABOUT THIS RUMOR IN HIS DIARY. THE ONLY REAL ARTISTIC LICENSE THAT I HAVE TAKEN IS TO CONFLATE THREE SERVANTS INTO ONE, THE WONDERFUL JOSÉ. SIMILARLY, LILLIAN WAS ABLE TO CONFLATE DEPICTIONS FROM ILLUSTRATIONS OF SERVANTS WORKING FOR HUMBOLDT FROM HIS BOOKS AND DESCRIPTIONS INTO THE VISUAL DEPICTION OF JOSÉ. THE KNOWLEDGE WE HAVE ABOUT HUMBOLDT'S SERVANTS IS SKETCHY — SOME ACCOMPANIED HUMBOLDT ONLY FOR CERTAIN PARTS OF THE JOURNEY AND WE DON'T KNOW ANYTHING ABOUT THEM, BUT MOST HUMBOLDT SCHOLARS AGREE THAT JOSÉ DE LA CRUZ WAS WITH HUMBOLDT AND BONPLAND FOR THE ENTIRE TIME OF THE EXPLORATION, AS WELL AS TRAVELING WITH THEM TO THE UNITED STATES AND POSSIBLY EUROPE. HUMBOLDT, WHO WAS SO METICULOUS ABOUT EVERYTHING, WAS NOT SO ABOUT HIS SERVANTS. HE REFERRED TO HIS SERVANTS VARIOUSLY AS "INDIO" (SUGGESTING AMERINDIAN), "MESTIZO" (SUGGESTING PART AFRICAN, PART AMERINDIAN HERITAGE) AND "MULATTO" (SUGGESTING PART AFRICAN, PART EUROPEAN HERITAGE). THE THREE SERVANTS WHO WE KNOW BY NAME ARE CARLOS DEL PINO, FELIPE ALDAS AND JOSÉ DE LA CRUZ.

The Adventures of Alexander von Humboldt IS BASED ON HUMBOLDT'S OWN PUBLICATIONS AS WELL AS HIS DIARIES, NOTES AND LETTERS. FOR THOSE

WHO WOULD LIKE TO KNOW MORE ABOUT HUMBOLDT (ESPECIALLY HIS YEARS BEFORE AND AFTER HIS FIVE YEARS IN LATIN AMERICA), PLEASE REFER TO MY BOOK *The Invention of Nature. Alexander von Humboldt's New World*, WHICH ALSO INCLUDES DETAILED ENDNOTES AND A LONG BIBLIOGRAPHY NOT INCLUDED HERE BECAUSE IT WOULD HAVE ENCUMBERED THIS BOOK UNNECESSARILY.

HUMBOLDT'S AMERICAN DIARIES AND NOTES ARE DEPOSITED AT THE STAATSBIBLIOTHEK BERLIN AND ARE AVAILABLE ONLINE. IT'S AN EXTRAORDINARILY RICH SOURCE. OVER THE PAST DECADES THE ALEXANDER-VON-HUMBOLDT FORSCHUNGSSTELLE AT THE BERLIN-BRANDENBURGISCHE AKADEMIE DER WISSENSCHAFTEN HAS PUBLISHED MANY VOLUMES OF HUMBOLDT'S CORRESPONDENCE AND DIARIES, WHICH HAVE BEEN EQUALLY INDISPENSABLE – IN PARTICULAR THE DIARY VOLUMES BY MARGOT FAAK. ALSO, THEIR ONLINE "HUMBOLDT CHRONOLOGY" IS A WORK OF GREAT SCHOLARSHIP, AND THEIR CURRENT RESEARCH PROJECT "ALEXANDER VON HUMBOLDT AUF REISEN – WISSENSCHAFT AUS DER BEWEGUNG" (2015-2032) WILL MAKE ALL DOCUMENTS THAT RELATE TO HUMBOLDT'S JOURNEYS (NOT JUST THE SOUTH AMERICAN EXPLORATION BUT ALSO THE RUSSIAN ONE) AVAILABLE ONLINE.

THERE ARE TOO MANY OF HUMBOLDT'S OWN PUBLICATIONS TO LIST THEM HERE, BUT HIS *Personal Narrative* (1814-1829), *Views of Nature* (1849), *Political Essay on the Kingdom of New Spain* (1811), *Cosmos* (1845-1852) AND THE OPULENT TWO VOLUMES OF *Vues des Cordillères et monumens des peuples indigènes de l'Amérique* (1810-13) WERE THE MOST IMPORTANT FOR THIS BOOK.

ALL THE HANDWRITTEN MANUSCRIPTS THAT ARE USED AS COLLAGES ARE HUMBOLDT'S OWN MANUSCRIPTS – PAGES FROM HIS DIARIES, LETTERS, NOTES AND SKETCHES. WE'VE ALSO USED MANY OF HUMBOLDT'S AND BONPLAND'S HERBARIUM SPECIMENS THAT ARE TODAY AT THE BOTANICAL GARDEN IN BERLIN. MIXED WITH THOSE ARE PLANTS FROM THE NEW YORK BOTANICAL GARDEN THAT WE RECEIVED FROM THEIR AMAZING LIVING SOUTH AMERICA COLLECTION AND THAT LILLIAN PRESSED AND DRIED (AND SOMETIMES PURPOSELY MADE MOLDY). WE'VE ALSO USED MANY OF THE MAPS, ENGRAVINGS AND ILLUSTRATIONS FROM HUMBOLDT'S OWN BOOKS – FROM HIEROGLYPHS AND INCA MONUMENTS IN *Vues des Cordillères* TO HIS SPECTACULAR MAPS IN *Atlas Geographique et Physique du Royaume de la Nouvelle-Espagne* (1811). FRIENDS AND STRANGERS KINDLY GAVE US PERMISSION TO USE THEIR PHOTOGRAPHS OF TREETOPS, RIVERS AND FORESTS. OTHER COLLAGES ARE MADE FROM PAINTINGS AND WATERCOLORS SUCH AS THOSE BY JOHANN MORITZ RUGENDAS (WHO WAS ENCOURAGED BY HUMBOLDT TO TRAVEL TO SOUTH AMERICA) OR FREDERIC EDWIN CHURCH (WHO WAS SO INSPIRED BY HUMBOLDT'S BOOK *Cosmos* THAT HE FOLLOWED HIS HERO'S FOOTSTEPS THROUGH SOUTH AMERICA). IN ADDITION, WE HAVE USED A WHOLE RANGE OF OTHER ENGRAVINGS AND ILLUSTRATIONS – MANY OF WHICH ARE PART OF THE FANTASTIC WELLCOME IMAGE LIBRARY OR AVAILABLE ON ONE OF THE MOST EXCITING NEW ONLINE IMAGE LIBRARIES, THE ARCHIVE OF EARLY AMERICAN IMAGES AT THE JOHN CARTER BROWN LIBRARY.

ONLINE LINKS AND SOURCES

FOR A SELECTION OF HUMBOLDT'S BOOKS THAT ARE AVAILABLE ONLINE:
HTTP://WWW.AVHUMBOLDT.DE/?PAGE-ID=469

HUMBOLDT PROJECTS AT THE BERLIN-BRANDENBURGISCHE AKADEMIE DER WISSENSCHAFTEN
HTTP://WWW.BBAW.DE/FORSCHUNG/AVH-R/PROJEKTDARSTELLUNG

INTERNATIONAL REVIEW FOR HUMBOLDT STUDIES HIN
HTTP://WWW.HIN-ONLINE.DE/INDEX.PHP/HIN

HUMBOLDT CHRONOLOGY
HTTP://EDITION-HUMBOLDT.DE/CHRONOLOGIE/INDEX.XQL

HUMBOLDT'S DIARIES AND NOTES AT THE STAATSBIBLIOTHEK ZU BERLIN, PREUSSISCHER KULTURBESITZ
HTTP://HUMBOLDT.STAATSBIBLIOTHEK-BERLIN.DE/WERK/

HUMBOLDT'S AND BONPLAND'S PLANT SPECIMENS AT THE BOTANISCHER GARTEN UND BOTANISCHES MUSEUM BERLIN
HTTP://WW2.BGBM.ORG/HERBARIUM/RESULT.CFM?SEARCHART=2

ARCHIVE OF EARLY AMERICAN IMAGES AT THE JOHN CARTER BROWN LIBRARY
HTTPS://JCB.LUNAIMAGING.COM/LUNA/SERVLET/JCB~1~1

WELLCOME COLLECTION
HTTPS://WELLCOMECOLLECTION.ORG/WORKS

IMAGE BANK OF PREUSSISCHER KULTURBESITZ BERLIN
HTTP://WWW.BPK-IMAGES.DE

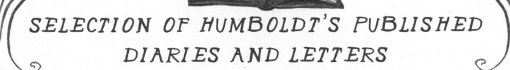

SELECTION OF HUMBOLDT'S PUBLISHED DIARIES AND LETTERS

Alexander von Humboldt. Reise durch Venezuela. Auswahl aus den Amerikanischen Reisetagebüchern, EDITED BY MARGOT FAAK, BERLIN: AKADEMIE-VERLAG, **2000**.

Alexander von Humboldt. Reise auf dem Río Magdalena, durch die Anden und Mexico, EDITED BY MARGOT FAAK, BERLIN: AKADEMIE-VERLAG, **2003**.

Alexander von Humboldt. Lateinamerika am Vorabend der Unabhängigkeitsrevolution: eine Anthologie von Impressionen und Urteilen aus seinen Reisetagebüchern, EDITED BY MARGOT FAAK, BERLIN: AKADEMIE-VERLAG, **1982**.

Briefe aus Amerika 1799–1804. Alexander von Humboldt, EDITED BY ULRIKE MOHEIT, BERLIN: AKADEMIE-VERLAG, **1993**.

Alexander von Humboldt und die Vereinigten Staaten von Amerika. Briefwechsel, EDITED BY INGO SCHWARZ, BERLIN: AKADEMIE-VERLAG, **2004**.

Alexander von Humboldt et Aimé Bonpland. Correspondance 1805–1858. EDITED BY NICOLAS HOSSARD, PARIS: L'HARMATTAN, **2004**.

PICTURE CREDITS

THE ARCHIVE OF EARLY AMERICAN IMAGES AT THE JOHN CARTER BROWN LIBRARY: 35, 56, 57, 84, 91, 121, 123, 126, 131, 138, 139, 192, 211, 212, 215, 240, 252.

BOTANISCHER GARTEN UND BOTANISCHES MUSEUM BERLIN: 13, 18, 32, 44, 48, 49, 53, 87, 88, 89, 96, 97, 173, 174, 177, 210, 219, 226, 236, 237.

DETROIT INSTITUTE OF ARTS: 204, 205, 206.

JOHN MUIR PAPERS, UNIVERSITY OF THE PACIFIC © 1984 MUIR-HANNA TRUST: 51.

LIBRARY OF CONGRESS: 253, 258, 259, 260.

METROPOLITAN MUSEUM OF ART, NEW YORK: 134, 135, 136, 138, 140, 143.

MINISTERIO DE CULTURA DEL ECUADOR, QUITO: 19.

NEW YORK PUBLIC LIBRARY: 252.

PRIVATE COLLECTION: 82, 126, 236.

PUBLIC DOMAIN: 28, 32, 190.

STIFTUNG PREUSSISCHER KULTURBESITZ, STAATSBIBLIOTHEK BERLIN AND BILDAGENTUR BPK: 6, 7, 9, 10, 19, 20, 21, 22, 24, 25, 30, 33, 34, 35, 36, 38, 45, 50, 55, 60, 61, 62, 78, 79, 82, 86, 87, 88, 89, 91, 94, 95, 96, 97, 98, 99, 102, 103, 108, 109, 110, 114, 115, 124, 126, 128, 129, 131, 138, 140, 141, 143, 151, 158, 162, 164, 165, 166, GATEFOLD, 170, 172, 174, 175, 176, 178, 180, 184, 185, 186, 188, 189, 191, 195, 196, 197, 198, 199, 202, 210, 217, 221, 222, 223, 224, 232, 233, 234, 235, 236, 237, 250, 251, 255, 262.

WELLCOME COLLECTION: 18, 19, 59, 61, 62, 74, 84, 86, 88, 89, 90, 95, 101, 126, 129, 139, 143, 144, 163, 169, 170, 174, 176, 180, 199, 204, 205, 206, 208, 209, 211, 212, 213, 214, 215, 216, 217, 218, 219, 220, 228, 229, 230, 231, 234, 236, 237, 238, 239, 240, 255, 259, 267.

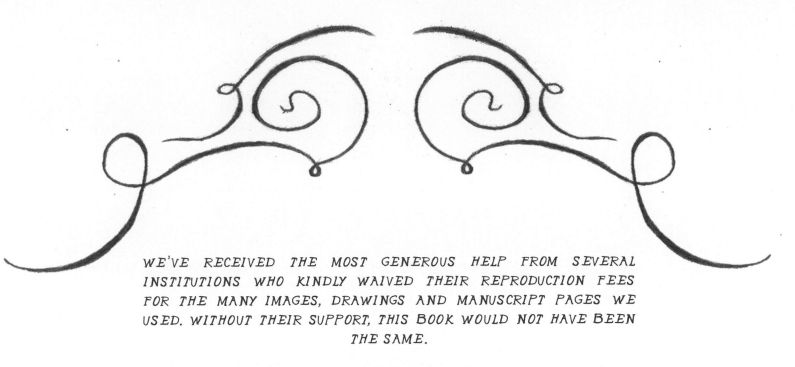

WE'VE RECEIVED THE MOST GENEROUS HELP FROM SEVERAL INSTITUTIONS WHO KINDLY WAIVED THEIR REPRODUCTION FEES FOR THE MANY IMAGES, DRAWINGS AND MANUSCRIPT PAGES WE USED. WITHOUT THEIR SUPPORT, THIS BOOK WOULD NOT HAVE BEEN THE SAME.

THE STIFTUNG PREUSSISCHER KULTURBESITZ, STAATSBIBILIOTHEK BERLIN AND BILDAGENTUR BPK ALLOWED US TO "RAID" THEIR HUMBOLDT ARCHIVES AND IMAGE LIBRARY. ALL THE MANUSCRIPT PAGES (BUT MANY OTHER IMAGES, TOO) IN THE *Adventures of Alexander von Humboldt* ARE FROM THEIR COLLECTIONS.

THE BOTANISCHER GARTEN UND BOTANISCHES MUSEUM BERLIN KINDLY GAVE US PERMISSION TO USE HUMBOLDT'S AND BONPLAND'S HERBARIUM SPECIMENS.

BG BM Botanischer Garten & Botanisches Museum Berlin

HERBERT RAMIREZ, THROUGH SERENDIPITY, WAS ABLE TO PROVIDE THE DRONE PHOTOGRAPHS OF TREES THAT WE USED FOR COLLAGE PAGES ALONG THE ORINOCO AND AMAZON. DAVID BOCKINO GAVE US PERMISSION TO USE THE IMAGE OF THE MAIPURES RAPIDS, AND THE MONTPELIER FOUNDATION SHARED THEIR PHOTOS OF JAMES MADISON'S LANDMARK FOREST.

THE ARCHIVE OF EARLY AMERICAN IMAGES AT THE JOHN CARTER BROWN LIBRARY AND THE WELLCOME LIBRARY PROVIDED MANY WONDERFUL ENGRAVINGS AND IMAGES TO ILLUSTRATE HUMBOLDT'S TRAVELS THROUGH SOUTH AMERICA.

THANK YOU ALL FOR YOUR EXTRAORDINARY GENEROSITY!!

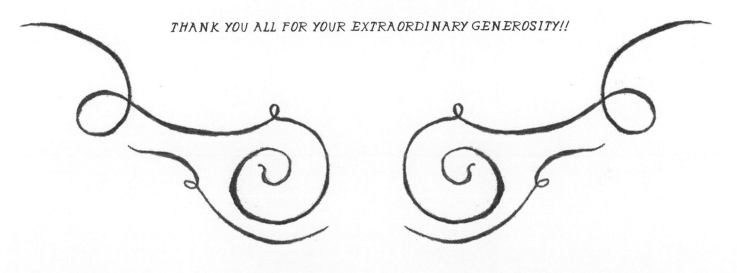

ACKNOWLEDGMENTS

THE MAKING OF *The Adventures of Alexander von Humboldt* WAS A TRULY HUMBOLDTIAN EFFORT— SO MANY PEOPLE AND INSTITUTIONS HELPED US. WITHOUT THEIR HELP, THIS BOOK WOULD HAVE BEEN IMPOSSIBLE. THANK YOU TO EVERYBODY, AND IN NO PARTICULAR ORDER OTHER THAN SPINNING ACROSS THE GLOBE: IN EUROPE: BARBARA SCHNEIDER-KEMPF, JEANETTE LAMBLE AND JUTTA WEBER AT THE STAATSBIBILIOTHEK BERLIN; HERMAN PARZINGER AT STIFTUNG PREUSSISCHER KULTURBESITZ; HANNS-PETER FRENTZ AND CHRISTINA STEHR AT BILDAGENTUR BPK; PATRICIA RAHEM-IPOUR AT THE BOTANISCHER GARTEN UND BOTANISCHES MUSEUM BERLIN; AND ONCE AGAIN THE FORMIDABLE CREW AT THE ALEXANDER-VON-HUMBOLDT-FORSCHUNGSSTELLEIN BERLIN: INGO SCHWARZ, ULRIKE LEITNER, ULRICH PÄBLER, AND TOBIAS KRAFT IN BERLIN. WE WOULD ALSO LIKE TO THANK JULIA BAYERL, FRANK HOLL AND JOHN HEMMING. IN THE UNITED STATES AND THE REST OF THE WORLD: DIANA CROHN AT PANTA RHEA FOUNDATION FOR THEIR GENEROUS GRANT; LESLIE BOWMAN AND JOSHUA SCOTT AT MONTICELLO AND THE THOMAS JEFFERSON FOUNDATION; MARY WOLTZ; THOMAS WOLTZ AND EVERYBODY AT NELSON BYRD WOLTZ LANDSCAPE ARCHITECTS; NEIL SAFIER AT THE JOHN CARTER BROWN LIBRARY; RICHARD PASELK AT HUMBOLDT STATE UNIVERSITY; VANESSA SELLERS AND FRANCISCA COELHO AT THE NEW YORK BOTANICAL GARDEN; STEVE HINDLE AT THE HUNTINGTON LIBRARY, ART COLLECTIONS, AND BOTANICAL GARDENS; KAT IMHOFF AND GILES MORRIS AT THE MONTPELIER FOUNDATION; MARIE ARANA; SANDRA NICHOLS; CHRIS NORTH, VICTORIA JOHNSON; DAVID BOCKINO; CESÁR ASTUHUAMAN. NICK SOUSANIS, PAT CUMMINGS, ALEXANDRA GLENN COLLINS; SAM SHEPHERD; DAIJA WASHINGTON AND CAELEIGH MACNEIL; MARGALIT CUTLER, JULLIAN KLEPPER, SCOTT SUTHERLAND, ROBERT AND CATHLEEN WHEELER.

THANK YOU TO MARVELOUS PATRICK WALSH AND JOHN ASH AT PEW LITERARY AGENCY; AND TO EVERYBODY AT CW AGENCY. THANK YOU TO EVERYBODY AT KNOPF AND PANTHEON, IN PARTICULAR EDWARD KASTENMEIER AND DAN FRANK FOR ALLOWING US TO GO BIG AND FULL COLOR (AND EVEN LETTING US HAVE A FOLDOUT). AND OF COURSE A BIG THANK-YOU TO EVERYBODY AT JOHN MURRAY AND THE WONDERFUL TEAM AT C. BERTELSMANN.

SPECIAL THANKS TO NATHALIE MORENO AND MARISSA BACA FOR ARTFULLY COMBINING OUR WORDS AND PICTURES WITH THEIR TYPESETTING.

AND LAST BUT NOT LEAST, A BIG THANK-YOU TO LAUREN REDNISS FOR BRINGING US TOGETHER.

THIS ONE IS FOR YOU, **THOMAS WOLTZ** — AND TO OUR FAST LANE. THANK YOU FOR EVERYTHING THAT YOU HAVE DONE AND CONTINUE TO DO.

TO MY MOTHER, **JENNIFER SUTHERLAND**, FOR SHOWING ME HOW FUN ART AND HISTORY CAN BE. AND TO MY FATHER, **DOUGLAS MELCHER**, FOR SHARING WITH ME HIS LOVE OF ALL CRITTERS FROM CREEPY TO CRAWLY.

ANDREA WULF WAS BORN IN INDIA, MOVED TO GERMANY AS A CHILD AND NOW LIVES IN LONDON. SHE IS THE AWARD-WINNING AUTHOR OF FIVE BOOKS. HER PREVIOUS BOOK, *The Invention of Nature,* WAS AN INTERNATIONAL BEST SELLER AND CHOSEN AS ONE OF THE **10** BEST BOOKS OF **2015** IN *The New York Times.* IT HAS BEEN PUBLISHED IN **26** COUNTRIES AND HAS WON **12** INTERNATIONAL LITERARY AWARDS. SHE IS AN INTERNATIONAL FELLOW OF THE EXPLORERS CLUB, A FELLOW OF THE ROYAL GEOGRAPHICAL SOCIETY AND A FELLOW OF THE ROYAL SOCIETY OF LITERATURE. FOR THE PAST YEARS, SHE HAS FOLLOWED HUMBOLDT'S FOOTSTEPS THROUGH EUROPE AND SOUTH AMERICA — FROM CHIMBORAZO AND THE MAIPURES RAPIDS AT THE ORINOCO TO THE ARCHIVES IN BERLIN.

LILLIAN MELCHER WAS BORN AND RAISED JUST OUTSIDE OF BOSTON, MASSACHUSETTS. SHE ATTENDED PARSONS SCHOOL OF DESIGN IN NEW YORK CITY. IN **2016**, SHE GRADUATED WITH A DEGREE IN ILLUSTRATION. SHE IS THE RECIPIENT OF THE SCBWI STUDENT ILLUSTRATOR SCHOLARSHIP. THIS IS HER FIRST BOOK. WHILE SHE HASN'T BEEN TO CHIMBORAZO OR THE ORINOCO, DIVING INTO THE DENSE UNIVERSE OF HUMBOLDT'S WORK OVER THE PAST TWO YEARS WITH ANDREA WULF AS HER GUIDE HAS BEEN A GREAT ADVENTURE. SHE HOPES YOU FEEL THE SAME WAY.

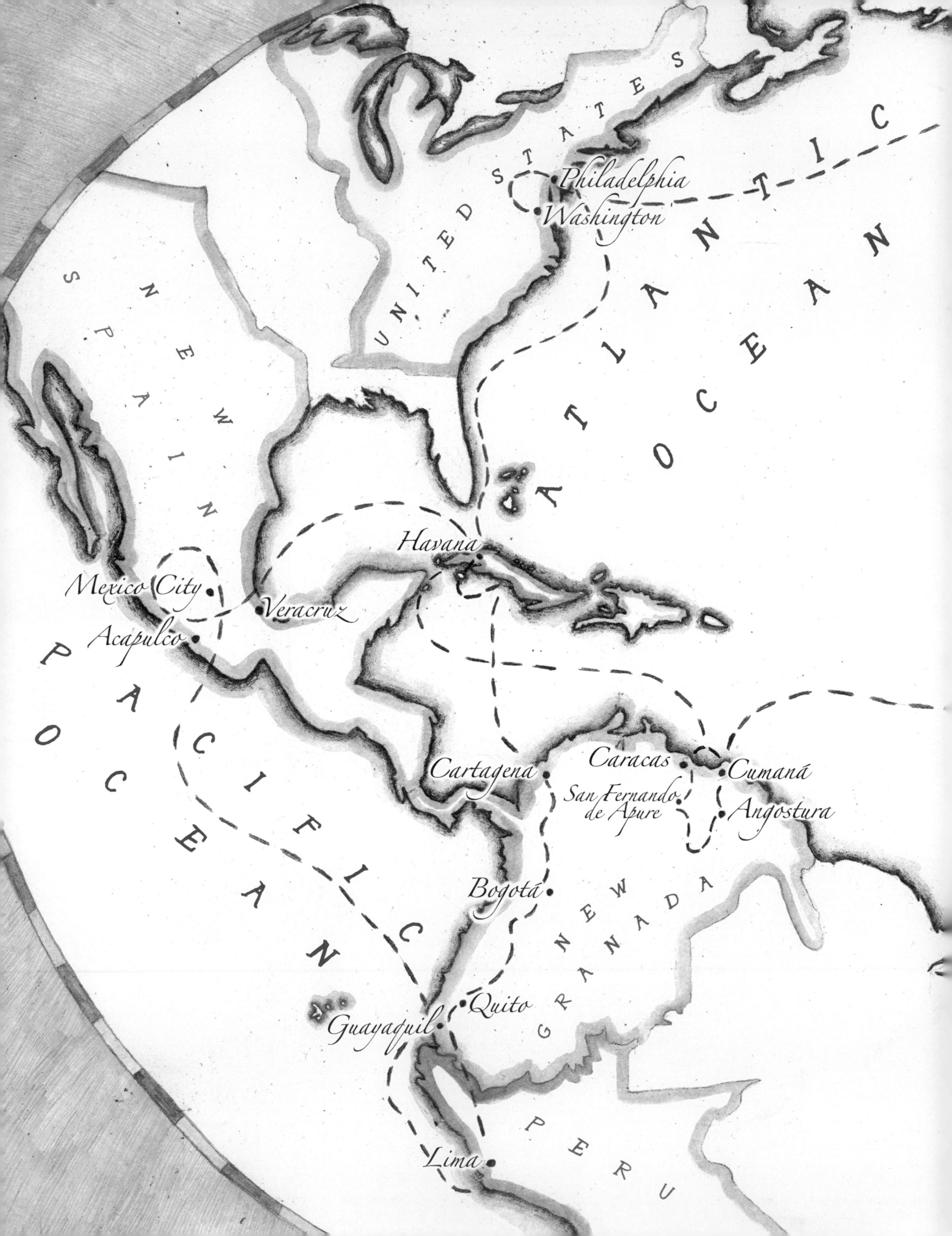
UNITED STATES
Philadelphia
Washington
ATLANTIC
ATLANTIC OCEAN
NEW SPAIN
Havana
Mexico City
Veracruz
Acapulco
PACIFIC OCEAN
Cartagena
Caracas
Cumaná
San Fernando de Apure
Angostura
Bogotá
NEW GRANADA
Quito
Guayaquil
PERU
Lima